Ethnic Families in America

PATTERNS AND VARIATIONS

Second Edition

Ethnic Families in America

PATTERNS AND VARIATIONS

Second Edition

Edited by

CHARLES H. MINDEL

Graduate School of Social Work
University of Texas at Arlington

and

ROBERT W. HABENSTEIN

Department of Sociology
University of Missouri, Columbia, Missouri

ELSEVIER
New York · Oxford

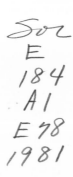

Elsevier North Holland, Inc.
52 Vanderbilt Avenue, New York, New York 10017

Sole distributors outside the United States and Canada:
Elsevier Science Publishers B.V.
P.O. Box 211, 1000 AE Amsterdam, The Netherlands

Library of Congress Cataloging in Publication Data

Main entry under title:

Ethnic families in America: patterns and variations.

   Includes bibliographies.
   1. Minorities—United States—Addresses, essays, lectures. 2. Family—United
   States—Addresses, essays, lectures. 3. United States—Social
   conditions—1960- —Addresses, essays, lectures. I. Mindel,
   Charles H. II. Habenstein, Robert Wesley, 1914–
E184.A1E78   1981   305.8′00973   81-7787
ISBN 0-444-99090-9 (pbk.)   AACR2

First edition designed by Loretta Li

Desk Editor   Louise Calabro Schreiber
Design Editor   Glen Burris
Cover Design   José García
Production Manager   Joanne Jay
Compositor   Publishers Phototype, Inc.
Printer   Haddon Craftsmen

Manufactured in the United States of America

Contents

Preface to the Second Edition

In the intervening five years since the publication of the first edition of *Ethnic Families in America* we have seen interest in the "ethnic" factor continue to increase and grow in American society. Ethnic solidarity among some groups is on the rise and ethnic conflict both here in the United States and abroad is an almost daily source of news in the mass media. These attachments of heritage, "blood," "peoplehood," "one's own kind," or whatever term chosen, remain highly salient for large numbers of people the world over. They may be dismissed as devisive, primitive, or vestigial by some but there is no doubt that they exist and will continue to exist for some time to come.

Part of the increase and growth in interest in ethnicity in recent years has been as a response to the widespread attitude that ethnic attachments and ethnic culture should be quickly disposed of so as to assimilate rapidly, painlessly, and melt into the larger American mass.

The melting pot metaphor has long been a cornerstone element in American intergroup relations, but recent authors are now apt to point out that the "melting pot" has not reflected the actual state of affairs with respect to how ethnics are accepted into the mainstream of American society. Today they are more than likely to reject the negative stereotypes and slurs that were once applied to their group. They now argue that ethnic culture and ties that exist and persist represent positive and useful modes of existence. Shame, embarrassment, or defensiveness are no longer appropriate responses to the awareness of ethnic differences, but rather pride, self-respect, and a sense of community are expected. As one prominent ethnic spokesman has pointed out, ethnic pluralists are not demanding that we "hold back the clock" or return to an earlier cultural era, but rather that we recognize the continuing importance of ethnic culture, identity, and community.

In this edition of *Ethnic Families in America*, the authors have attempted to examine more carefully the distinctions between those things identified as ethnic—and those other forces impinging on people's lives—as for example, social class and social mobility and other economic matters. We have asked our authors to distinguish between characteristics or changes in the ethnic family that are ethnic-cultural and characteristics or changes that are due to social class and social mobility trends, and how these two forces have interacted with each other.

We have also asked our authors to address the unique ways that various liberation movements have had an impact on the ethnic family. How, we asked, has the women's movement affected ethnic identity and, contrariwise, how has ethnic identity affected the women's movement? How have the elderly been treated in the ethnic family and how does this relate to the enormous increase in interest in problems of the elderly in the United States?

Finally, we have asked our authors to deal with the problem of persistence of ethnic diversity in the United States, with particular reference to their own group. Are they optimistic or pessimistic? Under what circumstances or situations will ethnic culture flourish or perish?

The new issues that we have attempted to grapple with in this edition are the result in large measure of the comments of many of the readers and reviewers of this work. We would like to thank the readers who have commented favorably and also those who have pointed out the gaps that we have tried to fill in this new edition. Special thanks for editorial assistance is extended to Gloria Mindel. Thanks are also extended to the Center for Research in Social Behavior at the University of Missouri and the Graduate School of Social Work for technical assistance provided, with a special nod to Donna Turner for her wonderful assistance.

A special note of appreciation to Bill Gum, editor, overseer, critic, and prodder. His encouragement has been invaluable.

A work such as this, on ethnic groups in America, reflects, certainly, our academic and scholarly interests, but also in large measure our own personal history. We, the editors, though several generations removed, are products of those great waves of immigration to the United States. Our ideas, behavior—our consciousness—have been shaped by these events, sometimes very consciously, other times on a more subtle level. Most of all, it has been within our families that we have learned to appreciate the heritage and the contributions of our respective ethnic groups, our "people." We therefore dedicate this work to our parents, Samuel and Freda Mindel, and Herman and Winifred Habenstein.

April 1981

CHARLES H. MINDEL
ROBERT W. HABENSTEIN

Preface to the First Edition

The idea for this book was first conceived several years ago with the inability of one of the editors to find readings and lecture material on family patterns of America's ethnic minorities. In searching out the material it became apparent that most of the recent textbooks on the sociology of the family had begun to pay attention to some minority family types, especially the black family, but that the overwhelming emphasis has been and probably will continue to be on the generalized white Protestant middle-class American family.

Considering the fact that America, a nation of immigrants, still contains large numbers of families who see themselves as members of ethnic groups and for whom ethnic culture still has important behavioral consequences it seemed appropriate that a volume on these distinctive family types might be organized.

In planning this book the editors decided to try to include most of the major American ethnic groups, but at the same time it became apparent that to write this book ourselves would be a near impossible task, certainly beyond our expertise as well as the range of our ethnic—Jewish and German—experience. In addition, one of the deficits we and others have noted about most writings on race and ethnic studies is a tendency to examine only the negative or "problems" of minority families. Most frequently this is the case because the writers are not members of the group about which they are writing. In this volume we decided to take a more positive approach, examining ethnic family strengths as well as weaknesses, and to lodge these characterizations in historical socioeconomic contexts. Consistent with this approach was our decision to seek out scholars who also happened to be members of the ethnic group about which they might be writing. The risk of getting an overly rosy picture of the ethnic group we felt to be more than offset by the benefits, which include a greater penetration into the subjective meanings that group members attach to certain cultural traits or behaviors, and a depth of understanding that might not be so apparent to an outsider. Although we were not totally successful in securing authors who were also members of the ethnic group they wrote about, in those chapters where we do not have correlative ethnic authors (Amish, North American Indian, and Puerto Rican) we do have experts who have worked for many years in and with their groups.

The decision was made at the outset to develop a common outline that each of the authors would follow so that a certain consistency would exist and that the book would be seen as an integrated whole rather than a collection of readings. To a large extent this goal was achieved but to a certain degree it was not. Rather than seeing this as a failing we prefer to see it as the consequence of the great heterogeneity of America's ethnic groups, and our agreement that contributing authors be allowed to develop those areas where they thought their respective ethnic group was most distinctive. If the chapters do not always follow the outline in every detailed respect we do not think on balance that it was necessarily a bad thing for the book.

Some contributors have raised the question of the use of "America" throughout the book. Inasmuch as the Western Hemisphere has been geographically divided into three "Americas," it may be questioned if our usage might not be erroneous at best, offensive at worst. Our decision rests on what we believe to be social usage and the common currency of "America" in everyday discourse to mean the country Kate Smith sings about in "God Bless America" and which graces the titles of thousands of books all referring, technically speaking, to the United States. Without our usage, most authors in the end would have difficulty in expressing the ethnic linkage to the host culture, as in Chinese American, Mexican American, Polish American, Greek American, and the like.

Attempting to acknowledge all those who over the last several years have facilitated our efforts would be impossible, but special thanks are in order first of all to all of the contributing authors who have worked patiently with us through the many edits and re-edits of their chapters. We also would like to specially thank Ellen H. Biddle for her extra contributions as well as Susan Elder and Jean Bailey for their assistance with the manuscript. To the staff of the Center for Research in Social Behavior we would like to acknowledge their cooperation in the task of typing, retyping, duplicating, and distributing the manuscript in its many forms.

A final word of thanks are in order for William Gum of Elsevier who without white horse or shining armor rescued this pristine work from ravaging editors in another part of the publishing forest.

November 1975

CHARLES H. MINDEL
ROBERT W. HABENSTEIN

List of Contributors

DAVID ALVIREZ is Dean of the School of Social Sciences and professor of sociology at Pan American University. He received his Ph.D. degree in sociology from The University of Texas at Austin. His major research interests are Mexican Americans and demography, and currently he is pursuing a study of the determinants and consequences of legal immigration of Mexicans to the United States. Among his major works are articles on the Mexican American worker, the effects of religiosity on the fertility patterns of Mexican Americans, and census data problems with respect to the conceptual definition of the Mexican American population.

FRANK D. BEAN is professor and Chairman of Sociology at The University of Texas at Austin. He received his Ph.D. degree from Duke University. His major research interests are in the areas of family and fertility, fertility differentials among ethnic groups, and the sociology of the family. He has published numerous articles, including several dealing with various aspects of fertility among Mexican Americans.

ELLEN HORGAN BIDDLE received a B.A. degree from Wellesley College (sociology) in 1950, an M.A. degree from Earlham College (community development) in 1952, and a Ph.D. degree from the University of Missouri at Columbia (sociology) in 1969. Her fields of interest are ethnic groups, family, gerontology, and social work. A book on urban Australian aborigines, *Look Forward, Not Back*, of which she is co-writer, was published in 1975. At present an assistant professor at the Kent School of Social Work, University of Louisville, Dr. Biddle has conducted studies of decision-making within families concerning long-term care relocation and housing and health-care patterns of older adults. She is Director of the Gerontology Center of the University of Louisville.

BRUCE L. CAMPBELL received his B.A. and M.A. degrees from Brigham Young University in child and family development. He received his Ph.D. degree in sociology at the University of Minnesota. His major research interests are aging and the family. Dr. Campbell is presently located at the Department of Home Economics, California State University, Los Angeles.

EUGENE E. CAMPBELL, professor of history, received his M.A. degree from the University of Utah in 1940 and his Ph.D. degree in history from the University of Southern California in 1952. On the faculty of Brigham Young University since 1956 and department chairman, 1959–1967, Dr. Campbell's major research emphasis is Utah and Mormon history. He is coauthor of *The United States: An Interpretative History* and a contributor to *History of a Valley: Cache Valley*. Among his other publications are articles on important figures and events in Mormon political and social history. Dr. Campbell has been elected as a fellow of the Utah State Historical Society.

ABDO A. ELKHOLY, a graduate of Princeton University, is considered an authority on the Arab Americans and Arab Canadians. He has written numerous articles, and his book, *The Arab Moslems in the United States: Religion and Assimilation*, is used by students of assimilation at many colleges and universities. He is well-known in the Arab world as a leading authority on "manpower" utilization and mobilization. For the academic year, 1973–1974, he was selected by both the Board of Foreign Scholarships and the Government of the United Arab Emirates to conduct sociological research in Abu Dhabi under the Fulbright-Hays Program of Senior Scholars. His current research interest is motivation of birth control in the Middle East. Dr. Elkholy is currently a professor of sociology at Northern Illinois University.

BERNARD FARBER received his Ph.D. degree from the University of Chicago in 1953. Since then, his major research interests have been in the sociology of the family and kinship. His books include *Family: Organization and Interaction* (1964); *Comparative Kinship Systems* (1968); *Mental Retardation: Its Social Context and Social Consequences* (1968); *Kinship and Class, A Midwestern Study* (1971); *Guardians of Virtue: Salem Families in 1800* (1972); *Family and Kinship in Modern Society* (1973); and *Conceptions of Kinship* (1980). He has also edited *Kinship and Family* (1966) and has written a series of monographs on the effects of retarded children on family relationships. Currently, he is a professor of sociology at Arizona State University, Tempe.

JOSEPH P. FITZPATRICK received his M.A. degree in philosophy from Fordham University and his Ph.D. degree in sociology from Harvard. Much of his research has been devoted to a study of the Puerto Rican migration. He has published *Puerto Rican Americans: The Meaning of Migration to the Mainland*; (with John Martin) *Delinquent Behavior: A Re-definition of the Problem*; and (with J. M. Martin and R. E. Gould) *The Analysis of Delinquent Behavior: A Structural Approach*. Dr. Fitzpatrick has been a faculty member at Fordham University in New York since 1949.

LAWRENCE FRENCH received his degrees at the University of New Hampshire in sociology and is completing a second Ph.D. in psychological and cultural studies at the University of Nebraska.

ROBERT W. HABENSTEIN began a delayed career in sociology after experiences in C.C.C. camps, armed forces, and industrial work in Cleveland, Ohio. His Ph.D. dissertation at the University of Chicago in 1954 dealt with funeral directing. And, at the University of Missouri, where he has been on the staff since 1950, he has conducted a number of studies in the family and occupations and professions. He is author of eight books. Although currently he is a professor of sociology and research associate in the University's Center for Research in Social Behavior, his plans for the immediate future focus on opening an art gallery and oriental rug shop in the artists' colony at Tubac, Arizona.

LUCY JEN HUANG, professor of sociology, was born in China. She received her Ph.D. degree at the University of Chicago in 1954. Before coming to her present position at Illinois State University in 1967, she taught sociology at Lake Erie College and Boston University. Her major interest in sociology is comparative family and alternate lifestyles in marriage and the family. Her major published works are in the area of changing family and sex roles in the Chinese family, especially the changing family in the People's Republic of China.

GERTRUDE ENDERS HUNTINGTON was born in Wooster, Ohio, on the edge of the largest Amish community in America. She did graduate work at Rochester University and received her Ph.D. degree from Yale, writing her dissertation on an Old Order Amish community. She has worked with religious minorities, particularly the Hutterites and the Amish. With John A. Hostetler she co-authored *The Hutterites in North America* (1967, Fieldwork edition, 1980) and *Children in Amish Society* (1971). Her special interests are in the areas of childrearing practices, the anthropology of education, the role of grandparents, and the interaction of the family with the community. Currently Dr. Huntington is a visiting lecturer in anthropology and in environmental studies at the University of Michigan.

AKEMI KIKUMURA is currently assistant professor of anthropology and ethnic studies at the University of Southern California in Los Angeles. She received her Ph.D. from the University of California, Los Angeles, and is the author of the forthcoming book, *Michiko: The Story of a Japanese Immigrant Woman*.

HARRY H. L. KITANO is currently professor of social welfare and sociology, academic assistant to the Chancellor, and Co-Director of the Alcohol Research Center, University of California, Los Angeles. He was formerly the Director of the University of California Tokyo Study Center. He received his Ph.D. degree from The University of California, Berkeley, and is the author of *Race Relations* (1980); *Japanese Americans: The Evolution of a Subculture* (1976); and *American Racism* (with Roger Daniels) (1970).

GEORGE A. KOURVETARIS received his Ph.D. degree from Northwestern University in 1969 and is currently a professor of sociology at Northern Illinois University and founder and editor of *The Journal of Political and Military Sociology*. His major academic and research interests include political and military sociology, social stratification, intergroup relations, and comparative sociology. Among his most recent publications are "The Greek Army Officer Corps: Its Professionalism and Political Interventionism," in Morris Janowitz and Jacques Van Doorn (eds.), *On Military Intervention* (1971); *First and Second Generation Greeks in Chicago: An Inquiry into Their Stratification and Mobility Patterns* (1971); and *Social Origins and Political Orientations of Officer Corps in a World Perspective* (1973). He is also co-editor of *World Perspectives in the Sociology of the Military* (1977); *Political Sociology: Readings in Research and Theory* (1980); and co-author of *Society and Politics: An Overview and Reappraisal of Political Sociology* (1980).

BERNARD LAZERWITZ did his graduate work at the University of Michigan and has specialized in survey research, the study of ethnic minorities, and the sociology of housing. He has taught at the University of Illinois, Brandeis University, the University of Missouri, and is now a professor at Bar-Ilan University in Israel. Among his major works are studies of religion and social structure, trends in fertility rates of Jews and Arabs in Israel, a book on the components and consequences of religioethnic identification, and the statistical design for the first large-scale national sample survey of the American Jewish population. At present, he is studying urban renewal in Israel.

HELENA ZNANIECKA LOPATA received her Ph.D. degree from the University of Chicago in 1954 and is currently a professor of sociology and Director of the Center for the Comparative Study of Social Roles, Loyola U iversity of Chicago. Formerly she served as Chairman of the Sociology Department at Loyola University, 1970–1972. Her major works include *Occupation: Housewife* (1971); *Widowhood in an American City* (1973); *Marriages and Families* (ed. 1973); *Polish Americans: Status Competition in an Ethnic Community; Women as Widows: Support Systems* (1979); and *Research on an Interweave of Social Roles: Women and Men* (ed. 1980). Currently Dr. Lopata is analyzing data from a study of identities and commitments of women to work, family, and other roles.

CHARLES H. MINDEL, born in New York City, received his B.A. degree at the State University of New York at Stony Brook and his Ph.D. degree in sociology at the University of Illinois in 1971. His research interests are in the areas of kinship, family, and aging. His recent works have included articles, "Extended Familism Among Urban Mexican Americans, Anglos and Blacks" and "Multigenerational Family Households: Recent Trends and Implications for the Future." He is currently writing two books on aging with Kyriakos Markides, *Cross Cultural Aging in America* and *Older People and Their Families*. Dr. Mindel is currently an associate professor of social work at The University of Texas at Arlington.

JOHN A. PRICE is a professor of urban anthropology at York University in Toronto. He received his Ph.D. degree at the University of Michigan and has done fieldwork in Japan, Mexico, America, and Canada. He has recently published two books on Indian life, *Native Studies: American and Canadian Indians* (1978) and *Indians of Canada: Cultural Dynamics* (1979).

JILL S. QUADAGNO is an assistant professor at the University of Kansas. She is the editor of the recently published book, *Aging, The Individual and Society* (St. Martin's Press, 1980). She spent 1980 at Cambridge University as a National Science Foundation Postdoctoral Fellow and is presently writing a book on aging and the family life cycle in 19th century England.

ROBERT STAPLES was born in Roanoke, Virginia, and educated in California. He received his Ph.D. degree at the University of Minnesota. His major research interests are in the area of ethnic family systems, human sexuality, race relations, and urban sociology. His most recent book is *The World of Black Singles: Changing Patterns of Male–Female Relations* (1981). Among his major works are 70 articles on black family life and the books, *The Black Family: Essays and Studies* (1978); *Introduction to Black Sociology* (1976); and *The Black Woman in America: Sex, Marriage and the Family* (1973). He is an associate professor in the graduate program in sociology at the University of California Medical Center at San Francisco.

DORIE WILLIAMS is a doctoral candidate in sociology at The University of Texas at Austin. Her major research interests are in the areas of family sociology, social psychology, and sex roles. She is currently involved in research on the effects of family configuration on unwanted fertility and a study of marital conjugality on the decision for male or female sterilization procedures.

Ethnic Families in America
PATTERNS AND VARIATIONS
Second Edition

Family Lifestyles
of America's Ethnic Minorities:
An Introduction

This is a book about patterned differences in American families—differences based on the national, cultural, religious, and racial identification and membership of groups of people who do not set the dominant style of life or control the privileges and power in any given society. These differences are embedded in what are generally known as "ethnic groups." Ethnicity is usually displayed in the values, attitudes, lifestyles, customs, rituals, and personality types of individuals who identify with particular ethnic groups. Had these ethnic identifications and memberships no other effect on peoples' lives than to provide interesting variety within a country, sociologists would long since have described them in their variety and moved on to other matters. But identification with and membership in an ethnic group has far-reaching effects on both groups and individuals, controlling access to opportunities in life, feelings of well-being, and mastery over the futures of one's children.

CHAPTER ONE
BY
CHARLES H. MINDEL AND
ROBERT W. HABENSTEIN

ANALYSIS AND METAPHOR

Ethnicity and the analysis of ethnic groups have long been topics of discussion in scholarly and popular literature. Terms such as "melting pot," the metaphor embodying the notion that immigrants from all over the world somehow fuse together here in America, producing a new and better amalgam, combining the best cultural contributions of each, was first coined by Israel Zangwill in a 1906 play of the same name. However, there have been avid discussions about the virtues of maintaining a "cultural pluralism," that is, becoming "American" while at the same time retaining one's cultural heritage, since 1915, when Horace Kallen first introduced the idea. Still others

1

have claimed that really what we have here in America is a highly ethnocentric coercion toward "Anglo conformity," implying the downgrading and elimination of ethnic culture and the incorporation of the dominant Anglo culture. The element of conflict and the transformation of ethnic groups into politically conscious ethnic minorities are central to this approach.

In recent years there has been a decline in "melting pot" theories of racial and ethnic assimilation, and the notion of American society as a conglomerate of "unmeltable ethnics"—existing in a somewhat tenuous societal pluralism has been gaining ground. The "salad bowl" metaphor has found favor in Canada where pluralism—the willingness of any one group to seek an amicable accord with any other, whatever hue or creed—has long been an article of national faith (Elkin, 1970; Ishwaran, 1971; Queen and Habenstein, 1974; Wade, 1960). Conflict theory has not yet developed an acceptable figure of speech to characterize American ethnic relations, but "cats in a bag" might not be totally inapplicable.

But the concept of assimilation historically has long enjoyed the status of what Gouldner (1970) has called a domain assumption, carrying with it a kind of value-laden ethnocentrism that presumes superiority on the part of the host culture in all respects and an inferior cultural baggage carried ashore by the newly arrived immigrants. True, "Americanization," the lingual epitome of an earlier 20th-century social movement to detribalize and de-ethnicize the ubiquitous foreign element, has long since left the sociologist's lexicon, although its presence may occasionally be noted in a Fourth of July or Memorial Day public address.

Some of the enthusiasm for denigrating ethnic groups has lost its national appeal. The long-term rise in the standard of living and the disappearance of much physically demanding, toil-ridden work has made for fewer "dirty-work" occupations being associated with particular ethnic groups (Fuchs, 1968). The material success of some ethnic groups *qua* ethnic groups, Chinese, Japanese, Jews, Irish, and recently Cubans, has helped explode the myth that ethnics are somehow best equipped genetically and culturally to remain at lower or, at best, middle levels of America's economy.

A more recent and spectacular development in the sociopolitical realm has been the impressive growth of the civil rights movement, punctuated by fire storms of political activism and violence, with attendant proliferation of legislation and court rulings aimed directly at discrimination in all its guises. An expanding black consciousness has for millions of Americans reversed the onus of color: "black" does not "stay back," "brown" is not "down," and "white" is not necessarily "right."

In reviewing these developments of long and short duration, it is evident that there has been a growth of ethnic awareness of a different genre in America, whether it expresses itself in the comfort that older ethnic groups can now feel when proclaiming their Old World heritage or in the troubled and troublesome abrasiveness of the long-subjugated ethnic minorities searching for a status yet to be won. Both the achievers and the achieving, it remains to be added, face the universal problem of searching for, finding, and maintaining roots and tradition in face of the appeals of modernity and homogenized living in the burgeoning mass society.

Though all of these contrasting and seemingly contradictory views concerning American immigrant and minority groups, "Anglo conformity," "melting pot," and "cultural pluralism," or as sociologists often refer to them, assimilation, amalgamation, and accommodation (Rose, 1974: 66) have taken on a new relevancy today. Only in the last few years have we begun to acquire knowledge about ethnic groups.

Most textbooks on the American family's attempt to meet the challenge of ethnic diversity include in their work examples of one or two distinctive families (Nye and Berardo, 1973; Burgess, Locke, and Thomes 1963; Kephart 1972; Cavan 1969; Reiss 1971). However, while ethnicity continues to act as an important determinant of behavior for a significant number of people, it has often been treated by scholars and textbook writers *en passant,* either as a historical or residual category.

It may well be that in the long run ethnic differences will disappear, as Glazer (1954) and others have argued, but as Greeley (1969: 21) notes, "Family, land and common cultural heritage have always been terribly important to human beings, and suspicion of anyone who is strange or different seems also deeply rooted in the human experience." It is the purpose of this book to examine a wide variety of American ethnic groups, probing the historical circumstances that impelled them to come to this country, focusing on the structure and functioning of their family life to determine or at least to raise clues as to how and why they have been able or unable to maintain an ethnic identification over the generations, and, finally, looking ahead to speculate on what the future has in store for these groups and their constitutive families.

WHAT IS AN ETHNIC GROUP?

What is it to be ethnic? In recent years it has often been suggested that ethnicity is unimportant, that "ethnic" ties are part of man's primitive past—a past out of which humans have been evolving over many years. As Greeley (1974:10) states,

In fact the conflicts that have occupied most men over the past two or three decades, those that have led to the most appalling outpourings of blood, have had precious little to do with ideological division. Most of us are unwilling to battle to the death over ideology, but practically all of us it seems are ready to kill each other over noticeable differences of color, language, religious faith, height, food habits, and facial configurations.

Greeley (1974:10) further points out that

> Thousands have died in seemingly endless battles between two very Semitic people, the Jews and the Arabs. The English and French glare hostilely at each other in Quebec; Christians and Moslems have renewed their ancient conflicts on the island of Mindanao; Turks and Greeks nervously grip their guns on Cyprus; and Celts and Saxons in Ulster have begun to imprison and kill one another with all the cumulative passion of a thousand years' hostility.

In addition, more recently the Persians of Iran and Arabs in Iraq serve as another example of "ethnic" conflict. It appears that perhaps the collapse of old colonial empires and the rise of nationalism in the post-World War II period have given rise to numerous conflicts at tribal, linguistic, religious, geographical, and cultural levels. The conflict appears to be increasing rather than decreasing.

What all these conflicts seem to share is not "an ideological character," especially the ideology of modern superpower conflicts, namely economic systems and social class, but rather these conflicts are all concerned in some sense with very basic differences among groups of people, particularly cultural differences. There are things reflected in these conflicts that are apparently important to people—matters for which they are willing to fight to the death to defend. Clifford Geertz (1963: 109) referred to these ties that people are willing to die for as "primordial attachments":

> By a primordial attachment is meant one that stems from the "givens"—or more precisely, as culture is inevitably involved in such matters the "assured givens"—of social existence: immediate contiguity and kin connection mainly, but beyond them, the givenness that stems from being born into a particular religious community, speaking a particular language, or even a dialect of language, and following particular social patterns. These congruities of blood, speech, custom, and so on, are seen to have an ineffable, at times overpowering, coerciveness in and of themselves. One is bound to one's kinsman, one's neighbor, one's fellow believer, *ipso facto*, as a result not merely of one's personal affection, practical necessity, common interest, or incurred obligation, but at least in great part by the virtue of some unaccountable absolute import attributed to the very tie itself. The general strength of such primordial bonds, and the types of them that are important, differ from person to person, from society to society, and from time to time. But for virtually every person, in every society, at almost all times, some attachments seem to flow from a sense of natural—some would say spiritual— affinity than from social interaction.

4

These attachments, these feelings of belonging to a certain group of people for whatever reason, are a basic feature of human condition. These ties are called "ethnic" ties and the group of people that one is tied to is an "ethnic" group. In this general sense, an ethnic group consists of those who share a unique social and cultural heritage that is passed on from generation to generation.

Gordon (1964), in slightly different terms, sees those who share a feeling of "peoplehood" as an ethnic group. But the sense of peoplehood that characterized most social life in the past centuries has become fragmented and shattered. This, it is suggested, has been occurring for a variety of reasons, including in the last few centuries massive population increases, the development of large cities, the formation of social classes, and grouping of peoples into progressively larger political units. However, many other writers have noted, there has been a continuing need for individuals to merge their individual identity with some ancesteral group—with "their own kind of people." Gordon proposes that the fragmentation of social life has left competing models for this sense of peoplehood; people are forced to choose among them or somehow to integrate them totally. In America, the core categories of ethnic identity from which individuals are able to form a sense of peoplehood are race, religion, and national origin or some combination of these categories (Gordon, 1964). It is these criteria emphasizing substantively cultural symbols of consciousness of time, that are used to define the groups included in this book.

Ethnicity in America

In the 1970s we have seen a growing interest in cultural pluralism, ethnic pluralism, and ethnic differences in the United States. This has not always been the case and it has been argued by some that the reason why examination of ethnic differences in the scholarly study of man has been lacking has much to do with the dominant assimilationist model of American society. According to this model, ethnic differences, while perhaps useful in the past in preserving the familiar or the *gemeinschaft* character of the old country for large numbers of people set adrift in alien America, are not particularly useful today in our more rational and class-oriented society. In addition, the divisive aspects of ethnicity are emphasized and seen as barriers to peaceful coexistence within the American social fabric. Integrative aspects of ethnic ties and ethnic culture have been almost entirely neglected. As a result large numbers of individuals with rich ethnic heritages have been encouraged, coerced and, in other ways, pushed toward giving up their heritage and becoming "Americanized." Stereotypes abound concerning the negative aspects and consequences of ethnic culture. Italians are corrupt; Polish are ignorant; white

5

ethnics are racist and warmongers; and any number of different ethnic groups are lazy and will not work. This kind of view has long been part of the general American culture. The implication is that as soon as one gives up his or her inferior beliefs and ties, and as soon as one leaves this life— this narrow, dull, provincial life—the better all these people will be.

That this view is now seen by many as ethnocentric and destructive reflects a major shift. As Greeley (1974) states, "Ethnicity is far from being a divisive force in society. It can be viewed as a constructive one, at least it is inevitable." This shift reflects a renewal of ethnic consciousness—a new awareness of distinctive ethnic culture, partly a consciously remembered one and partly a set of inherited customs and beliefs. Ethnics are now allowed to endorse the theme that they "have the right to be different." This new consciousness on the part of ethnic groups reflects the larger changes and upheavals that American society has gone through in the 1960s and 1970s, especially the various liberation movements that emerged during this period, most notably the black civil rights movement. These movements tended in their turn to re-new the ethnic consciousness of the so-called "white ethnics" or "unmeltable ethnics," as Novak has referred to them, inspiring renewed interest in cultural pluralism and a new sensitivity toward others and their differences. We have seen increases in the personal, conscious, self-appropriation of one's own cultural history and a willingness to share in the social and political needs and struggles of groups to which one is personally tied. The re-emergence of ethnic feelings and interests has not necessarily meant a return to old world culture. It does not, as Novak (1973) points out, represent an attempt to "hold back the clock"—rather it represents a defense of ties that are important to large numbers of individuals in this country.

The reason why these interests are seen as important to defend, and at times, as we have seen in various locales, to fight for, is that they are very important to individuals in their daily lives, not a mere nostalgic defense of some useless cultural artifact. There are (and were) many reasons for maintaining ethnic communal ties. Some were primarily useful at the time when members of ethnic groups were early immigrants to this country and others continue to be important into the present day. The utility of ethnic ties and ethnic groups is in large part the reason for their continued existence. It should be remembered that as Glazer (1973: 169) states:

> The immigrants . . . were as much in favor of the melting pot as native American nationals, indeed more so, because they thought the melting pot, if they really succeeded in dissolving into some American mass, would give them access to every position in society; while native American chauvinists trying to monopolize these positions were not nearly so much in favor of so complete a disappearance of the immigrant groups.

In fact, the melting pot never did succeed fully and large numbers of immigrant groups were forced to maintain ethnic communal ties almost as a matter of self-defense. Glazer and Moynihan (1970), in their work on ethnicity and their analysis of the evolution and persistence of ethnicity, argued that "the adoption of a totally new ethnic identity, by dropping whatever one is to become simply American, is inhibited by strong elements in the social structure of the United States." These inhibitions range from brutal discrimination and prejudice to the "unavailability of a simple 'American' identity" (Glazer and Moynihan, 1970: xxxiii). Most positively seen, ethnic communities provide individuals congenial associates, help organize experience by personalizing an increasingly impersonal world, and provide opportunities for social mobility and success within an ethnic context (Greeley, 1969: 30).

Glazer and Moynihan also offer some provocative suggestions to explain the increasing importance of ethnicity in recent years. They hypothesize that ethnic identities have replaced occupational identities, particularly working-class occupational identities that have lost much of their glamour in recent years. It is better to be Polish than to be known as a Polish assembly-line worker in a Detroit automobile plant. Second, they speculate that one's ethnic identity in America in large measure has become separate from events in the country of origin. Domestic happenings are more important than international events in evoking feelings of ethnic awareness. (They make an important exception for the Jews, a group whose ethnic identification increased dramatically in America with the creation of the state of Israel.) Third, they suggest, contrary to Greeley and Herberg, that religion as well as occupation and homeland have declined as a source of ethnic identification. That is due, they say, to declining religiosity in general and among the Catholics to the rather dramatic changes that have overcome the Catholic Church in the past decade. Ethnic groups (they concentrated on "Negroes, Puerto Ricans, Jews, Italians, and Irish of New York City") have become largely political, economic, and cultural interest groups (Glazer and Moynihan, 1970: xxxiv–xxxvi). Interethnic relationships, by the same token, become dynamic, tension laden, and carry seeds of potential conflict. The major cities remain the locus of interethnic unrest. Paraphrasing Max Weber, cultural relationships that are not power-centered give way to political relations that certainly are.

Minority Groups

Related, of course, but of a different genre is the concept of minority or minority group. "Minority" in the sociological as opposed to the statistical sense refers to a power or dominance relationship. Those groups that have unequal access to power, that are considered in some way unworthy of sharing power equally, and that are stigmatized in terms of assumed inferior traits or characteristics are minority groups. To be a member of a minority group, then, is to share a status relationship, and to act as a minority group member is to express power consciously. To be a member of an ethnic group, on the other hand, is to share a sense of cultural and historical uniqueness, and to act as a member of an ethnic group is to express feelings or call attention to that uniqueness. It should be understood that the same individual at any one moment may act in either capacity. The black student who complains about the student cafeteria food may be expressing (ethnically) a desire for dishes familiar to him from childhood, or he may be expressing (minority) resentment against being denied these foods on the basis of race and race alone.

ETHNICITY AND FAMILY LIFESTYLE

The maintenance of ethnic identification and solidarity ultimately rests on the ability of the family to socialize its members into the ethnic culture and thus to channel and control, perhaps program, future behavior. The manner in which the respective ethnic families carry out this function we refer to as family lifestyles. Consequently, the distinctive family lifestyles that developed as a consequence of historical and contemporary social processes become the focal concern of this work. Authors were asked to examine the relationships and characteristics distinctive of ethnic family life; to look to the past for explanation of historical or genetic significance; to describe the key characteristics of the ethnic family today; and to analyze the changes that have occurred to the family and speculate as to what lies ahead.

It bears repeating that the historical experience of the ethnic group both with respect to when the group arrived on these shores as well as the conditions under which the members of the group were forced to live is a vitally important factor in the explanation of the persistence of the ethnic family and the ethnic group as well. It is for this reason that each chapter contains an important discussion on the historical background of the respective ethnic groups. In addition to the old-country settings each author was requested to summarize the major characteristics of the family as it existed previously or as it first appeared in America, in order that the subsequent changes and adaptations could more clearly be seen.

One of the most significant ways in which an ethnic culture is expressed is through those activities that we identify as family activities. The family historically has been a conservative institution, and those cultural elements concerning family life, if not affected by outside forces, will tend to replace themselves generation after generation (Farber, 1964). Experiences within the family are intense, heavily emotion-laden, and are apt to evoke pleasurable ¬ainful memories for most individuals. For example, it is not accidental

8

that in many of the ethnic groups to be discussed here "eating" and particularly eating "ethnic" food remain a significant part of the ethnic identity. These are activities that occur in a family context. If traditional ethnic values are to be found anywhere, they will be found in the family.

In addition to developing historical context, the authors were asked to discuss four major areas relevant to ethnic family life in which ethnic culture might either be generated, sustained, or have an impact. First were the demographic characteristics of the ethnic family. How does the ethnic culture get specific expression in fertility, marriage, and divorce rates? How does the group cope with the cultural matter of intermarriage? Intermarriage can be viewed as an important indicator of assimilation for the ethnic group and ranges in incidence from very low among the black Americans and Amish to relatively high as among the Japanese Americans. Second is the question of the structure of the family, which involves the distribution of status, authority, and responsibility within the nuclear family and the network of kin relationships linking members of the extended family. Most discussions of ethnic family life have focused on this area because many ethnic groups have been characterized as patriarchal or matriarchal or as having very close knit extended family relationships. It is in this context that we hear comments about black matriarchy or the "Jewish mother." How much is cultural myth or ideology? How much is fact? What has been the effect of the American experience?

In addition to the cultural patterns that define family roles and statuses, rights and obligations, there are many attributes of an ethnic culture that are mediated through the family. These are cultural values that concern such issues as achievement, style of life, and educational or occupational aspirations. While many historical economic and other factors such as discrimination and prejudice have limited the mobility of individuals in many ethnic groups, for many the possession of a cultural reservoir of motivations and skills has worked to their distinct advantage. For others the lack of this reservoir has worked to their disadvantage. The cultural tradition of the Jews, with its emphasis on literacy and education, has helped them immeasurably from a socioeconomic standpoint. On the other hand, the Poles have only recently begun to emphasize the importance of education to their family members. These cultural distinctions, while existing to some extent outside the family context, are for the most part developed within the family.

Finally, in discussing ethnic family life, it is important to examine the family at different stages of the family life cycle. In this collection of essays authors were requested to analyze those aspects of child rearing, adolescence, mate selection, and the place of the elderly in which ethnic culture has had significant influence. The culture of many groups usually specifies what the most desirable end product of the socialization process should be. Whether this product should be a good Mormon or Amishman, the family as the major force of socializ ation, especially in the critical early years, is the most responsible ethnic ins itution.

Most of the large-scale immigration to America has ceased, although as in the case of the Puerto Ricans, the Greek Americans, Arab Americans, and most recently the refugees from C iba and Indo-China there has been a continuing or sudden large-scale migration to this country. Is it then true, as many writers have suggested, that ethnic differences may very well be on the decline, and in the future they may be relatively unimportant distinguishing features of individuals? In this book the authors will continue the chapters with a brief look into the future of ethnic groups. For some, such as black Americans and other racial groups, these differences and potential for tension and conflict appear destined to continue for some time. For others, such as Greek Americans, Irish Americans, or Polish Americans, these distinctions appear to be disappearing at a somewhat faster rate.

ETHNIC DIVERSITY AS THE CRITERION OF SELECTION

Although not randomly selected, the ethnic families presented in this book were chosen to represent a rather wide spectrum of distinguishable groups, ranging from the less than 100,000 Amish to the 22 million black people, whose ethnicity continues to be expressed through identifiable institutions and, significantly, the family. Nevertheless, there *are* large numbers of Americans who find it possible to trace descent to foreign nations and cultures such as Germany, Great Britain, and Canada, yet who retain little if any of an Old World cultural identity. Their lifestyles are largely indistinguishable from others of similar socioeconomic classes (except in certain isolated enclaves here and there), and for this reason they have been excluded from this work.

While the possession of an ethnic heritage that continues to be expressed in a distinctive family lifestyle is the common theme among all groups chosen in this work, the reasons both for their appearance in America (remembering that native American Indians had precedence!) and continued existence as an identifiable ethnic group remain to some extent unique. That groups migrating to America in great numbers in pre- and early 19th-century periods were responding to general social, economic, and class-oppressive pressures gave all immigrants of that time a measure of common status. Nevertheless, each has its own distinguishing features, contingencies, and value system to provide significantly different ethnic group life histories, and therefore, each has its own story to be told.

There is some justification, then, for adopting the kaleidoscope approach and simply jumbling all 15 family groups together without anything more ordered than what can be achieved by an alphabetical arrangement. Or, conversely, for those more compulsive about systematization, a set of formal ahistorical, all-inclusive categories might be constructed. We have chosen something less abstract through the pragmatically useful grouping of our ethnic families into four substantive categories: (1) early arriving ethnic minorities, (2) recent and continuing ethnic minorities, (3) historically subjugated but volatile ethnic minorities, and (4) socioreligious ethnic minorities.

These categories help sort out the groups, according to several dimensions, but they should in no way be taken as definitive, completely exclusive, or the only way to achieve a useful classification. The most important criterion in the minds of the authors has been that the categories appear to capture a particularly important contingency or group experience that has had a continuing influence upon its collective fate. Let us briefly discuss the scheme that we have chosen:

1. Early Arriving Ethnic Minorities

The importance of this category lies in the time dimension. Each of these ethnic groups has been in this country in substantial numbers for 75 to 100 years. Important questions for the study of these groups relate to the effects of time and generation on the cultural heritage but more particularly as they directly affect family life. The extent to which assimilation and acculturation has had an impact on ethnic identity and lifestyle remains one of the key problems encountered by these groups of people. The first group includes the Polish, Japanese, Italian, Irish, and Chinese American families. Religion plays an important role in all these families, but it is not such a determining factor as for others dealt with in the final section.

2. Recent and Continuing Ethnic Minorities

The three ethnic minorities in this category are the Arab, Greek, and Puerto Rican immigrants who arrived in the late 19th and early 20th centuries. These ethnic groups (who in small numbers may have come to America earlier) are characterized by a sizable number of recent as well as a continuing flow of immigrants. The problems they have faced include adjusting to a modern business cycle and war-plagued industrialized society and to constant infusions of new representatives from their respective countries of origin.

3. Historically Subjugated but Volatile Ethnic Minorities

These groups either preceded the arrival of the "Americans" or arrived later and were immediately or later placed in some form of bondage. Enslaved to the land, alienated from it, or bound in a latter-day peonage, blacks, native

Americans, and Hispanics have in America the darkest and least savory group life histories from which to build viable ethnic cultures. In at least two of these three groups it will be noted that the role of the family, whether truncated or extended, becomes crucial for ethnic survival.

4. Socioreligious Ethnic Groups

The last four groups, the Amish, the Jews, the Mormons, and the French Canadian Americans, are categorized together because their identity and experience have largely been a result of or strongly influenced, if not dominated, by their respective religions. By no means later arrivals, they all sought in America a place to live that kind of social existence in which religion could continue to be vitally conjoined with all aspects of their life and livelihood.

A NOTE ABOUT THE AUTHORS

When we originally conceived the idea of preparing a book on family lifestyles of American ethnic groups, one option was to write the book ourselves. However, the task of understanding and grasping the essence of the historical and cultural experiences of each of the suggested ethnic minorities appeared a virtual impossibility. Rather than embark on what would most likely end up as an exercise in futility, we felt a better choice would be to approach scholars in the field who themselves had researched and experienced the culture of some particular ethnic minority group. The success of this approach may be measured in the fact that in 12 chapters the authors themselves are members of the ethnic group they are writing about, and a number of these are widely recognized in the area of ethnic studies. In the other three ethnic family chapters the authors have spent many years in one way or another concerned about and as students of "the" American family in its common and diverse features.

REFERENCES

Burgess, Ernest, Harvey J. Locke, and Mary M. Thomes. 1963. *The Family* (3rd ed.). New York: American Book.
Cavan, Ruth S. 1969. *The American Family* (4th ed.). New York: Thomas Y. Crowell.
Elkin, Frederick. 1970. *The Family in Canada: An Account of Present Knowledge and Gaps in Knowledge About Canadian Families.* Ottawa: The Vanier Institute of the Family.
Farber, Bernard. 1964. *Family Organization and Interaction.* San Francisco: Chandler.

Fuchs, Victor. 1968. *The Service Economy*. New York: National Bureau of Research. Distributed by Columbia University Press.

Geertz, Clifford. 1963. "The Integrated Revolution," in Clifford Geertz (ed.), *Old Societies and New Societies*. Glencoe, IL: The Free Press.

Glazer, Nathan. 1973. "The Issue of Cultural Pluralism in America Today," in Joseph Ryan (ed.), *White Ethnics: Their Life in Working-Class America*. Englewood Cliffs, NJ: Prentice Hall, pp. 168–177.

———. 1954. "Ethnic Groups in America: From National Culture to Ideology," in Morroe Berger, Theodore Abel, and Charles H. Page (eds.), *Freedom and Control in Modern Society*. New York: Van Nostrand.

Glazer, Nathan, and Daniel P. Moynihan. 1970. *Beyond the Melting Pot* (2nd ed.). Cambridge, MA: M.I.T. Press.

Gordon, Milton. 1964. *Assimilation in American Life*. New York: Oxford University Press.

Gouldner, Alvin. 1970. *The Coming Crisis in Western Sociology*. New York: Basic Books.

Greeley, Andrew M. 1974. *Ethnicity in the United States: A Preliminary Reconnaissance*. New York: John Wiley.

———. 1969. *Why Can't They Be Like Us?* New York: Institute of Human Relations Press.

Ishwaran, K. (ed.). 1971. *The Canadian Family: A Book of Readings*. Toronto and Montreal: Holt, Rinehart and Winston of Canada Ltd.

Kephart, William M. 1972. *The Family, Society and the Individual* (3rd ed.). Boston: Houghton Mifflin.

Novak, Michael. 1973. "Probing the New Ethnicity," in Joseph Ryan (ed.), *White Ethnics: Their Life in Working-Class America*. Englewood Cliffs NJ: Prentice-Hall, pp. 158–167.

Nye, F. Ivan, and Felix Berardo. 1973. *The Family: Its Structure and Interaction*. New York: Macmillan.

Queen, Stuart, and Robert W. Habenstein. 1974. *The Family in Various Cultures* (4th ed.). Philadelphia: Lippincott.

Reiss, Ira. 1971. *The Family System in America*. New York: Holt, Rinehart and Winston.

Rose, Peter I. 1974. *They and We: Racial and Ethnic Relations in the United States* (2nd ed.). New York: Random House.

Wade, Mason (ed.). 1960. *Canadian Dualism*. Toronto: Toronto University Press.

EARLY ETHNIC MINORITIES
(circa 1850–1920)

Polish American Families

The main thrust of this chapter is upon the Polish American family as it exists within the developing and changing Polish ethnic community, an area Dr. Lopata refers to as Polonia. This emphasis is acknowledged to be different from much of the literature on ethnic groups, which is primarily concerned with individualistic assimilation and acculturation, and which attempts to determine the factors that impede or facilitate the absorption of peoples into a society. This chapter focuses on certain background characteristics of Old World Polish culture, especially in its peasant variations and of the historical trends in Polonia, which have created a unique ethnic community that persists into the 1980s. The Polish family must be seen in its relation to the continued existence of the Polish American community.

CHAPTER TWO
BY
HELENA ZNANIECKA LOPATA

HISTORICAL BACKGROUND

Introduction

In spite of the fragmentary and chronologically mixed nature of information about Polish Americans, many observers of the American scene, even social scientists, have drawn numerous generalizations about them and their families. Some of these generalizations contain negatively biased assumptions and statements, often bordering on stereotypes.[1] Such generalizations are especial-

---

[1]Janowitz (1966:xxiii–xxv) reports in his introduction to a collection of works by W. I. Thomas and from the Thomas and Znaniecki's (1918–1920) *Polish Peasant in Europe and America* that one of the main reasons Thomas became interested in studying the assimilation of Poles was "Polish murder," so labeled by the Chicago police. "Boys and young men who were law-abiding or at least conforming would suddenly, with little provocation and no forethought, engage in violent and explosive fights, including attacks on police officers. . . ." That is hardly a sociological analysis. He further states:

> In the lore about W. I. Thomas that grew up among graduate students at the University of Chicago there was a story of how he came upon the use of letters as a crucial research tool. . . . One morning, while walking down a back alley in the Polish community on the West Side of Chicago, he had to sidestep quickly to avoid some garbage which was being disposed of by the direct means of tossing it out the window. In the garbage which fell at his feet were a number of packets of letters. Since he read Polish he was attracted to their contents, and he started to read a bundle which was arranged serially. In the sequence presented by the letters he saw a rich and rewarding account and in time he was led to pursue the personal document as a research tool.

ly prevalent when applied to large numbers of foreign people whose behavior is witnessed from the outside and when its dramatic instances run counter to the value system of the observer. American society has been particularly concerned by the size of its immigration and even internal migration and has tended to label these with value-ladened terms. "Political" immigrations, or those accompanying political upheavals in other societies, are usually seen as involving only upper- and upper-middle-class people. The Cubans coming to America after Castro's revolution were called the "golden immigrants," although many had not been of the upper classes in Cuba. "White Russians" entering after the Bolshevik revolution were identified as mainly "counts and princesses." Migrations classified as "economic" tend to acquire a lower-class stereotype. Polish immigrants coming to America in waves between 1880 and 1914 were labeled as "landless peasants," although members of a variety of peasant subclasses and other major classes were contained in the stream (Szczepanski, 1970; Thomas and Znaniecki, 1918–1920). In addition, peasants were often portrayed as lacking in intelligence and passively obedient to the powers, including the priests (Brunner, 1929). Anyone familiar with Reymont's (1925) *The Peasants* or Thomas and Znaniecki's (1918–1920) description of peasant life in Poland would realize that such a picture of passive peasantry is simply untrue.

Characteristics of the Polish peasant immigrants are not so easily generalized. Although a third of the immigrants at the turn of the century were illiterate, this proportion dropped to 3 percent by 1924 (Lopata, 1976a: 16). The two-thirds who were literate and the 699,372 people who entered America with a Polish identity but without immigrant status cannot be ignored as sources of Polonian life and structure. Among the almost two million immigrants coming to America since 1882 who identified Poland as their country of origin or who were identified as "Polish race or people" were 297,590 people who came as immigrants and later returned to Poland. In addition, as Mostwin (1969, 1971) and others have repeatedly pointed out, the *nowa emigracja* (new emigrants) entering America during and after World War II added further heterogeneity to the population with origins in Poland. Polonia as a superterritorial, complex, and very active community could not have been built and survived for over 100 years had all the immigrants fit the stereotype of the passive peasant that is so often applied to the Polish Americans (Lieberman, 1978).

Now that I have established the impossibility, or at least the danger, of overgeneralizing about the "Polish American family," I proceed cautiously to examine some of the characteristics that different types of Polish families in America may have in common and to discuss some variations.

Polish American Families: Common Themes

Thomas and Znaniecki (1918–1920) were pessimistic about the future of Polish peasant families in America. They foresaw a growing loosening of the ties to the extended families of both the husband and the wife, the village and the parish, resulting in "hedonistic" and immoral behavior and individuated rather than family-based orientation. They witnessed and documented incidents of wives charging husbands in American courts for nonsupport and parents using the police and the courts in an effort to make their children obey and contribute to the economic welfare of the family. They distinguished the following problems (Thomas and Znaniecki, 1918–1920):

> 1. Demoralization of adults: a) economic dependency (on the American welfare system—cases from the archives of United Charities); b) break of the conjugal relation (materials chiefly of the Legal Aid Society): murder (Criminal Court and Coroner's office).
> 2. Demoralization of children (materials from the Juvenile Court): a) vagrancy and dishonesty of boys; b) sexual demoralization of girls.

Their focus upon disorganization, arising from their theoretical perspective and the obvious evidence of conflict in some families recorded by the American agencies, led to a failure to include in *The Polish Peasant in Europe and America* other aspects of Polish American family life. Unfortunately their work has been used by other social scientists and policy planners as reflective of the whole Polonian community.

Several researchers have demonstrated that the predicted dissolution of Polish American families did not take place, at least as far as divorce statistics are concerned. J. L. Thomas (1950), Rooney (1957), and Polzin (1973, 1976) concluded that the main reason high divorce and desertion rates are not true of Polish American families is the strength of the religion, but there appear to be other binding forces that were not dealt with by Thomas and Znaniecki (1918–1920). I will examine some of these forces and the roles of men and women in the Polish American families throughout the life course, as far as data allow.

Historical and Cultural Foundations for Polish American Family Life

Families do not live in a vacuum but within a community and the larger society. Their actions and interactions are patterned by family roles, with obviously idiosyncratic variations growing out of the family history.[2] Family life is embedded in a complex culture, each member holding beliefs, images, expectations, evaluations, and so forth concerning themselves, other family members and the world within which they are living.[3] It is, of course, impossible to determine what aspects of Polish American family life are a consequence of socialization into, and life within, Polish culture, migration experiences, settlement in America, or life in Polonian communities. The members of the *stara emigracja* (old emigration) who were of peasant origin came from rural and agricultural lifestyles, usually into an urbanizing and industrializing world. Some of their problems may be akin to those experienced by rural migrants to urban communities in Poland (Piotrowski, 1966). Yet, the country from which Poles migrated to America changed considerably over the years since the turn of the 20th century, as documented for the remaining population by many Polish rural sociologists (Jagiello-Lysiowa, 1976; Kowalski, 1976; Turowski and Szwengrub, 1976). Other emigrants never experienced Polish culture the way that the peasant segment of the *stara emigracja* had experienced it.[4]

The Polish immigrants to America came from two separated class subcultures, although they shared Polish language, the Polish version of Catholic religion, and many major cultural complexes. The subcultures were actually variations on the major themes, but variations that kept the two groups basically apart in Poland and in America until recent years. The common themes of the emigrants included beliefs in a national character, a system of status competition and the willingness and ability to build a complex ethnic Polonian community with horizontal strata and vertical lines of connection (Lopata, 1976b, Thomas and Znaniecki, 1918–1920). The two groups consisted of the combined, mutually influencing gentry or small nobility and intelligentsia, on the one side, and the various levels of the peasantry, on the other

---

[2]I am using here Znaniecki's (1965) definition of a social role as a set of patterned, functionally interdependent social relations between a social person and a social circle, involving duties and rights.

[3]Studies of the acculturation of a group of people limited to a few items, such as the use of language, religious celebrations, and so forth neglect a very important and more significant aspect of group identity, its feeling and definition of "national character." People who share a belief that they are similar transmit to younger generations this feeling of identity and their whole philosophy of life is incorporated in their child rearing procedures (McCready, 1974). Sandberg (1974) has an extensive set of measures of Polish American ethnicity, but even he does not deal with beliefs as to human nature, Polishness and child rearing methods.

[4]There are frequent comments in the Polonian press and made by social science observers concerning the vast difference in the way most of the *stara emigracja* and the *nowa emigracja* see their homeland, Poland. It would be interesting to compare sociologically family life of former peasants who migrated to Polish cities with that of emigrants to American cities. Bloch (1976) has done that for families remaining in a smaller community in Poland with their relatives in America.

(Szczepanski, 1970). Urban "bourgeois" and the "working class" lifestyles were not highly developed during the time of the mass emigration (Jawlowska and Mokrzycki, 1978). In the decades when most "old emigration" families left Poland, "the social cleavage between peasants and *szlachta* (gentry) was absolute and unbridgeable" (Benet, 1951:33). Each had its own image of the national character, status arenas, and hierarchies—as well as companionate circles of ethclass organization and informal association (Gordon, 1964; Lopata, 1976b).

NATIONAL CHARACTER. The socialization of children and the interaction among adults in Poland and Polonia were, and apparently still are, based upon a strong belief in a national character, admittedly with regional, even community, age, and sex variations. Each believer in the Polish national character affirms its existence, but careful perusal of the literature, including autobiographies, indicates that the content of this alleged character contains few common items when expressed by different people (Super, 1939; Szczepanski, 1970).

Szczepanski (1970: 167) elucidates some of the components of the ideal national character of the upper classes in his *Polish Society:*

> The traditional Polish personality ideal was derived from the culture of the nobility and was composed of such traits as readiness for the defense of the Catholic faith, readiness for the defense of the fatherland, a highly developed sense of personal dignity and honor, a full-blown individualism, an imposing mien, chivalry, intellectual brilliance and dash.

This image contains the moral obligation of members of the Polish national cultural society to develop and perpetuate its culture and to educate potential members into its literary base in an effort to fight denationalization (Znaniecki, 1952). The obligation to fight the three foreign states who partitioned and ruled the Polish political state for 125 years before World War I resulted in numerous uprisings which failed, adding a tragico-romantic element to the upper-class vision of the national character. The intelligentsia's variation on the major theme added a strong intellectual bent—the members of that class seeing themselves as "cultured men" familiar with all aspects of the national Polish culture as well as with the cultures of other nations (Lopata, 1976c; Szczepanski, 1962). This total image was shared by many political emigres and most of the immigrants to America who had been displaced by World War II. The attempt to nationalize the non-upper-class Polish Americans to gain assistance in the struggle for independence capitalized on this romantic image of the Pole.

Most of the peasants who emigrated prior to the First World War did not share the intellectual and nationalistic features in their view of the national character. In fact, they tended to be anti-intellectual, believing that human beings were created for hard physical work. They saw Poles through a mixture of magico-religious prisms, but as basically sinful and evil, or at least weak (Chalasinski, 1946; Finestone, 1964, 1967; Thomas and Znaniecki, 1918–1920). This belief in a basically sinful human nature—the men easily ruled by temper and both sexes by sexual desire and impulsive often unwise action—resulted in relatively harsh methods of socialization of children, different from the patterns evolving in America (Finestone, 1964; Thomas and Znaniecki, 1918–1920).[5]

In spite of these major differences between the upper-class and peasant images of the national character, there were many common elements. Super (1939) [quoted by Lopata (1976b: 114–115)], who considered himself an objective observer, listed characteristics all Poles felt were common to them:

> A strong emphasis on equality within the two main classes with a strong sense of individualism; tolerance of other groups; religiosity of predominantly Catholic identity; idealism, romanticism; love of the soil; a strong family orientation; hospitality; interest in good food and drink of an international flavor; stress on courtesy, etiquette and manner highly developed and strictly followed.

The anthropologist Benet (1951: 216) also pointed to this last-named characteristic, one which Poles are very conscious of, and one which is apparent in the letters contained in *The Polish Peasant in Europe and America* (Thomas and Znaniecki, 1918–1920):

> The Polish peasant is probably the most polite and well mannered man in Europe. Rural etiquette prescribes certain expressions and even certain dialogues for everyday life and it is not permissible to improvise substitutes.

A persistent theme, one constantly repeated in the Polish and Polonian mass media and among Poles when they talk of themselves, passed on from generation to generation, is the emphasis on individualism and competitiveness, within one's own stratum (Benet, 1951: 33):

> Within each class, however, there is an almost fanatical insistence on the equality of individuals. A Pole would rather bow to a foreigner than give authority to one of his own group.

---

[5]Thomas and Znaniecki (1918–1920) apparently believed this image of the Polish peasant in America since they predicted "hedonistic" and noncooperative behavior once the tight controls of village and extended family life were removed. Interestingly enough, there is little concern in sociological literature with the demoralization of upper- and middle-class immigrants.

This belief, in a basically competitive rather than solidified national group, is a basic component of the fabric out of which Polish and Polish American men and women weave their life course.

STATUS COMPETITION. The belief in individualism and competitiveness has evolved and been institutionalized into an elaborate system of status competition that regulates conflict, adds excitement (even joie-de-vivre), and has contributed to keeping the Polonian community and its families together and internally oriented in spite of the disorganization tendencies and gradual Americanization of the culture (Lopata, 1976b). Concern with and activity on behalf of one's "reputation," or position vis-à-vis other members of the community underlies much of traditional village and urban life of Poland, with the *okolica* expanding in size as villages become less isolated in recent years and villagers enter other occupations (Dziewicka, 1976; Jagiello-Lysiowa, 1976; Jawlowska and Mokrzycki, 1978; Kowalski, 1967; Slomczynski and Wesolowski, 1978; Turowski and Szwengrub, 1976). The *okolica* or area within which a person's and a family's reputation is contained can vary from a single village to the whole national culture society, and both Poland and the United States have provided not only arenas but also whole systems of status sources and hierarchies (Thomas and Znaniecki, 1918–1920: 144; Jawlowska and Mokrzycki, 1978). Traditionally, the major source of status has been property, especially land and buildings. Other means of attaining status came from less permanent economic goods, such as farm machinery, animals, products grown or handicrafted and money earned by family members who could gain paid employment. Finally, but also significantly, status evolves from a person's reputation derived from physical appearances, accomplishments, actions, and affiliations. The family is a very important source of status, locating the individual in the community at birth and continuing to contribute to status gain or loss throughout the life course. Spouses and children have a moral obligation to assist each member in the status-building or maintenance process of the family as a unit and individually. Members must continue to earn their right to the family's position and to the cooperative action through their own contributions throughout life. Finestone (1964, 1967) found this family system quite different from that of Italian families, whose right to cooperative membership is acquired at birth and never threatened, even in the face of societally disapproved behavior.

Polish immigrants of all classes brought with them to America this interest in status competition within a self-defined *okolica* and this characteristic may be one of the major reasons why predictions of complete "demoralization" and disorganization of the family and the immigrant group as a whole were not fulfilled. Simultaneously, being a major source of involvement in Polonia, this focus prevented interest in the community's reputation from developing outside of its social boundaries or the use of more popular external status symbols. Resources for upward mobility within American society as a whole were not used in the internal status competition if they did not have a traditional Polish base. This is especially true of the schooling of youth in place of immediate employment when legal requirements were met.

POLONIA AS AN ORGANIZED COMMUNITY. Although they devoted part of their set of volumes on *The Polish Peasant in Europe and America* to the organizations of Polonia, Thomas and Znaniecki (1918–1920) did not fully stress the importance of the local and larger community in providing an organized, normative base for individual and family life. Immigrants to America, even if they came from small villages to large urban centers, seldom arrived and lived as isolated beings in a sea of foreigners. Most came to friends, former neighbors, or kinfolk who were already partially established among other Poles (Lopata, 1976a). These people built churches and schools, organized parishes and neighborhoods, formed a multitude of voluntary organizations—pulling new members into the already existing life. The neighborhoods were woven into local communities in large cities, regional circles and superterritorial complexes (Lopata, 1976b). During the many decades of its growth, Polonia developed multiple webs of companionate circles and services, involving daily contact within local areas, at work, in the church, in stores, and in clubhouses. It is into this organized community that immigrants came. They involved themselves through various family members in all levels of community life, creating new groups through schisms or new interests while continuing interaction with kin and neighbor. Thus, the image of a totally disorganized slum with increasingly demoralized and isolated former peasants as drawn by Thomas and Znaniecki (1918–1920) ignores this fabric of social relations within which the Polish American family carried forth its life course (Suttles, 1968). Undoubtedly, marital and parental conflicts did exist; they were documented for Hamtramck (Wood, 1955), Sundeland (Abel, 1929), and Chicago (Thomas and Znaniecki, 1918–1920), but the families basically survived.

FAMILY LIFE. Families were needed by members not only for involvement in the status competition and for the maintenance of a social life within the *okolica*, but also in everyday existence. Families worked to create a home and a means for having and raising children. Abel (1929: 216) explained that the Polish immigrants who settled in the Connecticut Valley were able to buy up the land at astonishing rates:

The ability of the immigrant to establish himself so quickly and to pay off staggering mortgages in a short time was owing to the cheap labor offered by a numerous family and to the willingness to do hard work, and to his low standard of living.

The neighbors of these immigrants were horrified by this standard of living and the level of child care. The death rate of Polish children was much higher than in neighboring families. Yet, these immigrants and their children (with whom they fought constantly) not only bought land and homes, but built sturdy and sizeable "Polish houses" and parishes. The same was true of Polish families in other parts of America: Chicago (Ozog, 1942), Hamtramck (Wood, 1955), and Buffalo (Obidinski, 1968). In addition, and in spite of their original idea of working hard and saving all the money to return to Poland to buy land (or more land), these people contributed millions of dollars, clothes, and foodstuffs to the Polish fight for independence, Polish care during wars, and rebuilding of the country following wars. Much of that money went to families and home villages, but a considerable amount was sent to the national cultural society at large [see Znaniecki's (1952) discussion of this concept].

Polonian families were originally diversified by social class, region and type of community in Poland and they became increasingly diversified as the Polonian communities expanded in America (Golab, 1977). The more educated and/or affluent immigrants organized a whole range of services and businesses needed by newcomers deprived of the established social institutions "back home." Mobility, geographical and social, was possible, a step at a time, since the new environment freed individuals and families from restrictions imposed by past family reputations, regulations, and occupations. Lack of language skills and opportunities for training outside of a limited number of occupations, however, restricted this mobility for many (Duncan and Duncan, 1968; Hutchinson, 1956; Lieberson, 1963; Miaso, 1971). The insularity of the community prevented the use of American contacts, existing lines of mobility, and status symbols. Thus, the community was built with many layers and companionate circles, becoming relatively self-sufficient and opening opportunities for advancement, but mainly within its own boundaries (Breton, 1964). This community changed over time, modifying traditional family patterns and relations. Unfortunately, we do not know how the tensions and conflicts inevitably produced by migration, problems of settlement, and generational gaps were resolved. The community must have cushioned the effects of migration and change, focusing attention away from home problems, but there is insufficient knowledge available as to the scars and the strengths of family life in Polonia.

THE MODERN POLISH AMERICAN FAMILY

Roles of Women: Growing Up

Polish culture contained, as does any other culture, many assumptions as to the nature and proper roles of women in each major stage of their life course. At the time of the mass migrations, and particularly among the peasant classes many of these assumptions centered around them as sexual objects, actually or potentially. Parents were fearful of girls becoming pregnant before marriage or of developing "loose reputations." Thomas and Znaniecki (1918–1920) devoted a whole section of their Part III on the disorganization of the immigrant to the "sexual immorality of girls," equating it with criminal behavior and the vagabondage of boys.[6] Human character being weak, Polish women were expected to be constantly susceptible to sexual advances, even when married. Strict socialization and control throughout life was their traditional lot.

Peasant families expected girls to continue the work of their mothers—learning to keep house, sew, cook, and take care of younger children (Chalasinski, 1946: Ch. 12). Formal education was not considered important for them because the knowledge and skills they needed could be learned only at home. Furthermore, the girls, just as their brothers, learned to work early in life, contributing what they could to the economic welfare of the family and carrying out tasks around the home and farm (Thomas and Znaniecki, 1918–1920).

Many observers of the Polish American scene reported over the years that this attitude toward women's education was carried over by the peasants to this continent and by parents to their children (Abel, 1929; Obidinski, 1968; Wood, 1955). This does not mean that boys were encouraged to get as much education as possible—only that formal schooling was definitely discouraged for girls. If they had to go to school, it was the parochial, not the public, system that was encouraged. [Parents wanted their girls to be under the close supervision of nuns (Kuznicki, 1978; Miaso, 1971).]

The concern for the morality of Polish American girls extended to their work for pay outside of the home. Nonagricultural families faced a dilemma in that they were very interested in having each member bring in earnings and yet wanted to protect their daughters from temptation and even gossip by keeping them close to home or at least under close supervision. Domestic ser-

---

[6]Actually, this view of the delinquency of girls is not unique to Polonia. Lerman (1973) points out in "Child Convicts" that the American legal system has built its moral code into definitions of delinquent behavior, so that youths can be punished for behavior legally allowed adults. "The vast majority of the girls in the Home (The State Home for Girls) today, as in past years, were accused of misbehavior that would not be considered crimes if committed by adults."

vice was preferred as an occupation for young women because it provided good training for future home roles.

The result of the undervaluation of education for the women of Polish American families is evident in the types of occupation in which they are and have been found. In 1950, foreign-born Polish women in comparison to other foreign-born women, were disproportionately located in occupations such as laborer, operative in factories, and service worker, especially in private service (Hutchinson, 1956: 248). Comparatively few Poles were recorded as clerical workers and professionals. More detailed analyses of job specialization found them disproportionately among charwomen, janitors, sextons, meat cutters, and self-employed managers of wholesale and retail trade. Native-born females of Polish parentage were also disproportionately located among operatives and laborers, with few women in farming, either as farmers or farm laborers, or working in white collar jobs. However, this generation had moved out of service jobs in the private sector. Second-generation Polish American women displayed an even greater occupational concentration than did their first-generation counterparts, and more recent figures document a continuing lag in entrance into white collar occupations, particularly in the professions. Only Spanish and Italian women had lower rates in 1970 (U.S. Bureau of Census, 1971). These statements do not apply to the women of the new emigration, most of whom entered with at least a high school education, many going on to school in America and concentrating in white collar jobs. Throughout Polish history the upper classes have maintained themselves through higher education, often using college as a means of ensuring that their daughters have educated, higher-income-producing husbands. There is recent evidence that Polish American boys and girls have discovered higher education as a major means of upward mobility within American society and that their parents have modified their stance on such schooling (U.S. Bureau of the Census, 1971). One of the reasons for the increasing tolerance by parents of years spent in schooling on the part of the offspring, even daughters, is that the younger generations appear to have won the struggle over their right to keep the money they earn outside of the home for personal use, so that they no longer contribute to the family economic welfare anyway.

THE ROLE OF WIFE.[7] A frequent component of descriptions of Polish and Polish American families is their allegedly total authoritarian and patriarchal nature. Polzin (1976: 109) repeats this imagery as late as 1976: "The

---

[7]Of course, not all Polish women married, a relatively large number of them going instead into Catholic religious orders. Radzialowski (1975) studied the largest of the Slavic teaching orders, the Felician Sisters, and there were several Polish orders and Polish American nuns in mixed orders.

pattern of male dominance with corresponding unquestioning obedience by the wife and children belonged to the internalized norms on expected family behavior brought to this country." Yet, there is much evidence that the status of women in agricultural communities is not that of passive subordinates (Radzialowski, 1977). Their influence within the family is determined by their contribution to its welfare (Sanday, 1974). Farm women make a very visible and important economic addition to this welfare (Thomas and Znaniecki, 1918–1920: 82–83):

> In matters of reciprocal response we find among the Polish peasants the sexes equally dependent upon each other ... under conditions in which the activities of the woman can attain an objective importance more or less equal to those of the man, the greatest social efficiency is attained by a systematic collaboration of men and women in external fields rather than by a division of tasks which limits the woman to "home and children."

Bloch (1976: 5), comparing the situation of women in Polish villages in contrast to American cities, reinforces this point:

> The source of this equality and partnership between husband and wife can be located in the economic nature of the partnership, and particularly in two aspects of village economy. The first of these is the importance of village women to the operation of the house and farm. . . . But even more important than this contribution to subsistence is the strong position of women in terms of the basic wealth of the village—land and buildings.

During times of migration, whether for seasonal work in Europe or America, women were often left on the farms or in other economic situations in charge of economic decisions and property maintenance for extended periods of time without their husband or adult sons (Thomas and Znaniecki, 1918–1920). The pattern of household and family management without the "patriarch" was not unusual, as it had been repeated through centuries of the Crusades, wars, and traveling occupations of men (Origo, 1956).[8] Emigration, however, introduced two major changes in the roles of married women, especially if they moved across the ocean. In the first place, both the husband and the wife deprived themselves of rights of inheritable property, if there were any. Parents usually distributed the property they had inherited and, hopefully, contributed to through their work to the remaining offspring in Poland. The

---

[8]We have a collection of letters exchanged by my great-grandmother and her husband and sons, as well as two years of her diaries during the Franco-Prussian war, which detail her activities in managing the estate. Wars often removed all adult men from their families and businesses, which were then taken over by the women in addition to their usual labor in the home, land, and whatever other enterprises they were engaged in.

28

emigrating children were, in fact, expected to contribute to the family's status by sending money earned in America to be used for increasing property holdings by relatives in Poland. Coming to America with very few possessions, the emigrants faced a second major change of life circumstances, resulting in changes of roles and relationships. Both the husband and the wife, but especially the wife, were freed from the claims on their residence by the older generation whose home or land it had been before retirement. They were also freed from the daily observation and control by the elders of both families. They were independent of the constant supervision of their behavior found in extended kin village life. At the same time, they were deprived of the support network which exists in stable extended families and neighborhoods (Wrobel, 1979: 67–77).

Thomas and Znaniecki (1918–1920: 1705) pointed out that "economic ideals, when they exist, contribute, indeed to the maintenance of family life in general, since the immigrant can seldom imagine an economically perfect life without a family." Yet, these sociologists worried about what they considered to be an inevitable "Break of the Conjugal Relation" (Chapter Three, Volume II), mainly because American law "treats him (the husband) and his wife as isolated individuals, not as primary-group members" (pp. 1750–1751):

> The consciousness that she can have her husband arrested any time she wishes on charges of non-support, disorderly conduct or adultery is for the woman an entirely new experience. Though under the old system she had in fact a part in the management of common affairs almost equal to that of the man, yet in cases of explicit disagreement the man had the formal right of coercing her, whereas she could only work by suggestion and persuasion, or appeal to the large family. Now not only can she refuse to be coerced, since the only actual instruments of coercion which the man has left after the disorganization of the large family— use of physical strength and withholding the means of subsistence—are prohibited by law, but she can actually coerce the man into doing what she wants by using any act of violence, drunkenness or economic negligence of his as pretext for a warrant. No wonder that she is tempted to use her newly acquired power whenever she quarrels with her husband, and her women friends and acquaintances, moved by sex solidarity, frequently stimulate her to take legal action.

This image of the Polish peasant family in America neglects some of the forces actually present in social relations when physical coercion or economic dependence are removed. Divorce and desertion were negatively evaluated in Polonia, strong status handicaps occurring from such behavior. In addition, people needed their spouses, in many ways, even when not fully economically dependent on them.

The economic dependence of Polish and then Polish American wives on their husbands varied considerably. Many women were able to earn substantial economic goods by providing services or making goods even in urban settings. Boarding and rooming houses were kept by many women during the height of immigration since it was mainly men without families who came over and it was some time before they made enough money to send for relatives back home (Zand, 1956). Even new family units remained as boarders with their families, or other people, until they could afford their own dwelling. Davis (1971), writing about *Immigrant Health and the Community* reported that the Poles had the higher percent of households keeping boarders or lodgers of all ethnic groups, the total of 48.4 percent exceeding by far the 32.9 percent average for all foreign groups.

In addition to managing boarding homes for income, many Polish American women cooperated with their husbands in "ma and pa" stores, taverns, or restaurants specializing in Polish food. Each Polonian neighborhood had a number of such businesses requiring work from all family members. Seamstresses and beauticians, piano or English teachers, writers and readers of letters—all these were needed in Polonia and women of the various classes and skills were able to undertake such roles. Such activities were considered appropriate means of contributing to the family's economic status and some of the services were a source of prestige.

Of lower community approval was employment by wives and mothers outside of the home and its environs, especially among men and, worst of all, among people other than Polish Americans (Wrobel, 1979: 76). However, the wish for money was there: first, in order to return to Poland and buy land and homes; later, in order to help people back in the homeland; and, throughout, for material goods for their own use and status, and to offset some of the misgivings about the wife's employment away from the home. Interestingly, the employment of the women was seen by the Polonian community and the wider society as an individual choice so that few adjustments were made to help women manage the dual job of working for pay and managing the home and the family.[9]

THE ROLE OF MOTHER. It is possible that the heavy burdens of either the job–home combination or of full-time homemaking in a large family have taken their toll in the mother–child relation. McCready (1974: 168–169) uses

---

[9]Caroline Bird (1979) details in *The Two-Paycheck Marriage* the difficulties experienced by American women who return to the labor force after having managed the home full time. Their families usually do not distribute the functions of the role of housewife among all members in adjustment to the wife–mother's occupation outside of the home. Sokolowska (1964, 1977) lists extensive resources in Poland developed to help working mothers because that society, unlike America, ideologically wants such members to be in paid employment and because families really need two breadwinners. However, cultural norms of city life, which assigned to the woman the management of the home, still linger, and husband–fathers are reputedly less than egalitarian in sharing work, unless they are of the youngest married generation.

work by Radzialowski (1974) to support his conclusion drawn from a National Opinion Research Center sample that "the mother did not exert a strong influence in the raising of her children because of the dependence on the extended family in the peasant society." McCready found that the mother of Polish American college graduates of 1961 was not as "salient" a parent as she was for other ethnic groups, in that she was not mentioned as frequently as was the father. This was true even of the young women:

> The young Polish women rate themselves high on domestic skills, attractiveness, and sex appeal, indicating that they do espouse the traditional values for women in the society. Their low saliency scores for mother indicate that they have received these values from their fathers rather than emulating their mothers as role models. In other words, they think of themselves as attractive, competent women because their fathers told them they were.

POLISH AMERICAN WOMEN IN THE COMMUNITY. The first- and second-generation Polish American women did not limit their involvements to the home and the family. They were active organizers and participants in voluntary associations and the life of the community. They founded one of the major insurance and financial companies, the Polish Women's Alliance, with branches in many neighborhoods, a feminist newspaper called "The Voice of Polish Women" with "Faith, Enlightenment, Love of the Native Language, Concord, Perseverence" as its motto and education as its major function aside from the economic activity (Radzialowski, 1977: 197). The newspapers and local meetings taught members to be independent and also taught new ways of cooking, cleaning, child care, health, and hygiene (Radzialowski, 1977: 196):

> ... it urged on its members the wisdom of saving for the future, avoiding needless spending, acquiring training and job skills, shunning gambling and excessive use of alcohol and other traits usually subsumed under the misnamed "puritan ethic."

The Polish Women's Alliance had its own doctors, insurance adjusters, teachers and business leaders. It encouraged mothers to seek higher education for their children. Other organizations for women or branches of superterritorial associations and even local groups provided opportunities for leadership roles, help in the schooling of children into Polish language and culture, social contact, and activities. Again, this extensive activity at each level of Polonian life negates the image of passive Polish immigrant women.

THE LATER STAGES OF LIFE. In contrast to the situation which appears to have developed in Poland since World War II, the Polish American working woman does not seem to be able to depend on her mother or mother-in-law to help with the housework or care of the children (Mirowski, 1968; Lobodzinska, 1970, 1974; Piotrowski, 1963; Sokolowska, 1964). Although Polish American widows are more willing to live with a married child, usually a daughter, than are women of similar age and marital status situations among Americans in general, most elderly women who are able to do so choose to live only with their husband or alone if widowed (Lopata, 1977).

American society no longer expects the housing of elderly parents with younger generations, nor heavy household and child care obligations of older women to their adult children (Lopata, 1971, 1973). The history of the society does not provide an ideological base for such action, mainly because of its disapproval until recent years of the employment of married women who would then require babysitting assistance. In addition, older women are economically independent in many cases, albeit often living on very limited incomes and within narrow life spaces (Chevan and Korson, 1972; Lopata, 1973, 1979). Although often residing in the poorer sections of towns no longer inhabited by Polish Americans, due to death of older generations and the upward and outward mobility of younger ones, the older women tend to own their homes. These homes could not bring them sufficient monies to afford moving elsewhere, and their roots and unfamiliarity with life outside of the neighborhood preclude such resettlement. These elderly widows are often strongly involved with one of their children but in an "intimacy at a distance" manner typical of the one reported by Rosenmayr and Kockeis (1963) for the elderly in Vienna, Austria [see also Bild and Havighurst (1976) and Siemaszko (1976)].

The social class background of older Polish American women influences significantly their social life space and support systems, the middle- and upper-class women drawing on a much wider set of personal and community resources. However, even the lower-class women retain active involvement in voluntary associations, being thereby different from their counterparts in other ethnic and American communities. The lifelong habit of involvement in the community is broken only if friends and familiar neighbors die or move away; the church loses its Polish American parishioners, clubs move out of the area, and the family disperses (Lopata, 1977, 1979; Ozog, 1942; Sanders and Morawska, 1975; Wood, 1955). The consequences of the harshness of life for the immigrant and even the second-generation women is reflected in their health problems and in the inability to retain contact with siblings and children living at inconvenient distances (Lopata, 1973, 1979).

There is insufficient evidence as to the circumstances of the latter stages of the life course of the "new emigration" women to determine how they are different from other Polish women in America at the present time. The circumstances under which this immigration entered the United States would lead us to assume that few could bring their older parents over [see also Mostwin (1969, 1971)]. After all, ex-combatants and displaced persons came from places other than Poland during and after World War II, and immigration directly from that country has expanded only in recent years. The new emigration is aging, but we know little about this process, since it is numerically too small to be located through anything but selective sampling.

The Roles of Men

The lives of immigrant men in America also varied considerably according to the resources with which they entered. The masses of Polish immigrants entering at the turn of the 20th century were young men who came from a village background and with relatively little education. They obtained jobs in the mines of Pennsylvania, in the steel mills or meat-packing houses of Chicago, on farms, or in other locations in which knowledge of English and advanced skills in the industrialized or service sectors of the economy were not needed. Boarding at first in Polish homes in the community, they saved money and sent for their wives and children, or siblings. Some of the more affluent went back to Poland to help the migration process or to find a wife. Women of Polish background were scarce in America during the early years of Polish immigration. As late as 1920, there were 131 males per 100 females, but the ratio decreased to 116.1 in 1930, 110.4 in 1940 and 101.8 by 1950 (Hutchinson, 1956: 19). Men who married daughters of already established families received help in establishing themselves, but tended to develop an egalitarian, or at least not a strongly patriarchal family demeanor, since they did not have their own families to back them up (Zand, 1956).

HUSBANDS AND FATHERS. Polish male immigrants worked hard, long hours, often unable to spend much time with their children. The father's function as the main disciplinarian was the only one known to many children and his European style of relating to them often created strong conflict. The second-generation's young men were reputedly involved in street gang behavior (Thrasher, 1927; Fleis-Fava, 1950). Taft (1936: 723) felt obliged to point out to American criminologists that the first generation of Polish immigrants had very low criminal records and that the age distribution of the second-generation males pushed up the rate for the whole immigrant group. Polonia contained a disproportionate number of young men in the "criminally significant" ages. Conflict with the father arose not only from the son's delinquent behavior, but also from his unwillingness to contribute to the family's social status by turning over his earnings for family use (Thomas and Znaniecki, 1918–1920; Wood, 1955). Thomas and Znaniecki (1918–1920) reported fre-

33

quent and public disagreement between fathers and their children over economic matters. Finestone (1964, 1967) found that family members would completely ignore members who had been sent to prison for criminal activity. They had to reestablish their relations by promising not to disgrace the family again after they were released. This finding adds weight to the thesis of the importance of the status competition to Polish American families.

Polonia, as an organized community with many mass communication media, also completely ignored problems of juvenile delinquency or criminality. No organization was set up to help the youth or adults in serious trouble and the newspapers did not make mention of it, even in face of American reports. Wood (1955) documents facts of criminal activity never discussed in Polonia except as part of the natural flow of life. Yet, whatever gang fights or other juvenile delinquent behavior the second generation of Polonian young men were involved in, it seemed to have worked out by the time they reached adulthood.

The second-generation Polonian men remained organizationally active, although to a lesser extent in ethnic communities than had their parents (Emmons, 1971; Galush, 1975; Obidinski, 1968; Sandberg, 1974). Yet, Polish American men did not experience much intergenerational occupational mobility (Duncan and Duncan, 1968; Greeley and Rossi, 1968; U.S. Bureau of the Census, 1971). Hutchinson (1956: 248) found the foreign-born Polish males in service, operative, and laborer jobs in metal industries. Their specific occupations included, disproportionately, tailors and furriers, cleaners and porters, and self-employed managers. The native born of foreign-born parents were employed most frequently as operatives and laborers, less frequently than other groups as professional workers, managers, farmers and service employees, or sales workers. They were even more occupationally concentrated than the second generation of most other foreign-stock Americans. Duncan and Duncan (1968) concluded that the Poles "suffer a modest handicap" in achieving upward mobility from the first job to the current one by American standards. The main reason for this is that sons tended to follow their fathers in the type of job they entered among the Polish Americans more than among other ethnic groups currently in the work force (p. 362).

By 1961, Polish American fathers seem to have developed better relations with their children, or at least with daughters, than prior researchers indicated. As mentioned before, it was the father, not the mother, who was listed as having more influence upon the lives of female college graduates (McCready, 1974). McCready (1974: 167) seems to uphold the patriarchal image of the Polish American father:

All the members of the post-migration Polish family exhibited a concern for the well-being of the father, who seemed to have suffered most in the move from vil-

34

lage to city. The literature on the Polish family in America describes two types of Polish father. One was the man who had been a strong patriarchal figure in Poland, was unable to maintain that role in the new country, and became a dependent person. Warner reviewed literature that indicated that this type of Polish father eventually became a child to his own children. The children were his disciplinarians and protectors. The second type was the man who had been a strong patriarchal figure in Poland and was able to maintain that role in this country.

This is a strongly bifurcated picture of the Polish elderly man in America, seen in isolation from other relations and the community. However, Lieberman (1978) also reports high incidence of mental illness and withdrawal into passivity vis-à-vis the rest of the family on the part of men who expected to function as patriarchs in relations with their children, but who did not have the resources to carry off such relations. Wrobel (1979: 76) found Detroit men "feeling personally inadequate" because of the kind of work they did and their inability to better their "lot in life."

The "new emigration" men, who entered America with more education and occupational skills and who settled mainly away from the established Polonian communities, may have also experienced troubles with their offspring as the latter more rapidly absorbed American values, but the problems do not appear to be as severe as with former peasant families (Mostwin, 1969, 1971). The recorded violence of temper of Polish peasant and lower-class men, especially explosive when combined with alcohol, may easily have been the consequence of frustration over the lack of resources to lead the type of life and relate with others as they had been socialized (Thomas and Znaniecki, 1918–1920; Janowitz, 1966). More educated and culturally less insulated men may have had more resources and more tolerance of the changing behaviors of family members. Second-generation men of either emigration may have engaged in less conflict with their children because of the remembered problems with their fathers. At least, the few studies which focused on intergenerational family relations report less attitudinal and value differences than reported for the first-generation immigrants.

CHANGE AND ADAPTATION

There are many people living in the United States who could be called Polish Americans because their parents or grandparents, or great-grandparents came from Poland, but who have completely obliterated this identification. These people cannot be identified in any way by census-takers or sociologists, especially if they have changed originally Polish sounding names. Louis Adamic observed the name-changing tendency as early as 1942 in his *What's Your Name?* Several social scientists studied this behavior among

"Poles and Polish Americans [who] seem impelled to more changing than any other group" [(Kotlarz, 1963: 1); see also Borkowski (1963) and Zagraniczny (1963)]. Kotlarz (1963) estimated in 1963 that, of about 300,000 Polish Americans living in the Detroit area, about 3,000 modified their names annually (1963: 1–4). The Polonian press occasionally reports that this process has stopped and that some younger members of Polish American families are going back to the original name and its spelling. It is almost impossible to determine the extent of either direction of name change.

There is a second layer of Polish American families whose members have some identification with their ethnic group and who belong to some organizations within Polonia, but who otherwise lead ordinary "American" lives. Some studies pick up traces of familial or religious attitudes that harken back to prior generations' culture, but items and complexes vary by family. There are also Poles in America who identify themselves as both Poles and Americans but not as Polish Americans, who tend to have limited involvement in specialized organizations and friendships, but who otherwise live middle- or upper-middle class lives (Mostwin, 1969, 1971). Both types of this second layer of involvement in Polonian life are really peripheral to it because the community could not depend on these families to maintain itself. A third layer of Polish American families is more involved in more of the ethnic community activities than the other two, although this varies by age, education, generation, and area (Galush, 1975; Obidinski, 1968; Sandberg, 1974). Some Polish Americans still reside in the heart of the remaining neighborhoods, without speaking English and with restricted lives. Few middle-generation-controlled families are so located. Others live Polonian lives by being involved in superterritorial organizations, in informal contact with other leaders, living their "ethnicity" almost professionally. The families that have such strong ties are usually controlled by second-generation men or women, with occasional involvement and passing of status and ethnicity to the youth. Some of Polonia's life has been taken over by the families of the new emigration.

Conclusions

The heterogeneity of structure, interaction and cultural base for Polish American families lies in their original variation when they came to America and in the divergence of paths they followed. The tendency of most social scientists is to focus on the large mass of peasants who migrated before World War I and who brought over other family members before the closedown of the flood through American legislation. It is they who were studied through their processes of "adjustment" or "disorganization," with frequent reports of interfamilial and intrafamilial conflict. Relations of men and women at all stages of life underwent change, often against the wishes of participants, as such change rarely hits the whole family at the same time. Members who benefitted from the village family system had the most to lose when other persons refused to follow traditional norms. Yet family members needed each other rather desperately, and the growing community siphoned some of the hurt and conflict by drawing attention to the interfamily status competition. Life in Polonia was very involved and complex, providing many opportunities for individualistic as well as cooperative identity and status.

Little is actually known of the processes by which first-generation families worked out the conflicts or at least tensions between husband and wife and of each parent with each child. Second-generation children, especially the boys, often expressed their frustrations by moving out into the streets with peers. Most grew up leading "normal" lower- or lower-middle class lives within or outside of Polonian neighborhoods. The women tended to follow the traditional life course of American urbanites, except that many had to work outside of the home for financial reasons, in spite of community disapproval, and except that, at all class levels, they were more organizationally active than is generally true of their non-Polish counterparts. The status competition and community life, as well as their control over their own homes in the absence of a tightly controlling family gave them more independence and power in the family than is usually attributed to women in traditionally patriarchal cultures. Marital conflict appears to have been strong in some families, particularly of the first and early second generations, but it did not result in high divorce rates for a variety of reasons. The older generations of Polish Americans tend to live independently, although there appears to be a certain segment of the male population that suffers psychological problems from the strain of migration and adjustment to life in America.

Upward mobility within Polonia and out of it is increasing in recent years so that children or grandchildren of peasant families are joining the Polish-Americans who inherited, or built up in the past, higher status. Most third- and fourth-generation Polish American families are lost to sociological knowledge, especially when they do not identify with this ethnic group in responses to census and other survey questions. Some of the youth are now developing an interest in Poland and its national culture, an interest expressed in a desire to travel to their grandparents' or great-grandparents' homeland and the taking of Polish courses in schools.

REFERENCES

Abel, Theodore. 1929. "Sundeland: A study of change in the group line of Poles in New England Farming Community," in Edmund De. S. Brunner (ed.), *Immigrant Farmers and Their Children*. Garden City, NY: Doubleday, pp. 213–243.
Adamic, Louis. 1942. *What's Your Name?* New York: Harper and Brothers.

Benet, Sula. 1951. *Song, Dance and Customs of Peasant Poland.* New York: Roy.

Bild, Bernice R., and Robert Havighurst. 1976. "Senior citizens in great cities: The case of Chicago." Special issue, *The Gerontologist,* 16(1) (February), part II.

Bird, Caroline. 1979. *The Two-paycheck Marriage.* New York: Rawson Wade Publishers.

Bloch, Harriet. 1976. "Changing domestic roles among Polish immigrant women." *The Anthropological Quarterly,* 49(1) (January): 3–10.

Borkowski, Thomas. 1963. "Some patterns in Polish surname changes." *Polish American Studies,* 20(1) (January–June): 14–16.

Borun, Thaddeus (Compiler). 1946. *We the Milwaukee Poles.* Milwaukee: Mowiny Publishing Co.

Breton, Raymond. 1964. "Institutional completeness of ethnic communities and the personal relations of immigrants." *American Journal of Sociology,* LXX(2) (September): 193–205.

Brozek, Andrzej. 1977. *Polonia Amerykanska, 1854–1939.* Warszawa: Wydawnictwo Interpress.

Brunner, Edmund De. S. (ed). 1929. *Immigrant Farmers and Their Children.* Garden City, NY: Doubleday.

Chalasinski, Josef. 1946. *Mlode Pokolenie Chlopow.* Rzym: Wydawnicto Polskiej YMCA Przy APW.

———. 1976. "The young rural generation in the Polish peoples republic," in J. Turowski and L. M. Szwengrub (eds.), *Rural Social Change in Poland.* Ossolineum: The Polish Academy of Sciences Press, pp. 251–277.

Chevan, A., and H. Korson. 1972. "The widowed who live alone: An examination of social and demographic factors." *Social Forces,* 51: 45–53.

Cohler, Bertram, and Morton A. Lieberman. 1977. "Ethnicity and personal adaptation." *International Journal of Group Tensions,* 7 (3–4): 20–41.

Davis, Michael M., Jr. 1971. In William S. Bernard (ed.), *Immigrant Health and the Community.* Montclair, NJ: Patterson, Smith. (Originally published in 1921.)

Duncan, Beverly, and Otis Dudley Duncan. 1968. "Minorities and the process of stratification." *American Sociological Review,* 33(8) (June): 356–364.

Dziewicka, Maria. 1976. "Dual occupation in Polish agriculture," in Jan Turowski and Lili Maria Szwengrub (eds.), *Rural Social Change in Poland.* Ossolineum: The Polish Academy of Sciences Press, pp. 251–277.

Emmons, Charles F. 1971. "Economic and political leadership in Chicago's Polonia: Some sources of ethnic persistence and mobility." Unpublished dissertation. Chicago: University of Illinois, Circle Campus.

Finestone, Harold. 1964. "A comparative study of reformation and recidivism among Italians and Polish adult male criminal offenders." Unpublished dissertation. Chicago: University of Chicago.

———. 1967. "Reformation and recidivism among Italian and Polish criminal offenders." *American Journal of Sociology,* 72(6) (May).

Fleis-Flava, S. 1950. "The Relationship of Northwestern University Settlement to the Community." Unpublished Master's Thesis, Department of Sociology, Northwestern University.

Galush, W. T. 1975. "Forming Polonia: A Study of Four Polish-American Communities, 1880–1940." Unpublished dissertation, Department of History. University of Minnesota.

Golab, Caroline. 1977. *Immigrant Destinations.* Philadelphia: Temple University Press.

Gordon, Milton. 1964. *Assimilation in American Life.* New York: Oxford University Press.

Greeley, Andrew. 1971. "Ethnicity as an influence on behavior," in Otto Feinstein (ed.), *Ethnic Groups in the City.* Lexington, MA: Lexington Books.

———. 1974. *Ethnicity in the United States.* New York: John Wiley.

Greeley, Andrew M., and Peter H. Rossi. 1968. *The Education of Catholic Americans.* Garden City, NY: Anchor Books, Doubleday and Company.

Greene, Victor R. 1968. *The Slavic Community on Strike: Immigrant Labor in Pennsylvania Anthracite.* Notre Dame, IN: University of Notre Dame Press.

Hutchinson, E. P. 1956. *Immigrants and Their Children, 1950–.* New York: John Wiley.

Jagiello-Lysiowa E. 1976. "Transformation of the way of life of the rural community," in Jan Turowski and Lili Maria Szwengrub (eds.), *Rural Social Change in Poland.* Warszawa, Ossolineum: The Polish Academy of Sciences Press, pp. 123–138.

Jakubczak, Franciszek. 1968. "Pol wieku badan nad rodzina chlopska w Polsce." *Przeglad Socjologiczny,* Lodz 22, No. 2: 106–129.

Janowitz, Morris (ed.). 1966. *W. I. Thomas: On Social Organization and Social Personality.* Chicago: University of Chicago Phoenix Books.

Jawlowska, Aldona, and Edmund Mokrzycki. 1978. "Styles of life in Poland: A viewpoint on typology," in The Polish Sociological Association, *Social-Structure: Polish Sociology 1977.* Warszawa, Zaklad Narodowy Imienia Ossolinskich: Wydawnictwo Polsiej Akademii Nauk, pp. 93–107.

Kotlarz, Robert J. 1963. "Writings about the changing of Polish names in America." *Polish American Studies,* 20(1) (January– June): 1–4.

Kowalski, Mieczyslaw. 1967. "Basic directions of changes in rural life system in Poland." Acta Universitatis Lodziensis, *Zeszyty Naukowe Uniwersytetu Lodzkiego Nauki Ekonomiczne i Socjologiczne,* Seira III (10): 5–29.

Kusielewicz, Eugene. 1974. "On the condition of Polish culture in the United States." *The Kosciuszko Foundation Monthly Newsletter,* 29(2) (October): 2–6.

Kuznicki, Ellen Marie. 1978. "The Polish American parochial schools," in Frank Mocha (ed.), *Poles in America.* Stevens Point, WI: Worzalla Publishing Co.

Lerman, Paul. 1973. "Child convicts," in Helena Z. Lopata (ed.), *Marriages and Families.* New York: D. Van Nostrand, 285–294.

Lieberman, Morton A. 1978. "Social and psychological determinants of adaptation," *International Journal of Aging and Human Development,* 9(2).

Lieberson, S. 1963. *Ethnic Patterns in American Cities.* New York: Free Press.

Lobodzinska, Barbara. 1970. *Malzenstwo w Miescie.* Warszawa: Panstwowe Wydawnictwo Naukowe.

———. 1974. *Kodzina w Polsce.* Warszawa: Wudawnictwo Interpress.

Lopata, Helena Znaniecka. 1971. "Living arrangements of urban widows and their married children." *Sociological Focus,* 5(1): 41–61.

———. 1973. *Widowhood in an American City.* Cambridge, MA: Schenkman.

———. 1976a. "Polish immigration to the United States of America: Problems of estimation and parameters." *The Polish Review,* 21(4): 85–108.

———. 1976b. *Polish Americans: Status Competition in an Ethnic Community.* Englewood Cliffs, NJ: Prentice-Hall.

————. 1976c. "Members of the Intelligentsia as developers and disseminators of cosmopolitan culture," in Aleksander Gella (ed.), *The Intelligentsia and the Intellectuals*. Beverly Hills, CA: Sage Publications, pp. 59–78.

————. 1977. "Widowhood in Polonia." *Polish American Studies,* 34(2) (Autumn): 5–25.

————. 1979. *Women as Widows: Support Systems.* New York: Elsevier.

Lopata, Helena Znaniecka, and Kathleen Fordham Norr. 1979. "Changing commitment of women to work and family roles and their future consequences to the Social Security Administration." Chicago: Loyola University of Chicago.

McCready, William. 1974. "The persistence of ethnic variation in American families," in Andrew Greeley (ed.), *Ethnicity in the United States.* New York: John Wiley, pp. 156–176.

Miaso, J. 1971. "Z Dziejow Oswiaty Polskiej w Stanach Zjednoczonych." *Problemy Polonii Zajzanichzhej,* 4: 19–49.

Mirowski, Wlodzimierz. 1968. *Migracje do Warszawy.* Warszawa: Zaklad Narodowy im Ossolinskich, Wydawnictwo Polskiej Akademii Nauk.

Mostwin, Danuta. 1969. "Post World War II Polish immigrants in the United States." *Polish American Studies,* 26(2): 5–14 (Autumn).

————. 1971. "The transplanted family, a study of social adjustment of the Polish immigrant family to the United States after the Second World War." Ann Arbor, MI: University Microfilms.

Obidinski, Eugene. 1968. "Ethnic to status group: A study of Polish Americans in Buffalo." Unpublished dissertation. New York: State University of New York Microfilms.

Origo, Iris. 1956. *The Merchant of Prato, Francesco di Marco Datini: 1355–1410.* New York: Alfred A. Knopf.

Ozog, Julius J. 1942. "A study in Polish home ownership in Chicago." Unpublished master's thesis. Chicago: University of Chicago.

Piotrowski, Jerzy. 1963. "*Praca Zawodowa Kobiety a Rodzina.* Warszawa: Ksiazka i Wiedza.

Piotrowski, Waclaw. 1966. "Life and work of rural migrants in urban communities." *The Polish Sociological Bulletin,* 2:149–158.

Pohoski, Michael. 1974. "Interrelation between social mobility of individuals and groups in the process of economic growth in Poland," in *Polish Sociological Association: Polish Sociology.* Warszawa: Ossolineum.

Polzin, Theresita. 1973. *The Polish Americans.* Pulaski: Franciscan Publishers.

————. 1976. "The Polish American family." *The Polish Review,* 21(3): 103–122.

Radzialowski, Thaddeus. 1974. "The view from a Polish ghetto." *Ethnicity,* 1974. 1(2) (July): 125–150.

————. 1975. "Reflections on the history of the Felicians." *Polish American Studies* 32 (Spring): 19–28.

————. 1977. "Immigrant nationalism and feminism: Glos Polek and the Polish Women's Alliance in America, 1898–1917." *Review Journal of Philosophy and Social Science,* 2(2): 183–203.

Reymont, Ladislas. 1925. *The Peasants: Fall, Winter, Spring, Summer.* New York: Knopf.

Rooney, Elizabeth. 1957. "Polish Americans and family disorganization." *The American Catholic Sociological Review,* 18 (March): 47–51.

Rosenberg, Charles (ed.). 1975. *The Family in History*. Philadelphia: University of Pennsylvania Press.

Rosenmayr, Leopold, and E. Kockeis. 1963. "Propositions for a sociological theory of aging and the family." *International Social Science Journal*, 15: 410–426.

Sanday, Peggy R. 1974. "Female status in the public domain," in Z. Rosaldo and L. Lamphere (eds.), *Women, Culture and Society*. Stanford: Stanford University Press, pp. 189–206.

Sandberg, Neil C. 1974. *Ethnic Identity and Assimilation: The Polish American Community*. New York: Praeger Publishers.

Sanders, Irwin, and Eva T. Morawska. 1975. *Polish American Community Life: A Survey of Research*. Boston University: Community Sociology Training Program.

Siemaszko, Maria. 1976. "Kin relations of the aged: possible impact on social service planning." Unpublished master's thesis. Chicago: Loyola University of Chicago.

Slomczynski, Kazimierz, and Wlodzimierz Wesolowski. 1978. "Theoretical orientation in the study of class structure in Poland, 1945–1975," in *Polish Sociological Association, Social Structure: Polish Sociology, 1977*. Warszawa, Zaklad Narodowy Imienia Ossolinskich, Wydawnictwo Polskiej Akademii Nauk, pp. 7–31.

Sokolowska, Magdalena. 1964. *Kobieta Pracujaca*. Warsaw: Wiedza Powszechna.

———. 1977. "Poland: women's experience under Socialism," in Janet Zollinger Giele and Audrey Chapman Smock (eds.), *Women: Roles and Status in Eight Countries*. New York: John Wiley, 347–381.

Super, P. 1939. *The Polish Tradition*. London: Maxlove Publ. Co.

Suttles, Gerald. 1968. *The Social Order of the Slum*. Chicago: University of Chicago Press.

Symmons-Symonolewicz, Konstantin. 1978. "Polish contributions to American scholarship: The fields of sociology and cultural anthropology 1918–1976," in Frank Mocha (ed.), *Poles in America: Bicentennial Essays*. Stevens Points, WI: Worzalla Publishing Company.

Szczepanski, Jan. 1962. "The Polish Intelligentsia: Past and present." *World Politics*, 16(3) (April): 406–420.

———. 1970. *Polish Society*. New York: Random House.

Taft, D. 1936. "Nationality and Crime". *American Journal of Sociology* (August), 1–4, 724–736.

Thomas, John L. 1950. "Marriage prediction in the Polish peasant." *American Journal of Sociology*, 55 (May): 573–583.

———. 1956. *American Catholic Family*. Englewood Cliffs, NJ: Prentice-Hall.

Thomas, William I. and Florian W. Znaniecki. 1918–1920. *The Polish Peasant in Europe and America*. Boston: Richard G. Badger. (Reprinted, New York: Dover 1958.)

Thrasher, F. M. 1927. *The Gang: The Study of 1,313 Gangs in Chicago*. Chicago: University of Chicago Press.

Turowski, Jan, and Lilli Maria Szwengrub (eds.). 1976. *Rural Social Change in Poland*. Warsaw: Ossolineum, The Polish Academy of Sciences Press.

U.S. Bureau of the Census: Current Population Reports, Series P-20. 1971. *Characteristics of the Population by Ethnic Origin, November 1969*. Washington, DC: Government Printing Office.

Warner, Lloyd W. 1945. *Yankee City Series*, Volume III. New Haven: Yale University Press.

41

Wojniusz, Helen K. 1976. "Ethnicity and other variables in the analysis of Polish American women." *Polish American Studies,* 39 (Autumn): 26–37.

Wood, Arthur Evans. 1955. *Hamtramck: Then and Now.* New York: Bookman Associates.

Wrobel, Paul. 1979. *Our Way: Family, Parish and Neighborhood in a Polish-American Community.* Notre Dame IN: University of Notre Dame Press.

Zagorski, Krzysztof. 1974. "Social mobility in Poland," in *Polish Sociological Association: Polish Sociology.* Warszawa: Ossolineum.

Zagraniczny, Stanley J. 1963. "Some reasons of Polish surname changes" *Polish American Studies,* 20(1) (January–June): 12–14.

Zand, Helen Sankiewicz. 1956. "Polish family folkways in the United States." *Polish American Studies,* 13(3–4) (July–December): 77–88.

Znaniecki, Florian W. 1952. *Modern Nationalities.* Urbana, IL: University of Illinois Press.

———. 1965. *Social Relations and Social Roles.* San Francisco: Chandler Publ.

The Japanese American Family

The Japanese American family has been credited with providing the structure, the socialization and control that has resulted in remarkably low rates of dysfunctional behavior. The family has also been an important factor in encouraging a high achievement oriented population. Exposure to the American system has resulted in structural changes that resemble the American bilateral system. However, despite the increased acculturation of each generation, the importance of the family persists and in some cases has even increased. If past experiences can be taken as a guide, the Japanese American family will retain a style that will continue as a combination of the Japanese and the American cultures.

CHAPTER THREE
BY
AKEMI KIKUMURA AND
HARRY H. L. KITANO

INTRODUCTION

The Japanese American family is the product of the interaction of the Japanese and American cultures. The immigrants brought with them the culture of *Tokugawa* (1603–1868) and *Meiji* (1868–1912) Japan. They entered the United States in the late 19th and early 20th centuries, primarily along the Pacific Coast and Hawaii, immediately greeted by anti-oriental hostility. They came to the United States for the same reasons as most other immigrants: better jobs, better lives, and an escape from harsh home conditions. However, there was one factor that made them unique: They came from a nation that would eventually be at war with the United States. As a consequence, the Japanese immigrants and their children became victims of a mass incarceration, an episode unique in American immigrant history.

HISTORICAL BACKGROUND

The significant immigration of the Japanese to America began in the 1890s. Many came with the intention of staying for a few years and making enough money to return to their homeland. The young men came first, settling mainly along the Pacific Coast. The majority of available jobs were to be had in domestic services and farm labor. Others found jobs in contract gardening, canneries, railroad construction, lumber mills, mining, logging camps, fishing, and small, ethnic-oriented businesses like restaurants, hotels, markets, and barbershops.

Although an unknown number went back to Japan, a larger number gave up the sojourner status to make a permanent home in the United States. Prejudice, discrimination, the lack of opportunities to meet American women, and personal preference led the vast majority of these young males to "return" to Japan when thinking of marriage and a family: Those who were already married sent for their wives; others made a trip home to secure a bride. Another method was the "picture brides," a process which involved an exchange of pictures between potential spouses. Scrupulous care was taken by the go-between who checked the personal characteristics and family background of each party. This practice, which was essentially an extension of social customs in Japan and recognized by Japanese law, was seized upon as "immoral" by American exclusionists and the practice was terminated after 1921 (Ichihashi, 1969). The importing of Japanese women was a critical factor in shaping the Japanese immigrant toward a more "normal" family life. With a wife there would be children, making a stronger stake in remaining and adapting to the new country.

Other racial obstacles riddled the lives of the *Issei* (first-generation of Japanese immigrants) in their new country. The California Land Laws of 1913 and 1920 limited and later prevented the *Issei* from owning or leasing land. It was an effort by the dominant group to drive the Japanese out of agriculture (Ichihashi, 1969). Moreover, the *Issei* were prevented from obtaining United States citizenship, without which they could not even be tenant farmers. Many put their land holdings under the nominal ownership of their children but legal difficulties were abundant.

By 1924, the exclusionists were successful in their attempts to stop the flow of Japanese immigration. The suspension of Chinese immigration had already been accomplished by the Exclusion Act of 1882, and the Immigration Act of 1924, aimed at "aliens ineligible for citizenship," effectively prohibited further Japanese immigration to the United States.

The *Nisei,* or the second generation, were the American-born children of the *Issei.* They had an important advantage over their parents: American citizenship. However, this factor was of little significance after the Japanese attack on Pearl Harbor on December 7, 1941, as they were herded into concentration camps, along with their alien parents, under Executive Order 9066 issued by President Franklin D. Roosevelt on February 19, 1942. The decision to incarcerate 110,000 individuals of Japanese ancestry was supported by public sentiment and by the rulings of the U.S. Supreme Court so that most Japanese families lived under the control of first the United States Army and later the War Relocation Authority, from 1942 to 1945. (TenBroek, Barnhart, and Matson, 1968).

In spite of their early historical experiences, including discrimination, prejudice, and a forced wartime evacuation, by the 1970s the Japanese were looked upon as one of America's most "successful" minorities. Although there was disagreement within the Japanese American community as to the extent of this "success," some writers (Petersen, 1971) have referred to them as a "model minority."

Part of the economic mobility of the Japanese American family has been explained by the speed of their acculturation (Broom and Kitsuse, 1955; Caudill, 1952; DeVos, 1955; Kitano, 1976) and the compatibility of American and Japanese values, such as politeness, diligence, emphasis on long term goals, respect for authority and parental wishes, the importance of keeping up appearances, and the use of adaptive mechanisms such as sensitivity to cues from the external world and suppression of desires and emotional feelings (Caudill, 1952). It is important to emphasize that Caudill wrote about the compatability of the values, rather than their similarity.

The wartime evacuation was another factor in the Japanese American's speedy acculturation (Kitano, 1976). The incarceration broke up the ghettos in which the Japanese were previously concentrated, scattered them into parts of the country that formerly did not have a Japanese population, exposed them to American ways, dissolved old institutions and structures, and reordered the family structure by putting more power into the hands of the *Nisei*.

Perhaps the unit most responsible for integrating the conflicting demands of Japanese and American cultures is the family. To better understand the Japanese Americans and their present family structure and the cultural continuities and discontinuities from Japan, it will be useful to examine briefly the pre-War Japanese family system and the social structure in which the *Issei* were reared.

TRADITIONAL JAPANESE SOCIETY AND FAMILY

Feudal Japan

The *Issei*, for the most part, were the first generation to be born after the *Tokugawa* feudal era (1603–1868). Even in the wake of rapid industrialization and a conscious effort toward modernization, many of the old traditions and values were tenaciously preserved. It was these old customs and patterns of social behavior, developed over approximately 300 years of Japan's feudal period, that the *Issei* tried to impart to their children, the *Nisei.*

During the long period of *Tokugawa* feudalism, a rigid hierarchical social system similar to a caste system based on hereditary and occupational endowment had developed. Society was divided into three classes: The first was the ruling class, the warriors, and administrators; the second was the ruled class, which included farmers, independent and tenant landowners, artisans, and merchants; and the third were the outcastes, the *Eta* ("pollution abundant") and *Hinin* ("nonhuman"). This outcaste class engaged in the most "lowly" occupations of begging, entertainment, working for the police as prison guards and executioners, and makers of leather goods [in the Shinto religion, contact with anything dealing with death or blood was polluting (DeVos and Wagatsuma, 1966)].

This long period of feudalism, conditioned by a rigid class stratification, resulted in "the general disposition to accept authority, formalization of status, glorification of military values and codes of the *samurai* (warriors), collectivity-orientation, and an extreme 'other directed' definition of situations" (Iga, 1957:274).

The social values crystallized during this period were very important for the moral foundation of modern Japan. The *Meiji* government decided to readopt Confucian values as the foundation of moral education, in conjunction with universal education, so that these values permeated the lowest stratum of the Japanese population. Previously these values and education had been more or less limited to the *samurai* class and upper class farmers and merchants. Therefore, in spite of institutional and legal changes incurred by industrialization and westernization, behavioral patterns and psychological attitudes based on moral education continued to persist.

The backbone of the *Meiji* era was Confucian ethics, which emphasized duty, obedience, filial piety, ancestor worship, and *bushido*—the way of the warrior—which began in the 14th century and stressed *giri* (indebtedness). Codes of appropriate behavior in interpersonal relationships were rigidly prescribed according to role-status, age, and sex. Specific behavior was required between lord and subject, father and son, husband and wife, older and younger siblings, and friend and friend. The ultimate importance in a relationship was knowing one's role in relationship to others and thereby fulfilling the appropriate obligation, duty, and loyalty owed to others in each situation. Adherence to the required behavior was a sign of virtue.

The importance of status- and role-consciousness was also built into the Japanese language itself which has specific ways of addressing others depending on the role-status of the individuals. As Ruth Benedict observed, there was great security to be found by the individual in knowing precisely how one should behave in any given situation (Benedict, 1946:73–74):

> If the Japanese loved and trusted their meticulously explicit map of behavior, they had a certain justification. It guaranteed security so long as one followed the rules; it allowed protests against unauthorized aggressions and it could be manipulated to one's advantage. It required the fulfillment of reciprocal obligations.

The Traditional Family System

The traditional family system was a conceptualized set of behavioral patterns and standards against which actual conduct was measured; deviation from these prescribed standards was socially disapproved (Dore, 1958). It was a norm by which the Japanese family guided their behavior but it was not necessarily representative of what people actually did.

The following description of the family system illustrates what the Japanese family thought they should do prior to World War II (Wagatsuma, 1977). Central to the concept of the Japanese family system was the *ie* (family, household, house), the primary unit of social organization. As a legal and political organization it was based upon Confucian political principles, which stated that stable families ensured a stable society. The *ie* was an entity continuous through time, including all past, present, and future members of the family—of greater importance than any of its members and their individual interests and goals. It was a composite of the concrete and the abstract, the material as well as the spiritual and included such elements as the family name, occupation, property, tradition, family altar, graveyard, and family code, which listed expected behavior.

Since the continuation of the *ie* was of utmost importance to the family's future, marriage and the selection of prospective mates was a serious matter concerning the entire family. The social, psychological, and physical background of the prospective mates and their families were carefully scrutinized before arrangements actually proceeded. Marriages were made for the purpose of producing an heir; marriage for the sake of love was considered immoral because it was an assertion of individual interest and welfare above that of the *ie*. Continuation of the *ie* was so important that adoption (of a daughter, husband, or husband and wife) was practiced when there were no offspring. In cases where one's wife was unable to bear children, it was not unusual for the husband to find a mistress to bear his child without replacing his wife.

The moral as well as legal duty of continuing the *ie* was vested in the househead (*kachō*) who, as eldest son and heir to the property rights, had the

47

obligation of securing a stable environment for its members and of providing arrangements for marriage, occupation, food, and living comforts. The jurisdiction of his authority encompassed final decisions in matters concerning marriage, choice of occupation, place of residency, and expulsion from the family, for each member of the *ie*. However, his authority was to be enforced not for personal whimsy but for the good of the *ie*.

Dedication of one's life for the advancement and good reputation of the *ie* was an obligation not only observed by the household but also by each of its members. Respect, obedience, and filial piety to parents and ancestors (especially toward father) was highly emphasized along with observance of rank order within the family structure. Generally, respect was required from persons of lower rank to a person of higher rank: from younger member to older member, from children to parents, from wife to husband.

THE MODERN JAPANESE AMERICAN FAMILY

Attempts to preserve the *ie* ideal has continued to persist within the Japanese American family (Connors, 1974) but has been modified to suit the new country and situation. The *Issei* came alone and did not have their parents and extended family to whom they had to pay their obligations, duties, and responsibilities. Instead, the *ie* adapted to encompass a larger unit—the village or *ken* (prefecture) from which they came or the entire Japanese community itself. The larger unit functioned similar to the *ie* serving as an effective device for social control (Kitano, 1976).

Individual interest was subordinated to that of the community with the understanding that what an individual did (good or bad) would cast a reflection upon not only one's self and one's family but also the entire community. One of the major concerns was showing a "good face" to the *haku-jin* (Caucasian). Community solidarity was high when it came to dealing with the majority group. Individuals were encouraged and often socially pressured into behaving in a way that would benefit the reputation of the family and all Japanese. The Japanese community in turn furnished the security of the *ie* in Japan, providing a sanctuary from the often hostile majority group. Ethnic businesses and services, such as restaurants, markets, and Japanese language schools, flourished, offering employment, socialization opportunities, and recreation.

With the end of World War II and their release from concentration camps, the cohesiveness and housing concentration of the Japanese changed. Many took the opportunity to leave the camps and to settle in the east and midwest (New York, Cleveland, and Chicago); although, by 1970, of the 588,324 Japanese Americans, 217,175 were living in Hawaii and 213,277 were living in

California. Furthermore, their higher socioeconomic status through finding better jobs and gaining higher degrees, coupled with a lessening of discrimination, has allowed a high degree of housing and social mobility. This has been coupled with rapid acculturation (including facility with the English language and American styles of life) and a greater sense of security in dealing with the majority group. However, in areas with a high Japanese concentration (Hawaii and selected areas in California), ethnic community organizations remain, providing structurally pluralistic models for those who wish to participate within a Japanese setting.

Family Characteristics

A summary of current Japanese American family characteristics can be drawn from the 1970 Census (Office of Special Concerns). Eighty-six percent had both husband and wife, which was the same rate for the country as a whole. The percentage of children under six (27 percent) was also equivalent to the national rate. Japanese families were slightly above the national average in size (3.7 to 3.5 persons) and in extended family (16 to 12 percent). In general, it appears that Japanese Americans did not differ substantially from Americans as a whole. This reflects a high degree of acculturation.

One-third of all Japanese women have married out of the group, and the proportion rises to 46 percent among those in the 16-to-24-year-old group.

The mean family income (male head) was $13,511. Only 7.5 percent had incomes below the poverty level (as defined by the U.S. Census) with the preponderance of low incomes in the 65 years or older category (U.S. Bureau of the Census, 1973).

Although there were regional differences on variables such as income, housing costs, and the like, the overall picture is one of an ethnic group that has achieved a reasonable degree of economic security and is similar to the majority group on selected demographic variables.

Current Studies on the Japanese American Family

Levine and Montero (1973) have suggested that within the Japanese American community there flow two different streams (both in which the *Sansei* or third generation navigate): One is more traditional and the other is more assimilationist. They predicted that if the *Sansei*'s high educational training and skills and emphasis on socioeconomic success disperse them geographically into a widely scattered minority, then radical changes, such as the destruction of the more Japanese overtones of Japanese American family life, could be expected.

Connors's study (1974) of three generations of Japanese Americans in Sacramento provided evidence that despite the acculturation of each successive generation, the importance of family and the inculcation of dependency needs persisted.

Johnson (1977) studied Japanese American kinship relations in Honolulu. There was a persistence and even an increase in kin solidarity and sociability among the *Sansei* despite their social mobility and increased assimilation into extrafamilial institutions. This was made possible through the process of exchange based upon the traditional Japanese value system of sociocentricity, obligation to parents, reciprocity, and dependence. However, she found that within the Japanese American family, structural changes had occurred that resembled the American bilateral system. Among the *Nisei* parents and their *Sansei* offspring, the traditional rule of primogeniture has changed to equal inheritance, introducing more symmetry into sibling relationships. Obligation to parents was less burdensome and more easy to fulfill because the responsibility of aged parents was shared by the entire sibling group rather than being the province of the eldest son. She found that the sharing of filial responsibility and more symmetry into sibling relationships actually increased kin solidarity.

Yanagisako (1975) demonstrated that social structural changes in kinship patterns occur without changes in the cultural structure of kinship (referring to the system of symbols and meanings embedded in the normative system). Social structural changes can evolve without a modification in the symbolic structure itself or in the underlying traditional values. Therefore, equal inheritance and symmetry in sibling relationships occur without a modification in the traditional Japanese value system of sociocentricity, obligation to parents, reciprocity, and dependence.

Yanagisako (1977) also recognized the central role of the female in promoting household solidarity. She found that pairs of female kin (mother–daughter and sister–sister) had more frequent contact and affective solidarity with their primary kin (parents, children, and siblings) than pairs of male kin (father–son and brother–brother). Women maintained closer ties through telephoning, letter-writing, and visiting each other than the males; and especially through the arrangements and planning of family events and holiday gatherings. Whereas in the traditional Japanese family the female was presumed to have left her natal family at marriage to become a part of her husband's family, in the Seattle Japanese American family, the man was said to be the one who was lost to his wife's family.

Current studies on the Japanese American family indicate the process of acculturation is not a linear phenomenon, so that despite culture change, the

50

feeling of family solidarity and the retention of certain Japanese values still persist and in some cases increase. The elements of both cultural change and cultural persistance within the Japanese American family should be the target of further research.

Socialization

Caudill and Weinstein (1974) noted in their study on maternal care and infant behavior in Japan and America that there were different styles of caretaking between the two cultures and that by three to four months of age the infant in both cultures had become habituated to respond appropriately to the different styles of caretaking.

A follow-up study by Caudill and Schooler (1973) of the same sample of children and caretakers at different ages (two-and-a-half years old and six years old) demonstrated that the essential cross-cultural differences in behavior in the three-to-four-month-old infants were repeated at age two-and-a-half and again at age six. Caudill and Weinstein (1974) wrote that the basic difference in behavior is that in Japan "there is an emphasis on inter-dependence and reliance on others, while in America the emphasis is on independence and self-assertion" (p. 229). The Japanese were group-oriented and interdependent compared to the Americans who were more individual-oriented and independent. The Japanese were also more self-effacing and passive, whereas the Americans seemed more self-assertive and aggressive. The Japanese relied more on emotional feeling and intuition on matters that required a decision in contrast to the Americans, who emphasized rational reasons for their actions. Finally, the Japanese used more forms of silent, nonverbal communication in interpersonal relations through gestures and physical proximity in contrast to the Americans, who relied primarily on verbal communication.

Caudill and Frost (1974) conducted a study of everyday behavior with Japanese American mothers and their three-to-four-month-old infants to determine whether behavioral differences were due to genetic factors or cultural learning or conditioning, and to determine whether significant shifts in infant behavior would occur as succeeding generations of mothers cared for their infants in a different style within the context of social change. Their findings indicated that Japanese American mothers and infants were closer in their styles of behavior to the American than to their Japanese counterparts. The *Sansei* mother was more like the American mother than the Japanese mother in several respects: First, she engaged in a greater amount of chatting to her baby than the Japanese mother. Second, she did more positioning and less rocking than the Japanese mother. The *Yonsei* (fourth generation) baby was

51

more like the American baby than the Japanese baby in that it engaged in greater amounts of happy vocalization and physical activity with lesser amounts of unhappy vocalization.

However, the influence of cultural persistence was also demonstrated. The results indicated that the *Sansei* mother was more like her Japanese counterpart than the American mother in several respects: For example, she carried and coddled her infant more than the American mother. She also spent a greater amount of time playing with her child than the American mother.

There is other evidence to support the assumption that different emphases in family life and interpersonal relations continue to exist among the Japanese Americans. Johnson (1977) found interdependence expressed in various areas of Japanese American family life in Hawaii. Young people were expected to live with the family until marriage. Aged parents lived with a member of the family rather than in a nursing home. All age levels were usually integrated into the family and kin activities rather than age-segregated social networks.

The influence of cultural persistence is found in Kitano's data (1976:206–207). Kitano stated that although with each succeeding generation the trend is toward acculturation, the evidence supports ". . . a high degree of conformity, obedience, a manifestation of ethical behavior, and respect for authority, and a corresponding low degree of acting out, overt rebellion, and independence" (p. 136).

DEPENDENCE vs INDEPENDENCE. Doi (1962) claimed that the concept of *amae* (to depend on and presume another's benevolence) was essential in understanding the personality structure of the Japanese. Parental dependence is fostered and even institutionalized into its social structure. Physical and psychological dependence between mother and child was found to be well established among the Japanese infant by three to four months of age (Caudill and Weinstein, 1974). The basic alignment between the mother and child versus the father was noted by Vogel (1963:211) as a division within the family. Caudill's study (1952) indicated that parental dependence persisted among the Japanese Americans and that ". . . for *Issei* and *Nisei* alike, one never really breaks away from the mother as she continues to remain solidly internalized in the superego throughout life" (pp. 313–314).

One method that reinforces mutual dependence between parent and child is related to family sleeping arrangements. Caudill and Plath (1974) found that an individual in urban Japan can expect to co-sleep in a two-generation group for more than half of one's life, first as a child and then as a parent. Bathing and eating together were other forms of familial activities that fostered mutual dependence in a Japanese family. Co-sleeping arrangements no longer seemed to be the practice among Japanese Americans, although many

Nisei recalled sleeping first with their parents and then with other siblings. Whether this practice was carried over from Japan because of poverty and the lack of sleeping space or because of preference was not ascertained. But there was agreement that great comfort and security could be derived from such arrangements. Bathing together in a Japanese style *o-furo* (bath) was another family activity that many *Nisei* recalled from their early years, although this activity is no longer practiced among the younger generations.

The differing emphasis on dependence versus independence in American and Japanese cultures has been a source of conflict for many Japanese American families. The push for greater freedom of personal choice and expression of individuality by the *Nisei* was often challenged by the *Issei* with increased efforts to retain parental authority. DeVos (1955) feels that "the conflicts in the *Nisei* seem to be concerned with the problem of achieving greater self differentiation rather than accepting the personal submergence emphasized by the older Japanese ideal and the necessity thereby of assuming more rigid and constrictive controls" (p. 270).

Spiro's survey (1955) of literature on the acculturation of American ethnic groups acknowledged that parental authority was seriously diminished as the immigrant family slowly integrated into the social system of the larger community, forcing the parents to relinquish some aspects of their former educational, economic, and recreational roles. Efforts to retain former authority resulted in parent–child conflict.

A study conducted by researchers from Japan (Institute of Statistical Mathematics, 1979) indicated that Japanese American families in Hawaii placed a high priority on a child's obedience to parents when compared to a sample who came from the mainland. The researchers expressed concern about the emphasis on obedience since they felt that it was at the price of creativity.

ENRYO. *Enryo* (reserve, constaint) helps to explain much of the differences in styles of communication and behavior. As Kitano (1976) indicated, this concept originally referred to the deferential manner in which "inferiors" were supposed to behave toward their "superiors" but was adapted by the Japanese in America to apply to how one should behave toward the white man. One of the main manifestations of *enryo* was the conscious use of silence as a safe or neutral response to an embarrassing or ambiguous situation.

The manifestations of *enryo* in Japanese American social interactions are further illustrated by Kitano (1976:124–125):

For example, take observations of Japanese in situations as diverse as their hesitancy to speak out at meetings; their refusal of any invitation, especially the first time; their refusal of a second helping; their acceptance of a less desired object when given a free choice; their lack of verbal participation, especially in an integrated group; their refusal to ask question; and their hesitancy in asking for a raise in salary—these may all be based on *enryo.*

The interaction rules related to the norm of *enryo* are learned early in the Japanese family. A child quickly learns the importance of reticence, modesty, indirection, and humility and is punished for boastful, aggressive, loud, and self-centered behavior. The Japanese child is taught to be sensitive to the reactions of others, therefore in the ideal social interaction with one's peers, neither person dominates the other. To be boastful of one's achievements and to dwell too long on one's activities or interests is considered in bad taste. By "bad mouthing" one's self and complimenting others, modesty is preserved and self-validation is achieved by both partners.

According to Wagatsuma (1979), "If one speaks without reserve in a given circle or helps themselves [*sic*] uninvited to a person's material possessions, one may be blamed for having no *enryo.* Without *enryo,* one imposes too much of one's need and demands upon others." The social interactional rules related to the norm of *enryo* are not as explicitly defined as with the preceding generations, but one can still observe this pattern in a Japanese American social setting.

Utilizing the concept of *enryo,* Johnson and Johnson (1975) illustrated how the differences in interaction rules between Japanese Americans and *haoles* (Caucasians) in Hawaii can be the basis for potential difficulties in establishing close interpersonal relationships. Verbal behavior differed markedly between Japanese and the *haole* in the initial interaction process. The Japanese tended to exhibit quiet agreeableness, awareness of status of the other person, and formality; the *haole* displayed greeting behavior as typified by informality, casualness, heartiness, disclosure of personal information, and egalitarianism. While the Japanese may evaluate the *haoles'* heartiness as insincerity and quick disclosure of personal data as boastfulness, the *haole* may interpret the Japanese's formality, quiet agreeableness, and respect for status as being distant, unemotional, and inscrutable. These differences of styles often operated against establishing mutuality and was the basis of much misunderstanding.

MARRIAGE AND MALE–FEMALE RELATIONSHIPS. Male dominance had long been a social norm expected of the Japanese male but actually existed only among a small number of upper-class families (Wagatsuma, 1977). According to the social norm, at the head of the upper-class Japanese family was the "strict and stern" father making most of the decisions while the mother was said to be "loving and gentle," making certain that she fulfilled the family's dependency needs. Caudill (1952) stated that though outwardly more dominant, the Japanese male was emotionally more dependent on his wife than the American male. At home with his wife, he was allowed to be passive and dependent, whereas the American male, though outwardly less dominant, was faced at home with a wife who was more emotionally dependent upon him. Whether outside or inside his own home, the American male was expected to be in control of the situation.

The *Issei*'s ability to *gaman* (stick things out at all cost) was often what carried them through times of hardship, disillusionment, and loneliness (Gee, 1971; Ito, 1973); duty and obligation to husband, wife, and children were the bonds that kept the marriages together instead of love and romance. The practice of arranged marriages continued to be observed by many *Issei*, causing tension between parent and child (Iga, 1957). But as open rebellion against arranged marriages and the push for more personal freedom threatened to break the family's foundation, the *Issei* slowly backed down on their traditional demands. However, most were adamant in their demands for marrying within the ethnic group, but with time this practice, too, was breached.

Pressure from the *Issei* parents to pattern their daughters after the overtly submissive Japanese female has been a major source of conflict and dissatisfaction for the *Nisei* female. Caudill (1952) discovered that women directed their hostility toward and felt competitive with the male, and under the surface of conformity lay guilt conflicts that manifested themselves as masochistic and sadistic acting-out behavior. Meredith (1965) observed that among *Sansei* females there existed great conflict in balancing (tradition-directed) parental expectations and (present-directed) personal choices. But with the *Nisei* male, the (prescribed) cultural roles did not seem to come into conflict with personal goals. Instead the problem lay in the passive security found in conformity, which created a fear of leaving the protection of home to face the outside world.

Recent studies on interracial marriages show out-group rates approaching a 50 percent level (Kikumura and Kitano, 1973; Omatsu, 1972; Tinker, 1973). The Japanese American females continued to dominate the intermarriage statistics as they have in the past, although the gap appears to be closing. An important factor contributing to the historical preponderance of female intermarriage rates was personal dissatisfaction and conflict. Barnett's (1941) case studies of northwestern California Indians established that personal conflict and dissatisfaction played a critical role in culture change. He saw the acceptance of new patterns and standards as a means of relieving personal conflict and dissatisfaction. This was found to be the case among many Japanese American females who married out of their group in Los Angeles

County (Kikumura, 1975). Personal dissatisfaction among Japanese American women in their expected female roles may also be the primary reason that the females of this group appear to be acculturating more rapidly than the males (Arkoff, Meredith, and Iwahara, 1962; Caudill, 1952; DeVos, 1955; Fisher and Cleveland, 1958).

Although the high rate of outmarriage among the Japanese Americans attests to their greater interaction with the majority group, there is evidence that it is still accompanied with a degree of skepticism and anxiety (Kikumura, 1975). The fear of not being accepted by both spouses' families was often expressed by those who out-married. The comfort, rapport, and security that one Japanese American gets from another was something missed and longed for by many, and the feeling of guilt—of deserting "one's own kind" or of having done something deviant—was felt by others.

CHANGE AND ADAPTATION

The Japanese American family over the course of the generations has undergone, through acculturation, many changes, bringing it more into line with the family system of the dominant Anglo groups. However, the Japanese culture, in combination with the low power and high visibility of this group, has acted as a brake on total acculturation and assimilation.

It is appropriate, here, to summarize our view of the Japanese American family and the major directions in which it appears to be going:

1. It has remained an intact family unit with low rates of separation and divorce, although there are changes toward a more American model. The low past rates of separation and divorce are probably rising (1.3 percent in 1960; 4 to 6 percent in 1970).

2. The structure of the family was initially vertical, with father and males on top. It could be likened to a traditional family model, in contrast to the modern urban American family. Entertainment and recreation often took place in the family and extended family units. Families were larger; problems were often handled within the unit, and the use of outside professionals was a last resort.

3. The *ie* unit was adopted in America to include larger units, including village, *ken,* and even the entire Japanese community. It served as an effective social control device; it provided socialization opportunities through ethnic language schools, cultural and recreational opportunities. The Japanese community became a reference group; the functions were similar to those of an *ie.*

4. Socialization and child rearing took into account minority-group position, power, and the carrying on of the Japanese culture. Those values,

56

norms, and behaviors most likely to persist were those of the Japanese culture that interacted with the power position of the Japanese in America and their visibility in a race-conscious society. Many of these behaviors have also been reinforced by the majority group, so that they have become stereotypes of the Japanese. These include quietness, conformity, loyalty, diligence, maximum effort, good citizenship, high school achievement, and a group orientation.

5. The situational orientation has been an important part of Japanese American behavior. Learning how to behave to those above, below, and equal has meant learning appropriate styles. According to Kitano (1976: 106–107):

> There are elements of a "schizophrenic adaptation" on the part of the Japanese to life in the United States. But most physically identifiable groups are also faced with the same problem—the how-to-behave problem when interacting with the majority and the behaviors when with one's own group. Therefore, within one individual there is often the many personalities—the "Uncle Tom" to the white man, deferential and humble; the "good son" to his parents, dutiful, and obedient; and the "swinger" to his peers, wise-cracking, loud, and irreverent. And all of these behaviors are real so that none can be said to give a truer picture except in terms of time, place, and situation.

The situational approach is intimately related to power. The less powerful have to learn many adaptations; those with power can afford to use one style. Americans expect others to adapt to them, and with their power can often command or buy this recognition. Therefore, we often assume that there are social-science universals—"the personality" and "the truth," whereas our search may be more a reflection of our power position than a social-scientific reality.

6. Acculturation has been the most powerful single influence on Japanese behavior. But it has not been a simple linear movement; the variables of power and visibility have shaped differential styles so that Japanese Americans in Hawaii will be different in many instances from their peers along the Pacific and Atlantic seaboards. There is a current reawakening of an ethnic identity and a militancy among the *Sansei* (Kitano, 1976) that may slow the trend toward acculturation.

One of the most influential events hastening acculturation was the incarceration of the Japanese during World War II. It broke up the power of the *Issei* and the ethnic ghettos, altered family life, scattered Japanese throughout America through resettlement, sent many males into the armed forces and overseas, and made many renounce everything Japanese (Kitano, 1976).

7. Social class has always been a factor in the Japanese culture, but it is

difficult to transcribe into the American scene. The *ies* tried to make appropriate matches, and "good" families were class conscious. Although most of the immigrants started at the bottom of American class structure, they did not identify with the lifestyle of the lower classes. Rather, they brought with them many of the values associated with the middle class: high educational expectation for their children, respect for those in authority, including the police, desire to own property, emphasis on banking and savings, and a future orientation (Kitano, 1976). They seldom fully adopted a lower-class style even though their incomes and housing were clearly in the ghetto areas.

However, there is an increasing heterogeneity in the Japanese American community and development of a more formal social class system (e.g., debutantes, professional organizations). It remains much more open, but with continued differences in education and income, it may soon become much more crystallized.

8. Outside professionals have not been consulted as frequently by the Japanese Americans as might be expected. Psychiatrists, psychologists, social workers, and lawyers note that for a relatively affluent group with many of the concerns of the middle class, the Japanese use of such professional services has been limited. And often when turning for help, many Japanese have turned to members of their own ethnic group.

The Japanese American family has its roots in *Tokugawa* (1603–1868) and *Meiji* (1868–1912) Japan. Confucian values were highly stressed with male dominance and female submission, and clear role prescriptions for each member of the family. Individualism was submerged in favor of a group orientation and values such as duty and obligation were given precedence over preference and voluntarism.

Exposure to the American system has resulted in changes of the Japanese American family. Factors such as area of residence, group size, community cohesion, contact with the home country, the attitudes of the majority, and time have combined to change the old Japanese ways. Nevertheless, even the newer generations appear to have retained some of the old Japanese mannerisms.

The Japanese American family has been credited with providing the structure, the socialization, and control that has resulted in remarkably low rates of dysfunctional behavior such as crime, delinquency, and mental illness. It has also been an important factor in encouraging a highly educated, high achievement oriented population.

By the start of the 1980s there has been a wide diversity among Japanese Americans. Wide-scale intermarriage has taken place so that the variable of physical identifiability, probably the single most important factor in maintaining a Japanese identity, may also be affected. Nevertheless, if past experiences can be taken as a guide, the Japanese American family will retain a style that will continue as a combination of Japanese and American cultures.

REFERENCES

Arkoff, A., G. Meredith, and S. Iwahara. 1962. "Dominance–Deference Patterning in Motherland—Japanese, Japanese-American, and Caucasian-American Students," *Journal of Social Psychology,* 58: 61–66.

Barnett, H. G. 1941–42. "Personal Conflicts and Cultural Change," *Social Forces,* 20 (October–May): 160–171.

Benedict, R. 1946. *The Chrysanthemum and the Sword.* Boston: Houghton Mifflin.

Broom, L., and J. Kitsuse. 1955. "The Validation of Acculturation: A Condition to Ethnic Assimilation," *American Anthropologist,* 57 (February): 44–48.

Caudill, Wm. 1952. "Japanese American Personality and Acculturation," *Genetic Psychology Monographs,* 45(1): 3–102.

Caudill, Wm., and L. Frost. 1974. "A Comparison of Maternal Care and Infant Behavior in Japanese-American, American, and Japanese Families," in William P. Lebra (ed.), *Youth Socialization, and Mental Health,* Honolulu: The University Press of Hawaii.

Caudill, Wm., and D. W. Plath. 1974. "Who Sleeps by Whom? Parent–Child Involvement in Urban Japanese Families," in Takie Sugiyama Lebra and William P. Lebra (eds.), *Japanese Culture and Behavior.* Honolulu: The University Press of Hawaii, 277–312.

Caudill, Wm., and C. Schooler. 1973. "Child Behavior and Child Rearing in Japan and the United States: An Interim Report," *The Journal of Nervous and Mental Disease,* 157(5): 323–338.

Caudill, Wm., and H. Weinstein. 1974. "Maternal Care and Infant Behavior in Japan and America," in Takie Sugiyama Lebra and William P. Lebra (eds.), *Japanese Culture and Behavior.* Honolulu: The University Press of Hawaii, 225–276.

Connors, J. W. 1974. "Acculturation and Family Continuities in Three Generations of Japanese Americans," *Journal of Marriage and the Family,* 26 (February): 159–165.

DeVos, G. 1955. "Acculturation and Personality Structure: A Rorschach Study of Japanese Americans," Ph.D. dissertation for the University of Chicago, Illinois.

DeVos, G., and H. Wagatsuma. 1966. *Japan's Invisible Race.* Berkeley: University of California Press.

Doi, T. L. 1962. "Amae: A Key Concept for Understanding Japanese *Personality Structure,"* in R. J. Smith and R. K. Beardsley (eds.), *Japanese Culture: Its Development and Characteristics.* Chicago: Aldine Pub. Co.

Dore, R. P. 1958. *City Life in Japan.* Berkeley: University of California Press.

Fisher, S., and S. E. Cleveland. 1958. *Body Image and Personality.* Princeton: D. Van Nostrand.

Gee, E. 1971. "Issei: The First Women," in *Asian Women,* Berkeley: University of California, pp. 8–15.

Ichihashi, Y. 1969. *Japanese in the United States.* New York: Arno Press and New York Times.

Iga, M. 1957. "The Japanese Social Structure and the Source of Mental Strains of Japanese Immigrants in the United States," *Social Forces,* 35: 271–278.

Institute of Statistical Mathematics. 1979. "Toward the Development of Statistical Analysis for the Study of Comparative Culture And [*sic*]: Attitudinal Study of Honolulu Residents." Tokei-suri Kenkyuzyo, Tokyo, Japan: Research Report, General Series No. 47.

Ito, K. 1973. *Issei: A History of Japanese Immigrants in North America.* Seattle: University of Washington Press. pp. 247–288.

Johnson, C. L. 1977. "Interdependence, Reciprocity and Indebtedness: An Analysis of Japanese American Kinship Relations," *Journal of Marriage and the Family,* 39 (May): 351–363.

Johnson, C. L., and F. A. Johnson. 1975. "Interaction Rules and Ethnicity, The Japanese and Caucasians in Honolulu," *Social Forces,* 52(2): 452–466.

Kikumura, A. 1975. "Japanese American Outmarriages in Los Angeles County 1971–1972," unpublished master's thesis for the Department of Anthropology at University of California, Los Angeles.

Kikumura, A., and H. H. L. Kitano. 1973. "Interracial Marriage: A Picture of the Japanese Americans," *Journal of Social Issues,* 29(2): 67–81.

Kitano, H. H. L. 1976. *Japanese Americans: The Evolution of a Subculture.* Englewood Cliffs, NJ: Prentice-Hall.

Levine, G. N., and D. M. Montero. 1973. "Socioeconomic Mobility Among Three Generations of Japanese Americans," *Journal of Social Issues,* 29(2): 33–48.

Meredith, G. M. 1965. "Observations on the Acculturation of Sansei Japanese Americans in Hawaii," *Psychologia,* 8(1–2) (June): 41–49.

Omatsu, G. 1972. Nihonmachi Beat. *Hokubei Mainichi* (January 12).

Petersen, W. 1971. *Japanese Americans.* New York: Random House.

Spiro, M. E. 1955. "The Acculturation of American Ethnic Groups," *American Anthropologist,* 57, 1240–1252.

TenBroek, J., E. N. Barnhart, and F. W. Matson. 1968. *Prejudice, War and the Constitution.* Berkeley and Los Angeles: University of California Press.

Tinker, J. N. 1973. "Intermarriage and Ethnic Boundaries: The Japanese American Case," *Journal of Social Issues,* 29(2): 49–66.

U.S. Bureau of the Census. 1973. *Japanese, Chinese and Filipinos in the United States—1970.* Census of the Population, PC(2)-1G Washington, DC: U.S. Government Printing Office.

Vogel, E. F. 1963. *Japan's New Middle Class.* Berkeley and Los Angeles: University of California Press.

Wagatsuma, H. 1977. "Some Aspects of the Contemporary Japanese Family: Once Confucian, Now Fatherless?" *Daedalus,* 106(2): 181–210.

Wagatsuma, H. 1979. "Entries of Encyclopedia of Japan," Kodanshi: International Ltd.

Yanagisako, S. J. 1975. "Two Processes of Change in Japanese-American Kinship," *Journal of Anthropological Research,* 31(3) (Autumn): 196–224.

Yanagisako, S. J. 1977. "Women-centered Kin Networks in Urban Bilateral Kinship," *American Ethnologist,* 4(2): 207–226.

The Italian American Family

Italian Americans and their family system are a major component of the American ethnic mosaic. The migration of Italians, mostly from southern Italy, was one of the largest in terms of numbers of people, and they brought with them a close knit family system that is, to a large extent, the prototype of the "ethnic family." In spite of increasing social mobility, which came comparatively late to Italian Americans, they have retained a high degree of residential concentration and a strong sense of family cohesion, which serve to maintain ethnic pluralism.

CHAPTER FOUR

BY

JILL S. QUADAGNO

INTRODUCTION

While many scholars have been swayed by an assimilationist model of ethnicity, assuming that America's racial and ethnic groups will eventually be incorporated into the mainstream culture, others have challenged this assumption. Researchers have recognized that ethnic diversity may be a meaningful indicator of group differences, independent of social class (Greeley, 1974:22; Kantrowitz, 1973). Others argue that it is social class and not ethnicity that is the critical factor in group differences (Gans, 1962; Gordon, 1964; Lopreato, 1970).

The southern Italian immigrants who arrived around the turn of the century brought with them a culture that was in many ways antagonistic to a rapidly developing society—a society that needed their labor but rejected their seemingly incomprehensible customs. A glance through the literature of the times reveals this antagonism. The following excerpt from a popular magazine was written in 1890 (Morgan, 1890:260–261):

> Sooner or later, somebody in this country will be obliged to grapple with the problem of the "dago." Can he be kept out of jail? Can he be made a useful citizen by utilizing the leisure he spent in jails to educate him into some sort of comprehension of the new country in which he finds himself?

These racist and ethnic hostilities so vividly expressed, combined with cultural traditions that emphasized distrust of outsiders, contributed to the insulation of the Italian American community. The extent to which they remained insulated from the larger society can be seen by examining characteristics of Italian Americans today. While assimilation has certainly occurred, there are remnants of cultural traditions, maintained by strong family ties, which still clearly distinguish Italian Americans from other ethnic groups.

HISTORICAL BACKGROUND

Traditional Family Structure

The Italian immigrants in the United States brought with them a family structure that was different in many ways not only from American society but from other European cultures as well. The concept of the family that prevailed included all blood and in-law relatives, and the family was an inclusive social world in and of itself (Covello, 1967:149). Family was not necessarily limited to one household but embraced several households which were scattered over the villages or town. However, Italian households often contained extended kin rather than being comprised solely of the conjugal family. This contrasted with the pattern in western Europe in general, in which the small conjugal-family household predominated (Wrigley, 1977:78). Particularly among sharecroppers in which the labor of many people enhanced the whole family's economic situation, it was common for married brothers with their families to share a common household. Three-generation households, including aged parents, were likely to be found at the end of the life cycle, as widowed parents would move into the home of their married children and grandchildren (Kertzer, 1978:341).

Family solidarity was the basic code of family life, and this code encompassed the parents, grandparents, aunts, uncles, cousins and godparents (Covello, 1967:149). The strength of the norm of solidarity meant that the disgrace of one member of the family affected everyone. Thus, a disobedient child was the concern not only of the parents but of the extended kin as well. Within the family, a complex system of rules that regulated both an individual's relations and responsibilities to the members of his family and posture to the outside world was developed.

The concept of obligation was a distinctive aspect of family solidarity. The family council, headed by the *capo di famiglia,* usually the father, made decisions about such diverse matters as the education of a child, a cousin's dowry, or the funeral expenses of an aunt (Covello, 1967:151). A person in need of credit would apply first to family members and only if no help were forthcoming would he then turn to outsiders or *stranieri.*

While the Italian family has often been perceived as patriarchal, there were many limitations on patriarchal authority. First, since the southern Italian *famiglia* embraced many marriage units, the decision as to who was the head of the extended family was not reached without rivalry among several aspirants. Though authority was usually conferred upon the oldest married member, this was not always the case. Thus, in a broad sense the Italian male was not the sole or absolute authority. The fact that a system of orthodox patriarchy was not adhered to can be seen in the limitations on leadership that prevailed. As long as a man was the main provider, his leadership was not questioned. However, old age or feebleness definitely terminated his role as the representative of family tradition. Similarly, if he became a widower, he retained his leadership only if one of his sons were not married. As soon as a son, preferably the oldest, married, he assumed the leadership role of his widowed father (Covello, 1967:154). The father retained respect, but there was no longer blind obedience.

A second limitation on male dominance was the power and authority of the Italian mother. An important indicator of this was the fact that the wife had the right to possess property and dispose it without her husband's consent (Covello, 1967:206). The dowry was an economic weapon that she retained until her death and which upon her death went either to her children or, if childless, back to her own blood relatives. Another source of power for the peasant woman was the fact that she often contributed economically to the family by working part time in the fields. Thus, the husband was not the sole support of the family. In addition, cultural tradition granted a prestige to the mother that contradicted her assumed subservence to her husband (Covello, 1967:213). The major kinship ties were with the female relatives, and the nurturing of children was done by the mother and her female relatives. The mother was the center of the family in a society where nonfamilial relationships were secondary. In a world where the family status was judged not by the occupation of the father but by the signs of family well-being which emanated from the household, the mother played an important role in securing that status.

Traditional Ethnic Culture

The Italian family system formed the basis for the perpetuation of a set of beliefs and values that affected all areas of social life including work, education, and definitions of social status.

The necessity of family ties was of singular importance. One's personal identity was derived from his family, and family membership was essential in terms of defining one's place in society. The most shameful condition was to be without a family (Gambino, 1974:31). A man who violated the family code was not only an outcast from his family but an outcast from the larger society as well. He could only become a day laborer and even in this he was the last hired. For a female without a family the only options were to become a beggar or a prostitute. However, loyal kin were rewarded by always having a place within the family. The aged were cared for in the family and "no one went to poorhouses, orphanages, or other institutions of charity in the *Mezzogiorno* except those few unfortunates without any family intimates" (Gambino, 1974:29).

The strength of familial ties also affected the attitude of the *contadino* (peasant) toward work: "Work is regarded as moral training for the young. And among adults, it is regarded as a matter of pride. To work is to show evidence that one has become a man or a woman, a full member of the family" (Gambino, 1974:80). Thus work was not defined as abstract but as tangible—something that could be shown to others as a "visible" result of an individual's skills and efforts. The disdain for intangibles was also related to the *contadino*'s attitude toward education.

While the ideal of the *contadino* was to cultivate children who were *ben educato* (well-educated), the translation of this phrase is deceptive. Being educated did not refer to formal schooling but to being educated in proper behavior. "*Ben educato* meant raised with the core of one's personality woven of those values and attitudes, habits and skills that perpetuated *l'ordine della famiglia,* and thus one was attuned to the welfare of the family" (Gambino, 1974:225). In this sense, formal schooling was antithetical to proper training for manhood or womanhood, involving the influence of *stranieri* (outsiders) who might interfere with *la via vecchia* (the old ways) as well as keeping young people from the more important lessons they might learn from work.

The concept of *ben educato* was applied differently to male and female children. For a young boy, this meant first and foremost to be *pazienza,* patient. This is not to be confused with fatalism or stoicism; it meant more than that. According to Gambino (1974:119), "The idea of *pazienza* is an ideal of control of life. First and foremost, it is an ideal of inner control, of reserve." Thus, the Italian male was training to wait and react cautiously, evaluating the events of life rather than actively pursuing a particular course. This value was expressed in a popular game played by men and boys called *morra* or throwing fingers. The game doesn't stress competition or mere chance. "It stresses cleverness in the context of chance situations, a mini-model of life" (Gambino, 1974:139). A boy was also taught to show respect to those older than himself, to acknowledge their wisdom, and to model his behavior after his male relatives. The Italian's attitudes toward the purpose of childrearing can be summarized by the old saying, "Only a fool makes his children better than himself."

In southern Italy, the ideal of womanhood included not only bearing children and knowing household skills but having those supportive qualities that enable a woman to take her place as the center of the family. In raising a daughter, the family's ultimate goal was to see her settled and competent in her roles as a woman (Gambino, 1974:151). From the age of seven, girls were apprenticed in learning household skills and developing the qualities of womanhood under constant supervision. Thus, an Italian girl learned manner and style as well as the crucial economic and social roles of womanhood (Gambino, 1974:155).

Italian Migration: A Rationale

It is impossible to understand Italian Americans without understanding why the peasants, who made up the majority of the population of 19th century Italy, left their homeland. This was a behavior starkly antithetical to their own *cultura* and their essential ideological makeup, which required that they remain. Italy to the tourist is a land of milk and honey, alive with olive, almond, orange and sweet lemon trees, and grape vines. But from the perspective of the farmhand impoverished beyond hope, it was an impossible place of infertile, worn-out soil, of archaic and utterly impracticable agricultural methods and equipment, of living in stone and mud tombs (*sassi*), caves (*marni*), or huts (*baracche*), and sharing these, if one were lucky, with some livestock; of long hours of unrewarded toil in the oppressive heat and humidity of the *scirocco* and, finally of seeing much of what was grown taken by the wealthy landowners (Carlyle, 1962:88, 100; Chapman, 1971:12ff).

Pushed by economic necessity, many single or married men (traveling alone) came to the United States with the idea of going back as soon as possible. The United States represented a source of work and income for them that would support their families, who through the trying times must, by necessity, remain at home. This kind of emigration was not only acceptable but enouraged in Italy. Although the exact number is not known, Caroli (1973) has shown that of the millions who left there to come to the United States, one and a half million emigrants returned home during the years 1900 through 1914. Thus, there was substantial return migration. The wandering of these men was permitted by the economic and political leadership of the United States as long as the need for cheap labor outpaced the demands of the ever-growing native xenophobia. In the eyes of the peasant migrant, this expeditionary sojourn was the least radical of the migration possibilities.

The second migratory type of resettlement was by families who sought a fertile land where they could reestablish themselves and maintain as much of their old way of life, but on a higher economic level. For them, America represented a place where with hard work they could join the landed class. Here a *zappatore,* a farmhand, could hope to own acres. A *pescatore,* a fisherman, could work to own his own boat. The continuity of their lives came from the similarities they sought in work, government and social structure, there being little or no change permitted in their family or religion.

The Italian Immigration in America

Arriving on the shores of this country, the emigrants from the villages and cities of Italy, Sicily, Corsica, and Sardinia were collectively identified as Italians and Sicilians—later simply Italians.

In the case of the Italians who immigrated to the great cities of the eastern seaboard, the greatest cruelty, from their point of view, was administered by fellow Catholics, the Irish (Tomasi, 1970:163–193; Vecoli, 1969: 217–268). The Irish, who by this time had been in the United States for three or more generations, had largely internalized values including the xenophobia under which they themselves had suffered earlier. The fact that the Italians belonged to the same religion as the Irish might lead some to suppose that these groups would have united and that the Italians would have found in the Irish a source of solicitude and help. From the point of view of the Irish, however, many factors militated against this, and three important considerations must be noted: First, in spite of the fact that the Irish emigration had begun much earlier, there were many instances where the Irish and the Italians were in direct economic competition (Fieldstein and Costello, 1974; Foerster, 1919). Second, some Irish, after about 50 or 60 years, were reaching middle-class status, and they saw no advantage in being identified with these impoverished, illiterate, foreign newcomers who could only serve to hold them back or drag them down. Third, there were important differences in the religious styles of the Irish and the Italians with respect to both liturgical observance and the relationship between the priest and the people. These differences were sufficient to generate enormous resentment which precluded cooperation between the two groups. The subjective reactions of the Italians to Irish Catholicism in the United States have been dealt with more extensively elsewhere (Russo, 1970:195–213; Femminella, 1961:233–241). It must be emphasized here that from the point of view of the newly arrived *contadino,* those who might have been considered closest to him outside of his family and *paisani* were of little help.

In response, the newly arrived Italians reestablished their village life here as far as possible (Dore, 1968:95–122). Honest work for the Italian was honorable and was to be performed with a sense of dignity, whatever the type of work. Digging ditches, carrying garbage, sweeping streets, shining shoes or cleaning toilets were jobs that could bring a man money to feed his family here or in Italy. And if his wife and children were here already, he would manage to put some money aside to be sent back home to help his parents or other relatives who had remained in Italy. And they in turn, whenever they could, invested the money in land not only for their own use but for their sons in America in hope and preparation for their return (Vecoli, 1974:31–43).

THE MODERN ITALIAN AMERICAN FAMILY

Demographic and Ecological Factors

While people tend to associate Italian immigration with the late 19th and early 20th centuries, the immigration of Italians to the United States has actually been a continuing process, beginning much earlier and continuing to the present time. Four different periods of exodus can be identified, each having somewhat distinctive characteristics.

In the 18th and 19th centuries, small numbers of northern Italians came to the United States. These immigrants were scarcely visible in the population and did not identify themselves with the masses of southern Italians who came later. The 1870s were the starting date of the migratory flow from southern Italy, which increased rapidly during the next 50 years until the outbreak of World War I (Velikonja, 1977:68). In 1860, there were only 9,231 Italians in the United States; by 1904, there were 741,986 (Castiglione, 1974:53). The crest of the immigrant wave was between 1901 and 1914 when the yearly average totaled 616,000 (Gallo, 1974:25). In this second immigration period, young healthy males were the typical immigrants, with few old and even fewer women arrivals. Until 1925 the number of males remained three times greater than that of females as a result of the previously discussed phenomenon of return migration (Meloni, 1977:7).

In 1926, strict immigration quotas based on national origin were imposed by the United States government, and the flow of immigrants decreased to a trickle. The 1965 Immigration Act substituted the national origin quotas for a new set of preferences, helping new immigrants join close relatives who were already residents of the United States (Velikonja, 1975:191). Recently arrived immigrants are quite different from the peasants who entered the North American continent at the turn of the century. More exposure to the modern world has lessened their isolation in the old country, and they are more likely to be well educated, having been specifically selected for certain occupations and professions that would not replace indigenous workers. Since 1967 an average of 23,000 Italian immigrants have come to the United States annually (Gallo, 1974:45). These new arrivals help to strengthen and maintain the traditions and customs of *la via vecchia,* the old ways.

67

RESIDENTIAL MOBILITY AND KINSHIP TIES. In arguing for pluralism or assimilation, a key indicator used by both sides has been that of residential segregation. That is, to what extent do ethnic groups, regardless of social class, remain ethnically segregated and how lasting are these patterns of residential segregation?

Several studies have examined residential segregation among Italian Americans. From the very beginning of their immigration, Italians settled in what have been called "Little Italies," and these ethnic communities tended to be concentrated along the eastern seaboard, particularly New York and in the cities of Rhode Island, Connecticut, Massachusetts, and New Jersey (Lieberson, 1963:79: Lopreato, 1970:41). Americans of Italian descent make up more than one sixth of the population of New York City (Gallo, 1974:25). To a large extent these broad patterns of residential settlement have been maintained (Abramson, 1973:29; Lopreato, 1970:53). According to the 1960 census, nearly 70 percent of Italian Americans are concentrated in the northeastern portion of the United States.

While broad patterns of residential segregation have been maintained, a more significant indicator of ethnic pluralism is the maintenance of neighborhoods. There is evidence to suggest that for Italians the meaning of neighborhood transcends the physical characteristics of housing. Italians imbue neighborhoods with a special significance so that they become, in effect, extended families. In an early study of the Italian North End of Boston, Firey (1947) found that second-generation Italians were more inclined to move to the suburbs than the older first-generation Italians. He interpreted this to mean that they were seeking identification with American cultural patterns (Firey, 1947:200–209).

Years later when assimilationist theories were being challenged, Glazer and Moynihan (1963:187) noted that, "While the Jewish map of New York City in 1920 bears almost no relation to that in 1961, the Italian districts, though weakened in some cases and strengthened in others, are still in large measure where they were." They also noted two trends among second- and third-generation Italians. One was a tendency to redo old neighborhoods, so that social mobility did not necessarily mean moving to suburbs. They also noted that when Italians did move, it was often a two-generation process, with both children and parents moving to suburban neighborhoods together. Glazer and Moynihan's findings were confirmed by a detailed analysis of residential segregation by ethnicity in New York City based on 1960 census data (Kantrowitz, 1973). Kantrowitz (1973:7) concludes, "that ethnic segregation . . . has declined little over a generation."

The meaning of the maintenance of ethnic neighborhoods, particularly for Italian Americans, has been investigated in a comprehensive study of ethnicity from the National Opinion Research Center (Greeley, 1971). Greeley (1971:77) found that, "Of all the ethnic groups, Italians most often live in the same neighborhood as their parents and siblings and visit them every week." Further, he notes that, "When the same data are sorted out according to social class and the physical distance that separates the respondents from parents and relatives, Italians are still the most likely to visit both their parents and their siblings." Greeley (1971:78) concludes that among Italians, "ethnic differences seem to persist even when different social classes are examined separately." Similar data were reported by Abramson (1970). Studying ethnic communities in four Connecticut cities, Abramson found that more than 50 percent of Italians and eastern Europeans had friends and relatives in the immediate neighborhood, as compared with 10 to 15 percent for Jews, German Catholics, and Yankees.

Extending the analysis to visiting patterns as well as residential propinquity, Gallo, (1974:86) found that while first-generation Italians tended to live in closer proximity to kin than the second or third generation, the younger Italian Americans visited relatives and were in turn visited more frequently. Gallo (1974:86) concluded that, "the second and third generation respondents become increasingly active outside the family as they acculturate to urban values, but at the same time retain family contacts. The extended family plays a greater role for the second and third generation respondents than for those of the first."

In contrast to these findings, Lopreato's research of New Haven Italians indicates that middle-class Italians visit relatives only slightly more frequently than the general population, while working-class Italians visit twice as much. Lopreato (1970:51) concludes, "These findings seem to indicate that to a considerable extent the working class still adheres to old world habits and practices. The Italian-American middle class, on the other hand, is for all practical purposes indistinguishable from the American middle class as a whole."

Drawing data from household surveys in the state of Rhode Island, Kobrin and Goldschneider (1978) compared four Catholic ethnic groups with Protestants and Jews on a number of variables. In regard to the issue of residential concentration, they found, like Lopreato, that it was affected by social class. Working-class Italians were more likely than middle-class Italian Americans to reside in ethnically cohesive neighborhoods.

Obviously the relationship between social class and ethnicity is complex, and the final answer has not been provided. It seems unlikely that the upward social mobility of third- and fourth-generation Italians will lead to complete assimilation. Rather, evidence indicates that they will continue to maintain a distinct ethnic identity. In a study based on interviews with 100 Irish and

Italian Catholics, in Providence, Rhode Island, Goering (1971) found that third-generation Italians were more likely to think of themselves ethnically than first- or second-generation Italians and concluded that ethnic awareness may be increasing.

FAMILY SIZE AND FERTILITY. While the impoverished Italian immigrant women had exceptionally large families, their second-generation daughters reversed this pattern completely. As reported by Rosenwaike (1973:272), the 1910 census showed that women of Italian parentage constituted 4.9 percent of the female population in Boston between the ages of 15 and 44 and accounted for 15.3 percent of the births for that city. Data from New York indicate a similar pattern. Immigrant women generally had more children, but those from Italy were exceptional. This changed drastically with the second generation. Rosenwaike (1973:275) concludes, "Obviously very strong assimilationists pressures had been at work, for not only did the second generation Italian-American women, on the average, have fewer than half the children of the immigrant generation; they curtailed their childbearing to a level below that of Americans of native parentage."

Certainly, assimilationist pressures is one possible explanation for this intergenerational difference in fertility. However, Gambino (1974:163–4) offers an alternate explanation of this same phenomenon:

Large families were found in the *Mezzogiorno* not because the *contadini* confused womanhood with high fertility. Nor did they have large families to satisfy any religious views. They had large families for two reasons. First, they lacked effective birth control technology. Second, a large number of children was an asset to a family in the economic system of old southern Italy. . . . Italian-American women of the second generation had means of birth control available to them. They were free to exercise only the traditional criterion regarding children—the economic well-being of the family. . . . they had children in proportion to their family incomes in America, where economic realities punished families with many children. They and their husbands decided it was better for the family to limit its number of children. And they did so.

Thus, according to Gambino it was not assimilationist pressures that caused second-generation women to limit their family size, but a continuing tradition of primary concern for family well-being.

The birth rate for third-generation Italians still appears to be decreasing. In a study of three generations of Italians in New York City, Russo (1970:207) found definite generational variation in family size with third-generation Italians reporting the fewest number of children. In response to the question, "How many children do you have?", 42.2 percent of third-gener-

70

ation Italians reported two or less. In contrast, among first-generation Italians 54.7 percent came from families of five or more children. This trend is apparent in spite of the fact that most Italians are Catholic. In fact, in a national survey, Ryder and Westoff (1971) reported that Italian Catholics were most likely of all Catholic ethnic groups to use contraceptive methods other than rhythm. Thus, it would appear that the stereotype of the Italian woman burdened by large numbers of children due to her religious convictions is certainly not typical of the average second- or third-generation Italian woman.

ENDOGAMY. Rates of intermarriage are useful indicators telling us something about social amalgamation and the disposition to lose ethnic identification. Endogamy among Italian Americans has been the subject of several studies, dealing in various ways with each of the immigrant waves.

In one study, Kennedy (1952) investigated intermarriage among seven ethnic groups in New Haven, Connecticut, for the period 1870–1950. She found that after the Jews, the Italians had the highest in-group marriage rate of the seven ethnic groups considered. However, the rate of in-group marriage did show a decrease from first-generation to second-generation Italians. In 1900, 97.9 percent of Italian marriages were strictly endogamous, as they were for most newly arrived ethnic groups. By 1950 this rate had fallen to 76.7, a sizable decrease but still high compared to other ethnic groups.

More recently, Abramson (1973) studied endogamy among nine Catholic ethnic groups using NORC data that sampled the total white Catholic population of the United States between the ages of 23 and 57. He found that the Italians were the only ethnic group of those arriving prior to 1920 that still showed relatively high rates of endogamy. Sixty-six percent of the Italian-Catholics in his sample were endogamous compared to 50 percent or less for Polish, Lithuanian, eastern European, German, Irish, and English. The only groups with higher rates of in-group marriage were the Spanish-speaking Catholics and the French Canadians. However, these results were tempered by several factors. Among those factors influencing rates of intermarriage was region. Those Italians living in the middle Atlantic states with high concentrations of Italians had very low rates of intermarriage (only 27 percent), but this increased to a high of 49 percent in the north central portion of the United States where Italians are relatively few in number. Even more significant were the different rates of intermarriage when age was used as a control. While only 27 percent of Abramson's sample of Italian Americans between the ages of 40 and 50 married non-Italians, 42 percent of those between 20 and 30 intermarried. He also found level of education to have an effect on endogamy with those completing high school having much higher rates of intermarriage than those without a high school diploma. This indicates that education is a powerful influence on assimilation, and that rates of intermarriage for Italians may continue to increase as they obtain college degrees and are increasingly exposed to individuals of other ethnic backgrounds.

These findings were basically confirmed and further refined by Alva (1976), who used the same data to determine if there were a generational effect on rates of intermarriage. He found that rates of intermarriage increased in each generation, although they remained lower for Italians than for most other groups. Alva (1976:1039) concluded that "the most obvious finding. . . . is the universality of a trend toward increasing social assimilation."

Finally, in the extensive study of ethnic pluralism in American life discussed earlier in regard to residential concentration, Kobrin and Goldschneider (1978) found that Italians of all age groups were more likely than Irish, French Canadians and Portuguese to have a spouse of the same ethnic origin, even though this was less true for younger Italians than it was for the older ones. Kobrin and Goldschneider's (1978:230) conclusions about the meaning of ethnicity in American life disagree sharply with those of Alva:

> Overall, ethnic homogamy has declined as the most important distinguishing feature of ethnic groups. Ethnicity in America is much less based on marriage within narrowly defined ethnic communities and the role of the intermarried is apparently being redefined in such a way as to allow for the ethnic community identification. . . . These convergences and growing homogeneity among ethnic communities in marriage patterns do not necessarily imply similarities and uniformities. Substantial differences remain and continue to characterize ethnic communities. That these marriage differences reflect more than class and cohort variations among ethnic groups suggests that specific ethnic structural and cultural determinants are operating.

DIVORCE. Marriage was essential for the southern Italian as a source of social identity, and family stability still seems to be relatively intact. According to the 1973 Census report on ethnicity (U.S. Bureau of the Census, 1973), "There were 2.6 million families in March 1972 whose head was of Italian origin. Most of these families were composed of husband–wife families, eighty-seven percent, and only about ten percent were families with a female head." This was the smallest percentage of 11 major ethnic groups for women between the ages of 15 and 44.

The stability of the Italian family is reflected in the low divorce rates for Italian Americans. According to the U.S. Census, only about 3 percent of all Italian Americans are divorced, and the divorce rate for younger Italians is not significantly higher than that for those over 45 (U.S. Bureau of the Census, 1973). In a comprehensive study of ethnicity in the United States using data based on seven NORC surveys, Greeley (1974:46) found that Italian American Catholics had the second-lowest divorce rate (only 2.0 percent) of all ethnic groups. The only group with a lower divorce rate was the Irish Catholics (1.8 percent). Similar findings were reported by Kobrin and Goldschneider (1978:40) who found that Italians and Irish were not only least likely of all Catholic ethnic groups to divorce but that if they did terminate their first marriage, they were also least likely to remarry. While the effects of religion cannot be discounted, the relatively weaker ties of the Italians to the Catholic Church indicate that family influence is certainly playing some role in maintaining a low divorce rate. This can be illustrated by the fact that other Catholic groups that have stronger ties to the Catholic Church have higher divorce rates. For example, Polish, Slavic, and French Catholics all have divorce rates over 4 percent, and it is 6.6 percent for Spanish-speaking Catholics. Thus, Catholicism cannot be the only explanatory factor for the low divorce rate among Italian Americans. Strong familism is certainly a critical variable.

SOCIAL CLASS. The Italians came to this country basically illiterate and with few skills to offer except a willingness to work. The significance attached to work and the disdain of the *contadino* for the value of education, described earlier, was carried over into their life in American society by resistance to the educational institutions. This conflict was very conspicuous in the early part of this century when Italian children were perceived as "problems" in the school system (Covello, 1967:284). Second-generation Italian children were more likely than other children to be truant, to cut classes, to be late for class, and to be involved in disciplinary infractions (Covello, 1967:285). According to Covello (1967: 288–296), there were many aspects of southern Italian cultural patterns that contributed to resistance to education. First, there was a fear on the part of the parents of the indoctrination of alien concepts which might destroy family unity. This was coupled with the belief that all necessary skills could be learned in the parental home or through apprenticeships. Second, there was an economic aspect to the conflict. The southern Italian peasant was accustomed to economic contributions to the household from children as young as 12 years. The idea of adolescents remaining in school throughout their teenage years was perceived by the first generation as enforced idleness of no clear benefit (Covello, 1967:289). Girls, in particular, and less frequently boys, were actively discouraged from attending school, an attitude which put them directly in conflict with compulsory education laws.

This antagonism toward formal education expressed by first-generation

Italians has had long-range repercussions. In terms of level of education, the Italians have ranked behind other ethnic groups that came to the United States about the same time. According to a U.S. Census report based on 1972 data, the greatest change between Italian Americans over 35 and those under 35 was in the percentage graduating from high school. As shown in Table 1, although only 31.9 percent of those over 35 graduated from high school, 51.1 percent of the younger Italians finished high school, an increase of almost 20 percentage points. While only 16.5 percent of those under 35 graduated college, a relatively low figure, this still represents a marked increase over the 6 percent of college graduates over 35.

These specific beliefs regarding the value of formal education are part of a broader orientation toward life. Several studies have attempted to measure these beliefs and assess their impact on social mobility.

An early study by Rosen (1959) found that Italian Americans placed relatively low value on independence and achievement training and had relatively low aspirations in terms of expectations for education and occupational choice. In a more recent study of adult males, Featherman (1971) found that Italian and Mexican Catholics expressed a high "materialistic orientation" toward work, valuing work instrumentally for achieving other goals, rather than regarding work as intrinsically satisfying. However, Featherman cautions against using adult motivation as an explanatory variable for ethnic group achievement differentials and suggests that motivation to complete school may be the key intervening variable. Finally, in a study of college seniors, Gottlieb and Sibbison (1974) asked students to explain their reasons for attending college. Both male and female Italian American students rated job-training as the major reason over more abstract choices such as seeking knowledge.

One visible outcome is that Italians went into blue-collar work, a pattern that has begun to change only within the third generation. Table 2 compares the employment patterns of first- and second-generation Italian males from the 1950 Census and all males from the 1972 Census. There was very little

TABLE 1
Years of School Completed by Italian Americans by Age

| AGE | ELEMENTARY | | | HIGH SCHOOL | | COLLEGE | | MEDIAN |
| | 0–4 | 5–7 | 8 | 1–3 | 4 | 1–3 | 4 OR MORE | SCH. YRS. |
	(%)	(%)	(%)	(%)	(%)	(%)	(%)	(%)
25–34	0.9	2.4	3.3	13.0	51.1	12.3	16.5	12.6
35 and over	8.7	10.5	17.0	19.7	31.9	6.1	6.0	11.1

SOURCE: U.S. Bureau of the Census (1973).

TABLE 2
Employment Patterns of Three Generations of Italian American Males

	FIRST-GENERATION MALES (%) 1950	SECOND-GENERATION MALES (%) 1950	ALL ITALIAN MALES (%)[a] 1972
Professional	3	6	13
Managerial	13	10	14
Clerical and Sales	6	17	15
Craftsmen	24	22	22
Operatives	24	29	16
Laborers	14	9	9
Service Workers	14	6	10
Private Household Workers	0	0	0

SOURCE: Gambino (1974:83). U. S. Bureau of the Census (1973).

[a]The census report did not differentiate by place of birth but by ethnic identification, thus all three generations are included in this figure.

change between the first and second generations with men of both generations largely employed in blue-collar work as either craftsmen or operatives. As Meloni (1977:10) explains, "As many as two-thirds of the second generation have remained common labourers like their fathers. The gap between the first and second generation is still smaller for Italian Americans than for any other major European ethnic group in America." By the third generation a significant shift toward white-collar work accompanied by an increase in the ranks of professionals can be seen. However, much of social mobility that has occurred has been in the television industry, in newspaper reporting, and in sports (Meloni, 1977:10). This can probably be attributed to the lesser role of education in occupational mobility among Italians. Unlike many other ethnic groups, upward mobility among Italians has not necessarily been correlated with higher educational levels (Kobrin and Goldschneider, 1978:32).

In analyzing the work history of Italian women, some research has centered around the expected conflict between work and family life. A study of Italian immigrants in Buffalo, New York, in the early part of this century discovered that while most Italian women were employed, their employment was limited to certain types of work (Yans-McLaughlin, 1977). Specifically, they were likely to work as seasonal laborers for the fruit and vegetable processing companies. In contrast to Polish immigrants, they rejected domestic labor, which would take them out of the Italian community and into other people's homes. The author interprets this pattern of work choice as compatible with the family orientation of the immigrant, because it allowed the fam-

TABLE 3

Employment Patterns of Three Generations of Italian American Females

	FIRST-GENERATION FEMALES (%) 1950	SECOND-GENERATION FEMALES (%) 1950	ALL ITALIAN FEMALES (%) 1972
Professional	2	5	12
Managerial	4	2	6
Clerical and Sales	8	40	46
Craftsmen	2	2	1
Operatives	77	44	18
Laborers	0	0	1
Service Workers	4	4	15
Private Household Workers	1	0	2

SOURCE: Gambino (1974:84). U. S. Bureau of the Census (1973).

ily to continue as the basic productive unit. It was a situation that minimized family strain by permitting mother and child to work together. As Yans-McLaughlin (1977:189) notes, "While 90 percent of the American-born children came to the canneries as independent workers, all the Italian youngsters worked and travelled with their parents. This suggests the foreign parents' unwillingness to relinquish economic and familial control over their young." Seasonal work , in addition, was not an assault on male pride, since the women were then not working more steadily than their frequently unemployed husbands. Thus, they could contribute to the family income, while minimizing sex-role conflicts. Further, as a community activity, field work permitted strict familial and sexual control over women in comparison to domestic work.

More recently, the work patterns of Italian women have been similar to those of Italian American men. As shown in Table 3, first-generation Italian women were most likely to be operatives. The second generation shifted to clerical work, as did most women with the expansion of this sector of the labor force after World War II. Even so, a relatively high proportion remained operatives as opposed to most other women who were more likely to be service workers. Further, Italian women are least likely to be professionals of all ethnic groups with the exception of Spanish, although, like the males, they did show a significant increase in this category by 1972. Since professional occupations require more schooling as well as a stronger career orientation which might interfere with family life, both these factors have probably worked as impediments to the upward occupational mobility of Italian women.

Roles in the Nuclear Family

While the southern Italian family has been termed patriarchal, the limitations of this description have already been discussed. All authority did not adhere to the father largely because of the socioemotional leadership of the Italian mother which gave her considerable power and influence on her family's affairs. However, her power, like the father's, was circumscribed, and there was a distinct separation of roles for males and females. This division of labor was largely maintained by the first-generation immigrant to the United States, and even in the second there are indications that remnants of fictitious patriarchy remain. As one second-generation mother (and grandmother) describes her marriage: "The most important thing is, that a man wants to be head of the family, so he could be, but in a roundabout way, I get my own way. So he's the boss, but I get my way if I know how to work it. . . . But you have to work very hard to make a successful marriage. You have to be a saint sometimes."

Several writers have explored this theme, comparing attitudes toward familial roles of first- and second-generation Italians. One study (Ware, 1935) found quite different beliefs between those over 35 and those under 35 in regard to the interpretation of familial roles. Ware (1935:193) found that 64 percent of the younger Italians disagreed with the statement, "the husband's authority should be supreme" as opposed to 35 percent of the older group. Eighty-six percent of the younger group did not think large families were a blessing as opposed to 58 percent of the older group. Finally, 54 percent of the second generation disagreed that a child should sacrifice his personal ambition to the welfare of the family group as opposed to 31 percent of the older group.

In a comprehensive study examining changes between the southern Italian peasant and first- and second-generation Italian Americans, Campisi (1948) found major changes. He described the southern Italian peasant as patriarchal, the first generation as fictitiously patriarchal, and the second generation as democratic with the father sharing high status with the mother and children. He found little in-group solidarity among second-generation Italians and a general weakening of Italian culture, which was no longer transmitted by the family but by the larger society.

Both of the above studies were done during a time when researchers believed that assimilation was inevitable, and thus both were concentrating on differences. Other more recent studies have found more cultural continuity than was originally believed to exist. In a descriptive study of an urban, Italian neighborhood, Gans (1962) found that while some of the outward manifestations of Italian culture had disappeared, many traditional patterns remained. Specific among these was what Gans termed the "segregated con-jugal pattern" where husbands and wives had distinctly separate roles, duties, and obligations and turned to kin of the same sex for advice and compan-ionship so that the society was essentially sex-segregated. According to Gans (1962:52):

> The segregated conjugal pattern is closely associated with the extended family, for the functions that are not performed by husband and wife for each other are handled by other members of the extended family. In a society where male and female roles are sharply distinguished, the man quickly learns that, on many oc-casions, his brother is a better source of advice and counsel than his wife.

While Gans's findings have been criticized for being applicable only to second-generation working-class Italians, and not descriptive of suburban college-educated Italian Americans (Lopreato, 1970), some more recent em-pirical studies indicate that even among upwardly mobile individuals, tradi-tional patterns remain. In a survey of graduating college seniors in five schools in Pennsylvania, Gottlieb and Sibbison (1974:49) found that Italian Catholic students were more likely to have a traditional conception of sex-roles than any other ethnic group including Irish, Jewish, Polish, or black. They also found that Italian females were less traditional than the males, al-though still more so than the other ethnic groups.

Similar findings were reported by Greeley (1974:157) who attempted to de-termine "whether ethnic heritage continues to have an influence on the re-lationships within the contemporary American family despite the process of assimilation and homogenization that was the American context of the im-migrant family."

In measuring the source of identification for third-generation Italians, Greeley (1974:162) found that the males found their father to be their pri-mary source of identification, while the females were most likely to identify with their mothers. The identification with the mother was stronger for Ital-ian females than any other group except blacks. However, Italian females tended to reject traditional roles for women and to not consider domestic skills important. In contrast, Italian males' acceptance of the traditional role for women was particularly high.

Pursuing the issue of generational change in a study of three generations of Italian Americans, Gallo (1974:84) found increasing equalitarianism with each succeeding generation. While the father still maintained his primary sta-tus within the family in the first generation, 80 percent of the second-gener-ation respondents asserted that there was shared decisionmaking among all family members and that discipline was shared between mother and father.

This trend was increased among third-generation respondents who reported democratic decisionmaking within the family with the family performing primarily affectional functions.

Socialization of Children

The first generation of Italians who came to the United States and settled in insulated communities were able to resist encroachments of American culture in their own lives, but the beliefs and customs they valued were more difficult to instill in their second-generation children. The second-generation Italians were not able to maintain the same degree of isolation. They were socialized not only by their parents, but also by American institutions, particularly the school system, and what they were taught at home was frequently in conflict with what they learned at school.

The resistance to the school system has already been discussed. One solution to generational conflict taken by many young Italian men was to identify with peers rather than parents or school, and so for many youth their friends became an important source of socialization. In Gans's (1962:38) study of the West Enders of Boston, he describes the significance of the peer group:

> Before or soon after they start going to school, boys and girls form cliques or gangs. In these cliques, which are sexually segregated, they play together and learn the lore of childhood. The clique influence is so strong, in fact, that both parents and school officials complain that their values have difficulty competing with those being taught in the peer group. The sexually segregated clique maintains its hold on the individual until late adolescence or early adulthood.

Among the concerns of the male adolescent peer groups were self-control, independence, and a competitive sort of display involving games of skill, verbal bantering, as well as conspicuous consumption related to clothes or cars (Gans, 1962:83).

In Gans's study the actual responsibility for childrearing belonged to the mother, with formal discipline being provided by the father (Gans, 1962:59). He found the West End family to be adult-centered in the sense that the household was run to satisfy adult wishes first. Children were expected to act like adults and not interfere with adult activities. By the age of seven, girls were expected to assist their mothers, while boys were given more freedom to roam (Gans, 1962:56). Punishment tended to be physical but intermingled with verbal and physical signs of affection.

In a recent study, 76 families in which both spouses were Italian American were interviewed, and their responses were compared to families in nonhomogamous marriages. Distinctive patterns of childrearing among the Italians were identified. Specifically, the Italian mother was found to exhibit a high level of nurturance. As Johnson (1978:38) reports;

> Her total devotion to her children in material and emotional support, caresses, food-giving, and in fact, supportive extension of herself makes her an indispensible figure in her children's lives. Her love for her children has few contingencies, and other than diffuse expectations for respect and sociability, she has few strings attached to it.

A second distinguishing feature was the manner in which discipline as a means of social control was used (Johnson, 1978:38):

> In Italian-American families, discipline is frequently used, and it is physical, swift and directed at the external locus of control (rather than appeals to the child's conscience). . . . Italian parents value love and affection between themselves and their children. Love, enjoyable for its own sake, is also employed to manage and control the behaviors of their children.

According to the author, this use of both punishment and love as mechanisms of social control cements family solidarity while discouraging autonomy and independence.

The Extended Family

Researchers have described the ethos of *familism* as characteristic of the southern Italian family. The concept of familism refers to the domination of the kinship group over the other forms of social organization (Gallo, 1974:87). Because of this domination interaction with nonfamily members was limited, and in southern Italy few moral sanctions existed outside of the immediate family. One indicator of familism is the number of friendships formed outside the immediate family group. In a study of first- and second-generation Italian Americans, Palisi (1966:175) found that first-generation Italians were likely to have fewer friends outside the family and belong to fewer formal organizations than the second generation. However, the extent of participation in family affairs was still stronger for the second-generation Italians. He concluded that "individuals in the second-generation are likely to be more assimilated, and more outgoing and have more opportunities to make friends than do first-generation persons. Thus, they make friends fairly easily. But, they also retain some of the old world patterns of family participation" (Palisi, 1966:175).

The strength of extended family ties results in exceptional nurturance and support for aged family members. In comparing family interaction of Italian American elderly with data from a national sample, Johnson (1978:36) found that the Italian aged were more likely to be integrated into a family system, to have a larger number of surviving children, and to be in more frequent contact with their children, and that the widowed were less likely to live alone. Further, the younger married Italian families were four times more likely than non-Italians to endorse without reservation the thought of an elderly parent living with them (Johnson, 1978:37). They were also decidedly more likely than non-Italians to reject outright the choice of a nursing home as a last resort for an incapacitated parent. Johnson (1978:39) concluded that because Italian families are more likely to spend leisure time with relatives than friends, they viewed their obligation to aged parents as a natural outcome of the family cycle. Since the family operates as a source of nurturance, filling the dependency needs of all its members, the onset of dependency of an elderly member is merely an extension of a lifetime pattern.

CHANGE AND ADAPTATION

Some distinction should be made between the old family in Italy and the new family in the United States. The more important family unit among Italian Americans is the nuclear family, but ties to the extended family are retained (Tomasi, 1972:10). The pace of modern urban life and the pressures of our industrial society frequently militate against actively continuing these extended family relationships. However, when residential dispersion precludes daily visiting, kinship ties are maintained symbolically through such devices as regular gatherings at holidays or feasts, scrupulous attendance at wakes and weddings, the remembrance of the birthdays and anniversaries of at least the oldest members of the family, the casual felicity of occasional visits, and finally, the profound certainty of assistance if help is sought. As one third-generation Italian college professor stated, "You can't reject the family. You can't leave it, no matter what you do. . . . Your family comes first. No matter what crisis has ever occurred with me, no matter how hostile the conflict, at the end, after the initial explosion is over, the family is there."

Only in recent times have Italian Americans found their rightful place in American society. The question is whether they have paid a high price for social mobility, the price being the loss of their own unique identity. There are several indications which show that the Italians have maintained their uniqueness. They have higher rates of marriage and lower rates of marital separation than most other ethnic groups. While they have been upwardly mobile, the ways in which they have achieved upward social mobility are distinctive and focused in certain areas. They have maintained a relatively high degree of residential concentration which, in turn, has helped to keep rates of intermarriage comparatively low. In a general sense, although the Italians have achieved both physical and social mobility, in their movement upward they have tended to bring their institutions and social patterns with them.

How has this been achieved? Some writers have suggested that most of the costs of assimilation were born by the second generation. According to Hansen, (1958:139–144) second-generation Italians tended either to overidentify or reject their heritage. This was the marginal generation that was in America but not of it. These were the sons and daughters of immigrants who either preferred the old Italian ways and tried to maintain them, or spurned the ways of the past in exchange for what they considered a superior or at least more satisfying way of life—the American way. Often these latter individuals Anglicized their names, moved to non-Italian neighborhoods, and in subtle ways literally and figuratively denied their heritage. There was also the other group of Italian Americans, on the other hand, who overidentified with the past and idealized the old traditional Italian ways.

Child (1943) described the second generation in a similar way, including an additional category, which he termed the "apathetic" reaction. Two of his categories, the "rebel" and the "in-group" reaction, conformed roughly to those identified by Hansen. The "apathetic" reaction, which probably described the majority of second-generation Italian Americans (Lopreato, 1970:70), was apathetic only in the sense that this group did not take the strong position characteristic of either of the other groups. Instead, they attempted to gain acceptance in both cultures, having both Italian and non-Italian friends, most likely marrying neighborhood sweethearts and, in general, making the cultural transition rather painlessly. Thus, while the rebel rejected his heritage and the "in-group" Italian immersed himself in the traditional Italian ways, the "apathetic" second-generation individual adapted readily, accepting the best of both worlds.

In the third generation and beyond, the Italian Americans exhibit similar value orientation preferences. This is predictable on the basis of the Hansen theory of generations (Spiegel, 1972; Kluckholn and Strodtbeck, 1961), which derives from the Jewish proverb, "What the son wishes to forget, the grandson wishes to remember." Having been born in the United States, and with parents who were born here, the grandchild feels more secure in his Americanicity and is consequently more able to assert his Italianicity. But in identifying with his immigrant grandparents, his value orientations approximate those of middle-class America, which in its turn acquired these preferences from its immigrant forebears. In spite of the fact that changes have occurred, it is equally obvious that ethnic pluralism remains a continuing feature of American life. The specific content of Italian ethnicity has been altered in each generation but elements of continuity remain, and ethnic identification is still a major source of social differentiation. The modern Italian American is developing a real interest in both the classical as well as the more immediate aspects of his Italian heritage. Perhaps, all Americans can profit from a translated *campanilismo* and *familism* which would provide the much needed *gemeinschaft* relationships so lost by others in urban industrial society.

REFERENCES

Abramson, Harold J. 1970. "Ethnic Pluralism in the Central City." Storrs, CT: Institute of Urban Research, University of Connecticut.
————. 1973. *Ethnic Diversity in Catholic America*. New York: Wiley.
Alva, Richard D. 1976. "Social Assimilation Among American Catholic National Origin Groups," *American Sociological Review*, 41(December): 1030–1046.
Campisi, Paul J. 1948. "Ethnic Family Patterns: The Italian Family in the United States," *American Journal of Sociology*, 53 (May): 443–449.
Carlyle, Margaret. 1962. *The Awakening of Southern Italy*. London: Oxford University Press.
Caroli, Betty Boyd. 1973. *Italian Repatriation from the United States, 1900–1914*. New York: Center for Migration Studies.
Castiglione, G. E. Di Palma. 1974. "Italian Immigration into the United States, 1901–1904," in F. Cordasco and E. Bucchioni (eds.), *The Italians: Social Background of an American Group*. Clifton, NJ: Augustus M. Kelley, pp. 53–73.
Chapman, C. G. 1971. *Milocca: A Sicilian Village*. Cambridge, MA: Schenkman Pub. Co.
Child, Irwin L. 1943. *Italian or American? The Second Generation in Conflict*. New Haven: Yale University Press.
Covello, Leonard. 1967. *The Social Background of the Italo-American School Child*. Leiden, The Netherlands: E. J. Brill.
Dore, Grazia. 1968. "Some Social and Historical Aspects of Italian Emigration to America," *Journal of Social History*, 2(Winter): 95–122.
Featherman, David L. 1971. "The Socioeconomic Achievement of White Religio-ethnic Groups," *American Sociological Review*, 36(April): 207–222.
Feldstein, Stanley, and Lawrence Costello. 1974. *The Ordeal of Assimilation*. Garden City, NY: Anchor Books.
Femminella, Francis X. 1961. "The Impact of Italian Migration and American Catholicism," *The American Catholic Sociological Review*, 22(Fall): 233–241.
Firey, Walter. 1947. *Land Use in Central Boston*. Cambridge, MA: Harvard University Press.
Foerster, Robert L. 1919. *The Italian Emigration of Our Times*. Cambridge, MA: Harvard University Press.
Gallo, Patrick J. 1974. *Ethnic Alienation: The Italian Americans*. Rutherford, NJ: Fairleigh Dickinson University Press.
Gambino, Richard. 1974. *Blood of My Blood*. New York: Doubleday and Co.
Gans, Herbert H. 1962. *The Urban Villagers*. Glencoe, IL: The Free Press.

Glazer, Nathan, and Daniel P. Moynihan. 1963. *Beyond the Melting Pot.* Cambridge, MA: Massachusetts Institute of Technology Press.

Goering, John. 1971. "The Emergence of Ethnic Interests: A Case of Serendipity," *Social Forces,* 50(March): 379–384.

Gordon, Milton. 1964. *Assimilation in American Life.* New York: Oxford University Press.

Gottlieb, David, and Virginia Sibbison. 1974. "Ethnicity and Religiosity: Some Selective Explorations Among College Seniors," *International Migration Review,* 8(Spring): 43–58.

Greeley, Andrew M. 1971. *Why Can't They Be Like Us?* New York: Wiley.

———. 1974. *Ethnicity in the United States.* New York: Wiley.

Hansen, Marcus Lee. 1958. "The Third Generation: Search for Continuity," in H. D. Stein and R. A. Cloward (eds.), *Social Perspectives on Behavior.* New York: The Free Press, pp. 139–144.

Johnson, Colleen Leahy. 1978. "Family Support Systems of Elderly Italian Americans," *Journal of Minority Aging,* 3–4(August–June): 34–41.

Kantrowitz, Nathan. 1973. *Ethnic and Racial Segregation in the New York Metropolis.* New York: Praeger.

Kennedy, Ruby Jo Reeves. 1952. "Single or Triple Melting Pot? Intermarriage in New Haven, 1870–1950," *American Journal of Sociology,* 58(July): 56–59.

Kertzer, David I. 1978. "European Peasant Household Structure: Some Implications From a Nineteenth Century Italian Community," *Journal of Family History,* 3:333–349.

Kluckholn, Florence R. and Fred L. Strodtbeck. 1961. *Variations in Value Orientations.* Evanston, IL: Row, Peterson and Co.

Kobrin, Frances E., and Calvin Goldscheider. 1978. *The Ethnic Factor in Family Structure and Mobility.* Cambridge, MA: Ballinger Pub. Co.

Lieberson, Stanley, 1963. *Ethnic Patterns in an American City.* New York: The Free Press.

Lopreato, Joseph. 1970. *Italian Americans.* New York: Random House.

———. 1976. *Peasants No More.* San Francisco: Chandler Pub. Co.

Meloni, Alberto. 1977. *Italian Americans: A Study Guide and Source Book.* San Francisco: R and R Research Associates Inc.

Morgan, J. Appleton. 1974 (1890). "What Shall We Do with the 'Dago'?" in W. Mocquin and C. Van Doren (eds.), *A Documentary History of the Italian American.* New York: Praeger, pp. 259–262.

Palisi, Bartolomeo. 1966. "Patterns of Social Participation in a Two Generation Sample of Italian Americans," *Sociological Quarterly,* 7(Spring): 167–178.

Rosen, Bernard C. 1959. "Race, Ethnicity and the Achievement Syndrome," *American Sociological Review,* 24(February): 47–60.

Rosenwaike, Ira. 1973. "Two Generations of Italians in America: Their Fertility Experience," *International Migration Review,* 7(Fall): 271–280.

Russo, Nicholas J. 1970. "Three Generations of Italians in New York City: Their Religious Acculturation," in Sylvano M. Tomasi and Madeline H. Engel (eds.), *The Italian Experience in the United States.* New York: Center for Migration Studies, pp. 195–213.

Ryder, Norman B., and Charles F. Westoff. 1971. *Reproduction in the United States, 1965.* Princeton, NJ: Princeton University Press.

Spiegel, J. 1972. *Transactions: The Interplay Between Individual, Family and Society.* New York: Science House.

Tomasi, Lydio F. 1972. *The Italian American Family: The Southern Italian Family's Process of Adjustment to an Urban America.* New York: Center for Migration Studies.

Tomasi, Sylvano M. 1970. "The Ethnic Church and the Integration of Italian Immigrants in the United States," in Sylvano M. Tomasi and Madeline H. Engel (eds.), *The Italian Experience in the United States.* New York: Center for Migration Studies, pp. 163–193.

U.S. Bureau of the Census. 1973. *Population Characteristics: Characteristics of the Population by Ethnic Origin,* Series P-20, No. 249. April. Washington, DC: U.S. Government Printing Office.

Vecoli, Rudolph J. 1969. "Prelates and Peasants," *Journal of Social History,* 2(Spring): 217–268.

———. 1974. "The Italian Americans," *The Center Magazine,* 7(July/August): 31–43.

Velikonja, Joseph. 1970. "Italian Immigrants in the United States in the Sixties," in Sylvano M. Tomasi and Madeline H. Engel (eds.), *The Italian Experience in the United States.* New York: Center for Migration Studies, pp. 23–39.

———. 1975. "The Identity and Functional Networks of the Italian Immigrant," in Francesco Cordasco (ed.), *Studies in Italian American Social History.* Totowa, NJ: Rowman and Littlefield, pp. 182–198.

———. 1977. "Territorial Spread of the Italians in the U.S." in S. M. Tomasi (ed.), *Perspectives in Italian Immigration and Ethnicity.* New York: Center for Migration Studies, pp. 67–79.

Ware, Caroline F. 1935. *Greenwich Village.* New York: Harper and Row.

Wrigley, E. Anthony. 1977. "Reflections on the History of the Family." *Daedalus* (Spring): 71–86.

Yans-McLaughlin, Virginia. 1977. *Family and Community, Italian Immigrants in Buffalo, 1880–1930.* Ithaca: Cornell University Press.

The American
Catholic Irish Family

The writer of this chapter combines historical research, the sociological eye, and detailed memories of growing up in a Massachusetts Irish parish community to chronicle the dynamics of change and development of new meanings among one of the more successful ethnic groups to come to America. An early arriving group, the Irish immigrants successfully made the shift from living in a disorganized rural setting to that of an adaptive existence in the turbulence of the growing American cities.

In addition to distinctive cultural mannerisms, they brought with them to mid-19th-century America a well-structured variant of the stem family that emphasized familism, matched with a modified bilateral extended kinship system in which consanguineality (blood descent) and siblingship were stressed. The role of the church for most was central, and parish organization tended to define the limits of the local community. Following World War II a variety of family lifestyles emerged to make being Irish a complex human condition and to make the specification of the typical American Catholic Irish family difficult indeed.

CHAPTER   FIVE

BY

ELLEN HORGAN BIDDLE

INTRODUCTION

The assimilation of the Irish in American life has been extensive. As a consequence, writing of their family lifestyles is not easy. Consider that the immigration from Ireland to America took place over a period of at least 200 years—and that the heaviest immigration occurred after the middle and throughout the latter decades of the 19th century and, somewhat reduced, on into the 20th. Current books and articles on the American Irish, moreover, have concentrated little on the family, and detailed studies of the major cities in which the Irish settled are only now being published. Recent materials indicate that the Irish experience differed, depending on the economic opportunity structure, the characteristics of native-born persons in the area, and the nature of the ethnic and racial composition of the urban centers in which the Irish settled (Thernstrom, 1973:220–261). Finally there are contradictions within the scholarly literature as well as in more popular works.

People are accustomed to hearing or reading the terms Irish Catholic and Irish American applied to American Catholic Irish, but I have chosen to use the phrase American Catholic Irish in the title and text of this chapter. In explanation, first, when the phrase used for the ethnic identity of the Catholic Irish in this country has the nationality of the group as the adjective and another ethnic identity (American) or a religion (Catholic) as a noun, the emphasis in the term falls not on Irish ethnicity but rather on American or Catholic. Second, in spite of the many attempts to create a community of Catholics of diverse nationalities, pancatholicism has not often been a popular concept among lay people in this country.

The use of the term American Catholic Irish in no way implies dislike of diversity nor disapproval of aspirations for a pluralistic society in the United States. In fact, I agree with Robert E. Kennedy, Jr. (1976) that the Catholic Irish group is one that demonstrates the success of pluralism. The use of the phrase American Catholic Irish reminds the reader that the ethnicity of the group has roots in Ireland and in its past.

HISTORICAL BACKGROUND

The first notable characteristic of American Irish families is that in matters concerning the history of the immigration and early experiences here, Irish families failed to pass information on much beyond the second generation[1] except in the case of an important relative or a few startling events. Families, most of whose members were nonliterate on arrival, also taught little to their children about the history of Ireland. Yet pride in being Irish and of so identifying is characteristic of most American Irish.

The history of Ireland is complex. The most significant political fact is that Ireland was ruthlessly subjugated by England, which maintained the country as an agricultural colony for its own interest and that of the minority Protestant citizens of Ireland. Declared under the lordship of Henry II (of England) in 1169, the Irish have a turbulent history of battle, rebellion, intrigue, settlement, suffering, terrorism, and pauperism. Independence was attained in 1922: the (now) Republic of Ireland, independent of England and populated

---

[1]The numbering system for generations may be confusing. First generation refers to the immigrants; second generation to the children of the immigrants; third generation to the grandchildren of immigrants, and so on.

heavily by Catholics, and northern Ireland, still tied to the English Parliament and dominated by Protestants. This portion of the chapter will focus only upon the socioeconomic and familial contexts in which the emigrants made their decisions to come to this country.

Socioeconomic Background to Irish Migrations

The reasons for the Irish emigration were many,[2] but the interaction of the patterns of rural Irish society with political, economic, and demographic catastrophes were the most important. Briefly, England kept Ireland as a rural colony, taking steps to destroy beginning industrialization. The population increased from approximately four-and-a-half million in the last half of the 18th century to over eight million by 1845 (Adams, 1932:3–4; Brody, 1974:49). The excess could not be funneled into a growing industrial economy; in fact, urban growth declined from 1851 to 1891 (Kennedy, 1973:156–157). Concomitantly with this large population increase, subdivision of the land became prevalent, facilitated by the widespread use of the potato for subsistence.[3] From 1695 to 1746 a set of Penal Laws was passed that resulted in legal discimination against the Catholic majority, forging in the minds of the Irish a belief that their national identity and religion were one. During the 18th and 19th centuries the peasants tried several times but failed to rid themselves of the oppression both of England and of the Irish Protestant minority. In addition, famines caused by the infamous potato blights occurred in 1800, 1807, 1816, 1822, 1839, 1845–1848 (the "Great Famine"), 1863, and 1879 (Kennedy, 1973:27). These exacerbated what was already a situation of declining living standards. In the more difficult economic periods, the peasants turned on their landlords and the landlords' agents. These proximate causes for the resulting emigrations were bound up with the ownership and use of land.

LANDLORDISM. By the 18th century most of the land in Ireland was owned either by the gentry or by a landlord class, most of whom were Protestant and many of whom lived in England. Another class was made up of small farmers who held long leases and whose holdings were large enough to

---

[2]For details, see Beckett (1966) for a concise history of Ireland, Adams (1932) for the coalescing of reasons for emigration from 1815 to 1845, and Schrier (1958), Kennedy (1973), and Brody (1974) for short summaries of relevant 18th- and 19th-century history. Also see Marx and Engels (1970).

[3]The population increase (aided by a decrease in the age of marriage for men) and the subdivision of land occurred when the use of the potato became widespread, but the cause and effect relationships between these changes are disputed by scholars. See Adams (1932:4) and Brody (1974:49–53) for brief discussions of the problem.

make a small profit for themselves. These, too, were primarily Protestant. But about 80 or 90 percent of the population, mostly Catholic, were peasants who leased land and raised grain to pay the landlords' rent. During the famines the blight of the potato led to the near starvation of the peasantry who dared not eat the grain for fear of eviction.

In the latter half of the 18th century, when the cheap, easily raised potato became a staple, peasants began living on smaller amounts of land. Laws favoring landowners encouraged further subdivision of holdings. By the early half of the 19th century subdivision had gone too far, chronic malnourishment was common, and the huts built to house the increased population were inadequate. By the time landlords and peasants realized that land would have to be consolidated, it was too late to halt overpopulation and economic misery, and the peasants stampeded out of Ireland.

STEM-FAMILY CHARACTERISTICS. When peasants attempted to increase their standard of living by increasing the size of their farms, their method was a familial one. Under the Penal Laws, at the death of the owner or tenant, land had to be subdivided so that *all* sons inherited the land equally. When these laws were no longer in force, farmers reverted to a stem-family system of impartible—not to be divided—land holdings, with only one son inheriting the land, or if there were no sons, only one daughter.[4]

Since there was no principle of primogeniture (eldest son inherits) nor ultimogeniture (youngest son inherits), fathers were free to designate among their sons the one who would inherit the land and family home. When the parents retired, the heir married and brought his wife to live in the family home, the young couple establishing themselves as the household heads. The wife brought a dowry usually about equal in value to the worth of the groom's father's farm. The dowry was given to her father-in-law, *not* her husband. The patronym went with the farm. Other children usually had to move out when the heir married. Their father then used the bride's dowry to make provisions for these children, sometimes arranging a marriage for a daughter with a neighbor's son, using the dowry from his daughter-in-law. If a daugh-

---

[4]Le Play (1871) provided the classic description of the stem family; Zimmerman and Frampton (1935) [reprinted in Farber (1966)] interpret passages from Le Play on types of families. For description of the Irish stem family after it was revived, the reader is referred to Arensberg (1937 copyright, reprinted 1950), Arensberg and Kimball (copyright 1940, reprinted 1968), Messenger (1969), and Brody (1974). For a study of families that migrated from rural Ireland to Dublin, see Humphreys [published in the United States (1966); the field work was done from 1949 to 1951]. See Kennedy (1973) for a demographic theory based on the Irish stem family. Glazer and Moynihan (1963:226–229) point out parallels between Irish rural society and the American Irish political machine of New York City. Stein (1971) uses materials from descriptions of the Irish stem family to interpret stressed behavior of young American Irish males. Scheper-Hughes (1979) updates personal dilemmas of stem family members in Ireland.

ter were the heiress, the in-marrying son-in-law brought money to the bride's father, in excess usually of the dowries paid by brides, but the name of the farm remained that of the bride's father for a generation.

The father and his successor wrote a contract concerning the rights of the retired couple. These often included space for sleeping, provision of food, land to cultivate, perhaps a cow, depending on the wealth of the farm, and care for the surviving parent when the other died. Fathers understood that the relationship of mother-in-law and daughter-in-law might be strained; the contract specified that if conflict should occur, the parents would be cared for elsewhere.

The two fathers arranged the marriage. The details of the match were often completed within a week. The most important aspect of the arrangements was that the fathers should agree on the value of the groom's father's farm, a decision that affected the size of the bride's dowry. The status of the groom changed from that of boy or lad to adult when he married.[5]

There were several negative consequences for family members arising from this system. The successor was sometimes 40 or possibly 50 years old when the farm was inherited, so that almost-compulsory delayed marriage and singleness became common. Fathers often waited until near retirement before choosing an inheritor, increasing the probability of rivalry among the sons or, if there were no sons, among the daughters. The wife/mother hoped to have a daughter-in-law (son-in-law) with whom she would get along, yet her interest in harmony within the household might not coincide with the desires of her husband to receive a large dowry from the heir's bride (or a large sum of money if his daughter were the inheritor). Unless there were only two children in the family, there was no structural way in the system for the other children to obtain an inheritance equal to that of the inheritor. There was, however, a strong norm that the father should make some provision for the other children, however unequal this might be.[6] Additionally, the heir and his wife (or the heiress and her husband) were placed in the difficult situation of living with parents; consequently, their marriage was more regulated than those of their siblings (Mattis, 1975).

The major effect of the system, however, was to disperse the unmarried siblings of the inheritor of the land from rural Ireland, a pattern of neolocal residence. At the time of the Great Famine, when land holdings were small, and

---

[5]Messenger (1969:68) reports that male age grading in Ireland is conceptualized as follows: until age 40, a boy or lad; until age 60, an adult; until age 80, middle-aged; and after that, old age.

[6]Mattis (1975) sees the role of the bride as crucial since the other children could not be provided for unless the bride brought the dowry to her father-in-law. She terms the bride the "grand liberator."

the stem family was being reinstituted, migration to an industrializing nation became an acceptable solution to poverty and overpopulation. Two possible solutions were available for the dispersed siblings: a move to an urban area of Ireland, although economic conditions were little better in the cities, and a decision to become a landless laborer with no economic security (Kennedy, 1973:154–155).

Counterbalancing the problematic aspects of the system was a positive strength. Familism developed—a set of beliefs in which the family placed its welfare above the idiosyncratic wishes of any one person. The father accepted responsibility for the economic welfare of members of the family, and children accepted differential treatment in the interest of family loyalty. All members shared the value that the land or leasehold should remain in the family. Sibling solidarity was a natural outgrowth of familism. And, in fact, both the emigration out of Ireland to this country and the continuing economic stability of the farms from which the migrants came were supported to a large extent from the savings of siblings and relatives in this country who sent money home even though they were partially destitute themselves (Schrier, 1958:111).

WORK, AUTHORITY, AND THE SEXES. The Irish believed that married women should not go out to work, also a church view. This was reinforced by the belief that a working wife diminishes the status of her husband, that women should stay home and rear children, and that jobs in a marginal economy should go to others. But unmarried daughters were permitted to leave home to go to work. In an economic class with rising material aspirations, some daughters remained single all their lives. Since the maintenance of an acceptable standard of living had become a dominant value in Ireland, more important than marriage and a family, the numbers of single people increased over time (Kennedy, 1973:159–160).

This increase in single persons was also a function of the low status of women in rural Ireland compared with urban women in America and England. Within the family, the father was dominant. He made decisions, controlled the money, operated the farm, and did no domestic work. The mother, meanwhile, was in charge of all domestic matters, but she was also in charge of the ecological area around the hut (the haggard) and of any animals the family owned. She also did heavy farm work with her husband and sons when needed. Boys worked with their fathers and did no housework; they were treated by their mothers in a warm, supportive manner. Daughters helped their mothers, establishing a no-nonsense quasi-instrumental relationship with them. In the evenings fathers and sons relaxed, but mothers and daughters worked. The women were also subservient to the men, caring for their needs before their own; for example, they served the fathers and sons first at meals and gave them not only more food but more nutritious food (Kennedy, 1973:52).

Male domination had serious consequences for women. As early as 1841 in rural areas, men had a higher life expectancy than women (Kennedy, 1973:45). After 1870 life expectancy for women in both rural and urban Ireland was only slightly higher than that for men and not as much higher than the same rates for women in America and England (Kennedy, 1973:55). From 1871 until 1940, moreover, age- and sex-specific death rates indicate that more Irish females than males died among children over five years old and up to 19 (Kennedy, 1973:60). Daughters would have been unaware of these indices, but they were not unaware of their low status vis-à-vis their brothers and their future low status as wives. Daughters left rural Ireland not just for a job but for higher status as women and for independence (Kennedy, 1973:7). The uncommonly high number of single women in the Irish immigration may be seen as an early example of feminism.

Migration Periods

There seem to have been three distinct periods in the Irish immigration (Adams, 1932:68).

1. *Colonial Period to 1815.* By 1790 the U.S. Census listed 44,000 Irish immigrants (Adams, 1932:70), with an estimate of about 150,000 people of Irish descent (Shannon, 1963:29). After that, the numbers arriving fluctuated (Adams, 1932:69–70) but were few. Migrating were small farmers of an economic class above the peasantry (Adams, 1932:34–35). They were young, often single, and mostly Protestants from northern Ireland who were English and Scottish in descent.

2. *1815 to the Great Famine of Ireland in 1845–1848.* Although statistics are unreliable for this period,[7] numbers arriving were approximately 50,000 to 60,000 through 1819, about 15,000 between 1820 and 1826, around 45,000 to 50,000 from 1827 to 1828, and at least 400,000 between 1829 and 1845. The total for the period was probably over a half million (Adams, 1932).

   The types of immigrants in this transition period changed little at first. Most were small farmers, but others were tradesmen, weavers,

---

[7]See Adams (1932:410–428) for a discussion of the difficulties of gathering statistics of immigrant arrivals and the kinds of estimate possible from different sources. The figures are taken from Adams. The writer, however, does not endorse Adams's view of the Irish immigration nor his biased reporting of the Irish poor.

spinners, deep-sea fishermen, shopkeepers, domestic servants, and by 1818 and 1819 a number of peasants from southern Ireland, the first large exodus of Catholic Celts (Adams, 1932:104–111). By 1835 these latter had changed the character of the immigration. Fifty to 60 percent were Catholics from southern Ireland (Adams, 1932:191–192;222). And while in the early 1830s women were about 35 percent of immigrants, the proportion rose to 48 percent in 1835. More of these latter were married, for it seems that peasants came first as intact families (Adams, 1932:194–195). Single women continued to migrate; those who spoke only Irish increased (Adams, 1932:223).

3. *Immigration After 1845, Great Famine Period.* About 120,000 Irish immigrants arrived in 1845 and 1846. Then in only eight years, 1847 to 1854, about one-and-a-quarter million people, mostly Celtic Irish, came (Schrier, 1958:157).

Those who came in this period were mostly Catholic peasants from south and west Ireland. From 1850 to 1877, about 66 percent were between the ages of 15 and 35; for the rest of the century the proportion aged 15 to 35 was never less than 80 percent (Schrier, 1958:4). Except for the early Great Famine years, married immigrants were rarely over 16 percent (Schrier, 1958:4). After the 1870s the number of single women increased (Kennedy, 1973:76–85). The immigration of the 20th century seems to have followed much the same pattern except that more women than men arrived (Ferenczi, 1929:432–443).

Summarized and based on U.S. Census materials: From 1821 to 1850 about a million Irish entered this country; from 1851 to 1900 about three million arrived (Schrier, 1958:159); and from 1901 to 1924 700,000 came (Ferenczi, 1929:432–443). After 1924, the Irish immigration declined.

Social Context of the Lifestyles of the American Catholic Irish

Readers should be aware of the social context in which the Irish settlement and adjustment were embedded.

First, the Irish went to cities and stayed in cities. They congregated in Boston, New York, Jersey City, Philadelphia, Pittsburgh, St. Louis, Chicago, and San Francisco (Wittke, 1956:23–24; Schrier, 1958:6–7). That a rural people became urban is not an anomaly, for the migrants did not enter as intact families nor as experienced farmers. They did not, for example, have the technology for horse-drawn methods of farming (Kennedy, 1976:358). They were, instead, the young, single, dispersed children of poor, rural Irish.

Second, the Irish established the Catholic Church as a powerful institution in this country. Protestant, native-born people feared and hated the church for reasons rational and irrational. The church absorbed some of the hatred directed toward the Irish and provided the immigrants and their children a clear personal-salvation theology to help them with life-cycle stressors.

Third, the Irish had startling success as have other ethnic groups in building parallel institutions to provide services for their mutual benefit (Handlin, 1941:156–183: Kutzik, 1979:32–65). Kutzik points to these five ways in which the Irish helped one another, including the aged poor: informal aid from kin and neighbors, trade associations (not yet unions), fraternal organizations, creation of their own welfare system through political activities, and homes for the aged, with nuns staffing and priests overseeing (Kutzik, 1979:49–57). These mutual-aid groups and organizations helped the immigrants and protected them from the hurt of exclusion from associations of native-born people. But, they also isolated the Irish and impeded rapid acculturation. The Irish, moreover, coopted urban political machines and major influence centers in the Democratic party, in the growing labor movement, in the police and fire departments, and in civil services in several cities.

Fourth, the Irish changed reference groups. Immigrants first compared themselves to their relatives in Ireland and considered themselves fortunate. Later they compared themselves with other American Irish, congratulating themselves on success—or else resenting failure. Socially mobile Irish used double comparison groups—other American Irish and native-born people— and were vulnerable to an ambivalence engendered thereby, with the less successful Irish putting the more successful down, and native-born people not accepting them.

Fifth, the work experience of the Irish was harsh. On arrival, they did menial, manual labor, as did most of the second generation. They did pick-and-shovel work, building streets and railroads and were, for instance, the main construction workers on every canal in the north up to the Civil War (Adams, 1932:151). In the cities men were, for example, hod carriers, dock workers, stable hands, street cleaners, waiters, bartenders, and porters. Women were servants, cooks, charwomen, laundresses, and aides to the semiskilled (Wittke, 1956:25). Hours were long, pay was lower than that for native-born people, work was wearying, and employers often unfriendly. The stability of the family was fragile when work was insecure.

Sixth, social class was a factor in the social context of American Catholic Irish lifestyles as has been documented often (Warner and Srole, 1945; Greeley, 1972; Birmingham, 1973; Rose F. Kennedy, 1974). Matza (1966), Thernstrom (1973), and Esslinger (1975) report, however, the slow rise of American Catholic Irish in the class system. The reasons suggested for the slow rise are the following: the pauperization of the Irish before they migrated (Matza); the low level of skill for work on arrival (Thernstrom); the discrimination against them because of their ethnicity, especially their religion (Thernstrom); values learned and perpetuated within the family such as the need for security and lack of interest in risk-taking (Thernstrom); and the large number of people who were economically mobile downward (*skidding* is the term Thernstrom used). This slow upward mobility is a fact of history that tied the American Catholic Irish to their cultural past. Colloquial terms (some are negative labels) have been used for years to describe American Catholic Irish socioeconomic classes. These include shanty Irish, lace curtain Irish, venetian blind Irish, oriental rug Irish, and Birmingham's contribution, "real lace" Irish (1973), used in the title of his book.

Early Adaptation of the American Irish Family

America was ill prepared for the arrival of the Irish. Squalid living conditions existed in all major cities. Those of Boston described by Handlin (1941:93–127) were more than matched, for instance, by the miseries in New York of which McCague wrote (1968:20–27). The immigrants found housing wherever they could: lodging houses; older, larger, subdivided houses; warehouses; shanties (huts); flats; and cellars and attics of old buildings. Sanitation was inadequate or absent, smells deplorable, and the water supply uncertain. Roofs leaked. Walls were damp. Garbage rotted. Privacy was limited. Cleanliness was next to impossible.

Under these conditions, family and community life were often turbulent. Men left for work early and returned late, as did many women; children and young teenagers roamed the street. In the neighborhoods, pawnbrokers thrived; greengrocers (fruit and vegetable shops) often sold more inexpensive rye whiskey than other items (not exclusively to men); saloons flourished; idle men stood around, hoping for work; fights started easily and spread quickly; prostitution occurred. Handlin (1941) reported that in Boston after the Irish came, infant mortality rates rose (p. 199), Irish longevity decreased (p. 199), marriage and fertility rates increased (p. 121), pauperism rose (p. 121), and emotional stress increased (p. 126) as did the rate of non-legitimate births (p. 126). Norms of rural family life and social forms such as drinking, argumentation, and visitation lost much of their meaning in a social context of high-density urban living.

In Buffalo, from 1855 to 1875, some carryover of structural elements of the Irish family were found by Mattis (1975). Delayed marriage remained a salient factor in the Irish immigrant community; when both partners were from Ireland, the average age at marriage for males was 35 and for females, 31. The average age for male native-born people was 26, and for females, 23. Some Irish, females more so than males, remained single throughout their lives. [For 1950, Heer (1961:236–238) reports that both Irish males and females, immigrants and second-generation people, were more likely to marry late or not at all compared with 12 other ethnic groups and native-born people. These findings are for the end of the Irish immigration.] These patterns in Buffalo may be seen as consistent with the need for the Irish to establish themselves economically before marriage and with the relatively high number of women who came here seeking increased independence. That Mattis found more Irish men marrying non-Irish women rather than the reverse pattern is consistent with her finding that some Irish women did not marry at all. [But by 1920 Irish immigrant men were more likely to have an Ireland-born wife, 71 percent, than Ireland-born women were to have Ireland-born husbands, 61 percent (Carpenter, 1927:234–235).]

HOUSEHOLDS HEADED BY WOMEN. A significant form of adaptation in family organization appeared in the first decades after arrival of the Irish. Mattis (1975) reports that households headed by women appeared high—18 percent in 1855, 14 percent in 1865, and 16 percent in 1875. Most of these heads of households were widows, the latter partly a consequence of men marrying younger women than themselves (Mattis, 1975) and partly a consequence of the dangerous occupations of men and of their early deaths. As another adaptive aspect, Mattis also notes that *most of the households expanded to include relatives were headed by women,* a finding noticed in other urbanizing minority groups (Pauw, 1963; Rainwater, 1966; Smith and Biddle, 1975). At the height of the Irish immigration in 1855, families expanded to include parents, siblings, nieces, nephews, and some in-laws. By 1875 the added relatives were mostly grandparents, a finding that might be interpreted as a partial return to the traditional stem family or, more simply, as a reflection of the passage of time during which other relatives found different housing.

Additionally, in both 1855 and 1875 about one-fifth or one-fourth of the immigrant households had someone *not* related by blood or marriage living in the house (boarders and *their* relatives). This pattern is one of adaptation to the economic and social exigencies faced by women who headed these households. Women needed money obtained from rent and assistance with their families. But they also provided service for others who had recently migrated.

THE ESTABLISHED AMERICAN CATHOLIC IRISH FAMILY AND PARISH LIFE: 1920–1950

Over several decades after the mass migration and the introduction of further Irish immigrants of a slightly more stable background, the structure, values, and behavior of the Irish stem family combined into an amalgam of the old and new. The immigrant quasighetto neighborhoods in the cities tended to

96

disappear and were replaced by the parish as the unit of community living.[8] Although not a large number were involved, some American Irish families moved as single units into the economically better neighborhoods. But the majority remained ethnically and ecologically nucleated, building community and family solidarity around the parish which was organized by the church. The extensive depiction of family life in one mid-Massachusetts parish that follows represents a form of marshaling ethnographic data through the personalized and extended sociological anecdote as experienced by the writer of this chapter who grew up in the parish described.[9] Apart from the lack of a parochial school, there was little to differentiate this parish from others in Massachusetts.

No justification need be made for the style of reporting, for there are few sociological sources of information about American Irish family life. Novels, biographies, and works on aspects of the American Irish experience other than the family abound, yet none of these provides the kind of sociological information readers may wish to know. The time period of the parish described is approximately 1920 to 1950.

THE PARISH

The parish was an ecological unit, a community of families and an organized church membership. It was an enclave of American Irish families of the second, third, and sometimes fourth generation living dispersed among native-born people and a few families from other ethnic groups. Church administrators drew boundaries so that families of about the same economic level were included and built the church near the center. Shops were close to the church and included a drugstore, a laundry, two or three proprietor-run grocery stores, a gasoline station, variety store, a shoe repair shop, a bakery, a liquor store, and a tavern. Some of the stores had delivery service. Many women shopped daily. Three public schools and a park were found in the parish, not always contiguous to the parish center. The parish served during the week as the unit within which social interaction took place.

CONTROLS

The parish was compact enough that some of the children knew almost everyone and at least half the adults knew one another personally and knew more by sight.

---

[8] The use of the parish as a neighborhood unit is common when writing of the American Irish, for the coalescence of residence, church, and parochial school (or public elementary school) within a small geographically closed area was a feature of the Catholic parish that the church administrators wisely fostered in the first half of the 20th century. The parish as a unit has been used most recently by Greeley (1972) when he described the neighborhood of "Beverly." Farrell's *Studs Lonigan* (1938) also took place in a parish and Curran's novel, *The Parish and the Hill* (1948), contrasts a poor Massachusetts Irish parish with a Yankee neighborhood.
[9] Parish people ranged from working class to lower-middle and middle-middle in the United States system.

People with problems and children with handicaps were enveloped in a relatively closed community. Priests were a familiar sight on the streets talking with adults and watching the young. Some men would go the tavern at night although a few might be there all day. Older teenagers and young adult men would gather at the shops in the evenings and teenage girls in groups would find some reason to shop or to visit the church. There were informal cliques among all age groups and, harking back to Ireland, most of these were age and sex graded. The pace of life was not fast. Small talk passed back and forth. Those in need were visited by the priests. Women individually and voluntarily helped other families at times of crisis.

Lest this sound like the mythical village, strains should be noted. While small talk kept people informed, it also made family happenings public knowledge quickly, it worked to induce conformity of behavior, and it reaffirmed prevailing attitudes. As a result, new ideas, different values or changes in custom were slow to occur. Constraints on behavior were as much external as internal.

Families were, however, quite private about family matters; children were usually sent outside while family business was discussed. Adult parishioners kept private within the family how they voted, the size of family income, expenditures planned, gossiped-about sexual behavior, the beliefs of those who left the church, public events on which there might be controversy, job changes, and the futures of children. The conversations to which children might listen involved general discussions about politics and politicians, family events being planned, news about relatives, and comments about those persons whose public behavior was not approved.

CHURCH MEMBERSHIP

The parish was an organized church membership. The priests knew every family. The activities of the family revolved around the church calendar as much as the school schedules of children and the work hours of men (and some women). Most religious activities and rituals took place in the church. Mothers were responsible for the religious education of children at home. Boys were expected to serve at mass as altar boys. Girls participated in services on Holy Thursday and Good Friday. Children, if they did not attend parochial school, went to religious instructions on week afternoons and were separated into groups by school grade and sex. Catechisms were memorized and lessons listened to, with nuns as the usual teachers. Children were expected to go to confession on Saturday afternoon and, after fasting from midnight, to receive communion on Sunday morning. At the children's mass, the same nuns who taught religious classes supervised and, again, children were seated by school grade and sex. High school students went to religious instruction on a week night, were taught by priests, and, by custom now, segregated themselves by gender.

Families were urged to attend mass on weekdays and to make short visits to the church when close by, although few did. Attendance at Sunday mass and the special holy days was required and those who did not attend committed a mortal sin, serious enough to send one's soul to hell if one died before confessing. Most parishioners attended these masses. Those who aspired to attend mass as a family, as Protestant families attended their services, were disappointed. Priests insisted upon school children attending their own mass, and parents often went individually to separate masses so that the younger children might be attended by the other, if no kin lived nearby to watch the children.

CHURCH AND FAMILY

The most important aspect of the church was the underpinning it gave to the structure of the American Irish family and the clear dogma of personal salvation it gave to members. The de facto theology, the beliefs which the laity thought the church taught [Osborne (1969:40) uses this term] was passed from parents to children. The chief points of the doctrine were the following: each individual had an immortal soul; people were born with original sin which could only be removed by Catholic baptism; God was three people, the Trinity, God the Father, God the Son, and God the Holy Spirit but yet only one; Mary, the mother of Jesus was a virgin and, when she died, her body went to heaven; Jesus became a man to provide an opportunity for people to reach Heaven and to create a church that would show people the way to live; the Catholic Church was the only true church and adherents of other religions, even if they led exemplary lives, could only go to limbo, a pleasant place but one in which God never appeared; all sins committed in one's lifetime had to be suffered for in purgatory before one's soul went to heaven; the difficulties of life were to be borne as best one could; unequal talents and socioeconomic success or failure were unimportant to God; mortal sins on one's soul at the time of death prevented one from going to purgatory or heaven so that regular confession was necessary; the list of mortal sins was long but included not only those of murder, lying, and theft but also disobedience of parents and others in authority, sinful thoughts, the use of contraceptives, adultery, fornication, abortion, divorce, marriage in a non-Catholic ceremony, suicide, lack of attendance at Mass on Sundays or holy days—and others; if one were a good Catholic and died in the grace of God, one went eventually to heaven to be with God forever.[10]

The sinfulness of people was stressed but the way to salvation was clear; follow the teachings of the church; participate in the sacraments and pray—to keep one's faith. Children were admonished to obey their parents, believe in their church and show their faith in such ways as not saying the Protestant end of the Lord's Prayer at school, by blessing themselves before batting in a ballgame or going swimming, and by wearing a "miraculous" medal. When children misbehaved, mothers suggested they confess their sins and, if they raised questions about Catholic beliefs, they talk to the priest. When children, especially girls, were required to do something they found unpleasant, mothers suggested they offer their difficulties to God as a gift.

FATHER'S AND MOTHER'S POSITIONS

The church affected family life by supporting the traditional Irish family's way of doing things. When the man lost the tangible sign of the farm as a basis for

---

[10]The writer wishes to stress that this is the theology as understood by lay people in the parish, circa 1920–1950, to remind readers of the extensive literature created by scholars and philosophers who have astutely interpreted Catholic thought through the centuries, and to note that the Catholic Church in the United States has changed extensively since the Second Vatican Council.

family cohesion, he did not forfeit his authority and status as head of the family responsible for the economic welfare of all. Because fathers' work hours were long, mothers were in charge of daily domestic activities within the family and some believed they had effective influence. Even so, husbands made most major decisions alone or perhaps after a brief discussion with their wives. Most importantly the husband was in charge of money and provided a set sum to his wife, usually on a weekly basis. Few children had allowances, including those in high school and even some in college.

Men often decided on the children's occupations and educations and, although the children's abilities were taken into account, their wishes were sometimes ignored. The fathers were deeply involved in decisions about children's marriages but mothers' views were often heard that daughters should be socially mobile by making a good marriage and that marriages for both sons and daughters should be delayed as long as possible, certainly until the young people established themselves economically. In fact, both mothers and fathers emphasized good marriages for their children—in economic terms as well as in terms of the character of the future spouse. This was not spoken about openly.[11] Going steady was discouraged, as was dating a non-Catholic. The father's position was recognized by the expectation that an aspiring groom would ask him for his daughter's hand, not always a ritual matter, for some men were rejected. But, apart from the mother's input concerning marriage, fathers decided when and how the family should move, buy items of furniture, purchase a car, and take a vacation. No matter how quiet, inarticulate, or unassuming the father might have been, nor how kindly he exercised his authority, he made the decisions.

There were, of course, some women who *did* make major family decisions. Some of these had mild husbands who allowed them to do so. There were other women who might not have chosen to head the family, but whose husbands did not through default of character, overuse of alcohol, or desperation in the face of an indomitable woman. These were relatively rare. The more usual case was the gentle, friendly, hardworking husband who quietly headed the family and a competent, industrious but mild wife who accepted her husband's authority. It is unfortunate that the family in Ireland and this country has sometimes been portrayed as dominated by women (Greeley, 1972:110–113; McCready, 1974: 164–165), as this view hides the real difficulties of energetic and instrumental American Irish women who accepted a subordinate role within the family. One problem was that some men acted at home in an arbitrary or authoritarian manner.[12]

Women were in charge of domestic activity with some assistance from their husbands, who might take a child for a walk on Sunday, or dry a few dishes, or, more rarely, help prepare a meal. Living in tenements and apartments or rented houses, women no longer were responsible for the haggard, and gardening was not common. Women gained independence in spending the family's money. They also had the responsibility of rearing their sons through the teenage years. They kept up the homes and seldom questioned the family's economic status over which they worried but had little control.

---

[11]See Humphreys (1966) for a discussion of the openness of Dublin families on this issue.
[12]Studs' father is an example (Farrell, 1938).

As in Ireland, single women were free to work. Despite some stigma, expressed by married women, which attached to remaining single, some women chose not to marry, as did some men.[13] Widows, too, went to work but not always full time in a regular job. Some became the itinerant helpers of parish families, helping out when life course events occurred in others' families. Married women usually did not work, either in regular paid jobs or with their husbands, except in small proprietary businesses at busy times of the year. The exceptions to this were women who helped establish the family economically and then stopped [as in Buffalo, see Mattis (1975)] or when their husbands were unemployed during the Great Depression or when the country needed workers during World War II (although, even then, few did). American Irish women behaved very much like their counterparts in Ireland and, out of each cohort of women, some decided to marry and rear a family (having relatively high fertility rates); others delayed marriage or remained single and worked. Widows had little choice. They ran their homes, reared their children, and worked. Widows, although treated deferentially by men, were not usually considered eligible as marital partners. Widowers often married single women, sometimes younger than themselves. Motherhood was considered virtuous; wifehood was rarely mentioned.

CHILDREN

Children in American Catholic Irish homes were treated as children, not small adults. Mothers were firm and moralistic but also kind, sentimental, and active. Children learned to be subordinate, obedient, and respectful. Children were also taught to be respectable—to do the right thing and to be polite. A spoiled, whiny, or bold child was unacceptable to mothers and fathers. Punishment for disobedience of children was external and expressed by parents, parishioners, and priests. Shame and ridicule, appeals to the embarrassment caused one's parents (especially one's mother), and mocking were used interchangeably by all. Success of children, however, was underplayed, was assumed a part of life, and, when told to others, was understated.

Mothers emphasized physical activity for children and often suggested they go outside and play or exercise rather than stay inside the home and read, hang around, or pursue hobbies. Participation in sports was emphasized, especially for boys. Achievement in school was encouraged. Since success in educational and occupational spheres had not been an experience of mothers, they pointed to people they admired in the parish and encouraged children to make something of themselves.

In one area of parenting, fathers stepped in—they taught sons to fight. Mothers disapproved of boys' fighting and hoped their sons would not become involved in neighborhood arguments. Fathers were ambivalent. They, too, did not want their boys to fight but, even more, they did not want their sons to be beaten up or not to stand up for their rights. As a result, many fathers taught their sons to fight; and the boys fought, often over the issue of whether or not they would

---

[13]Kennedy (1973:152) points out that in Ireland there was little or no stigma attached to remaining single throughout one's life.

do so. It was also a part of the youth culture for a boy to be known as a good fighter; girls knew which boys would stand up for their rights and which would not.

Differential treatment by mothers of their sons and daughters continued, as in Ireland. Boys were treated more affectionately than girls. The importance of the boys' work future was stressed while the learning of how to run a household was emphasized for girls. Children knew from an early age that the resources of the family could not provide for all. If their brothers were older or equally talented, or almost so, daughters knew that the resources of the family would go first to their brothers. In the less well-off families, older sons and daughters went to work and younger brothers, and sometimes their sisters, might benefit from the increased status of the family. In the better-off families, the older sons were provided opportunities, the younger waited their turn, and daughters hoped to be helped.

The concept of equal treatment of each child remained subordinate to the concept of providing as best one could for all within the context of limited resources. However different one might consider such familism by today's standards of the enhancement of each individual, there was the advantage that a family in which each looks out for the others has cohesion. Sibling loyalty is not necessary when there are adequate resources but, when they are scarce, some system of allocation *without* rivalry is needed [see Greeley (1972:115–116) on sibling relationships]. Families, who in the usual course of events had a relatively capable father and a responsible mother who was reasonably warm toward her children, were strengthened by the concern of children for one another. When these were absent, difficulties occurred.[14] In the parish, adult siblings kept in touch, assistance was given to one another when needed. All cared for elderly parents but in different ways, depending on their resources—paying bills, shopping, visiting, and having the parents live in their homes.

Sons may have been confused by being the recipients of both affective and instrumental behavior from their mothers in a way in which daughters were not. As long as sons could look forward to being heads of families catered to by their wives and children, major problems were avoided. If daughters could find a husband who would head the family and achieve economic viability, few difficulties occurred. Change the admixture slightly or lessen the priests' support of the traditional family, and some sons would remain bachelors, some would become priests, some would marry a less demanding woman from another ethnic group, and some might simply drink too much. Likewise, some women would remain single, some would become nuns, some would marry but have no children, some would try to dominate their husbands, and some might marry a man from another ethnic group.

KINSHIP

Kinship among the American Irish follows that of Ireland. Kin were people related by descent (blood) or marriage to whom one owed mutual assistance and among whom some marriages were tabooed. A modified bilateral system pre-

---

[14]See Stein (1971) for a discussion of stress reactions among American Irish *male* adolescents.

vailed. In Ireland, the kinship bond extended, as an example on the paternal side, from a husband to his father's father's father (great grandparent) and all the kin in the descending generations were kin of the husband (ego); thus, kin on the male side of the family were father's father's brother, and father's father's brother's son and the son of the last. But all possible roots were counted, *female* as well as male, so that the number of consanguineal (blood) kinship *positions* came to 32 in ego's generation of first and second cousins. The church but not the people tabooed marriage with third cousins but dispensations for these marriages were evidently easily obtained. Affinality (kinship by marriage) was limited somewhat, as the spouses of the siblings of one's parents were not considered kin, nor were the spouses of father's and mother's parents' siblings.

The importance of kinship to the Irish cannot be overstated. Although the household in Ireland was both the unit of economic production and of the family (nuclear and husband's parents), farmers needed help from others at times of planting and reaping, especially, and the families needed assistance or support for some events, such as childbirth, illness, or death. The help was given by consanguineal kin who by so doing established a "claim" against the household helped and who could expect that when they were in need the household members they had assisted earlier would reciprocate. Household members were ambivalent about giving and seeking help, however, for household self-sufficiency was a matter of great pride. But knowing that the day would come when the household members could not alone solve some problems, families assisted others and stored up "claims" for the future. For minor matters, the immediate families of the spouses helped one another but, for major crises, the wider extended kindred were on hand.

At marriage, both husband and wife acquired the full consanguineal kindred of the new spouse but only the spouses did so, not their kindred; the wife's parents and the husband's parents, then, did not become kin to one another. After marriage, the immediate families of each spouse were treated by both spouses as if they were consanguineal kin. Members of the immediate family were father-in-law and mother-in-law, brother-in-law and sister-in-law, and son-in-law and daughter-in-law. Again, however, the spouses of one's spouse's siblings (sister-in-law's husband, brother-in-law's wife) were not included as kin although there were often warm relationships between them. The extended kin of one's spouse were less important than the immediate ones, but in times of need mutual help was given, and on ritual occasions kin ties operated more extensively.

In the Massachusetts parish, the immediate families of both husband and wife were the close kin: For the couple, these included the four parents, siblings of both spouses (brothers-in-law and sisters-in-law), and the children of the siblings (nephews and nieces). For the children of the couple, the relatives were grandparents, aunts and uncles, and cousins. And, although from the viewpoint of one's parents, spouse's siblings' spouses were ambiguously treated, children used the American system and made no such distinction between aunts and uncles in terminology or gift-giving but did know which of these aunts and uncles were relatives by descent and which by marriage. In most matters, kinship relations took place between members of immediate families and more distant relatives attended weddings, wakes, and funerals. When godparents were chosen, one usually came from the father's side of the family and one from the mother's, symbolizing the bilaterality of the kin system.

Marriages in the parish took place at a mass before noon and usually on a Saturday so relatives and friends could attend. They ranged from the simple with only immediate families present, to formal with several bridesmaids and ushers. Festivities included a meal before which toasts were made, and sometimes dancing after the meal. Because of the expense, the custom arose of sending invitations of two types: one for the church service only and one which also included the reception. Families followed closely the usual American strictures about which family paid for various expenses of the wedding. Those marrying non-Catholics usually had a private service, not always in the parish. The non-Catholic was asked to take instructions in which the tenets of the church were learned and signed a contract with the priest present in which it was agreed that the children of the couple would be reared as Catholics. Almost as often, the non-Catholic was urged to convert to Catholicism. Couples were often engaged for a year or more in order to get to know one another and, as importantly, to get to know one another's families. The wait also permitted the young couple to save money to furnish their home. Premarital sex was absolutely forbidden and so serious was the situation of a pregnant bride that the marriage took place in great haste, often outside the parish, and usually without announcement from the altar.

The American Irish wake is somewhat unusual. In the parish the family waked the dead person at home after the body had been prepared at a funeral home. The body was raised up in a casket with the upper half of the body showing, a rosary entwined in the hands. Flowers were banked around the casket. Usually for one or two afternoons and two evenings the family was home to meet friends and relatives. The rosary was said around ten o'clock. There were sherry or red wines for the women, whiskey for the men, and food for all. The women often stayed in the livingroom or parlor with the casket, and the men moved to the kitchen. Much of the talk was of happy or humorous events concerning the dead person and the reminiscing helped families to mourn publicly and without embarrassment. Drunkenness and raucous joking were not as common as alleged; the usual case was that a few women had a little too much sherry or a few men had too much rye. Two male relatives often stayed up all night in the room with the body. For the religious services, the funeral home took over and brought the body in a hearse and the family in limousines to the church for the funeral mass. Burial was at a Catholic cemetery. Afterward all returned to the family home for a luncheon. Very young children did not attend wakes but by their teen years children in the family were expected to attend. The cars in the funeral procession were assigned by degree of closeness of the kin relationship or of friendship and of children by birth order. Many persons made contributions for masses to the church for the deceased relative or friend. Cremation was taboo. For people who committed suicide or who were apostates, there were no public services and their graves were located in unblessed land in the cemetery.

Baptisms were less ritualized and usually celebrated with a party at the parents' home. The infant was taken to the church by the godparents for baptism by the priest who usually performed the ceremony on a Sunday afternoon. Children were given one saint's name. But the naming was deemed less important than the sacrament that removed original sin. Guests usually brought small gifts for the baby, sometimes money to start a savings account. Being a godparent carried with it the responsibility to see that the child was not only reared as a Catholic but also remained so until marriage.

The American Catholic Irish family, then, adapted to conditions in this country and succeeded in creating strong, loyal family units. Entering as the least experienced of the immigrant groups who arrived about the same time historically, they moved slowly into solid working-class jobs and the lower levels of bureaucracies, while some became upper-middle-class professionals and others successful owners of companies (Birmingham, 1973) or corporation executives. The family of the parish exists in an attenuated degree in enclaves in several of our large cities today. Others who were more successful have made the exodus to the suburbs, bringing with them many of the attitudes of the parish. The children who grew up in the parish are the parents of today's young adults and teenagers. Some of these young people may go on to complete integration in this country, not knowing much about their Irish ancestors.

THE MODERN AMERICAN CATHOLIC IRISH FAMILY: CHANGE AND ADAPTATION

If one assumes a 30-year period for a generation, then the young people today are the fifth generation descended from the Great Famine immigrants and the fourth generation descended from those who entered this country in the 1870s. Some immigrants arrived later, of course, and there are some young people today whose grandparents came from Ireland but few compared to the total population descended from Irish immigrants. To write about the new generations in general terms is difficult, for there are few data on family lifestyles of American Irish of different generations and differing social classes with the exception of the now outdated Warner and Srole work (1945), Thernstrom's study (1973), and Esslinger's book (1975). There are, however, a few types that may be briefly described.[15]

The Enclaved American Catholic Irish Families

There are those who remain in enclaves in our large cities or in nearby suburbs and work in blue collar jobs or in the lower echelons of government and business bureaucracies. This group still lives in parishes but now side-by-side with those from other ethnic groups. The family is still highly important, as

---

[15]The types described here are not Weberian ideal types and cannot be, for the criteria distinguishing them are too many and the data on which to construct them too few. In fact, the difficulties encountered in trying to present even a few types leads the writer to commend Nancy Scheper-Hughes on her proposed study in Massachusetts of American Catholic Irish families.

is their religion. The father has a tendency to make decisions for the family, but the participatic n of wives and children has increased significantly. Intergenerational mobih y aspirations are slightly less than in preceding generations. Married women are more likely to work to maintain the economic viability of the family, and the number of permanently single women has declined. While home ownership re nains important, education of children is stressed equally. Some of the children attend parochial schools; some go to Catholic colleges. The views of the Catholic Church are heard equally with those of the secular society. The group identifies as Irish, usually votes Democratic, and sometimes ignores the beliefs of their church, especially regarding use of contraceptives, although some young people believe contraception introduces an unnatural aspect to sexual behavior. Delayed marriage is a matter of the past, since both spouses work; women often work before the last child enters school. Marriage to non-Catholics is more common. Family schedules are less organized by the church now, while church schedules are more flexible.

Most have become members of working-class America but retain Irish identification. Structural differences in families have disappeared, but many of the characteristics of the group have not. These include the lesser amount of overt affection, the favoritism toward sons, the attitudes of male authority, the preference for action, the use of alcohol to increase sociability, the obligations of families to care for one another, and the gathering of family members for rituals and holidays.

Although this group has not risen high economically, its members form an important part of our industrial society. They also remain a slightly controversial group in our national life. The issue of separation of church and state, for example, is not seen as one of civil liberties but as one of unfair taxation, especially in regard to education. Some are resistant to alternate lifestyles for families.

They are loyal to this country and patriotic. When convinced that an activity is for the country's good, they are enthusiastic. When they believe that they are being wronged by government action, they will feistily resist. One need only recall the vehemence of opposition from South Boston Irish to bussed racial integration of the school system to underscore the importance of their neighborhoods.

Middle Class American Catholic Irish Families

Among those who have risen economically, there is diversity of lifestyles. A few types emerge. *First,* out of the strength of parish families, in which fathers and mothers stressed economic and educational advancement, and in which the children grew up during the Great Depression and the strains of World War II, have come professional and business men and women whose lifestyles vary little from those of other successful urbanites and suburbanites. Many have degrees from private Protestant colleges, from state universities, and from Catholic colleges. They are integrated into American life, live in neighborhoods of professional and business families, understand well the philosophical underpinnings of the country, and have close friends among many groups.

Their orientations are to their organizations, companies, professions, and communities first—their church and neighborhood, second. The new Catholic Church does not surprise them. They sometimes complain about the poor quality of parochial schools, which they help maintain, but which their children often do not attend. Although not living and interacting with many Irish people on a daily basis, they nevertheless identify as Irish, they seem not to accept the pancatholic attitudes of the church, and they note the ethnic backgrounds of those with whom they work. They are also identified as Irish by others.

This group is mixed with respect to political party affiliation, perhaps more of the lawyers and teachers remaining Democrats and more of the bankers, physicians, and business men and women becoming Republicans. There is little favoritism of sons over daughters. Their children appear less interested in striving for achievement or excellence in professions and business; some are downwardly mobile. Affection within the family is open, especially by mothers. Some of the women work after marriage; others return to work when the last child enters school.

Second, there is a subgroup of successful middle-class American Catholic Irish families begun in the 1950s and early 1960s, in the era of togetherness, who have had five, six, seven, or more children *by choice.* Mothers are affectionate, worry little about their matter-of-fact child-rearing styles, and identify positively with *traditional* American Catholic Irish families. The men are likely to be preoccupied with their work. They take small part in the rearing of children, express most concern when it is time to choose colleges for and with the children, although they insist on the best available precollege education for them, and, having succeeded themselves, worry little about an improvement in the economic welfare of their children.

Third, there is a group among American Irish middle-class people who maintain close ties to the Catholic Church but in a new way. Many of these were educated in parochial schools and Catholic colleges. They orient their family life around the church, and they bring the church into their homes, celebrating church holidays with family rituals or days of special significance for the family with religious rituals. Expectably, they are active in churches, both with formal councils and groups, and with informal groups that join together in one another's homes to discuss issues, perhaps adding a semiritualistic aspect by sharing wine and bread. Some are active in the ecumenical movement.

The comfort of this third group of middle-class American Irish as Catholics and their serious concern with religion seem paradoxical when they state that many of the tenets of the Catholic Church are not applicable to their lives. Many are in favor of abortion, sterilization, the use of contraceptives, and vasectomy. Others think the celibacy of priests is not necessary. Some think women should be priests. Divorce is considered an alternative to stressed marriages. The Bible is read and interpreted by themselves. Many participate in communion and in the weekly mass when in a spiritual mood. Many talk of situation ethics regardless of any universal system of morality. Some have little understanding of more traditional Catholics, seem not to know the meaning of heresy and find it difficult to understand why anyone would be an apostate, now or in the past. At issue, however, is whether they can transmit their religious loyalty to their children.

The family life of this third group of middle-class American Catholic Irish is one of togetherness. There usually are two or three children; women do not work until the children enter school, although some obtain college or professional degrees while rearing their children. Men work hard but are more integrated into family life than other American Catholic Irish men. Children are reared with a mixture of American flexibility overlaid with learning of complex family rules. Some fathers in these families are less successful economically than those in the first and second middle-class groups.

Other American Irish

Many American Catholic Irish do not fit the types described. There are those who are third, fourth, or fifth generation married to members of other American ethnic groups—some of whom were educated in Catholic colleges, some not—whose pancatholicism seems more important than their ethnicity: some live in mixed ethnic enclaves, some in surburbia. There are second-, third-, fourth-, and fifth-generation American Catholic Irish at all class levels who married descendents of native-born people, who have children who do not know of their Irish ethnic past. There are those who drifted away from Catholicism and the Irish parish without much concern; their descendents have little knowledge of their ethnic heritage. There are apostates from the Catholic Church. Of these, some have joined other religious groups; others, who are not religious, term themselves renegades, apostates, agnostics, or atheists. There remain people of second-, third-, and fourth-generation American Catholic Irish who remained single or who married late and had no children.

There are many American Catholic Irish in the midwest and west, and some in the south, who were not reared in ethnic parishes, have little identification with the Irish, and are unfamiliar with the ethnic rivalries of their compatriots. Yet there are others in the midwest and west, a few in the south, who were reared in Irish enclaves and who share much with their northeastern counterparts.

Issues of Serious Concern to the American Catholic Irish Family

As an ethnic group, the American Catholic Irish find issues which are problematic for their family life. Particularly difficult are those concerning care of the elderly, marital disruption, feminism, and divisiveness within the Catholic Church.

THE ELDERLY. Among American Catholic Irish, care of older adults is an issue. As in colonial United States (Fischer, 1978), older males in Ireland controlled the family and the land, constructing a legacy of ambivalent response and wary distrust among the children. Stivers (1976:51–74) writes that male noninheritors of the farms in Ireland joined with their nephews in an avunculate, often symbolized by joining one another in drinking behavior. In this country, the pattern varied in that the male family head was away working while the woman reared children, including the sons, for a longer time period than in Ireland. Sibling loyalty, familism, and the strength of both parents led to behavior in the United States in which kin cared for older adults. Some older siblings lived with one another. Now, there is a preference by some middle-aged children for expanding families to include older adults, by others for care within a long-term care residence managed by Catholic orders, and by some for use of public or private long-term care settings.

Acceptance of Medicaid funds is difficult for some—not for others. Sons and daughters both share concern for older adults, although their functions sometimes differ, men more often being instrumental and daughters affective. Care for older nuns, brothers, priests, and monks has been resolved by some orders establishing their own long-term care residences. Not quite ready to relinquish the familial system of care and yet not always able to pay the costs of in-home and community-based services and residences, American Catholic Irish remain ambivalent and their behavior diverse concerning older adults.

MARITAL DISRUPTION. A set of problematic issues for Catholic Irish are those of marital status and of parenting after separation, divorce, or desertion. In many urban areas there are groups of single Catholics, made up largely of divorced people but which sometimes include widows, widowers, and people single by choice. Of those divorced, separated, or deserted, many seek annulments of their former marriages so that they may remarry within their religion. Joint custody of children is sometimes sought by those divorced. Single-parenting and step-parenting are common among separated and divorced people and among widows and widowers. Remarriage is relatively common, sometimes within the Catholic Church—sometimes, without. Men often marry younger women, thus creating a cohort of women who find a dwindling group of same-aged men to marry. (Norms remain that proscribe women marrying younger men.) Postmarital sexual behavior without the bond of marriage has increased, as has the number of people living together without formalizing the relationship. Problematic for single American Catholic Irish people is the link between their behavior, proscribed by their religion, and maintenance of membership in their church. Celibacy is not welcomed by many nor are homosexuality, lesbianism, and bisexuality.[16] While some masturbate, this solution is also not a permanent nor satisfying one for many.

FEMINISM. Another issue for the American Catholic Irish is the place of feminism in their lives. Although strong, directed women have always been a part of the group, authority in the family both in Ireland and in this country had remained with men. With the reemergence of feminism, several issues have arisen which have yet to be resolved, the three most controversial being passage of the Equal Rights Amendment, equality of women with men in decisionmaking within all areas of family life *and* choice concerning whether or not to have children and/or choice concerning the timing and the number of children. Catholic Irish women are in many ways prepared to respond to these issues in terms of the history of the group. Yet the close link of the Catholic Church with national identity has juxtaposed the issues in a way which makes it difficult for women in the group to ally with one another to gain equality. There would be small controversy over ERA among the Catholic Irish, for example, were not the issue of choice regarding contraception and abortion a serious concern of the Catholic Church, and egalitarianism within the family would not remain problematic were women socialized within the family and within the Catholic Church to take an active stance about control of their bodies. But in the present situation where the three issues are intertwined with concepts of sin and with calls to become or remain traditional wives and mothers, it is difficult for women to differentiate their roles as women, as Catholics, as workers, as wives, as mothers, as citizens and as

---

[16]Heterosexual orientation has been the norm among American Catholic Irish. This does not imply, however, that sexual behavior of individuals has usually followed the norm nor that there is an absence of bisexual, lesbian, and homosexual behavior among American Catholic Irish.

quite fallible people.[17] As a result, ERA, equality within the family, and choice regarding family planning remain divisive with Catholic Irish families.

DIVISIVENESS WITHIN THE CATHOLIC CHURCH. A final issue of concern for the Catholic Irish is the Catholic Church itself. Many nuns, priests, brothers, and monks have left their orders with sorrow. Participation in the ecumenical movement is somewhat ambivalent particularly after the papal visit in 1980 and after the papal notice for withdrawal from political office by those with priestly, sisterly, and brotherly callings. Feminists within the Catholic Church and within the orders of sisters find their activities proscribed to more traditional behavior than now expressed and their hopes for equality within the church may not be met. Tightening of rules about the ritual aspects of religion has led to some dismay. Calls for noncelibacy of priests (on principle and on grounds of assistance in the recruitment of priests) continue, although the same calls have not been made for orders of sisters. At issue for Catholic Irish in this country is the response of those affected by divisiveness within the Catholic community, functionaries and laypeople alike who hold alternate realities to those held officially by the Catholic Church. Alienation from one's traditional religion is more than difficult.

Conclusion

For every family characteristic described, some Catholic Irish person will find his/her experiences at variance with those depicted. Yet, there are some cultural and structural tendencies that came from the stem family in Ireland and the established families in the United States which remain.

Despite numerous exceptions, American Irish families are still predominantly Catholic. Fathers remain heads of families but egalitarian spouseship is rapidly increasing. Mothers continue to work at home and, now, with full time paid jobs. Familism is still prevalent; sibling loyalty continues. Extended kinship gatherings still occur. Children receive sensible rearing. Loyalty to the family unit, even with separated and divorced parents, is emphasized. Enthusiasm for feminism has increased.

American Catholic Irish are still very much concerned with the economic welfare of the total family unit. Men and women appear to work for achieved status. Entry to active rather than contemplative occupations remains the norm. Many still seek secure jobs. Catholic Irish women appear to maintain

---

[17]Mary Daly (1968, reprinted 1975; 1973; 1975; 1978), who is distinctively American Catholic Irish, has presented an ideological background or metaethics for radical feminism which illustrates the dilemmas of choice for American Catholic Irish women as well as for women of all groups nationally and internationally.

resistance to the concept of work being more important than family. Interest in politics is little abated. Higher education is valued. Considerably less regulated now are the marriages of children by parents. Sexual behavior now more closely matches that of other people in this country, premarital, marital, postmarital, and nonmarital. Other tendencies have diminished.

American Catholic Irish families retain differences from other groups, a striking example of cultural pluralism. It would be facile, then, to predict full structural and cultural integration in the future, particularly in view of the new ethnic assertiveness. If economic conditions turn downward and the gap widens between those who are economically successful and those who are not, ethnic competitiveness might increase. Such an eventuality would be tragic, for the American Catholic Irish have tried to transmit to their descendents a belief in the ability of those with differing backgrounds to live in peace with one another in this country.

R E F E R E N C E S

Adams, William Forbes. 1932. *Ireland and Irish Emigration to the New World, from 1815 to the Famine.* New Haven: Yale University Press.

Arensberg, Conrad M. 1950. *The Irish Countryman: An Anthropological Study.* New York: Peter Smith.

Arensberg, Conrad M., and Solon T. Kimball, 1968. *Family and Community in Ireland.* Cambridge: Harvard University Press. (Original copyright, 1940.)

Beckett, J. C. 1966. *The Making of Modern Ireland, 1603–1923.* New York, Knopf.

Birmingham, Stephen. 1973. *Real Lace: America's Irish Rich.* New York: Harper & Row.

Brody, Hugh. 1974. *Inishkillane: Change and Decline in the West of Ireland.* New York: Schocken Books.

Carpenter, Niles. 1927. *Immigrants and Their Children, 1920.* Census Monographs VII. Washington, DC: U.S. Government Printing Office.

Curran, Mary Doyle. 1948. *The Parish and the Hill.* Boston: Houghton Mifflin.

Daly, Mary. 1968. *The Church and the Second Sex.* New York: Harper & Row.

———. 1973. *Beyond God the Father: Toward a Philosophy of Women's Liberation.* Boston: Beacon Press.

———. 1975. *The Church and the Second Sex: With a New Feminist Postchristian Introduction by the Author.* New York: Harper & Row.

———. 1978. *Gyn/Ecology: The Metaethics of Radical Feminism.* Boston: Beacon Press.

Esslinger, Dean R. 1975. *Immigrants and the City: Ethnicity and Mobility in a Nineteenth Century Midwestern City.* Port Washington, NY: Kennikat Press.

Farber, Bernard (ed.). 1966. *Kinship and Family Organization.* New York: Wiley.

Farrell, James T. 1938. *Studs Lonigan: A Trilogy Containing Young Lonigan, The Young Manhood of Studs Lonigan and Judgment Day.* New York: Random House.

Ferenczi, Imre. 1929. *International Migrations.* Vol. I. "Statistics." Compiled on behalf of the International Labour Office, Geneva. With Introduction and Notes.

Edited on Behalf of the National Bureau of Economic Research by Walter F. Willcox. New York: National Bureau of Economic Research, Inc.

Fischer, David Hackett. 1978. *Growing Old In America: The Bland-Lee Lectures Delivered at Clark University, Expanded Edition.* New York: Oxford University Press.

Glazer, Nathan, and Daniel Patrick Moynihan. 1963. *Beyond the Melting Pot.* Cambridge: M.I.T. Press.

Greeley, Andrew M. 1972. *That Most Distressful Nation: The Taming of the American Irish.* Chicago: Quadrangle Books.

Handlin, Oscar. 1941. *Boston's Immigrants, 1790–1865: A Study in Acculturation.* Cambridge: Harvard University Press.

Heer, David M. 1961. "The Marital Status of Second-Generation Americans," *American Sociological Review,* 26(2):233–241.

Humphreys, Alexander J. 1966. *New Dubliners: Urbanization and the Irish Family.* New York: Fordham University Press.

Kennedy, Robert E., Jr. 1973. *The Irish: Emigration, Marriage, and Fertility.* Berkeley: University of California Press.

———. 1976. "Irish Americans: A Successful Case of Pluralism," in Anthony Gary Dworkin and Rosalind J. Dworkin (eds.), *The Minority Report: An Introduction to Racial, Ethnic, and Gender Relations.* New York: Praeger Pub. pp. 353–372.

Kennedy, Rose Fitzgerald. 1974. *Times to Remember.* Garden City, NY: Doubleday and Co.

Kutzik, Alfred J. 1979. "American Social Provision for the Aged: An Historical Perspective," in Donald E. Gelfand and Alfred J. Kutzik (eds.), *Ethnicity and Aging: Theory, Research, and Policy.* New York: Springer, pp. 32–65.

Le Play, Frederic. 1871. *L'Organisation de la famille selon le vrai modèle signalé par l'histoire de toutes les races et de tous les temps.* Paris: Tequi.

Marx, Karl, and Frederick Engels. 1970. *Ireland and the Irish Question: A Collection of Writings by Karl Marx and Frederick Engels.* (This is a relatively recent organization of the writings of Marx and Engels which has been "gleaned from handwritten notes and fragments" (p. 15) taken from the "Introduction" by L. I. Golman (Moscow). New York: New World Paperbacks.

Mattis, Mary Catherine. 1975. *The Irish Family in Buffalo, New York, 1855–1875: A Socio-Historical Analysis.* Unpublished dissertation, St. Louis, Washington University.

Matza, David, 1966. "The Disreputable Poor," in Reinhard Bendix and Seymour Martin Lipset (eds.), *Class, Status and Power: Social Stratification in Comparative Perspective* (2nd ed.). New York: The Free Press, pp. 289–302.

McCague, James. 1968. *The Second Rebellion: The Story of the New York City Draft Riots of 1863.* New York: Dial Press.

McCready, William C. 1974. "The Persistence of Ethnic Variation in American Families," in Andrew M. Greeley, *Ethnicity in the United States: A Preliminary Reconnaisance.* New York: Wiley, pp. 156–176.

Messenger, John C. 1969. *Inis Beag: Isle of Ireland.* New York: Holt, Rinehart and Winston.

Osborne, William A. 1969. "The Church as a Social Organization: A Sociological Analysis," in Philip Gleason (ed.): *Contemporary Catholicism in the United States.* Notre Dame: University of Notre Dame Press, pp. 33–50.

Pauw, B. A. 1963. *The Second Generation: A Study of the Family Among Urbanized Bantu in East London.* Cape Town: Oxford University Press.

113

Rainwater, Lee. 1966. "Crucible of Identity: The Negro Lower-Class Family," *Daedalus: The Negro American—2*, 95(1):172–216.

Scheper-Hughes, Nancy. 1979. *Saints, Scholars, and Schizophrenics: Mental Illness in Rural Ireland.* Berkeley: University of California Press.

Schrier, Arnold. 1958. *Ireland and the American Emigration 1850–1900.* Minneapolis: University of Minnesota Press.

Shannon, William V. 1963. *The American Irish.* New York: Macmillan.

Smith, Hazel M. and Ellen H. Biddle. 1975. *Look Forward, Not Back: Aborigines in Metropolitan Brisbane 1965–1966.* Canberra: Australian National University Press.

Stein, Rita F. 1971. *Disturbed Youth and Ethnic Family Patterns.* Albany: State University of New York Press.

Stivers, Richard. 1976. *A Hair of the Dog: Irish Drinking and American Stereotype.* University Park: Pennsylvania State University Press.

Thernstrom, Stephen. 1964. *Poverty and Progress: Social Mobility in a Nineteenth Century City.* Cambridge: Harvard University Press.

———. 1973. *The Other Bostonians: Poverty and Progress in the American Metropolis, 1880–1970.* Cambridge: Harvard University Press.

Warner, William Lloyd, and Leo Srole. 1945. *The Social Systems of American Ethnic Groups.* New Haven: Yale University Press.

Wittke, Carl. 1956. *The Irish in America.* Baton Rouge: Louisiana State University Press.

Zimmerman, Carle C., and Merle E. Frampton. 1935. *Family and Society.* Princeton: Van Nostrand.

The Chinese American Family

This chapter's title might well have been expanded to read "The Chinese American Family: A Neglected Ethnic Minority Group." Exploitation and intermittent violence, ghettoization, and the development of values for survival have marked the Chinese American experience. Particularly interesting has been the use of the cultural ideal of a familism built around ancestor worship, filial piety, and patriarchal authority while nevertheless developing a closely knit nuclear family as the central agency of socialization.

Buttressed by clan and other forms of community organization plus a solid array of extended kin, the nuclear Chinese American family retains a remarkable viability as an operating agency of socialization and refuge, and as a center for social intercourse. The adaptiveness of Chinese Americans has been tested by adversity and oppression of earlier decades; they now face the cultural discontinuities produced by a new influx of migrants from Taiwan, Hongkong, and recently the People's Republic of China, the opened gates of social and geographic mobility, and the siren call of American mass lifestyle. The neglected silent minority is no longer silent judging from the recent protests of the Yellow Power movement.

CHAPTER SIX
BY
LUCY JEN HUANG

HISTORICAL BACKGROUND

It is reported that a few Chinese were known to have been in America as early as 1785. Hong Neck Woo arrived in Philadelphia in 1855, settled in Lancaster, became a U.S. citizen in 1860, and volunteered in the Pennsylvania militia during the Civil War. By January 1849, there were about 800 Chinese in San Francisco, including two women. In 1852 more than 20,000 arrived. Except those who had jobs in San Francisco, they went to the mining districts. The number of Chinese immigrants increased steadily in subsequent years. In the 1860s it reached 50,000. Du Pont Street (now Grant Avenue) replaced Sacramento Street as the hub of the burgeoning Chinese community with 33 stores, 15 restaurants, five butchers, five barbers, and two silversmiths. (*Newsletter of the Midwest Chinese Student and Alumni Services,* 1976).

One may surmise the main motive for the Chinese to enter the United States by the nickname they gave to San Francisco, i.e. the "Gold Mountain" (Saxton, 1971:18):

> Colville's Gazeteer of San Francisco, published in 1856 but referring to the year 1851, described the Chinese as "unique." Their appearance seemed devised "to make people wonder"—the writer thus established a dichotomy between *Chinese* on one hand and *people* on the other—"to make people wonder that nature and custom should so combine to manufacture so much individual ugliness." On the same page he spoke of Chinese women as "the most degraded and beastly of all human creatures." He has apparently not yet made up his mind whether Chinese were or were not of the human condition; but that they were different and "degraded" was beyond question.

According to this author, the words assimilable, white, and the pseudoscientific term *Caucasian,* just then coming into fashion, would be taken as equivalents. And before the decade of the 1870s ended, there would be California workingmen, styling themselves brothers in the Order of Caucasians, who would undertake the systematic killing of Chinese in order to preserve their assimilable fellow toilers from total ruin (Saxton, 1971:18).

The arrival of the Chinese laborers came about in a precipitous manner; only 42 were residing in San Francisco in 1853, but two years later there were between three and four thousand. Prior to the enactment of the exclusion legislation of 1882 the number of Chinese immigrants rocketed to 40,000. Kearny, a leader of the anti-Chinese movement in California, estimated the Chinese population to be 200,000 in 1876, with 75,000 in San Francisco alone. However, in October of the same year a joint committee of Congress placed the figure at 117,449. Whether or not the figures quoted were accurate, the major point is that the Chinese did come in such great numbers as to arouse the concern of a large number of Americans (McClellan, 1971:5). The concern of the host group gradually turned into fear, animosity, and atrocities so well documented in reports of the last century.

The Chinese laborers were invited to this country by railroad agents who went to China, promising plentiful work, high wages, and free passage. In 1868 the Chinese merchants of San Francisco were present at a banquet honoring their contributions to the life and well-being of that city. In the same year the Burlingame Treaty was applauded in that city as the keystone of a new era of prosperity based on Chinese immigration. In 1869 the Central Pacific met the Union Pacific in Utah. Nine years later the Nevada mines collapsed. Suddenly the presence of the Chinese had changed from a blessing to a curse in the minds of most Californians (McClellan, 1971:10).

It was during this period that ethnic slurs were given to the unwelcome immigrants. The Chinese were referred to as "Chinamen," "Yellow lepers,"

"Yellow perils," or "the Chinks." On Broadway, the Chinese were burlesqued and ridiculed for the amusement of American audiences. "A Trip to Chinatown" played for 650 consecutive performances between November, 1891 and August, 1893. "Chin-Chin Chinaman" and "Toy Monkey" were two songs from these dramatic efforts which lampooned the Chinese and achieved popularity beyond Broadway. Other productions at the end of the century bore titles like "A Night in Chinatown," "The King of the Opium Ring," "Chop Suey One Lung," "Chinatown Charlie," and "Queen of Chinatown." In 1899 "The Singing Girl" appeared with a score by Victor Herbert containing the song "Chink! Chink!" A musical comedy entitled "A Chinese Honeymoon" and several more comic operas contributed many popular songs about the Chinese during the next few years (McClellan, 1971:46).

Thomas J. Geary, a representative from California, submitted additional provisions to the old Chinese Exclusion Act of 1883, requiring all Chinese in the country to register and submit an identification card with a photograph, thus reducing somewhat the confusing phenomenon that "all Chinese look alike anyway." The Geary Law was enacted in 1894 with strong public support, but the resentment of the Chinese against unfair laws had in the most part brought them closer together in joint efforts and cooperation.

"In our American cities the ghetto refers particularly to the area of first settlement i.e., those sections of the cities where the immigrant finds his home shortly after his arrival in America" (Wirth 1956:4). It represents a prolonged case of social isolation, a form of accomodation between divergent population groups. It is one historical form of dealing with a dissenting minority within a larger population. The ghetto, in general, was not the product of design, but rather the unwitting crystallization of needs and practices rooted in the customs and heritages, religious and secular. This was as true in the case of the Chinese as in the case of Jews, as Wirth described it.

Faced with the racial prejudice and discrimination from the host society, as described in this section, the Chinese immigrants became scapegoats as a consequence of the heated economic competition with white railroad and mine workers, especially when Irish miners began to invade the west coast. Under hysterical attacks from all sides, the Chinese began to withdraw from competitive labor and entered occupations that other immigrants were not so eager to perform. Table 1 gives an eloquent picture of this change of occupations.

Once Chinese laborers left work at the railroads and the mines, they moved to low rent districts of urban centers. They kept to themselves, living under extremely crowded conditions, like most new immigrants. The presence of the Chinese was feared because the part of the city or town where they congregated soon took the character of a foreign settlement. Hostile writers and reporters described the Chinese in Chinatown in terms of animal-like inferi-

TABLE 1
Selected Occupations for the Chinese in the United States 1870–1920

OCCUPATION	YEAR	NUMBER OF CHINESE	PERCENTAGE INCREASE OR DECREASE
Miners and Laborers	1870	27,045	−99.45
	1920	151	
Domestic Service Workers	1870	9,349	+280.00
	1920	26,440	
Traders and Dealers	1870	779	+960.00
	1920	7,477	

SOURCE: Cheng (1949:59) in Yuan (1965:277–284).

ority and viciousness. The eccentricities of Chinatown caught the eye of many a visitor. The clothing, the written language, and even the local apothecary (with its "beetles, snake bones, lizards, toadsblood, and other tonics") highly amused the Americans. Funerals were a source of curiosity and amusement, as were the local religious temples or joss houses. The idols, the incense, and the corpulent resident priest all strengthened the impressions of the Chinese as heathens (McClellan, 1971:34–35).

In a study of New York's Chinatown, Yuan formulated hypothetical stages of the development of Chinatown. The first stage was *involuntary choice* due to the host society's prejudice and discrimination toward the Chinese. The second stage was *defensive insulation* for the Chinese needed mutual help and cooperation against the hostile world. The third stage then became *voluntary segregation* in which a strong sense of group identification and *we-feeling* developed among the Chinese. The Chinese population in the New York metropolitan area was about 25,000 in the 1960s with 8000 living in and around New York's Chinatown, evidence of the "institutionalization" of the voluntary segregation of Chinatown. The fourth stage is then *gradual assimilation,* a process which may not be easy due to voluntary segregation and social isolation from the majority group (Yuan 1965:277–284). It is against this historical backdrop of discrimination, alienation, and ghettoization that the characters in the drama of Chinese family life play their parts.

THE MODERN CHINESE AMERICAN FAMILY

Size and Location of the Chinese American Population

The total number of Chinese in the United States, the U.S. Census Bureau shows, has been increasing. From 77,000 in 1940; 118,000 in 1950; 237,000 in 1960; there were 435,000 in 1970. The Chinese in the United States are

118

a largely urban group. Of the 435,000 Chinese in the United States in 1970, 419,000 lived in urban areas. The largest number, 170,131, resided in the state of California. New York State was next with 81,378. The state with the third largest Chinese population was Hawaii, where 52,039 lived in 1970. Illinois and Massachusetts each had over 14,000 Chinese. (U.S. Bureau of the Census 1977).

Intermarriage

Informants among Chinese professional families confirm the fact that most parents prefer their chidren to marry Chinese, in spite of the fact that many of them are fighting a losing battle. One family with three daughters born in China was sure that at least the older daughters would marry Chinese, while the youngest, who was totally Americanized, would probably marry an American. After the marriage of the eldest daughter to an American, the mother lost all hope. "I never expect Number One would marry a foreigner, for she has always been so reserved and quiet. I can't understand it. There are so many nice Chinese boys on campus, and she had to marry a foreigner," the mother complained.

Chinese young people, though born in the U.S., tend to be socially less aggressive and more conservative than their Caucasian counterparts. One may hypothesize that in the future intermarriage between second-generation Chinese and non-Chinese will increase. Since they are socialized in the Chinese household with relative inhibitions, most young people may find it difficult to initiate emotional expressions in dating situations. If Winch's theory of complementary needs is our guide, it is psychologically more satisfying for active "chasers" to approach reticent and yet interested mates. A Chinese mother of a Caucasian daughter-in-law informed this writer, "She chased after him for over two years. Everyday she would declare that she was going to marry my son, even in front of me." It is possible that most young Chinese in America are socially more subtle and thus less expressive than their American dates, who, in the process of courtship do most of the active pursuit, thus saving the efforts of the Chinese partner. The average Chinese girl born in the United States would not have shown her apparent liking for a fellow in her action—let alone verbalize it prematurely. Whether or not it is true as some males contend that "there is a shortage of good-looking Chinese girls," the fact seems to support one Barnard College coed's comment that a good many Chinese American boys seem to be attracted to "those short petite blonds" (*The Wall Street Journal,* 1969).

In the 1940s and 1950s, intermarriage among Chinese professionals might still be considered to have been "deviant" and "unconventional." Good friends and relatives of the Chinese partner, in the process of defending such "exceptionally untraditional" behavior, or in consoling the "culprit" for entering into such a daring marital contract, would comment, "But he is so Chinese in his behavior." Thus the parents of today's American-born children still hold the concept that Caucasian Americans are in general "wild," "flippant," "irresponsible," "childishly unsubtle," and worst of all, "foreign," while their children in the 1960s and 1970s may have considered marrying a Caucasian socially sophisticated and "with it." Hsu (1970:338) believes that the Chinese objection to interracial marriage is that it is "socially inconvenient," for communication would be difficult between spouses, families, and friends. But from the point of view of the young Chinese of 1960s and 1970s, marrying a Caucasian may turn out to have been more convenient and natural than marrying another Chinese.

Lee (1960:251) suggested that the earlier immigrants from Kwangtung objected to intermarriage in order to maintain racial homogeneity, and to avoid hostile situations and general feelings of marginality. Gordon (1964:227) discusses intermarriage among the Chinese in the United States by tracing it back to the anti-Chinese feeling in the 19th century. This social distance between them and the whites and a strong adherence to a family loyalty pattern contributed to the discouragement of intermarriage. Therefore, despite the high ratio of males to females, the number of Chinese intermarriages has not been large, if we accept Gordon's reference to Schwartz's (1951) data from the 1930s. On the other hand, Beaudry (1971:59–67) found that the degree of acculturation and assimilation had a great deal to do with whether one would approve of intermarriage or not, the more assimilated being more likely to approve of intermarriage. He found females to be less assimilated and thus less approving of intermarriage. Consistent with this author's observations and interviews among midwest Chinese professionals, Beaudry found that a majority of foreign-born Chinese professionals were undecided or disapproved of intermarriage. However, from Huang's (1956) research in the 1950s and her interviews and observations in the 1970s, the female students and professionals from China proved to be more sensitive to acculturation and assimilation processes in the U.S. and thus more approving of intermarriage. It is assumed that even if both male and female professionals are equally Americanized, the male may be more hesitant in entering intermarriage because of the tradition of patrilineal descent of the Chinese family and the possible problem of adjustment in case he returns home to China with a non-Chinese wife. Barnett (1963:426) reported there was a slight trend in direction of more intermarriage by females than by males based on his data from 1955 to 1959 in California. This trend seems to be consistent with this author's findings in Chicago in the 1950s, in which there were three females to one male who entered into an intermarriage. Hsu (1971) agrees that the rate of intermarriage among Chinatown-based Chinese is much lower than among the children of professional Chinese families. His report also shows that more Chinese females than males marry non-Chinese.

Barron (1966:116–119) found that in Los Angeles of 97 marriages involving Chinese in the decade from 1924 to 1933, 23.7 percent were interracial marriages. In the same period in New York City, among 650 marriages involving Chinese, 150, or 23 percent, were contracted with a marriage partner who was non-Chinese.

Loh (1944), in his study of 81 Chinese families in Philadelphia, found that 22 were mixed marriages. In another study, Schwartz (1951:562–568) found that of 254 marriages among Chinese males in New York City from 1931 to 1938, 26 percent were with non-Chinese brides. This proved to be a significant drop from earlier years. For the sake of comparison, the author found that from 1908 to 1924, one out of every two marriages involving a Chinese was a mixed marriage.

In recent years, both sexes among the second-generation Chinese of professional families have increasingly married non-Chinese, as one male stated (Chen, 1972:7):

> Certainly one of the most tangible evidences of an individual's assimilation into a culture is for that individual to take a spouse of that culture. The members of our group have until now so unanimously married non-Chinese persons that it was a standing joke among us that a fifty-dollar prize would be awarded to the first one to take a Chinese mate.

The future of intermarriage among the Chinese in the United States may be a function of such factors as propinquity, sex ratio, foreign-born or native-born, and level of education. Increasing dispersal of Chinese away from the Chinatown ghetto and the propinquity of residence of similar social classes (Heer, 1966) may prove to be important facilitative factors.

Attitudes Toward Divorce

Traditionally the Chinese considered divorce as a great shame and tragedy, especially for the woman. Grounds for divorce were mostly in favor of the husband, for a wife could be divorced if she happened to be disrespectful to her parents-in-law, especially if she was quarrelsome toward her mother-in-law (Hsu, 1970:142). Moreover, if a wife did not give birth to a son, there was a danger of her being divorced unless she was willing to accept concubines for her husband in the hope that secondary wives might bring male offspring to bless the family and thus continue the male line.

The Chinese, in general, disapprove of divorce, no matter how openminded or educated they are. This attitude is not related to any religious convictions (unless they are extremely pious Catholics); it is rather a serious social ostracism that few could afford to experience, even at the risk of having an unhappy household. Few Chinese young men today, either American-born or foreign-born, would consider going with a woman who had been engaged to or gone steady with another man before, let alone a divorcée. It would be very difficult for the Chinese to understand why an American bachelor would marry a divorcée with several children. He would be seen as mentally deranged or a social misfit to consider marrying "used merchandise."

The divorce rate, therefore, is relatively low among the Chinese families. Only the very courageous and independent individuals dare accept divorce as a solution to marital difficulties. Thus, it is not uncommon for unhappy couples to remain together for fear of public opinion and social disgrace. However, the younger generation born in the United States may not be as conservative as their foreign-born parents, especially when they are brought up in a culture where individual love and happiness are more important than what other people would say.

Lee (1960:10–26) however, found a surprisingly high divorce rate of 8.5 percent among the Chinese in the San Francisco Bay Area. For those couples who were married by the "picture bride" arrangement, in which men went to China for a few weeks to complete the wedding ceremony, the only thing in common was they were both Chinese. The women from Hong Kong were much more westernized than their Chinatown husbands. Divorce therefore is higher in these trans-Pacific marriages.

Furthermore, there is much stress and strain in Chinese families, especially in the the adjustment of newly married couples. For the more traditional-minded wives, discord and unhappiness are generally turned inward toward the self and are reflected in a high suicide rate rather than in divorce statistics. As Sung (1967:162) observes:

> The suicide rate among the Chinese in San Francisco is four times greater than that for the city as a whole, and it is predominantly the women who decide to end it all. Suicide has been the traditional form of protest for Chinese women who find life unbearable within their matrimonial bonds.

In addition, the author further reported that the divorce rate is also kept low because some wives are not sophisticated enough to seek legal severance of their marriage. They merely run away and form another union by the de facto act of cohabitation.

We have observed that, as most evidence shows, interracial marriages tend to have a higher rate of divorce. In a small community in Illinois in 1979 there were 12 cases of intermarriage: five Chinese American men married Caucasian wives, and seven Chinese American women married Caucasian husbands. Of the 12 intermarriages there were five divorces. Three cases were G.I. warbrides from Taiwan and two cases were Chinese men married to American wives.

Role, Status, and Authority in the Nuclear Family

Chinese families of the first or second generation in the United States are mostly of the nuclear type. Since many Chinese students arrived in the United States in the 1940s, the changing political regime on mainland China made it impossible for them to want to return. These individuals have since completed their education, become United States citizens, and held professional careers. By the 1970s they have become grandparents to their American-born children. In recent years, Chinese families from Taiwan and Hong Kong have had grandparents, especially widowed grandmothers, visit in the United States. They are, without exception, included in the extended family, often serving as helpful babysitters and housekeepers for their careerwomen daughters and daughters-in-law. Since early 1979 friendly relations between the People's Republic of China and the United States have reunited an increasing number of family members after over 30 years of separation.

Chinese families who have been in the United States for four or five generations can be structurally termed, "semiextended." Many grandparents prefer to establish their own household even though they prefer to live in the same house or in the same block. "My grandmother is very independent," reported a third-generation American Chinese girl. "She has her own apartment in our home, cooking her own meals, and coming and going as she sees fit. But at the same time my parents are able to look in on her and see to it that she is well and happy."

CHANGING WOMEN'S ROLES. Confucius once observed that women and uneducated people are most difficult to deal with. For centuries the position of women had not changed from the old shackles of custom and tradition. Female infanticide was known in the poverty-stricken families as well as in rural villages. Girls were sold as slaves and prostitutes. Polygyny was practiced for centuries in the old country.

In the United States, for decades there was a tremendous problem of shortage of women due to discriminating immigration laws. The Immigration Act of 1924 virtually condemned the Chinese in the United States to a life of forced celibacy, bachelorhood, or trans-Pacific marriages.

123

The status of women in the Chinese American family is determined by various factors. Were they China-born or were they born in the United States? Are they married to the China-born husbands or native-born husbands? What level of education do they have? Is there a scarcity of women of marriageable age? In general, the higher the education, the more Americanized the women are, the higher the status of women in the family. However, there is still a tendency of the wife to assume the role of the co-pilot and helper to her husband rather than be totally equalitarian in relationship.

Increasing numbers of Chinese women are combining a career with their traditional wife and mother role. For those women who are in the professional group or blue collar group, the combination of a career and wife–mother role is not the easiest task, especially because the Chinese men, in general, are not socialized to be very helpful with household chores.

Childrearing: Socialization Style and Methods

In general, Chinese children grow up in the midst of adults, not only their parents, but also members of the extended family. In contrast to the American family in which a child's world is socially and structurally segregated from the world of his parents and other adults as houses are built with "the children's wing" away from their parents (Lear 1965:16–30), Chinese children as a rule are seldom left at home with babysitters or other adults (Hsu, 1972:84):

> Chinese parents take their children with them not only to wedding feasts, funeral breakfasts, and religious celebrations, but also to purely social or business gatherings. A father in business thinks nothing of bringing his boy of six or seven to an executives' conference.
>
> This pattern is still adhered to by the majority of second, third and fourth generation Chinese-Americans in Hawaii. . . .

This sharing of the same world of reality between Chinese children and their parents may be one of the more crucial factors in the process of socialization. Ruth Benedict pointed out some time ago that American children suffered from cultural discontinuity, that whatever they learned from their parents had to be unlearned or relearned later as they reached different stages of their life cycle (Benedict, 1938:161–167). The childrearing practices of the Chinese may help to facilitate the socialization process and render relatively smooth transition from childhood to adulthood.

Having been exposed to the companionship of adults, Chinese children are more aware of what socially approved patterns of behavior should be, as well as what other people think of them. In the process of childrearing, contrary to the American emphasis on the sense of guilt, Chinese children experience shame which "supposes that one is completely exposed and conscious of being looked at: in one word, self-conscious" (Erikson, 1963:252). It arises from being out of touch with one's social relationship, a mistake in any prescribed convention. The person involved is much concerned with what he does in the presence of others (Hsu, 1949:223–242). Living in the Chinatown ghetto, social control may have been derived chiefly from public opinion rather than an inner sense of guilt, a voice from the superego.

One aspect of socialization is the strict control of aggression. Sollenberger (1962) in his study found that 74 percent of Chinese parents demanded their children to show no aggression under any circumstances. Not one single parent strongly urged their children to defend themselves or punished them for running home for help in case of encountering attacks by other children. Sibling rivalry and aggression were in general discouraged. Relationships among siblings is seasoned with the Chinese concept of *jang* in which older children are encouraged to set an example for their siblings in gentleness, manners, and willingness to give up pleasure or comfort in favor of someone else. It is a sentiment encouraging one to give in during a quarrel or a polite refusal in favor of someone else (Sollenberger, 1962:18–19). Cattell (1962:63) reported that Chinese children were picked on by other children, mostly Puerto Ricans and Italians. "They get beaten up, and the Chinese ways they have been taught don't help them in dealing with that sort of problem."

Sue and Sue (1971) found Chinese American students at the University of California at Berkeley to exhibit characteristics similar to their cultural and historical background. They tended to evaluate ideas on the basis of their immediate practical application, while their American counterparts evaluate ideas on an abstract, reflective, and theoretical orientation. The Chinese students are more comfortable in well-structured situations, less autonomous, less independent from parental controls and authority figures, more obedient, conservative, conforming, inhibited, socially introverted, and more likely to withdraw from social contacts. They tend to score lower in verbal sections of their college entrance examination than their American counterparts partly due to the limited communication patterns between parents and children. In the Chinese household, Chinese culture rewards one for silence and inconspicuousness while punishing for outspoken behavior. Broverman, Broverman, and Clarkson (1970:1–7) find the traits of "not at all aggressive," "very submissive," "very passive," and "very quiet" to be female-valued stereotypic items. Thus, the Chinese American female socialized in a Chinese household finds her socialization compatible with American female socialization, whereas the passive males, who are not "competitive," are at a disadvantage. The

Chinese males are not characterized as "very dominant," "very independent," "very active," and "very talkative." On the contrary, they are characterized as "inadequate" and a "failure" at the American dating game. They are described as "shallow," "egocentric," "childish," "sexually inept," and demonstrating a "lack of advances." This is in contrast to the male's role in the American dating situation—"mature," "sophisticated," "suave," "cool," "swinging," and "sexy" (Weiss, 1969:86–94). It may take time for the Chinese men in the United States to overcome effects of the traditional Chinese values and personality so deeply rooted in their culture.

SEX ATTITUDES. Sex education in the Chinese family has been somewhat a mystery. The segregation of the sexes had been practiced for thousands of years. The only members of the opposite sex one was able to meet were cousins within the same extended family. The classic novels *Dreams of the Red Chamber* by Chao Shueh Ch'in (1929) and *The Family* by Pa Chin (1972) illustrate many of the secret love affairs among cousins and other members of the same consanguineal family. Informants from China related incidents that may shed some light on the question of sex education. It was reported that whenever there was a bride-to-be, she would invariably be sleeping with some older female members of the family weeks or months before the wedding. It was suspected that certain sex instruction might be going on during these last minutes before the wedding. This writer once came across a Chinese brass mirror on the four corners of which were etched figures of four sexual positions presumably for the benefit of the newlyweds.

Most Chinese families, like the average American family, do not engage in frank discussions of sex with their children, either foreign-born or American-born. Somehow, it is assumed that as they grow up, the younger generation will automatically learn about such subjects as sexual relations from their peers. Parental instruction in such intimate relations between the sexes is far from adequate. One may assume because of higher educational levels that among professionals there is greater communication between parents and children in this area than among Chinatown-based families.

A distinct characteristic of the Chinese family is the lack of external expression of affection among the members. Many Chinese children have never seen their parents kiss or hug one another. One does not express such emotions in public except with small infants or children who are often hugged or smell-kissed (burying one's nose in a baby's cheek and inhaling) but never directly on the mouth. The average Chinese is seldom seen hugging and kissing at an airport or railroad station, either when seeing relatives off or welcoming them. There is a great deal of smiling and handshaking accompanied by shouts of joy or other verbal expressions of farewell. A good example is an incident recounted by a female college student. "When I went to New York to meet my brother who arrived in the United States two years after I did, all we did was shake hands. I felt awkward, for I thought I wanted to express more in the American fashion, but we are Chinese, so that's what we did." Hsu (1970:10) contrasted the prominence of emotions in the American way of life to the tendency of the Chinese to underplay all matters of the heart. He analyzed it by stating that the American is more individual-centered while the Chinese is situation-centered. Being situation-centered, the Chinese is inclined to be dependent socially or psychologically on others, for he is tied closer to his world and his fellowmen. His happiness and his sorrow tend to be mild since they are shared. Regardless of what the reason is, public demonstration of affection tends to embarrass the Chinese, both professionals as well as nonprofessionals, American-born or foreign-born. When non-Chinese demonstrate their affection publicly, it is accepted with understanding, but when the Chinese do that, it is considered poor taste or unnecessarily childish. Therefore, at times it is relatively awkward for American-born children who have been away to college among non-Chinese peers to return home after a year's absence merely to greet their parents with "Father, Mother," whereas they would hug and kiss their casual friends after a week's absence. "When I tried to hug my close relatives after years of absence, they behaved very stiffly. Not that they don't care, but it is just not the way they are used to," an Americanized Chinese girl said. The Caucasian spouse of the family soon learns to repress his or her affectionate expressions in front of Chinese relatives.

Adolescence and Problems of Parent–Child Interaction.

Pearl Buck (1956:312–313) once pointed out that to move from an old established society into an effervescent and a fluid new society, such as the American one, and remain for many future decades or perhaps centuries is more than simply changing countries—it is changing worlds and epochs.

Due to the strong emphasis on filial piety and strict obedience to parents in the Chinese family, one may expect value conflicts between Chinese-born parents and American-born children to be relatively subtle and hidden. In a study on the changing personality traits of second-generation Orientals in America, Smith states that because there is greater opportunity for self-expression, there is also a greater range of personality types. He classifies them into three types: the conformist type, the rebellious type, and the philosophic type. The conformist type consists of those who are very conservative, living close to parents, accepting their ideas and traditions and venturing no change. The rebellious type tends to react violently against the old system and yet has not worked out any consistent scheme of behavior. To be emancipated from the old seems to be more important than to develop any new mode of life organization. The philosophic type consists of those who appreciate their parents values as well as those of the American culture. They serve as mediators between the two cultures, not rejecting wholesale the culture of their parents nor adopting everything American. They are able to work out a life organization embracing elements from both cultures and adjust themselves with considerable success (Smith, 1928:922–29).

One major difficulty in the intergeneration adjustment is that the old Chinese family system, which is still dominant in the villages in Kwangtung, and which lives on in the minds of the "old skulls" of American Chinatowns, is strongly patriarchal (Hayner, 1957:633). This trend has not changed through the years, in spite of the fact that certain major revisions have occurred in the old country. It is not only those who were brought up in the New World of the United States who experienced difficulties and conflicts with their parents, but also those who were sent back to China for education or those who arrived in this country in their late teens. "Most were better educated and [more] sophisticated than their parents. Accustomed to more westernized Chinese cities, they rebelled against the prescribed life and the conservatism of Chinatowns" (Lee, 1960:208).

Writers and journalists also observe the disparity in the lifestyle and culture between generations among the Chinese. They realize that Chinatown is not quite China, nor is it quite America. Within its blocks one civilization is in transition, and another is not yet acquired. The elders celebrated birth with ancient ceremonies and kept their wives in upstairs seclusion. After funerals they held banquets where it was rude to appear sad, and went only to Chinese restaurants, where everyone at a table ate from the same bowl as a symbol of fraternity. They read only Chinese papers and periodicals, while their sons who hardly spoke or read Chinese, preferred the city tabloids (*The New York Times,* 1946:4).

In the urgent interest to bring up their children with knowledge of Chinese history and culture, many parents send their children to Chinese schools daily after public school is out. As stated in her autobiography, an eight-year-old Chinese girl, Jade Snow, was ordered by her father to enroll in Chinese evening school to learn about China's great river, T'ang poetry, provincial differences, and compete in class essays. "Studying Chinese at school was quite like studying at home with Daddy, except that it was easier. Instead of individual response to a watchful father, it was group response to a teacher. . . ." However, she added, "after public school there was scarcely an hour left for folding diapers and getting something to eat before starting for the Chinese school. School was not dismissed until 8:00 p.m., after which there were more lessons at home" (Wong, 1945:33–34). Like many other Chinese families the father had decided to send her to China for further studies and for her brother to finish medical training and serve as a medical doctor there (Wong, 1945:95).

It was the practice of many Chinatown-based families to send their teenage children back to China for Chinese education before 1949, the year the People's Republic of China took control of the China mainland. Furthermore, with the onset of the depression in the 1930s and discriminatory practices in the United States, many young Chinese returned to China in search of economic betterment, especially in large metropolitan cities where the knowledge of English was mandatory. More recently, in the 1960s and the early 1970s, many Chinese parents, professional and otherwise, began the old practice of sending their teenage children back to Taiwan, either for the summer months or for the whole year, to get acquainted with Chinese culture. (*Newsletter of the Midwest Chinese Student and Alumni Services,* 1967, 1968).

However, cultural conflict and the inconsistency experienced by the younger generation cannot be denied, no matter how eager parents would like their children to accept some of the Old World values.

The young Chinese grew up in a brand new world. Finding their parental generation full of obsolete precedents and out-of-date responses, they had to resort to looking for new models among their peers. "These peers present them with more practical models than those of the elders, whose past is inaccessible to them and whose future it is difficult for them to see as their own" (Mead, 1970:31).

Mate Selection: Husband and Wife Interaction

The old Chinese saying that "one should marry a spouse whose front door faces his own" indicates the traditional emphasis on homogamy. Parents in traditional China often frowned on their children marrying someone out of the province, let alone out of one's country or race. These attitudes have long historical precedence and were transplanted to the new country. However, in spite of miscegenation laws and general apprehension against exogamy, Chinese men in Chinatown did resort to intermarriage. Because of the extreme unbalanced sex ratio and the difficulty of returning to China to obtain a "picture bride," Chinese merchants, restauranteurs, and laundrymen were found to have non-Chinese wives.

In a study of mate selection among New York City's Chinese males, Schwartz (1951) found that in the years between 1931 to 1938, there was a pronounced difference among various occupational groups in the patterns of mate selection. During the decade between 1930 and 1940, the sex ratio was 80 percent male to 20 percent female according to the U.S. Census report. Among 254 Chinese grooms in New York City, the most common type of interracial marriage was between restaurant worker grooms and white brides, numbering 24 cases, while 19 cases of "merchant group" grooms married white brides. In marriages with Negro brides, nine restaurant workers and five laundry workers married black brides.

However, American-born Chinese girls were not considered as desirable as those born in the old country. The following sentiment was very typical among Chinatown-based Chinese [quoted from Pacific Coast Relations Survey, Document 242 in Hayner and Reynolds (1957:360)]:

> Chinese girl I think very much better than American-born Chinese. No spend much money. I no like go shows. All they think about stay home, help husband, save money. American-born Chinese girls, My God, spend lots of money buy all the time, pretty clothes, fancy shoes. American girls, no know Chinese custom, no like big family. Yes, I think China boy better marry girl in China.

The Immigration Act of 1924, the so-called Second Exclusion Act, "tightened" the enforcement of the earlier regulation that American-born males of Chinese descent could not bring their foreign-born wives to the United States after they had gone to China to select them. As a result, many husbands and wives were separated on opposite sides of the Pacific Ocean for years even though their minor children could be admitted.

Discriminatory immigration laws were crucial factors in producing the sex ratio imbalance, not to mention marital and familial dislocations. It was during this period that falsification of birth records of children born in China was widespread. The birth of a daughter was reported as a son. This "slot" on the family tree had saleable values to those who would like to enter the country and yet had no derivative citizenship rights. Through the sale of those "slots" many male immigrants arrived in the United States, taking the family names of the owners of the "slots".

Thus, the sex ratio imbalance continued to create problems for the Chinatown-based men who were either single or whose wives were left in China. A relatively typical case was a successful restaurant administrator who had never brought his family to the United States, living a bachelor's life for over 30 years except for periodical visits to China. Upon learning that he had cancer, he bought an airplane ticket and headed for home. He died in China surrounded by his wife and semistranger families.

CHINATOWN CHINESE. Chinese women born in China or in the United States have for many years been in great demand, especially among Chinatown-based men. Informants have revealed many cases of American-born Chinese women, capitalizing on the unbalanced sex ratio and exploiting lonely men and young bachelors behind their husbands' backs. One may say that these women had "secondary husbands" or "concubines-in-reverse" except for the fact that the latter not only provided extramarital sexual opportunities but also bribery in gifts and money. In some cases the husbands, usually older than the wives, knew about such arrangements but could or would not do anything about them since a Chinese woman was hard to find.

Interviews of educated Chinese women who became citizens in America show the great difficulties they have in accepting the attentions of lonely Chinatown-based bachelors. Except for the fact that they were both Chinese there was very little in common. During such dating situations there was no common reference for discourse or common interest to share with one another except in enjoying a Chinese dinner at the best restaurant in Chinatown. "Besides the delicious dishes which remind me of home, the date was a total disaster," a female informant confided. "All through the dinner he was reading the racing form, and as if that was not enough, he went to the telephone five times to check with his bookie." Since they did not speak the same dialect, they spoke English to each other. Having come from a large cosmopolitan city and therefore speaking fluent English herself, the young woman said there was nothing worse than being courted by a man who spoke pidgin English with attitudes and behavior patterns of her grandfather's generation or perhaps even her great-grandfather's generation.

Differential degrees of acculturation on either side of the Pacific Ocean thus creates difficulties in heterosexual associations, either before or after marriage. Those who were born in Chinatowns or grew up there since childhood do not seem to be more "westernized" than individuals born and raised in coastal metropolitan cities of Asia, in fact they may be less "westernized." The traditional practices brought over by early immigrants in the last century continued to survive among the Chinatown-based Chinese in spite of the fact that culture in China had undergone great changes. When a China-born wife was brought over to America, she was shocked by the attitude of Chinatown Chinese. She thought that the Chinatown population had "stood still" while Asia was progressing. At the same time she was further shocked at the superficial conduct and loose attitudes and behavior found among some Chinese Americans. As a consequence, documentary evidence strongly suggests that the Chinatown-based husband in America is not always the "boss." A product of traditional values he is characteristically puzzled and disillusioned by the activities of a spouse who often no longer shares those values, but he tries to be reasonable and makes the best of a difficult situation (Hayner and Reynolds, 1957:635).

TAIWANESE. Students and professionals from Taiwan appear to have problems relating to love and marriage resembling those of Chinese students and professionals in the 1950s. However, their affairs of the heart are further complicated by the ousting of the Republic of China from the United Nations in 1971, leaving citizens of Taiwan in a state of anxiety and worry for their own safety. The international setback has further intensified parental requests for their children to stay in the United States, become American citizens and settle in this country. It is no wonder that an ideal mate for Chinese from Taiwan consists of the "Three P's": permanent residence, a Ph.D, and property. Taiwan students and professionals tend to be very practical and rational when it comes to mate selection. It is not unusual for someone to ask his or her first date whether she or he has received a "green card" yet. According to a report by the Chinese consulate in Chicago in the 1970s, only 5 percent of Taiwanese students returned to Taiwan after they completed their education in the United States.

Having been brought up to think that early dating was wrong, most Chinese from Taiwan seldom date before they are 20 or older. Consequently, whenever they meet someone they become very emotional and serious, often leading to a premature marriage. On the other hand, since many Chinese have little experience in dating, when they are ready to get married they solicit professors and married couples to arrange "casual" dinner meetings at their homes in order to meet eligible women. For those who are unsuccessful in finding mates in this way, many return to Taiwan during winter or summer vacations, line up 20 or 30 young women to interview by arrangement, and select one before the vacation is over. Others might put an advertisement in a Chinese newspaper either in Taiwan or in the United States. An example of one of these advertisements runs as follows: "A 37 year old overseas female student, divorced, with children, hopes to meet a gentleman around 45 years of age, possessing gentle and honest character. Friendship before marriage."

Under the circumstances that Chinese young people meet and get married, we may assume that in comparison to the American practice, they tend to have a relatively limited period of time to get to know one another. Whether it is a "picture bride" engagement, Taiwan interview, arrangement by friends or relatives, or by independent choice, the Chinese tend to have a short period of premarital association. Chinese married couples, therefore, in general, lack knowledge and understanding of their spouses. The most frequent statement by young Chinese wives is, "I didn't know he was like that." Consequently, the adjustment process after marriage may often be a traumatic one.

Elders in the Ethnic Family

One of the traditional values of the Chinese family is the great respect and obedience shown toward elders of the family. One does not have to be very old to command respect; it is enough for one to be slightly older than the other. The high regard the Chinese hold for a teacher can be explained by how they address him, *Shien-Sheng,* meaning one who was "born first." Filial piety, therefore, is one of the values that has united the Chinese family for centuries.

Both the Chinatown-Based Chinese and the Chinese in professional groups still show respect to the older members of the family. This is evidenced by the use of appropriate kin terms of address between individuals in different age groups. In the family, for example, one addresses siblings as "Older Brother, Oldest Sister, Second Older Sister, Third Older Sister and Fourth Older Sister" (Wong, 1945:2).

The early Chinese who arrived in America in the 19th century did not intend to stay. They came as laborers in order to make enough money to send home and later return to enjoy the fruits of their toils. Many wonder why the Chinese, who came from a rural background in south China, entered such untraditional occupations as restaurateurs and laundrymen. According to Mead (1955:239), they were working for the family they had left behind, either for a sister's dowry, a brother's education, or for additional family land, which gave them a sense of stability and a feeling of personal freedom, which explains how Chinese immigrants, with the thought of sustained family continuity, as an ever-present value, were able to withstand the hardships of racial prejudice, persecution, and low-status occupations.

Before 1949 when the People's Republic of China assumed control of mainland China, it was the practice of many older immigrants to return to China after they retired, to enjoy the glorious period of old age surrounded by children and grandchildren, many of whom they had never seen. For those unfortunate enough to die in America before they left for home, the various clan, district, or benevolent associations would see to it that their bodies were shipped home for burial in the family plot, or they would even have their bones dug up and shipped overseas, sometimes even eight or ten years after death. Since 1949 this luxury of being buried in their homeland has been taken away from the elders among Chinese immigrants.

America is a youth-oriented country. Being old and poor is one of the greatest fears of many of its people. Many elderly Chinese Americans have retired to room at association headquarters, living on the generosity of friends and relatives. It is an unspoken charitable gesture for Chinese restaurants in Chinatown to offer free meals to the old and deprived. The elderly can frequently be observed walking straight into the kitchen of a restaurant around mealtime to receive a hot bowl of rice from their fellow countrymen.

Most sojourners could not qualify for Old Age Assistance or other forms of relief until the 1940s. However, even if they were qualified, many refused to accept public relief and charity, partly due to the loss of "face" or pride, and partly because they were afraid to be deported as public charges. There has been a gradual change of attitude, especially with regard to accepting Social Security, to which many had contributed during the productive years of their lives. The breakdown of the mutual-aid system provided by the clan and family associations and the indifference of kinsmen in times of genuine need has also forced a change in attitudes toward accepting public aid. Neurotic and psychotic disorders have been found among the rejected, lonely, and deprived older people in Chinatown (Lee, 1960:329–331).

Retired immigrants appear to have few pleasures unless they are relatively wealthy. The unsuccessful ones may live at the company houses, several to a room, with limited modern conveniences or comfort. They may gamble at a social club or one of the numerous one-room gambling dens. In the early 1950s the New York Community Service Society and the Department of Welfare initiated a Golden Age Club, and attendance exceeded expectations. The membership in 1962 was well over 1000, which indicated the great need this group had for recreational activities as well as the fact that their respective family-name associations had not made them welcome. The traditional function of the family-name association may be declining, judging from the fact that there are many older Chinese seeking help from the Chinatown nursing office of Community Service of New York and other public social agencies (Cattell, 1962:48).

On the other hand, few immigrant professionals who arrived in this country in the 1940s are at retirement age. Some of them had brought their aged parents to America after they became citizens or received permanent-resident status. Most of their parents and elders, however, are still in mainland China and are not able to leave the country. By the time this post-1940s professional group reaches retirement age, they may not suffer the same problems of the Chinatown-based retirees due to their higher educational background, greater intellectual and economic resources, and, most important of all, a family of American-born children and grandchildren well rooted in the new society.

Having been socialized in China in the most formative years of their lives, they may encounter some difficulty adjusting to their increasingly Americanized children and grandchildren, whose ways of treating parents and grandparents are not appropriate to the Chinese tradition. Recently a mother confided in this writer that she and her husband were shocked to receive a letter from their son and Caucasian daughter-in-law. They were happy to hear from them, but not to be addressed as "Dear Jeanie and Jack." "At least she could address us as Father Wong and Mother Wong," she stated, meaning that undoubtedly it was the American daughter-in-law who instigated such a big dose of democracy in their new relationship.

Due to rapid social change in the American society, one may assume that it will take several generations before elders from Chinatown-based families and professional suburban families accept the attitude and behavior of the

134

younger generations. The basic central theme of respect for the elders from the traditional Chinese values may linger on in the minds of most members of the older generation regardless of educational background or length of residence in America. One often hears Chinese Americans express that it is better to live in America when one is young. When one grows old, one should return to the old country where age is respected and catered to. The generation gap in the average American family has been a frequent topic of discussion in recent decades, but the gap between generations in the Chinese American family is many times more dramatic, especially between foreign-born parents and American-born offspring. Resignation among the younger generation, rather than rebellion, has been the pattern as an open confrontation in human relationships is much frowned on in the Chinese culture.

The attitude of Chinese Americans toward their elders may show greater concern and devotion than in the average American family. The lot of the older people in America, however, may compare unfavorably with that traditional China in which age was not regarded as a problem so long as the pattern of continuity between the generations was maintained. In both Chinatown-based families and Chinese suburban families, one usually expects elderly helpless parents to be included in the household, especially when the parent is widowed. The professional group tends to be more resourceful and independent, and the retired group among them have already organized the Chinese Retirement Association of America, an affiliate of Midwest Chinese Student and Alumni Services (*Newsletter of the Midwest Chinese Student and Alumni Services,* 1976). The major function of the association is to promote the welfare of the retired members.

CHANGE AND ADAPTATION

The Effects of Immigration on Ethnic Solidarity

For over 30 years since 1949 there was practically no Chinese immigration from the People's Republic of China (PRC). Since the renewed friendly relations between the United States and the PRC in 1979, American citizens have attempted to apply for visas for relatives. However, informants report that even though permission had been granted for long-lost relatives to enter the country, there is a waiting period of several years because they also have to process all the applications for those who wish to come from Hong Kong and Taiwan. Regardless of the political circumstances of the cases, the United States Immigration and Naturalization Service considers them all Chinese and will process entrance to the United States in the order of the date of application.

Chinese ethnic identity and ethnic solidarity is based primarily on origin of birth as well as on spoken dialect. In various universities, for example, Chinese students are usually divided into such groups as Hong Kong students, Taiwan students, or those who speak Mandarin, Shanghai dialect, or Cantonese. In general, the Chinatown residents have very little to do with those who come from Taiwan, and the professional groups have little contact with the businessmen. Furthermore, those who came from Taiwan have very little to do with those who are sympathetic to the People's Republic of China.

Furthermore, some Chinese Americans have been found to group their fellow Chinese by their origin of birth and the length of time they have been in the United States. The name distinction between such groups as A.B.C.s (American-born Chinese), F.O.B.s (Fresh off the boat), H.I.Ps (Hong Kong Instant Product), and M.I.T.s (Made in Taiwan) indicates certain divisions if not discrimination among Chinese themselves. But when bullied by other minority groups in the neighborhood, Chinese youths began to organize into gangs in order to protect themselves (*Newsletter of the Midwest Chinese Student and Alumni Services,* 1969).

With the renewed friendly relations between the United States and the People's Republic of China, it can be assumed that there will be new immigrants trickling in from the mainland China after over 30 years of isolation. It remains to be seen with the political and sociocultural differences of the new immigrants whether there is any possibility of increasing ethnic solidarity among the Chinese Americans in the United States.

The social and cultural orientations and sentiments of Chinese in America are gradually shifting from the ethnic subculture to the larger American society. As Caucasian society continues to become a positive reference group, its norms and values begin to guide as well as modify the behavior and perspectives of the Chinese (Fong, 1965:271).

However, being racially different from the Caucasian host group, most Chinese Americans find it difficult to be totally accepted by the host society. One eloquent native-born Chinese expressed his conflict and dilemma (L. Yee, 1974:3):

> In the case of Chinese Americans the whites call him "Chink" while the Chinese call him "jook sing," meaning the hollow part of the bamboo stick, in reference to his lack of Chinese culture. Not knowing anything about Chinese culture or how to read and write or even speak Chinese, the "jook sing" doesn't feel Chinese. Unlike the Chinese from China who learns to become American, the "jook sing" who never leaves the United States must work hard to become something he is not.

Because of the racial difference, Chinese Americans, no matter what their ethnic identity may be, are forever regarded by others as foreigners in their own country. No matter how many generations of one's family have been in

136

the United States and how American one feels, the Chinese American is for-ever being asked, "How long have you been in this country?" It is not likely the ethnic factor will disappear among the Chinese in the United States unless it is through generations of intermarriage with the host group. Even for those who are thoroughly assimilated Chinese American citizens, they are said to suffer from the "banana" syndrome, yellow on the outside and white on the inside (L. Yee, 1974).

Chinese American Alienation and the Yellow Power Movement

Asian Americans may be considered the silent minorities, and among them Chinese Americans have been known to be a relatively peaceful and quiet group of citizens. However, recent reports seem to indicate that the 1970s may be entitled the decade for emerging Yellow Power as the voices of Asian Americans began to speak out for justice and equality for their members. In 1971 a group of concerned Chinese Americans organized the ad hoc Chinese American Leadership Council. The purpose of this organization was to in-fluence the White House, various executive agencies, Congress, and state and local governments, for improvement in the basic well-being of Chinese Americans, a neglected minority in the United States (Wang, 1973).

In May of 1973 the first national meeting was held in Washington, DC. For the first time Chinese leaders were concerned not only with the neglected plight of some Chinese in Chinatowns, but also with the increasing number of Chinese entering the United States. The Chinese American population had grown from 237,000 in 1960 to 435,000 in 1970. Problems of immigrants, such as language difficulty, unemployment, juvenile delinquency, and family dislocation have begun to alarm authorities in and out of Chinatowns.

In the summer of 1974, the Organization of Chinese Americans, Inc. held its first young adults conference at Camp Arrowhead, Delaware. The confer-ence was conceived by four Chinese American students at Harvard Univer-sity and Radcliffe College under the leadership of K. L. Wang. Members of the conference were exposed to discussions on issues of Asian American iden-tity, history, political action, and social action.

Young Chinese Americans have begun to realize through historical records that the Chinese American minority has long suffered prejudice and discrim-ination silently. Since the visit of ex-President Nixon to Peking in the early 1970s many universities and schools have begun to emphasize Asian studies and Chinese language classes. Chinese American students that were inter-viewed admitted that they have been able to lift up their heads in pride, em-phasizing their own heritage and identity (A. H. Yee, 1975). The new pride has spread from college campuses to the Chinatown in San Francisco where Chinese Ameircans began to celebrate China's "Liberation" on October 1, the date of the change to the Chinese Communist regime in 1949. "Some of the youths were wearing bright blue, cotton Mao tunics" (M. S. Yee, 1972:19). Though the Chinese in general are not very political in orientation, the new emergence of the People's Republic of China on the international scene as well as the changing attitude of the United States government toward China has given Chinese Americans a new sense of worth and dignity in their national origin and cultural heritage.

In recent years, Chinatown parents in San Francisco have been registering protests against the massive transfer of Chinese American children away from their neighborhood schools. They stated that the neighborhood school system gave their children the opportunity to obtain an education in Chinese language, art, and culture through additional facilities maintained by the Chinese American community with classes beginning at the close of the public school classes (*The New York Times,* 1971:12). The most recent expression of the Yellow Power movement consisted of the mass protest by Chinese Americans in New York City against the beating of a Chinese engineer by the police (*The New York Times,* 1975:41). The protest group marched on City Hall; such a protest has never before been witnessed among the Chinese Americans who closed all the businesses and offices in their effort to register their angry sentiment in unity. The quiet minority is no longer silent.

The Yellow Power movement further expressed itself in the open confrontation of Chinese Americans in protesting the use of the name "Chinks" by a Pekin, Illinois, high school athletic team. Several Chinese American civic groups have tried to persuade the school authorities and city fathers to change the name of the football team, without success (*Pantagraph,* 1974:A10).

In general, the parental generation tends to be relatively philosophical and less willing to make waves in the face of prejudice and discrimination. "I don't worry whether my children feel 'banana' or not as long as they are 'top banana' in this rat race" (Anonymous, 1974:3). A rather typical attitude of parents is illustrated by the following statement (A. H. Yee, 1975:10):

> Observing our three children and responding to them with greater time and education than our elders, my wife and I must help them understand persistent myths of and prejudice against Asians and the concern of the children with identity.

With or without parental support or approval, the current generation of Chinese American youth has shown a deep sense of conviction that it is about time to get organized with other Asian Americans to fight for equal rights and justice as citizens in the United States. Today, most of the larger universities have Asian American Associations, to be distinguished from the Chinese Student Association, which consists of mostly foreign students from Hong Kong and Taiwan. The charter organization of the Asian American Association of Ohio State University initiated as objectives, among others, group identity, self-awareness, self-evaluation and promotion of the Asian American image and subculture through public education. It is implied in the rationale of the organization "although Asian Americans are American citizens [OSU Asian American Association], they must develop within this country a new set of values and ideals consistent with their dual cultures." It is indeed this sensitive issue of the marginal man status that young Asian Americans consider most crucial. Not to be outdone by the Black Power Movement of the 1960s and women's liberation of the 1970s, Asian American youth all over the U.S. on university campuses have begun to organize the Yellow Power Movement in the 1980s. Instead of fighting a tug-of-war between parental culture and the American culture, young Americans of Chinese heritages have begun to search for harmony in the synthesis of two highly divergent cultures. Since the People's Republic of China began to rise on the international scene, Chinese Americans have begun reevaluating the importance of their Chinese cultural heritage. This, in turn, raises their consciousness in the search for a new identity through group unity and combined efforts with other Asian Americans.

The contributions of the Yellow Power movement consist in the reeducation of the white majority as well as in raising the consciousness of all Asian Americans in search of a new identity. The group unity and strength of the Yellow Power movement will not only reduce the psychological alienation of Asian Americans in different degrees of the "banana" syndrome but also will promote social and economic welfare of the disenchanted minority groups through political participation. The alienation of Chinese American youth will continue to endure unless the conscious effort of the Yellow Power movement can help them in the search for harmony in their identity crisis. According to Cooley's looking-glass-self theory, one's self-concept comes from how others perceive him. The image of the alien will be perpetuated if Chinese Americans do not attempt to destroy the myths and stereotypes that surround the citizens of Chinese heritage.

R E F E R E N C E S

Anonymous. 1974. *Newsletter of the Midwest Chinese Student and Alumni Services,* 16(4).
Barnett, L. D. 1963. "Students' Anticipation of Persons and Arguments Opposing Interracial Dating," *Marriage and Family Living,* 25 (August): 355–357.
Barron, Milton L. 1966. *People Who Intermarry.* Syracuse, NY: Syracuse University Press.

Beaudry, James. 1971. "Some Observations on Chinese Intermarriage in the United States," *International Journal of Sociology of the Family,* Special Issue (May), pp. 59–68.

Benedict, Ruth. 1938. "Continuities and Discontinuities in Cultural Conditioning," *Psychiatry,* 1 (May): 161–167.

Broverman, I. K., D. M. Broverman, and F. E. Clarkson. 1970. "Sex-role Stereotype and Clinical Judgments of Mental Health," *Journal of Consulting and Clinical Psychology,* 34(1): 1–7.

Buck, Pearl. 1956. *My Several Worlds.* New York: Pocket Books.

Cattell, Stuart H. 1962. *Health, Welfare, and Social Organization in Chinatown.* New York: Community Service Society.

Chao, Shueh-Chin. 1929. *Dreams of the Red Chamber.* New York: Doubleday.

Chen, Clarence. 1972. "Experiences as an American in Disguise," *Newsletter of the Midwest Chinese Student and Alumni Services,* 14(Summer): 4–8.

Cheng, David Te-Chao. 1949. *Acculturation of the Chinese in the United States—A Philadelphia Study.* China: Fukien Christian University Press.

Erikson, Erik H. 1963. *Childhood and Society* (2nd ed.). New York: Norton.

Fong, S. L. M. 1965. "Assimilation of Chinese in America: Changes in Orientation and Perception," *American Journal of Sociology,* 71:265–273.

Gordon, Albert. 1964. *Intermarriage.* Boston: Beacon Press.

Hayner, Norman, and Charles M. Reynolds. 1957. "Chinese Family Life in America," *American Sociological Review,* 22(October): 630–37.

Heer, David. 1966. "Negro–White Marriage in the United States," *Journal of Marriage and the Family,* 27(August): 262–273.

Hsu, Francis L. K. 1949. "Suppression Versus Repression: A Limited Psychological Interpretation of Four Cultures," *Psychiatry,* 12: 233–242.

———. 1970. *Americans and Chinese.* Garden City, NY: Doubleday Natural History Press.

———. 1971. *The Challenge of American Dream: The Chinese in the United States.* Belmont, CA: Wadsworth.

———. 1972. *American Museum Science Book* (2nd ed.). Garden City, NY: Doubleday Natural History Press.

Huang, Lucy. 1956. "Dating and Courtship Innovations of Chinese Students in America," *Marriage and Family Living,* 18(February): 25–29.

Lear, Martha Weinman. 1965. *The Child Worshippers.* New York: Pocket Books.

Lee, Rose Hum. 1952. "Delinquent, Neglected, and Dependent Chinese Boys and Girls of the San Francisco Bay Region," *Journal of Social Psychology,* 36(August): 15–34.

———. 1960. *The Chinese in the United States.* Hong Kong: Hong Kong University Press.

Loh, Homer. 1944. "Americans of Chinese Ancestry in Philadelphia," Ph.D. thesis, University of Pennsylvania.

McClellan, Robert. 1971. *The Heathen Chinese.* Athens, Ohio: Ohio University Press.

Mead, Margaret. 1955. *Cultural Patterns and Technical Change.* Garden City, NY: Doubleday Natural History Press.

———. 1970. *Culture and Commitment: A Study of the Generation Gap.* Garden City, NY: Doubleday Natural History Press.

Newsletter of the Midwest Chinese Student and Alumni Services. 1967. 10(December).

———. 1968. 11 (March, July, and December).

———. 1969. 12(Winter).

———. 1976. 19(Winter).

Pa, Chin. 1972. *The Family.* New York: Anchor Books.

Pantagraph. 1974. "Chinese Protest Use of Chinks by Pekin," (July 11), p. A 10.

Saxton, Alexander, 1971. *The Indispensable Enemy.* Berkeley: University of California Press.

Schwartz, Shephard. 1951. "Mate-Selection Among New York City's Chinese Males 1931–38," *American Journal of Sociology,* 56(May): 562–568.

Smith, William. 1928. "Changing Personality Traits of Second Generation Orientals in America," *American Journal of Sociology,* 23: 922–929.

Sollenberger, Richard T. 1962. "Chinese-American Child-Rearing Practices and Juvenile Delinquency," *The Journal of Social Psychology,* 74: 13–23.

Sue, Stanley, and Derald W. Sue. 1971. "Chinese American Personality and Mental Health," *Roots,* Regents of University of California, pp. 72–81.

Sung, Betty Lee. 1967. *Mountain of Gold.* New York: Macmillan.

The New York Times. 1946. Section VI (December 15), p. 60.

———. 1957. Section VI (October 6), p. 49.

———. 1965. (July 11), p. 43.

———. 1968. (June 29), p. 31.

———. 1971. (August 18), p. 12.

———. 1975. (May 20), p. 41.

The Wall Street Journal. 1969. (January 28).

U.S. Bureau of Census. 1977. *Statistical Abstract of the U.S.* Washington, DC: U.S. Government Printing Office.

Wang, King Lee. 1973. "An Open Letter to All Concerned Chinese-Americans," *Newsletter of the Midwest Chinese Student and Alumni Services,* 15 (Spring):10.

Weiss, Milford S. 1969. "Inter-Racial Romance: The Chinese Caucasian Dating Game," paper presented at the Southwestern Anthropological Association, Las Vegas, April.

Wirth, Louis. 1956. *The Ghetto.* Chicago: University of Chicago Press.

Wong, Jade. 1945. *Fifth Chinese Daughter.* New York: Harper & Row.

Yee, Albert H. 1975. "Identity Crises for Asian-Americans: A Personal View," revised from a paper presented at the Annual Convention of Asian Studies, San Francisco, March 26.

Yee, Lawrence. 1974. "Banana," *Newsletter of the Midwest Chinese Student and Alumni Services,* 16 (4)(Summer).

Yee, Min S. 1972. "Red Star over San Francisco," *Saturday Review* (October 28), p. 19.

Yuan, D. Y. 1965. "New York Chinatown," in Arnold M. Rose and Caroline B. Rose (eds.), *Minority Problems.* New York: Harper & Row, pp. 277–284.

RECENT AND CONTINUING ETHNIC MINORITIES
(circa 1920–present)

The Arab American Family

The Arab world, with its huge oil reserve, emerged in 1973 as an area of enormous importance to America and the Western world. It may come as a surprise for many Americans and Canadians to learn that there are sizeable Arab communities in their countries. It is also a fact that few sociological studies have been conducted on these Arab American and Arab Canadian communities and their family patterns. Although the chapter presented here does suffer from a relatively scant amount of knowledge of this ethnic group, Dr. Elkholy has relied on two field studies separated by 20 years, one conducted in 1957 and the other in 1977. In addition, the participant-observation technique has aided his interpretation of the statistical data gathered on these Arab communities in the United States and Canada.

Understanding the Arab Americans and their styles of family organization may enable us better to comprehend the Middle East. This chapter provides us with a spectroscopic examination of the family patterns of an old people in a new land, and by inference, a picture of an enigmatic people who may nevertheless, through our scientific and sociological probing, provide us with the knowledge requisite to achieve an overall pattern for assimilation of Middle Eastern nations into a world community of peoples.

CHAPTER SEVEN
BY
ABDO A. ELKHOLY

HISTORICAL BACKGROUND

Arab Americans and Arab Canadians proudly mention their ancestors crossing the Atlantic from Spain and arriving at Brazil in the year 1150 A.D. Before that, in the 10th century A.D. (according to the Arab geographer Al-Sharilf (Al-Idrisi), eight adventurous Arabs sailed from Lisbon, Portugal, trying to discover what lay beyond the sea of darkness, the Atlantic Ocean (Audat, 1956:5–17). It is said that they landed in South America. Some historians suspect that Al-Idrisi's story inspired Columbus to try to reach the East through the West, which led to the great discovery of America. In 1955, when Italy celebrated the five hundredth anniversary of the birth of Columbus, there was a fair at which many of Columbus's belongings were displayed.

Among them was an Arabic book, said to be the Idrisi book, in which the story of the eight adventurers was mentioned. It suffices to state that migration remains one characteristic of the Arabs because of their nomadic history. If those early migrations were initiated by personal curiosity, the late ones have been initiated by social causes.

South America captured the attraction and imagination of the early Arab emigrants, who went there in large groups to form sizable and influential ethnic communities. Perhaps the cold climate and the Europeanization of the United States and Canada made them less attractive to the early Arabs than South America, since the Arabs only started to migrate to the United States and Canada in the last quarter of the 19th century. One distinct religious feature dominated the early Arab emigrations of the 19th century: The great majority were Christians. Fear of losing their religion in the Christian, missionary-minded New World delayed the immigration of the Arab Moslems to America by about 25 years, until the start of the 20th century (Makdisi, 1959:970). The head-start migration thus achieved by Christian Arabs increased their ratio to the Moslem Arabs up to the start of World War II by nine to one.

The Arab migration to North America resulted from two causes (Warner and Srole, 1945:105): "forces of attraction exerted by the expanding American economy and forces of expulsion exerted in the lands of emigration." Prior to 1950, only 2 percent of Arab Americans left their native land for political reasons and less than 1 percent for education in America. Driven by poverty and attracted by wealth, most of them came from the peasant sector in Greater Syria, politically recognized now as Lebanon. It is not surprising that with unfavorable demographic characteristics such as low socioeconomic and educational status, the early waves of immigrants did not fare well in the New World. One-fourth of them ended their journey in the southern states where farm labor was welcomed, and many became successful farmers in Georgia, Texas, Tennessee, Mississippi, New Mexico, and Arizona, and (in Canada) Nova Scotia, New Brunswick, Quebec, Ontario, Manitoba, Saskatchewan, and Alberta. About 50 percent of the early immigrants stayed on the east coast, in New York, New Jersey, Pennsylvania, the New England states, and Nova Scotia, New Brunswick, and Quebec. They peddled dry goods and started grocery stores. The remaining 25 percent moved to the midwestern states of Ohio, Michigan, Indiana, Illinois, Iowa, and Ontario and Manitoba to work as unskilled laborers in the railroad, steel, and auto industries in addition to dry goods peddling and grocery stores. As some pioneers recalled, they often were sponsored by successful businesspeople who had migrated earlier from the same region. Upon their arrival in U.S. or Canadian ports, immigration officials pinned name tags on them, put them on

146

the train, and called the sponsor to announce their arrival at their destination. In most cases their passage was paid by either relatives in the old country or the sponsors, who generally assumed responsibility of finding them living quarters and providing them with employment. The sponsors were mainly dry goods wholesalers who relied on the immigrants to sell their goods from door to door. This arrangement was mutually satisfactory in the short run. The immigrant, who lacked funds and knowledge of the English language, found suitable and ready employment in a strange environment, and the wholesaler found squadrons of laborers who contributed to the prosperity of his business.

Whether Moslem or Christian, the Arabs who formed the first waves of immigrants from the last quarter of the 19th century up to World War II never intended to spend the rest of their lives in America. They only wanted to accumulate the most money possible in the shortest time and then return home. Sixty percent of those early immigrants came unmarried. Because of economic uncertainty, only 12 percent of those married came with their families (Elkholy, 1966:83).

Though attracted to America, as reported by 97 percent of a sample of the early immigrants, they were handicapped by their lack of knowledge of English: "Learning the English language was the most difficult adjustment to make" (Elkholy, 1966:84). Coming from the lower educational class and having acquired no knowledge of English prior to their emigration, those of the earlier waves found everything strange in America. The majority of the first immigrants had to cluster around pioneers in order to solve the critical linguistic handicap, which has been one of the most influential factors in erecting ethnic clusters all over the world. The less English-speaking an ethnic community in America, the more clannish it is, and the more it segregates itself from American life. Such segregation delays the process of acculturation.

The early immigration waves between 1880 and 1939 carried the Arabs to the agricultural southern states as well as to the large cities of the east coast, New England, and the midwestern states, and forced them to congregate in small as well as large communities. The second immigration waves, which started in the 1950s and are still continuing, scattered the educated elites and technicians almost randomly across the United States and Canada.

The sharp demographic contrast between the first- and second-immigration waves is the function of two dramatic episodes in the Middle East: First, the creation of Israel in 1948 resulted in the expulsion of about two million Palestinians to make room for the European and Russian Jews, who have been coming to Israel ever since. Most of those Palestinian refugees who had the chance to come to America for one reason or another remained here permanently. Some were professionals and skilled workers. The majority acquired their higher education in American and Canadian universities when scholarships were plentiful and an unprecedented expansion of higher educational institutions took place. The second dramatic episode was the Egyptian Revolution in 1952, which grew out of the Arab world's frustration over the loss of Palestine, and which instigated a series of similar military coups d'etat and revolutions in other Arab and Moslem countries and disrupted the status quo in the social structure of the entire Middle East. Those Egyptians and other Arabs with professional and financial means, who did not fare well under the military regimes, started to look around for a way out. A great proportion of them have been emigrating to America since 1952; especially after 1956 and 1967, the late arrivals, the intellectual elite of the Arab society, were highly educated and skilled (*Arab Youth,* 1975:6). Seventy-three percent were educated in the United States, Canada, or Europe. This put them in favorable bargaining positions in the expanding educational, research, and technological markets, especially since they had no linguistic barrier to restrict their mobility. They sought employment as university professors, school teachers, engineers, technicians, and physicians. Some have already acquired national fame and prominence.

Many new Arab communities have sprung up over the United States and Canada during the 1950s and 1960s. From Jersey City, New Jersey, to St. Louis, Missouri, and Los Angeles, California, and from London, Ontario, to Edmonton, Alberta, the newly immigrated Arabs settled in either new concentrations or as individuals, depending on their professions. During the so-called "brain-drain" period, which labeled those two decades, 90,915 Arabs, most of them professionals, immigrated to America. Between 1962 and 1972, 68,305, or about 90 percent of the total immigrants admitted to America from seven Arab countries, were professionals. Again, the majority of them came from Egypt. Added to these 90,915, another 2080 nonimmigrants were naturalized between 1950 and 1971. Although there is no religious census taken in America of these new waves of Arab immigrants, it is estimated that 78 percent are Moslems. High professionalism and Moslem majority characterized the second-wave immigration in contrast to the early waves prior to World War II.

To speak of this professional category as a social group or an ethnic community gives a misleading impression, for there was no single institutional organization prior to 1960 under which they could be sheltered. It was only after the creation of Israel that a number of Arab American organizations were started mainly for the purpose of defending themselves against what they considered Zionist propaganda and defamation practices. In 1952 the Federation of Islamic Associations in the United States and Canada was

148

formed, followed by the American Arab Association in 1961, the Association of Arab American University Graduates in 1967, and the Association of Egyptian American Scholars in 1970. However, these organizations attracted only a small percentage of the Arab elites in America.

The family lifestyle of this professional category approximates that of the typical middle-class WASP family style. In the absence of distinct racial characteristics betraying their ethnic origin, the members of this professional category are fully accepted by American society. Their intention to make America a permanent home facilitated the process of adaptation. In the Elkholy study, 68 percent of the men were found to be married to American, Canadian, or European spouses whom they met on university campuses at the time they were studying. The remaining 32 percent of Arab wives of these professionals belong to the upper-middle socioeconomic class in the Arab world. They are not handicapped by linguistic barriers, compared with the previous waves of less educated wives, and thus have easy access to higher education and employment. The professional, economic, and social prosperity of this category with Arab wives made assimilation to and acceptance by the American society as easy and speedy as it was for those 68 percent Arabs with Western spouses. The average number of children is 2.27. Birth control and family planning are practiced by 87 percent of the couples. Their American-born children are typical Americans with only scant knowledge of the Arab world and its problems.

While it is difficult to identify the product of the second waves of immigration as being members of Arab communities (due to their professional commitments and their high rate of mobility), it is quite easy to find concentrated communities that are the product of the early immigration waves.

THE MODERN ARAB AMERICAN FAMILY

The structure as well as the socialization processes of the Arab family in America oscillate generally between preservation of traditional culture and acculturation, depending on a number of variables, one of which is intermarriage with Westerners. From the perspective of intergroup relations, the problem can be seen through the eyes of the ethnic minority looking toward the larger society and its various groups. The intergroup relations are affected by the stereotyped images that the minority and dominant groups develop toward each other. The stereotype, which creates social distance, is extended to the members of a given group, and thus the interaction becomes biased. Overcoming the mutually unfavorable images of East and West requires strong personal sentimental preference in the face of traditions of both the minority and dominant groups. Intermarriage is viewed here from the standpoint of the minority spouse as a strong agent of assimilation, because the spouse who belongs to the dominant culture facilitates the cultural transformation of the offspring.

The difference between assimilation and acculturation may be made clear here. Acculturation cannot occur without assimilation. When the minority members assimilate the prevailing values of the host society and prefer them over the traditional values of their cultural background, one of two things takes place: The minority community rejects the assimilated members and makes their presence in the community unwelcome, often forcing them to leave, becoming a total loss to the minority community. However, when the minority community retains its assimilated members, they become a gain to the overall community acculturation. In the first instance, the community will ultimately dissolve by the time the last member leaves or dies. In the second case, the community may remain distinct, although acculturated. Intermarriage between Arabs and Westerners is in general neither desired nor encouraged by the Arab communities in the United States and Canada. Nevertheless, there are two variations in these atittudes which are related to religion and education.

Intermarriage and Religion

Although intermarriage with Westerners is desired by neither Moslem Arab nor Christian Arab communities, it is more strongly resisted by the Moslems than by the Christians. Since it was indicated before that intermarriage facilitates the processes of both assimilation and acculturation, it is to be expected that the Christian Arab communities will be more acculturated than their Moslem counterparts. In either case the process of interreligious marriage is not always smooth. Various cultural barriers intervene, one of which is the Arab family lifestyle, which differs from the American lifestyle.

Our sample study has shown that more than 68 percent of the Moslem immigrants came to the New World unmarried. Less than 12 percent of the married immigrants came with their families. The pattern, then, was for the immigrants to come alone. Aside from the few female students who marry in the New World and decide to remain, the entire stock of the single Moslem immigrants is composed of young men. These young men are faced with a problem: Whom do they marry?

Marital choice differs between the two types of immigrants. The great majority of the unmarried pioneers married within their own ethnic groups by importing their wives from the old countries. Approximately 67 percent of the late arrivals, however, married Europeans, Americans, or Canadians.

Thus, despite the relatively short time span the Moslems have been in the New World, they have generally adopted a liberal attitude toward interreligious marriages. This seems to be true for both males and females, and most particularly true for Moslem immigrants coming to this country after World War II. Liberal attitudes toward intermarriage are related to education, which is related to professionalism.

Aside from the fear of diluting their communities in the long run via intermarriage, Arabs desire that their young men marry only their young women. Marrying outside the group, even when the wives are brought to the community, means that an equal number of young Arab women will either stay unmarried or marry outside, thus leading to undesirable consequences. Intermarriage always brings to the community unpredictable members whose values, customs, and habits are not in accordance with those of the community. As one member put it to the author (Elkholy, 1966):

> With our people, we can drop by at any time, day or night, whenever we feel like it. We can go to the kitchen and icebox to help ourselves with no hesitation. We feel welcome and the wives do not resent us. They are our sisters. They understand what we talk about, for there is a common theme which cannot be taught. A lot of things can be taken for granted and do not require the cautions we have whenever we visit one of our unlucky brothers who married outside. We are hesitant to eat at their homes. The wife cannot follow our conversation. She gets frustrated. We feel embarrassed and soon the atmosphere becomes boring. Some of those wives are snobbish and feel superior. I don't know whether they really feel this way or just play it that way to keep a certain distance from the rest of the community. We feel sorry for the children. They do not have the joy our children have. We also feel sorry for those foolish husbands. We suspect that they are not happy at home. They miss our food, our conversation, gossip, and our entire atmosphere.

This might be an exaggerated image reflecting attitudes of some members toward such marriages. However, such an image constrains the social relations and restricts the interactions between the community and the families of intermarriage.

A REVERSE SITUATION: AN AMERICAN WIFE. From the viewpoint of the non-Arab wife, the story might be somewhat different. The pattern of the Western family hardly coincides with that of the Arab one. The wide gulf of hard reality between the immediate family and the extended one is not easy for the Western wife to comprehend. When she has to cross that rugged gulf to the extended family pattern of her husband, she finds herself aggravated and lost in an infinite number of relationships, each of which is traditionally prescribed and requires a set of specific mutual obligations. The following case study reported to the author (Elkholy, 1966) illustrates the predicament:

An American wife married to an Iraqi professor when interviewed tried to illustrate the sources of her agony in Iraq which led her husband to immigrate to the United States. As is often the case, she met him on the American campus where they were attending the same university. They left the States for Iraq with their 6-month old child, immediately after the husband received his Ph.D. degree. All that she knew about the Middle East came to her mind through the fantasies of the book One Thousand and One Nights, plus the Western image of the sleepy, rosy medieval conditions. She did not find Bagdad the golden city she imagined. Rather, she found in it clusters of confusion emanating from social and ecological changes. Although her husband was given a university teaching position, his salary could hardly sustain the lifestyle of their Americanized household.

Her anxieties started as soon as they strove to find a suitable apartment. The landlords did not desire to rent out their nice places to natives like her husband. They preferred foreigners, perhaps to get higher rent, or to be more sure of better maintenance. Her husband, for the first time, felt discriminated against in his own country. It was some time before they acquired a suitable apartment whose rent they could afford. With one car, which they had brought with them, they could hardly manage. The heavy teaching schedule of the husband, the imposed consultations with government circles for very little reward, and the endless favors the husband had to render daily to acquaintances, friends, and relatives in getting them positions or work here and there, to write them letters of recommendation, or to call influential people in their behalf—all this hardly left any of the husband's time for her or household affairs.

Managing household affairs without a car, she had to use public transportation which she found frustrating. For help, she had to rely on unreliable maids. After she had half-trained the maid, the girl would quit or was attracted elsewhere by higher wages. She found it a losing battle which, however, she could not afford to stop fighting. During the three-year period the couple spent in Iraq, her husband hardly had time to eat dinner with her at the regular time more than a dozen times. Normal family life was quite often interrupted by unscheduled visits of demanding relatives who felt they had an indisputable right to use the house as if it were their own. The concept of hotels and restaurants was alien to them. Gradually, the social burden became unbearable. Finally, the informant said, "we had to quit and return to the States."

The experiences of the Western wife in the native land of her Arab husband are not the most pleasant. She cannot grasp or bear the burden of the complexity of kinship outside the Western world. In the West, for example, there is only one term, cousin, to denote different types of kin relationships. All of them are equal in one respect: remoteness. There are, in the Middle East, eight different categories of cousins. Each category has a definite set of mutual rights and obligations that are legally acknowledged and traditionally carried out and maintained. The following illustrates the eight different categories of cousins.

	CHILD
Father's side: Brother of the father	1. Son of brother of the father 2. Daughter of brother of the father
Sister of the father	3. Son of sister of the father 4. Daughter of sister of the father
Mother's side: Brother of the mother	5. Son of brother of the mother 6. Daughter of brother of the mother
Sister of the mother	7. Son of sister of the mother 8. Daughter of sister of the mother

When these eight categories are considered by age in relation to the child's age (i.e., younger, same age, older), the net result of the cousin categories alone adds to 24, for each category may contain persons who are older, younger, and equal in age to child. If a child died without leaving a spouse or children, his belongings are legally distributed among some of these categories, not in equal shares but according to a precise legal formula. If members of some of these cateogires are alive, they prevent some other categories from inheriting. By the same token, if a child survives some of these categories, he is apt to inherit a prescribed portion of their belongings. Extended kinship relations constitute the principal fabric of the social structure outside the Western world. They have the greatest functions in societies with little bureaucratic experience in which secondary institutions have not yet taken deep roots. The Western wife finds it difficult to function in this complex kinship system, which is a comfortable social world for the one reared in it, even in America.

Lifestyle of the Arab Family

The Arabs brought to the New World certain traditional family lifestyles that are more closely adhered to by the early immigrants than by the more recent professional immigrants. Four features are identified:

1. The Arab family was traditionally patriarchal and generally oriented toward older family members. The elders had a controlling voice in family affairs including approval of marriage partners for their children.

Screening of possible mates for a suitable one lay in the hands of the mother, the father making the final arrangements. Islam as well as Christianity still considers the father the head of the household, the manager of the affairs of the family.

2. Traditionally, a boy had the privilege—even right—of marrying the daughter of his father's brother. While this practice has declined, it still occasionally may be claimed as a right, or the girl and her parents may feel that she has been slighted if the cousin does not seek her in marriage.

3. Moslem women may not marry non-Moslems unless the non-Moslem becomes converted to Islam prior to marriage. This prohibition is not explicit in the Quran but is implied in the Traditions. It is felt that almost certainly the woman who marries a non-Moslem, as well as her children, will be lost to Islam.

4. Men may marry non-Moslems provided they are members of either Jewish or Christian faith—both groups being considered of the Heavenly Books and kin to the Moslems. It is anticipated that the wives will enter Islam, and their children will be reared as Moslems.

These traditional policies create many problems in the social situation of the New World and especially for American-born children of Moslems who tend to adopt the romantic-individualistic pattern of mate selection.

There are two general lifestyles of the Arab family, depending on the degree of education one or both of the Arab parents have acquired. However, those with no college education, whether Moslems or Christians, are the backbone of the Arab communities whose lifestyle is depicted here.

Through intimate contacts with their playmates and schoolmates, under the compulsory school system, second-generation members have had the chance to compare two different cultures and ways of life. The unfavorable socioeconomic conditions in the old countries at the time their parents came to America leave no doubt in the judgment of the second-generation members. They prefer the American socioeconomic and political structure over that of the old country. In fact, they consider themselves more fortunate than their parents to have been born in this country. The parents share this view. The first-generation immigrants are proud to hear their children speak English fluently—like any American or Canadian. It is also very common for the first-generation members to give their children American nicknames. In one family there are Mike, Ralph, Ronald, Fred, Dennis, Vicki, Stephen, and Churchill for outside identification, while the Arabic names are kept for the family and community identification.

The second generation plays a transitional role between the old and the new cultures and thus is often the victim of both. The members of the second generation teach the members of the first generation a great deal about the American culture. But it is hard for the first-generation members, who are dominated by a patriarchal family image, to accept the reversal of roles, which makes them pupils of their own children. This widens the cultural gap between the two generations. Most of the second-generation members, in response to the question, "About what things do you most frequently disagree with your father?", mention that their fathers are slow at making decisions and have a habit of arguing over little things. Among the common complaints against the mother are that they "interfere" in their children's personal affairs, are too absorbed in the social life of the immigrant women, and engage in too much malicious gossip in the style of the old country.

The two generations, therefore, live in two different social atmospheres with separate outlooks on life. The first-generation members are affected by the memories of their great efforts to make their way in a strange land. Looking forward, they realize that socially, as well as religiously, they have lost their offspring to America. They admit that they have gained economic wealth, but they doubt whether that wealth compensates for their loss.

Authority Relations in the Family

Most of the first-wave immigrants have had little or no formal education. The family in the old country performed many functions that, in the more complex societies, are performed by separate specialized institutions. Although the school was the formal educational institution, difficult economic conditions prevented that institution from serving as large a group as in the more economically advanced countries . The agrarian family needed the complete participation of all its members on the farm. The children simply could not be spared for formal education. Thus, the main education a child could obtain was in the tradition transmitted from one generation to another. The parents functioned in roles of vocational trainer and educator.

Since the emphasis in knowledge and wisdom was on the past, parents achieved status in the family through experiences that were associated with maturity. The traditional admiration for the aged in less literate societies derives from that association between experience and old age, accentuated in folklore. In more literate, industrialized societies, the emphasis in knowledge is on science and technology. Knowledge is not tied to the past. The machine and space era, with its emphasis on scientific achievement for the future, has shifted family status from the aged to the young. The function of traditional education in the home, to solidify the family under the control of the aged, has given way to a new concept of education.

The tradition-oriented first-wave Arab in America was puzzled by the independence and the disobedience of his children. He often expressed his disappointment about the new pattern of family relations by saying, "We lost our children in America," for they still dream of the patriarchal pattern, which they imagine (incorrectly) to be unchanged in the old country. The attitudes of the first generation puzzle the second generation, too. According to Warner and Srole (1952:125):

> Not only does the child resent the fact that his parents do not act after the American behavioral norms; not only does he resent pressure to act after the ethnic behavioral modes, but, infused with American social logics, he implicitly questions the right of his father to dominate and control his behavior.

The demand for freedom by the second generation conflicts with the desire of the first to retain control. This is the cornerstone of generational conflict. The more traditional the first-generation members, the more they demand control over the second generation, and the wider the differences become.

The progeny of the first-wave immigrants is born into two different cultures and grows up under both influences. In time the influence of his family is outweighed by the influence of the American culture. Once the children go out to play with American children, they encounter the fear and fascination of a new language. By the time they go to school, the English language is dominant. The different symbols of the English language (especially slang concerning dates, girlfriends, and boyfriends) convey lighter, easier values, which differ from the more ponderous values of their family.

Communication among generations in the family is manifested in the language both generations use at home. Linguistically, the family pattern has become heterogeneous: The first generation speaks in Arabic, while the second generation answers in English. Not only is English easier for the second-generation members, it is superior. They see the struggles of their parents to express themselves in English and use English words in Arabic constructions. Though the children laugh at their efforts, parents learn a great deal of English from their children—and much, as well, about the American way of life. The crucial point comes, as Warner (1953:126) says, when "the child, not the parent, becomes the transmitting agent of social change."

Education is, therefore, a major reason why the younger generation of the Arab community has become the catalyst for social change. The sharp educational difference among generations, especially between the first and second, is one of the factors responsible for family conflict in the Arab community. The family has become less integrated as each generation views the other from its own position and values.

Also associated with family conflict is the first generation's strong resistance to the social change introduced by the younger generation. Since the new environment continuously strengthens the value standards of the younger American- and Canadian-born generation over those of the first-wave immigrants, the latter group is frustrated in a losing battle. The unbalanced opposite forces between generations in the family relations have resulted in the father's failure to maintain tradition. "He does not know how to control the children" is the common complaint of the Arab wife against her husband. "The children," she continues, "don't listen to us. They spend most of their time out. They just come home to eat and sleep."

Arab new-generation members complain about the failure of traditional family structure to interest them and hold their loyalty. The disintegration of the traditional family structure manifests itself in numerous patterns, ranging from conversation to food. The parents' conversation is centered around persons and families taking the concrete shape of gossip. The children's conversation is centered around cars, nights, pleasures outside the home, and even general social problems. The parents continue to relish Arabic dishes, which the children do not enjoy. Very often, the housewife cooks *mijaddara* or *kebba nayya* for herself and her husband and something else for her children. A second-generation member summed up in three words the view of his generation toward their parents: "They neglect life," he said. Asked to elaborate, he replied to the author in a personal communication:

> I don't remember that my parents ever took us out to dinner, movies, or theater. They never invited any American family or accepted any American invitation. The reason is that my mother does not speak English. When I bought my car they were angry at me. I don't have complete freedom to spend my money. I work for my father. He gives me much less than what I could get working outside. Despite this they watch what I spend as if I were spending their money. Next year I'll be 30 years old but they still deal with me as if I were a child. If I buy a new suit or spend my vacation in Florida with some American friends they cry that I'm spoiled, that I spend too much on my friends, and so on. I'm sick of this life.

The Status of the Aged

Contrary to what might be expected, when the Arab American parents retire and cease to be economically productive, they are taken care of by their American- or Canadian-born children. Usually the parents live alone in the homes they own, and their married children, if nearby, look after them. The pattern is that they spend Sundays and holidays with their parents. The old folks look forward to these occasions, when two or three generations meet.

The "nursing home" is still an unknown institution to senior Arab Americans whose homes are social centers for an extensive network of relatives and friends. Even those who go back to retire in the old country return to the United States and Canada because they find that they miss their children, friends, and the lifestyle of the New World.

It is a Western cultural *norm* that this category of the elderly belongs in nursing homes, away from the loving, affectionate, vivacious, enthusiastic atmosphere of the younger generation. And here comes the great difference between the Western cultural norms and their counterparts in the culture of the Middle East, which are still adhered to by the Arab immigrants in the United States and Canada (Quran: Al-Isra', Sura XVII,23–24):

> And your Lord has decreed that you worship none but Him and always be kind to your parents. Whenever one or both of them attain old age, never say to them a word of contempt, nor repel them, but address them in terms of honor. And treat them with extreme humbleness and compassion, and say: "My Lord, bestow on them Your mercy for they cherished me in childhood."

The Quran is full of these moral instructions which have become an integral part of Islam and have influenced the culture of the Middle East. To cherish one's parents is second only to the worship of God. There is no ceiling to the reverence accorded the position of the mother. The Tradition states: "Paradise is under the feet of mothers." It is inconceivable of a Middle Easterner to think of sending his parents to a nursing home or similar public institution. As a matter of fact, no such institutions exist in the Middle East. Parents and grandparents are considered a valuable asset to the family, a means to blessings manifesting themselves in secular prosperity and reward in the hereafter. Senility among the aged appears to be a rare occurrence in the Middle East and could be looked upon as a Western phenomenon resulting from the feeling of worthlessness and from inactivity among the elderly.

While in the technological industrial culture of the West, the focus is on the future and changed values have given the young a higher status for their prospective accumulative achievement, the traditional agrarian culture of the Middle East reveres the past, stresses stability and continuity, and gives the aged the highest status for their accumulation of experiences. This accumulation of experiences, acquired with the passage of time, is assumed to have given the elderly wisdom beyond the grasp of the young.

Mental health is associated with self-esteem which, among other things, is the function of one's perception of one's worth. When the aged in the Western societies believe that they are useless and experience the negative attitudes of their culture as well as their families, they lose self-esteem and a sense of self-worth and start to suffer mental and psychological disintegration.

The social problems of the aged and the aging are among the awesome and bitter fruits of industrialization, technology, and modernization—all of which weakened the traditional extended family structure in which the aged were the responsibility of the younger members. Nowhere has the sociological theory of "exchange" been violated more than in the modern family, whose pattern is toward neglecting the aged rather than reciprocating the maintenance, care, and upbringing provided by them.

With the rapid medical advancement and health care programs that will ultimately prolong life expectancy, the problems of the aged and the aging will become increasingly acute. These are not merely physical or socioeconomic problems, which the modern state can handle, but rather emotional, psychological problems, which require education in the moral obligation toward the aged.

Islam, as a social system, addressed itself to these social-psychological problems and managed to form one of the more durable patterns of the family structure which took care of its aged by equating the care of one's aged with one's worship of God.

The West might find a solution for its disintegrating family pattern in the Middle Eastern traditions of the Arab American and Arab Canadian family style.

CHANGE AND ADAPTATION

Arab Americans and Arab Canadians refer to the New World as a paradise for women and children because the Arab family has become dominated by the mother and children. This has resulted because parents attempt to provide children with opportunities they never had. Parents desire to care for their children and control every aspect of their present and future lives. It is the wife who often initiates invitations and entertainments at the home, a sharp contrast from tradition. In fact, the community affairs are to a large degree sustained and run by women.

Marriage is no longer arranged. It follows the American pattern of dating, courtship, and romantic love—a concept and experience totally alien for the older members of the community. At colleges, as well as at work, Arab boys and girls meet other young people and start dating. Arab boys generally dislike dating the Arab girls or vice-versa, for family connections and relationships preclude any misbehavior, making for dull dates. Times of togetherness, or dates, might be interpreted by the elders in the community, especially the parents of the girl, as engagement. If marriage does not follow, ill feelings pervade the families involved. Christian Arabs and Moslem Arabs, as a rule, do not intermarry. Neither do the two Moslem sects of Sunni and Shia nor the two Christian sects of Maronites and Melkites encourage intersectarian marriage. If intermarriage takes place, it is between Arabs and non-Arabs. The Christian Arabs are more lenient in this respect than the Moslem Arabs. This is a factor contributing to the higher rate of acculturation of the Christian Arab communities in comparison to their Moslem counterparts. In the former communities, assimilation aids acculturation. In the latter, Moslem Arab girls (who are left without ethnic religious partners as a result of the tendency of the boys to date American girls) marry Americans and move outside their community. This further delays the process of acculturation among the Moslem Arab communities, which still preserve a great deal of traditional Middle Eastern values. Similar to Jews who managed to preserve traditional values on the basis of their religion, the Moslem Arabs in America have succeeded in perpetuating their religious institution around the mosque, an organization that has flourished and increased tremendously during the last two decades. Surprisingly, the mosque organization is sustained mainly by the third Moslem Arab generation, a matter that may usher in a pattern of a religiocultural revivalism similar to the pattern that occurred prior to World War II among the German Americans and the Japanese Americans. The response of Arabs in America following the creation of Israel was a revival of pride in their original culture, which they saw being deprecated by a religious minority. Here we find that religion became a utility for politics, and the mosque started to serve new functions to cater to the Sunday-oriented Moslem Arab American communities, which are gradually shifting from the traditional Friday religious activities in order to adapt to the working conditions of the American environment.

The speed and degree of assimilation of Arab Americans and Arab Canadians and acculturation of their communities will also depend on the diplomatic and economic relations between their new countries and the Arab world, which is, after all, the homeland of their ancestors and a hidden source of their personal pride.

The accidental or intentional migration of the Arabs to the New World hardly severed their ties with their motherlands in the Middle East. Even those who married non-Arabs to constitute mixed family patterns managed to blend their family style with that of the exotic Middle East by exposure through visits, nostalgia, cultural norms, and relatives.

In contrast to the nuclear American family, the Arab family in the United States and Canada is still inclined toward the extended style. In a strange land, the psychological tendency is toward mutual support, and the family network pattern serves such needs. The inflated stories of the actual or imaginary successes of early Arab immigrants to the New World quickly spread among the relatives and friends left behind. The early immigrants paved the way and served as receiving stations to distribute newcomers to centers of economic opportunity, where the Arab communities started to take roots, to widen the circle, and attract yet more people from the homeland. During the last 15 years, as a result of the "Fifth Preference" which allows any permanent resident to bring, off quota, his spouse and/or unmarried children, and allows any citizen to bring, off quota, his parents, brothers, sisters with their entire families, there have been more than one million additional Arabs who entered the New World to make it their permanent residence. This new wave of relocated families (not individuals) has revitalized the traditional structure of the Arab American family.

RECENT INTERNATIONAL EVENTS

Since the Arab-Israeli October War of 1973, in which the Arabs restored some of their pride and international reputation, and as a result of an embargo that demonstrated the energy dependence of the free world on Arab oil, American foreign policy became less anti-Arab. The American and Canadian media reflect a changing attitude toward the Arabs, and thus the Arab Americans and Arab Canadians are coming to feel less frustrated and more American- and Canadian-affiliated. However, cultural regression or revivalism, which awakened a sense of tradition among the Arab Americans and Arab Canadians as a self-defensive mechanism, is likely to be enhanced by the new international prestige the Arab world occupies nowadays. The oil bonanza, which spurred economic development and technological progress in the "homeland," seems likely to inspire Arab American and Arab Canadian youth to learn or perfect their Arabic and direct their professional aspirations toward the Middle East. The hitherto illiterate Arab states, for example, Kuwait, the Gulf states (United Arab Emirates), Libya, and Saudi Arabia, are launching vigorous programs in developing science, technology, education, and every aspect of their societies to catch up to the approaching 21st century.

There is a possibility that the recruitment of those of Arabic background who have American and Canadian technical knowledge will strengthen the Arab ethnic solidarity in the New World. A sense of self-redefinition and ethnic reidentification similar to that which swept the heart of the American Jews and revived the Jewish family lifestyle in America will emerge among the Arab Americans and Arab Canadians. The impact of the actual or exaggerated "reverse brain drain" on the Arab American family lies in the amount of inspiration developing among Arab American youth. However, it is too early to assess the psychological impact of the Middle Eastern Arab prosperity and the emerging new international image on either the Arab American personality or the Arab communities in the United States and Canada.

R E F E R E N C E S

Arab Youth. 1975. (April 7), p. 6.

Aruri, Naseer H. 1969. "The Arab-American Community of Springfield, Massachusetts," in Hagopian and Paden (eds.), *The Arab-Americans: Studies in Assimilation.* Wilmette, IL: Medina University Press International, pp. 50–67.

Audat, Yacub. 1956. *Al-Natigun bil-dad li Amirika al-Ganubiyya.* Beirut: Dar Rihani.

Elkholy, Abdo A. 1966. *The Arab Moslems in the United States: Religion and Assimilation.* New Haven: College and University Press.

———. 1971. "The Moslems and Inter-religious Marriage in the New World," *International Journal of Sociology of the Family: Special Issue,* I(May):69–84.

Glazer, Nathan. 1954. "Ethnic Groups in America: From National Culture to Ideology," in Morroe Berger, Theodore Abel, and Charles H. Page (eds.), *Freedom and Control in Modern Society.* Princeton, NJ: Van Nostrand, pp. 158–76.

Makdisi, Nadin. 1959. "The Moslems of America," *The Christian Century* (August 26), pp. 969–971.

Warner, W. Lloyd. 1953. *American Life.* Chicago: University of Chicago Press.

Warner, W. Lloyd, and Leo Srole. 1945. *The Social System of American Ethnic Groups.* New Haven: Yale University Press.

———. 1952. *Structure of American Life.* Edinburgh: University Press.

The Greek American Family

In this chapter, Professor Kourvetaris discusses the Greek American family in terms of an "ethnic generational frame of reference," covering three chronological generations of Greeks and Greek Americans in America. Within this generational framework he first presents a concise institutional profile of Greeks in America, followed by a discussion of certain normative patterns, lifestyles, and changes of three generations of the Greek family in America. Finally, he presents a model of transgenerational change with a prognosis for the future of the Greek American family in the context of the larger and changing society.

CHAPTER EIGHT
BY
GEORGE A. KOURVETARIS

HISTORICAL BACKGROUND

Greeks along with other immigrant groups from southeastern and central Europe made up the "late immigrants" vis-à-vis the "early immigrants" from countries of northwestern Europe. While most other European immigration to America has declined and almost ceased, Greek immigration, excluding the interwar years, has never really done so. Continued Greek immigration has given the larger Greek American community a graduated scale of ethnicity and continual doses of "Greek cultural transfusion." At one extreme of the continuum are those Greeks who are totally "Americanized," while at the other extreme are those who can hardly speak a word of English. It is only proper that one differentiates between "early" immigrants, or those who came prior to the 1920s, and the "late" Greek immigrants, or those who came in the 1950s and 1960s and continue. Although no exact figure of either group is known, a reasonable combined estimate of the present population would be somewhere between 2,000,000 to 2,500,000 Greek-born and Greek-descended Americans.[1]

---

[1]The Greek embassy estimates the Greek American population to be 2,000,000 while the Greek Archdiocese estimates it to be about 3,000,000.

The overwhelming majority of the early Greek immigrants were working class and came from southern Greece (Peloponesus). For example, it has been reported (Fairchild, 1911:3,35; Xenides, 1922:81; Saloutos, 1964; Moskos, 1980) that early Greek immigrants, as a rule, were poor, had limited education and skills, came primarily from agricultural communities, and consisted of young males. Included in this group was a small number of Greek school teachers, priests, journalists, and other professionals who became the apostles of ideals and values of Greek culture and society. Like most southern European immigrants, particularly Italians, early Greek immigrants did not come as families because they did not expect to stay in America. Despite their working-class and rural origins, the early Greek immigrants had a middle-class work ethic. They were industrious, independent, and thrifty. They had a sense of determination and cultural pride coupled with a sense of ethnic consciousness and community.

Although a number of early Greeks came from different parts of Greece or from the islands, by far the majority of early Greek immigrants to America came from the southern regions of Greece, especially from the peninsula of Peloponesus, which has a terrain that is more rocky and mountainous than the central and northern parts of Greece. Other Greeks came from Asia Minor (modern Turkey) when one-and-a-half million Greeks were uprooted in the 1910s and 1920s. Immigration was and still is looked on as a source of social and economic mobility particularly for the farming and lower classes.

By contrast, the late Greek immigrants were more educated and did not come exclusively from small agricultural communities; many came as families, sponsored by friends and relatives among the early immigrants. Included in this group was a substantial number of students and professionals[2] who came to America either to practice their profession or pursue an education in American institutions of higher learning. The education of the late Greeks, however, should not be exaggerated. By and large late Greek immigrants followed similar occupational patterns (e.g., restaurant owners) as the early Greek immigrants.

As a rule, both groups brought with them a lifestyle that was folk-oriented, ethnocentric, familistic, and traditional. The provincialism and traditional ways of life were a carryover from the village subculture in Greece that were and still are maintained in America especially in the early years of immigrant

---

[2]In a study on the "Greek Brain Drain," I found that Greece is among the few countries that lose a considerable number of her talented and professional people annually (Kourvetaris, 1973). For example, in the decade between 1962 and 1971 Greece lost to America alone 4,517 of her professional, technical, and kindred people; 4.4 percent of the total members of professional occupations admitted to America in the same decade were Greek.

life. One finds a proliferation of small ethnic village fraternal societies in America that reflect the values and traditions of agricultural communities and regions in Greece. The purpose of these *gemeinshaft*-type societies was and still continues to be ethnic and benevolent in nature: to maintain the group ideals and raise funds for their respective communities in the homeland. These village subcultures were transplanted to the New World and enabled the immigrant to keep in touch with his home community, find solace and relief from an urban way of life, and facilitate his transition and adjustment to the larger American society. They also reflected the regional diversity, particularism, and individualism of the Greeks.

Unlike the old, northwestern European immigrants who generally settled in small towns and rural areas, most late southeastern European immigrants, including the Greeks, settled in cities in which opportunities for employment and entrepreneurial activities were greater and ethnic communities flourished. These ethnic communities became the marketplace in which intraethnic, informal, social, cultural, religious, kinship, and business transactions took place.

From the very beginning, the early Greek immigrant was ambivalent about his permanent settlement in the New World. His original intention was to amass his fortune and return to his place of birth. Because of indecisiveness, the scarcity of Greek women, job insecurity, and the problems of social adjustment and acceptance in the host society, the Greek male was reluctant to commit himself to marriage and to raising a family. While he was physically in America, sentimentally and emotionally he was in his land of birth. (This is also somewhat true of the late Greek immigrants.) Although a substantial number of early Greek immigrants (over 120,000) returned to Greece, the vast majority remained in America.[3] Only when the Greek male felt reasonably secure in his job or business did he decide to settle down, get married, and have a family. Then he found it difficult to return to his native country. In fact, for many immigrants, marriage was the turning point that not only provided them with a feeling of permanence but made it more difficult, if not unthinkable, for them to return to Greece (Saloutos, 1964:85).

During the late immigration, feelings of xenophobia, properly cultivated by

---

[3]Somewhat similar patterns of repatriation are followed by the late Greek immigrants. Since the early 1970s a number of new Greek immigrants returned to their homeland. The extent of repatriation is not known. However, as a result of inflation, the Greek American relations over the Cyprus and Aegean issues (which have politically alienated and angered many Greeks toward the American foreign policy in the area), and the higher standard of living and socioeconomic and political improvement in general for Greece, many Greeks have been convinced to return. In this respect the Greek government has also encouraged repatriation especially the more skilled and technically trained Greeks. [See Terlexis, 1979.]

a prejudiced press, raised questions of contamination and lowering of standards of the Anglo-Saxon culture or the *Herrenvolk* by the so-called unassimilated and inferior stocks of southeastern European immigrants. Indeed, in 1924, Congress enacted a racist and discriminatory law with a quota system based on the 1870 U.S. Census, limiting sharply the number of southeastern Europeans entering America. The act, which was the official U.S. Immigration and Naturalization policy until 1965, conspicuously favored immigrants from countries of northwestern Europe (Simpson and Yinger, 1972:121). Thus, like other late ethnic groups, Greeks encountered problems of social discrimination. Omaha and Salt Lake City were just two extreme examples in which riots and strikes occurred where some immigrants, including Greeks, were killed (Saloutos, 1964; Papanikolas, 1970; Moskos, 1980). However, the tough beginnings, coupled with problems of adjustment and ethnic prejudice, galvanized the characters of the early Greek immigrants and made them more determined to master and overcome their lowly social and economic origins. Despite the success and *embourgeoisement* of many Greeks, many thousands of Greeks did not make it in America.[4]

Despite considerable variation between the early and late Greek immigrants and between generations, a number of students of Greek culture (Tsakonas, 1967; Sanders, 1962; Capanidou Lauquier, 1961) maintain that family and religion seem to be the two social institutions largely responsible for preserving the traditions, values, and ideals of modern Greek culture among the Greeks of the diaspora. For the Greek immigrant, as for other late immigrant groups, religion and family became the differentiating ethnic institutions that set them apart from the early northwestern European immigrant groups. Despite the importance of religion and family to the early Greek immigrants, these very institutions have been challenged by the Greek American younger generations and indeed some of the late Greek immigrants. Ideally, every Greek ethnic community in America was a spiritual community. A Greek church signified the existence of an ethnic colony and that every Greek was potentially a member of his church. To this effect, the admonition of Athenogoras—Archbishop of the Greek Orthodox Church in the Americas and later the Patriarch of Constantinople—that the Greeks of America should unite around the Church was clear in the 1920s and early 1930s.

In reality, however, and despite a considerable number of Greek Orthodox churches in America (about 425), only a small sustaining number of dues-

---

[4]For the *embourgeoisement*, success, and struggle of Greeks in America, see Moskos (1980). The book is a second-generation view of Greeks and Greek Americans. It somewhat exaggerates the success and *embourgeoisement* thesis and underemphasizes the failure and problems. Moskos draws primarily from English writings and not from Greek sources written by the Greek immigrants.

paying members are actively interested in church affairs. Furthermore, while Greek communities and churches were established early in the present century, 1922 marks the beginning of organized ecclesiastical life of the Greek Orthodox Archdiocese of the Americas. The average Greek, both in Greece proper and in America, does not perceive his church and/or religion in institutional/organizational terms. A parish priest is closer to the Greek immigrant than the hierarchical structure of the Church. A Greek church is a personalized extended family system of relationships interwoven with such events of the life cycle as births, baptisms, weddings, and religious and national holidays.

During the 1920s, the Church, following the political development in Greece proper, was divided along two political lines, the Royalists (supporters of constitutional monarchy) and the Republicans/Liberals (supporters of a Greek Republic) (Saloutos, 1964). Although this cleavage is no longer present in the Church, it has nevertheless been replaced by cleavages along generational lines (first versus second generation, early versus late immigrants), social class, and what Gordon calls "ethclass"[5] subcultures (self-employed versus employed, educated versus uneducated, professionals versus small businessmen), and those divided along nationality (Greekness, language) versus orthodox (religion) forms of cultural and ethnic identification. Most Greek American (church) communities are run by second-generation and some early Greek and late Greek immigrants. Most of them are business and some professional classes who tend to be more conservative in political and civil rights issues.

When the Greek Orthodox Church was formally organized, a group of early Greek immigrants met in Atlanta, Georgia (1922) and established the American Hellenic Educational Progressive Association (AHEPA). Its original purpose was to combat ethnic prejudice and discrimination including the activities of the Ku Klux Klan; later its scope was broadened to include educational, social, political, cultural, and benevolent activities. It endorsed a policy of "Americanization" and urged all its members to become American citizens. Although AHEPA is a secular organization, it maintains close ties with the Greek Orthodox Church in America and has become the formal linkage between the Greek and the larger American communities. Despite a proliferation of Greek American federations and organizations (over 60 in America alone), AHEPA is by far the largest Greek American organization,

---

[5] By "ethclass" Gordon (1964) meant that primary-group relationships tend to be generated within one's social-class segment of one's ethnic group or the intersection between ethnicity and behavioral-class similarities.

with an estimated membership of between 28,000 and 30,000 members in America.

Greeks established other ethnic institutions, schools, and ethnic professional societies including the ethnic mass media (over 100 ethnic radio and TV stations, newspapers, and magazines in both Canada and America) and the Greek Orthodox parochial school system (over 20 Greek American daily elementary schools) (Greek Orthodox Archdiocese of North and South America, 1972). Usually most of these ethnic institutions are managed by late Greek immigrants and patronized by those who are active in the church affairs and/or other ethnic organizations. The ethnic press is often the spokesman of the businessmen, the *nouveaux riches,* of the larger Greek American community.

Three types of Greek American communities can be discerned at the present time: a predominantly post-World War II Greek community made up of late Greek immigrants and their families, a mixed Greek American community of early and late Greek immigrants and their progenies, and a Greek American community made up of second- and third-generation American-born Greeks. The first two are by and large ethnic urban communities. Their members are characterized by working- and lower-middle-class lifestyles, with a substantial number engaged in small service-oriented establishments, particularly restaurants, taverns, and groceries, and low white-collar occupations, especially among second-generation Greeks. As a rule, they reside in close proximity to their churches. The third type, which is increasingly a suburban Greek American community, is characterized primarily by middle- and upper-middle-class lifestyles, or their members are professionals and businessmen. The latter increasingly follow the patterns and lifestyles of the tripartite Catholic, Protestant, and Jewish suburban ethnoreligious groups. Although most Greek churches are bilingual, in the third type Greek is gradually but steadily being replaced by English, and the priests are exclusively recruited from the second-generation American-born Greeks. In the last analysis, language has become the differentiating issue between first and second generation. Greek language is supported mostly by late Greek immigrants, while the second generation tends to support Orthodox religion conducted in English not in Greek.

THE MODERN GREEK AMERICAN FAMILY

First-Generation Greek Family

Although the first-generation Greek family includes both the early (1900–1920s) and late Greek immigrants (1950s to date), here the emphasis will be on the former. In analyzing the lifestyles of the first-generation Greek family, one should keep in mind the sociocultural and economic antecedents in Greece proper and those in America at the time of early Greek immigration.[6]

Coming from agricultural communities in which a large and extended kinship family system was more conducive to an agrarian economy, the first-generation family in America wanted to follow patterns similar to those in rural Greece. However, this was not normally the case. There were many reasons for this. First, the socioeconomic conditions of the immigrants and the problems of adjustment and hardships they encountered did not allow them to replicate the Greek village patterns of extended families. Second, the presence of many siblings in the immigrants' family of orientation in Greece forced them to migrate in the first place. Immigrants wanted to see their children succeed and projected their own unfulfilled aspirations to them. In this instance the smaller the family unit the more economic resources could be used for each child's benefit. Third, the immigrants had many obligations and promises to fulfill in their home communities such as to provide for their sisters' or nieces' dowries[7] or pay their fathers' debts. (Indeed, many never married for this reason.) Fourth, most early immigrants were males with no firm decision to settle in the United States. Fifth, the majority of early Greek immigrants settled in the cities. Finally, the immigrants had to support their own families in America.

As noted previously, early Greeks did not come together as family units:

---

[6]Similarly, when one refers to the late first-generation Greek family lifestyles, one must consider the changes both in Greece proper and those in America at the time of late and present Greek immigration. On the contemporary Athenian urban family, for example, see studies by Safilios-Rothschild (1965, 1967a, b, 1969a, b, 1971–1972) whose repertoire of topics is extensive and includes, among others, research on fertility and marital satisfaction; social class and family; deviance and mental illness; morality, courtship, and love in Greek folklore; and sex roles. Also, see the study by Vassiliou and Vassiliou (1966) on social attitudes, stereotypes, and mental health in the Greek family.

On the rural and semiurban Greek family see studies by Lambiri-Dimaki (1965) on dowry and the impact of industrial employment on the position of women in a Greek country town. Also, see studies by Friedl (1962) on dowry, kinship, and the position of women in rural Greece. In addition, Bardis (1955, 1956, 1967), Campbell (1964), and Sanders (1962, 1967) have also written on various aspects of the rural Greek family.

[7]The dowry system is an extension of the arranged type of marriage whereby the bride's family has to provide their future son-in-law a negotiated amount of cash or property in exchange for marrying their daughter. The dowry system is part of the economic and stratification systems in general in which marriage becomes a vehicle of class mobility or immobility for the parties concerned and favors the higher socioeconomic classes. For example, the higher the socioeconomic class or social origins of the groom, the greater the amount of expected dowry. The dowry system has brought tragedy to many poor families in Greece particularly those with large numbers of girls. In recent years, however, this practice has been challenged and it is not practiced as widely as it used to be in the past, particulary in cities, if both of the future spouses are working and are educated. While in the United States the institutionalized form of dowry as practiced in Greece was discontinued among the Greeks, nevertheless, vestiges of this practice continued to exist in more informal ways in terms of gifts and elaborate wedding ceremonies by the bride's parents.

primarily, young males migrated. Vlachos maintains that "very few females crossed the ocean in the early years of Greek immigration and their small percentage increased significantly only after 1923" [quoted in Kardaras (1977)]. The scarcity of first-generation women, for example, forced a substantial number of Greek males to marry non-Greek women (Mistaras, 1950). These outmarriages were neither encouraged nor accepted by the more ethnocentric Greeks. Thus the more tradition-bound the Greek male was, the more strongly he needed a mate of his own nationality and religion. Many of the early Greek males returned to Greece in search of a bride. Some had prospective brides arranged and vouched for by relatives and friends waiting for them in Greece or simply had arranged a marriage through an exchange of photographs (Saloutos, 1964:85). The arranged type of marriage should be understood in the context of the Greek kinship system where mate selection was an affair that goes beyond the immediate parties concerned. It was also a matter of economics, for many early Greek male immigrants could not afford to travel to Greece searching for a bride. Furthermore, many of the prospective grooms had known the young woman's family prior to coming to America.

Another important dimension of family organization involves the structural sex role differences and decisionmaking processes traditionally vested in different family statuses and occupied by different members of the immediate family. Thus, one can speak of father versus mother, male versus female, husband versus wife relationships. The majority of fiction and nonfiction writers (Bardis, 1955, 1956; Safilios-Rothschild, 1967b; Vlachos, 1968; Saloutos, 1964; Petrakis, 1966; Chamales, 1959; Stephanides, 1972; Koty, 1958; Lambiri-Dimaki, 1965; Capanidou Lauquier, 1961) have suggested that the early Greek family both in America and Greece was a male-dominated, patriarchal, and close-knit social unit. In most of these writings the Greek father is portrayed as an imposing figure whose authority over the rest of the family members, particularly the wife, was absolute. The Greek wife was depicted as a submissive and powerless creature whose major role was homemaking and catering to the rest of the family. This imagery of the Greek family authority and sex-role relationships was a carryover from Greece and it was not unique to the Greeks only. However, one can argue that these sex roles were contingent upon the social-economic conditions and prevailing ethos in male–female relationships in the United States and Europe.

That there is an "ideal" and "real" dimension culturally and socially prescribed for every sex role and family member is well documented. However, one finds the tendency among students of the sociology of marriage and the family to describe normative/ideal patterns of sex-role differentiaton as empirical/real facts. Most studies tend to deemphasize the conflict and pathology of the Greek marriage and the family. With the exception of some studies conducted by Safilios-Rothschild and those conducted by Friedl (1967) and Campbell (1964) in Greece proper, no systematic studies have been conducted on the sex-role differentiation and authority relationships in the Greek family at the level of role performance and conflict.

A more realistic analysis of role differentiation in the Greek family would entail a network of role complementarity rather than strict differentiation on the basis of widely held beliefs of male-dominated (instrumental) versus female-subordinate (expressive) roles. In other words, in most cases a Greek husband/father could assume both expressive and instrumental roles simultaneously whenever the primary group (family) interests were served and family contingencies demanded it. The early Greek immigrant father was as a rule older than his wife. Most first-generation Greek men take an active role in the household chores including shopping, cooking, and so forth. Some of these roles were learned in restaurants, in the old country, or by the immigrant men who came alone to America and had to improvise to save money.

Ideally, the father was the head and authority figure of the family unit, and he expected respect and cooperation from his wife and children. In reality, however, his authority was contingent on his ability to prove himself and be a good provider for his family, a compassionate husband, and an understanding father. Masculinity alone, based on arbitrary exercise of authority without considerations of fairness, family unity, and common good, could not sustain the first-generation immigrant family. The Greek father was as compassionate and good-natured as the Greek mother, particularly in times of adversity and life crises. While he was primarily a provider for the entire family and had to work incredibly long hours outside the home, he helped whenever he could in the household chores, in the discipline and socialization of his children.

The discrepancy between the "ideal" and "real" aspects of husband–wife and mother–father roles is also evident if one examines what Friedl (1967) and Campbell (1964) refer to as the "public" versus "private" domains of behavior in the rural family in Greece. In the public/social sphere, both husbands and wives put on a facade and behave according to the prevailing societal cultural norms. These norms depict Greek husbands–fathers as if they were the true masters and dominant figures within the family unit. The wives–mothers, however are expected to behave in a modest and submissive manner, particularly in public places when their husbands are present. However, in a more private family setting, husbands–fathers and wives–mothers change considerably and behave more naturally. What seems to the outsider to be the unequivocal dominance exercised by the husband over the wife is in reality not so in more informal family settings. In some instances the Greek wife–mother was the most dominant figure in the Greek immigrant family. Her presence and influence were felt not only in the family but in the larger

171

ethnic community affairs. As a rule, early first-generation women did not work outside the home and this gave them more time to run the household.

To an immigrant husband who left his parents at a young age, his wife was more than the sociological sex-role partner. She was the wife, the adviser, the partner, the companion, and the homemaker. She also assisted her husband in his business and the family decisionmaking. Wives–mothers usually exercised their influence in the family decisionmaking indirectly through the processes of socialization of the children because the Greek father had to work incredibly long hours away from the home. Children were attached to the mother, not the father, particularly in the formative years of immigrant life. Later, it was the wife–mother who had to approve or disapprove of her daughter's marriage, and then she would convince her husband. Furthermore, it has been reported by Tavuchis (1972) that among his "respondents and a large unknown proportion of second-generation Greek Americans, the father emerges as a shadowy, distant figure throughout childhood and adolescence but his sociological presence was always felt. . . ." In addition, the relatively higher status and freedom enjoyed by the American women vis-à-vis Greek women in Greece benefitted the Greek women more than the Greek men in America.

Greek immigrant women have played an important role not only in the family but in the Church and Greek American community in general. Moskos (1980:27) argues that the arrival of Greek women contributed greatly to the cohesion of the Greek American family and indeed the Greek American community and the Church at large. As a rule, immigrant women—married and unmarried—did not work outside the house. This contrasts sharply with post-world War II Greek immigrant women who, by and large, work outside the house—either in the family restaurant or in some other capacity as seamstresses, beauticians, and factory workers.

As in the American family in general, one of the primary functions of the Greek family is procreation. A family without children was, and still is, thought to be incomplete. It is not by accident that the formal ideology of the Greek Orthodox Church (and other religions for that matter) encourages procreation within a marital context. The birth of a child is not only an affair of the family but of the Church as well. Motherhood is highly esteemed in the Greek Orthodox religion. Those couples who have children are looked upon by the Church as fortunate and blessed.

Childless couples were and still are made uncomfortable in the Greek community, especially the husband. Not having children was suspicious and impinged on the Greek male image. In many instances the childless immigrant family or the old bachelor uncle would support a nephew or niece, but adoption of Greek or non-Greek children was not an accepted practice.

172

It has been reported (Stephanides, 1972; Tavuchis, 1968) that first-generation Greek parents tended to overprotect their children, even to the extent of wanting to find marriage partners for them. This should be interpreted in the context of the traditional ideal norms of a family and kinship system. Parents underwent personal sacrifices for their children and therefore expected their children to meet their high expectations even after they reached maturity. Ideally, first-generation Greek parents worked and strived to give their children happiness, love, and material comforts. Parents regulated and guided their children's behavior to a certain point. In return, children were expected to respect their parents, develop a sense of responsibility and self-reliance, and become a credit to their family unit and the larger ethnic and American communities. Like their immigrant parents, the children had a minimum of leisure time. They were exposed to the vicissitudes of life at a tender age and were socialized to postpone their immediate gratifications for a future goal. For a majority of the Greek parents that goal was to see their children happily married, maintain certain ethnic traditions, and move up the social ladder through the avenue of education, business, and commerce outside the Greek ethnic community.

In general, the Greek immigrant family was adult- rather than child-centered. The child had to learn to respect his parents and the elderly. It has also been reported (Vlachos, 1968; Capanidou Lauquier, 1961) that there was a differential preference for boys in the immigrant family. This pattern is still true to some extent in Greece because of the institution of dowry. One can argue however that this preferential treatment was not as pronounced in America because:

1. There was no dowry system in America;
2. girls incorporated the Greek traditional norms and ideals more readily than boys;
3. girls were more attached to their parents, particularly to the mother; and
4. above all, it was the daughter, not the son, who would look after her elderly parents even after she was married.

Despite the similarities, however, the early and late first-generation Greek families had the following differences, which created many conflicts between the early and late generations and their progenies:

1. In contrast to the earlier, the late immigrant arrived when there was a more equal number of males and females in their age groups.
2. In contrast to the earlier, the later first-generation Greek women (both

married and nonmarried), particularly from blue collar and working classes, are gainfully employed outside the household.

3. Late Greek immigrant families more than early Greek families visit Greece via cheap charter flights.

4. The late Greek immigrants are less integrated in the Greek ethnic (church) community than are the second- and-third-generation (children of the early arrivals).

5. In contrast to the earlier, the late Greek immigrant families tend to be more educated, more diverse in social class background, less religious-oriented, less conservative, more materially and exogamously oriented, more likely to divorce and dissolve the marriage bond, less tradition-oriented, more business-oriented, and more ethnically oriented through Greek language and nationality identification rather than Orthodox religious identification.

Some of these differences and conflicts stem from generational, age, class, regional, and cultural differences in general. Despite many differences between the two groups of the first-generation Greek family, both groups, however, share the Protestant work ethnic, strong ethnic family ties, material and success orientation and competition and ethnic pride.

Second-Generation Greek Family

The second-generation Greek family is that social unit in which both parents are American-born of Greek extraction or mixed parenthood (one parent Greek from Greece and the other either non-Greek or American-born Greek). As in other ethnic groups, the second-generation Greek family is a transitional-type family. Children were born and raised in two social worlds or subcultures. One was particularistic, with an ethnic subculture made up of the Greek immigrant parents and relatives, immigrant priests and school teachers, Greek religious and national holidays, and Greek peers. These agents of socialization shared similar experiences and attempted to socialize the children to traditional norms and values of the Greek subculture. The other was a more universalistic world (American) made up of public schools, non-Greek peers and friends, and institutional norms and values of the dominant society and culture. The second generation emerged as a product of a Greek subculture and an American culture and social structure, a sociocultural hybrid with a dual identity.

In many respects, members of the second generation shared similar experiences and lifestyles with their immigrant parents throughout their formative and adolescent years. However, pressures from within and from outside the family unit made them somewhat ambivalent and marginal. They were torn between two ways of life. The emphasis on family ties, the Greek language, and the Greek Church shaped their attitudes and behavior (Saloutos, 1964:311). These early attitudes and behaviors changed, however, as the children came of age, went to public schools, began to work, moved away from the original settlement, were married, and started a family. However, it must be pointed out that the influence of the first-generation (immigrant) family on the second generation was not uniform in all Greek American families throughout the United States. For example, in small towns and communities where fewer Greeks were found, the process of assimilation and convergence (including intermarriage) with the rest of the population was greater than in larger cities with larger numbers of Greek ethnic colonies.

Three types of family lifestyles seem to be prevalent in second-generation Greeks (Vlachos, 1968:150–151). From a somewhat different perspective these family lifestyles appear to be phases along a continuum of assimilation–acculturation. One type represents a complete abandonment of the traditional Greek way of life. A substantial number in this group Anglicized their names and moved away from the Greek colony; some changed their religion; and many minimized their interaction with their foreign-born parents and relatives. This group is more concerned with social status and acceptability by their peers and other Americans rather than maintaining their Greek nationality and incorporating the ideals and norms of Greek culture as perceived and represented by their parents and relatives in America. Their intent is to assimilate the values and norms of American culture as soon as possible. In many respects, this type of second-generation family passes for an American family, and it is rather atypical. It is more prevalent in small towns and suburbs with dispersed Greek ethnic populations.

A second type of the second-generation Greek family is one of "cultural atavism," an inward retrogressive orientation and identification with what are perceived to be, by second-generation Greeks, ethnic Greek lifestyles. Ideally this type of family is economically, culturally, socially, and psychologically tied up with the Greek community and its ethnic institutions. This type is more working-class- or blue-collar-oriented. It is found close to Greek immigrant colonies. Many of these families can be described as "stables" or "downward mobiles."

A third type of second-generation Greek family shows marginality at the structural, cultural, and social-psychological levels. Norms and values are of a "hybrid" nature. Social interaction and networks of social relationships are neither genuinely American nor Greek. The family is likely to move out of the original settlement, and its members are less likely to engage in primary-group interaction with members of the first-generation Greeks outside the immediate intergenerational kinship group. In most instances, this type of family finds some midpoint of accommodation between the two worlds by taking what its members perceive to be the best of the two lifestyles. This type appears to be more representative of the majority of the second-generation Greek families, a contention supported by the existing literature on the second-generation Greek Americans.

In addition to these three types one can suggest a fourth one where ethnicity and class intersect, or what Gordon referred to as "ethclass." In a study of ethclass (Kourvetaris and Dobratz, 1976), it was found that second- and third-generation Greek Americans follow ethclass rather than ethnicity or class alone in patterns of interpersonal and primary relations including marriage. Thus, if a second-generation male/female marries with his/her ethnic group (religious), the tendency is that he/she will marry within his/her social class in the Greek American community. This type of ethclass marriage is also prevalent in the first generation. It is more characteristic, however, in the second-generation Greek American family.

As in other ethnic groups, second-generation Greeks had certain advantages over the first generation. First, they did not have to start from scratch as did their parents. Second, they grew up in a fairly close knit Greek family in which rudiments of Greek ethnic subculture were transmitted to them, particularly those pertaining to courtship, marriage, language, religion, and respect for mother, father, and the elderly. Third, the values of aspiration, hard work, the Greek *philotimo,* and family honor were implanted in them by their parents. Achievement and success were a pride and credit not only to their immediate families and kin but also to the entire Greek community. It is within this frame of reference that the organization of the second-generation Greek family emerged in America. With the exception of the first, these advantages may not distinguish the two generations, but they contributed to the mobility of the second generation.

Several writers (Saloutos, 1964; Sanders, 1962, 1967; Friedl, 1962; Vlachos, 1968) have reported that Greeks traditionally display a high degree of family cohesion and extended kinship relationships within and across generational lines. It has also been reported (Rosen, 1959; Handlin and Handlin, 1956; Kourvetaris, 1971a, b; Tavuchis, 1972; Chock, 1969; Moskos, 1980) that this intergenerational kinship system is coupled with a strong ideological commitment to social mobility and achievement in the American social structure. Tavuchis (1972) in his study of 50 second-generation male family heads, found an elaborate system of kinship and ethnic ties coupled with strong intergenerational patterns of vertical class mobility.

Unlike other social scientists, particularly family sociologists who have lamented the weakening of kinship bonds and the demise of family as a viable institution, Tavuchis found no evidence of such trends among the second-generation Greek family. In fact, Tavuchis argues that the stronger the kinship ties, the more highly mobile its members were found to be: "Differential class mobility was not found to be a detriment to close ties with parents, siblings, and affines. . . ." Tavuchis (1972:296–297) mentions five mechanisms that in his judgment prevented potential strains: a strong commitment to kinship values, a close propinquity to relatives, extraclass criteria of ranking, identification with successful kinsmen, and gross status differences neutralizing invidious distinctions.

Although Tavuchis' finding is not unique among Greek Americans (Jewish Americans display similar patterns), it is somewhat contrary to the prevailing notion among sociologists who believe that extended kinship relationships are a detriment to intergenerational social mobility (e.g., the Mexican Americans). More recently a somewhat similar finding has been reported by Kardaras (1977) who found no relationship between different types of modernity (marital, sexual, and educational) and structural/psychological assimilation. The second generation were found to be conservative or traditional in one dimension and modern in another. Somewhat surprisingly, the higher the social class among the second generation the greater the tendency to espouse a more traditional (conservative) view in sex roles.

Three trends of authority relations seem to be prevalent in the emerging literature on the second-generation Greek family:

1. The "quasipatriarchal" model or a trend toward lessening the patriarchal orientation in which ultimate authority in decisionmaking no longer is exercised by the father (Tavuchis, 1972);
2. the "equalitarian" model in which the father shares his status and authority with his wife (Capanidou Lanquier, 1961:225; Kardaras, 1977); and
3. the "patriarchal" model (Vlachos, 1969:162) in which the father is still the ultimate authority with final responsibility for providing for his family and for the discipline of his children, partly because that is a father's duty and partly because he is a man and men are economic providers (Chock, 1969:38).

Sex roles of the siblings are also viewed in normative terms by most writers and not in actual role performances. For example, the traditional Greek cultural norms and ideals of filial piety and respect for one's parents and the elderly persist in the second-generation Greek American family. Unlike the first generation, the father is not perceived as a fearful and distant person, but the father–son relationship is one of mutual understanding and respect

177

(Tavuchis, 1972; Chock, 1969; Capanidou Lauquier, 1961; Moskos, 1980). According to Chock, "Greek children are expected to love their parents, to respect them and to assume some care for them if they need it in their old age. . . ." Despite the respect between first and second generation, as a rule second generation do not live in the same household with their parents and in-laws. More and more immigrant generations (especially widows) live alone or are placed in homes for the aged. The immigrant family, particularly the father, has a sense of pride that does not accept living with one's children or son-in-law. This is especially true of the second-generation family in a mixed marriage.

As in the first generation, both parents in the second generation share in the responsibility for the care, education, and well-being of their children. Second generation tend to have fewer children than the first generation. However, many second-generation parents tend to spoil their children and to be possessive. Second-generation Greek women are inclined to take a greater interest in the Greek Orthodox Church and religion rather than in the Greek language. Second-generation Greek women tend to be more conservative than first-generation Greek men. As in the first generation, second-generation families show respect for their parents and the elderly. Grandparents (*papa* and *yiayia*) are important figures in the Greek American family.

Recently, due to the Women's Liberation movement, many sex roles in the second generation have changed. Safilios-Rothschild, Constantakos, and Kardaras (1976) and Kardaras (1977) have found that both husbands and wives in the upper-class second-generation families in the Detroit metropolitan area share somewhat similar views on marriage and the family. Thus, both husbands and wives are against the double standard on sexual matters, disapprove of infidelity and extramarital relations, and approve of divorce on grounds of brutality. They also believe that each member should have the right both to initiate and refuse sexual activity. Although we do not know the extent to which these findings are uniform among all second-generation Greek American families, one can suggest that "ethclass" and "generation" are more important variables in explaining ethnic family patterns than ethnicity, class, or generation taken singly.

Greek Americans regardless of generation tend to be more conservative on civil rights and economic issues. Moskos (1980) contends the conservativism of the Greek Americans is an attitude of mind rather than a body of ideas— a distaste for confrontation politics and a suspicion of collective action for social improvement. Greek Americans, Moskos argues, "search not for a better world, but for a better life." The conservative ethos of Greek Americans reflects the individualistic orientations of the Greek entrepreneur, the influence of the Greek Orthodox Church, the cohesiveness of the family, and the rural origins of the early Greek immigrants, the majority of whom came from the southern part of Greece (Peloponesus), which is the most traditional and conservative region. One can also conclude that second-generation Greek American families tend more often to be church-goers on Sunday than first generation (especially the late Greek immigrants). In short, Greek American families maintain an ethnic identification through their membership in the Greek Orthodox Church and only secondarily to the language and Greek nationality.

Third-Generation Greek Family

The third-generation family consists of grandchildren of the first generation or the children of the second-generation Greek family in America. This group also includes the offspring of intermarriages of second-generation couples. By third generation, there is a significant decrease in Greek ethnic identification (as measured by language and Greek family norms); but some vestiges of ethnic social behavior remain, particularly those pertaining to politics (Humphrey and Brock, 1972), Greek religion, and Dionysian aspects of modern Greek culture (Kourvetaris, 1971c).

As a rule, members of the third generation have incorporated the values, attitudes, and norms of the American middle- and upper-middle-class subcultures. Social class lifestyles are more important to them than ethnicity and religion. Despite the lack of empirical studies, both education and professional achievement seem to be highly valued among members of the third generation. In an empirical and comparative study of six ethnic groups, it was found (Rosen, 1959:47–60) that a high level of aspiration and achievement exists among members of third-generation Greeks. Rosen argued that the cultures of white Protestants, Jews, and Greeks stand out as being more individualistic, activistic, and future-oriented than Italians, blacks, and French Canadians.

Unlike the first and second generations, members of the third generation are not preoccupied with ethnic prejudice and discrimination. Viewed in this way, they can afford to be proud of their ancestry. However, they consider themselves primarily American and only symbolically manifest an interest in and liking for Greek food, music, and dancing. This Dionysian cultural atavism in things Greek was stimulated by the new influx of Greek immigrants following World War II and the popular movies, *Zorba the Greek* and *Never on Sunday*, whose theme songs became worldwide favorites. Furthermore, the marriage of Jacqueline Kennedy to Aristotle Onassis, the Nixon–Agnew ticket in 1968 and 1972, the resurgence of ethnic studies and programs, and summer excursions to Greece have further awakened their interest in modern

Greek ethnicity and culture. In addition, the new influx of post-World War II Greek immigrants brought a new awareness of Greek ethnic identity. However, one finds little or no interest among members of the third generation in maintaining the ethnic institutional aspects of Greek culture, such as language, family traditions, and endogamous marriage—with the exception of the Americanized form of the Greek Orthodox Church.

It has been argued by some Greek American writers that the new influx of Greeks following World War II would retard the Americanization and assimilation processes of the third generation. However, American-born Greeks (even post-World War II Greeks who have been in America for a longer period of time) do not usually associate with the newcomers. This is especially true in the patterns of dating and marriage. For example, in dating patterns on college campuses there is a tendency for members of ethnic groups to seek dates outside their ethnic group. This is primarily because dating within one's own group has a constraining influence on him or her. Greek American women are no different from other American women—especially when they date non-Greeks. When Greek American women date Greek American men, they tend to be more restrained, especially if they are members of the same community. It is also a matter of availability of both sexes of the same ethnic group in a college population. In general, the more ethnically oriented the Greek man or woman, the greater the tendency to date someone with similar ethnic background. Furthermore, the more assimilated the Greek, the less likely he/she is to place importance on dating Greek women/men. This is also true in terms of ethnic endogamous patterns of marriage.

If ethnicity (nationality) is the single most important characteristic in the first generation and religion in the second generation, it appears that social class is characteristic of the third generation (Kourvetaris, 1971a, b). Thus, the oncoming of the third generation is followed by a concomitant decline of ethnoreligious factors and the increase in importance of social class as a factor in marriage. However, those who maintain their ethnic (nationality/religiosity) identification tend to date and marry within their class segment of their ethnic group (ethclass). In a more recent study (Safilios-Rothschild, Constantakos, and Kardaras, 1976), ethnic generation and class were found to be the most differentiating variables between traditional Greek culture and third-generation Greek Americans. Thus, the higher the social class, the more removed is a Greek American woman from her Greek cultural heritage and sex role restrictions. As a rule, the third generation is a college-oriented generation. It is a status- and class-conscious generation rather than an ethnic-conscious generation.

At the same time, while intermarriage in the first and second generations was not an accepted norm in the Greek American family, by the third generation it is not only accepted but in some Greek American communities it is the norm rather than the exception. It has been estimated that one in five Greeks entered a mixed marriage by 1926 [Saloutos (1973) quoted in Moskos (1980)]. By the 1960s, intermarriages accounted for three out of ten church marriages and by the mid-1970s, it was about half (Moskos, 1980: 73). In some communities it is even higher.

CHANGE AND ADAPTATION

The movement from the early first-generation Greek family lifestyles to those of the third generation is accompanied by an attenuation of the Old World family ideals and norms (as exemplified in the first-generation Greek family) to those more symmetrical with the American middle-class family lifestyles (as exemplified in the third-generation Greek family). "Greekness" (nationality) as a form of ethnic identification in the first generation gives way to the "orthodoxy" (religion) in the second generation, which in turn gives way to "class" lifestyles (behavioral identification). It is suggested by this author that by the third generation the "Greekness" of the first generation might be transformed to philhellenism (friend of Greece). This generational transformation might be genuinely conceptualized as following more or less five processes and/or phases of acculturation initially suggested in part by Park (1950): the *initial* contact phase, the *conflict* phase, the *accommodation* phase, *assimilation*, and *pluralist* phases.

The Initial Contact Phase

In the first decade of Greek immigrant life in America, the organization of the Old World family was still fairly well intact. As a result of pressures from within and outside the family structure, the Old World ideal was challenged. Some of the most salient factors were the physical/ecological separation from the parental and kinship system and village subculture in general, the necessity of physical survival and social-psychological adjustment of the immigrant to a different sociocultural and urban ecological environment, the separation of work and residence, and the exposure of the immigrant's children to the lifestyles of the American community and public schools, which in many ways meant ethnic prejudice and discrimination against those ethnic groups and families that were culturally different from the Anglo-Saxon group. All these made the first-generation immigrant family extremely ethnocentric and highly cohesive as in the Old World. In this phase of initial contact the immigrant family was socially and culturally insulated in the Greek colony and did not seriously feel the pressures of American society. Despite its many problems, the first-generation Greek family was stablized by its strong desire to return to Greece. It drew social and psychological support from the family unit, the family and kinship relationship, the Church and the Greek community in general. However, this initial phase gave way to both the conflict and accommodation phases with the coming of the second generation.

The Conflict Phase

With the oncoming of the second generation, the highly ethnocentric, traditional, and folk-oriented outlook of the first-generation subculture was challenged. Although culture conflict between parents and children was not inevitable, in many instances it did take place. Out of this generational conflict, three major subtypes of first-generation Greeks emerged: the ethnic subculturalists (pluralists), the social assimilationists, and the mixed type (in some respects ethnic pluralists and in other respects social assimilationists).

The ethnic subculturalists (pluralists) were faced with major difficulties in carrying out their intent to socialize their children in the Greek ways of life. These difficulties and their fear of losing control over their children were intensified when the children came into contact with the larger American society, particularly when they entered public schools, began working, dating, and came of marital age. This exaggerated fear by the Greek immigrant of losing control over his children was further aggravated by the Greek Orthodox Church and the family kinfolk. Furthermore, it stemmed from the inability of the immigrant himself to adjust more readily to the nonmaterial and subtler aspects of American culture and thus be able to understand his children. This group proved unyielding and was usually found in cities with large Greek colonies. They insisted on preserving their ethnic institutions, particularly those pertaining to religion, language, endogamous marriage, and a close-knit family. They attempted to convince their children of the mystique of the Greek ancestry, warned them against the dangers of intermarriage, and made an effort to instill in them a sense of ethnic consciousness and peoplehood. According to Papajohn and Spiegel, clinical studies of mentally disturbed second-generation Greek American children indicated that these children came from families where an extremely traditionalist Greek form of childrearing was attempted. In fact, those immigrant parents who were more open to American influences were more successful in passing Greek ethnicity than those parents who tried to resist totally all American encroachment [quoted in Moskos (1980;94)].

The social assimilationists (known also as environmentalists) believed that their children must grow up as Americans but wanted them to retain membership in the Greek Orthodox Church, maintain their Greek name, and learn some Greek (Saloutos, 1964:312). This group felt that the assimilation process could not be stopped but only temporarily delayed. They were more realistic, experienced less conflict with their children, and were more aware that powerful social and cultural forces operate in the American social structure and culture that exert an unprecedented influence on their children toward Anglo conformity and Americanization. This assimilation process has been challenged by the ethnic resurgence of the 1960s and early 1970s. This is especially true among Greek-born, post-World War II, Greek immigrants, students, and professionals. The lack of support in American foreign policy for the Greek-Cypriot position in Cyprus has alienated many Greeks and Greek Americans. For many Greeks and Greek Americans, Cyprus became the catalyst for ethnic solidarity and consciousness.

The social assimilationist process began roughly during the second decade of first-generation family living in America, especially when the first-generation immigrant family abandoned its intent to return to Greece. It was during this period that both the organizational structure of the Orthodox Church and by far the largest ethnic association—AHEPA (American Hellenic Educational Progressive Association)—launched an all-out effort to organize the Greeks in America, facilitate the transition and Americanization processes, and maintain the ethnic institutions of church and family, which in many ways became complementary to each other. Nationality gradually was giving way to religion, particularly during the 1920s when Greeks, along with other southern and eastern European immigrants, were targets of prejudice and discrimination. Second-generation Greeks were discovering that to be of Greek ancestry did not indicate particularly high social status. This phase gave way to a new realization and intergenerational relationship.

A number of the first generation, especially the more educated (both early and late), followed a mixed approach; it was a compromise between the two polar opposites. This was compatible with the pluralist ideology of ethnic groups, which replaced the Americanization and assimilation models. It started in the 1940s but was more evident in the 1950s and 1960s with the influx of new immigrants. Also the ethnic resurgence of the 1960s gave new impetus to ethnic consciousness in American society. The defeat of the Italian forces by the Greeks in October 1940 gave a new ethnic pride and ethnic consciousness to the second-generation Greeks in America. This ethnic pride, along with the rise of a professional and commercial class of second-generation Greeks and the post-World War II Greeks, contributed to a new status of the Greeks in America.

It must be stressed that conflict between the first and second generations was always there, but both groups worked out a modus operandi and followed a pattern of accommodation.

The Accommodation Phase

An effort was made to broaden the base for continued and meaningful interaction between the two generations (Tavuchis, 1972). On the one hand, the first generation realized that they had to modify the Old World family lifestyles for the sake of retaining the affection of their children and maintaining the unity of the family. On the other hand, the second generation came to the realization that complete repudiation of the parents' way of life would hurt their parents and leave them isolated. Both generations searched for points of compatability, mutual levels of tolerance, complementarity of lifestyles, individuality, and family unity.

This period of accommodation between first- and second-generation family units led to a more stable form of family relationships. The parents came to realize that life in the United States was to be permanent. They also recognized that social and economic status and success could come to their offspring as the latter became more and more socialized into the dominant Anglo-American culture. A parallel effort was made on the part of the second generation to resocialize their parents to their own generational values and lifestyles. The interdependence between parents and children gave way to the dependence of parents on their children as interpreters and informants of the American scene (especially those whose English was not proficient enough). This dependence led to the conscious and unconscious willingness on the part of the parents to forego and sacrifice certain norms and ideals of the Old World family for the sake of their own happiness and that of their children. Finally, it was a matter of realism and convenience.

As the first generation was dying out, the conflict and accommodation phases between first and second generations gave impetus to new forms of social and generational change. By the late 1950s and 1960s the coming of the third generation Greek American was caught between an ongoing process of assimilation and *embourgeoisement* and an ethnic resurgence spearheaded by blacks and later by Chicanos. Added to these ethnic movements was the new Greek immigrantion of the mid-1960s and early 1970s, which brought a new cultural transfusion and a new ethnicity to Greek Americans. It is my contention that neither the rise of ethnic/racial consciousness in the United States nor the late Greek immigration arrested the Americanization of the third generation Greek Americans. By the late 1950s and early 1960s second- and third-generation Greeks had joined by and large the lower-middle-, middle-, and upper-middle-class lifestyles. While "ethnicity" had been there all along, it was giving way to class and ethclass lifestyles and patterns of behavior.

Third- and later-generation Greek Americans retained mostly the hedonistic (like most American youth for that matter) and/or Dionysian aspects of the Greek culture but with a few exceptions had very little knowledge and understanding of the contemporary nonmaterial or Apollonian aspects of the Greek culture. Greek cuisine, dancing, and music were more appealing to them than the more abstract and remote notions of *philotimo* (honor, generosity), *philoxenia* (hospitality), Greekness (ethnicity), nationality, the Greek language, poetry and prose, family traditions, history, and the like. The Greek American youth, like American youth in general, were disenchanted with the institutional forms of religion. The Greek American youth complained that they could not understand the almost mystical and highly ritualistic practice of Orthodox Christianity. Many turned to more socially minded religions or were converted through intermarriage to other religions.

Assimilation or Pluralism?

By third generation the Greek American family lifestyles became more and more symmetrical with those of the larger American middle class family. This, however, does not mean that all vestiges of ethnic subcultural lifestyles are lost. In some respects the Greek American family is more American but in other respects it maintains some of its unique ethnic features. For example, names, religion, food, holidays, trips to Greece, intergenerational family ties, and to some extent, endogamous marriages remain. Assimilation, a multidimensional process itself, does not have to be complete. It has been suggested (Kourvetaris, 1971c) that Greek Americans maintain their ethnic identity through their religion. As the subsequent generations of Greek Americans remove themselves from the original generation, nationality/language is replaced by religion for those who support the organization of the Greek Orthodox Church in the United States. The Greek American family lifestyles are both assimilative and pluralistic. It is a blending but not necessarily a perfect or equal blending of the two.

The transformation and gradual change from the Greek rural traditional type (first-generation immigrant) family to one Greek American urban middle class is somewhat coterminous with those changes brought about by urbanization and internal migration processes in Greece proper. Since the 1920s and especially the 1940s these processes have been accelerated. By the third generation, even Greeks in Greece have changed family lifestyles and mores from those found in the traditional rural-type family to those more symmetrical with the contemporary middle-class urban Athenian families. The difference is found in linguistic, national, and cultural forms but the values and norms are not that different. In short, unless Greek immigration continues, the Greek family in America by third and subsequent generations will retain

185

mostly the organizational and institutional aspects of Greek American sub-culture, particularly religion, family, and the success ethic but not the more subtle aspects of Greek culture and ethnicity. The generational family ties will be somewhat attenuated but they will not lose respect for those institutions that sustained them throughout their long history and culture.

REFERENCES

Bardis, Panos. 1955. "The Changing Family in Modern Greece," *Sociology and Social Research,* 40 (October): 19–23.

———. 1956. "Main Features of the Greek Family During the Early Twentieth Century," *Alpha Kappa Delta,* 26 (Winter, November): 17–21.

———. 1957. "Influences on the Modern Greek Family," *Social Science,* 32 (June): 155–158.

Campbell, J. K. 1964. *Honor, Family, and Patronage.* Oxford: Clarendon Press.

Campisi, J. Paul. 1948. "Ethnic Family Patterns: The Italian Family in the United States," *American Journal of Sociology,* 53 (May): 443–449.

Capanidou Lauquier, H. 1961. "Cultural Change Among Three Generations of Greeks," *American Catholic Review* (now *Sociological Analysis*), 22 (Fall): 223–232.

Chamales, Tom T. 1959. *Go Naked in the World.* New York: Scribner.

Chock, P. Phyllis, 1969. "Greek-American Ethnicity," unpublished Ph.D. dissertation in the University of Chicago Library, Department of Anthropology, Chicago, IL.

Cutsumbis, N. Michael. 1970. *A Bibliographic Guide to Materials on Greeks in the United States 1890–1968.* New York: Center for Migration Studies.

Fairchild, H. P. 1911. *Greek Immigration to the United States.* New Haven: Yale University Press.

Friedl, Ernestine. 1962. *Vasilika: A Village in Modern Greece.* New York: Holt.

———. 1967. "The Position of Women: Appearance and Reality," *Anthropological Quarterly,* 40 (July): 97–108.

Gordon, Milton. 1964. *Assimilation in American Life: The Role of Race, Religion and National Origin.* New York: Oxford University Press.

Greek Orthodox Archdiocese of North and South America. 1972 *Yearbook.* New York: Graphic Arts Laboratory.

Handlin, F. Oscar, and Mary F. Handlin. 1956. "Ethnic Factors in Social Mobility," *Explorations in Entrepreneurial History,* 9 (October): 4–5.

Humphrey, R. Craig, and Helen T. Brock. 1972. "Assimilation, Ethnicity, and Voting Behavior Among Greek-Americans in a Metropolitan Area," paper presented at the 1972 Annual Meeting of the Southern Sociological Society, April 5–8, New Orleans.

Kardaras, Basil P. 1977. "A Study of the Marital and Familial Options of the Second Generation Greek-Americans in the Detroit Metropolitan Area," M.A. thesis, Department of Sociology, Wayne State University, Detroit, MI.

Koty, John. 1958. "Greece," in Arnold M. Rose (ed.), *The Institutions of Advanced Societies.* Minneapolis: University of Minnesota Press, pp. 330–383.

Kourvetaris, George A. 1971a. *First and Second Generation Greeks in Chicago.* Athens, Greece: National Center of Social Research.

———. 1971b. "First and Second Generation Greeks in Chicago: An Inquiry Into Their Stratification and Mobility Patterns," *International Review of Sociology* (now *International Review of Modern Sociology*), 1 (March): 37–47.

———. 1971c. "Patterns of Generational Subculture and Intermarriage of the Greeks in the United States," *International Journal of Sociology of the Family,* 1 (May): 34–48.

———. 1973. "Brain Drain and International Migration of Scientists: The Case of Greece," *Epitheoris Koinonikon Erevnon (Review of Social Research),* Nos. 15–16.

———. 1977. "Greek-American Professionals: 1820s–1970s," *Balkan Studies,* 18:285–323.

Kourvetaris, George A., and Betty A. Dobratz. 1976. "An Empirical Test of Gordon's Ethclass Hypothesis Among Three Ethnoreligious Groups," *Sociology and Social Research,* 61 (October): 39–53.

Lagos, Mary. 1962. "A Greek Family in American Society," unpublished eight page transcript, Franklin and Marshall College, Lancaster, PA.

Lambiri-Dimaki, Ioanna. 1965. *Social Change in a Greek Country Town.* Athens: Center of Planning and Economic Research.

Mistaras, Evangeline. 1950. "A Study of First and Second Generation Greek Outmarriages in Chicago," unpublished Masters Thesis in the University of Chicago Library, Department of Sociology. Chicago, IL.

Moskos, Charles C. Jr. 1980. *Greek Americans: Struggle and Success.* Englewood Cliffs, NJ: Prentice-Hall.

Papajohn, C. John. "The Relation of Intergenerational Value Orientation Change and Mental Health in An American Ethnic Group," a manuscript in the Florence Heller Graduate School for Advanced Studies in Social Welfare, Brandeis University.

Papanikolas, Z. Helen. 1970. *Toil and Rage in a New Land: The Greek Immigrants in Utah.* Salt Lake City: Utah State Historical Society.

Park, Robert E. 1950. *Race and Culture.* Glencoe, IL: The Free Press.

Petrakis, Harry Mark. 1966. *A Dream of Kings.* New York: McKay.

Plous, F. K. Jr. 1971. "Chicago's Greeks: Pride, Passion, and the Protestant Ethic," *Midwest Sunday Magazine of the Chicago Sun Times* (April 25), pp. 22–26.

Rosen, Bernard. 1959. "Race, Ethnicity, and the Achievement Syndrome," *American Sociological Review,* 24 (February): 47–60.

Safilios-Rothschild, Constantina. 1965. "Mortality, Courtship, and Love in Greek Folklore," *Southern Folklore Quarterly,* 29 (December): 297–308.

———. 1967a. "Class Position and Success Stereotypes in Greek and American Cultures," *Social Forces,* 45 (March): 374–383.

———. 1967b. "A Comparison of Power Structure and Marital Satisfaction in Urban Greek and French Families," *Journal of Marriage and the Family,* 29 (May): 345–352.

———. 1969a. "Patterns of Familial Power and Influence," *Sociological Focus,* 2 (Spring): 7–19.

———. 1969b. "Family Sociology or Wives' Family Sociology? A Cross-Cultural Examination of Decision-Making," *Journal of Marriage and the Family,* 31 (May): 290–301.

——. 1971–1972. "The Options of Greek Men and Women," *Sociological Focus,* 5 (Winter): 71–83.

Safilios-Rothschild, Constantina, Chrysie Constantakos, and Basil P. Kardaras. 1976. "The Greek-American Woman," paper presented at the Greek Experience in America Symposium 1976 at the University of Chicago, October 29–31.

Saloutos, Theodore. 1956. *They Remember America.* Berkeley and Los Angeles: The University of California Press.

——. 1964. *The Greeks in the United States.* Cambridge: Harvard University Press.

Sanders, Irwin. 1962. *Rainbow in the Rock: The People of Rural Greece.* Cambridge: Harvard University Press.

——. 1967. "Greek Society in Transition," *Balkan Studies,* 8: 317–332.

Seder, L. Doris. 1966. "The Influence of Cultural Identification on Family Behavior," Ph.D. dissertation in Brandeis University Library, Department of Social Work, Boston, MA.

Simpson, George, and J. Milton Yinger. 1972. *Racial and Cultural Minorities: An Analysis of Prejudice and Discrimination,* 4th edition. New York: Harper and Row.

Stephanides, C. Marios. 1972. "Educational Background, Personality Characteristics, and Value Attitudes Towards Education and Other Ethnic Groups Among the Greeks in Detroit," Ph.D. dissertation in Wayne State University Library, Department of Sociology, Detroit, MI.

Stycos, J. M. 1948. "The Spartan Greeks of Bridgetown," *Common Ground* (Winter, Spring, Summer), pp. 61–70, 24–34, 72–86.

Tavuchis, Nicholas, 1968. "An Exploratory Study of Kinship and Mobility Among Second Generation Greek-Americans," Ph.D. dissertation in Columbia University Library, Department of Political Science, New York, NY.

——. 1972. *Family and Mobility Among Greek-Americans.* Athens, Greece: National Centre of Social Research.

Terlexis, Pantazis, 1979. "Metanastefsi Kai Epanapatrismos: 1 Prosklisi to 1980" (Immigration and Repatriation), *Review of Social Sciences* (in Greek), July–September.

Tsakonas, Demetrios. 1967. *Koinoniologia Tou Neou-Hellenikou Pnevmatos (Sociology of the New Hellenic Spirit).* Athens: Ellinika Grammata.

Vassiliou, George, and Vasso Vassiliou. 1966. "A transactional Approach to Mental Health," Contribution to the International Research Conference on Evaluation of Community Mental Health Programs of N.I.M.H.

Vlachos, C. Evangelos. 1968. *The Assimilation of Greeks in the United States.* Athens, Greece: National Center of Social Research.

——. 1969. *Modern Greek Society: Continuity and Change.* Special Monograph Series No. 1, Department of Sociology and Anthropology, Colorado State University.

Xenides, J. P. 1922. *The Greeks in America.* New York: George H. Doran.

The Puerto Rican Family

Professor Fitzpatrick, a Roman Catholic priest who has studied Puerto Ricans in America and on the island of Puerto Rico for many years, discusses the Puerto Rican family from the perspective of migration from the island to the mainland. Puerto Ricans are a unique group because of the status of Puerto Rico as a commonwealth. An important implication of this fact is that Puerto Ricans are citizens of America and thus can move to and from the island freely. Because of the movement in both directions Professor Fitzpatrick has found it especially imperative to discuss the family as it is found on the island of Puerto Rico. Its continual and reinforcing influence on Puerto Ricans on the mainland make it the key to understanding the Puerto Rican family in America.

CHAPTER NINE
BY
JOSEPH P. FITZPATRICK

INTRODUCTION

The Puerto Ricans now constitute one of the major minority groups in the eastern part of the United States. They come from a small island in the Caribbean, one of the Greater Antilles, about a thousand miles southeast of Florida. Puerto Rico was a Spanish colony from the time of its discovery by Columbus on his second voyage, 1493, until 1898 when it was ceded by Spain to America after the Spanish–American war. The indigenous peoples, now generally called Tainos, disappeared soon after the Spanish conquest either by death, flight, or absorption. The first African slaves in the Western world were brought to Puerto Rico in 1511. As a result, the population of Puerto Rico is a mixture of Tainos, Caucasoid Europeans, and blacks.

Puerto Ricans were granted American citizenship in 1917. In 1948, they were granted the right to elect their own island governor. In 1952, the present political status was approved by the U.S. Congress and inaugurated; this is the constitution of the island known as the *Estado Libre Asociado*, the Free

Joseph P. Fitzpatrick, PUERTO RICAN AMERICANS: The meaning of Migration to the Mainland. (c) 1971, pp. 77–100. Revised and updated by permission of Prentice-Hall, Inc., Englewood Cliffs, NJ.

Associated State of Puerto Rico, officially identified in English as the Commonwealth of Puerto Rico. Puerto Ricans enjoy most of the rights of American citizens, including that of completely free movement between the island and the American mainland. They do not vote for the President, nor do they have elected representatives in Congress. They pay no federal taxes.

A small colony of Puerto Ricans lived in New York City in the last century, mostly political leaders active in the movement for independence for the island. After 1898 a small but steady migration of Puerto Ricans began. This increased during the 1920s, diminished during the Depression of the 1930s and World War II, and increased to sizable proportions in the late 1940s, which has continued to the present. Many Puerto Ricans now return to the island; the migration is a two-way phenomenon of people migrating from the island to the mainland and others migrating back to the island.

The 1970 U.S. Census reported 1,454,000 Puerto Ricans living on the American mainland: 811,000 of these were born in Puerto Rico, 636,000 were born on the mainland of Puerto Rican parentage, and 7000 were born elsewhere. Approximately 60 percent (872,471) reside in New York State, the great majority in New York City; close to 10 percent (135,676) live in New Jersey, with sizable numbers in Connecticut, Massachusetts, Pennsylvania, and Ohio.

Puerto Ricans are the ethnic minority with the lowest income of all groups in New York City. As a result, many of them must seek public assistance, a source of income but a source of problems that complicate their lives enormously. As a people, they are a mixture of many colors, from completely Negroid to completely Caucasoid and face the difficult problem of adjusting to racial prejudice. Their children find it difficult to achieve well on the standardized English and math tests in the schools; many drop out before finishing high school. There is a high rate of drug addiction among Puerto Rican youth, and the community faces many complicated problems in the area of physical and mental health. Although most are baptized Catholics, it is estimated that less than 30 percent are in effective contact with any religious group in New York City, Catholic or Protestant. Many of them are attracted to the small, neighborhood Pentecostal sects.

Nevertheless, the Puerto Rican community continues to struggle for stability and development. In 1980, it had one elected representative in Congress, two in the New York City Council, two members in the New York State Senate, and five in the State General Assembly. Effective agencies are developing strength and influence: *Aspira* in the area of education, the Puerto Rican Forum in the area of community affairs, the Puerto Rican Family Institute in social service, the Puerto Rican Merchants Association in commerce, the Association of Home Town Clubs in the area of social and community life, and many others. In their migration and adjustment to New York City, Puer. Ricans face the experience of millions of newcomers who preceded them into a city that has been formed by the continued migration of people; they face the conflict and collaboration, the strain and satisfaction, the frustration and achievement that results from stranger meeting stranger in the most complicated city in the world.

In this experience, the family is the institution that faces the most direct shock of cultural change; it is also the institution that provides the greatest strength for its members in the process of change. Puerto Ricans bring with them a style and a structure of family life that has been formed by four centuries of tradition on the island. In order to understand this family as it faces the adjustment to the mainland, the family as it exists on the island must be clearly understood. Many features of the family continue as the context of Puerto Rican life on the mainland. The consequences of cultural transition will be explained after a detailed description of the family in the tradition of Puerto Rico.

HISTORICAL BACKGROUND

Four major influences have contributed to the structure of family life, kinship patterns, and the patterns of family living of the Puerto Ricans[1]: (1) The culture of the Borinquen Indians, now generally referred to as the Tainos, the natives on the island when it was discovered, (2) the influence of Spanish colonial culture, (3) slavery, and (4) the American influence and economic development.

Very little is known about the culture of the Borinquen Indians. Unlike

---

[1]The literature on the Puerto Rican family is extensive and uneven. Steward (1957) is one of the best presentations of varied types of Puerto Rican families. Mintz (1960) is a life history that is really a study of family life in a small *barrio* on the southern coast of Puerto Rico in an area in which rates of consensual union have been high. It is probably the finest single book on this kind of Puerto Rican family. Landy (1959) is a study of socialization and life cycle among poor families in a town in the northeast section of the island. It is an excellent study of family life and socialization. Roberts and Stefani (1940) is out of date, but it has detailed descriptions of many family habits and practices that are still common among the poor and rural families of the island. Stycos (1955) was part of a study of attitudes toward birth control but actually presents extensive information about the Puerto Rican family, particularly in attitudes toward marriage, children, and sex. Rogler and Hollingshead (1965) is a study of the causes of schizophrenia in Puerto Rico, but it provides an excellent and detailed analysis of family experience, especially among poor Puerto Ricans. Lewis (1965) is a vivid and detailed picture of the day-to-day experiences of a family with a history of prostitution in a slum area of San Juan. The introduction, which presents a lengthy analysis of what Lewis calls the "culture of poverty," is important as a setting for the rest of the book. Fernandez-Marina (1961) is an analysis of a form of hysteria common among Puerto Ricans, but the analysis involves a study of the changes in the values of Puerto Rican families under the influence of the mainland. See also, Hill (1955), an example of family change.

areas of the Spanish empire, the indigenous people in Puerto
have disappeared as an indentifiable group early in the history
y. Some speculations are available about their culture and family
le of it is reliable. New studies are now in progress.

Spanish Colonial Culture

The great influence in the past and present on all levels of Puerto Rican family life was the Spanish colonial culture, the important features of which will now be discussed.

PREEMINENCE OF THE FAMILY. As in most cultures of the world, the individual in Latin America has a deep consciousness of his membership in a family. He thinks of his importance in terms of his family membership. This is not a matter of prestige (as in belonging to the Ford or Rockefeller family), but a much more elemental thing, and it is as strong among the families of the very poor as it is among those of the very wealthy. The world to a Latin consists of a pattern of intimate personal relationships, and the basic relationships are those of his family. His confidence, his sense of security and identity are perceived in his relationship to others who are his family

This is evident in the use of *names,* the *technonomy* of Puerto Rican and Latin families. The man generally uses two family names together with his given name, for example, José Garcia Rivera. Garcia is the family name of José's father's father; Rivera is the family name of José's mother's father. Thus the name indicates that José comes from the family of Garcia in his father's line and from the family of Rivera in his mother's father's line. In Spanish-speaking areas, if the man is to be addressed by only one family name, the first name is used, not the second. José would be called Mr. Garcia, not Mr. Rivera. The mixing of these names by Americans is a source of constant embarrassment to Spanish-speaking people. The former governor of Puerto Rico, Luis Muñoz Marin was regularly referred to in American publications as Governor Marin. It should have been Governor Muñoz. Referring to Muñoz Marin as Governor Marin would be similar to referring to John Fitzgerald Kennedy as President Fitzgerald.

On some formal occasions, Puerto Ricans, like other Spanish-speaking people, will use the names of all four families from which they come. If José were announcing his wedding, or an important official appointment, he might write his name: José Garcia Diaz y Rivera Colon. By this he is telling the world that he comes from the families of Garcia and Diaz on his father's side, and Rivera and Colon on his mother's side. The Puerto Ricans are not as familiar and informal with their public figures as Americans are. They may refer to a person as Don[2] Luis, Señor Muñoz, Señor Muñoz Marin, or as Muñoz, but they would not refer to him with the equivalent of "Louie" the way Americans refer to Ike and Dick and Jack or Harry. Americans are more sensitive to the importance of the individual—it is Harry who is important, or Ike, or Dick—but Puerto Ricans emphasize the importance of presenting themselves in the framework of the family of which they are a part.

The wife of José writes her name Maria Gonzalez de Garcia. She retains the family name of her father's father, Gonzalez, and she adopts, usually with the "*de*," the first name of her husband, Garcia. She may use both his names and present herself as Maria Gonzalez de Garcia Rivera. On formal occasions she may retain both her family names and would then present herself as Maria Gonzalez Medina de Garcia Rivera. The children of José and Maria would be Juan Garcia Gonzalez and Carmen Garcia Gonzalez; in formal situations, they would be Juan or Carmen Garcia Rivera y Gonzalez Medina.

The family is much more involved in the process of courtship than would be the case with an American family. In America, boys and girls mingle freely, date each other, fall in love, and by various means ask each other to marry. If they agree to marry, they will advise their parents. If the parents agree, the marriage proceeds happily; if the parents disagree with the couple, they may go ahead and get married regardless. In Puerto Rico, intermingling and dating is much more restricted. A young man interested in a young woman is expected to speak to the parents of the girl, particularly the father, to declare his intentions. A serious courtship may never get started if the families disapprove. As one Puerto Rican sociologist explained personally to the author: In America courtship is a drama with only two actors; in Puerto Rico, it is a drama of two actors, but the families are continually prompting from the wings. Marriage is still considered much more a union of two families than it would be in America.

Finally, Puerto Ricans have a deep sense of family obligation. One's primary responsibilities are to family and friends. If a person advances in public office or succeeds in business enterprises, he has a strong sense of obligation to use his gains for the benefit of his family. Americans also have a sense of family loyalty, but to a much larger degree, they expect to make it on their own. Success does not make them feel obliged to appoint family members to positions, share their wealth with relatives, or use their position for the benefit of the family. They expect selection in business and government to be on the basis of ability and effort, not personal or family relationships. This is an

---

[2]Don is a title of respect used generally in direct speech toward a man (Doña for a woman). It has no class implication. Very poor and humble people use it of their own family members or friends as a sign of respect. It is generally used with the first name (Don Luis or Doña Maria), never without it (Don Luis Muñoz, perhaps, but never Don Muñoz).

oversimplification, since family influence operates in America and people in Puerto Rico are increasingly chosen on the basis of ability and effort. But in Puerto Rico the sense of family is much deeper. As economic development proceeds on the island, or as its citizens adjust to American life, the need increases to sacrifice family loyalty and obligation to efficiency. The Puerto Rican finds this a very difficult thing to do.

SUPERIOR AUTHORITY OF THE MAN. A second feature of the Puerto Rican family is the role of superior authority exercised by the man. This is not peculiar to Latin cultures; it is the common situation in most cultures of the world. The man expects to exercise the authority in the family; he feels free to make decisions without consulting his wife; he expects to be obeyed when he gives commands. As a larger middle class emerges in Puerto Rico, the role of the woman is in the process of being redefined. But in contrast to the characteristics of cooperation and companionship of American families, the woman in Puerto Rico has a subordinate role.

This must not be interpreted as meaning that women do not have subtle ways of influencing men. The influence of mother over son is particularly strong in the culture of the Puerto Ricans. Furthermore, women have played an unusually important role in public and academic life. In 1962, of the 76 *municipios* in Puerto Rico, ten had women as mayors, the most famous being Doña Felisa Rincon de Gautier, who was mayor of the capital city of San Juan for 20 years. Women play an important role on the faculty of the University of Puerto Rico. Oscar Lewis (1965) found the Puerto Rican women among the families he studied to be much more aggressive, outspoken, and even violent than the women in Mexican families. Nevertheless, the role is culturally defined and ordinarily maintained as subordinate to the authority of the husband. Until recently, and still to a surprising extent, women will not make such decisions as consultation of a doctor or sending children for medical treatment without seeking permission of the husband.

The superior position of the man is also reflected in what Americans call a double standard of morality in reference to sexual behavior.[3] In Latin cultures, as in most cultures of the world, a very clear distinction is made between the "good" woman, who will be protected as a virgin until marriage, and then be protected as a wife and mother, and the "bad" woman, who is available for a man's enjoyment. Puerto Ricans are concerned about their girls, and fathers and brothers feel a strong obligation to protect them. On the other hand, a great deal of freedom is granted to the boys. It is rather

---

[3]See references to *machismo* in Stycos (1955).

194

expected, sometimes encouraged, that a boy have sexual experiences with women before marriage. After marriage he may feel free to engage in what Puerto Ricans sometimes jokingly refer to as "extracurricular activities." These patterns of protection of the woman and freedom for the man are changing, but they are still quite different from patterns of sexual behavior on the mainland. It is also true that patterns of sexual behavior that are going through a revolution to greater sexual freedom in America involve boys and girls equally and thus draw us even further away from the style of life in Puerto Rico.

COMPADRAZGO. Another consequence of the influence of Spain on the Puerto Rican family has been *compadrazgo*,[4] or the institution of *compadres*. These are people who are companion parents, as it were, with the natural parents of the child; the man is the *compadre*, the woman is the *comadre*. Sponsors at baptism, for example, become the godparents (*padrinos*) of the child, and the *compadres* of the child's parents; this is also true of sponsors at confirmation. Witnesses at a marriage become *compadres* of the married couple. Sometimes common interests or the intensification of friendship may lead men or women to consider themselves *compadres* or *comadres*. The *compadres* are sometimes relatives, but often they are not. They constitute a network of ritual kinship, as serious and important as that of natural kinship, around a person or a group. *Compadres* frequently become more formal in their relationships, shifting from the familiar "*Tu*" to the formal "*Usted*" in speech. They have a deep sense of obligation to each other for economic assistance, support, encouragement, and even personal correction. A *compadre* may feel much freer to give advice or correction in regard to family problems than a brother or sister would. A *compadre* is expected to be responsive to all the needs of his *compadre*, and ideally, he supplies assistance without question. When Sidney Mintz was doing his anthropological study of a *barrio* of Santa Isabel, Puerto Rico, his principal informant was a remarkable man, Taso Zayas, a farmworker who cut sugar cane. Mintz reached a degree of close friendship with Taso and later decided to do his life history. Mintz describes the relationship that had developed between himself and Taso. Taso had reached a point at which he felt free to ask Mintz for money. "In his own words he would not 'dare ask' if he were not sure I would respond; and failure to do so, if it were a matter of free choice would end our friendship" (Mintz, 1960). In other words, Mintz and Taso had become *compadres*.

---

[4]There is some evidence that *compadrazgo* may have existed among the indigenous people. Some traces of it have been found among the Mayans. But it definitely was a significant Spanish institution that the colonizers either implanted or reinforced when they arrived.

Slavery

Another influence on family life in Puerto Rico was that of slavery. Slavery was a milder institution in Puerto Rico than in America. But slavery in the Western world has had a devastating effect on family life. Little effort was made to provide for the stability and permanence of the slave family, men and women, relatives, children, were bought, sold, exchanged, and shifted with little or no regard for permanent family union. Slave women were defenseless before the advances of free men.

The usual consequences of slavery in the broken family life of blacks have been as evident in Puerto Rico as elsewhere. A number of features of Spanish culture modified the effects to some extent. Consorting with a woman who was not one's wife was a practice of upper-class men in the Spanish colonial tradition and was not confined to black women. Therefore, the extramarital relationships of white men and black women tended to follow a pattern similar to that of white men with white women. Cultural patterns formed around these relationships that provided some advantages to the women and children involved in them. However, the mother-based family—the family with children of a number of fathers and no permanent male consort—has been a common phenomenon in Puerto Rican history.

America and Economic Development

Within recent years, two other major influences have become important: (1) the influence of America on the educational system, which for many years after annexation was in the hands of Americans and conducted on the American model, and (2) religious influence from the mainland. Most of the Catholic priests, brothers, and nuns working among Puerto Ricans during the past 50 years have come from America. Protestant denominations have been established on the island since the turn of the century, and Pentecostal sects have preached a strong and effective gospel among the poor. Finally, and most important, Puerto Ricans returning from the mainland either to visit or to stay bring with them a strong and direct influence of mainland culture in relation to the family. The consequences, particularly of this last influence, will be indicated later.

THE MODERN PUERTO RICAN FAMILY

As a consequence of the above influences, a fourfold structural typology can be identified among Puerto Rican families.

1. EXTENDED FAMILY SYSTEMS. These are families in which there are strong bonds and frequent interaction among a wide range of natural

or ritual kin. Grandparents, parents, and children may live in the same household, or they may have separate households but visit frequently. The extended family is evident regardless of the type of marriage (regularized or consensual), and it is a source of strength and support. Traditionally, this was by far the most common pattern of family life.

2. THE NUCLEAR FAMILY. With the rise of the middle class, the conjugal unit of father, mother, and children, not living close to relatives and with weak bonds to the extended family, is becoming more common. It is difficult to get reliable evidence on the number of these families, but observant Puerto Ricans are noticing that with migration and upward mobility their number is rapidly increasing. This is an expected response to social and economic development.

3. FATHER, MOTHER, THEIR CHILDREN, AND CHILDREN OF ANOTHER UNION OR UNIONS OF HUSBAND OR WIFE. This is not an uncommon phenomenon among Puerto Rican families. New Yorkers have complained about the difficulty of understanding the differing names of children in some Puerto Rican households. In places on the island in which this phenomenon is common, children will identify themselves accordingly. If a visitor asks a boy if the girl with him is his sister, he may respond: "Yes, on my father's side," or "Yes, on my mother's side."

4. THE MOTHER-BASED FAMILY, WITH CHILDREN OF ONE OR MORE MEN, BUT WITH NO PERMANENT MALE CONSORT IN THE HOME. According to the 1970 census, 18.5 percent of families in Puerto Rico were of this type.

These four types of family structure are evident among Puerto Ricans on the mainland.

Consensual Unions

Important in relation to family structure is the phenomenon of consensual unions,[5] which in former years have been common on the island but have been rapidly declining. A consensual union is a relatively stable union of a man and a woman who have not gone through a religious or civil marriage ceremony. They began living together and raising their family and may live this way throughout their lives. At some later date they may regularize the union in a civil or religious ceremony.

---

[5]The phenomenon of consensual union is widely discussed in the literature. The best insight into this cultural practice is found in Mintz (1960). A broader but less detailed description is found in Mintz's chapter, "Canamelar," in Steward (1957). A more detailed study of different rates of consensual unions in different parts of Puerto Rico is found in Dohen (1967). Some lengthy descriptions are also found in Lewis (1965) and Rogler and Hollingshead (1965).

This is not the "common law" marriage, which is an institution in English common law. The Roman law tradition, which has prevailed in Puerto Rico, never recognized a union as a marriage unless it was regularized, but Roman law always acknowledged the situation in which two people would live together without getting married. This state was defined as *concubinatus* or *concubinage*. Concubinage has unfavorable connotations in the English language, but it never had these in the Roman law tradition. Puerto Ricans who live consensually, or in concubinage, refer to themselves as *amancebados*, living together without marriage. The U.S. Census reports consensual unions as a recognized "civil status" and consequently asks people if they are living consensually. According to the decennial census, of all couples "living together" on the island, the following percentages were reported as "living consensually":

1899	34.7 percent of all unions
1920	26.3 percent of all unions
1950	24.9 percent of all unions
1960	13.5 percent of all unions
1970	6.5 percent of all unions

It is a status, therefore, that has always been culturally and officially acknowledged, and Puerto Ricans, unless they are speaking with strangers who they think may not understand, are very open about admitting that they are living consensually. They do not look on this as an immoral state, as it would be considered in many other parts of the Christian world. The partners generally are not well instructed in any religious faith and consequently have no guilt feelings about living without religious marriage.[6] In addition, they are usually poor people with no property rights related to marriage. These simple people recognize that a man needs a woman, and a woman needs a man, and they begin to live together and bring up the children resulting from their union or from other unions that either one might have led. They judge the moral quality of the union in terms of their relationship to each other. He is a good man if he works to support the woman and children, treats them respectfully, and does not abandon them. She is a good woman if she keeps his house, cooks his meals, keeps his clothes, and raises his children properly. In fact, people in consensual unions are sometimes more concerned about the basic moral relationships than are people preoccupied with the regularization of the union.

---

[6]This does not mean they do not respect religious marriage. Many of them do not enter religious marriage because they understand its binding character and do not wish to commit themselves this way until they are sure they mean it.

The percentage of existing consensual unions has been declining sharply. It dropped from 25 percent in 1950 to 13.5 percent in 1960, and to 6.5 percent in 1970. A number of factors help to explain the decline. First, the increase in religious and spiritual care has created a wider concern for religious marriage. Second, important economic benefits have come to be associated with regularized unions; for example, widow's pensions, family benefits, social security, and, in former years, particularly in New York City, admission to public housing projects. Finally, the rapid emergence of the middle class has been important. Consensual union has always been a phenomenon of the poor population. As persons from the poorer classes advance to middle-class status, they become aware of regularized marriage as a middle-class value, and so they marry. Increased education and the gainful occupation and changing status of women have also contributed to the decline. In other words, the social conditions in which it was functional have disappeared.

Illegitimacy

Related to consensual unions is illegitimacy, about which at least brief mention must be made. International reports of population use the term "illegitimate" to designate the children of parents who are not married. Children of consensual unions are included in this. This is a misleading designation. In Puerto Rico, as in the Roman law tradition generally, the term "illegitimate" was never used.[7] A child of a marriage that was legalized, and whose rights before the law were thus protected, was called "legitimate." He was a "legal" child. "Natural" was the term used for all other children. This had a much less pejorative connotation than that associated with the term "illegitimate" A third term has come into use in Puerto Rico, the *hijo reconocido,* the recognized child.[8] In Puerto Rico, if the father of a child is known, whether he is living consensually with the mother, or whether the child resulted from a casual union, he is required by law to recognize the child. This gives the child a number of rights before the law, including the right to use the father's name, the right to support, and some rights of inheritance. Therefore, in examining statistics on legitimacy from areas like Puerto Rico, it is important to note that many of the children reported as illegitimate may actually be the children of stable consensual unions.

---

[7]In contrast to English common law, which was concerned with illegitimacy, Roman law always acknowledged that some people would live together without getting married, in a state of concubinage. English common law, however, had the principle of common-law marriage: If a couple lived together long enough, it recognized the union as legal.

[8]In the late 1960s the vital statistics reports do not use the category "recognized child" as they once did. As a result, it is difficult to determine how many there are. They had also ceased using the term *hijo natural* and began to use the standard international category "illegitimate" for children of parents not in regularized unions.

FERTILITY. Fertility has generally been high in Puerto Rico, although it appears to be dropping in recent years.[9] This may be due largely to the migration of large numbers of young people to the mainland during their most fertile years. In any event, the rate of population increase on the island has been declining. Puerto Rico has been one of the classic examples of "population explosion," and efforts to control the population increase have been widespread, well known, and at times very controversial. The estimated natural increase of the population during the period 1887–1899 was 14.3 per 1000 population; the crude birth rate during the same period was 45.7, and the crude death rate was 31.4. The introduction of better hygiene caused the death rate to decline consistently but the birth rate to remain high, so population increase has been rapid. The average annual increase during the period 1930–1935 was 18.9 per 1000; during the period 1940–1945 it was 24.9; in 1950 it was 28.6; in 1965 it had declined to 23.4; in 1975 it had declined to 16.2. Crude rates such as these are not very helpful in explaining population changes, but they give a general picture of increases and decreases. Actually, the continuing migration of Puerto Ricans to the mainland has been the safety valve of population increase. Had all the migrants remained in Puerto Rico, the population would be doubling every 20 years, a rate of growth that would have caused major problems on the island.

Family Values

Some aspects of the values of Puerto Rican family life have already been mentioned in relation to the influences that have helped to form it. In the following paragraphs, the range of values will be indicated that distinguish the Puerto Rican family from the predominant middle-class family values of the mainland.[10]

PERSONALISM. The basic value of Puerto Rican culture, as of Latin cultures in general, is a form of individualism that focuses on the inner impor-

---

[9]The problem of population policy and birth control has been a troublesome issue between the government and the Catholic bishops on the island. For an analysis of the problem up to 1950, see Perloff (1950: Chapters 12 and 13). For the more modern period, Vasquez (1964) brings the data up to date. An intensive study of backgrounds of fertility was done during the 1950s in Puerto Rico. The first publication, Hatt (1952), was a survey of public attitudes toward large or small families. This was followed by Stycos (1955), which sought to determine why people said they preferred small families but continued having large ones; the final study was Hill, Stycos, and Back (1959), which reports the results of various methods to bring people to the practice of birth control. Sterilization has been the most common method of birth control in Puerto Rico. More than one-third of the women of child-bearing age have been sterilized, the highest rate by far of the entire world. See Presser (1973) for detailed analysis.

[10]One of the best brief treatments of Latin values that are shared by Puerto Ricans can be found in Gillin (1960). Another good treatment is found in Wells (1969: Chapters 1 and 2).

tance of the person. In contrast to the individualism of America, which values the individual in terms of his ability to compete for higher social and economic status, the culture of Puerto Rico centers attention on those inner qualities that constitute the uniqueness of the person and his goodness or worth in himself. In a two-class society in which little mobility was possible, a man was born into his social and economic position. Therefore, he defined his value in terms of the qualities and behavior that made a man good or respected in the social position in which he found himself. A poor farm laborer was a good man when he did those things that made a man good on his social and economic level. He felt an inner dignity *(dignidad)* about which the Puerto Rican is very sensitive; he expected others to have respect *(respeto)* for that *dignidad.* All men have some sense of personal dignity and are sensitive about proper respect being shown them. But this marks the Puerto Rican culture in a particular way. Puerto Ricans are much more sensitive than Americans to anything that appears to be personal insult or disdain; they do not take to practical jokes that are likely to embarrass or to party games in which people "make fools of themselves." They do not "horse around," as Americans would say in an offhand, informal manner; they are unusually responsive to manifestations of personal respect and to styles of personal leadership by men who appeal to the person rather than a program or a platform. Although the old two-class society in which these values developed has been disappearing, the values themselves are still very strong.

PERSONALISM AND EFFICIENCY. It is this personalism that makes it difficult for the Puerto Rican to adjust easily to what Americans call efficiency. For a Puerto Rican, life is a network of personal relationships. He trusts persons; he relies on persons; he knows that at every moment he can fall back on a brother, a cousin, a *compadre.* He does not have that same trust for a system or an organization. The American, on the other hand, expects the system to work; he has confidence in the organization. When something goes wrong, his reaction is "Somebody ought to do something about this." "Get this system going." Thus, an American becomes impatient and uneasy when systems do not work. He responds to efficiency. The Latin becomes uneasy and impatient if the system works too well, if he feels himself in a situation in which he must rely on impersonal functions rather than personal relationships.

THE PADRINO. Related to personalism is the role of the *padrino.* The *padrino* is a person, strategically placed in a higher position of the social structure, who has a personal relationship with the poorer person for whom he provides employment, assistance at time of need, and acts as an advocate if the poor person becomes involved in trouble. The *padrino* is really the intermediary between the poor person who has neither sophistication nor influence, and the larger society of law, government, employment, and service. He is a strategic helper in times of need, but the possibilities of exploitation in this relationship are very great. The poor person can become completely bound to the *padrino* by debt or by obligations to personal service to such an extent that his life is little better than slavery. The role of the *padrino* has decreased in Puerto Rico, but the tendency to seek a personal relationship in one's business affairs is still strong.

MACHISMO. Another aspect of personalism is a combination of qualities associated with masculinity. This is generally referred to as *machismo*, literally, maleness. *Machismo* is a style of personal daring (the great quality of the bullfighters) by which one faces challenge, danger, and threat with calmness and self-possession; this sometimes takes the form of bravado. It is also a quality of personal magnetism that impresses and influences others and prompts them to follow one as a leader—the quality of the *conquistador*. It is associated with sexual prowess, influence, and power over women, reflected in a vigorous romanticism and a jealous guarding of sweetheart or wife, or in premarital and extramarital relationships.

SENSE OF FAMILY OBLIGATION. Personalism is deeply rooted in the individualism that has just been described; it is also rooted in the family. As explained above, the Puerto Rican has a deep sense of that network of primary personal relationships that is his family. To express it another way, he senses the family as an extension of the person, and the network of obligations follows as described above.

SENSE OF THE PRIMARY OF THE SPIRITUAL. The Latin generally refers to American culture as very materialistic, much to the amazement of Americans, who are conscious of human qualities, concerns, and generosity in American culture that are missing in the Latin. What the Latin means is that his fundamental concerns are not with this world or its tangible features. He has a sense of spirit and soul as much more important than the body and as being intimately related to his value as a person; he tends to think in terms of transcendent qualities, such as justice, loyalty, or love, rather than in terms of practical arrangements that spell out justice or loyalty in the concrete. On an intellectual level, he strives to clarify relationships conceptually with a confidence that if they can be made intellectually clear and precise, the relationships will become actualities. He thinks of life very much in terms of ultimate values and ultimate spiritual goals, and expresses a willingness to sacrifice material satisfactions for these. In contrast, the American preoccupation with mastering the world and subjecting it to man's domination, through technological programs, gives him the sense of reversing the system of values, of emphasizing the importance of mastering the physical universe rather than seeking the values of the spirit. It is striking to note how many important political figures are also literary men with a humanistic flair. Former Governor Muñoz Marin is a poet and is affectionately called *El Vate,* the Bard, in Puerto Rico; the former resident commissioner in Washington, Santiago Polanco Abreu, is a literary critic; some of the best known figures in public service in the Puerto Rican community in New York, such as Juan Aviles, Carmen Marrero, and Luis Quero Chiesa, are accomplished writers and artists.

FATALISM. Connected to these spiritual values is a deep sense of fatalism in Puerto Ricans. They have a sense of destiny, partly related to elemental fears of the sacred, partly related to a sense of divine providence governing the world. The popular song, "Que será, será," "Whatever will be, will be," is a simple expression of it, as is the common expression that intersperses so much of Puerto Rican speech: *Si Dios quiere,* "If God wills it." The term "destiny" recurs frequently in Puerto Rican popular songs. This quality leads to the acceptance of many events as inevitable; it also softens the sense of personal guilt for failure. If, after a vigorous effort, an enterprise does not succeed, the Puerto Rican may shrug his shoulders and remark, "It was not meant to be."

SENSE OF HIERARCHY. The Puerto Ricans, like other Latins, have had a concept of a hierarchical world during the whole of their history. This was partly the result of the two-class system, in which members never conceived of a world in which they could move out of the position of their birth. Thus, they thought of a relationship of higher and lower classes that was fixed somewhat as the various parts of the body were fixed. This concept of hierarchy contributed to their concept of personal worth as distinct from a person's position in the social structure.

The Puerto Rican Family on the Mainland

The institution that faces the most direct shock in the migration to the mainland is the family, and the progress of Puerto Ricans can be measured to a large extent by a study of the family. First, a statistical description of Puerto Rican families can be presented, followed by an analysis of the effect of migration on the family.

It has long been recognized that the migration of Puerto Ricans is a family migration, in the sense that they either come as families ⌣ expect to stay and found their families here. This is reflected in the percentage of the population on the mainland that is married. According to the 1960 Census, of all Puerto Rican males over 14 years of age, 70 percent were married; of females, about 80 percent (Fitzpatrick, 1966). Age at marriage shows a sharp decline from first generation to second generation, indicating an adaptation to mainland patterns of younger marriage.

One of the most serious differences between Puerto Rican families on the mainland and on the island, revealed in the 1970 Census, is the high rate of "families with female head." On the mainland 28 percent of Puerto Rican families were reported as having a female head, almost as high as the rate for American blacks; even more surprising is the fact that this high rate continues in the second generation: almost 26 percent of the families have a female head. This is in contrast to the 18.5 percent of families in Puerto Rico with a female head. No one has yet found a satisfactory explanation of this phenomenon. It will certainly affect Puerto Rican family life in the future.

The phenomenon of "out-of-wedlock" children is also steadily increasing in New York State. In 1957, only 11 percent of Puerto Rican births in New York State were out of wedlock; this increased to 22 percent in 1967 and 30 percent in 1969. This was considerably higher than the rate of about 20 percent in Puerto Rico in 1970.

Type of Ceremony

Another indication of change can be found in the type of religious ceremony of Puerto Rican marriages on the mainland. Comparison of type of religious ceremony for all marriages in Puerto Rico in 1975 with type of religious ceremony for Puerto Rican marriages in New York City gives results as shown

TABLE 1
Type of Religious Ceremony for all Marriages in Puerto Rico, and all Puerto Rican Marriages in New York City for Selected Years

	CIVIL (%)	CATHOLIC (%)	PROTESTANT (%)
Puerto Rico, 1949	24.3	61.4	14.3
Puerto Rico, 1975	43.6	31.2	25.0
New York City, 1949[a]	20.0	27.0	50.0
New York City, 1975	42.0	26.0	32.0

SOURCE: Fitzpatrick (1966); Fitzpatrick and Gurak (1979: Table 18).

[a]A few other type ceremonies are omitted.

204

in Table 1. The pattern of marriage ceremony has changed substantially in Puerto Rico between 1949 and 1975. The pattern in New York in 1975 closely approaches that of Puerto Rico. The rate of Catholic ceremonies remains low; the rate of Protestant ceremonies has declined while civil ceremonies have increased. The decline in Protestant ceremonies from 1949 to 1975 appears to be a decline in marriages performed by Pentecostal ministers. This tends to confirm the theory that association with sects and storefront religious groups is a first-generation phenomenon. As numbers in the second generation increase substantially, in their growing familiarity with American life, they tend to withdraw from the sects.

The Role of Religion

Religious identity has played a major role in the adjustment of immigrant groups to American life. It is not clear what role religion will play in the experience of the Puerto Ricans. They come from a Spanish colonial type of Catholicism: Most are baptized Catholics; religious practice frequently takes the form of communal celebrations and processions; folk practices are common such as veneration of saints, use of medals and personal devotions, small family shrines, and religious promises to saints in return for favors.

Puerto Ricans enter a very different religious environment in New York where Catholicism is highly organized, emphasizes individual practice of the faith by attending mass and receiving the sacraments, and which is dominated by religious leaders from European ethnic backgrounds, many of whom find it difficult to understand the Puerto Ricans. Furthermore, the Puerto Ricans are the first large group of Catholic newcomers to migrate to the mainland without their own clergy. Extensive efforts have been made by mainland dioceses to respond to the religious needs of the Puerto Ricans. Thousands of priests and religious personnel have been trained in Spanish and in an understanding of Puerto Rican culture. But the effort still falls short of the need.

Probably the most important religious development among Puerto Ricans on the mainland has been the *Cursillo*, a short two- or three-day period of prayer and intensive self-examination, and the development of small supporting groups who meet regularly to enable the group members to be faithful to their resolutions and their dedication to a more deeply religious life. The *Cursillistas*, as they are called, tend to be the most active members of the parishes.

Pentecostal and Evangelical sects are numerous in Puerto Rican areas. These are small, grass-root congregations, generally operating in storefronts, in the heart of the neighborhoods which they serve, and in a religious style in which the Puerto Ricans feel at home. In the midst of a world that often appears "cold" to Puerto Ricans, the Pentecostal congregation is a community experience that provides psychosocial satisfaction as well as a familiar form of religious practice. Within recent years, strong Pentecostal movements have appeared among Catholic groups.

Folk religious practices are widespread. *Botanicas,* small stores that sell candles, medals, and all the paraphernalia for folk religious practices or for spiritism, dot the Puerto Rican neighborhoods. Spiritism is a common practice, rooted in the conviction that one can communicate with the spirit world, especially with the dead. The practice ranges from highly sophisticated seances to folk-style gatherings, from manipulations of the spirit world that can result in anxiety or harm, to invocations of the spirits that can be helpful in maintaining support for persons who appear to be mentally disturbed.

Thus the role that religion plays in the experience of Puerto Ricans on the mainland remains obscure. It is now estimated that one-half or more of the Catholics of the New York Archdiocese and the Brooklyn Diocese are Hispanics, mostly Puerto Ricans. Most of them have no contact with any church—Catholic, Protestant or Pentecostal. The vitality of those associated with the Church is strong and impressive.

Intermarriage

The most significant evidence of adjustment to life on the mainland has been the increase of marriage of Puerto Ricans with non-Puerto Ricans. In his study of New York marriages for the years 1949 and 1959, Fitzpatrick (1966) established that there is a significant increase in the rate of out-group marriage among second-generation Puerto Ricans over the first. The data are presented in Table 2.

The increase in the rate of out-group marriages among Puerto Ricans in both 1949 and 1959 between the first and second generation was as great as was the increase for all immigrants in New York City in the years 1908 to 1912.[11] It is legitimate to conclude from this that if out-group marriage is accepted as an index of assimilation, the assimilation of Puerto Ricans in New York is moving as rapidly as the assimilation of all immigrants during the years 1908–1912. However, the replication of this study in 1975 indicated an increase in out-group marriage for first-generation Puerto Ricans, and a decline in out-group marriage for the second generation. This may be a function of population density (many more second-generation Puerto Ricans, and concentrated in Manhattan and the Bronx); it may also reflect a resistance to as-

---

[11]The data for marriages of immigrants, 1908–1912, which were used in the Fitzpatrick study were taken from Drachsler (1921).

TABLE 2
Rate of Out-Group Marriage of Puerto Ricans in New York City, 1949, 1959, and 1975, by Generation; and of All Immigrants in New York City, 1908–1912

	1ST GENERATION		2ND GENERATION		INCREASE IN 2ND GENERATION
	%	No.	%	No.	
Grooms					
Puerto Rican, 1949	5.2	3079	28.3	378	23.1
Puerto Rican, 1959	3.6	7078	27.4	638	23.8
Puerto Rican, 1975	9.4	4003	21.3	2344	11.9
1908–1912	10.39	64,577	32.4	12,184	22.01
Brides					
Puerto Rican, 1949	8.5	3077	30.0	523	21.5
Puerto Rican, 1959	6.0	7257	33.1	717	27.1
Puerto Rican, 1975	12.9	3606	20.7	2943	7.8
1908–1912	10.1	61,823	30.12	14,611	20.02

SOURCE: Fitzpatrick (1966); Fitzpatrick and Gurak, (1979: Table 12).

similation. However, for Puerto Ricans outside New York City, out-group marriage rates remain high.

Changes in Values

Much more important than the statistical description of the Puerto Rican families in America or in New York City is the study of the changes in values that they face. Probably the most serious is the shift in roles of husband and wife. There is abundant evidence that this is a common experience of immigrants. It is provoked by a number of things. First, it is frequently easier for Puerto Rican women to get jobs in New York than Puerto Rican men. This gives the wife an economic independence that she may never have had before, and if the husband is unemployed while the wife is working, the reversal of roles is severe. Second, the impact of American culture begins to make itself felt more directly in New York than on the island. Puerto Rican women from the poorer classes are much more involved in social, community, and political activities than they are in Puerto Rico. This influences the Puerto Rican wife to adopt gradually the patterns of the mainland.

Even more direct and difficult to cope with is the shift in role of the Puerto Rican child. Puerto Rican families have frequently lamented the patterns of behavior of even good boys in America. Puerto Rican parents consider them to be disrespectful. American children are taught to be self-reliant, aggressive, and competitive, to ask, "Why," and to stand on their own two feet. A Puerto Rican child is generally much more submissive. When the children begin to behave according to the American pattern, the parents cannot understand it. A priest who had worked for many years with migrating Puerto Ricans remarked to this writer: "When these Puerto Rican families come to New York, I give the boys about forty-eight hours on the streets of New York, and the difference between his behavior and what the family expects will have begun to shake the family."

The distance that gradually separates child from family is indicated in much of the literature about Puerto Ricans in New York. In the autobiography of Piri Thomas, *Down These Mean Streets* (1967), it is clear that his family—and it was a good, strong family—had no way of controlling him once he began to associate with his peers on the streets. The sharp contrast of two life histories, *Two Blocks Apart* (Mayerson, 1965), also demonstrates the difficulties of a Puerto Rican family in trying to continue to control the life of a boy growing up in New York. His peers become his significant reference group. A considerable number of scholars and social workers attribute much of the delinquency of Puerto Ricans to the excessive confinement that the Puerto Rican families impose in an effort to protect their children. Once the children can break loose in the early teens, they break completely. When Julio Gonzalez was killed in a gang fight on the Lower East Side in reprisal for the murder of a black girl, Theresa Gee, in 1959, he was buried from Nativity Church. Julio's father, a poor man from a mountain town in Puerto Rico, was like a pillar of strength during the wake. He was a man of extraordinary dignity and self-possession. After the funeral mass, he went to the sacristy of the church, embraced each of the priests who had participated, and thanked them. Here was a man who sought to pass on to his son the qualities of loyalty, dignity, and strength. But when the son reached the streets, different definitions of loyalty and dignity took over. As Julio was dying, after the priest had given him the last rites of the Catholic Church, he fell into unconsciousness, mumbling: "Tell the guys they can count me; tell them I'll be there."[12]

Probably the most severe problem of control is the effort of families to give their unmarried daughters the same kind of protection they would have given them in Puerto Rico. When the girls reach the early teens, they wish to do what American girls do: go to dances with boys without a chaperone and associate freely with girls and boys of the neighborhood or school. For a good Puerto Rican father to permit his daughter to go out unprotected is a serious

---

[12]For a lengthy discussion of this change of values and its relation to delinquency, see Fitzpatrick (1960). This is reprinted in Tyler (1962:415–421).

moral failure. In a Puerto Rican town, when a father has brought his daughters as virgins to marriage, he can hold up his head before his community; he enjoys the esteem and prestige of a good father. To ask the same father to allow his daughters to go free in New York is to ask him to do something that the men of his family have considered immoral. It is psychologically almost impossible for him to do this. The tension between parents and daughter(s) is one of the most difficult for Puerto Rican parents to manage. It is frequently complicated because Americans, including school teachers and counselors, who are not aware of the significance of this in the Puerto Rican background, advise the parents to allow the girls to go out freely.[13]

Finally, the classic tension between the generations takes place. The parents are living in the Puerto Rican culture in their homes. The children are being brought up in an American school where American values are being presented. The parents will never really understand their children; the children will never really understand the parents.

Weakening of Extended Kinship

Apart from the conflict between generations, the experience of migration tends to weaken the family bonds that created a supporting network on which the family could always rely. To a growing extent, the family finds itself alone. This is partly the result of moving from place to place. It is also due to the fact that the way of life in mainland cities is not a convenient environment for the perpetuation of family virtues and values. The Department of Social Services provides assistance in time of need but not with the familiar, informal sense of personal and family respect. Regulations in housing, consumer loans, schools, and courts create a requirement for professional help, and the family is less and less effective.

Replacement of Personal Values

Closely related to all the above difficulties, and creating difficulties of its own, is the slow and steady substitution of impersonal norms, norms of the system rather than norms of personal relationships. The need to adjust to the dominant patterns of American society requires a preparation to seek employment and advancement on the basis of merit or ability. To people for whom the

---

[13]Protection of the girls generates its own problems in Puerto Rico, a form of "cloister rebellion" that may lead to escape from the home or elopement. It is well described in Stycos (1955: Chapter 5).

world is an extensive pattern of personal relationships, this is a difficult adjustment.

The process of uprooting has been described before in the extensive literature about immigrants. It leads to three kinds of adjustments. The first involves escape from the immigrant or migrant group and an effort to become as much like the established community as possible in as short a time as possible. These people seek to disassociate themselves from their past. They sometimes change their name, they change their reference groups, and seek to be accepted by the larger society. They are in great danger of becoming marginal. Having abandoned the way of life of their own people, in which they had a sense of "who they were," there is no assurance that they will be accepted by the larger community. They may find themselves in a no-man's land of culture. In this stage, the danger of personal frustration is acute.

A second reaction is withdrawal into the old culture, a resistance to the new way of life. These people seek to retain the older identities by locking themselves into their old way of life.

The third reaction is the effort to build a cultural bridge between the culture of the migrants and that of the mainland. These are the people who have confidence and security in their own way of life, but who realize that it cannot continue. Therefore, they seek to establish themselves in the new society but continue to identify themselves with the people from whom they come. These are the ones through whom the process of assimilation moves forward.

CHANGE AND ADAPTATION

In view of the above discussion, it is important to discover at what level of assimilation the Puerto Rican family now stands, and how it is affected by the problem of identity. In terms of intermarriage, national data indicate a high rate of out-group marriage among Puerto Ricans. According to the 1970 Census, in New York State 34 percent of second-generation Puerto Rican men and 32 percent of second-generation Puerto Rican women married and living with their spouses are married to non-Puerto Ricans. Nationally, this is higher: 68 percent of second-generation Puerto Rican men and 65 percent of the women married and living with their spouses were married to non-Puerto Ricans. The 1970 Census reports do not discriminate between non-Puerto Rican spouses who are Hispanic and those who are not. The data in Fitzpatrick (1966) and Fitzpatrick and Gurak (1979) are confined to Puerto Ricans marrying non-Hispanics. As indicated above this rate of intermarriage among second-generation Puerto Ricans in New York City declined between 1959 and 1975.

Second, in view of the character of the migration from Puerto Rico (i.e., the return of many Puerto Ricans from the mainland and the continuing movement of large numbers of new migrants to the mainland), there continue to be large numbers of Puerto Rican families in the early and difficult stages of adjustment to New York, struggling for a satisfactory cultural adjustment as defined by Gordon (1963) and Eisenstadt (1955).

The increase in the number of second-generation Puerto Ricans indicates that the classical problems of newcomers (e.g., adjustment to new environment, disruption of ties) are very likely at a serious level and will continue to be so for a considerable length of time. It is not clear just how family difficulties contribute to these larger problems, but it is certain that these problems contribute immeasurably to family difficulties. In the early 1960s, a group of Puerto Rican social workers founded the Puerto Rican Family Institute in an effort to assist Puerto Rican families in New York. The objective of the institute was not simply to provide family casework but to identify well-established Puerto Rican families in New York and match them as *compadres* to newly arrived families that showed signs of suffering from the strains of adjustment to the city. This was an attempt to use the traditional forms of neighborhood and family help that were characteristic of Puerto Rico. When families could be matched, the program has been very helpful. But recently the institute has found that the percentage of families with serious and immediate problems has been increasing. This may reflect the fact that as agencies around the city learn of a Puerto Rican institute, they refer their Puerto Rican problem cases to it; it may also reflect the shock of uprooting upon the newly arriving families or the disruption that occurs as the numbers in the second generation increase. The growth of militancy among the young will be another factor that will increase tension. However, in the demonstrations at City College of New York in the spring of 1969, in which militant Puerto Rican students played a major part, observers commented that the parents of the Puerto Rican students were very much on hand, supporting their sons and daughters, bringing them food, clothing, and supplies.

The treatment of upward mobility in the second generation would require an article in itself. The evidence is clear that, educationally and occupationally, second-generation Puerto Ricans have reached a higher level than the first generation. According to the 1970 Census, second-generation Puerto Rican men, 18–24 years of age, had completed a median average of 11.5 years of schooling. This is almost as high as the median for the total U.S. population. The 1970 Census reported 8 percent of second-generation Puerto Rican men in professional and managerial positions in contrast to 3.2 percent of the first; 28.6 percent of the second-generation men were in white-collar employment in contrast to 16.8 percent of the first; for women the advance was from 32 percent of the first generation in white-collar employment to 64 percent of the second. However, the second generation is still so young that its socioeconomic advancement has not yet had an impact on the total Puerto Rican population. The median age of second generation Puerto Ricans in 1976 was 9.2 years; half the second generation are small children. For example, of all Puerto Rican men in the labor force, only 13 percent are second generation. It will be years before the impact of the second generation will be felt.

Rogler and Cooney (1979) found a strong continuity of ethnic identity among second-generation Puerto Ricans who had finished high school. The organizational participation of these graduates tended to be strong and in associations related to Puerto Ricans. The Rogler and Cooney study was based on a sample of stable, intact families in which the marriages of the children were in-group (Puerto Rican with Puerto Rican.) The authors concluded their study with the remark: ". . . we are left with the need to modify the original postulate . . . that the host society uniformly represents a non-ethnic force. If San Juan is being Americanized, it is no less true that New York City is being Hispanicized." The main source of the continuity of culture they found in the family.

Finally the strength of the Puerto Rican family is seen in the condition of the aged. Due to the youthfulness of the Puerto Rican population, the number of aged is still relatively small in New York City and the mainland; and many of the aged Puerto Ricans return to the island. A study by Cantor (1973) of a representative sample of all the aged (over 60 years) in the poverty areas of New York City found that the Hispanic elderly (mostly Puerto Rican) are the "youngest" among the aged in the City. They have the highest percentage (43%) living with a spouse. Their educational level is low, and they find themselves out of employment at an earlier age than the average aged person in New York City or the nation. The Hispanic elderly live closest to their children, and 80 percent see their children at least once a week. They are still part of an extended family which encompasses frequent interaction and much direct mutual support. If this continues it can have a significant influence on the situation of the Hispanic aged in the City.

In the period during which the Puerto Ricans struggle for greater solidarity and identity as a community, the family remains the major psychosocial support for its members. In many cases, it is a broken family; in others, it is hampered by poverty, unemployment, and illness, but it remains the source of strength for most Puerto Ricans in the process of transition. In the turbulent action of the musical *West Side Story,* when Bernardo, leader of the Puerto Rican gang, sees Tony, a youth of another ethnic group, approaching his sister Maria, Bernardo pulls Maria way from Tony to take her home; he then turns to Tony in anger and shouts: "You keep away from my sister. Don't you know we are a family people!"

During 1966, the first presentation in New York of *The Ox Cart* took place. This is a play by a Puerto Rican playwright, Rene Marques, which presents a picture of a simple farm family in the mountains of Puerto Rico, struggling to survive but reflecting the deep virtues of family loyalty and strength. Under the influence of the oldest son, the family moves to a slum section of San Juan in order to improve itself. But deterioration sets in as the slum environment begins to attack the solidarity and loyalty of the family members. The family then moves to New York; there the strain of the uprooting becomes worse, the gap between mother and children more painful, and the virtues of the old mountain family seem even more distant. After the violent death of the son, the play ends with the valiant mother setting out to go back to the mountains of Puerto Rico; there she hopes to regain the traditional values of Puerto Rican family life that were destroyed in San Juan and New York.

This is an ancient theme, and it may be as true for Puerto Ricans as it was for earlier newcomers. But if the Puerto Ricans make it on the mainland, it will be through the same source of strength that supported the immigrants of earlier times—the solidarity of the family.

REFERENCES

Cantor, Marjorie H. 1973. *The Elderly in the Inner City.* New York: Institute on Gerontology, Fordham University.

Dohen, Dorothy M. 1967. *The Background of Consensual Union in Puerto Rico.* In *Two Puerto Rican Studies.* Cuernavaca, Mexico: Center of Intercultural Documentation.

Drachsler, Julian. 1921. *Intermarriage in New York City.* New York: Columbia University Press.

Eisenstadt, S. N. 1955. *The Absorption of Immigrants.* New York: The Free Press.

Fernandez-Marina, R. 1961. "The Puerto Rican Syndrome: Its Dynamics and Cultural Determinants," *Psychiatry,* 24 (February): 79–82.

Fernandez-Marina, R., E. D. Maldonado Sierra, and R. D. Trent. 1958. "Three Basic Themes in Mexican and Puerto Rican Family Values," *Journal of Social Psychology,* 48 (November): 167–181.

Fitzpatrick, J. P. 1960. "Crime and Our Puerto Ricans," *Catholic Mind,* 58:39–50.

———. 1966. "Intermarriage of Puerto Ricans in New York City," *American Journal of Sociology,* 71 (January): 401.

———. 1971. *Puerto Rican Americans: The Meaning of Migration to the Mainland.* Englewood Cliffs, NJ: Prentice-Hall.

Fitzpatrick, J.P., and Douglas Gurak, 1979. *Hispanic Intermarriage in New York City,*

1975. Monograph No. 2. Bronx, NY: Hispanic Research Center, Fordham University.

Gillin, John, 1960. "Some Signposts for Policy," in Richard N. Adams et al. (eds.): *Social Change in Latin America Today.* New York: Vintage, pp. 28–47.

Gordon, Milton. 1963. *Assimilation in American Life.* New York: Oxford University Press.

Hatt, Paul. 1952. *Background of Human Fertility in Puerto Rico.* Princeton, NJ: Princeton University Press.

Hill, Reuben, 1955. "Courtship in Puerto Rico: An Institution in Transition," *Marriage and Family Living,* 17 (February): 26–34.

Hill, Reuben, J. Mayone Stycos, and Kurt W. Black. 1959. *The Family and Population Control: A Puerto Rican Experiment in Social Change.* Chapel Hill, NC: University of North Carolina Press.

Landy, David. 1959. *Tropical Childhood.* Chapel Hill, NC: University of North Carolina Press.

Lewis, Oscar. 1965. *La Vida: A Puerto Rican Family in the Culture of Poverty—San Juan and New York.* New York: Random House.

Mayerson, Charlotte Leon (ed.). 1965. *Two Blocks Apart.* New York: Holt, Rinehart and Winston.

Mintz, Sidney. 1960. *Worker in the Cane,* New Haven: Yale University Press.

Perloff, Harvey S. 1950. *Puerto Rico's Economic Future.* Chicago: University of Chicago Press.

Presser, Harriet B. 1973. *Sterilization and Fertility Decline in Puerto Rico.* Berkeley, CA: Institute of International Studies, University of California.

Roberts, Lydia, and Rose Stefani. 1940. *Patterns of Living in Puerto Rican Families.* Rio Piedras: University of Puerto Rico Press.

Rogler, Lloyd, and Rosemary Santana Cooney. 1979. *Intergenerational Change in Ethnic Identity in the Puerto Rican Family.* Unpublished Manuscript. Bronx, NY: Hispanic Research Center, Fordham University.

Rogler, Lloyd, and A. B. Hollingshead, 1965. *Trapped: Families and Schizophrenia.* New York: Wiley.

Steward, Julian. 1957. *People of Puerto Rico.* Champaign-Urbana: University of Illinois Press.

Stycos, J. Mayone. 1955. *Family and Fertility in Puerto Rico.* New York: Columbia University Press.

Thomas, Piri. 1967. *Down These Mean Streets.* New York: Knopf.

Tyler, Gus. 1962. *Organized Crime in America.* Ann Arbor: University of Michigan Press.

Vasquez, Jose L. 1964. *Fertility Trends in Puerto Rico.* Section on Bio-Statistics. San Juan: Department of Preventive Medicine and Public Health, School of Medicine of Puerto Rico.

Wells, Henry. 1969. *The Modernization of Puerto Rico.* Cambridge, Harvard University Press.

HISTORICALLY SUBJUGATED
BUT VOLATILE
ETHNIC MINORITIES

The Black American Family

Robert Staples's chapter on black families in America is an attempt to introduce a new perspective to this controversial and at times politically explosive subject. Analysis of the black family has until recently concentrated on the weaknesses and problems of black people and their families. The "pathological" black family has received the lion's share of attention.

Concentrating on the strengths of black families, Dr. Staples emphasizes the historical importance of family and kinship among black people, first in African society and later in the slavery and postemancipation period. The family, whatever its weaknesses, has been a survival mechanism serving as a refuge for affection, companionship, and self-esteem.

CHAPTER TEN

BY

ROBERT STAPLES

INTRODUCTION

As the United States' largest visible minority, the black population has been the subject of extensive study by behavioral scientists. Its family life has been of particular concern because of the unique character of this institution, due to a history that is uncharacteristic of other ethnic groups. There are four traits of the black group that distinguish it from other immigrants to the United States. These differences are cultural in the sense that (1) blacks came from a country with norms and values that were dissimilar to the American way of life; (2) they were composed of many different tribes, each with its own languages, cultures, and traditions; (3) in the beginning, they came without females; and, most importantly, (4) they came in bondage (Billingsley, 1968).

The study of black family life has, historically, been problem-oriented. While the study of white families has been biased toward the middle-class family, the reverse has been true in the investigation of black family patterns. Until relatively recently, almost all studies of black family life have concentrated on the lower-income strata of the group, while ignoring middle-class families or even "stable" poor black families. Moreover, the deviation of black families from middle-class norms has led to the definition of them as "pathological." Such labels ignore the possibility that while a group's family form may not fit into the normative model, it may have its own functional organization that meets the needs of the group (Billingsley, 1970).

One purpose of this description of black family lifestyles is to demonstrate how it has changed in the decade of the 1970s. Additionally, the forces that black families encounter, which create the existence of large numbers of "problem" families, must be carefully examined. Out of this systematic analysis of black family adaptations may come a new understanding of the black family in contemporary American society.

HISTORICAL BACKGROUND

The Preslavery Period

There are several historical periods of interest in determining the evaluation of black family life in the United States. One era is the precolonial one of the African continent from which the black American population originated. The basis of African family life was the kinship group, which was bound together by blood ties and the common interest of corporate functions. Within each village, there were elaborate legal codes and court systems which regulated the marital and family behavior of individual members (Brown and Forde, 1967).

The Slave Family

In attempting to get an accurate description of the family life of slaves, one has to sift through a conflicting array of opinions on the subject. Certain aspects of the slave's family life are undisputed. Slaves were not allowed to enter into binding contractual relationships. Since marriage is basically a legal relationship that imposes obligations on both parties and exacts penalties for their violation, there was no legal basis to any marriage between two individuals in bondage. Slave marriages were regulated at the discretion of the slavemaster. As a result, some marriages were initiated by slaveowners and just as easily dissolved (Genovese, 1974).

Hence, there were numerous cases in which the slaveowner ordered slave women to marry men of his choosing after they reached the age of puberty. They preferred a marriage between slaves on the same plantation, since the primary reason for slave unions was the breeding of children who would become future slaves. Children born to a slave woman on a different plantation were looked upon by the slaveholder as wasting his man's seed. Yet many slaves who were allowed to get married preferred women from a neighboring plantation. This allowed them to avoid witnessing the many assaults on slave women that occurred. Sometimes the matter was resolved by the sale of one of the parties to the other owner (Blassingame, 1972).

Historians are divided on the question of how many slave families were involuntarily separated from each other by their owners. Despite the slaveholder's commitment to maintaining the slave families intact, the intervening events of a slaveholder's death, his bankruptcy, or lack of capital made the forceable sale of some slave's spouse or child inevitable. In instances where the slavemaster was indifferent to the fate of slave families, he would still keep them together simply to enforce plantation discipline. A married slave who was concerned about his wife and children, it was believed, was less inclined to rebel or escape than would a "single" slave. Whatever their reasoning, the few available records show that slaveowners did not separate a majority of the slave couples (Blassingame, 1972).

This does not mean that the slave family had a great deal of stability. While there are examples of some slave families living together for 40 years or more, the majority of slave unions were dissolved by personal choice, death, or the sale of one partner by the master. Although individual families may not have remained together for long periods of time, the institution of the family was an important asset in the perilous era of slavery. Despite the prevalent theories about the destruction of the family under slavery, it was one of the most important survival mechanisms for African people held in bondage (Blassingame, 1972; Fogel and Engerman, 1974).

In the slave quarters, black families did exist as functioning institutions and as models for others. The slave narratives provide us with some indication of the importance of family relations under slavery. It was in the family that the slave received affection, companionship, love and empathy with his sufferings under this peculiar institution. Through the family, he learned how to avoid punishment, to cooperate with his fellow slaves, and to retain some semblance of his self-esteem. The socialization of the slave child was another important function for the slave parents. They could cushion the shock of bondage for him, inculcate in him values different from those the masters attempted to teach him, and represent another frame of reference for his self-esteem besides the master (Abzug, 1971).

Much has been written about the elimination of the male's traditional functions under the slave system. It is true that he was often relegated to working in the fields and siring children rather than providing economic maintenance or physical protection for his family; but the father's role was not as insignificant as presumed. It was the male slave's inability to protect his wife from the physical and sexual abuse of the master that most pained him. As a matter of survival, few tried, as the consequences were often fatal. But, it is significant that tales of their intervention occur frequently in the slave narratives. There is one story of a slave who could no longer tolerate the humiliation of his wife's sexual abuse by the master right before his eyes. He choked him to death with the knowledge that it meant his death. He said he knew it was death, but it was death anyhow, so he just killed him (Abzug, 1971:29).

One aspect of black family life frequently ignored during the slave era is the free black family. This group, which numbered about half a million, was primarily composed of the descendants of the original black indentured servants and the mulatto offspring of slaveholders. For this minority of black families, the assimilation and acculturation process was relatively less difficult. They imitated the white world as closely as possible. Because they had opportunities for education, owning property, and skilled occupations, their family life was quite stable. Some of them even owned slaves, although the majority of black slaveholders were former slaves who had purchased their wives or children. It is among this group that the black middle-class was early formed (Frazier, 1932).

After Emancipation

There has been a prevailing notion that the experience of slavery weakened the value of marriage as an institution among Afro-Americans. Yet, the slaves married in record numbers when the right for a freedom to marry was created by governmental decree. A legal marriage was a status symbol, and weddings were events of great gaiety. In a careful examination of census data and marriage licenses for the period after 1860, Gutman (1976) found that the typical household everywhere was a simple nuclear family headed by an adult male. Further evidence that black people were successful in forming a bi-parental family structure are the data that show 90 percent of all black children were born in wedlock by the year 1917 (Bernard, 1966:3).

The strong family orientation of the recently emancipated slaves has been observed by many students of the reconstruction era. One newspaper reported a black group's petition to the state of North Carolina asking for the right "to work with the assurance of good faith and fair treatment, to educate their children, to sanctify the family relation, to reunite scattered families, and to provide for the orphan and infirm" (Abzug, 1971:34).

It was during the late 19th century that the strong role of women emerged. Males preferred their wives to remain at home, since a working woman was considered a mark of slavery. But, during a period described as the "the most explicitly racist era of American history" (Miller, 1966), black men found it very difficult to obtain jobs and, in some instances, found work only as strikebreakers. Thus, the official organ of the African Methodist Episcopal Church exhorted black families to teach their daughters not to avoid work, since many of them would marry men that would not make on the average more than 75 cents a day (Abzug, 1971:39). In 1900, approximately 41 percent of black women were in the labor force, compared to 16 percent of white women (Logan, 1965).

What was important, then, was not whether the husband or wife worked, but the family's will to survive in an era when blacks were systematically deprived of educational and work opportunities. Despite these obstacles, black families achieved a level of stability based on role integration. Males shared equally in the rearing of children; women participated in the defense of the family. As Nobles (1974) comments, a system where the family disintegrates due to the loss of one member would be in opposition to the traditional principles of unity, which defined the African family. These principles were to be tested during the period of the great black migration from the rural areas of the south to the cities of the north.

The rise of black illegitimacy and female-headed households are concomitants of 20th century urban ghettos. Drastic increases in these phenomena strongly indicate that the condition of many lower-class black families is a function of the economic contingencies of industrial America (Anderson, 1971:276). Unlike the European immigrants before them, blacks were disadvantaged by the hard reality of northern segregation along racial lines. Furthermore, families in cities are more vulnerable to disruptions due to the traumatizing experiences of urbanization, the reduction of family functions, and the loss of extended family supports.

In the transition from Africa to the American continent, there can be no doubt that African culture was not retained in any pure form. Blacks lacked the autonomy to maintain their cultural traditions under the severe pressures to take on American standards of behavior. Yet, there are surviving Africanisms that are reflected in black speech patterns, esthetics, folklore, and religion (Herskovits, 1958). They have preserved aspects of their old culture that have a direct relevance to their new lives. And, out of the common experiences they have shared has been forged a new culture which is uniquely Afro-American. The elements of that culture are still to be found in their family life.

THE MODERN BLACK FAMILY
Demographic Characteristics

The black population in the United States had a growth rate more than twice as large as that of the white population between 1970 and 1979. In the decade of the 1970s, there was a 6.3 percent population increase among whites, from

179 million to 190 million, whereas the black population went from 23 million to 26 million—a 14.4 percent increase. The median age of the black population (24.6 years) is younger than that of the white population (30.9 years) (U.S. Bureau of the Census, 1980b). A larger proportion of blacks continue to live in urban areas than do whites. In 1979, 90 percent of all black families lived in metropolitan areas and over 50 percent resided in central cities. Among middle-income blacks, a greater percentage moved to the suburbs in the last decade than did their white counterparts. Some discernible changes in black migration patterns emerged in the last decade. The proportion of black families in the northeast and north central region of the United States decreased while it increased in the west and south. This is the first time in several decades that the southern region experienced a net gain in black migration (U.S. Bureau of the Census, 1979b).

The majority of black families still adheres to the nuclear family model. In 1979, approximately 52 percent of black families had both the husband and wife present (U.S. Bureau of the Census, 1980a). A significantly larger percentage of black households were headed by a female than in white families. While white families had a woman head in 13 percent of all such families, 45 percent of black families were headed by a woman. Moreover, this was an increase of 82 percent from 1970 to 1978. This large number of female-headed households is mostly a result of socioeconomic forces. As the level of income rises, so does the number of male-headed families. At the upper-income level of $15,000 and over, the percentage of male-headed households is comparable to that for white families. Slightly less than 50 percent of all black children live in single-parent families. Black mother-only families have an average of 2.0 children as compared to 1.4 children for husband–wife families (U.S. Bureau of the Census, 1979a).

One of the most significant changes in the period 1970–1979 was the change in the black fertility rate. In 1978, the black birth rate continued to decline. However, the white birth rate declined even more rapidly (11 percent white versus 2 percent black), and the total fertility rate in 1979 of 21.5 children per 1000 black women is still higher than that (14.4 per 1000) of white women (U.S. Bureau of the Census, 1980b). The black fertility rate is influenced by a number of factors including regional variations, rural–urban differences, and, significantly, socioeconomic levels. In 1979, black women in the south had more children than those who lived in the north, and the birth rate of urban black women was lower than that of black women in rural areas. Significantly, college-educated blacks have the lowest fertility rate of almost every demographic category in the United States, whereas middle-class Catholics and Mormons have the highest. College-educated black women actually have a lower birth rate than college-educated white women (U.S. Bureau of the Census, 1979b).

One of the more significant events of the last decade was the steady increase in the out-of-wedlock births to black women, while the birth rate among married black women has shown a steady decline. The illegitimacy rate among whites went from 1.7 to 7.3 (per 1000 unmarried women, 15–44 years old) between 1950 and 1975, while the rate among blacks increased from 17.9 to 48.6 during the same time span (Bianchi and Farley, 1979). Some of this racial difference in the illegitimacy rate increase can be attributed to the more frequent and effective use of contraceptives and abortions among white women. The official data show that black women married before the child was born in only 32 percent of the cases, whereas 63 percent of white women married before the child was born (U.S. Bureau of the Census, 1976). Another reason has been the substantial decrease in legitimate fertility rates among married black women over the age of 24. Almost a third of all births to black women occur to those under the age of 19, the majority of them illegitimate. In 1978, 34 percent of black mother-only households were maintained by never-married women (U.S. Department of Health Education and Welfare, 1978). Based on past trends, the majority of unmarried mothers will eventually wed. At least in 1969, that occurred with 87.6 percent of white women and 76.6 percent of blacks who were single when their first child was born (U.S. Bureau of the Census, 1976).

As reported earlier, about 45 percent of black families are headed by women. About 52 percent of these families, in 1977, had incomes below the official "poverty" level. This is true, despite the fact that many of these women heads of black households work—most of them full time. When not employed, three out of four mother-only black families have incomes below the poverty level. Slightly less than 50 percent of them receive welfare assistance (National Urban League, 1980). These female-headed households include widowed and single women, women whose husbands are in the armed forces or otherwise away from home involuntarily, as well as those separated from their husbands through divorce or marital discord. The majority of them came about through separation or divorce, while 10 percent of them involve widows, and 34 percent were never married (U.S. Bureau of the Census, 1979b).

Employment, Income and Education

Over the past 40 years, the rate of unemployment among blacks has been steadily twice that of whites. In January 1980, black unemployment (11.8 percent) was higher than it was in 1969. Over all, 11.7 percent of blacks were officially unemployed in 1979, compared to 5.2 percent for whites (U.S. Department of Labor, 1980). The black unemployment rate increased considerably among married men who were the main breadwinners in their households between 1974 and 1976, increasing from 153,000 to 225,000, a rise of from 4.3 percent to 6.5 percent (National Urban League, 1978). There is some evidence that the unemployment of black men is a significant factor in their high rate of marital breakup. Moynihan (1965) found that blacks made up one-third of all unemployed males who were married but not living with their wives.

In a comparison of the median income of blacks with whites over the past decade, one notes a slow but steady widening of the income gap between the two races. Blacks earned only 57 percent of the income of whites in 1977, compared to 59 percent in 1976. This method of comparison is quite misleading because more black families (75 percent versus 67 percent for whites) derive their family income from sources other than the husband's income. The income gap between black and white families with the husband as sole breadwinner did not significantly close in the last decade. According to the U.S. Bureau of the Census (1979c), when both the young (under 35) black husband's and working wife's annual incomes were totaled, it achieved parity with that earned by a white working couple, in the north and west. Of course, those young, dual-career black couples comprised a small proportion (6 percent) of all black families in this country (U.S. Bureau of the Census, 1979b).

Education and occupation make little impact on this racial gap in income levels. In education, for example, the proportion of blacks graduating from high school and college increased slightly, but it had little effect on the income gap between them and their white counterparts. Indeed, the relative income gap between blacks and whites increases with education. College educated black men earn less vis-à-vis college educated white men than do black high school graduates. Black women college graduates earn less than white men with high school diplomas (National Urban League, 1978). Some years ago, Siegel (1965) estimated that the black elementary school graduate would earn 64 percent of his white peer's lifetime income, but the black college graduate's lifetime earnings would be only 50 percent of his white counterpart's lifetime income. Hence, highly educated blacks suffer the brunt of income discrimination more intensely than those with less education.

Education and gender have significant impact on the opportunities for marriage and risks of divorce. Failure to marry, among black men, tends to be linked to income and employment potential. Black men whose incomes are below the poverty level are the most likely to remain unmarried, while college-educated black males have the greatest chance of being married. As incomes rise, so does the number of black men who marry. The reluctance of lower-income black men to marry is understandable, given the fact that they have the highest rate of marital dissolution of all sex-race groups in the United States. However, black female college graduates are less likely to marry, or remarry if divorced, than their less-educated counterparts, both black and white (U.S. Bureau of the Census, 1977a). It seems that educational and occupational success adds to a man's desirability as a mate but detracts from a woman's. Conversely, the low-income black male has difficulty attracting a mate because of his poor employment and income potential.

Social Structure

It is generally acknowledged that the black kinship network is more extensive and cohesive than kinship bonds among the white population. The validity of this assumption is born out by the U.S. Census data (1979b) that show a larger proportion of black families taking relatives into their households. Billingsley (1968) divides these subfamilies into three general categories. They include (1) the "incipient-extended family," composed of a husband and wife who are childless and take in other relatives; (2) the "simple extended family," a married couple with children who have other relatives living with them; and (3) the "attentuated extended family," a household composed of a single, abandoned, legally separated, divorced, or widowed mother or father living with his or her own children, who takes into the home additional relatives. According to Hill (1972), these subfamilies constitute 6 percent of all black families. Approximately 75 percent of black subfamilies are headed by women with children under the age of 18. And, more than 75 percent of these female heads of households reside with one or both of their parents (or parents-in-law). Recent trends indicate that the woman with children is more likely to head her own family instead of living with relatives (Bianchi and Farley, 1979).

There is some disagreement on the reason for the stronger kinship bonds among black families. Adams (1970) has suggested that minority status tends to strengthen kin ties because of a need for mutual aid and survival in a hostile environment. Others have attributed it to the individual's general distrust of neighbors and neighborhoods, the prevalence of large female-headed households receiving public assistance, and the high rate of residential mobility, which makes long-term friendships difficult (Feagin, 1968; Stromberg, 1967). In opposition to the above theories is the argument by Matthews (1972) and Nobles (1974) that contemporary black kinship patterns are but a variant of the extended family system found in African societies.

Whatever the source of black kinship bonds, they provide a very valuable service to black families. A number of studies have revealed that kinsmen help each other with financial aid, child care, advice, and other forms of mutual aid (Aschenbrenner, 1975; Martin and Martin, 1978; Shimkin et al., 1978; Stack, 1974). Another important function of the kinship group is to enhance the emotional relationships within the kinship network and beyond.

Kinship groups perform this function by the high frequency of social interaction members have with each other. Hays and Mindel (1973) found black families interacted with more of their extended kin in almost every category of kinship than did white families.

With the possible exception of elderly parents, black families rely more heavily on extended kin than white families. The range of the kin network is extensive and includes parents, siblings, cousins, aunts, and uncles. A unique feature of the black kinship network is the inclusion of nonblood relatives who are referred to and regarded as kinsmen. Among lower-class black males, for instance, males who are unrelated to one another "go for" brothers and interact on that fraternal basis. Usually, this is a special friendship in which the normal claims, obligations, and loyalties of the kin relationship are operative (Liebow, 1966; Shimkin et al., 1978). These para-kinship ties seem to be a facilitating and validating agent of black life in the United States.

Although extended family living arrangements seem to be declining statistically among black Americans, this does not mean that the crucial functions of an extended family remain unfulfilled. When they do not live in the same household, or in close proximity, many blacks remain in close contact with extended family members. Through the use of the mail and telephone, they continue to exchange financial and emotional support. The percentage of black children in an extended family living arrangement increased from 22 to 33 percent between 1969 and 1974, primarily due to a deterioration of the economic situation among single-parent families (National Urban League, 1978). It is possible that children living in extended families have an advantage over those youngsters who are primarily confined to the nuclear family. In the nuclear family, a child must find love and support from two adults or none at all. The child within an extended family network has a much richer variety of roles from which to choose. Moreover, it appears that even middle-class blacks have retained this part of their roots. McAdoo (1975) found that they keep in close touch with their parents, siblings, and other kin—exchanging substantial kinds of services. Her conclusion was that these helping patterns were more common among middle-class blacks than among the families of Catholic and Jewish immigrants.

Within the black nuclear family, there is a fluid interchanging of roles. This role flexibility is assumed to have emerged out of the economic imperatives of black life. Although family theorists have stated that men carry out instrumental (i.e., economic support) functions in the family and women are assigned expressive (i.e., domestic and emotional) functions, Billingsley (1968) noted that these tasks were interchanged by black husbands and wives. It was not at all uncommon for the males to engage in expressive functions in regard to the maintenance of family solidarity and assistance in childrearing and

226

household tasks. The instrumental role of many black women is well known. A large number of working wives help to keep their families in the middle-class category—or at least out of poverty. Even the youths participate in family affairs by caring for younger siblings and occasionally working to supplement the family income (Jackson, 1972).

One finds no special status or authority associated with roles in the black family. Contrary to theories about the black matriarchy and the dominance of women, most research supports the fact that that an equalitarian pattern typifies most of these families (Mack, 1974; Scanzoni, 1975). In a succinct summary of authority patterns in the family, Hill states that: "The husbands in most Black families are actively involved in decision making and the performance of household tasks that are expected of them. And, most wives, while strong, are not dominant matriarchs, but share with their husbands the making of family decisions—even in the low-income Black families" (Hill, 1972:20).

Social Class and Lifestyle

When it comes to describing social classes and lifestyles among the black population, the task is made difficult for a number of reasons. Among them is the fact that social class is an analytical concept that is neither (1) universally accepted in the social sciences, (2) conceived in precisely the same way by all students of social stratification, nor (3) commonly designated by the same label (Hodges, 1964: 12–13). This difficulty is magnified when attempting to delineate the class structure. Among the difficulties encountered is the massive amount of mobility occurring in the class structure, with a fairly large number of upwardly mobile blacks. Another is the number of middle-class blacks who want to preserve their cultural traditions and thus adopt values and lifestyles that are commonly associated with the lower class (Kronus, 1971).

If income and educational levels are used, approximately 25 percent of black families would be in the middle-class category. The rest would fall in some level of the lower-class stratum, with only a negligible number in the upper-class group. In 1977, about 25 percent of black families had an income over $17,000. About 9 percent of black families had incomes greater than $25,000. Over 63 percent of blacks, 25 to 34 years old, had completed high school in 1975. About 21 percent of young blacks were enrolled in college in 1977. Most of these black members of the middle-class have only recently emerged from the lower-class group (National Urban League, 1978).

But, the concept of social class refers to more than a person's educational and income levels. It is measured just as well by cultural values and behavioral patterns, summed up as a class lifestyle. Bernard (1966) divides black families into two strands: the "acculturated" and "externally adapted." The former term describes those who have internalized western norms and, the latter, those who have adapted to these norms superficially. It is my belief that most middle-class blacks belong in the externally adapted group. Instead of internalizing white values, most new members of the black middle-class have adopted certain middle-class practices as a strategy for obtaining a decent life.

The paucity of research on middle-class black families does not provide many data for this assumption (Kronus, 1971). But, if one examines the dynamics of middle-class black behavior, a certain pattern emerges. For example, the sexual behavior of upwardly mobile females is more conservative because a premarital pregnancy can mean dropping out of school and ruining one's chances of gaining entrance into the middle class (Christensen and Johnson, 1978; Staples, 1978a). When the middle-class female becomes pregnant before marriage, she is more likely to get an abortion than her lower-class counterpart (Gebhard et al., 1958). Middle-class black families have a significantly lower family size than low-income black families, not because they place less value on children, but because they perceive a very direct link between low income and large families. These class differences in marital and familial behavior reflect pragmatic choices—not different values.

Courtship and Marriage

Studies on black dating and sexual patterns are few and unreliable (Allen, 1978). As with the research on other aspects of black family life, the focus has been on problems allegedly resulting from the "different" dating styles of Afro-Americans. Thus, one rarely finds a study of black sexuality that does not associate this aspect of black behavior with the problems of illegitimacy, female-headed households, and welfare dependency. The sexual relationship of blacks is rarely, if ever, investigated as an element of the normal functioning of the families. The intricate meaning and emotional dynamics of the sexual relationship are seldom captured in most black family studies (Johnson, 1977).

Heterosexual relationships develop at an early age in the communal setting of social relationships. Within the households there exists a variety of joyous adult activities in which children participate (Rainwater, 1970). This is a time of feasting, drinking, and dancing. Even very young children are often matched with members of the opposite sex at this time. Males and females learn to interact with one another on the romantic level, usually associated with the postadolescent stage for whites. Hence, one study of black students found that black males were more oriented toward love and romance than their white male counterparts (Larson et al., 1976).

Within the same-sex peer group, black males and females are socialized into their future pattern of sex-role interaction. Males learn the technique of "rapping," a linguistic pattern designed to convince the female that he is worthy of her interest, and as a verbal prelude to more intimate activity. The female acquires the ability to discriminate between men who are "with it," and how to unmask a weak rap. When the male petitions her for sex, she may accept if interested or if she has other motivation. Whether she agrees to participate in premarital sexual activity will not be based on the morality of such behavior, but on the practical consequences (pregnancy) which may ensue (Ladner, 1971).

This lack of moral emphasis on sexual behavior will be in opposition to the teachings of her parents. Most parents (usually the mother) urge their daughters to remain chaste until an adult—not necessarily until marriage. They are rarely told that premarital coitus is sinful, but that sexual relations before marriage can result in out-of-wedlock pregnancy. The black female's reference group, however, is her peers, and they are more supportive of the philosophy that losing one's virginity is a declaration of maturity—of womanhood. Those who refuse to indulge are often subordinating peer group approval to their desire for upward mobility. Yet, they do not condemn others who decide to participate in premarital sex, even when their decision is to refrain (Ladner, 1971; Rainwater, 1970).

It can be said that much dating behavior is ipso facto sexual behavior. In fact, among many black youth, there is no such thing as the dating pattern found among the white middle-class. Young people meet in their neighborhoods and schools and soon begin to go out with one another. However, Dickinson (1975) found that between 1964 and 1974, the dating behavior of blacks became more like that of whites while white dating behavior changed less in the same decade. Sexual involvement may begin shortly afterward (Rosenberg and Bensman, 1968). In one investigation of black females aged 15–19, it was reported that, by the age of 19, five out of six unmarried women had engaged in premarital intercourse. However, while the proportion of comparable white nonvirgins was lower (50 percent), it was the white group that had increased twice as much as the black group (Chilman, 1978).

While the black woman has an intrinsic appreciation for the sexual relationship, it is laden with an emotional meaning for her. Once sex has taken place, the intensity of the emotional relationship begins. As her association with her sexual partner becomes routinized, the emotional aspect is increased, and the male is ultimately expected to limit his close relationships with other women (Ladner, 1971). In one study, about 50 percent of the subjects said their relations had been confined to a single partner and half of the females had not engaged in sex within the four weeks prior to being interviewed (Chilman, 1978). Christensen and Johnson's (1978) comparison of black and white premarital sexual standards revealed that, although relatively permissive, blacks are not generally promiscuous: They tend to require affectionate relations as a basis for sexual behavior.

Most black women desire a stable, enduring relationship—ultimately marriage. This feeling is not always reciprocated by the males (Broderick, 1966). Many black men apparently evade the institution altogether, as a fairly large proportion of them never marry at all (U.S. Bureau of the Census, 1980a). Males, traditionally, have been less oriented toward marriage and the domestic responsibilities it entails. In the case of the black male, his reluctance to marry is reinforced by the unhappy marriages around him and the abundance of women available for companionship in his environment. For the female desirous of marriage, these facts of black life all work to her disadvantage.

When it comes to finding a compatible mate, she faces a number of obstacles. One of the biggest hurdles is the excess number of black women *vis-à-vis* black men. In the age group over 14, there are approximately a million more females than males listed by the U.S. Bureau of the Census (1979b). Although the number of males is really higher due to their underenumeration in the census, the number of black men available and acceptable to black women for marriage is actually fewer than the census figures would indicate. This low number of eligible males is due to their higher rate of mortality, incarceration, homosexuality, and intermarriage (Staples, 1978b; Stewart, and Scott, 1978). Once all these factors are considered, there may be as many as two million females without a male counterpart. This fact is particularly important when the reasons are sought for the large number of female-headed households in the black community. There is simply no way of establishing a monogamous, two-parent household for many black women within a racially endogamous marriage.

Still, most black women maintain an ideal concept of the man they would like to marry. These idealistic standards of mate selection, however, must often be subordinated to the realities they encounter. In the lower-class group, they frequently will settle for a man who will work when he is able to find employment; avoid excessive gambling, drinking and extramarital affairs; provide for the children; and treat her with respect. Even these simple desires cannot be met by lower-class husbands who are unable to find work and retreat into psychologically destructive behavior such as alcoholism, physical abuse of their wives, and so forth (Drake and Cayton, 1945; Rainwater, 1970; Staples, 1976a).

The middle-class black woman has no advantage over her lower-class counterpart when it comes to finding a mate. There is a ratio of two single women for every eligible man among black college graduates. And, the ratio will be lower in the future, based on the fact that, in 1979, there were a hundred thousand more black women enrolled in college (U.S. Bureau of the Census, 1979b). Among middle-class women, their requirements for a mate will include economic stability, status homogamy, emotional and sexual satisfaction, and male participation in childrearing. One aspect of traditional marriage expectations that is absent is the nonworking wife. In order to achieve income parity with white families (where the wife is increasingly likely to work), the middle-class black wife must be a joint earner. Most research indicates the black male accepts his wife's holding an outside job and is not particularly threatened by her employment (Scanzoni, 1975).

Marriage, however, has proven to be a fragile institution for blacks—even in the middle class. The divorce and separation rate for blacks as a group is double that of whites. While marriages are dissolving in record numbers for all racial groups, the rate of dissolution has been particularly high for blacks. In the last decade, the annual divorce rate has risen 82 percent. For white women between the ages of 27 and 32, the probability of their marriages ending in divorce is one in three. For comparable black women, the chances are one in two. In 1975, 30 percent of black women who had ever been married were separated or divorced, compared to 20 percent of similar white women (U.S. Bureau of the Census, 1977a).

The problems of being black in a racist society have their ramifications in the marriage arena. It seems quite evident that whatever difficulties lower-class black spouses have in their interpersonal relations are compounded by the problems of both poverty and racism. The middle-class black marriage is threatened less by poverty than by the shortage of black males, especially in the higher educational brackets. There are approximately 60 college-educated black males available for marriage to every 100 black female college graduates. Many black college women—especially those at black institutions—remain single (Bayer, 1972). Others may marry men with less education, and this type of hypogamous marriage has a greater statistical probability of ending in divorce. One result of the male shortage in the black middle class has been the tendency of women seeking educated, high status black professionals to pursue men who are married as fair game. This type of female competition becomes a direct assault on a man's marriage and increases the risk of divorce (Rosow and Rose, 1972; Staples, 1981). Such demographic pressures do not pose as great a threat to white marriages.

Another factor decreasing the available supply of educated black males is the tendency of males in the middle-class to date and marry white women, while white males are less involved with black women (Porterfield, 1977). In the period between 1970 and 1977, there has been a one-third increase in interracial marriage (U.S. Bureau of the Census, 1978). Public opinion polls support the notion that there is a growing tolerance of interracial marriage by both blacks and whites (Bontemps, 1975). The most common interracial marriages involve a black male and white female, and some studies document this via an examination of marriage records (Heer, 1974; U.S. Bureau of the Census, 1978). The Bureau of the Census in 1977 reported 125,000 known black–white marriages, and 75 percent consisted of a black man and white woman. This is double the number reported for that particular duo in 1970, but they still account for less than five percent of all married black men. Some concern has been evidenced over the fact that a disporportionate number of black men in interracial marriages are members of the middle-class and the dissolution rate for such unions is higher than for intraracial marriages (Heer, 1974).

Whereas certain problems exist in black marriages, high separation and divorce rates are not necessarily a valid measure of the stability and functionality of black families. What is important is whether they meet their functional obligations. There are many female-headed households, for instance, that socialize their children into successful adult roles. The biggest problem they face is the economic and employment discrimination against women, which hinders their children (Peters and deFord, 1978). In this endeavor, they frequently have the support of a black male who may not be the legal husband–father. Schulz (1969) and Stack (1974) have reported that the lower-class black male contributes to the welfare of his woman more than is commonly acknowledged and plays an important role as a substitute father to her children.

Childhood and Childrearing

One of the most popular images of the black women is that of "Mammy," the devoted, affectionate nursemaid of white children who belonged to the slavemaster or employer. This motherly image of black women has some validity. Motherhood has historically been an important role for black women, even more meaningful than their role as wives (Bell, 1971). In the colonial period of Africa, missionaries often observed and reported the unusual devotion of the African mother to her child. The slave mother also developed a deep love for, and impenetrable bond to, her children (Ladner, 1972). It would appear that the bond between the black mother and her child is deeply rooted in the African heritage and philosophy that places a special value on children because they represent the continuity of life (Brown and Forde, 1967).

Many studies have conveyed a negative image of the black mother because she does not conform to middle-class modes of childrearing. Yet, black mothers have fulfilled the function of socializing their children into the multiple roles they must perform in this society. They prepare them to take on, not only the appropriate sex and age roles, but a racial role as well. Children must be socialized to deal with the cold reality of white racism that they may encounter. Black females are encouraged to be independent rather than passive individuals because many of them will carry family and economic responsibilities alone (Iscoe et al., 1964). Taking on adult responsibilities is something many black children learn early. They may be given the care of a younger sibling and some will have to find work while still in the adolescent stage. The strong character structure of black children was noted by child psychiatrist Robert Coles (1964) as he observed their comportment under the pressure of school integration in the south during a volatile era.

The black mother's childrearing techniques are geared to prepare her children for the kind of existence that is alien to middle-class white youngsters. Moreover, some white middle-class socialization patterns may not be that desirable for the psychological growth of the child. The casual upbringing of black children may produce a much healthier personality than the status anxieties associated with some rigid middle-class childrearing practices (Green, 1946). Using threats of the withdrawal of love if the child fails to measure up to the parent's standards is much more common among white parents than black parents of any class stratum. One result of the black child's anxiety-free upbringing is a strong closeness to his parents (Nolle, 1972; Scanzoni, 1971).

While black parents are more likely to use physical rather than verbal punishment to enforce child discipline than white parents, this technique is often buttressed by the love they express for their children. Moreover, as Billingsley (1969:567) has noted, "Even among the lowest social classes in the black community, families give the children better care than is generally recognized, and often the care is better than that given by white families in similar social circumstances." One indication of the decline in this attitude is found in the statistics which show that child abuse has become more common in black families than in white families (Gil, 1971). Some of the racial differences can be attributed to reporting bias but much of it may reflect the effect of poverty and racism on black parent–child relationships (Staples, 1976a).

The most undesirable aspect of the black child's life is reputed to be the absence of a positive male figure (Moynihan, 1965; Rainwater, 1966). A plethora of studies have found that the black child has a low self-esteem because of both his blackness and the fact that often he grows up in homes without a male model. A number of studies have emerged that are in opposition to the theories of low self-esteem among blacks. In reviewing the literature on black self-esteem this author has found that much of it is invalid. Others have concluded that blacks are less likely to suffer from low self-esteem because of countervailing influences such as religion, reference groups, group identification, and positive experiences in the extended family (Staples, 1976b: 82–84).

Problems in black child development are alleged to be a function of the father's absence or ineffectiveness. There has yet to be found a direct relationship between father absence and child maladaption. And, a few studies (Hare, 1975; Nobles, 1973; Rubin, 1974) have concluded that the fatherless child does not noticeably suffer from the absence of the male parent. In part, the black child continues to have male role models among the male kinsmen in his extended family network, and as Stack (1974) points out, the mother generally regards her children's father as a friend of the family whom she can recruit for help rather than as a father failing his parental duties. However, we must be careful not to overly romanticize the single-parent family as a totally functional model. They are the poorest families in the United States and are overrepresented among the society's failures in education, crime, and mental health.

The ineffective black father has been assumed to be pervasive among black families. Much of the more recent literature suggests that black fathers have warm, nurturant relationships with their children and play a vital role in their children's psychological and social development (Lewis, 1975; Scanzoni, 1971). How well they carry out the paternal role may be contingent on the economic resources available to them. Hence, we find better patterns of parenting among middle-class black fathers who have the economic and educational resources, and, consequently, participate more in child care, are more child-oriented, and view their role as different from the mother's (Cazanave, 1979a; Daneal, 1975). As far as the male child's sex-typed identity is concerned, Benjamin (1971) discovered that black male youth had a better conception of the male role when the father had one or more years of college education, indicating a strong relationship between the opportunity to play a role and the actual playing of that role.

The Aged

As a result of the declining fertility rate among blacks, the elderly represent a larger proportion of the total black population than in previous times. By 1979, blacks over the age of 65 comprised 8 percent of the black population in contrast to half the corresponding proportion in 1910. Increasingly, the black elderly population is disproportionately female. As a result of the growing gap in mortality rates between black men and women, widowhood occurs

234

at an earlier age for black than for white women. For example, during the years 1939–1941, there was only a difference of two years in the life expectancy rate of black men and women. As of 1979, that gap had widened to 12 years (U.S. Bureau of the Census, 1979b). Based on his calculations from 1975 fertility and mortality data, Sutton (1977) estimated that the chances of becoming a widow among ever-married black women prior to age 65 are nearly one in two. Those who become widows could expect to have a tenure of 9.0 years in that status before their 65th birthday. Their chances of remarriage are undermined by the extremely low sex ratio among blacks 65 years and over. For every 100 black females in that age category, there were only 72 males in 1976 (U.S. Bureau of the Census, 1977b).

Compounding the problems of early widowhood among the black elderly is the lingering problem of poverty. In 1977, about 36 percent of the black elderly were poor, compared to only 12 percent of elderly whites. Moreover, while the proportion of poor elderly decreased from 13 to 12 percent between 1975 and 1977, the number of poor black persons 65 years and over increased by 110,000 during the same period, maintaining the same percentage in poverty in 1975. One result of this overwhelming poverty is that a much larger percentage of elderly black wives continue to work after reaching the age of 65 than their white counterparts (U.S. Bureau of the Census, 1979b).

Despite their poverty, the extended kin network manages to buttress the problems attendant to aging among its elderly members. When Hutchinson (1974) compared black and white low-income elderly, his results indicated that blacks and whites were identical on their expectations for the future, feelings of loneliness, amount of worrying, perception of others, and general life satisfaction. Moreover, the black elderly were more likely to describe themselves as being happier. One of the reasons the black elderly do not experience serious adjustment problems with growing old is that they continue to play a vital role in the extended family. Very few, for instance, are taken into the households of younger relatives. Only 4 percent of black families have relatives 65 years and over living with them. Instead, young black children often are taken into the households of elderly relatives, usually a grandmother. This process of informal adoption is so common that half of all black families headed by elderly females have dependent children, not their own, living with them (Hill, 1977).

CHANGE AND ADAPTATION

One of the most fluid institutions in American life is the family. Probably in no other sphere of our society have such rapid and profound changes taken place. While the changes are most significant for white Americans, blacks, too, are influenced to some degree by the same forces. Among the most visible trends are the increase in sexual permissiveness, challenges to the traditional concept of woman's role, the increase in singlehood, more divorces, and reductions in the fertility rate. Although blacks are part and parcel of these dynamics, their different history and socioeconomic status indicates that they will be affected more by economic and sociocultural forces unique to them.

There is considerable disagreement over whether a revolution in sexual behavior has occurred. Some argue that only the public acknowledgment of past sexual behavior has transpired, which gives the appearance of actual changes in what people are doing sexually. Yet, it is impossible to refute the fact that the openness of sexual permissiveness reflects a revolution in attitudes. The most significant change is in the sexual liberation of white women. There are many indications that the double standard of sexual conduct is disappearing or being modified. This change in male attitudes about female sexuality has little effect on lower-class black female sexuality, since they have rarely been subjected to the same sexual restrictions as white women.

Previously, the sexual liberation of black women had been the source of white American stereotypes of Afro-Americans as morally loose. In reality, black women escaped the fate of many white women who were condemned to premarital chastity and marital frigidity. The healthy attitudes blacks have toward sex have aided them in avoiding some of the "deviant" sexual actions more common to whites. One finds a much lower incidence of mate swapping, sex crimes, transvestism, pornography, and incest in the black population. However, blacks have shared in the general sexual freedom of whites, especially the black middle class. There is more of an acceptance of sexual cohabitation, different forms of sexual expression, out-of-wedlock births, etc., among the black middle class today (Cazanave, 1979b; Staples, 1981).

Much of the sexual revolution is caused by challenges to the traditional concept of woman's role in society. White women are demanding equality in employment opportunities, legal rights, shared responsibility for raising children, and to be freed of the liabilities only women face in the United States. Few black women are involved in the women's liberation movement because many of its demands seem irrelevant to their needs. They, particularly, cannot relate to the desires of white women to enter the labor force, to cease being viewed as sex objects, to be freed from child care responsibilities, or their view of marriage as an oppressive institution.

These demands of white women do not relate to the reality of black women. They have always been in the labor force, whether they wanted to or not. Black women have not been depicted as sex objects as much as they have been *used* as sex objects. Motherhood and marriage were two institutions that were denied to them in the past. Because they had to work, many were deprived of the time to enjoy their children. Marriage was a luxury many could not afford or the conditions of their lives would not provide. To the many black women who are heading households, a husband would be a welcome figure.

But, many of the methods and goals of the women's liberation movement are of importance to black women. As a result of women declaring their independence from the domination of men, there will be a greater acceptance of women heading families by themselves. Only then will society make provisions for eliminating some of the problems incurred by female-headed households (e.g., increasing the availability of child care facilities). The demand for equal employment opportunities for women and income parity for women in the same jobs as men is very important to black women. It is black women who are the most vicitimized by employment and income discrimination against women. They are most likely to be heads of households who will earn the low salaries paid women on the assumption that they do not have families to support.

The shortage of black males available for marriage may force black women to rethink the idea of a monogamous marriage that will last forever. There are simply not enough black males around to permit fulfillment of this desire. Perhaps some convergence of white and black marital patterns is possible. White women, too, face a shortage of five million males due to the higher infant mortality rate for males and earlier death rates in general. It appears that many white females have abandoned heterosexual relationships for the homosexual world. Black women, in the main, remain more committed to an exclusive male–female dyad. However, the continued shortage of black males could bring about a willingness to consider more radical lifestyles than heretofore (Smith, 1978).

Based on present trends, it appears that a dichotomy is emerging among blacks, largely determined by class and gender. College-educated black males will continue to have a high rate of marriage and those unions will probably be more egalitarian than in the past. While middle-class black women have not affiliated organizationally with mainstream feminist groups, the equalitarian ideology has had an impact. Moreover, it is quite possible that college-educated black women will reach economic parity with their black male cohort by the year 1985. Their income is increasing at twice the rate of similar black males and had reached 90 percent of this income in 1978 (U.S. Bureau of the Census, 1979b). One mitigating factor in the black woman's push toward sex-role equality is the limited pool of males eligible for marriage in her class level. Middle-class black males may opt for a mate who does not demand total equality, when they are in a position to pick and choose. Whatever the character of their marriage, the excess number of black female col-

237

lege graduates presages that large numbers of them will remain without a spouse (Staples, 1981).

However, lower-class families have been attenuated by the pervasive economic forces that plague them. Almost a third of black children are born to women under the age of 19—most of them out of wedlock. More than half the black children born in the United States are born out of wedlock and a minority of black children live with two parents. Those lower-income blacks who do marry have one of the highest rates of marital dissolution in the country. Many of the men cannot afford to marry or find a woman who will take a chance on marrying them. Fortunately, lower-income blacks have other structures to buttress the effects of those changes in family patterns. Boyfriends, and often the biological father, play very supportive roles in the financial and emotional support of mother and child. The process of informal adoption means that most black children will be placed in homes where they receive affection and the appropriate socialization. While the structure may be different, the functions of the nuclear family are still carried out.

Internal Adaptations

The changes in the interior of the black family, while ideologically in the direction of nativism, are statistically in the direction of assimilation and acculturation. Examples of this phenomena are seen in the diffusion of blacks into predominately white suburbs, the increase in interracial dating and marriage, higher incidences of suicide and mental illness, and a decline in the extended family pattern. But, these patterns reflect the variation in the black community. What is surprising is that, given the pace of racial integration in American society, more blacks have not become assimilated into the majority population's mode of behavior. The integration of the school systems, desegregation of suburbia, and greater access to knowledge of majority cultural norms through the mass media have provided, without precedent, opportunities for black acculturation.

Instead, we find blacks in separate facilities and organizations on white university campuses. Those blacks who moved to the suburbs continue their social lives in the inner cities. While the extended family may not exist together in the same household, its functions of providing emotional solidarity and other kinds of assistance are still carried out.

Moreover, the concept of the extended family is broadened to include all members of the black community. These are among some of the internal adaptations made by the black community to prevent the trend of racial integration from diluting their cultural unity.

Another most important adaptation under consideration is the adoption of polygyny as the black marriage system. The assumption here is that there are not enough black males to go around and that the sharing of husbands could stabilize black marriages and provide certain legal benefits to women now deprived of them. At least one study has confirmed the existence of informal polygyny among blacks in the United States (Scott, 1979). The actual number of black polygamous marriages is negligible. Such marriages are illegal in this country, and, thus, no legal benefits can accrue to the second wife. Moreover, in African society, the practice of polygamy is closely related to the economic system, and people are socialized to accept it.

Problems and Prospects

The problems black people face are essentially the same as in the past century. Those problems are not related to family stability, but the socioeconomic conditions that tear families asunder. In general, the problems are poverty and racism. While the past decade had produced a decline in racial segreagation and white stereotypes of black inferiority, blacks are still singled out for discriminatory treatment in every sphere of American life. Moreover, any national effort to further remedy these racist practices has a low priority among white Americans.

A low socioeconomic status continues to plague many black families. Whereas some blacks have achieved a higher standard of living as a result of the civil rights movement, large numbers of blacks continue to live below the poverty level. A disproportionate number of these blacks will be female heads of families. They will have more responsibilities and less income than any other group in American society. Yet, no effective programs are being proposed to meet the needs of one-half of all black families. Obviously, there is a need for a public policy and program to meet the needs of women who cannot find employment. Even if they could find jobs, the child care facilities in the black community are few and inadequate. The persistence of employment and salary discrimination against women will continue to handicap black women in their struggle to maintain a decent life for their families.

However, poverty is not the only reason for the high breakup rate of black marriages. The increase in the black divorce rate in recent years is due to sociopsychological factors as well. A primary cause is the economic independence of black women. Marital stability among whites in the past was based on the subordinate status of women. Once white women were emancipated from the economic domination of men, their divorce rate increased radically. Black women have been independent—economically and psychologically— for a much longer period of time. Equality of sex roles in the family may be desirable for women, but when men are socialized to expect unchallenged leadership in family affairs, conflict is an inevitable result.

The increased rate of interracial marriages will continue because more blacks and whites will meet as peers. Some black men will marry white women because the society's standards of beauty are still white. More black women will marry white men because they can provide them with a greater amount of economic security and because they have become disenchanted with black men. Whatever the reason, these marriages will face many obstacles. In an era of unabated white racism and a shortage of black males, many interracial couples will face resistance from both black and white communities. The normative problems of marital conflict will be compounded by external pressures as well.

It is difficult to project the future of black families because there are several parallel trends occurring at the same time. Many blacks are entering the middle-class as a result of higher education and increased opportunities. At the same time, the future is dim for those blacks in the underclass; the forces of automation and cybernation are rendering obsolete the labor of unskilled black men who are in danger of becoming a permanent army of the unemployed. The status of black women is in a state of flux. Some welcome the liberation forthcoming from male control, while others urge a regeneration of black male leadership. Easier and cheaper access to contraceptives and abortions may mean a continued decline in the black fertility rate. Whatever the future of black families, it is time to give recognition to the crucial role of this institution in the black struggle for survival.

REFERENCES

Abzug, Robert H. 1971. "*The Black Family During Reconstruction,*" in *Key Issues in the Afro-American Experience* (Nathan Huggins et al., eds.). New York: Harcourt, Brace and Jovanovich, pp. 26–39.

Adams, Bert N. 1970. "Isolation, Function and Beyond: American Kinship in the 1960's," *Journal of Marriage and the Family,* 32 (November): 575–598.

Allen, Walter. 1978. "Black Family Research in the United States: A Review Assessment and Extension," *Journal of Comparative Family Studies,* 9 (Summer): 167–189.

Amos, Wilson. 1978. *Developmental Psychology of the Black Child.* New York: Africana Publ.

Anderson, Charles H. 1971. *Towards a New Sociology.* Homewood, IL: The Dorsey Press.

Aschenbrenner, Joyce. 1975. *Lifelines: Black Families in Chicago.* New York: Holt, Rinehart and Winston.

Bayer, Alan E. 1972. "College Impact on Marriage," *Journal of Marriage and the Family,* 34 (November): 600–610.

Bell, Robert. 1971. "The Relative Importance of Mother and Wife Roles Among Lower-Class Women," in R. Staples (ed), *The Black Family: Essays and Studies.* Belmont, CA: Wadsworth, pp. 248–256.

Benjamin, R. 1971. *Factors Related to Conceptions of the Black Male Familial Role by Black Male Youth.* Mississippi State University Sociological–Anthropological Press Series.

Bernard, Jessie. 1966. *Marriage and Family Among Negroes.* Englewood Cliffs, NJ: Prentice-Hall.

Bianchi, Suzanne, and Reynolds Farley. 1979. "Racial Differences in Family Living Arrangements and Economic Well Being: An Analysis of Recent Trends," *Journal of Marriage and the Family,* 41 (August): 537–552.

Billingsley, Andrew. 1968. *Black Families in White America.* Englewood Cliffs, NJ: Prentice-Hall.

———. 1969. "Family Functioning in the Low-Income Black Community," *Social Casework,* 50 (December): 563–572.

———. 1970. "Black Families and White Social Science," *Journal of Social Issues,* 26 (November): 127–142.

Blassingame, John. 1972. *The Slave Community.* New York: Oxford.

Bontemps, Alex. 1975. "National Poll Reveals Startling New Attitudes on Interracial Dating," *Ebony,* 30 (September): 144–151.

Broderick, Carlfred. 1966. "Social Heterosexual Development Among Urban Negroes and Whites," *Journal of Marriage and the Family,* 27 (May): 200–203.

Brown, A.R. Radcliffe, and Darryle Forde. 1967. *African Systems of Kinship and Marriage.* New York: Oxford University Press.

Brown, Prudence, et al. 1977. "Sex Role Attitudes and Psychological Outcomes for Black and White Women Experiencing Marital Dissolution," *Journal of Marriage and the Family,* 39 (August): 549–562.

Cazanave, Noel. 1979a. "Middle-Income Black Fathers: An Analysis of the Provider Role," *The Family Coordinator,* 28 (November).

———. 1979b. "Social Structure and Personal Choice in Intimacy, Marriage and Family Alternative Lifestyle Research," *Alternative Life Styles,* 2 (August): 331–358.

Chavis, William M., and Gladys Lyles. 1975. "Divorce Among Educated Black Women," *Journal of the National Medical Association,* 67 (March): 128–134.

Chilman, Catherine. 1978. *Adolescent Sexuality in a Changing American Society.* DHEW, Washington, DC: U.S. Government Printing Office.

Christensen, Harold T., and Leonor B. Johnson. 1978. "Premarital Coitus and the Southern Black: A Comparative View," *Journal of Marriage and the Family,* 40 (November): 721–732.

Clayton, Richard, R., and Harwin L. Voss. "Shacking Up: Cohabitation in the 1970's," *Journal of Marriage and the Family,* 39 (May 1977): 273–284.

Coles, Robert. 1964. "Children and Racial Demonstrations." *The American Scholar,* 34 (Winter): 78–92.

Daneal, Jealean Evelyn. 1975. "A Definition of Fatherhood as Expressed by Black Fathers." Unpublished Ph.D. Dissertation, University of Pittsburg.

Dickinson, George E. 1975. "Dating Behavior of Black and White Adolescents Before and After Desegregation," *Journal of Marriage and the Family,* 37 (August): 602–608.

Drake, St. Clair, and Horace Cayton. 1945. *Black Metropolis.* Chicago: University of Chicago Press.

Feagin, Joe R. 1968, "The Kinship Ties of Negro Urbanites," *Social Science Quarterly,* 49 (December).

Fogel, William, and Stanley Engerman. 1974. *Time on the Cross*. Boston: Little, Brown and Co.

Frazier, E. Franklin. 1932. *The Free Negro Family*. Nashville: Fisk University Press.

Gebhard, Paul, et al. 1958. *Pregnancy, Birth and Abortion*. New York: Harper.

Genovese, Eugene. 1974. *Roll, Jordan, Roll*. New York: Pantheon Books.

Gil, David. 1971. "Violence Against Children," *Journal of Marriage and the Family,* 33 (November): 637–648.

Green, Arnold. 1946. "The Middle-Class Male Child and Neurosis," *American Sociological Review,* 11 (February): 31–41.

Gutman, Herbert. 1976. *The Black Family in Slavery and Freedom 1750–1925*. New York: Pantheon Books.

Hare, Bruce R. 1975. "Relationship of Social Background to the Dimensions of Self-Concept," unpublished Ph.D. Dissertation, University of Chicago.

Hays, William, and Charles, Mindel. 1973. "Extended Kinship Relations in Black and White Families," *Journal of Marriage and Family,* 35 (February).

Heer, David. 1974. "The Prevalence of Black–White Marriage in the United States, 1960 and 1970," *Journal of Marriage and the Family,* 36 (May): 246–258.

Herskovitz, Melville. 1958. *The Myth of the Negro Past*. Boston: Beacon Press.

Hill, Robert. 1972. *The Strengths of Black Families*. New York: Emerson-Hall.

———. 1977. *Informal Adoption Among Black Families*. Washington, DC: National Urban League Research Department.

Hodges, Harold. 1964. *Social Stratification*. Cambridge: Schenkman.

Hutchinson, Iran. 1974. "Life Satisfaction of Lower Income Black and White Elderly," paper presented at the National Council on Family Relations Meeting, St. Louis, MO.

Iscoe, Ira, et al. 1964. "Age, Intelligence and Sex and Variables in the Conformity Behavior of Negro and White Children," *Child Development,* 35: 451–460.

Jackson, Jacquelyn. 1972. "Comparative Life Styles and Family and Friend Relationships Among Older Black Women," *The Family Coordinator,* 21 (October): 477–486.

Johnson, Leonor Boulin. 1977. "The Sexual Oppression of Blacks," in H. Gochros and J. Gochros, (eds.), *The Sexually Oppressed*. New York: Association Press: pp. 173–191.

Kronus, Sidney J. 1971. *The Black Middle Class*. Columbus, OH: Charles V. Merrill.

Ladner, Joyce. 1971. *Tomorrow's Tomorrow: The Black Woman*. Garden City, NY: Doubleday.

———. 1972. "The Legacy of Black Womanhood," *Tuesday Magazine* (April), pp. 4–5, 18–20.

Larson, David L., et al. 1976. "Social Factors in the Frequency of Romantic Involvement Among Adolescents," *Adolescence,* 11 (Spring): 7–12.

Lewis, Diane R. 1975. "The Black Family: Socialization and Sex Roles," *Phylon,* 36 (Fall): 221–237.

Liebow, Elliot. 1966. *Tally's Corner*. Boston: Little Brown and Co.

Logan, Rayford. 1965. *The Betrayal of the Negro*. New York: Collier.

Mack, Delores E. 1974. "The Power Relationship in Black Families and White Families," *Journal of Personality and Social Psychology,* 30 (September): 409–413.

Martin, Elmer P., and Joanne Martin. 1978. *The Black Extended Family*. Chicago: University of Chicago Press.

Matthews, Basil. 1972. "Black Perspective, Black Family and Black Community," paper delivered to the annual Philosophy Conference, Baltimore, MD (April).

McAdoo, Harriette. 1975. "The Extended Family," *The Journal of Afro-American Issues,* 3 (Summer/Fall): 291–296.

Miller, Elizabeth. 1966. *The Negro in America: A Bibliography.* Cambridge, MA: Harvard University Press.

Moynihan, Daniel Patrick. 1965. "Employment, Income, and the Ordeal of the Negro Family," *Daedalus,* 94 (Fall): 745–770.

National Urban League. 1978. *The State of Black America 1977.* New York: National Urban League.

———. 1980. *The State of Black America 1979.* New York: National Urban League.

Nobles, Wade, 1973. "Psychological Research and the Black Self-Concept: A Critical Review," *Journal of Social Issues.*

———. 1974. "African Root and American Fruit: The Black Family," *Journal of Social and Behavioral Sciences,* 20 (Spring): 52–64.

Nolle, David. 1972. "Changes in Black Sons and Daughters: A Panel Analysis of Black Adolescent's Orientation Toward Their Parents," *Journal of Marriage and the Family,* 34 (August): 443–447.

Peters, Marie, and Cecile de Ford. 1978. "The Solo Mother" in R. Staples (ed.), *The Black Family, Essays and Studies,* 2nd ed. Belmont, CA: Wadsworth. pp. 192–200.

Porterfield, Ernest 1977. *Black and White Mixed Marriages.* Chicago. Nelson-Hall.

Rainwater, Lee. 1966. "The Crucible of Identity: The Lower Class Negro Family," *Daedalus* 95 (Winter): 258–264.

———. 1970. *Behind Ghetto Walls: Negro Families in a Federal Slum.* Chicago: Aldine Pub.

Rosenberg, Bernard, and Joseph Bensman. 1968, " Sexual Patterns in Three Ethnic Subcultures of an American Under-class," *Annals of the American Academy of Political and Social Science* (March), pp. 61–75.

Rosow, Irving, and K. Daniel Rose. 1972. "Divorce Among Doctors," *Journal of Marriage and the Family,* 34 (November): 587–599.

Rubin, Roger H. 1974. "Adult Male Absence and the Self-Attitudes of Black Children," *Child Study Journal,* 4, 33–44.

Scanzoni, John. 1971. *The Black Family in Modern Society.* Boston: Allyn and Bacon.

———. 1975. "Sex Roles, Economic Factors and Marital Solidarity," *Journal of Marriage and the Family,* 37 (February): 130–144.

Schulz, David. 1969. "Variations in the Father Role in Complete Families of the Negro Lower-Class," *Social Science Quarterly,* 49 (December): 651–659.

Scott, Joseph W. 1979. "Polygamy: A Futuristic Family Arrangement for African-Americans," *Black Books Bulletin.*

Shimkin, Demitri, et al. (eds.). 1978. *The Extended Family in Black Societies.* The Hague: Mouton Publishers.

Siegel, Paul M. 1965. "On the Cost of Being Negro," *Sociological Inquiry,* 35: 52–55.

Smith, Marie. 1978. "Black Female's Perceptions on the Black Male Shortage," unpublished Masters Thesis, Howard University.

Stack, Carol. 1974. *All Our Kin.* New York: Harper & Row.

Staples, Robert. 1976a. "Race and Family Violence: The Internal Colonialism Perspective" in L. Gary (ed.), *Crime and the Black Community.* Washington, DC: Institute for Urban Affairs and Research, pp. 85–97.

———. 1976b. *Introduction to Black Sociology.* New York: McGraw-Hill.

————. 1978a. "Race, Liberalism, Conservatism, and Premarital Sexual Permissiveness: A Bi-racial Comparison," *Journal of Marriage and the Family*, 40 (November): 733–742.

————. 1978b. "Race and Masculinity: The Black Man's Dual Dilemma," *Journal of Social Issues*, 34 (Winter): 169–183.

————. 1978c. *The Black Family: Essays and Studies (Volume 2)*. Belmont, CA: Wadsworth.

————. 1979. "Beyond the Black Family: The Trend Toward Singlehood," *Western Journal of Black Studies*, 3 (Fall): 150–157.

————. 1981. *The World of Black Singles: Changing Patterns of Male/Female Relations*. Westport, CN: Greenwood Press.

Stewart, James B., and Joseph W. Scott. 1978. "The Institutional Decimation of Black American Males," *Western Journal of Black Studies*, 2 (Summer): 82–92.

Stromberg, Jerome. 1967. "Kinship and Friendship Among Lower-Class Negro Families," paper presented to the Society for the Study of Social Problems Annual Meeting, San Francisco, CA (June).

Sutton, Gordon F. 1977. "Measuring the Effects of Race Differentials in Morality upon Surviving Family Members," *Demography*, 14 (November): 419–429.

U.S. Bureau of the Census. 1976. *Premarital Fertility*. Series p-23, no. 63. Washington, DC: U.S. Government Printing Office.

————. 1977a. *Marriage, Divorce, Widowhood, and Remarriage by Family Characteristics, June 1975*. Series p-20, no. 312. Washington, DC: U.S. Government Printing Office.

————. 1977b. *Population Estimates and Projections*. Series p-25, no. 643. Washington, DC: U.S. Government Printing Office.

————. 1978. *Perspectives on American Husbands and Wives*. Series p-23, no. 77. Washington, DC: U.S. Government Printing Office.

————. 1979a. *Divorce, Child Custody and Child Support*. Series p-23, no. 84. Washington, DC: U.S. Government Printing Office.

————. 1979b. *The Social and Economic Status of the Black Population in the United States: An Historical View, 1970–1978*. Series p-23, no. 80. Washington, DC: U.S. Government Printing Office.

————. 1979c. *Money Income in 1977 of Families and Persons in the United States*. Series p-60, no. 118. Washington, DC: U.S. Government Printing Office.

————. 1980a. *Marital Status and Living Arrangements: March 1979*. Series p-20, no. 323. Washington, DC: U.S. Government.

————. 1980b. *Estimates of the Population of the United States by Age, Race, and Sex: 1976 to 1979*. Series p-25, no. 870. Washington, DC: U.S. Government Printing Office.

U.S. Department of Health, Education, and Welfare. 1978. "Advance Report, Final Natality Statistics, 1976," *Monthly Vital Statistics*, 26 (March 29).

U.S. Department of Labor. 1980. Bureau of Labor Statistics. *Employment and Earnings*, 26 (1) (January).

North American Indian Families

As Professor Price makes clear in this chapter on family lifestyles of North American Indians, the large-scale cultural diversity of American Indians prevents us from discussing a single American Indian type. However, the experience of the American Indian since the appearance of the European settlers, which includes the wholesale slaughter of Indians and their movement to reservations, has brought some similarities to their family lifestyles. The American Indians differ from most other ethnic groups by virtue of their precedence on this continent, their primarily rural residence on reservations, and the historically paternalistic attitude of the American government. The consequences of these factors have produced a group that has proved to be highly resistant to assimilation and incorporation into mainstream American society.

CHAPTER ELEVEN

BY

JOHN A. PRICE

HISTORICAL BACKGROUND

American Indians arrived in the New World in waves of migration from northeastern Asia over a period of some 30,000 years. By the time of Columbus, they had spread throughout North and South America and evolved cultures that ranged in complexity from such simple hunting bands as the Eskimo to such agricultural states as the Inca empire. At that time there were several hundred linguistically separate societies. In the area of the United States and Canada there were 161 distinct languages, and the majority of these languages are still spoken. The populations of the advanced agricultural areas of Central American and western South America were comparable to some European areas at the time, each being over several million in size. North of Mexico, however, the aboriginal population counted only about two million, with concentrations in the agricultural south, and along coasts, especially the Pacific Coast with its rich marine resources (Price, 1978, 1979).

The center of American Indian civilization in North America, and the historical source for many innovations and most cultivated plants, embraced southern Mexico and Central America. The areas of the United States and Canada were at the far periphery or frontier of this civilization. In the three milennia prior to the arrival of the Europeans, maize agriculture had slowly spread north from Mexico through southern and eastern America, and reached its ecological limit in southeastern Canada. North and west of the agricultural area, hundreds of diverse primitive bands, tribes and chiefdoms carried on their specific cultural adaptations to their ecological niches: gathering plants and shellfish, land-mammal hunting, fishing, or sea-mammal hunting. The famous horseback-riding and buffalo-hunting cultures of the Plains evolved only after the Europeans arrived and introduced the horse to the New World.

American Indians are racially as differentiated as the Europeans and far more diverse culturally and linguistically. In the United States and Canada there are nine major language groups: Eskimo-Aleut, Na-Dene, Siouan, Algonquian, Uto-Aztecan, Hokan, Penutian, Salish, and Wakashan.

In line with this cultural diversity in the New World, almost all of the world's major variants of marriage, incest prohibitions, postmarriage residence customs, and in-law relations were practiced by one native North American society or another. This wide variation represents great historical depth and diverse adaptations to natural and cultural environments. In comparison, the Europeans who came to North America had more uniform marriage and family practices deriving from a relatively shallow and common history of an agricultural and then an industrial adaptation in Europe.

North American Indian vs European Practices

Before going into this New World diversity, it is useful to make several broad comparisons between aboriginal North American Indian and European practices. Indian marriages were invariably public and customary, while European marriages could be private, even secret, and were legal and in the nature of a contract between individuals. Indian marriages were more in the nature of a contract between kin groups. Indian cultures tended to be far more tolerant, and variant forms of marriage were more acceptable. Thus, for example, monogamy, polygyny, and polyandry were all acceptable forms of marriage in most societies. Polyandry, or plural husbands, was a very rare practice, usually fraternal; it was brought on by special circumstances, such as the crippling of an older married brother with the subsequent additional marriage of the younger brother to the older brother's wife. This tolerance of diversity within Indian societies tended to be greater than in modern European and American societies, which have a rather limited set of familial rules emphasizing monogamous marriage, the neolocal independent nuclear family, postmarital residence, and bilateral rules of descent and inheritance.

Polygyny was "common" among Indians of the Great Plains and northwest coast, occurring in more than 20 percent of the marriages. Monogamy, however, was almost the exclusive form among certain agriculturalists, such as the Hopi, Iroquois, and Huron. Matrilocal postmarital residence and matrilineal descent were common among Indian agriculturalists in eastern and southwestern America, where women played a major role in food production. With the intensification of agriculture, such as in Mexico, men were the predominant food producers, and postmarital residence and rules of descent shifted to patrilocal and patrilineal, as in premodern Europe.

Puberty reckoning, particularly related to a girl's first menstruation, was universal among Indian societies and usually associated with some ceremony. At the time of initial menstruation, the girl was held to be in a potentially dangerous state of close contact with supernaturals and therefore had to behave properly. The girl's conduct at this time tended to predetermine her behavior for the rest of her life. Typically, she was secluded, fasted, learned the duties of a wife and mother from an older sponsor, worked for other women, and finally ended her taboo period by bathing and dressing in new clothing.

Premarital sexual relations were less of a problem to Indian societies than to those of Europe. The age of marriage tended to be young, usually between 15 and 20 years of age. Most Indian societies were also more permissive toward premarital relations except when it violated rules of incest, endogamy, or adultery. Premarital pregnancies were accepted, and the child was usually reared by the mother's kinfolk.

Such customs as bride price and bride service were common in the Great Plains and northwest coast. Interfamilial exchange marriage, when two families exchange daughters to marry sons in another family, existed in areas in which there were few marriage formalities, such as the Great Basin in Nevada, Utah, and Subarctic. In families without sons, adopting a son to marry a daughter to inherit the family property and carry on a line of descent existed in several patrilineal areas. First cross-cousin marriages were permitted or even preferred in some strongly lineal societies, where the father's brother's daughter or mother's sister's daughter was in a different descent line than the groom. This was common, for example, among such wealthy fishing matrilineal chiefdoms as the Tlingit, Tsimshian, and Haida of coastal British Columbia and the Alaskan panhandle.

The Development of Kinship Systems

Simple hunting and gathering, "band" level societies tend to have a small-scale, flexible, and bilateral kinship system, similar in many ways to the modern American system. Social flexibility itself is adaptive in both the simplest and the most complex societies. In simple societies household units can easily detach themselves from a social group with failing food resources and move to join a more prosperous group. In complex societies we must move away from our relatives for opportunities in education, jobs, housing, and so forth.

The U.S. and Canadian Indian societies ranged in evolutionary levels from bands (Arctic, Subarctic, Great Basin, and Plateau) to tribes (northeast, plains, southwest, and U.S. west coast) and finally to chiefdoms (southeast and Canadian west coast). Bands were extremely egalitarian, generally bilateral in kinship, had little plural marriage, and had small residential households. Tribes were moderately egalitarian, generally strongly lineal in kinship, had much more plural marriage than bands, and often had large residential structures with households grouped together in lineages (as in the northeast "longhouses" or southwest "pueblos"). Chiefdoms had class systems, often with slaves at the bottom of the class structure. They were lineal, polygynous, and had the largest and most elaborate houses. Multifamily houses existed in societies all along the Pacific coast from California through Alaska and in most of the eastern part of the United States.

Kinship terms are the terms of reference, rather than of address, that one uses for one's relatives. These terms form a system because of the association between terms and behaviors. These terms are related to a society's social rules pertaining to incest prohibitions, marriage eligibility and preferences, and so forth. The distinctions between several kinds of systems show up, for example, in the terms that Americans call aunts, uncles, and cousins. Technically speaking, the English term "cousin" is classified as "Eskimo" because it is bilateral, that is, it ignores the line of descent as well as the sex of the relative.

The Hopi have "Crow" cousin terms and "bifurcate merging" aunt terms. Crow cousin terms are found in strongly matrilineal systems where fine distinctions are made between members of one's matrilineage. The father's relatives are placed together in broad-lumping categories, even across generations. For example, a man would have one term that lumps together his father and his father's sister's son. In this kind of society the father is not a "relative", so that a boy's discipline is monitored by his mother's brother, who is a very close relative in the same lineage as the boy. The mother's brother is a pivotal relationship in other ways as well, because in these systems a man often marries his mother's brother's daughter (who of course is in a different lineage) and receives his inheritance from his mother's brother.

To "bifurcate" means to split apart the mother's and father's sides into separate lineages and to "merge" means to lump relatives of the same sex and generation together under the same term. Thus "bifurcate merging" aunt terms means that a person uses the same term for his mother and his mother's sister. Among the Hopi, the mother's sister is close and behaves somewhat the same toward the child as the biological mother, so they are merged together with the same word, but bifurcated away from the father's sister, who belongs to a different lineage and lives in a different place.

The Kwakiutl have "Hawaiian" cousin terms, which lump together people of the same generation, and "lineal" aunt terms like our American English that distinguishes between "mother" and "aunt." This implies that kinship terminology was not very important to the Kwakiutl, because few distinctions are made. Lineages and clans were important: kinship terminology was not. Of great importance to the Kwakiutl was the elaborate social ranking system.

TABLE 1
Three Kinship Systems

	ESKIMO (NUNAMIUT)	HOPI	KWAKIUTL
Evolutionary level	band	tribe	chiefdom
Culture area	Arctic	southwest	northwest coast
Language family	Eskimo-Aleut	Uto-Aztecan	Wakashan
Subsistence	hunting	horticulture	fishing
Settlement pattern	seminomadic	permanent	permanent
Settlement size	20–100	200–400	400–1000
Stratification	absent	absent	hereditary aristocracy
Slavery	absent	absent	common
Warfare	absent	rare	common
Kinship			
Premarital sex	permitted	permitted	prohibited
Marriage mode	groom may work for family	gifts to bride	gift exchange
Polygamy	rare	absent	common
Postmarital residence	variable	matrilocal	patrilocal
Descent	bilateral	matrilineal	patrilineal
Lineal groups	absent	clans	clans
Cousin terms	Eskimo	Crow	Hawaiian
Sex roles			
Hunting	men	men	men
Fishing	both	absent	both
Gathering	women	women	women
House building	both	both	men
Weaving	absent	men	women
Pottery	absent	women	absent

Thus a person would lump together various kinfolk in their terms of reference, but these same individuals were carefully distinguished in the degree of deference of speech and manners according to their rank. A chief's family lived in the high-status parts of the great house, along the rear wall. People of high rank directed most activities, dressed with ornaments and trim on even their working clothing that signaled their high status, and were trained as speech-makers, warriors, and dramatists in privileged secret societies.

Mode of subsistence and sex roles tend to pattern the form of postmarital residence and the child's environment of socialization. Thus, for example, if women stay together with their sisters in the area of their natal home so that they can farm together, then their husbands will come to live with them and their children will grow up in a community dominated by the mother's relatives. Such children then acquire a matrilineal orientation about their descent, lineage and clan, succession, and inheritance. In Table 1, the three case studies illustrate some of these developmental correlations.

The Impact of European Cultures

The horse was introduced into the Great Plains from Spanish settlements in New Mexico in the 17th and 18th centuries. Many tribes of Indians then migrated into the Great Plains to take up the highly productive hunting of buffalo. This ecological shift brought on an initial convergence of social structures. Highly integrated societies that had previously been horticultural "regressed" to more flexible hunting tribes and emphasized "generational" kinship, while previously very simple gathering societies tended to build up their structures with more decisive military and political organization. Finally, the Plains Indians, defeated by whites and with the demise of the buffalo herds, relocated on reservations and began to acculturate to European forms of social structure.

As an example of the impact of European culture, missionaries, teachers, and government agents to the Choctaw of Mississippi, concerned that Indian women worked in the fields (the usual practice in horticultural societies), failed to understand that the fathers' disinclination to provide materially for their own children was in accordance with the matrilineal system of inheritance (Eggan, 1966:29):

New regulations regarding land were introduced that emphasized the position of the man as head of the family. Marriage was regulated by law, widows were entitled to dower rights, and children could inherit the father's estate. The leaders no longer came from the clans but were elected by the adult male members of the district, and the old town rituals were largely replaced by the church and its activities.

250

These changes broke down the clan and kinship structures, emphasized nuclear families and territorial ties, and shifted kinship from a matrilineal system to a patrilineally biased bilateral system. Similar historic shifts occurred among other southeast societies, such as the Creek and Cherokee.

Indians were forcibly removed from most of American lands east of the Mississippi River except in isolated spots: Cherokees in the North Carolina mountains, the Seminoles of the Florida Everglades, some Iroquois in northern New York, and some Algonquins in the northern woods. Total removal occurred later and was not as complete west of the Mississippi River. As a result, this is where most of the Indians live today, particularly in Oklahoma, the Dakotas, Montana, New Mexico, Arizona, and along the west coast. The pattern of displacement was similar in Canada, but the European population was much smaller, so that the extent of displacement and deculturation was less. Also, in the long period of fur trapping and northern exploration there was more use and respect for native skills than in the United States. However, the Beothuk were extinguished by the French and Scotch fishermen of Newfoundland. Wars between Indians were actively promoted by competing French and British interests in the Canadian fur trade, and Indians were generally displaced and enclaved in "reserves" in the east-to-west sweep of European immigrant agriculturalists across Canada.

Differences between Europeans who arrived in the New World played an important role in determining the nature of Indian–European relations. For example, the French, Spanish, and Portuguese were more tolerant of intermarriage with the natives than were northern Europeans. Thus, since early historical times there have been significant populations of Spanish-Indian *mestizos* and French-Indian *métis,* but few British-Indian "half-breeds", considering the size of the British population in North America. A major reason for this seems to be that in the 16th and 17th centuries the French, Spanish, and Portuguese came largely as single men, while the British tended to come as families. It also appears that southern European discrimination has been largely based on differences of culture and social class, while northern European (Germanic and British) discrimination has been more racial.

Perhaps more important than the foregoing intimate relations are the differences among Europeans in their colonial designs on the land and the people of the New World. Spaniards colonized basically to exploit the New World for gold and exports—and to convert the natives to Christianity. French ends seem to have been similar except that the wealth was in the fur trade in their northern territory. Some northern Europeans engaged in this exploitation as well, but large numbers of northern Europeans came looking for land to settle on and to farm themselves. Northern Europeans tended to force the Indians off the farming lands, while the Spaniards kept the natives working on the land, but now under European feudal-style haciendas and encomiendas.

The kinds of Indian culture that the Europeans met were also crucial in determining the character of European–Indian relations. Simple band-organized societies were nonagricultural and without tribalwide political organization or leadership. Thus, the Europeans had no significant military resistance from band-organized peoples, but they were also incapable of using them as agricultural workers. True tribes and chiefdoms often gave military resistance but were still difficult to rule as an internal agricultural peasantry. Thus, there was often bitter warfare between them and the Europeans until the Indians were finally displaced from the land. Where the Europeans conquered Indians from native agricultural-state societies, however, they were far more successful at simply replacing the existing state leadership with Europeans and keeping the natives working the land as agricultural peasants. With this situation, there was then no need for reservations.

The natives' states existed in the areas of Spanish colonization, particularly in Mexico and Peru. The modern state cultures in these areas have, in turn, been more strongly influenced by the Indian component in their heritages. This is particularly true of Mexico, which looks back with pride to its Indian foundations and to the heroic resistance of the Aztec leaders to Cortez and the Spaniards. Montezuma and Cuhuatemoc are the national heros, not Cortez.

Europeans imposed their concepts of proper marriage and family relations on the Indians, particularly through the preaching of Christian missionaries and through laws that were applied to Indians. In countless ways Europeans impressed their particular social system on Indians. One example of European bias is that when the Spanish priests contacted the Pima of southern Arizona, they gave bead necklaces to women and tobacco to men, but both men and women wear necklaces and smoke tobacco among the Pima. In more destructive fashion, Christian missionaries usually tried to eliminate plural marriages and matrilineal customs without understanding the crucial roles these practices had in the normal functioning of native societies. In Canada the potlach ceremonies of the Pacific coast that were so crucial in validating titles and bringing order to the kinship systems were outlawed because of Protestant concerns about wasteful feasts.

In Canada there are 290,000 "registered" or "status" Indians and about an equal number of persons who are not "registered" but still identify themselves as Indians. The registered Indians belong to 570 "bands" and live primarily on 2301 separate "reserves". The nonregistered Indians have been historically excluded from government programs, band membership, and residence on reserves largely because of the biases against interracial marriage and against matrilineal systems in the Indian Act of Canada. Since the turn of this century Canadian law has generally accepted Indian custom marriages, but has never accepted Indian custom divorces or polygamy, although these practices are still followed (Corrigan, 1974).

The Indian Act of Canada was written by Euro-Canadians who applied the assumptions that household heads should be male and wives should be dependent on them, that inheritance should be patrilineal, and that families should be nuclear. This act has been destructive of the social structure of matrilineal and bilateral Indian societies and supportive of patrilineal Indian societies. "Indian status" is essential to inclusion in rights to Indian band lands and to programs of the Indian Affairs Branch, but an Indian woman can lose this status if her husband loses his status, or if she ever marries a person without Indian status. Thus, for example, 585 Indian women lost their Indian status in 1974 through their marriages (D.I.A.N.D., 1975). That was 29 percent of the marriages of status Indians that year, one indication of the extent of interracial marriages. A man with Indian status does not lose his status if he marries a nonstatus woman; instead, his wife acquires Indian status even if she is Euro-Canadian. If a status woman marries a nonstatus person, thus losing her status, and later divorces that person, she still cannot reacquire status except by marrying a status Indian. The law supports patrilocal postmarital residence because at marriage a woman becomes a member of her husband's band. In spite of these inequalities, some Canadian Indians have been in favor of retaining the act as it is. They are critical of any changes in the act that would allow more whites (husbands in this case) to move onto the reserves. In a similar way in the United States, Jones (1974: 27) reports that Bureau of Indian Affairs welfare aid was refused in Anchorage to Indian women who had married whites, even though they were separated.

Cruikshank's (1971) study of the Indians of the Yukon Territory indicated the development of a frequent pattern of matrifocal families as a result of cultural disruption. Because native men have been economically displaced by the Euro-Canadian society, and the traditional (sexual) division of labor has broken down, women and their children may now be economically better off without a permanent male spouse. For example, Indian women's work in the Yukon, such as domestic service and waitressing, tends to be steady, whereas the men work in seasonal jobs. Indian women can easily relate socially and sexually with the Euro-Canadian men who come in the summer, and tend to be treated better by them than by Indian men. There are factors, however, that discourage Indian marriage to Euro-Canadians, such as the transient nature of Euro-Canadians' visits to the north and Canada's policy of taking official "Indian status" away from Indian women who marry non-Indians. Stanbury and Siegel (1975) reported a high, increasing level of common law marriages and matricentered families among Indians in British Columbia: 40 percent of all "single" Indian women in 1971 had one or more children, 57 percent of status and 38 percent of non-status Indian births in 1972 were "illegitimate."

Acculturation and the Formation of an Ethnic Group

Several acculturation hypotheses have been employed to analyze historical Indian culture continuity and change. Isolation on reservations is seen as a factor supporting their cultural continuity. Some cases of forced acculturation may have led to resistance toward change and the development of effective institutions that have helped to preserve cultural continuity—such as techniques to ward off religious and government agents of social change. This seems to have occurred especially when the native community has had a strongly bonded "corporate" structure, such as among the Hopi. Also, racist attitudes by Europeans concerning Indians set up a barrier against Indian assimilation, even to the extent of making Indian–European marriages illegal in the early legislation of several western states.

Another hypothesis holds that material aspects have changed more readily than social and ideological aspects, so that Indians are still able to revitalize some social and ideological dimensions of their cultures. The individual wage employment and entrepreneurship of industrial society tend to disrupt the cooperative, communalistic, pooling kind of economic arrangements that are an integral part of tribal kinship economics. In fact, these mutual ties of rights and obligations are seen as deterrents to economic advancement in an industrial society; kinfolk claims reduce the individual incentives that bring healthy competition into a capitalist society.

The modern law of state societies is universalistic. It applies to every sociocultural unit within the geographical jurisdictions of the law and thus reduces their diversity to common practices. Not only is the society-by-society diversity that existed among the hundreds of Indian societies reduced to conform with national and state laws, but the tolerant diversity that existed within single Indian societies must conform as well. Polygyny, for example, was almost universally allowed by Indian societies and is eliminated through the law. Indian children by law must attend school, so traditional education is undermined. Marriages must now be legally registered. Marital differences that were once handled by kinship councils can now come before the courts. However, it is very hard for even the postindustrial state society to control the nonempirical or ideological world of its internal subcultures, and it has no reason to control the ineffectual facades of cultural difference. Thus, we are allowed the myth of a legitimately plural society. The customs that survive are those innocuous ones that escape the conforming crush of law, such as religious practices, music, and tastes in food. These, then, become the hallmarks of ethnic difference—the stereotypes, remnants of once truly different cultures.

The basic pattern of cultural retention is that as separate sociocultural entities are integrated into expanding nation states, they are converted into ethnic subcultures. Assuming some continuity rather than outright destruction, the first significant changes tend to be material, economic, and some legal elements of integration with the dominant society. Internal adjustments, as well as direct pressures by missionaries and government agents, then tend to produce a variety of social and political changes. Finally, there is typically not only a survival but a creative readjustment of ideology, identity, religion, and other materially unimportant symbols of ethnic uniqueness: tastes in food, ethnic costumes, music, dance, art, etc. Language acculturation takes place over the whole period of acculturation, usually with the forms of bilingualism during the phase of significant social and political changes, and is complete when all that is left of the original language for most people are the ethnic words and phrases that have been incorporated into the dominant language as used by speakers of that ethnic group.

Societies that are native to a country have many differences with those that are migrants to the country. Thus, Indians identify with no other land, while all other immigrant groups have other geographical identities. Indians live more widely scattered across North America than any other sizable ethnic population. Along with their identification with the land, scattered distribution, and predominantly rural residence, Indians are probably more opposed to assimilation and integration into majority society and culture than any sizable ethnic population.

MODERN INDIAN FAMILIES: FOUR CASE STUDIES

Cultural continuity in the family lifestyles of Indians has been greater where European influences come later, as in the tropics and the Arctic, or less destructive, as in Mexico and Peru. Certain reservation enclaves have also provided sufficient isolation from European influences to adapt family structures gradually and with continuing social integration. Sketched below are four brief case studies from the United States to illustrate the changes occurring in modern Indian families in different settings of contact and ecology: (1) Eskimo of North Alaska, (2) Hopi of northern Arizona, (3) Menomini of Wisconsin, and (4) Indians of Los Angeles. The four case studies are presented in an order based on the extent of change from aboriginal family lifestyles, beginning with the more conservative Eskimo and ending with the largest urban settlement in North America of people who identify themselves as Indians.

It is only in reference to the more acculturated Indians, such as the Menomini and urban Indians, that we can accurately speak of an active membership in an *"American Indian* ethnic group" that would be comparable to the European ethnic minorities in North America. That is, the Eskimo and Hopi tend to be still so involved with their own cultures that they do not actively participate in a self-conscious, integrated, Indian ethnic minority even though they may be racially and culturally defined as members by the majority society. In fact, specific tribal identities are almost universally stronger and more important than identity as a Native American.

The Eskimo of North Alaska

There are dozens of different Eskimo cultures from across the varied ecological niches of their homelands in Siberia, Alaska, Canada, and Greenland. There are only two Eskimo languages, Yuit in southern Alaska and Inuit everywhere else. This case study is just about the several cultures of north Alaskan Inuit.

The traditional life cycle of the Alaskan Inuit began with an isolated and ignored birth, away from the family residence (Oswalt, 1967). The mother was prohibited from eating fresh foods and she used her own containers, to prevent ritually defiling those of the rest of the family. After the birth, she purified herself by bathing and putting on new clothes before she returned to her household. There was no community-wide recognition of the birth, leaving to her the choice of whether the infant was to live or die. Infanticide was common, usually by exposure to a freezing temperature, particularly of girl babies, and justified on the grounds that the infant was malformed or simply that the parents could not support another child.

It was common for the child to nurse for as long as three years and infancy was highly indulgent. Children were given toys, such as balls and dolls made from caribou skin, miniature kayaks, and spinning tops of wood. Girls were usually given decorative facial tattoos around the time of puberty, often a series of lines from the lower lip to the chin. The girl's first menstruation was marked by isolation, restrictions on her behavior, and food taboos. After this, the girl could marry. When a boy killed his first animal he was honored by a small feast and a distribution of gifts.

Sexual intercourse between unmarried people was accepted as normal and even adultery was tolerated much more than it is in American society. Homosexuality was unknown. Marriage often grew out of teenage love affairs, but the parents pressured the girl to select a good hunter. There was little in the way of marriage rituals, other than an exchange of gifts, and divorces occurred with little social disruption.

Hunters told each other the stories of their successes and failures in their hunts: the shifting weather conditions, tracking the movements of land animals, the long waits to spear seals at their breathing holes in the sea ice. Women excelled as seamstresses, making the warmest clothing in the world and sewing watertight skin covers for the men's kayaks. In mid-winter there was often a festival with singing, dancing, sports competitions, shamanistic demonstrations, and puppetry.

Even if we ignore the high infant mortality, the average life span of traditional Native Americans was usually less than 40 years, and accidental death was particularly frequent among hunters such as the Eskimo. Thus people were considered quite old when they were in their 40s. The older people helped with crafts and tended their grandchildren. When they died the funeral ceremony was just a family affair, as in birth and puberty, so the whole community was not involved. The body was removed through the house skylight, rather than the door, and placed with a few purposely broken burial goods as sacrificial offerings in a shallow rock-covered grave.

Traditionally Eskimo infants had intense, continuous, and warm maternal care. The infants were carried in a parka hood on the mother's back with skin-to-skin contact much of the time. They were breast fed as often as they wished. A crying or fussy infant was disciplined in nonverbal ways, such as the mother stiffening her body, which presented the child lying on the mother's back with some feeling of separation from the mother. This kind of extreme nurturance generated a strong sense of security in the child. With this kind of socialization the Eskimo developed an egocentric but optimistic personality that needs others, expresses friendliness with everyone, and is ambivalent about violence (Hippler, 1974).

People actively avoided verbal or emotional expressions of anger and aggression, but aboriginally the society had a very high murder rate. Later, under the colonial administration with communal village councils from 1920 to 1950 there was a near absence of mortal violence. Since 1950, under a neocolonial system, with state troopers and a magistrate rather than the councils, accessibility to alcohol, and unemployment, the rate of interpersonal violence has returned to the high level found at the earliest contact times. Eskimos have now been relocated into large communities where they can receive the modern services of medicine, education, retailing, policing, and courts.

Chance's (1966) study of the modern Eskimo of north Alaska showed that large families are welcomed, that children enjoy much love and affection, and that adoption between kin is easy and widespread. Children are often named after a deceased person, and some of the qualities or even the spirit of the original person continues in the namesake. Children are packed or carried in the back of a parka a great deal until about two years old. Weaning may not be completed until the third year, while toilet training begins before the first birthday. There is generally no shame or secrecy about excretory functions.

Childhood training emphasizes egalitarian social cooperation and skills of survival. Boys may begin to shoot a rifle as young as seven years, and girls begin to learn the techniques of butchering at a very young age. The sexual division of labor, however, is not extremely rigid. For example, boys may occasionally cook and girls may go fishing or bird hunting. Storytelling, wrestling, and hand games now combine with such western games as volleyball, Monopoly, and Scrabble. Children from six to 16 are required to attend the local Bureau of Indian Affairs School, in which use of the native language is now allowed. Eskimo adolescents become more peer-centered in social groups and in many ways emulate Euro-American teenagers in dress (denims and black leather jackets), slang ("Man, I don't go for parkas"), music, and dance steps.

Whale, seal, and caribou are still the main sources of food. They are now usually served on the western three-meals-a-day plan. Government control has removed the need for mutual protection of kin during feuds. Individual wage labor has decreased the economic interdependence that operated in the traditional bilaterally extended family. Sharing is now more common in such secondary economic activities as babysitting, butchering meat, and the distribution of household items. Young people today are freer from parental restrictions on selecting marriage partners, but the tradition of first-cousin marriage is still fairly common in some communities. Formal wife exchanges between friends is no longer practiced, but sexual mores are still relatively permissive. There is little display of emotions between husband and wife, although the mutual bond may in fact be close, affectionate, and satisfying. Hippler (1974) writes that in the traditional culture Eskimo men treated women cruelly and as inferiors, that their interest in women was more for sexual gratification than the development of intense interpersonal contacts with women. Couples rarely go visiting together or entertain friends together, and nonkin adult social gatherings are usually same sex only. However, very casual visiting between same-sex friends is a feature of daily family life. A friend may come in, watch the activities of the household for some time, and leave again without anything more being said between the host and visitor than a brief exchange of greetings.

Chance (1966: 85–87) wrote that in Kaktovik and other new small Eskimo villages relatively smooth adjustments to modern culture have occurred because of such things as (1) their intensive interaction and communication, (2) the kinship system remaining stable enough to support individuals in stressful

258

situations, (3) most of the newly defined goals, particularly for material goods, having been successfully realized, and (4) traditional leadership and pride having been maintained. Middle-aged and older women were the most alienated and isolated from the modernizing changes and had less contact with the American culture than their husbands, many of whom worked at a radar site, or their children, who went to the American schools. In larger communities, such as Barrow, there have been more problems related to the residential and social separation of Euro-Americans and Eskimos, that is, a marked lower status of and discrimination against Eskimos. In the south Alaskan city of Anchorage, "an Eskimo woman recounted the humiliating experience of walking down the street and having white men grab her buttocks and call her *klootch* (squaw woman) and salmon cruncher." (Jones, 1974:16).

The Hopi of Northern Arizona

Pueblo cultures have had fewer disruptions in their histories than most Indian cultures in the "lower 48" states of America. The western Pueblos (Hopi, Zuni, Acoma, and Laguna) tend to have matrilineal exogamous clans and extended matrilocal households, while the eastern Pueblos of the Rio Grande are primarily bilateral with moieties. The isolation of the Hopi has particularly shielded them from some of the pressures of change, although they have periodically faced extinction through drought, disease, and warfare. Each Hopi village tends to be endogamous and independent, except for intermarriage with nearby "colony villages." The history of the matrilineal clans in the village according to their order of arrival, occupation of the clan house, ceremonial possessions, and clan lands is important in determining village social relations.

Marriage is monogamous. Men join their wives' households and economically support them but retain ritual, leadership, and disciplinary roles in their natal households. Thus, they discipline their sister's children and play a passive role in their wife's household. The Hopi say that "The man's place is on the outside of the house." The tension in these contrasting roles contributes to a high divorce rate among the Hopi (Eggan, 1966:126). Another tension exists in the conflict between the basically theocratic organization of the Hopi and the modern demands for decisive political action that have been imposed on them. While community welfare is highly valued, there is competition between clans and villages in terms of such things as ceremonial performances.

Pueblo socialization is permissive, with gradual weaning and toilet training and little explicit discipline of children until they are over two years of age

(Dozier, 1970). Admonitions then center on such things as learning the civilized "Hopi way" of hard work, enduring discomforts, and not wasting food. The Hopi ideals are (1) peacefulness, (2) responsibility, (3) cooperation, (4) humility, and (5) self-reliance (Schlegel, 1973: 450). Masked disciplinarians with whips are used to threaten disobedient children. Initiation of girls and boys into a *kiva* or religious society occurs between the ages of six and nine with rigid physical and dietary restrictions. According to Schlegel (1973:449), "the Hopi girl follows a set life plan, and she is subjected to no cultural dilemmas," like the trauma-free Samoan adolescents described by Margaret Mead. However, the Hopi girls still go through a period of adolescent crisis because, after early mixed-sex socialization to the Hopi way, it is a time of strict sex-role socialization.

There is little opportunity for privacy, particularly in those villages that are still constructed as compact, adobe, apartmentlike pueblos. Gossip, ridicule, and the discipline of *kiva* societies keep down social deviancy, maintaining a quietistic solution to social relations. In the past, Hopis executed witches and evicted other deviants, but today the rebellious individuals tend to move to the freer life of cities and just visit their villages to renew kinship and ceremonial ties. One example of a semiurban adaptation is that about 600 Hopi live a suburban type of life at Moenkopi with such appliances as refrigerators, gas ranges, running water, and automobiles. These people often drive into the city of Flagstaff, Arizona, for shopping and visiting.

Religious ceremonialism, with its rich traditions of costumes, dance, music, and theology, is still at the center of Hopi life and is more attractive to the Hopi than the Christian alternatives. Developing within a context of Spanish and then Euro-American curiosity and pressures to change, the Hopi religious societies developed defensive secrecy and theological adjustments that rationalized Hopi religion in relation to Christianity and American culture. Hopi is an Indian society that has had sufficient autonomy from Euro-American pressures to gradually evolve a modern culture with a consistently high level of internal integration. Wages, work, western education, automobiles, electrical appliances, western dress, weekend supermarket shopping, etc., are now accepted practices, but the aboriginal language is being retained as a second language to English, and the Hopi religion has never been replaced by Christianity.

The Menomini of Wisconsin

The aboriginal Menomini ("wild rice people") were divided into two equal and exogamous moieties. One half belonged to the Earth People and they always married the Sky People in the other half. Members of one moiety also acted as the undertakers and mourners for the deceased members of the alternate moiety. The Menomini, although simpler than the Hopi, were also of a tribal level of cultural evolution and thus had social institutions that helped to bind the society together, such as clans, chiefs, councils, and a religious association.

Spindler and Spindler (1971a) found five social segments along a continuum of sociocultural adaptation among the Menomini living in a Wisconsin reservation: (1) native-oriented, (2) Peyotists, (3) transitionals, (4) lower-status acculturated, and (5) elite acculturated. The native-oriented group receives a definition and identity through maintaining the Dream Dance and other formalized dances and rituals. The Peyotists are involved in the pan-Indian "Native American Church," a religion that serves to resolve some of the ideological conflicts between the Christian and Indian traditions. The transitionals lack a firm identity and religious affiliation, but individuals in this large category are moving to either native-oriented or "whiteman" identity and religion. The more acculturated people tend to have a significantly higher economic status and no affiliation with either the aboriginal religious practices or the historical Peyotist movement. The acculturated, especially the elite, are usually Catholic in religion.

The native-oriented group tend to have the personal qualities of equanimity and, under duress, control of overt emotionality and aggression, autonomy, a sense of humor, and hospitality. They believe in having supernatural power, from a guardian spirit through a vision while fasting or simply through a displaying of quiescent receptivity to power, and that dreams can be used to predict the future.

Children in the native-oriented group are received as reincarnated elders and, like old people, are close to the supernatural power that pervades all things. Naming is ceremonious and very important. Children are treated with tolerance and permissiveness, with gradual weaning, casual toilet training, and mild discipline. When a boy kills his first game, he is given a feast, and praises are sung to him. When a girl fills her pail with wild berries, she is praised. Children participate in the important social happenings, such as the dances. They are told stories by the elders, including formalized "preachings" about proper behavior. The group is child-oriented because the transmission of traditional culture is a central purpose of the group. This results in a quite different kind of family life than that found among the "acculturated" Menomini. The Spindlers see the native-oriented cultural system as a conscious attempt to maintain a way of life that is dying, a reaffirmation of the traditional way while attempting to exclude the foreign way. This is similar to the Hopi *kiva* societies, the Long House Society people among the Iroquois, and the Guardian Spirit Dancers among the Salish of British Colombia and Washington.

The elite acculturated tend to live in a community different from that of the traditionals, in homes like business and professional people in nearby Euro-American communities. They are active in the Catholic Church, often play golf, bowl, or go snowmobiling, do not speak Menomini, and are consciously oriented toward Euro-American culture, but still derive some pride and identity from their Menomini heritage.

"The disruptions created in rapid culture change hit the men more directly, leaving the women less changed and less anxious. . . . Menomini women continue to play the affective, supportive, 'expressive' roles of wife, mother, and social participant in a more or less traditional Menomini fashion, unhampered by rigid role prescriptions." (Spindler and Spindler, 1971b: 398, 406). Landes (1971) made a similar point for the neighboring and culturally related Ojibwa, concluding that although traditionally women had a position of low prestige, they had far more freedom and latitude in their roles than men. Women could even go to war, hunt, and doctor as men do, as well as continue their domestic and child-raising activities, without disturbing the conventional ideals of the normal women or the sexual division of labor.

In 1961, the U.S. Bureau of Indian Affairs terminated its relations with the tribe, and the reservation became a county of Wisconsin, and Menominee Enterprises, Inc., became the tribal management. The American government had decided that the Menomini were sufficiently acculturated to entirely operate their own affairs. They found the costs of taking over the formerly free social services to be very high. Also the determination to keep Menomini identity and land intact was strong. After years of political action their termination was partially rescinded in 1974.

The Indians of Los Angeles

Of the approximately 965,000 Indians in the United States, about 500,000 live on or near reservations in rural settings. The remaining 465,000 live in towns and cities largely as a result of an urban migration that began as a significant movement after about 1955. Los Angeles today, by all estimates, has the most Indians of any urban area in America or Canada, somewhere around 45,000.[1] Anchorage, San Francisco, Tulsa, Oklahoma City, Minneapolis, Chicago, and Phoenix all have over 10,000 Native Americans. Albuquerque, Denver, and Seattle in America and Vancouver, Edmonton, Regina, Winnipeg, Toronto, and Montreal in Canada also each have several thousand or more In-

---

[1]Spanish America is excluded from discussion here because its extreme syncretism of European and Indian cultures led to fundamentally different patterns. Also, there is far more continuity of Indian cultures, so that, for example, over ten million people still speak Indian languages in Spanish America.

dians.[2] Research on urban Indians so far has focused on their migrations to cities and on urban ethnic institutions, so that little is known of their day-to-day family life.

Indians came to Los Angeles from all over North America but generally in the same proportions as the U.S. national distributions of Indians by state or by tribe (Price, 1978). Thus, for example, about 15 percent of the Indians in America live in Arizona, and 15 percent of the Indians in Los Angeles are from Arizona. Only about 6 percent of the Indians in Los Angeles were born in California. A similar correlation is found for tribal representation. Individuals from over one hundred tribes live in Los Angeles, but the larger the tribe, the more migrants it will tend to have move into Los Angeles. Thus, nationally and in Los Angeles, there are about 14 percent Navaho, 12 percent Sioux, and so on, to dozens of tribes with less than 1 percent.

A major force behind the urban migration of Indians in America was the Employment Assistance Program of the Bureau of Indian Affairs, which helped about 100,000 Indians relocate from reservations to urban areas and provided urban-oriented vocational training for over 25,000 household heads. Whether supported in their migration by the government or not, whether in the United States or Canada, the urban migration of Indians has a large number of parallels. The incentive is primarily economic, such as to find a job or higher wages and to improve physical living conditions. They miss the social contacts and activities of the reservation and, when possible, spend weekends or vacations back visiting on their reservation. As the years in the city go by, they tend to withdraw from reservation social contacts, idealize traditional reservation life, and perhaps talk of retiring or otherwise returning to their reservations, in which as members of the tribe they have a right to reside.

In a study by this author, a significant shift was found from traditional practices toward marriages outside the tribe to other Indians (about one-third) and outside the race (about one-third). More Indians went to church in the city (70 percent) than did on the reservation (53 percent). About 20 percent of the Indians were active in formal Indian associations, such as Indian athletic leagues, one of the ten Indian Christian churches, Indian dance clubs, and Indian social centers. In informal associations, some 29 percent of our sample reported their usual association as being only with other Indians, 67 percent mixed, and 4 percent exclusively with non-Indians. The vast majority preferred living in mixed neighborhoods and found no housing discrimination. Indians are, in fact, much more widely scattered residentially than

---

[2]Indians in Canada constitute a higher proportion of the total population (about 2.5 percent) than in America (about 0.4 percent), but a higher proportion in Canada live on or near their reserves (about 65 percent of status Indians) and retain a native first language (about 65 percent).

TABLE 2
Emotional Concerns

	MEN	WOMEN
1. Kinfolk, family, marriage	43	59
2. Employment, money, material life	64	27
3. Law breaking, arrest, police	31	13
4. Personal achievement, failure	17	13
5. Religious, mysterious, nature	12	14
6. Health, illness	13	11
7. Ethics	11	11
8. Friends	10	12
9. Drinking	11	9
10. City rewards, problems	10	9
11. Social success, failure	15	4
12. Sex	5	13
13. Recreation or lack of it	7	10
14. Politics	8	4
15. Fighting	10	2
16. Prejudice, discrimination	2	8
TOTALS	269	219

blacks or Mexican Americans. Recent arrivals tend to live first in the central city and then, usually after about two years, move to the suburbs.

We studied the emotional concerns of 13 men and 11 women. Table 2 is a classification of their responses, in interviews showing a tendency for the women to be concerned more with kinfolk, family, and marriage and the men to be concerned more with employment and material matters.

Indians tend to retain reservation attitudes that one should not spend much on clothes or housing, with large proportions of their budgets going toward travel and entertainment. Sports, television, Indian dancing at *powwows,* and socializing at Indian bars are major sources of recreation. We found that active involvement with Indian sports leagues and Indian dance groups was correlated with a positive and permanent adaptation of city life. Most urban Indians visit their home reservations so frequently that it has been characterized as a specialized kind of "commuting," but some finally settle in to a fairly permanent commitment to city life and actively work toward creating a new pan-Indian ethnic culture.

In the city, meeting Indians from over 100 different tribes, the Indian still finds many cultural commonalities and many common problems, as well as a common racial identity that becomes important in a racially sensitive society. This cultural pan-Indianism and a political awareness of the problems of Indians from other tribes flourishes in the city and becomes a stabilizing and integrating force for this new ethnic group. That is, individuals from hundreds of separate bands, tribes, chiefdoms, and states are in the process of creating a North American Indian ethnic group, and the large urban centers, such as Los Angeles, play a key role in that process of creation.

CHANGE AND ADAPTATION

A number of simultaneous processes are at work among Native American peoples: (1) a high population increase, (2) government programs to bring Indians out of their poverty lifestyle, (3) convergent social adaptations to the dominant society, (4) urbanization, and (5) an ethnic renascence that involves (a) the creation of a general pan-Indian ethnicity, (b) several special political and religious pan-Indian movements such as Peyotism and the Sun Dance, (c) the cultural revitalization of certain tribal and regional customs, and (d) a renewed interest in native history, literature, crafts, art, dance, foods, etc.

The future of native people is first one of *population expansion.* With an annual increase rate now of about 2 percent, they are growing somewhat faster than the population as a whole. This is in spite of high rates of infant mortality (about twice the American average), certain diseases (tuberculosis is seven times more frequent than the American average), and death (average life expectancy is some ten years less than the American average).

Indian life is still generally one of poverty. Some cultures define a life of poverty as nonmaterialistic, spiritual, noncompetitive, and in tune with the natural environment, but in North America it is defined as a sign of ignorance and without value. Indian life does look poor in terms of such majority society criteria as employment, income, housing, education, and health standards. In a city with severe problems such as Anchorage, the proportion of U.S. natives below the poverty line is about three times greater than whites. Also the proportion of native families receiving public assistance is seven times higher than whites (Jones, 1974:14). About one-third of all adult Indians in America are classified as illiterate, and only one adult male in five has a high school education.

We should not, however, project too much misery into our conceptions of the day-to-day life of Indians. Where the non-Indian visitor might suffer cultural shock in perceptions of reservation uncleanliness, drinking, fighting, and so forth, the person raised there usually looks back with loving warmth to his childhood in a close-knit community. Indian societies have values that, if used as criteria of evaluation of the majority society, could in turn make the lifestyle of the majority look "poverty stricken." These values differ somewhat from one Indian society to the next, so that Eskimo, Hopi, Menomini, and the Indians of Los Angeles would all judge the pathologies in our styles of life in different ways.

The majority North American society in the past received mostly material rather than social or ideological elements of culture from native societies: cultigens such as corn, tomatoes, potatoes, chocolate, pineapple, tobacco, and rubber; and artifacts such as the parka, toboggan, hammock, and moccasin. Today, however, there is some evidence that Indian social and ideological culture is influencing the majority society. Vine Deloria, an Indian spokesman, claims that "American society is unconsciously going Indian" in its search for individual freedom within a socially tolerant community that is in ecological harmony with its environment. The evidence of the history of cultural change, however, is that the major direction of influence will be that of drawing Indians out of their "poverty" into the clean, healthy, materialism of the majority society.

We examined the process of convergent social adaptation through acculturation. In family life we have seen this in the increasingly predominant pattern of the monogamous, bilateral patrilineal-biased, nuclear family. Kinship networks are still strong and supportive but there has been an abandonment of polygamy, multifamily residences, traditional ideologies of lineal descent, and corporate kinship groups such as lineages and clans. There are some residual differences in family life between even urbanized American Indians and the majority society. Indian families seem to be less child-centered and have less emphasis on such things as toilet training, cleanliness, punctuality, competition, and worldly achievement. Another social feature is that, compared with non-Indians, modern Indian political processes tend to work slower and less aggressively, have more consensus, and involve more personal rapport between leaders and their constituency.

I have discussed the process of urbanization in reference to the Los Angeles Indians. As the process of urban migration has proceeded, the reservations themselves have been changed. When the urbanization has already become extreme, as in California, many small reservations that are distant from cities have been abandoned, have become retirement communities for the older generation who stayed on while the younger people moved into the cities, or have become summer-vacation areas for their Indian owners. Among the Cupeño and Luiseño Indians of San Diego County, California, we found one reserve that had been essentially abandoned, one reserve with only a few older people left, two other reserves with a moderate population in farming, and a fifth that was increasing in population because it was close enough to the surrounding white farms and towns for the residents to commute to wage work (Price, 1978). We can expect to see many of the small tribes become assimilated, while other larger, more isolated, or more well-defended tribes survive as distinct sociocultural units. That is, the Hopi should survive indefinitely because they have a relatively large population, they have some physical and social isolation from the majority society, and they have created defense against assimilation. The Menomini, even though they have a large population and a large territory, have had difficulty developing defenses against assimilation, and still have poor prospects for survival as a distinct sociocultural unit.

The ethnic renascence of Indians has had about a century of significant pan-Indian developments but became a major movement only after the Chicago Indian Conference in 1961, if one had to pick a time and place. Since then, in addition to existing reservation and band administration, about 200 Indian political organizations have developed in the United States and Canada. Most of these organizations publish periodicals, and collectively these periodicals form an information network because the various editors read and report news from each other's papers (Price, 1978). Thus, an important news item can spread rapidly throughout the network of periodicals. This "common cause" literature in turn fosters the integration of an Indian ethnic group in spite of the great tribal diversity and the isolated, rural, and scattered residence of Indians.

Indian organizations have pressed all levels of government for action on their behalf, bringing changes in everything from the treatment of Indians in history books to support for the economic development of reservations. Even urban Indians are generally involved with the ethnic renascence, although it may mean no more than such things as reading books about Indians, attending a local Indian ceremonial *powwow* or fair "so that the children will know their heritage," or engaging in traditional Indian crafts. One of the ways this revitalization affects family life is in the "elder's movement," where older people are actively sought out to provide religious leadership and personal counseling. There has always been a special grandparent–grandchild relationship in native societies, but even adults today are widely encouraged in the native communications media (which now includes native-produced radio and television programs, as well as newspapers) to maintain a continuing apprenticelike relationship with an Indian religious elder. The social position of older people is also enhanced because they are being sought out now as narrators of local traditions and folk stories by the schools in Indian communities.

The latest step in the long history of the native peoples seem to be the creation for the first time in history of an American Indian ethnic group. As with ethnic groups generally, they are sensitive about what they are called.

The Yuit of southern Alaska do not care whether they are called Yuit or Eskimo, but the Inuit across the north and particularly in Canada prefer to be called Inuit, which means "people" in their language while *eskimo* is a Cree term for "raw meat eaters." The Eskimo in Greenland prefer to be called Greenlanders. Some Indians do not like to be called "after a land in southern Asia because of some stupid mistake of Columbus." Instead, many leaders prefer the term "Native," because it emphasizes the aboriginal heritage of the indigenous people, and it distinguishes them apart from all other ethnic groups in America.

REFERENCES

Association on American Indian Affairs. 1979. *Indian Family Defense* 11. New York.

Chance, Norman A. 1966. *The Eskimo of North Alaska.* New York: Holt, Rinehart and Winston

Corrigan, Samuel W. 1974. "A Note on Canadian Indian Marriage Law," *Western Canadian Journal of Anthropology,* 4(2)17–27.

Cruikshank, Julie. 1971. "Matrifocal Families in the Canadian North," in *The Canadian Family: A Book of Readings.* Toronto: Holt, Rinehart and Winston of Canada.

D.I.A.N.D. 1975. *The Canadian Indian: Statistics.* Ottawa: Indian Affairs

Dozier, Edward P. 1970. *The Pueblo Indians of North America.* New York: Holt, Rinehart and Winston.

Eggan, Fred. 1966. *The American Indian: Perspectives for the Study of Social Change.* Chicago: Aldine

Hippler, Arthur E. 1974. "The North Alaska Eskimos: A Culture and Personality Perspective," *American Ethnologist,* 1 (August): 449–469.

Jones, Dorothy M. 1974. *The Urban Native Encounters the Social Service System.* Fairbanks: Universityof Alaska.

Landes, Ruth. 1971. *The Ojibwa Woman.* New York: W.W. Norton.

Murdock, George P. 1967. "Ethnographic Atlas: A Summary." *Ethnology* 6 (April).

Oswalt, Wendell H. 1967. *Alaskan Eskimos.* San Francisco: Chandler.

Price, John A. 1978. *Native Studies: American and Canadian Indians.* Toronto: McGraw-Hill Ryerson.

———. 1979. *Indians of Canada: Cultural Dynamics.* Toronto: Prentice-Hall of Canada.

Reasons, Charles. 1972. "Crime and the American Indian," in *Native Americans Today.* New York: Harper & Row.

Schlegel, Alice. 1973. "The Adolescent Socialization of the Hopi Girl," *Ethnology,* 12 (October) 449–462.

Spindler, George, and Louise Spindler. 1971a. *Dreamers Without Power: The Menomini Indians.* New York: Holt, Rinehart & Winston.

———. 1971b. "Male and Female Adaptations in Culture Change," in *Man in Adaptation: The Institutional Framework.* Chicago: Aldine-Atherton.

Stanbury, William T., and Jay Siegel. 1975. *Success and Failure: Indians in Urban Society.* Vancouver: University of British Columbia Press.

Thomas, Robert K. 1979. "Position Paper (on the Definition of an Indian)," 24-page unpublished manuscript. Detroit: Wayne State University.

The Mexican American Family

Authors Alvirez, Bean, and Williams in their chapter on the Mexican American family illustrate the importance of analyzing the ethnic factor in understanding family lifestyles. Mexican Americans constitute one of the largest ethnic groups in America, and as the authors point out, certain cultural patterns that have been thought to carry great weight in family life among Mexican Americans do not in actuality uniformly characterize their family patterns. The most noticeable feature of the Mexican American family is its size relative to other groups of Americans. The fertility of Mexican Americans is substantially higher than other groups. However, as the authors indicate, the traditional Mexican family structure has been influenced by the forces of urbanization, female labor force participation, and geographical and social mobility.

CHAPTER TWELVE
BY
DAVID ALVIREZ, FRANK D. BEAN, AND DORIE WILLIAMS

HISTORICAL BACKGROUND

Although the number is uncertain, it is probable that about seven million persons of Mexican origin or descent inhabit the United States, making Mexican Americans the second largest minority group in the country.[1] The vast majority (more than 86 percent) live in five southwestern states close to Mexico—California, Texas, New Mexico, Arizona, and Colorado (U.S. Bureau of

Some of the information in this chapter is from material gathered in the Austin Family Survey, which was conducted with support of a grant from the U.S. Public Health Service, National Institute of Child Health and Human Development (Grant HD 04262) to the University of Texas at Austin. The survey supported by that grant was directed by David Alvirez, Frank D. Bean, Benjamin S. Bradshaw, and Harley L. Browning.

[1]The more neutral term "Mexican American" will be used throughout this chapter to designate the white population of Mexican origin or descent in America. Included under this term are many who identify themselves as Chicanos, Spanish American, Hispanos, Mexicanos, Californios, and Latin Americans. The term "Anglo" will be used to designate the white population of non-Mexican origin. The actual number of Mexican Americans in this country is very hard to determine and could run as high as ten million or more, depending on the number of undocumented immigrants and how many of them are included in the population estimates of the

(continued)

the Census, 1979b, Table 1). Because of continuous immigration and an unusually high birth rate, the size of the Mexican American population relative to the total population in America has been increasing over the past 30 years. This growth has been accompanied by more active and visible efforts on the part of Mexican Americans to improve their civil rights and economic opportunities. In turn, this has brought about the realization, throughout the nation as well as the southwest, that Mexican Americans are a large and important ethnic group in this country.

The historical experience of Mexican Americans in the southwest has shaped their contemporary social position and to a lesser extent their family patterns. An excellent discussion of this experience is provided by McLemore (1979: 207–215), who gives a more detailed account than can be presented here of the events and conflicts occurring in the 18th century that have influenced contemporary relationships between Mexican Americans and Anglos. For our purposes, the unique Mexican American heritage may be divided into several periods. The first, following the Spanish Conquest, is the period of colonization, beginning with the subjugation of the indigenous natives in the 16th century and lasting until 1821 when Mexico achieved her political independence. The explorers and settlers of the southwest during this time were the Spanish and the Indians, and thus are retrospectively referred to as Mexicans even though Mexico did not exist as a sovereign nation before that time.

The first settlements were in New Mexico, in which Juan de Onate established 25 missions between 1598 and 1630. Later, in 1769, a series of missions were established in California and to a much lesser extent in Texas and Arizona. By the end of the Spanish period, McWilliams (1968: 26) notes that the Spanish settlements in the southwest "consisted of a firmly rooted colony in New Mexico; an easily held and fairly prosperous chain of missions in coastal California; and a number of feebly garrisoned, constantly imperiled settlements in Texas and Arizona." No matter what the earlier warring and proselytizing proclivities of the Spanish, it is clear that their contributions to the southwest and to America are many, including language, names of places, cuisine, systems of irrigation, and methods of raising cattle.

(continued)
U.S. Bureau of the Census. The Environmental Fund in its population estimates for 1979 gives an estimate of the total population of the United States (based on its lowest estimate of undocumented immigrants) that is 5.1 million greater than the Bureau of the Census estimate. It also adds a footnote to its estimate for Mexico that indicates that the population of Mexico may be approximately 4 million *less* than the estimate provided (Environmental Fund, 1979). For discussions of problems in identifying the Mexican American population, see Buechley (1961, 1967), U.S. Bureau of the Census (1963), Hernandez, Estrada, and Alvirez (1973), and U.S. Commission on Civil Rights (1974).

But there were Mexican and Indian contributions as well. McWilliams (1968: 34) writes:

> While the form or model was often Spanish, the ultimate adaptation showed unmistakable Mexican and Indian influences. If the Spanish were the carriers of seeds and plows, Mexicans and Indians were the planters and plow hands. Beyond all doubt the culture of the Southwest was a trinity: a whole consisting of three intricately interwoven, interpenetrated, thoroughly fused elements. To attempt to unravel any single strand from this pattern and label it "Spanish" is, therefore, to do a serious injustice to the Mexicans and Indians through whom, and only through whom, Spanish cultural influences survived in the region.

Following Spanish colonization, the period from 1821 to 1848 is of interest for events that took place primarily in Texas, though these influenced the lives of all Mexicans in America. After gaining independence from Spain in 1821, Mexico encouraged the colonization of Texas through immigration from other nations. Colonists came in large numbers, mostly from America, but also from Germany, Norway, Czechoslovakia, and other European countries. Mexico tried unsuccessfully to stop the flow in 1830, but by 1834 Anglos outnumbered Mexicans in Texas by six to one, setting the stage for Texas' War for Independence. The Texas Revolution, in which incidentally many Mexican Texans fought for independence from the dictatorship of Santa Anna, brought on a decade of increasing hardship for the Mexican Texans. During this period there gradually evolved a pattern of conflict that more and more placed "Mexicans" against "Americans." As relationships between Mexican Texans and Anglos became more strained, tensions were compounded by language and legal, religious, cultural, and socioeconomic differences.

Hence, the Mexican War (1846–1848), while provoked by the annexation of Texas by America in 1845, was in part the culmination of 25 to 30 years of rising cultural conflict. In summary, the outcome of the war with respect to the social position of Mexican Americans in Texas has been aptly noted by McLemore (1973: 667):

> The consolidation of the systems within which "Mexicans" were subordinated to "Americans" in Texas was accomplished through the Mexican–American War, 1846–1848. In the Treaty of Guadalupe Hidalgo, Mexico finally recognized the loss of Texas and accepted the Rio Grande as the boundary. Although Mexico displayed great concern for the welfare of her citizens who were left within the territory of the United States, and even though the terms of the treaty made clear that Mexico's former subjects were to enjoy the rights, privileges, and immunities of the other citizens of the United States, the subordination of those of

Spanish-Mexican-Indian descent to those of Anglo-American descent had been largely achieved in Texas by the middle of the nineteenth century.

The hostility and conflict of the Mexican War continued on a lesser scale during the conquered era from 1848 to 1900. The prevalent attitude then was one of Anglo supremacy. In Texas, especially between the Nueces and the Rio Grande rivers, there was frequent conflict between the two groups. Outbreaks of violence and lynchings of Mexican Americans were not uncommon, and not the least among the instigators of such hostilities were the Texas Rangers, who to this day are still feared and hated by many lower-class Mexican Americans. In constant retreat and retrenchment, many Mexican Americans also lost their lands, both legally and illegally, during this time.

New Mexico stood above such conflagrations, with violence never assuming the proportions that prevailed in Texas. Until recently, Mexican Americans constituted a majority of that state's population, and while many were exploited, the exploitation was practiced by wealthy Mexican Americans as well as by Anglos. By contrast, Mexican Americans in California were held in contempt and often became the objects of violence. Only the *gente de razon,* the *Californios,* enjoyed immunity. In general, it can be said that in the southwest, this was a period of the birth (or reaffirmation) of the stereotype that Mexican Americans, as a conquered people, were inferior.

Migration to America

The turn of this century marked the advent of mass migrations from Mexico to this country. This influx heightened the visibility of Mexican Americans already in this country and worsened the conditions of both old and new Mexican American residents. Poverty and political instability in Mexico enhanced the lure of jobs and economic betterment in the north, and these factors acted as a strong magnet (a magnet still operating today) for immigration. It is impossible to ascertain how many persons migrated between 1900 and 1930, but the number was probably well over a million. Those who came were generally the poor and the unskilled who labored primarily in jobs of farming, mining, and railroads. Though faced with considerable discrimination in America, many of the newcomers thought their situation to be favorable in comparison to previous living conditions in Mexico. However, despite gains in relative material well-being, once they became aware of generally superior conditions among American workers, Mexican Americans were not docile and apathetic, as evidenced by the attempts of laborers to organize between 1915 and 1940—efforts that were quickly and effectively quelled by employers and law-enforcement agencies.

World War II marked a turning point in the lives of many Mexican Americans, accounting for much of the variability that may be found among Mexican Americans and their families today. Many opportunities, previously closed, became accessible. For some of the 300,000 to 500,000 men who served in the armed forces, military service provided their first contact with Anglos on other than a subservient basis. The experience among Mexican Americans that they could compete with Anglos on equal terms undoubtedly contributed to their open opposition to discrimination after they returned from the war. Also, exposure to other countries and cultures diminished some of their own ethnocentrism. They became increasingly politically conscious. Furthermore, for those who had served in the armed services, new vocational and educational opportunities became available. Even those who remained at home benefited in terms of occupational openings created by the labor shortages of a country at war. All those opportunities and new outlooks gave rise to what Alvarez (1973: 931) calls the "Mexican American generation," one whose cultural orientations and loyalties are tied to America and whose members expect to participate fully in American society.

Finally, in the mid-1960s there was the birth of the Chicano generation, a group of more active, militant Mexican Americans no longer willing to wait patiently for the rights that they believe are guaranteed by the U.S. constitution. Although it is not known what percentage of the Mexican American population identifies with this movement, there is little doubt that it has created a new pride among Mexican Americans in their own Spanish-Mexican-Indian heritage, a feeling that ultimately may prove to be a factor in preserving some of the traditional patterns of the Mexican American family.

The Traditional Mexican American Family.

In speaking of the "traditional" Mexican American family, one must realize that the heterogeneity among Mexican Americans thoughout America means that generalizations based on such a label must be made with caution: The "traditional" family type should not be taken to imply inferiority to a more modern type or to a more Anglo form. Rather, it refers to a family pattern that is different from what may be considered the prevalent or "typical" Anglo pattern, to the extent that such a depiction is possible. Moreover, the presentation of a "typical" Mexican American family in no way implies that such a pattern is "pathological" in the sense that such a family pattern is responsible for many problems Mexican Americans face. What is presented is an "ideal cultural type" that is partially reflective of the stereotypes held by Anglos as well as some of the ideas held by Mexicans and Mexican Americans.

Several traits are often imputed to Mexican Americans that are also thought to affect and/or reflect their family patterns (Murillo, 1971). These are frequently presumed to be cultural traits, although they may be partially derived from the conditions of poverty common among the majority of the people in this population. First, Mexican Americans are more person-oriented than goal-oriented. A great emphasis is placed on interpersonal relationships, and the roles played therein appear to make Mexican Americans more warm and emotional than Anglos, whom the former often see as cold and unfeeling.

Second, Mexican Americans tend to be less materialistic and competitive than Anglos and as a result probably enjoy greater emotional security. Tied in with this is a present-time orientation for which Mexican Americans have been criticized. Yet, as Murillo (1971: 100) notes, "Today much of our Anglo society's psychotherapy is aimed at developing or rekindling a *here* and *now* time orientation in the client as a means to improved mental health." For the Mexican American, material goods are not an end in themselves but only a means to an end. Other activities in life, particularly interpersonal relationships, are considered to be more important (Murguia, 1975: 9). Whereas the Anglo practices openness, frankness, and directness in his relationships with others, the Mexican American is likely to practice manners, politeness, courtesy, and deference, which may cause the Anglo to misinterpret the actions of the Mexican American.

Structural Features of the Traditional Mexican American Family

Turning to the Mexican American family itself, three main characteristics have been emphasized by Mexicans [see Penalosa (1968) for a review of their ideas], Mexican Americans, and Anglos as especially typical, although the interpretations given to these characteristics have varied. The first is *familism,* the importance of the family to all its members, including in many instances members of the extended family (Grebler, Moore, and Guzman, 1970: 351). The second is the idea of *male dominance,* in which the males assume superordinate roles. The third characteristic is the *subordination* of *younger* persons to *older* persons, accompanied by a great degree of respect for one's elders. The rest of this section will examine in more detail each of these three main characteristics.

The importance of familism can be seen in many different ways. For one thing, the needs of the family collectively may supersede individual needs (Grebler, Moore, and Guzman, 1970: 351). The family is one of the strongest areas of life activities, a closely knit unit in which all members enjoy status

274

and esteem (Ulibarri, 1970: 31). It may be the only place of refuge for the individual, providing both emotional and material security. When one needs advice or help, the person one will most often go to is another member of the family.

The importance of the family is reflected in the idealized role given to the extended family among Mexican Americans. Close relationships are not limited to the nuclear family but include aunts and uncles, grandparents, cousins, in-laws, and even *compadres* (godparents). Hence, those on whom one can rely for support form a numerically large group. Although it has been noted (Grebler, Moore, and Guzman, 1970: 351) that familism may operate as a hindrance to mobility because it cultivates attachments to people, places, and things, it can also be a supportive force in which members help and sustain each other in attaining goals that would be difficult for the individual to achieve by himself. For example, it has been common for Mexican Americans to care for aged parents within their household, a practice that would be otherwise difficult given the economic status of many Mexican Americans. Also, several cases are known in which large, closely knit families have helped each other in achieving such goals as acquiring a car or providing higher education for children. Only a person who has never experienced the warmth of the Mexican American family would tend to see it primarily from a negative perspective. Furthermore, such a view fails to recognize that for Mexican Americans, particularly those of lower status, the family is often the primary source of refuge from what is often seen as a hostile world. In fact, an historical function of the Mexican American family structure has been to protect individuals from the hostilities of the dominant Anglo white society (Baca Zinn, 1975: 18). Moreover, as some Mexican Americans improve their socioeconomic status, a strong familistic orientation may forestall the development of strong social-class cleavages within the ethnic group (Grebler, Moore, and Guzman, 1970: 353).

The idea of male dominance and male superiority is probably the characteristic most emphasized in the literature, both in Mexico and in America. The father is seen as the head of the family with absolute authority over wife and children. All major decisions are his responsibility, with part of the wife's role involved in seeing that the father's decisions are carried out. Power and prestige are the absolute prerogatives of the male head, and generally delegations of this authority are through the male line. Hence, when the father is not present, the oldest son often assumes considerable authority, and the sisters and younger brothers are expected to carry out his orders.

The concept of *machismo* forms part of the concept of male dominance. The most emphasized aspect of *machismo* has been sexual virility or maleness. From early childhood male children are given much more freedom than females and are socialized into the male role. In the adolescent years they are expected to begin at least verbalizing their sexual prowess, and stories involving the "conquest of women" often occupy a dominant place in their conversations. According to the narrow interpretation of *machismo,* the pursuit of extramarital sexual relations is condoned and even encouraged. Furthermore, such behavior is sometimes presumed not to generate husband–wife conflicts nor to interfere with a man's role as a father and provider (Madsen, 1964: 22). Such interpretations fail to recognize that *machismo* is more than sexual virility and that there are some inherent contradictions in the idea. Many would argue that it is difficult to conceive how a man may carry on after marriage the same as before without "a diminution in the husband's felt responsibility to his family or a loosening of his firm ties to it" (Hayden, 1966: 20). But *machismo* also consists of manliness in a broader sense than just sexual prowess. It includes the elements of courage, honor, and respect for others, as well as the notion of providing fully for one's family and maintaining close ties with the extended family. Murillo (1971: 103) points out that an important prescriptive aspect of the *machismo* role encourages the use of authority within the family in a just and fair manner. Misuse of authority may result in a loss of respect not only from the family but from the community at large, and hence such misuse is strongly avoided. The public pursuit of extramarital sex might often conflict with the fulfillment of these latter forms of *machismo.* The observations of the first author of this chapter lead him to conclude that while some extramarital sexual behavior (about which so much has been written) is characteristic of some Mexican American husbands, the majority do not fall into this pattern.

FEMALE AND SIBLING ROLES. Complementary to the expectation of male dominance in the Mexican American family is that of female submissiveness. Generally speaking, the woman is supposed to be subservient to the husband, and her primary roles are those of homemaker and mother (bearer of children). Drawing from other studies, Grebler, Moore, and Guzman, (1970: 366) note that "the bearing and rearing of children continue to be seen as perhaps the most important function of a woman, symbolizing her maturity." This is one explanation for the large families characteristic of Mexican Americans, an explanation that is combined with one that sees large families as evidence of the husband's *machismo.* In a more ideal sense, the mother is depicted as a naive, rather childlike, saintly woman who is very religious (Grebler, Moore, and Guzman, 1970: 360). Her personal needs occupy a place secondary to those of her husband and all other family members.

Early in life the female child begins to learn her proper role. She is given much less freedom than boys and begins to play the role of mother and homemaker by helping to care for younger brothers and sisters and by assisting with the housework. As she reaches adolescence, she is carefully chaperoned to protect her from suitors intent on sexual advances. Then, by the time she marries, the young woman is ready to fulfill the same role that was fulfilled by her mother.

In male–female relations within the family, children form an important and indispensable part. Early in life children are assigned real responsibilities necessary for the welfare of the family (Murillo, 1971: 104). Children are expected to get along with each other, with the older taking care of the younger and the brothers protecting the sisters. Generally speaking, there is probably less sibling rivalry in these homes than in Anglo homes. Children are expected to be models of respect, which indicates why discipline is so important in the family. Each child knows his place in the family scheme and does not trespass in spheres of life in which he has no business. Within this scheme sibling relationships are more important than parent–children relationships, a pattern different from that in Anglo homes and a possible explanation of why two boys and two girls may be considered the minimum ideal family size among Mexican Americans. With such a family composition, children of both sexes would have the desired companionship.

One last characteristic of the traditional Mexican American family is the subordination of the younger to the older. Older people receive more respect from youth and children than is characteristic in Anglo homes. There is even a familiar form of address that older people use with younger ones and that close friends use with each other, while the formal form is used always by children in speaking to their elders. Anglos may oftentimes offend Mexican Americans without realizing it by trying to become intimate with them before the Mexican Americans feel sufficient closeness has been established.

This pattern of subordination of the younger to the older is partially sex differentiated within the family. The older male children have some authority over the younger children *and* over their sisters. During the father's absence the older son assumes authority, and he is expected to be obeyed as if he were the father. Sometimes the range of authority includes the mother, particularly when the son is close to manhood.

The description that has been presented thus far portrays an idealized family form that may be far from the real or actual situations in many Mexican American families. It does provide, however, a starting point from which to consider the present Mexican American family. The next section will outline the demographic characteristics of the Mexican American family, comparing it to the American family, in general, or to the Anglo family, in some cases. After that we will leave the "typical" family and consider some of the bases of heterogeneity among Mexican American families.

THE MODERN MEXICAN AMERICAN FAMILY
Sociodemographic Characteristics

An examination of certain social, economic, and demographic characteristics of the Mexican American population highlights some of the more apparent differences between the Mexican American and Anglo populations and provides further indication of the subordinate status that many Mexican Americans occupy in the social structure of America. These characteristics also describe both the Mexican American family and the context within which Mexican American family life occurs.

FERTILITY. One of the most distinctive characteristics of Mexican Americans is their unusually high fertility. Census materials on children born show that the fertility of the Mexican American population, compared with the total white population, has been high and remains so, and that their fertility is as high or higher than the black population. Although current information will not be available until results from the 1980 census are published, we can examine the pattern based on 1970 data (Table 1). According to these data the average number of children born per 1000 Mexican-origin women, aged 35 to 44, was 4232, about 43 percent higher than the number for all women of this age, and 46 percent and 25 percent higher, respectively, than for all white and black women. Fertility of Mexican-origin women was also greater than that of any of the national origin groups shown.

Put in terms of the number of children per family, the average family size of Mexican Americans (4.2) is more than one person per family larger than that of the total American population (3.0). The larger size of Mexican American families is also indicated by the fact that 28.6 percent of their families have no children of their own under 18 compared to 48.2 percent for the white American population and by the fact that 4.7 percent of Mexican American families have five or more children compared to 1.5 percent for white America as a whole (U.S. Bureau of the Census, 1979a). The higher fertility characteristic of Mexican American women holds at all ages. And, compared to Anglo women, Mexican American females during their childbearing years will give birth to an average of nearly one and one-half more children.

To what extent the differences in fertility between Mexican American and Anglo populations are the result of cultural differences as compared to socioeconomic differences is difficult to judge. While more research is needed, available evidence does not rule out the idea that as education increases, the fertility of Mexican Americans will more closely resemble that of other

TABLE 1
ldren Born for Women 35–44, by Race and Ethnicity: 1970

GROUP	CHILDREN BORN PER 1000 WOMEN
otal	2958
White[a]	2891
Native	2913
Urban	2783
Urban native	2803
Rural	3179
Spanish Origin	3443
Mexican	4232
Puerto Rican	3240
Cuban	1932
Other Spanish	3041
Black	3489
American Indian	4267
Japanese	2149
Chinese	2833
Filipino	2981
Hawaiian	3940
Korean	2891
Other	3222

SOURCE: U.S. Bureau of the Census (1973: Tables 8 and 13).

[a]Includes persons of Spanish origin.

whites. If, however, larger families act as a hindrance to upward mobility, then a cycle may be operative that makes it difficult for Mexican Americans to escape the poverty in which many of them live.

Other evidence, however, would seem to show a cultural factor among Mexican Americans sustaining their higher fertility. Grebler, Moore, and Guzman (1970: 185–196) found that Mexican Americans had larger families than Anglos in every income bracket and hence conclude that differential family size does not seem to be simply a function of low-income status (and, by implication, of low assimilation). Roberts and Lee (1974), in a more detailed analysis, discovered that the relationship between fertility and ethnic status persisted even after controlling socioeconomic status. However, Lopez and Sabagh (1978) found that "cultural" variables, such as the tendency to speak Spanish in the home, did not account for high fertility among Mexican Americans as much as did "structural" variables, such as the degree of residential segregation. And Sabagh's (1980) recent research showing that Mexican Americans plan their fertility just as effectively as Anglos indicates that Mexican Americans do not have higher fertility because they are less effective users of contraception, but rather because they want more children. Thus, to understand Mexican American desired and actual fertility, further research must be done to disentangle the relative effects of both cultural and structural factors.

MARRIAGE AND DIVORCE. Turning to patterns of marital status, the percent married with spouse present among persons 25 to 64 years old is nearly the same among Mexican Americans (81 percent) as among all whites (84 percent), with blacks (66 percent) exhibiting a somewhat different pattern (U.S. Bureau of the Census, 1971). Also, the percentage of families with a female head of household among Mexican Americans (12 percent) is similar to that for whites (9 percent). One can say that the majority of Mexican Americans live in families in which both parents are present, but one cannot say from this evidence that their families are more cohesive than those of Anglos.

Evidence concerning divorce, however, shows somewhat greater stability among Mexican Americans, particularly among men (U.S. Bureau of the Census, 1971). The number of divorced men per 1000 currently married is 16 for Mexican Americans and 39 for other whites. Among the women the numbers divorced per 1000 currently married are 50 and 57, respectively, with the level for Mexican American women being only slightly lower than that for all white women. This pattern of perhaps somewhat greater family stability among Mexican Americans is also supported by the results of analyses by Frisbie, Bean, and Eberstein (1978) that control for other variables that might be thought to account for the pattern of less instability among Mexican Americans.

INTERMARRIAGE AND ASSIMILATION. Despite socioeconomic differences between Mexican Americans and Anglos the social assimilation of Mexican Americans, as measured by the incidence of intermarriage between them and Anglos, appears to be increasing somewhat (Table 2). Generally speaking, however, the figures indicate fairly strong patterns of in-group marriage, particularly in Texas. In Albuquerque, Los Angeles, and to a lesser extent in San Antonio, this is changing. In these cities, the latest available figures show as many as one in three Mexican Americans marrying an Anglo. Even these rates, however, demonstrate that Mexican Americans are a long way from complete assimilation into the larger society. Furthermore, with cultural pluralism increasingly becoming a viable option, acculturation may increase without a corresponding rise in intermarriage.

TABLE 2

Percent Exogamous Marriages of Mexican Americans, Various Places and Times

	LOS ANGELES		ALBUQUERQUE					SAN ANTONIO			CORPUS CHRISTI		EDINBURG, TEXAS (HIDALGO COUNTY)	
	1924–1933[a]	1963[a]	1924–1940[a]	1953[a]	1964[a]	1967[b]	1971[b]	1940–1955[a]	1960[d]	1973[c]	1960–1961[b]	1970–1971[b]	1961[b]	1971[b]
For individuals[e]	9	25	8	13	19	32	24	10	11	16	8	9	3	5
For marriages[f]	17	40	15	23	33	48	39	17	20	27	15	16	5	9

[a]Results from several studies summarized in Grebler, Moore, and Guzman (1970).

[b]Data gathered by David Alvirez and Edward Murguia.

[c]From Murguia and Frisbie (1977).

[d]From Bradshaw and Bean (1970).

[e]Refers for the time period to the percentage of individuals marrying exogamously among all individuals marrying.

[f]Refers for time period to the percentage of exogamous marriages among all marriages.

SOCIOECONOMIC STATUS. An area in which substantial differences between Mexican Americans and Anglos emerge is in socioeconomic status as measured by education, occupation, and income. The levels of education achieved by Mexican Americans are much lower than those of Anglos and contribute to their overall lower socioeconomic status and to limitations on upward social mobility. In 1978, among Mexican American males 25 years and older, 21.9 percent had completed less than five years of school, compared to 3.9 percent for the total male population. Comparable percentages for females were 24.4 and 3.4. The percentage completing 12 years or more of school showed the same disparity, with the figures favoring the total population. Among the total population over 25 years old, 66.8 percent of the males and 65.2 percent of the females had completed high school. Only 36.6 percent of Mexican American males and 32.1 percent of Mexican American females achieved this level of education. And only 4.8 and 3.9 percent of Mexican American males and females, respectively, completed college compared to 19.7 and 12.2 percent for the total population of males and females (U.S. Bureau of the Census, 1979b). These low levels of education, although up somewhat from past levels, affect labor-force participation, occupational opportunities, income, and poverty status (and hence influence family lifestyles and life chances).

Family socioeconomic status also depends on labor-force participation, and in this regard Mexican American males of working age are just as likely as other whites to be in the labor force, the rates of participation being 87 percent and 86 percent, respectively, while Mexican American females (39 percent) are less likely than Anglo women (50 percent) to be in the labor force (U.S. Bureau of the Census, 1972a). However, Cooney (1975) showed that almost all of the lower participation rate for Mexican American women was due to their lower socioeconomic status. Hence the idea that the greater absence of Mexican American women in the labor force is probably due to their traditional preference for staying home fails to receive support from her data; although the larger families characteristic of Mexican Americans, which allow less time for employment outside the home, may be a contributing factor in explaining the lower participation rate.

It is the examination of the occupational distribution of Mexican American men compared to other whites that most clearly demonstrates the disadvantaged position of Mexican American men (and, by extension, of Mexican American families) within the job structure of American society. Mexican Americans are greatly underrepresented in white-collar occupations, particularly at the top levels. Both among professional and technical workers and among managers and administrators Mexican American men have about one-third as many persons in these occupations as do other whites. On the other hand, they are overrepresented among blue-collar, farm, and service workers (U.S. Bureau of the Census, 1979b). This unequal occupational distribution, which is partly a result of lack of education and partly a result of discrimination, results in income disparities that heavily penalize Mexican American families.

In 1970, the median family income for Mexican Americans was $7117, compared to $10,236 for other whites—a difference of over $3,000 in annual income (U.S. Bureau of the Census, 1971). By 1975, Mexican American median family income had increased to $11,742 while the income of persons not of Spanish origin had increased to $16,284, a difference of over $4,000 (U.S. Bureau of the Census, 1979b). Hence little, if any, progress relative to the total U.S. population has been made.

Furthermore, when one recalls the larger family sizes of Mexican Americans and considers per capital income, it is fairly obvious that Mexican American families and their individual members are seriously handicapped by their low income levels. While per capita income for Mexican American male-headed households increased from $1334 to $2130 between 1970 and 1975, the per capita income for Anglo male-headed households increased from $2601 to $4333, which meant that per capita income for Mexican American households remained at 50 percent that of such Anglo households. Mexican American female-headed households per capita income was $808 and $1228 in 1970 and 1975, respectively, and actually represented a slight decline relative to Anglo male households, going from 31 to 28 percent of the Anglo male household per capita income (U.S. Commission on Civil Rights, 1978).

The result of all this is much higher levels of poverty for Mexican Americans than for Anglos with all the resulting disadvantages that poverty brings. Among all families and unrelated individuals, the percent of Mexican Americans below poverty was 28 percent in 1970 and 24 percent in 1975, compared to 13 percent and 9 percent, respectively, for Anglo male-headed families and unrelated individuals. Among female-headed families and female unrelated individuals the percentage below the poverty line was 53 percent in 1970 and 46 percent in 1975 (U.S. Commission on Civil Rights, 1978). One must keep in mind, however, that these differences are not the same throughout the United States. Poverty seems to be more prevalent in the southwest than in other portions of the country, yet it is less prevalent in California than in the other southwestern states. Even within states, there are large differences, with the greatest amount of poverty being found in southern Texas and in northern New Mexico. Yet in spite of regional differences, Mexican American families are always overrepresented among the population in poverty. Conditions will have to improve considerably before the socioeconomic position of Mexican American families reaches parity with other American families.

Social-Class Differences in Lifestyles

In speaking of social-class differences among Mexican Americans, it is well not to forget the complexity in social-class structures created by combinations of ethnicity and class. Gordon's concept of ethclass (1964) has been put to good use in previous chapters. Occupying a given position in the status hierarchy of a society inevitably structures the economic and lifestyle possibilities of families. Being a family in certain ethnic groups may enhance or diminish such possibilities. That is, Mexican Americans may not reflect all the characteristics of a given socioeconomic status in the larger society due to the fact they are Mexican Americans. This is particularly applicable to Mexican Americans with higher socioeconomic status who may both retain the cultural heritage of their ethnic group and face discrimination from the larger society. At the same time, it should be recognized that a status hierarchy exists as well among Mexican Americans. Hence, a Mexican American family may have relatively high status within the ethnic group than outside it. Moreover, the status of the Mexican American family may vary according to the length of time the family has been in this country, ranging from families of newly arrived immigrants to those of persons who trace their ancestors back as much as ten or 15 generations in this country. With these qualifications in mind, it can be said that social-class differences among Mexican American families are in many instances similar to those of American society in general. The higher the education of the main breadwinner, the better the job and the higher the income, hence the better the living conditions for the family as a whole.

Scarcely any studies have been conducted into the lifestyle consequences for Mexican Americans of attaining different levels of education or of holding different kinds of occupations. One exception is a study carried out in Austin, Texas, in which 348 Mexican American couples were interviewed to investigate the possible relations of social and cultural factors to family and fertility characteristics (Bradshaw and Bean, 1972). We will present some of the data from this study that pertain to social-class differences in lifestyles. As an indicator of social status, we divide the sample into two groups on the basis of education—one in which the husband had at least a high school education (higher socioeconomic status [SES]) and one in which the husband's level of schooling was less than 12 years (lower SES).

As would clearly be expected, SES affects where a family lives. Most importantly, it is of interest to note whether Mexican American families are or are not *barrio* (roughly the equivalent of a black ghetto) residents. Mexican American families with higher SES are more likely to be living outside the barrio than those low in SES. Seventy-four percent of the better educated Mexican American families lived outside the *barrio,* compared to 27 percent of the less educated ones. Though impossible to verify, the tendency as SES improves may be to move from the predominantly Mexican American *barrio* to a more mixed neighborhood, and then in turn to a predominantly Anglo, middle-class neighborhood.

Families with higher SES are more likely to have a working wife (52 percent) than are those with less education (42 percent). The higher percentage of working wives is probably due to a combination of two factors: the larger family sizes of the poorer Mexican Americans, together with a more personally materialistic orientation on the part of the women of higher SES. Indirect confirmation of this is provided by the fact that 62 percent of the working women whose husbands had not completed high school saw themselves as working due to family economic needs, compared to 43 percent of the working wives with better educated husbands.

Such economic conditions are also translated into role expectations. In respect to whether the wife expects her husband to be primarily instrumental (to mow the grass, to keep the home in good repair, etc.) or primarily expressive (to be sensitive to her needs, to be affectionate, etc.), wives with higher education living outside the *barrio* have the lowest rate of predominantly instrumental or materialistic expectations from their husbands (10 percent), whereas wives with low education living in the *barrio* have the highest instrumental expectations (35 percent). The indications are fairly strong that the wives of poor families are very much aware of their economic needs, and that such needs often take precedence over the expressive or socioemotional expectations that are often thought to be important to women in marriage, even those who may find themselves in poverty.

Given the better education and income of the higher SES families, one would hypothesize more homeownership among them. This was the case. Among the Austin families, only 38 percent of the low SES families owned or were buying their homes, compared to 71 percent among the higher SES families. These differences, however, should not be interpreted as being due to a lack of interest in homeownership among the poor but should be seen primarily as a reflection of their low SES.

In terms of friendship patterns and relationships with Anglos, greater contact with Anglos occurred among Mexican Americans with higher SES, suggesting more friendships and greater feelings of equality with Anglos among such persons. Several things in the Austin data lend support to this idea. The higher SES families were less likely to have only Mexican Americans among their close friends compared to the lower SES families—70 percent compared to 87 percent—although even among the higher SES males less than 5 percent had *only* Anglos as their closest friends. Probably the most noteworthy thing is that regardless of SES, or where the respondent lived, one's closest friends were likely to be all Mexican Americans. At least in Austin, ethnic ties are still quite strong and should continue to exert strong influences on most Mexican Americans.

The higher SES families are also more likely to have friends or relatives married to Anglos, 86 percent falling into this category, compared to 58 percent for lower SES families. This increased experience with intermarriage is probably a function both of SES per se and of place of residence and work, in which higher SES Mexican Americans have increased contact with Anglos. Hence, to this extent one might say that higher SES does tend to weaken ethnic ties.

Interestingly enough, however, higher SES respondents are just about as likely as lower status respondents to oppose their children marrying Anglos, 21 percent and 23 percent, respectively. In both cases it indicates that less than one-fourth of the respondents would oppose their children marrying Anglos, another factor that might weaken ethnic ties. Whether the militancy among Mexican Americans today will increase the opposition to intermarriage or cause more of one's ethnic heritage to be carried over into a mixed marriage is a matter that cannot be answered definitely.

Retention of the Spanish language is much more likely to occur among lower SES respondents. Forty-two percent of them used primarily Spanish in the home, compared to 8 percent among high SES families. The same finding is also reported by Grebler, Moore, and Guzman, (1970: 332). Conversely, 24 percent of lower SES respondents spoke primarily English, compared to 61 percent of the higher SES respondents. Given the new emphasis on bilingualism, it would appear that children of lower SES have a better chance of maintaining two languages and the benefits that come with being bilingual.

One last area to be mentioned in which social-class differences may appear is in that of husband–wife relationships. A more egalitarian relationship might be hypothesized (or expected) in the higher SES homes. On the assumption that an important aspect of an egalitarian relationship is open and free communication between spouses, the couples were asked a series of questions about how often they discussed with one another such matters as religion, birth control, child discipline, sex, and the number of children to have. Forty-nine percent of the higher SES couples indicated they talked frequently with each other about such things versus 38 percent of the lower SES couples. Overall, the percentage of couples with high levels of communication is below

50 percent. In the absence of comparative data for other groups, however, it is difficult to say whether this amount of husband–wife communication is typical of what might be expected from any group of married couples, or whether it reflects some degree of adherence to traditional patterns of husband–wife separation of roles.

A study by Hawkes and Taylor (1975) of Mexican and Mexican American farm laborer families is of some relevance to this question. It found that the most common pattern of conjugal decisionmaking among the husbands and wives in their sample tended to be joint-egalitarian instead of either husband- or wife-dominant. Since the couples in this study were lower SES couples, and since a joint-egalitarian approach to decisionmaking presupposes a high degree of interspousal communication, their findings suggest that it is probably inappropriate to interpret the low levels of communication observed in the Austin data as reflecting a greater tendency for Mexican Americans to prefer traditional patterns of husband–wife role separation.

The degree to which the findings for Mexican American families in Austin, Texas, can be applied to all Mexican Americans is something that cannot be answered at the present time. One would expect differences according to region of the country and to the percentage of the population that is Mexican American in that particular region. For example, findings would probably vary in California, in which Mexican Americans hold a slightly higher socioeconomic status than they do in Texas. They might also vary in border regions with high concentrations of Mexican Americans and a heavy influence from Mexico. We have no reason to feel, however, that results from other regions would be radically changed, rather, different only in degree.

CHANGE AND ADAPTATION

At various points in the discussion above we have mentioned and at times documented that considerable diversity and heterogeneity occurs among Mexican American families. Our attempt to describe the "typical" Mexican American family, of course, inevitably obscured this to some extent. In discussing the variation that occurs around some central pattern, two points in particular need to be emphasized. The first is that Mexican Americans have never very closely fit the stereotypes assigned to them. As noted in our treatment of the history of Mexican Americans in America, the Mexican American people do not all come from the same sociocultural backgrounds. The Spanish, Mexican, and Indian influences in the sociocultural background of Mexican Americans have always been and continue to be present in varying degrees in different parts of the population. To base descriptions of Mexican American family patterns on observations made only on poor families of predominantly Mexican backgrounds is to ignore cultural strains that perhaps better characterize other segments of the population and thus to risk perpetuating ethnic stereotypes (Madsen, 1964; Rubel, 1966).

Furthermore, the interpretation of Mexican American family life in terms of monolithic stereotypes implicitly assigns too great a role to the influence of cultural factors in shaping the family patterns of Mexican Americans. It invites the idea that certain patterns are derivative of beliefs and values passed from generation to generation rather than functional adaptations to a difficult environment. For example, the notion that such family patterns as living in extended family households, taking in poor relatives, and doubling up with other families in a single residence are reflections of the importance of familism does not on the face of it recognize that these patterns, as well as familism itself, may at least in part be responses to historical conditions of economic deprivation.

More significantly, when such ideas have been put to empirical test, they usually have been found wanting, as when Sena-Rivera (1979) in a study of Mexican American family structures found that the nuclear rather than the extended family prevailed as both the normative and actual pattern. This pattern is repeated in the results of the survey of Mexican Americans in Los Angeles and San Antonio (Grebler, Moore, and Guzman, 1970), which showed a virtual absence of extended-family living arrangements among the respondents at the time of the survey as well as for quite some time previously. It seems clear from the responses to the survey questions that many families felt an *obligation* to help others in time of need, and that such times had often occurred, but that their *preference* was to discard such living patterns as material welfare improved. These results suggest that the occurrence of extended family patterns has often been an adaptive response to the social and physical environment in which families have found themselves rather than a cultural prescription (Baca Zinn, 1975). Further support for this idea also comes from other studies that have observed that familism among Mexican Americans does not appear to be as pronounced as has often been assumed (Farris and Glenn, 1976; Bean, Curtis, and Marcum, 1977).

A second and very important factor increasingly renders it difficult to speak of Mexican American families in all-encompassing terms. In addition to the fact that the "traditional Mexican family" was never uniformly present in the population, family patterns among Mexican Americans have been involved in processes of change related to generation, class differences, regional differences (including distance from the border), and increasing urbanization. An especially relevant indication of the changes impinging on the Mexican American family can be discerned in changing patterns of intermarriage.

Based on marriage-license data in Los Angeles County, a recent study indicated that the social distance between generations of Mexican Americans was even greater than that between some Mexican Americans and Anglos. Third-generation Mexican Americans tended to marry out more than first-generation persons, and as Mexican Americans moved into the middle class, they tended to marry more on the basis of class than ethnic considerations (Grebler, Moore, and Guzman, 1970: 408–409). The importance of generation for intermarriage has also recently been reaffirmed (Schoen and Cohen, 1980), as has the significance of generation for modifying fertility patterns (Marcum and Bean, 1976) and self-concepts (Dworkin, 1970) among Mexican Americans. All of these studies suggest that the family patterns among later-generation Mexican Americans are likely to be different from those of earlier generations.

As Mexican American families have become exposed to and participants in the urban middle-class lifestyle and culture, the internal structure of the family has also changed. The brunt of this change seems to have been borne by the husband's role. The traditional patriarchal role of the man was especially suited for life in the rural past when there was plenty of work to be done outside as well as inside the house. Men did the former, and women the latter, and associated with this sexual division of labor was the patriarchal assumption of power, prestige, and prerogatives in decisionmaking. Considerable doubt has been cast on the notion that this pattern has ever been a behavioral norm (Grebler, Moore, and Guzman, 1970: 360). Certainly a sexual division of labor has lost much of its force in an urban milieu in which the ratio of the number of "masculine" tasks outside the house to the number of "feminine" tasks inside the house has declined. The Los Angeles study (Grebler, Moore, and Guzman, 1970: 362) found that this and other changes such as the "changing work situation, exposure to new values of both masculinity and femininity, and higher levels of living" have brought about changes in the definitions of the roles of husband and wife, but especially the husband. Comparing the responses of Mexican Americans to questions regarding who performs certain sex-typed household tasks to those of a sample of the general population of Detroit revealed that Mexican Americans are close to "typical Americans" and suggest "that egalitarianism occurs more in the masculine sex-typed tasks than in the feminine, just as there is more loosening in the norms regarding the husband's role than in those regarding the role of the wife" (Grebler, Moore, and Guzman, 1970: 362). Yet these changes in male roles and behavior have not always been surrendered willingly by Mexican American males. They are in part the result of a new awareness among some Mexican American women who have demanded not only new roles for themselves but have challenged what they consider the more negative aspects of certain male roles and behavior patterns (Mirande and Enriquez, 1979: 115–117).

Just as the role of the husband in the Mexican American family seems to be changing, the Mexican American family in general is changing in adaptation to new situations and opportunities. Although little research has been done in this area, the change cannot be occurring without some conflict, between new immigrants and "old" Mexican Americans, between members of one class and those of another. Yet vestiges of the more traditional Mexican American family linger on, especially in rural areas and in the more isolated *barrios*. And in some ways they perhaps are being strengthened by the continuing influx of Mexican immigrants. Perhaps these traditions may even become rejuvenated and more widespread in the wake of the Chicano movement, which emphasizes the positive features in the Mexican American sociocultural heritage. As the Mexican American family becomes subjected to these many different social forces and situations, one thing seems certain. It will become increasingly difficult to speak of "the" Mexican American family.

REFERENCES

Alvarez, R. 1973. "The Psycho-Historical and Socioeconomic Development of the Chicano Community in the United States," *Social Science Quarterly*, 53 (March): 920–942.

Baca Zinn, M. 1975. "Political Familism: Toward Sex Role Equality in Chicano Families," *Aztlan*, 6 (Spring): 13–26.

Bean, F., R. Curtis, and J. Marcum. 1977. "Familism and Marital Satisfaction Among Mexican Americans: The Effects of Family Size, Wife's Labor Force Participation, and Conjugal Power," *Journal of Marriage and the Family*, 39 (November): 759–767.

Bradshaw, B.S., and F.D. Bean. 1970. "Intermarriage Between Persons of Spanish and Non-Spanish Surname: Changes from the Mid-Nineteenth to the Mid-Twentieth Century," *Social Science Quarterly*, 51 (September): 389–395.

———. 1972. " Some Aspects of the Fertility of Mexican Americans," in C.F. Westoff and R. Parks, Jr. (eds.), *Demographic and Social Aspects of Population Growth*. Commission on Population Growth and the American Future, Research Reports, Volume 1. Washington, DC: U.S. Government Printing Office, pp. 139–64.

Buechley, R.W. 1961. "A Reproducible Method of Counting Persons of Spanish Surname," *Journal of the American Statistical Association*, 56 (March): 88–97.

———. 1967. "Characteristic Name Sets of Spanish Populations," *Names*, 15 (March): 53–69.

Cooney, R. 1975. "Changing Labor Force Participation of Mexican American Wives:

A Comparison with Anglos and Blacks," *Social Science Quarterly,* 56 (September): 252–261.

Dworkin, A. 1970. "Stereotypes and Self-images Held by Native-Born and Foreign-Born Mexican Americans," in John H. Burma (ed.), *Mexican Americans in the United States.* New York: Holt, Rhinehart and Winston.

Environmental Fund, 1979. "1979 World Population Estimates" (Chart). Washington, DC: The Environmental Fund.

Farris, B., and N. Glenn. 1976. "Fatalism and Familism Among Anglos and Mexican Americans in San Antonio," *Sociology and Social Research,* 60 (Summer): 393–402.

Frisbie, W.P., F. Bean, and I. Eberstein. 1978. "Patterns of Marital Instability Among Mexican Americans, Blacks, and Anglos," in F. Bean and W. P. Frisbie (eds.), *The Demography of Racial and Ethnic Groups.* New York: Academic Press, pp. 143–164.

Gordon, M. 1964. *Assimilation in American Life.* New York: Oxford University Press.

Grebler, L., J.W. Moore, and R.C. Guzman. 1970. *The Mexican American People.* New York: The Free Press.

Hawkes, G., and M. Taylor. 1975. "Power Structure in Mexican and Mexican American Farm Labor Families," *Journal of Marriage and the Family,* 37 (November): 807–811.

Hayden, R.G. 1966. "Spanish Americans of the Southwest," *Welfare in Review,* 4 (April): 14–25.

Hernandez, J., L. Estrada, and D. Alvirez. 1973. "Census Data and the Problem of Conceptually Defining the Mexican American Population," *Social Science Quarterly,* 53 (March): 671–687.

Lopez, D. and G. Sabagh. 1978. "Untangling Structural and Normative Aspects of the Minority Status-Fertility Hypothesis," *American Journal of Sociology,* 83 (May): 1491–1497.

Madsen, W. 1964. *Mexican-Americans of South Texas,* 2nd edition. New York: Holt, Rinehart and Winston.

Marcum, J. and F. Bean. 1976. "Minority Group Status as a Factor in the Relationship Between Mobility and Fertility: The Mexican American Case," *Social Forces,* 55 (September): 135–148.

McLemore, S.D. 1973. "The Origins of Mexican American Subordination in Texas," *Social Science Quarterly,* 53 (March): 656–670.

———. 1980. *Racial and Ethnic Relations in America.* Boston: Allyn Bacon.

McWilliams, C. 1968. *North From Mexico.* New York: Greenwood Press.

Mirande, Alfredo, and Evangelina Enriquez. 1979. *La Chicana, The Mexican-American Woman.* Chicago: University of Chicago Press.

Murguia, E. 1975. *Assimilation, Colonialism and the Mexican American People.* Mexican American Monograph Series #1. Center for Mexican American Studies. The University of Texas at Austin. Austin: University of Texas Press.

Murguia, E., and P. Frisbie. 1977. "Trends in Mexican American Intermarriage: Recent Findings in Perspective" *Social Science Quarterly,* 58 (December): 374–389.

Murillo, N. 1971. "The Mexican American Family," in N.W. Wagner and M.J. Huag (eds.), *Chicanos: Social and Psychological Perspectives.* St. Louis: Mosley, pp. 97–108.

Penalosa, F. 1968. "Mexican Family Roles," *Journal of Marriage and the Family,* 30 (Fall): 13–27.

Roberts, R., and E.S. Lee. 1974. "Minority Group Status and Fertility Revisited," *American Journal of Sociology,* 80 (September): 503–523.

Rubel, Arthur J. 1966. *Across the Tracks: Mexican Americans in a Texas City.* Austin: University of Texas Press.

Sabagh, G. 1980. "Fertility Planning Status of Chicano Couples in Los Angeles," *American Journal of Public Health,* 70 (January): 56–61.

Schoen, R., and L. Cohen. 1980. "Ethnic Endogamy Among Mexican American Grooms: A Reanalysis of Generational and Occupational Effects," *American Journal of Sociology* (forthcoming).

Sena-Rivera, J. 1979. "Extended Kinship in the United States: Competing Models and the Case of La Familia Chicana," *Journal of Marriage and the Family,* 41 (February): 121–129.

Ulibarri, H. 1970. "Social and Attitudinal Characteristics of Spanish-Speaking Migrants and Ex-Migrant Workers in the Southwest," in J. Burma, (ed.), *Mexican-Americans in the United States.* Cambridge: Schenkman, pp. 29–39.

U.S. Bureau of the Census. 1963. "Persons of Spanish Surname," *United States Census of the Population: 1960, Subject Reports,* Final Report PC(2)–1B. Washington, DC: U.S. Government Printing Office.

———. 1971. "Selected Characteristics of Persons and Families of Mexican, Puerto Rican, and Other Spanish Origin: March 1971," *Current Population Reports,* Series P-20, no. 224. Washington, DC: U.S. Government Printing Office.

———. 1972a. *Census of Population: 1970. General Social and Economic Characteristics,* Final Reports PC(1)–C6 California and PC(1)–C45 Texas. Washington, DC: U.S. Government Printing Office.

———. 1972b. "Selected Characteristics of Persons and Families of Mexican, Puerto Rican, and Other Spanish Origin: March 1972," *Current Population Reports,* Series P-20, no. 238. Washington, DC: U.S. Government Printing Office.

———. 1973. *Census of Population: 1970. Subject Reports,* Final Report PC (2)–3A. Washington DC: U.S. Government Printing Office.

———. 1979a. "Household and Family Characteristics: March, 1978," *Current Population Reports,* Series P-20, no. 340. Washington, DC: U.S. Government Printing Office.

———. 1979b. "Persons of Spanish Origin in the United States: March, 1978," *Current Population Reports,* Series P-20, no. 339. Washington, DC: U.S. Government Printing Office.

U.S. Commission on Civil Rights, 1974. *Counting the Forgotten: The 1970 Census Count of Persons of Spanish Speaking Background in the United States.* Washington, DC: U.S. Commission on Civil Rights.

———. 1978. *Social Indicators of Equality for Minorities and Women.* Washington, DC: U.S. Government Printing Office.

SOCIORELIGIOUS ETHNIC MINORITIES

The Amish Family

The Old Order Amish, as described by Dr. Huntington, are an example of an ethnoreligious group that has had great success in preserving its traditions and preventing wholesale assimilation. The primarily rural Amish are, as Dr. Huntington points out, probably contrary to popular opinion, a growing population that has managed to resist the onslaught of modern technology and major social change. Their ability to resist change is grounded in their religious commitment, which is expressed in their major social institutions. In this chapter we see how the family institution helps maintain Amish culture and society.

CHAPTER THIRTEEN
BY
GERTRUDE ENDERS HUNTINGTON

HISTORICAL BACKGROUND

The Old Order Amish Mennonites are direct descendants of the Swiss Anabaptists of the 16th century. "Anabaptist" is a historical and theological term used to designate a number of different theologies and social groups (Littell, 1964) that represent the left wing of the Reformation (Bainton, 1952). Those Anabaptist groups who survive emerged between 1525 and 1536 and are today represented by the Amish, the Mennonites, and the Hutterites. These churches are characterized by the maintenance of a disciplined community, pacifism, separation from the world, adult rather than infant baptism, and an emphasis on simple living.

The Amish developed between 1693 and 1697 as a dissenting conservative wing of the Swiss Mennonites. Their leader, Jacob Amman, introduced shunning (the avoidance of all normal social intercourse with a member who is under the ban), foot washing as a part of the communion service, communion twice a year instead of only once, the excommunication of persons who attend the state church, and greater uniformity of dress and hairstyle. The Amman group, or Amish, continue to this day to abide by rules established by Jacob Amman and interpreted by each local congregation.

Although the Amish family as we know it is an American phenomenon, its roots go back to the early days in Europe. Persecution was severe in Europe; the Amish were forbidden citizenship and thus could not own land. Therefore, they were generally unable to establish permanent, stable communities or to develop a distinctive social structure. Their livelihood, their place of residence, even their lives were subject to the whim of rulers and neighbors. Families often had to live at considerable distance from coreligionists; religious services were held irregularly and unobtrusively in the home of a church member. This mobility, isolation, and limited community interaction placed the emphasis for producing Christians directly on the family. To this day, the family has remained the smallest and strongest unit of Amish culture, the central social institution.

Anabaptist theology, which emphasized adult baptism, also supported the role of the family in child development. Protestant religious leaders such as Martin Luther and Philipp Melanchthon were suspicious of parents' ability to rear their children without the help and intervention of the state (Schwartz, 1973:102–114). In contrast, the Anabaptists never equated childrearing with schooling, nor did they believe that the child or the parent was morally subservient to some outside civil or religious authority. Childrearing was the parents' major responsibility. Menno Simons (about 1496–1561), an early leader in Holland after whom the Mennonites are named, wrote, "For this is the chief and principal care of the saints, that their children may fear, God, do right, and be saved" (Simons, 1956:950). He also taught that parents were morally responsible for the condition of their children's souls. "Watch over their souls as long as they are under your care, lest you lose also your own salvation on their account" (Simons, 1956:391).

In addition to urging parents to set an unblamable example for their children and to teach, instruct, admonish, correct, and chastise their children as circumstances require, parents were also to protect their children from worldly influences and from wrong companions. "Keep them away from good-for-nothing children, from whom they hear and learn nothing but lying, cursing, swearing, fighting, and mischief" (Simons, 1956:959). Parents were to direct their children to reading and writing, that they might learn from the Scripture what God teaches. They were to instruct them to spin and to earn their bread by the labor of their hands. One example from the *Martyr's Mirror*[1] of

---

[1] *The Bloody Theater*, or *Martyr's Mirror*, was first published in Dutch in 1660 and has periodically been reprinted in German and in English. It is a large book containing over 1500 pages and recounting, often with vivid details, the deaths of over 4000 men and women who remained steadfast to their faith in spite of branding, burning, stoning, sessions on the rack, the severing of tongues, hands and feet, live burials and drowning. No one who recanted is considered a martyr, nor is one a martyr if he survived his torture. The *Martyr's Mirror* helps strengthen members "to make every preparation for steadfastness in our faith," (preface to fifth English Edition, 1950) whether in the face of an inquisition, school officials, or universal conscription.

practical instruction for child care was written by Jacob the Chandler shortly before he was burned at the stake (Braght, 1951:798–799):

> Furthermore, I pray you, my dear and much beloved wife, that you do the best with my children, to bring them up in the fear of God, with good instruction and chastening, while they are still young. . . . For instruction must accompany chastisement: for chastisement demands obedience, and if one is to obey, he must first be instructed. This instruction does not consist of hard words, or loud yelling; for this the children learn to imitate; but if one conducts himself properly towards them they have a good example, and learn propriety; for by the children the parents are known. And parents must not provoke their children to anger, lest they be discouraged; but must bring them up with admonition and good instruction.

During their years in Europe, the Amish lived in Switzerland, Alsace-Lorraine, the Palatine, France, Holland, Austria, Germany, and Poland. Lack of religious toleration meant that the Amish in Europe remained renters, and that families had limited choice as to where they could settle, frequently being forced to move to new locations as political situations changed. Although an effort was made to stay near members of the faith—an old Amish hymn (*Ausbund*, 1564: Hymn No. 44) quoted a martyr writing to his son: "Live, only where the believers live,"—it was impossible for the Amish to establish discrete communities. In some areas they continued for many years as a religious sect, but they never formed a self-perpetuating subculture. Today there are no people left in Europe who are distinctly Amish (Hostetler, 1955).

There is some disagreement as to when the first Amish landed in America. A 1709 letter of William Penn's pertaining to the Palatinate immigrants mentions "diverse Mennonites" (Smith, 1920:214), which could be construed as a reference to the Amish. The Amish immigrated to this continent in two major waves: The first wave from about 1727 to 1770 settled in Pennsylvania, and the second wave from 1815 to 1860 went primarily to Ohio and Indiana. (Luthy, 1973: 14).

The first Amish to arrive in America settled in Pennsylvania; there they formed discrete clusters, separate from the Mennonites as well as from the "English."[2] In contrast to their experience in Europe, the Amish immigrants to America found cheap land and religious toleration. They responded by electing to purchase farms near fellow churchmen, away from the influence of cities. This has continued to be the basis of their settlement pattern. The

---

[2]A term used for all non-Mennonites (and sometimes for all non-Amish) even those who are German speaking.

297

TABLE 1
Old Order Amish Population by State and County (1980)

STATE	DATE OF FIRST AMISH SETTLERS[a]	PRESENT SETTLEMENT[e]	DISTRICTS[b]	BAPTIZED MEMBERS (ESTIMATED[c])	TOTAL MEMBERSHIPS (ESTIMATED[d])
Ohio	1808		165	13,035	27,720
Pennsylvania	c. 1720		132	10,428	22,176
Indiana	1839		102	8058	17,136
Missouri	1856	1947	22	1738	3696
Wisconsin	1908	1925	20	1580	3360
Iowa	1840		19	1501	3192
Illinois	1829	1864	13	1027	2184
Michigan	1895		12	948	2016
New York	1833	1949	11	869	1048
Delaware	1915		6	474	1008
Tennessee	1872	1944	6	474	1008
Minnesota	c. 1890	1972	5	395	840
Kentucky	1958		5	395	840
Maryland	1772	1850	4	316	672
Kansas	1883		4	316	672
Oklahoma	1892		3	237	504
Virginia	1895	1942	1	79	168
Florida	1925		1	79	168
Arkansas[d]	1927	1976	—	—	—
Montana[d]	1903	1970	—	—	—
Nebraska[d]	1880	1975	—	—	—
Canada	1824		15	1185	2520
TOTAL			546	42.186	91,728

[a]Information supplied by David Luthy, Alymer, Ontario.

[b]J.A. Raber (1980).

[c]Data calculated using Hostetler's estimate of 79 baptized members and 168 total Amish individual per church district. (Hostetler, 1980: 80–81). Cross, using data from Ohio, determined the number of baptized members to be 86 and the total membership per district to be 199. (1967:42). Smaller, less densely settled Amish communities have small church districts.

[d]Not listed in Raber. Listed as having Amish community schools in *Blackboard Bulletin.* New settlements do not always have a complete church structure nor is the population as high as 79 baptized members per district.

[e]Hostetler (1980:100).

Ohio Amish community was started in 1808; this community in central Ohio is the largest and in many ways the most conservative of the large Amish communities. In 1839 settlers in Indiana formed what was to become the third largest Amish settlement. More than three-fourths of the Amish live in these three states. Smaller settlements are found in Illinois, Iowa, Wisconsin,

Missouri, Delaware, Florida, Kansas, Kentucky, Minnesota, Oklahoma, Maryland, New York, Michigan, Tennessee, Arkansas, Montana, and Nebraska. At one time, there were Amish settlements in Oregon, North Dakota, California, Colorado, North Carolina, Georgia, Texas, New Mexico, Mississippi, Alabama, and Mexico.[3] In 1968, small Old Order Amish communities were established in Honduras and Paraguay. These communities are still in existence. However, the Honduras community has not remained typically Old Order, and that of Paraguay has only three families and one minister.

Table 1 gives the 1980 Amish population and the dates of the Amish settlers in each state. In some instances the first settlements were not successful, and present Amish population is the result of later immigrations. In other cases regular church districts were not established until a considerable time after the earliest settlement.

The Old Order Amish are a tradition-oriented, conservation branch of the Mennonite Church. The term Old Order came into usage during the last half of the 19th century when more liberal congregations separated from them. The Old Order are also known as "House Amish" because they hold their church services in their homes, or "Horse and Buggy Amish" because they do not own cars. The Old Order Amish are distinguished by prohibitions against owning automobiles, telephones, and high-line electricity. They have strict dress codes and forbid rubber-tired tractors (if tractors are used at all), central heating, and cameras. They speak a German dialect known as Pennsylvania Dutch in their homes, read the German Bible, and do not permit attendance at state schools beyond the eighth grade. In this chapter the discussion will be limited to the Old Order Amish.

THE MODERN OLD ORDER AMISH FAMILY
Demographic Characteristics

FERTILITY. Many people think of the Amish as a shrinking remnant whose days are numbered, but they are in actuality a growing church. Because the Amish do not proselytize, their growth depends primarily on biological increment combined with the ability to hold their children in the faith. The Old Order Amish have increased from a population of about 8200 in 1905 to 92,000 in 1980; from 43 church districts to 547 districts (Table 2). Household size varies from those married pairs who have no children to those having 15 children or more.

Studies of family size show that for completed families the average number of children born alive is about seven. This greatly exceeds the national av-

---

[3]Personal correspondence, December 21, 1973, Interview March 10, 1980, David Luthy, Aylmer, Ontario.

TABLE 2

Old Order Amish Population and Districts, 1905–1970

YEAR	POPULATION	NUMBER OF DISTRICTS
1905	8200	43
1920	13,900	83
1930	18,500	110
1940	25,800	154
1950	33,000	197
1960	43,000	258
1970	59,304	353
1980	91,900	547

SOURCE: Hostetler (1980:80) and Raber (1970, 1980).

erage for white rural households. Cross (1967:108) reported the annual natural increase of the Holmes County, Ohio Amish population to be 3.0 percent, or a potential doubling of the population every 23 years. Assuming this growth rate to be representative and constant, it is interesting to compare the potential population growth of the Amish with the observed population growth. Taking the estimated 1920 population to be 13,900, the 1943 potential population would be 27,800, and the 1966 potential population would be 55,600. Hostetler (1980:81) gives the actual estimated total population for 1966 as 49,371. This would represent a loss to the church of possibly about 6000 individuals over a 46-year period and an observed increase of about 35,500. These estimates would indicate that the Amish are successful in perpetuating their own subculture.

Recent demographic studies of the Amish (Hostetler, E. Ericksen, J. Ericksen, and Huntington, 1977, and J. Ericksen, E. Ericksen, Hostetler, and Huntington, 1979) have shown that there has been no reduction in Amish fertility over time; in fact, there may have been a slight increase in fertility. Sterility among Amish women appears to be lower than among the general American population. [Ever-married American women in the birth cohort 1922–1926 had a sterility rate of 7.5 percent while for ever-married Amish women in the birth cohort 1919–1928, it was 4.4 percent, and in the cohort 1928–1938, it was 2.6 percent (J. Ericksen, E. Ericksen, Hostetler, and Huntington, 1979:258)]. Twinning, which seems to be high, may be related to the longer reproductive history of Amish women and the larger number of children born—both of which factors seem to be related to frequency of twinning (Enders and Stern, 1948; Cross, 1967). Not only do the Amish continue to maintain a high birth rate with no indication of contraceptive practices but they are also successful in maintaining their grown children within the religious community. Detailed interviews with Amish women in Pennsylvania indicated that over 90 percent of their grown children remained Old Order Amish. [The 61 women interviewed had already produced a total of 385 grown children of whom 347 were Amish (Hostetler, E. Ericksen, J. Ericksen, and Huntington, 1977:39–40)]. An analysis of an Amish genealogy (Fisher, 1957) listing all the descendants of Christian Fisher, who was born in Pennsylvania in 1757, indicated that during the ensuing 200 years there had been no reduction in Old Order Amish fertility. However, there had been an average loss to the religious community (by individuals leaving the church) of about 22 percent. (J. Ericksen, E. Ericksen, Hostetler, and Huntington, 1979:272). Given the high birth rate of the Amish, even if they sustained a loss of one-quarter of their children, they would still maintain a substantial growth rate.

The Amish have a high standard of living, good medical care, and prohibit birth control. Therefore, except for the relatively late age of marriage, their birth rate resembles that of nonindustrialized countries, while their death rate resembles that of industrialized countries. When plotted by age and sex, the Amish population forms a wide-based pyramid, with over half the Amish under 20 years of age. This is in contrast to the population pyramid of the American rural farm population, which has a relatively narrow base. Within the typical American farm population, there are a disproportionate number of old people in relation to young people. The demographic structure of the Amish makes it relatively easy for the youthful population to carry the burden of supporting the aged; there are many productive young people to care for the relatively few old people.

DIVORCE. The Old Order Amish are strictly monogamous. The individual's first commitment is to God; his second is to his spouse. There is no divorce, and under no circumstances may an Amishman remarry while his spouse is living. Except for widows, the head of the household is always a man. The rare unmarried farmer will have a sister or perhaps a married nephew who lives in his household and helps out.

SEXUAL TRANSGRESSION. The Amish are strongly opposed to extramarital coitus, and any transgression must be confessed to the total membership of the church whether or not pregnancy results. The male and female have equal responsibility to confess fornication. However, after a period of punishment, during which the transgressor is under the ban, both repentant individuals are welcomed back into full church membership, and they are completely forgiven. Although pregnancy is not always considered sufficient reason to marry, if the couple decides to get married, an effort is made to have the wedding before the birth of the baby. The degree of community pressure to marry applied to a couple who has fornicated or conceived varies from one settlement to another. If the parents do not marry, the mother may keep the baby, or it may be adopted by an Amish couple.

MATE SELECTION. The Amish are endogamous; marriage must be "in the Lord," that is, within the church membership. Any Amish person who marries outside the church loses his membership and becomes non-Amish. Even within the Old Order Amish church there are breeding isolates resulting from preferred marriage patterns. Marriage between members of noncommuning churches is discouraged, and marriages tend to take place within one settlement or between closely related settlements. Although first-cousin marriages are forbidden, second-cousin marriages are common. The total Amish population has such a small genetic base that marriage partners are frequently as closely related as second and third cousins. Parents have considerable influence as to which group of young people within the settlement their children will "go with," for whom their children will work, and which communities they will visit. By this means young people are directed into preferred social groups and thereby into preferred marriages.

The Amish perceive the family as a religious and a social unit. Therefore, it is not surprising that Amish weddings are community affairs that fit into the general cycle of activity. The majority of weddings occur during the winter months after harvest and before spring planting—November and December being the most popular months. In Lancaster County, Pennsylvania, over 90 percent of the weddings occur during these two months. Outside of the Lancaster County settlement, there seems to be an extension of the wedding season, with more couples being married in late winter. In Ohio, two-thirds of the weddings occur between October and January. Indiana, the least traditional settlement, has only a few more than half the weddings occurring during these four months. The variation in season of marriage may be related to the trend away from farming. Of the three communities, Indiana has the largest number of family heads engaged in nonfarming occupations. In addition to holding weddings at specific times of the year, almost all Amish weddings are on Thursday, with a few being held on Tuesday, and occasionally a second marriage may be incorporated into a Sunday church service. Thursday is the most convenient day of the week to hold an elaborate, day-long celebration, considering the prohibition against all unnecessary work on Sunday. Thursday gives the host family four days in which to "set up" for the wedding and two days to clean up afterward without infringing on Sunday.

Not only have wedding customs remained traditional, the age of marriage has also been relatively stable among the Amish for the past 50 years. (Huntington, 1956:897; J. Ericksen, E. Ericksen, Hostetler, and Huntington, 1979: 257–258). The median age of first marriage for Amish women aged 45–49 in 1966 was 22.1, and 24.7 for their husbands.

SOCIAL STRUCTURE. All Amish communities are rural. Although there is a fairly wide variation in family income there are no extremes of poverty or affluence. The Amish in America have developed a distinctive social structure consisting of the settlement, the church district, the family, and the affiliation or network of communing church districts.

The settlement consists of all the Amish living in a given geographically contiguous area. A single Amish family cannot be considered to form a settlement; even a small group of Amish families is not considered to be a settlement until they organize a church district. There is a minimum size necessary for a settlement to be able to sustain itself. This size is related to the number of church officials in the settlement (there must be at least two) and to the distance from the nearest communing church district, as well as the actual number of families and the size of the families that make up the settlement. Those Amish who are isolated geographically and socially from other Amish for too long a period lose their Amish identity. The Amish realize this, and if a new settlement does not attract other Amish settlers quickly enough, it will disband. History shows that those individuals who remain where there is no organized church become absorbed into the surrounding culture (Umble, 1949).

A church district is composed of a contiguous cluster of Old Order Amish families who worship together. Typically, each church district has a bishop, two ministers, a deacon, and 25 to 35 nuclear families. The number of families is determined by the density of the Amish in the area and the size of the homes; when the group becomes too large to meet in a home or barn for the worship service, the district divides. The geographical area of a single church district is almost never settled exclusively by Amish. The area is crossed by paved roads, perhaps interrupted by a village, and is interspersed with "English" farms and homes. Although there are geographical boundaries, neither the Amish church district nor the Amish community is territorial; it is a cultural, social, and religious grouping. The community is not necessarily made up of one's neighbors but rather of one's fellow church members, who are bound together by an ideology and a way of life.

The family, rather than the individual, is the unit of the church. When one asks an Amishman how big his church district is, he always answers you by stating how many families belong, never by how many individual members there are. The *Ohio Amish Directory* lists the families in each district, with no indication as to which individuals have been baptized into the church; un-

303

married baptized members are not listed unless they own their own home. Growth of the church is related to number of weddings, not number of baptisms.

Due to the congregational structure and the strict rules of discipline, differences that may seem minor to the outsider often arise within the larger settlements. These differences are the basis of various affiliations. Church districts that are "in fellowship" with one another interpret the *Ordnung* (discipline) similarly and exchange ministers for Sunday services. All those churches whose ministers "help out" one another form a single affiliation. The affiliations are informal, often unknown to non-Amish, and frequently changing. The tendency is to divide into more affiliations rather than to coalesce. This functions to keep the groups small, to limit social interaction, and to protect tradition. In the central Ohio community there are at least seven different Old Order Amish affiliations that are not "in fellowship" with one another. These range along a conservative–liberal continuum from churches whose members will not ride in a private car (except to attend a funeral or go to the hospital) to churches in which young men drive cars until they actually join the church. Affiliations extend beyond settlement boundaries and, combined with kinship ties, help to bind different geographic Amish settlements together.

Kinship Relations

Kinship ties are maintained throughout the life of the individual. Excerpts from newsletters in *The Budget,* a weekly paper that goes to almost every Amish settlement, illustrate the importance of kinship ties both to the families and to the community (*The Budget,* August 7, 1973):

> The children grandchildren and great-grandchildren of Levi L. Slabach of Berlin were together for Sunday dinner at Bish. Roy L. Slabach's. All were present but three grandchildren. This was in honor of Levi's birthday which is August 6.
>
> Mother and us sisters were together at Benuel Stoltzfous, Jr. (sis. Mary). Mother Fisher is having quiltings this week and next to finish the quilts grandmother Fisher had started.

Extended families gather to celebrate birthdays and Christmas; brothers and sisters meet to work together, to help one another with church, to sew rags for woven rugs, to put up a milk house. And in the case of illness or any other stress, the extended family, the members of the church district, and other Amish neighbors rally round to help. Members of the Amish settlement are always identified by kinship groups. Husband and wife names are used together, Joe-Annie to signify Annie, the wife of Joe, or Annie-Joe meaning Joe, the husband of Annie; or father's name is used, Menno's Annie to identify Annie, the daughter of Menno. Traditionally, the Amish children in Ohio were always given their father's first name as a middle initial to help identify them. In some settlements the initial of the mother's first name or maiden name is used for an identifying middle initial. There are generally so few last names in a given settlement that first names are used more frequently than last; thus, families are identified as "the Raymonds" and "the Aden Js" instead of "the Millers" and "the Detweilers." In the central Ohio Amish settlement 12 names account for 85 percent of the families. There are only 124 different Amish surnames found in a population of about 90,000. Therefore, it is not surprising that nicknames are also widely used to distinguish individuals: "Barefoot Sam" or "Turkey John." Individuals are always identified by their families, by their *Fruendschaft.*.

Children in the Amish community schools introduce themselves by giving their father's first name . Young people quickly tell who their father and their mother are so that they can be placed genealogically. The signers of some Amish guest books are asked to indicate their date of birth and, if they are unmarried, to add their father's name. Kinship networks function to tie distant settlements together. Families visit married sons and daughters; brothers and sisters visit one another to "help out" or for a family get-together. Marriages, when outside the settlement, tend to take place between settlements that are closely related by kinship ties. Amish both publish and purchase genealogies, and family reunions are widely attended. *The Budget* has a section in the classified ads, "#23-Reunions," and in the late summer many of the columns from different communities mention reunions.

The kinship network, especially that involving parents of married children and brothers and sisters, plays a crucial role in establishing young Amish families on farms. In a study done in 1976 in Lancaster County, Pennsylvania, 76 percent of the young Amishmen who were farming had obtained their farm from relatives and the same percentage had obtained loans from family members. Seventy-four percent of the renters were renting land owned by relatives and only 10 percent were renting from non-Amish. The typical pattern is for an Amish couple to marry before obtaining a farm. For a short time the groom continues to work for wages, saving his money so he can rent a farm and, ideally, within a few years he buys his own farm. Although each nuclear family will eventually achieve economic independence, this is not expected of the newly married family. In spite of a strong community, Amish norms stress dependency on the family, especially on the extended family, for normal economic support. For catastrophic events, such as fire or unanticipated hospital expenses, the community supplements the kinship.

Family Roles

Roles are well defined in the Amish family. The man is the head of the woman (I Cor:3) as Christ is the head of the Church. Although the wife is to be subject to her husband, her first commitment is to God, and her second is to her husband. Because she has an immortal soul, she is an individual in her own right. She is not a possession of her husband, nor is she merely an extension of her spouse. Husband and wife become one flesh, a single unit separable only by God. She follows her husband, but only in that which is good. At council service before communion she decides, as an individual, if she is ready for communion. Should her husband transgress to the extent that he is placed under the ban, she, too, will shun him, as he will her in a similar situation. For the Amishman, the question of sacrificing his family for his job never comes up. The family comes first. A job is of no intrinsic importance; it is necessary because it supplies the economic basis for the family. The work of the household should provide vocational education for the children and fulfill the biblical standard, "In the sweat of thy face shalt thou eat bread." The wife's relative position is illustrated by her position in church, where she has an equal vote but not an equal voice. Farms are owned in the name of both husband and wife. Important family decisions are made jointly. Unlike the corporation wife, the Amish wife participates actively in any decision to move to a different locality. And unlike the corporation wife, the Amish farm wife makes as active contribution to the production of the household. She may help with the farm work, produce most of the salad material and vegetables consumed by her family, make more than half the clothing, help with the butchering, preserve much of the meat that they eat, and perhaps make soap, in addition to producing an average of seven children who in turn help with the farm work. Thus she has an essential role in the economic survival of the family and of the Amish community. Although Amish women appear docile and submissive, this does not mean that their contribution is not valued. Nor do they have a low self-esteem. Most Amishwomen are happy in their role and confident about the contribution they make to the family. In response to a formal interview question as to how much money she had made last year, an Amish wife would sometimes list one-half of her husband's income from the farm saying, "We're in it together. We're partners." [Abigail Mueller in Hostetler, E. Ericksen, J. Ericksen, and Huntington (1977:107).]

Parents present a united front to their children and to the community. In dealing with their children, Amish parents should be of one mind, discussing any differences privately and prayerfully. Admonitions to parents in sermons and in Amish writings are directed not to fathers as such, or to mothers alone, but to parents. Couples are never to disagree in public. The wife is expected to support her husband in all things, especially in his relationship with other people, whether it be their children, their parents, or friends and neighbors. The husband, in turn, should be considerate of his wife with respect to her physical, emotional, and spiritual well-being. The ideal is to be individuals to one another, making decisions jointly, and to be of one mind to all others.

The major role of Amish adults is childrearing. Parents of growing children have no individual rights, only responsibilities and obligations for the correct nurture of their children. They are to be examples to their children in all things, so that the children may become good Amishmen and eventually, through the grace of God, achieve life everlasting.

The role of the children within the family is more closely related to age than to sex. The older children are to care for and help the younger, while the younger are to obey the older in any reasonable demand. Older children do not physically punish younger children but cajole them into obeying. Although there is a division of labor by sex, children help one another and their parents as they are needed rather than strictly dividing the work by sex.

On the small, labor-intensive farms the children make a major economic contribution. Typically a child is not paid for his labor until he is 21 and if he works away from home his wages are returned to his father until he reaches that age. In turn, the parents try to set up each child in farming. Austerity must be practiced by the whole family in order to help the next generation become established economically. Children do not have a low status, although they are expected to be obedient and polite to those older than they. They are highly valued as "the only possessions we can take to heaven with us," and also, as contributors to the family, both economically and emotionally. Children function as socializing agents for the parents for as parents strive to be good examples for their children, they become better Amishmen themselves.

Grandparents, as parents of young married couples, have an important role in the Amish community. They are often instrumental in helping their married children get established on farms. They have a great influence as to where their children will settle. They help the young people with advice, labor, materials, and loans, Very often, the parents own the land onto which the young couple moves. The parents support their grown children with frequent visits. In Lancaster County, almost 90 percent of the parents saw all of their grown children at least once a month—in a culture in which car ownership is forbidden. Grandparents act as a buffer between the young couple and "the world." They help with labor and supply information as to where within the community the young couple can get produce they do not yet grow themselves. They teach the young family about community networks and help them interact within the community. And, as the young couple's children become old enough to help with the labor, the supportive role of the grandparents diminishes, but they continue to advise and admonish. At some stage the older couple will retire from farming, passing the farm on to one of the children and, depending on his age, the grandfather may run a small business of his own, for a few years.

Social Class and Lifestyle

The Amish are a small, homogeneous group within which social class has no meaning. They are exclusively rural, operating small family farms and, in some instances, working in small nonunion factories or on small carpenter crews. In relation to the outside society, these occupations would probably place them in the rural working class. Although there is considerable range in family income, and some families have a higher status than others, there are no class distinctions within the community, and lifestyle is as important as income level. No matter what the income, the need to accumulate capital to buy land for the next generation reinforces the simple living patterns prescribed by the *Ordnung*. Family farming is both the typical and the ideal occupation for a head of household with growing children. In each Amish settlement of any size there are Amishmen who own small businesses that are related to farming and the Amish way of life. Thus there will be a blacksmith, a harness maker, a buggy shop, a shop for adapting tractor-drawn farm equipment to horse-drawn, and there will be specialized carpenters who do cabinet work and make the Amish coffins. The Amish build and remodel their own homes and barns with the help of Amish construction crews. There are Amishmen who can draw up plans, lay brick, and install plumbing. Due to the increasing cost and scarcity of land, a growing number of Amish are accepting employment in small, nonunion factories that have sprung up in Amish areas: aluminum plants, small sawmills, trailer factories, and brick yards. Farming continues to be the preferred occupation. Many types of employment are forbidden as incompatible with their way of life. Nevertheless, a growing number of Amish heads of households are working in nonfarming occupations.

The Amish lifestyle is distinctive and consciously maintained. In an effort to build a "church without spot or blemish" and to remain a "peculiar people," strict disciplinary codes have been developed and are observed by members and their children. Most of these rules are unwritten, vary slightly from one church district to another, and are only completely known to participants. Most of the rules are taken for granted, but those pertaining to borderline issues, about which there might possibly be some disagreement, are reviewed twice a year by all baptized members of the church district. This allows for slow, orderly change in details of their lifestyle that is necessary for group survival. Only if consensus on the rules (*Ordnung*) is achieved, and if there is a unanimous expression of peace and good will toward every fellow member, is communion celebrated. Most church districts reach this degree of integration twice a year.

The Old Order Amish style of life is characterized by separation from the world, voluntary acceptance of high social obligation, symbolized by adult baptism, the practice of exclusion and shunning of transgressing members, and a nurturing attitude in harmony with nature and maintained on a human scale. The Amish interpret separation from the world quite literally. They have a distinctive dress, somewhat similar to that worn by European peasants of several centuries ago. They speak a distinctive language—an Amish form of Pennsylvania Dutch—that separates them from outsiders. Physically, too, they prefer to have some distance between themselves and non-Amish, between their households and non-Amish households. "Be ye not unequally yoked together with unbelievers; for what fellowship hath righteousness with unrighteousness? and what communion hath light with darkness?" (II Cor. 6:14). The Amish may not be union members or form partnerships with non-Amish, for both would join the believer with the unbeliever. In spite of this created distance, the Amish are not self-righteous nor judgmental in their relations with outsiders, whom they consider to be so different that the same criterion of conduct does not apply to them as it would to a fellow Amishman. "My kingdom is not of this world; if my kingdom were of this world, then would my servants fight"(John 18:36). Observing this teaching, the Amish may not serve in the military. Formerly, if they were called, they paid fines or served prison sentences; now they perform alternative service as conscientious objectors. All forms of retaliation to hostility are forbidden. An Amishman may not physically defend himself or his family even when attacked. He may not defend himself legally even when his civil rights have been violated. He is taught to follow the New Testament teaching of the Sermon on the Mount and the biblical example of Isaac. After the warring Philistines had stopped up all the wells of his father Abraham, Isaac moved to new lands and dug new wells (Genesis, 26:15–18). The Amish take this advice, and when they cannot remain separate from the world according to their own definition of separate, they move to new locations.

The adult Amishman voluntarily accepts a high degree of social obligation. His willingness to take on this responsibility is symbolized by the rite of baptism. Prior to baptism the future communicant renounces the world, the devil, his own flesh and blood, and acknowledges Christ as the Son of God and the Lord and Savior. He accepts a personal willingness to suffer persecution or death in order to maintain the faith. In addition, he promises to abide by the *Ordnung* and not to depart from the discipline in life or death. Each young man promises to accept the duties of minister should the lot ever fall on him. Applicants are warned not to make these promises if they cannot keep them, for once made, there is no turning back. It is not unusual for young people, during the period of instruction, to drop out. Generally they join a year or two later. No one may be married in the Amish church without first being baptized.

When deemed necessary, the Amish use excommunication and shunning (*Bann und Meidung*) to enforce the discipline and to keep the church pure and separate from the world. The full church membership participates in the decision and in the ceremony, in which the erring one is rebuked before all and purged out as a leaven. An Amishman in good standing may receive no favors from an excommunicated person; he may neither buy from nor sell to him, nor may he eat at the same table with the excommunicated person. The ban applies also between husband and wife, who may neither eat at the same table nor sleep in the same bed. The *Bann und Meidung* is used both to protect the individual and to protect the church. An erring member is shunned in order to help him realize the gravity of his sin and his need to return to the church. It is also used as a necessary step in the process of forgiveness, and thus helps the individual deal with guilt. The *Bann und Meidung* serves to protect the church by removing, both from ceremonial and social participation in the community, those individuals who will not follow the *Ordnung,* thus protecting the true believers from disruptive influence and temptations to modify their lifestyle. In some communities, individuals that leave the Old Order Amish to join other Amish churches are put under a limited ban and are no longer shunned forever. These individuals generally maintain kinship ties.

The Amish have an attitude of nurturance for their land, their children, and their people. The Amish nurturing lifestyle is in harmony with nature and functions to keep "the machine out of the garden." Wendel Berry (1978:7–8) contrasts the exploiter or individual who considers land a commodity with the nurturer, who considers land a trust.

> The standard of the exploiter is efficiency; the standard of the nurturer is care. The exploiter's goal is money, profit; the nurturer's goal is health—his land's health, his own, his family's, his community's . . . .Whereas the exploiter asks of a piece of land only how much and how quickly it can be made to produce, the nurturer asks a question that is much more complex and difficult: What is its carrying capacity? (That is: How much can be taken from it without diminishing it? What can it produce *dependably* for an indefinite time?) The exploiter wishes to earn as much as possible by as little work as possible; the nurturer expects, certainly, to have a decent living from his work, but his characteristic wish is to work *as well* as possible. The competence of the exploiter is in organization;

that of the nurturer is in order—a human order, that is, that accomodates itself both to other order and to mystery. The exploiter typically serves an institution or organization; the nurturer serves land, household, community, place. The exploiter thinks in terms of numbers, quantities, "hard facts"; the nurturer in terms of character, condition, quality, kind.

The prohibition against electricity holds the Amish work day to the solar day. The Amish home has neither air conditioning nor central heating, yet by modifying their daily routine, they manage to live comfortably with the changing seasons, relatively oblivious of energy crises. They do not exploit their environment, but care for it. The pea pods are put back on the garden, not thrown down a garbage disposal. There is a human scale to all of Amish life. Within the settlement distances are not too great, social groups are not too big, farms can be managed by a single family, and Amish schools have one or, at the most, two rooms. People know one another and identify with the physical environment in which they worship, live, and work. After a day visiting in a large city, an Amish farmer commented as we turned off the highway onto an unpaved road in his home county, "I know myself around here." He is the very antithesis of alienation.

By exercising a personal and a community discipline that excludes those who will not follow the dictates of the group and that stresses a voluntary commitment to a nurturing life in harmony with nature and socially separated from the outside culture, the Amish have been able to determine to a remarkable extent the style of their lives.

Family Life Cycle and the Socialization Process

The goal of the Amish family is the achievement of eternal life for each member. On an existential level, the goal is to teach children right from wrong, to be socially responsible as defined by the Amish community, to join the Amish church, and to remain faithful in the *Ordnung* until death.

In Amish society, a person passes through a series of six distinct age categories or stages of socialization as he progresses through life. Different behavior is demanded of him at each stage. The stages are: infancy, preschool children, school children, young people, adulthood, and old folks. [For a more detailed treatment of socialization, see Hostetler and Huntington (1971)]. Infancy covers the period from birth until the child walks. Children of this age are generally referred to as "babies." Preschool children are referred to as "little children;" they know how to walk but have not yet started school, which is generally entered at age 6 or 7. School children are called "scholars" by the Amish. They are fulfilling the eight years of elementary

311

schooling required by the state. They attend either public schools or Amish schools and are between the ages of 6 and 16. Young people are in the period between school (completed at 14 to 16, depending on the state) and marriage. Adults are traditionally married. An unmarried woman, no matter what her age, is referred to as "an older girl." Old folks have all their children married or independent, and they generally live in a "Dawdy House," the grandfather house on the "home place."

INFANCY. Babies are enjoyed by the Amish; they are believed to be gentle, responsive, and secure within the home and the Amish community, but vulnerable when out in the world. Babies are not scolded or punished, and there is no such thing as a bad baby, although there may be a difficult baby. A baby may be enjoyed without fear of self-pride, for he is a gift from God and not primarily an extension of the parents. If he cries, he is in need of comfort, not discipline. It is believed that a baby can be spoiled by wrong handling, especially by nervous, tense handling, but the resultant irritability is the fault of the environment, not the baby; he remains blameless. Old Order Amish parents give generous attention to their babies' needs, both physical and social. An Amish baby is born into a family and into a community. He is never spoken of as "a little stranger" but is welcomes as a "new woodchopper" or a "little dishwasher." Each baby is greeted happily as a contribution to the security of the family and the church.

CHILDHOOD. Amish children are taught to respect authority, and respect is shown by obedience. The Amish do not strive for blind obedience but for obedience based on love and on the belief that those in authority have deep concern for one's welfare and know what is best. Most traditional Amish parents teach obedience by being firm and consistent rather than by violent confrontations or single instances of breaking the child's will. The switch is used freely but not harshly. The prevailing attitude is matter-of-fact rather than moralistic in dealing with their children. Not only is the child taught to respect and obey those in authority, but he also learns to care for those younger and less able than he, to share with others, to do what he is taught is right, and to avoid that which is wrong, to enjoy work, and to fulfill his work responsibilities pleasantly. The parents create a safe environment for their children. They live separated from the world, maintaining the boundary for their children that protects them from malevolent influence. The parent has the responsibility to punish transgressions but also the power to forgive. Punishment is used primarily to ensure the safety of the child; for his physical safety ("stay away from that nervous horse"), for his cultural safety ("be respectful to older people"), for his legal safety ("don't fish without a fishing license"), for his moral safety ("be obedient"). Rewards are used to develop the right attitudes in the child: humility, forgiveness, admission of error, sympathy, responsibility, and appreciation of work. Children are motivated primarily by concern for other people and not by fear of punishment.

Although children are primarily the responsibility of their parents, the community plays an important part in their socialization. Families attend church as a unit every other Sunday. The children sit through the long service, learning to be considerate of others, quiet, and patient. Until they are about 9 years old, the girls sit with the mothers or grandmothers, and the boys with their fathers. After the service, the children share in the community meal, and the youngest may nap on a big bed with other babies. The rest of the time the children play freely and vigorously about the house and yard, safe in the presence of many adults who care for them and guide them. If a small child suddenly feels lost, someone quickly returns him to a member of his family. The Amish child experiences the community as being composed of people like his parents, all of whom know him and direct him. He is comfortable and secure within the encompassing community. In many settlements the community also participates in the socialization of the child through the Amish "parochial" school, which supports the teaching of the home.

Throughout his childhood the Amish child spends the greatest part of his time interacting with members of his family. Unlike the typical suburban school child, the Amish child is usually in a mixed age group rather than isolated with his peers (Bronfenbrenner, 1970:96–102). The Amish child's parents and siblings play a central role in his development. Although the Amish generally consider childhood to end with the graduation of the child from the eighth grade or on his 16th birthday, they do not feel that their task as parents is even near completion. The desired end product will not be achieved until much later.

YOUNG PEOPLE. The age category known by the Amish as "young people" covers the years between 14 or 16 and marriage. It corresponds roughly to adolescence. This is the most individualistic period in the life of an Amishman or Amishwoman and is considered to be the most dangerous. If an individual is to become Amish, he must be kept within the Amish community, physically and emotionally, during his crucial adolescent years. Yet at this time the family's control of the young person is somewhat limited, the community's control is informal, and the lure of the world is most strong.

During adolescence the peer group is of supreme importance, for during these years more of the Amish young person's socialization takes place within this group than within the family or the church. If the young person's peer group remains Amish, he has a reference point, a buffer, and a support. Even though as an individual or as a member of this Amish peer group he transgresses many rules and crosses most of the boundaries between the Amish community and the world, he will eventually return to the church to become a lifelong Amishman. However, if during this stage he makes "English" friends and identifies with an alien peer group, even though he is well behaved, he will probably leave the Amish church, never to return.

A certain degree of adolescent rebellion has become institutionalized among the Amish. The Amish child is raised in a carefully protected environment by relatively authoritarian parents. However, during this stage, the young Amish person will make the two most important commitments of his life: He will decide if and when to join the church and whom to marry. Both of these commitments he must make as an individual, albeit an individual who has the help of God, the concern of his parents, and the support of the community. In order to make such important decisions, he must establish a degree of independence from his family, and to some extent from his community, in order to develop his own identity. This is done in many ways, most of them carefully institutionalized. The family relaxes some of its tight control over the young person. He goes to social gatherings of his peers rather than having all of his social life with the family. The young person is learning what it means to be Amish. He may test some of the boundaries of the Amish community, sampling the world by such means as owning a radio, having his photograph taken, attending a movie, and occasionally wearing clothes that are outside the *Ordnung*. As long as these forays into wordliness remain discreet, they are ignored by the parents and the community, for it is believed that the young person should have some idea of the world he is voluntarily rejecting. One of the reasons courtship is secretive is that it is a means of achieving privacy in a closely knit community and within a large family. The young person is protected by a degree of institutionalized blindness on the part of adults, who thereby give him freedom—within safe boundaries.

The community indirectly counteracts youthful rebelliousness by providing social activities and vocational training for the adolescents. The Sunday evening singing is an important social event in most Amish settlements. Young people generally begin attending when they have finished day school and are about 16 years old. The family that "has church" has "singing" for the young people in the evening. Generally brothers and sisters go together to the singing, although they frequently return home in couples. In some of the larger settlements there will be Saturday night singing, or the young man may visit his girlfriend in her home. Weddings, wiener roasts, and work bees, will provide occasions for the young people to gather.

Proper vocational training is essential if the young person is to become an Amish Christian. Both the young Amishman and young Amishwoman work for a number of different people during these years, learning various acceptable vocational roles and, through their jobs, gaining a knowledge of other Amish families and other Amish settlements, and sometimes even a glimpse of the world by working for "English" people. The skills the Amish need are best learned by doing, and they have worked out an informal community apprentice system that serves the needs of the individual and the culture.

The relative freedom to test the boundaries of his culture, to make mistakes, to become aware of human weakness, counterbalanced by the individual's growing ability to be economically productive, and perhaps his interest in marriage, all function to make him think seriously about joining the church. When he finally makes this commitment in his late teens or early twenties, the parents have fulfilled their moral duty to the child, to the church, and to God. However, although in a theological sense they have completed their task as parents, in practice the parent–child relationship continues. Marriage, which even more than baptism is considered the beginning of adulthood, modifies the parent–child relationship but does not basically change it.

ADULTHOOD. Marriage is the beginning of social adulthood, but full adulthood is attained with parenthood. The adult Amish are responsible for the maintenance of their culture. They produce the children, who are expected to become Amish, they raise them in such a way that they want to become Amish, and they teach them the skills and attitudes that will enable them to remain Amish. The adult Amish watch over the boundaries of their culture, participating in the selective acculturation that is necessary for their survival as "a visible church of God" in 20th century America. Economically they must be sufficiently successful to support a large family and to help their children become economically independent after a few years of marriage. The Old Order Amish community is economically self-sufficient, and church members do not accept social security or welfare. Socially they are also self-sufficient, caring for those who are ill and old within the community. The adult Amishman or woman has no set retirement age. Retirement is voluntary, usually gradual, and related to the individual's health and the needs of his family. It generally takes place some time after the youngest child is married and has started to raise a family.

OLD FOLKS. Old folks normally signify their retirement by moving into the grandfather house adjacent to the main farmhouse. This may occur while the grandfather is still young and vigorous, but he moves to a new occupation, such as running a shoe repair shop, in order to free the land for his child. With retirement or semiretirement the role of the parents is modified, but still continues, for the old people remain physically and emotionally close

315

to their children and grandchildren. The young farmer discusses problems of farm management and sales prices with his father; the young mother asks advice about the children. The old folks still engage in the process of helping their youngest children become established economically.

Also, the old people have an increased obligation to attend funerals and to visit the sick and bereaved. When they are ill, members of the community visit them. As long as health permits, old folks spend a considerable amount of time visiting children, nieces, nephews, and friends in different parts of the settlement and in other settlements. They form an important link in the network of informal communication that ties the larger Amish community together. They are often reliable sources of news, as well as of local history and of genealogical relationships. They exert a conservative influence as they fulfill their accepted roles of admonishing the young. As they grow older, and perhaps become senile or bedridden, they are still cared for at home, sometimes by one child, often, with the children taking turns having them in their homes. With a large number of children available, this responsibility can be more easily shared.

Typically, dying takes place in the home, the person surrounded by family and friends—not in the lonely, impersonal, mechanical environment of a hospital (*The Budget,* August 2, 1973):

> On June 19th she . . . was admitted and put under oxygen. . . . She seemed to be losing out fast, as she had to labor to breathe even with oxygen. On Fri. we pleaded to go home. So arrangements were made with an ambulance to take her home, she being under oxygen all the while.
> . . . At daybreak in the mornings for the last 3 mornings were her hardest and on the morning at 4:45 of the 26th of June she easily and peacefully faded away.

When death occurs, neighbors and nonrelatives relieve the family of all work responsibility, leaving the relatives free for meditation and conversation with the guests who come to see their departed friend and to talk to the bereaved family. Funerals, especially of elderly people, are large, and often 500 mourners may be present. After burial in an Amish graveyard, the mourners return to the house of the deceased for a meal. With this meal, normal relationships and responsibilities are restored. The family circle has been broken by death, but the strong belief in eternal life indicates that the break is only temporary.

CHANGE AND ADAPTATION

The rapid social changes since the Depression have broken down the isolation of the Amish. Specific threats to their community structure and family organization have been posed by (1) social security, (2) consolidation of elementary and junior high schools, (3) lengthening of the compulsory-attendance period and consequent required high school attendance, (4) conscription, and (5) scarcity of farmland. Minor, more subtle threats are the availability of motorcycles and cars, the cheapness and small size of transistor radios and phonographs, televisions blaring in every store, the ease of travel, and the use of telephones. These are all dangers inherent in our technologically sophisticated mass culture. Technological competition for land use and invasion of farmland also pose problems. In Lancaster Country urban uses are pressing hard on land once available for farming. In Ohio, Amish communities have moved because of the intrusion of power plants and the risk that high power transmission lines may be strung across Amish farms, bringing onto Amish family lands, noise pollution, corona discharge, the danger of electrical shock, and intrusive personnel who patrol the lines to spray herbicides and perform other maintenance chores. A specific threat to the Amish young people is variants of the Billy Graham type of religious fundamentalism. Fundamentalist radio programs are one of the means for introducing these dissident ideas into the community; local revival meetings are another. The more liberal branches of the Mennonite church also offer a ladder to those who want to climb into "higher" churches step by step, changing their lifestyle more than their theology.

SOCIAL SECURITY. Although the five abovementioned specific threats to the Amish culture have been somewhat mitigated during the past few years, in every instance certain Amishmen bore the brunt of the encroachment by the state and paid fines, spent time in prison, and moved to other localities. The Amish do not believe in life insurance or old-age insurance. They live separate from the state, which they will support with taxes but not with their vote or with their lives. They believe that the Christian brotherhood should care for its own, and they are forbidden by the *Ordnung* to accept any form of survivors' insurance. Because they do not and will not accept social security payments from the state, they refuse to pay the social security tax to the state. After years of conflict, during which some Amish witnessed the sale of their horses and farms at public auction, the Amish were finally granted an exemption from the self-employment social security tax. This was a crucial issue for the Amish because both their family and their church structure, with the strong emphasis on social responsibility, would be weakened by reliance on outside funds.

ELEMENTARY SCHOOLING. The Amish in many settlements have responded to school consolidation and to rapid changes in the rural American culture by withdrawing further from the mainstream (see Table 3). It is not

TABLE 3
Amish Community Schools 1979–1980ᵃ

STATE	DATE OF FOUNDING OF OLDEST SCHOOL	NUMBER OF SCHOOLS	NUMBER OF TEACHERS	NUMBER OF PUPILS	SCHOOLS NOT REPORTING ENROLLMENT
Pennsylvania	1938	146	150	4022	
Ohio	1947	97	132	3235	
Indiana	1951	58	99	2423	
Wisconsin	1960	26	28	594	
Missouri	1950	26	29	581	
Iowa	1966	20	28	439	
New York	1949	14	17	398	3
Michigan	1960	12	14	254	1
Delaware	1925	6	10	211	
Tennessee	1975	7	7	187	
Illinois	1966	6	11	160	
Maryland	1967	4	4	135	
Kentucky	1969	3	5	130	
Minnesota	1975	8	8	44	4
Arkansas	1975	1	1	15	
Montana	1976	1	1	14	
Nebraska	1978	1	1	11	
Ontario	1953	18	24	476	—
Totals		447	561	13,293	8

ᵃAmish community schools listed by state. Number of pupils given only for schools reporting enrollment (*Blackboard Bulletin,* November 1979: 11–22).

that they want to be more different from their non-Amish neighbors; it is that they do not want to change so rapidly; they want to keep the old ways. Large, modern consolidated schools are not suitable agents of socialization for the Amish child. Many of the Amish children still attend public schools. Some of these are rural schools that were not caught in the net of consolidation, some are relatively small village schools, and some are large, sprawling elementary schools. When their children attend public school, the parents attempt to isolate its influence and to counteract the disruption it may cause. Over half of the Amish children attend community schools designed, built, and staffed by members of their own church. In 1979–1980, there were 447 parochial schools with an enrollment of over 13,000 children. These schools were located in 17 states and in Canada (*Blackboard Bulletin,* November 1979). In the community schools the Amish children learn the three Rs in an environment in which they are protected from the assumptions of 20th-century America, in which they can learn discipline, humility, simple living, and cooperation. The Amish schools emphasize shared knowledge rather than individual knowledge, the dignity of tradition rather than the importance of progress. The Amish schools do not teach religion, rather a style of living. The school's task is to cooperate with the parents to preserve the faith taught by the parents, for it is the role of the family, not of the school or even the church, to make Amish Christians of the children. The Amish family constellation will change if the school-age children cannot participate in the ongoing work of the home and farm. When the children are removed from the home for many hours each day, as is the case when they must spend long hours on the bus in addition to the hours spent in class, when the school year interferes with the agricultural season, and when the children are physically and ideologically removed from their community, they cannot be taught the skills and attitudes needed to become Amish.

COMPULSORY HIGH SCHOOL ATTENDANCE. High school attendance is no longer a problem for the Old Order Amish because the Supreme Court ruling of May 15, 1972, protects the religious freedom of the Amish by permitting Amish children who have graduated from the eighth grade to participate in community-based vocational programs in lieu of attending high school. The students spend half a day a week in school under the direction of a teacher and four-and-a-half days working in a modified apprentice system, generally under the direction of their parents. They learn technological skills in a social context as participants in the economy of the community. While working on a family farm, Amish children of high school age learn not only how to perform a task, such as how to harrow, but also when to harrow, and how to integrate harrowing into all the other work that is required of the vocation "farmer." They also learn wider community work roles by helping in threshing rings and at barn raisings, getting ready for church, and helping care for neighbors' children. Of great importance to the success of the Amish vocational training is the fact that the vocational expectations of the young people coincide with the vocational opportunities available to them.

CONSCRIPTION. Since the beginning of World War II the draft has taken young men outside of the Amish community at a most vulnerable stage in their development. The I-W program, which provided an alternative to military service, functioned in such a manner that young Amishmen spent two years outside the community, often alone in a city, perhaps wearing non-Amish clothing while at work. These measures separate the young men from community control and to a limited extent made them non-Amish. The draft was never incorporated into the Amish lifestyle. It interfered with two of the most important rites of passage among the Amish: baptism and marriage. Baptism signifies total commitment to the believing church community, physically and spiritually separated from the world. If the drafted young man were baptized before his alternative service, he could not live physically separated from the world as he was pledged to do. If he were not baptized before his service, he had not committed himself to the church community and so was more vulnerable to outside influence. Was it best for a young man to marry before, during, or after his alternative service? If he went into the world without a wife, he might form friendships with non-Amish girls, and because marriage must be with a coreligionist, such friendships were dangerous. If he had a wife, she helped protect him from worldly influences, but they started their married life with modern conveniences, electricity, and telephones, which are hard to give up when they return to an Amish way of life. During I-W or alternative service, both the Amishmen and their wives learned non-Amish work patterns, and many received training they could never use on an Amish farm.

The most traditional Amish refused even alternative service when it required them to live in a city or to wear non-Amish garb. As one Amish father explained, "God did not mean for the Amish to take the way of I-W service. It is better for the Amish to go to prison, though it is hard. God is with them there." At the time of writing, the selective service act is still in effect and registration for selective service is required. It is not clear presently whether the draft will once again disrupt the lives of young men. Certainly the Amish community will continue to be affected by the experiences of those young men who have already spent two years outside the protective boundaries of their culture.

SCARCITY OF LAND. The Amish prohibition against contraception, their positive attitude toward high fertility, and their insistence on labor-intensive, diversified family farming as the ideal means of livelihood, coupled with the belief that all one's grown children should settle near the parents (ideally within two miles) places tremendous pressure on farmland in and near Amish communities—even if there are not competing uses for the land. The rate of growth of the Amish community has been increasing while the limits of farmland available are finite. This is especially true for the Lancaster County Amish. They constitute the oldest Amish community in the country, having settled on land along major transportation routes between the expanding urban centers of Philadelphia and Harrisburg. They must compete with factories, shopping centers, and tourism as well as with one another. The Amish in Lancaster have responded to this problem by paying increasingly high prices for their land, subdividing their farms, establishing new communities in other parts of the state (often on poorer farmland), occasionally moving to other Amish communities outside the state, and, less acceptably, leaving the Old Order to join other branches of the church that do not put such a high premium on farming. Very few of the individual families in any state who leave the Amish church are successfully engaged in labor-intensive, general farming at the time they leave. Some Amish young people never join the church, but in Lancaster, it is more typical for young Amish to join the church, marry, start a family, and then leave.

In a detailed analysis of the Lancaster Amish population conducted in 1976 (Hostetler, E. Ericksen, J. Ericksen, and Huntington, 1977) it was determined that the rate of leaving was not related to a breakdown of family ties but was more closely related to the economic success of the parents which, because it was accompanied by austere living patterns, contributes to the likelihood of the younger generation becoming established in labor-intensive, family farming (E. Ericksen, J. Ericksen, and Hostetler, 1980). Among the Lancaster Amish, heads of households who are farmers are generally more successful economically than those who have other types of employment (except for a few of the self-employed Amish businessmen). Heads of households who are farmers are considered the most successful by their fellow churchmen for they are able to practice a style of life consistent with Amish values. Among a sample of Lancaster Amish it was observed that the likelihood of leaving the Old Order Amish was five times as great for children of nonfarmers as for children of farmers. This would indicate that there is a connection between the survival and growth of the Amish subculture and the ability of the parents, and to some extent the community, to get their young adults established in farming. Lack of farmland bodes ill for the community. But as it becomes more expensive to get established on a farm, more family heads look for other types of suitable employment. Near Amish and Mennonite settlements, small factories have been built to take advantage of the cheap (nonunion), skilled, reliable labor supply. The trend from farming to nonfarming occupations may have a profound effect on the Amish culture. The Amish family and Amish patterns of childrearing are built on the concept of shared parental responsibility, on the expectation that both parents work together caring for the farm and the children, that both parents are almost always in the home and available to support one another and to guide and teach their children. For example, family devotions are led by the father, but it is difficult to have these when the father has to punch a timeclock rather than being able to adjust his farm chores to the sleeping patterns of his growing family. The authority patterns within the family change when the father is absent during most of the day. A sick baby or a fussy three-year old are minor inconveniences when both parents are available. On an Amish farm the boys spend most of the time, when they are awake and not in school, working with or under the direction of their father. In no other occupation can the father so consistently teach, instruct, admonish, and correct his children.

The social structure of the Amish community is based on the availability of brethren and sisters to gather for work bees, for barn raisings, for day-long weddings, and day-long funerals. The Amish share labor within the family, between families, and among church members whenever there is extra or special work to be done. This combination of mutual aid and social interaction keeps the community strong and of one mind. This interaction can be relatively easily achieved in a church district in which most of the household heads are farmers; it is almost impossible when most of the men work in factories or on construction crews. The traditional Amish culture is dependent on both parents working in the home, that is, being available to each other and to the children and to the community any hour of the day, on any day of the week. Although the Amish are tied to the American market system, their culture mitigates these ties and functions to isolate the Amishman by circumscribing his economic options in such a way that the Amish family-centered culture can be perpetuated both socially and physically.

OTHER AREAS OF CHANGE AND ADAPTATION. The *Ordnung* protects the Amish from the encroachment of technology, from a throwaway mentality, and from the overstimulation of the individual (Toffler, 1970) The *Ordnung* further specifically forbids members to have highline electricity, which means that all electrical conveniences, from clothes dryers to vacuum cleaners to toasters, are unavailable. All musical instruments are forbidden, and radios and television sets can come under this prohibition. Telephones connect one with the outside world and "cause women to waste time," because "you can work and talk when you are both in the same room, but neither of you can work while talking on the telephone." In addition, telephones within the home intrude into the family, disrupting meals, work, and conversation.

Cars, and to a lesser degree motorcycles, are threatening because they enable people to travel too far, too fast, and to go beyond the face-to-face community in which everyone is known and everyone is noticed. Movies are forbidden but offer little threat to the community because there is no interest in them; they are too far from the individual's experience and value system to do more than elicit passing curiosity. In many ways the Amish culture is oral rather than literary, and though they have kept out the medium, and along with it the message (McLuhan, 1962), they are not really threatened by the printed word, by radio, or even by television. Consistent with the oral tradition, the Amish stress shared knowledge and the importance of meaningful social interaction. They are so far outside the mainstream of American culture that they have little shared knowledge with the average American citizen and little reason to interact socially with him. The area in which they may be the most vulnerable is that of religious fundamentalism, for here the familiarity with the Bible gives a degree of shared knowledge that may open the way for outside influence. Although the Amish are relatively immune to changes in their world view and basic thought patterns, they are more open to change in the area of economics. They know they must survive economically in order to survive culturally, but they also believe that it is better to suffer economic and physical hardship than to lose their unique religious orientation. There is more pressure to accept telephones and electricity than to permit radios and movie attendance. Those aspects of the outside culture that can enhance Amish family life and can reinforce community ties and community economic strength are tempting and will continue to be accepted if they can be incorporated without changing the family roles or the social structure and without permitting encroachment of worldly ideas and worldly ways.

During the 250 years the Amish have been in America they have successfully obtained good farmland that would produce high yields on small acreage when cultivated intensively by a large nuclear family. Farms needed to be small and of high quality in order to be worked by one family and to support a relatively dense farming population so that the characteristic social structure, stressing strong kinship and community ties and isolation from the surrounding culture, could be established and maintained. During these 250 years the Amish have successfully resisted the lures of mass consumption and mass communication, they have maintained their emphasis on limited gratification and limited consumption, stressing economy, savings, and cash payments. While the urban villagers of Boston argue that money earned should be spent immediately to make daily life more pleasant, because "life is too short for any other way of behavior" (Gans, 1962:187), the Amish argue that "no one would want such a beautiful home here on this earth if they hoped for heavenly home after this time" (*Family Life,* June 1973:11). Life is too short to risk losing one's soul just for comfort or pleasure. "Only one life, t'will soon be past; Only what's done for Christ will last."

The Amish stress on the individual's total commitment to God, thus his responsibility to live according to the Amish *Ordnung,* has enabled the Amish culture to survive, sometimes at tremendous personal expense to the individual. In the early years of their history, some individuals were martyred, and the total group was strengthened by the payment of the few. In recent times certain individuals have lost their farms and savings; they were in a sense economically martyred, and again the total group profited by the payment of the few. The steadfastness of the Amish as individuals finally resulted in changes in the enforcement of various laws, for example, social security, high school attendance, noncertified teachers in Amish schools, and alternative forms to military service. The Amish culture will continue to change as it adjusts to economic, technological, and social changes in the surrounding culture, but as long as the Amish are able to maintain their basic cultural figuration, their unique world view, and their own social structure, they will persist even though the details of their lives change.

REFERENCES

Ausband, Das ist: Etliche schöne christliche Lieder. 1564. First edition.

Bainton, Roland H. 1952. *The Reformation of the Sixteenth Century.* Boston: Beacon Press.

Berry, Wendell. 1978. *The Unsettling of America: Culture and Agriculture.* New York: Avon Books.

Blackboard Bulletin. Aylmer, Ontario: Pathway Publishing Corporation. A monthly published "in the interests of Amish Parochial schools."

Bronfenbrenner, Urie, 1970. *Two Worlds of Childhood: U.S. and U.S.S.R.* New York: Russell Sage.

Budget, The. Sugarcreek, Ohio. "A Weekly Newspaper Serving The Sugarcreek Area And Amish-Mennonite Communities Throughout The Americas."

Braght, Thieleman J. van 1951. *The Bloody Theatre or Martyr's Mirror of the Defenseless Christians Who Baptized Only Upon Confession of Faith, and Who Suffered and Died for the Testimony of Jesus, Their Savior, From the Time of Christ to the Year A.D. 1660.* Scottdale, PA: Mennonite Publishing House.

Cross, Harold E. 1967. "Genetic Studies in an Amish Isolate," Ph.D. dissertation, The Johns Hopkins University.

Enders, Trudy, and Curt Stern. 1948. "The Frequency of Twins, Relative to Age of Mothers, in American populations." *Genetics* 35: (May), 263–72.

Ericksen, Eugene P., Julia Ericksen, and John A. Hostetler, 1980. "The Cultivation of The Soil as a Moral Directive: Population Growth, Family Ties, and the Maintenance of Community Among the Old Order Amish," *Rural Sociology,* 44:49–68.

Ericksen, Julia, and Gary Klein. 1978 "Women's Roles and Family Production Among the Old Order Amish," paper given at the National Council of Family Relation, Philadelphia.

Ericksen, Julia, Eugene P. Ericksen, John A. Hostetler and Gertrude E. Huntington. 1979. "Fertility Patterns and Trends Among the Old Order Amish." *Population Studies,* 33,2:255–276.

Family Life. Aylmer, Ontario: Pathway Publishing Corporation. A monthly "dedicated to the promotion of Christian living among the plain people, with special emphasis on the appreciation of our heritage."

Fisher, John M. 1957. *Descendants and History of Christian Fisher Family.* Privately published by Amos L. Fisher, Route 1, Ronks, PA.

Gans, Herbert J. 1962. *The Urban Villagers.* New York: The Free Press.

Hostetler, John A. 1955. "Old World Extinction and New World Survival of the Amish," *Rural Sociology,* 20 (September–December):212–219.

———1980. *Amish Society,* Third Edition. Baltimore, MD: Johns Hopkins Press.

Hostetler, John A., and Gertrude Enders Huntington. 1971. *Children in Amish Society: Socialization and Community Education.* New York: Holt, Rinehart and Winston.

Hostetler, John A., Eugene Ericksen, Julia Ericksen, and Gertrude Huntington. 1977. "Fertility Patterns in an American Isolate Subculture." Final report. NICHD grant No. HD-08137-01A1.

Huntington, Gertrude Enders. 1956. "Dove at the Window: A Study of an Old Order Amish Community in Ohio," Ph.D. dissertation, Yale University.

Littell, Franklin H. 1964. *The Origins of Sectarian Protestantism.* New York: Macmillan.

Luthy, David, 1973. "The Amish in Europe." *Family Life* (March), pp.10–14. Aylmer, Ontario: Pathway.

———. 1974. "Old Order Amish Settlements in 1974," *Family Life* (December), pp. 13–16. Aylmer, Ontario: Pathway.

Marx, Leo. 1964. The Machine in the Garden: Technology and the Pastoral Ideal in America. New York: Oxford University Press.

McLuhan, Marshall. 1962. *The Gutenberg Galaxy.* Toronto: The University of Toronto Press.

Mennonite Encyclopedia. 1955. Scottdale, PA: Mennonite Publishing House; Newton, KS: Mennonite Publication Office; Hillsboro, KS: Mennonite Brethren Publishing House.

Ohio Amish Directory. Millersburg, Ohio.

Raber, J.A. (ed.). 1970, 1973, 1980. *Der Neue Amerikanische Calendar.* Baltic, OH.

Schwartz, Hillell. 1973. "Early Anabaptist Ideas About the Nature of Children," *Mennonite Quarterly Review,* 47 (April): 102–14.

Simons, Menno. 1956. *The Complete Writings of Menno Simons.* Scottdale, PA: Herald Press.

Smith C. Henry. 1920. *The Mennonites: A Brief History of Their Origin and Later Development in Both Europe and America.* Berne, IN: Mennonite Book Concern.

Toffler, Alvin. 1970. *Future Shock.* New York: Random House.

Umble, John. 1949. "Factors Explaining the Disintegration of Mennonite Communities," *Proceedings of the Seventh Annual Conference on Mennonite Cultural Problems.* North Newton, KS: Bethel College. Published under the auspices of the Council of Mennonite and Affiliated Colleges.

RECOMMENDED FILMS

The Amish: A People of Preservation. John L. Ruth, producer; Burton Buller, cinematographer; John A. Hostetler, consultant. Available through Encyclopedia Britannica, 425 N. Michigan Ave., Chicago, IL 60611, in 28-minute and 53-minute versions.

The French Canadian American Family

Unlike most ethnic groups discussed in this book, the French Canadians have had a long tenure in the New World and currently share minority status in two North American countries: Canada and America. The French Canadians are unique for several reasons. First, they have retained their minority status for nearly 400 years, and second they have done this without the aid of any visible racial or physical stigma. Many who have studied the French Canadians would argue that the main reason for their minority status is due more to internal resistance than to external hostilities. The universal presence of the Catholic Church in the French Canadian culture is more than just an added consideration.

This selection looks at the French Canadian as an ethnic entity, tracing its traditional culture historically through both Canada and New England. The family and the parish (French Canadian community) are the most important aspects of both the traditional and contemporary French Canadian culture. One type of family, that of the working-class mill worker, is focused upon. Granted, not all French Canadians fall into this category, but it is these people nonetheless who seem most responsible for the continuation of the traditional French Canadian culture among the numerous mill towns scattered throughout northern New England.

CHAPTER FOURTEEN
BY
LAURENCE FRENCH

HISTORICAL BACKGROUND
The French in the New World

Unlike most minority groups discussed in this volume, the French Canadians were initially a minority group. In this respect French Canadian culture in America actually reflects a sub-subculture in that the Canadian French are themselves a subculture of 17- and 18th-century France. Relevant parallel developments in both French subcultures will be discussed since open lines of communication and influence continue to facilitate the cultural development and identity of French Canadians in both countries.

The French Canadians represent a unique minority in that their cultural heritage in the New World equals that of the English dominant group. A French colony, New France, was established in eastern Canada in 1534, 86 years before the pilgrims landed at Plymouth and two centuries prior to American independence. One might ask why they are still ascribed a minority status in both Canada and America when most other Caucasian ethnic groups have overcome this stigma, integrating into the larger dominant culture. The answer to this perplexing question rests in part on the religious ideals and those of the dominant Protestant ethnic. This, coupled with the unusual circumstances surrounding the transfer of French Canada from French to British control, accounts for the unique phenomenon concerning the French Canadian's minority status. Relevant to these circumstances are numerous historical occurrences that further solidified and polarized the two cultures (French and English). It is in the context of these unique situations that the French Canadian family and social life have emerged.

The major attributes, then, that distinguish the French Canadians as a minority group are (1) they have the longest tenure of any Caucasian minority group in the New World; (2) they hold minority status in two countries in the New World, Canada and America and (3) the communication channels with the mother country (Canada) are still strong. The general historical background is especially important in that it provides the framework on which the French Canadian family style emerged.

The family is the basic economic and socializing unit, while the parish is the religious and civil community in which the family functions. The original French in Canada were affiliated with the trading companies, which more or less isolated them from the influence of the European industrial revolution. This enabled them to retain the medieval and feudal lifestyle they brought with them to the New World. The quasifeudal system that emerged in colonial Canada was patterned after the agrarian family system in France and consisted of (1) government officials, (2) landlords (*seigneurs*), (3) the priesthood (*curé*), and (4) the peasants (*habitants*).

The wars with England during the 18th century greatly altered the status of the French colonies in the New World. This in turn had an effect on the lifestyle of those French Canadians stranded on the American continent. The 1713 Treaty of Utrecht ended the War of the Spanish Succession, granting England important colonies that were previously owned by France (to become Nova Scotia, Newfoundland, and the Hudson Bay territory). A consequence of this treaty was the dispersion of the Acadian French, who previously populated these areas. And in 1755 the English authorities finally expelled the remaining Acadians (some 7000) from Nova Scotia. The Catholic Church refers to this incident as "one of the greatest crimes against civilization known in the annals of America" (Byrne, 1899). According to Church sources, families were separated in the most cruel manner, and many were forced to migrate to the French territory in America, later known as the "Louisiana Territory," while others fled to the 13 colonies. Only 500 escaped removal, illegally residing in their Canadian homeland. The hostility between the French and English reached such intensity at this time that a major manhunt occurred throughout the 13 colonies during the years 1755–1766 in an attempt to rid the colonies of French Canadians.

In 1763, the Treaty of Paris ended the Seven Years War, more commonly known as the French and Indian War. This document provided for French cession to England of Canada and all the territory east of the Mississippi River. After the defeat of 1760, French government officials left for France, leaving the leadership role to the Catholic Church. The French outnumbered the British 14 to one (70,000 French Canadians and only 5000 British) at this time, forcing the British to delegate French Canadian control to the Catholic Church. With the departure of both government officials and *seigneurs* (landowners), the Catholic Church conveniently filled the ensuing power vacuum. This endowed the Catholic Church with both sacred and secular powers—a situation closely resembling that of medieval France. With ties of communication severed with France and a lack of British concern, the French Canadians continued to maintain their traditional preindustrial lifestyle.

From the beginning, conflict emerged between the normative values of these two Canadian groups. The French Canadians spoke French, were Catholics, and belonged to an agrarian economic system. The British spoke English, were Protestant, and developed a progressive industrialized society. What resulted was a communication and cultural lag between the French majority and the ruling British government. This situation is reflected in French Canadians' dissatisfaction over their political impotence, which began in the early 1700s and continues today.

Local autonomy was established, however, when the Treaty of Paris temporarily united North America under the British flag. The British authorities, faced with growing unrest in the 13 colonies, gave up an early attempt to assimilate the French Canadians. Instead, they established the Quebec Act of 1774, recognizing the major institutions of the French-speaking community, especially the Church and the French language. By doing such, the efforts of the rebelling colonies to ally the French Canadians to their cause failed. Again, in 1791, the Canada Act was enacted to divide Canada for better representation by ethnic background. Yet, by 1834, the French Canadians, comprising three-quarters of the total population, still held less than one-quarter of the public offices. In 1837 a series of small-scale revolts were staged by the French Canadians in reaction to the Ex-Quebec Act, which advocated forcible assimilation. The Ex-Quebec Act attacked the Catholic Church indirectly by outlawing the use of the French language and curtailing the parochial education system. This act also encouraged migration to other areas of Canada in an attempt to disperse the French and weaken their solidarity. In 1840 the Union Bill, which established the Province of Canada, proved to be the main vehicle of forced assimilation. In 1867, the British North American Act created the Dominion of Canada. This act reduced some of the harshness of the Ex-Quebec Act by recognizing the French language and allowed each province certain powers of its own, such as educational control.

Migration to America

Meanwhile, during and immediately after the Civil War, the textile industry's rapid growth in New England provided the impetus for French Canadian immigration to America. In the mid-19th century hundreds of mills were built along New England's many rivers. The Civil War, low status associated with mill work, and westward migration caused a shortage of indigenous laborers. The mill owners desired a readily available, docile, easily controlled, low-salaried work force. Southern blacks, Filipinos, and other "minority" groups were under consideration, but initial cost of transportation and sensitive racial issues made these groups less desirable to the mill owners than the Caucasian French Canadians. The French Canadians met all the ideal prerequisites, while remaining racially invisible.

The motive for migrating was economic, for in Canada the French Canadians' traditional values and mores kept them out of commercial and industrial activities, and at the same time, their own economic system of farming, lumbering, and trapping began to decline. The large patricentric stem family could no longer absorb and support the excess labor force ushered in by the depression of 1873. The New England textile industry's labor needs seemed at the time to offer the best solution to this crisis. The French Canadians proved to be an ideal labor source, with their large available work force, their willingness to work for low wages, and the relatively short distance necessary to migrate. The French Canadians proved to be docile laborers, submissive to authority—with families, following tradition, often working together in the mills.

The French Canadians' migration and the development of a new French American subculture had an adverse effect on both the prevailing Quebec and

New England cultures. The French Canadian family system in Canada was, and still is, predominantly large and patriarchal, constituting a strong influence on the roles of the individual members. When the French Canadians came to New England to work in the factories, they did not originally intend to make the host state their permanent residence. Their main intent was that of economic exploitation with plans eventually to return to Canada. Their initial purpose was to work in New England during the Canadian depression in an attempt to alleviate the economic strain on their families left in Canada. While many did not plan to remain, only 10 percent returned to Canada. The peak influx of the French Canadians into New England was the decade 1890–1900. The rate dropped off thereafter, and in 1930, during our own depression, the border was closed.

The French Canadians' ethnocentricity in New England was strong. While they tried to retain their total ethnic background, they succeeded only in producing a subculture apart from their mother Canadian culture. One reason for this occurrence was that the ethnic code was supported by three diverse classes of people with different motivations: (1) the priesthood, (2) the businessmen, and (3) the bulk of the French Canadian laborers. The clergy knew from previous experience in Canada that when the French identity was separated from the Catholic Church, the people were prone to reject Catholicism. A case in point was the French Canadians who had migrated to Canada's western provinces. The businessmen, however, backed ethnic unity because it was profitable. They held a virtual monopoly on the business in the French Canadian ghetto communities in the mill towns. Most of the businessmen sent their children back to Canada for their education so they would be properly exposed to and supportive of the Quebec culture. Consequently, because they tended to gain from the situation, the French Canadian business group as a whole supported the Church's doctrine advocating cultural separatism. The third group, the mass of the French Canadian laborers and mill hands, nourished nostalgic ties with their mother country through frequent contact with relatives and friends from Quebec and (until 1930) by contact with the renewed supply of immigrants from Quebec.

Ethnic identification was also kept alive by various organizations and institutions that were established to provide for the needs of the immigrants. The organizations took the form of mutual-aid corporations and ethnic activities such as drama clubs and credit unions. The first French Canadian credit union in America, for example, was established in Manchester, New Hampshire, in 1907. The French newspaper was another medium by which ethnic unity was preserved. The major institution promoting ethnic identification was the Catholic Church with its parishes and parochial schools. The

Church was the focal point of all organizations, and the priest had influence in both religious and secular matters. Many organizations were established in conjunction with the local parish, since the Church's approval often determined their success or failure. French Canadian parochial education was and still is closely related with the Catholic Church. Most parishes provided at least primary-school facilities. The purpose of the parochial school has been to educate the children within the context of the ethnic culture, hence providing a major vehicle for the preserving and perpetuating of that culture.

In spite of numerous attempts to preserve the French Canadian culture, the system has undergone change. The old rural family system was threatened by the mechanisms of rational capitalist enterprise and economic organization. The mills were situated in towns and cities, and some 80 percent of the French Canadians migrated to urban areas in New England. The people who retained their old traditions were those who kept their old occupations, such as farmers and lumberjacks. Thus, it is ironic that the French Canadians should be one of the last groups of western European heritage to be exposed to industrialism, capitalism, and urbanization. After all, it was the French who initially influenced the rest of the world with their own capitalistic and democratic ideas.

The Early French Family in North America

Extended families combining into small parish communities (*rangs*) provided the nucleus of an early French Canadian society, which to a large extent still exists in rural Quebec province and in the Gaspé Peninsula. These families consisted of the ruling patriarch, his immediate family of procreation, and those of his married sons. In this respect the early French Canadian extended family was both patriarchal and patrilocal. Not only did the eldest male dominate the family, but married sons were expected to take up residence with, or near, their fathers. The patriarchs, in turn, were answerable to the parish priest and the priest to the bishop.

A general characteristic of these extended families was their large constituent families of procreation. Incentives were provided by the French crown to stimulate large families, thus strongly supporting the Catholic doctrines regarding procreation and providing a strong cultural value that still persists among French Canadians. Women were sent from France to become the wives of settlers, while incentive bounties were allotted males who married prior to age 16. Special compensations were given families with ten or more children, and, *au contraire,* patriarchs who failed to marry off their children at the prescribed ages were fined.

The parish community, which as noted was comprised of extended families, approached an autonomous socioeconomic unit. In such a community the priest, not the landlord, became the center of community life, and the Church pervaded all aspects of French Canadian life from birth to death. Miner (1967:91) writes:

> The philosophy of this religion is ingrained in the people from childhood. Emulation of the socially powerful individuals in the community means the acceptance of Catholic ideology and behavior patterns. All methods of orienting the child in the society are employed to develop in him emotional attachment to this particular set of beliefs. Lack of contact with persons of other convictions and the relative lack of functional problems in the mode of living mean that the particular native belief is seldom questioned.

Religious ritual became an indispensable part of community and family life. All records were kept by the parish priests, and all decisions awaited their approval. Until British rule the only taxes the peasants paid were tithings to the Church. Religion and education were inseparable. The only formal education (primary school) was and still is parochial. In short, the Church both defined and provided the French Canadians with their social, cultural, and normative systems.

The family provided the real basis of rural life in the parish. In the early extended family all members, regardless of sex and age, shared in the family enterprise. The females did the spinning, weaving, knitting, sewing, cooking and serving of meals, washing, gardening, milking, and housekeeping, while the males tended the farm. All profit, whether it be capital gain or material objects, was received and handled by the family patriarch. When the patriarch died, the management of the family holdings was transferred to the next eldest male, while the moral leadership of the clan remained entrenched in the patriarch's wife. Daily prayers and compulsory church attendance helped weld the family into a sacred unit. Mores and folkways provided effective informal modes of control both within the family and the larger parish community. Marriages were arranged with the payment of dowries and were closely controlled so as not to disrupt the community balance. The Church, in turn, exerted considerable control over the family not only morally but economically. Villages (*rangs*) were autonomous with government policy determined by the *curé* (parish priest) and the *famille souche,* or council of family patriarchs. The upkeep of the parish was paid by a yearly *dime* or tithe by which every 26th minot of grain belonged to the Church.

High occupational, political, and social aspirations were not emphasized. Sons took on the occupation of their fathers, such as farming, logging, trapping, or fishing. The women and children held subservient positions in the family scheme. In a hierarchy of control and dominance within the parish community, the priest ranked highest, the extended family patriarch second, his married sons next, while women and children ranked last, playing submissive, subordinate roles. The Catholic Church itself provided the highest aspirations for the French Canadians. Nearly every family had at least one member in the Church, occupying the role of priest, brother, or nun. All this helped strengthen the interrelatedness and autonomy of the parish community. But even in the Church women played subservient roles. Nuns or sisters either performed servitude roles for the priest and brothers or taught in the parish parochial schools.

Mill-Town Subculture of Early French Canadian Americans

The migration of French Canadians to New England had a tremendous influence not only on those who migrated but on the lifestyle of their countrymen who remained in French Canada. The open American–Canadian border from the 1860s to 1930 allowed cultural dissemination not only from Canada to New England but also vice versa. The areas most resistant to these influences were the small farm parishes along the lower St. Lawrence, both in Quebec province and in the Gaspé. In the rest of French Canada there was a trend toward urbanization and industrialization, which eventually replaced the archaic agrarian lifestyle. The new French American lifestyle became the focal point of social change among French Canadians. By the same token it provided a new French Canadian subculture. The mill ghettos became autonomous social units, bringing with them their own parish priest, and while the migrants did succeed in retaining a distinct ethnic identity, their lifestyle nevertheless changed considerably. The new economic lifestyle, the exposure to other types of social institutions, and the relatively higher standard of living altered the French Canadian's social system such that it eventually emerged into a distinct New England, French American subculture.

In the early French American family, French was still the primary language, but contrary to the Canadian situation English was often learned as a second language. Education still consisted of primary parochial education provided by the Church. The priest and Church still had a strong influence, but the patriarch's dominance diminished as the extended family often broke into conjugal units and no longer remained patrilocal. The male head of the conjugal but usually large family became the dominant figure, while women and children still played subservient roles and often spent long hours in the mills themselves.

THE MODERN FRENCH CANADIAN AMERICAN FAMILY

Once the French Canadian immigration to America began, an interesting social phenomenon occurred that altered the lifestyle of French Canadian families in both countries. The new family structure created in the New England mill communities soon had a reverse effect on the lifestyle of French Canada, providing impetus for Quebec province to industrialize and urbanize, something the British Canadians had tried in vain to initiate for decades. The irony of this situation is that the lines of communication between French Americans and French Canadians were better established than were those between the dominant British Canadians' culture and the subordinate French Canadians. What has emerged is a dual French Canadian subculture along rural-urban lines, with similar characteristics in each subculture in both countries.

The older, rural subculture still exists virtually unchanged in the farm parishes along both banks of the St. Lawrence, while in northern New England (Vermont, New Hampshire, and Maine) French American farmers and loggers still maintain a rural existence. Today, however, the rural French Canadians represent a distinct minority of the French population in both areas. It is estimated that less than a quarter of the residents of both Quebec province and northern New England reside in rural areas. The major difference in the population composition between the two areas is that in Quebec 90 percent of the population is French Canadian, while it is estimated that approximately 30 to 40 percent of northern New England's population is of French Canadian descent. In southern New England the proportion is somewhat smaller, comprising 15 to 20 percent of the population. Most of the French Canadian population, in both areas, reside in urban, industrialized settings. This does not necessarily imply large urban settings, for relatively small mill towns with populations varying from 2000 to 10,000 fall into this category. Interestingly enough, northern New England, which is considered to be an industrialized area, has no cities with a population exceeding 100,000. It is the French family living in these mill-town industrial areas in both Canada and New England that represents the new French Canadian subculture that has emerged within the last hundred years and that remains the focus of this chapter.

Indeed, the 1970 U.S. Census shows that New England and Louisiana have the greatest proportion of francophones (French, Acadian, and French Canadian) in the United States (Giguere, 1979; St. John-Jones, 1973; Lines, 1978).

Tables 1 and 2 show that the French Mother-tongue is better preserved among the Acadians in Louisiana than it is in New England. Much concern has been focused upon this phenomenon, i.e., the increasing decline of the

French *patois* among French Americans. These concerns have been voiced by both traditional groups such as the *Association Acadienne d'Education* and the *Association Canado-Americaine,* as well as by more recent political and/or educational groups—the *Front de Liberation du Quebec* (FLQ) and the *Franco-American Resource Opportunity Group* (FAROG).

This is an interesting phenomenon, given the closer proximity of New England French Canadians to their mother country, Quebec, Canada. However, the Acadians have managed to retain many of their cultural attributes—including their language, within their isolated, *gemeinschaft* sense of commu-

TABLE 1
French-Speaking Populations in the United States—by State[a]

AREA	STATE POPULATION	FRANCOPHONES	PERCENTAGE
Maine	993,663	141,489	14.2%
New Hampshire	737,681	112,278	15.2%
Vermont	444,330	42,193	9.5%
Massachusetts	5,688,903	367,194	6.4%
Rhode Island	948,844	101,270	10.7%
Connecticut	3,031,705	142,118	4.7%
Louisiana	3,640,442	572,262	15.7%
New York	18,236,882	208,801	1.1%
New Jersey	7,168,143	44,445	.6%
Pennsylvania	11,793,864	33,723	.3%
Ohio	10,650,903	32,014	.3%
Illinois	11,109,450	51,942	.5%
Indiana	5,193,665	14,777	.3%
Michigan	8,875,063	81,684	.9%
Wisconsin	4,417,731	24,317	.6%
Minnesota	3,804,971	28,413	.7%
Missouri	4,676,495	13,980	.3%
Maryland	3,922,391	22,072	.6%
Virginia	4,648,470	22,693	.5%
Florida	6,789,383	64,378	.9%
Texas	11,195,416	90,902	.8%
Washington	3,409,161	24,540	.7%
California	19,957,304	200,784	1.0%
United States	203,302,082[b]	2,598,408[b]	1.3%

[a]U.S. Bureau of the Census (1970). Franco-American Files, University of Southern Maine.

[b]Total reflects 50 states.

TABLE 2

Major French-Speaking Populations in the United States[a]

AREA (COUNTY/PARISH AND STATE)	PROPORTION OF FRANCOPHONES	RANK
St. Martin, LA	79.1%	1
Evangeline, LA	75.9%	2
Vermilion, LA	69.3%	3
La Fourche, LA	62.5%	4
Acadia, LA	53.4%	5
Lafayette, LA	52.1%	6
St. Landry, LA	48.0%	7
Iberia, LA	43.9%	8
Terrebonne, LA	39.4%	9
Androscoggin, ME	39.4%	10
Aroostook, ME	29.2%	11
Hillsborough, NH	23.9%	12
Calcasieu, LA	23.8%	13
York, ME	23.5%	14
Jefferson, LA	13.6%	15
Providence, RI	13.3%	16
Bristol, MA	12.6%	17
Worcester, MA	12.4%	18
Hampden, MA	10.8%	19

[a]Each county has at least 20,000 French-speaking people in residence (U.S. Bureau of the Census, 1970). Franco-American Files, University of Southern Maine.

nity in Louisiana. At any rate, the influx of immigrants is greater for the French Canadians where strong contacts remain between French descendants on both sides of the border.

Family Structure

Today's French American family is basically a conjugal unit, although strong intergenerational kinship ties are maintained. The family hierarchy of social positions and responsibilities still focuses on the "earthly trinity" analogy, whereby the father, like God, dominates, controls, and protects the family interests, while the mother's role, like that of the Virgin Mary, is to be compassionate to the family while remaining subordinate and submissive to the father. Her specific role is to provide moral support for the family. The religious aura encompassing and binding the family together through the use of daily ritual is analogous to the binding effect of the "Holy Spirit."

In the French American family model the dominant socioeconomic role is ascribed to the father, while the role of socialization agent is left to the mother. However, unlike the normative conjugal family model, which portrays small family units, the French American family is often large. A generation ago it was not uncommon for there to be ten members within a French American family unit. Currently, family sizes seem to be decreasing. This phenomenon can be attributed to trying economic conditions and new child-labor and minimum-educational laws that place excessive children as economic liabilities. Nevertheless, children seek to help the family economy, often leaving school as early as possible, seeking employment, and contributing to the household until they themselves marry and set up their own family unit. This system functions because of the unique socialization process and kinship structure of the French American family. French Americans, like their French Canadian cousins, establish complex primary relationships within their parish communities, whereby reciprocal family, kinship, and religious obligations still supersede the individual's self-interest.

This phenomenon is best explained within the context of French Canadian kinship. Piddington (1971) noted that French Canadian kinship patterns more closely resemble those of folk cultures than they do other western societies. The French Canadians have a wide range of priority kin, coupled with a large number of prescribed social relationships, while in most western societies the priority of kin are fewer, most being restricted to the closed conjugal family unit. The French Canadian family is distinguished as a discrete residential and economic unit through its constellation of kinship relationships. And through these kinship networks parish communities in both Quebec and New England are closely linked. The interparish linkage serves to provide acceptable mates and does much to offset the disruptive effects of migration. It also provides facilities for social contacts and economic opportunity. From the standpoint of religious organization, the kinship network has long been the handmaiden of a French Canadian Catholicism that has managed to easily transcend international boundaries in the maintenance of its Quebec and New England parishes.

Male dominance in the French American family and community is readily evident in both Canada and New England. Family status and identity is transferred through the male lineage. Informal nicknames, passed down from father to son for generations, play an important role in the preservation of family status, while at the same time providing a secure identity for the male child. Females assume their husbands' status upon marriage. In this fashion, family and community status is preserved through the male lineage. Even children born out of wedlock trace their status and identity to the biological father if his identity is known.

Early marriages are common among the French Canadian Americans, mainly because they lack the restraints their Canadian relatives employ, such as matched marriages and dowries. The absence of these controls and the Church's continued opposition to birth control have produced a situation among the lower-class French American families in which pregnancy is often the determining criterion for a decision to marry. Accordingly, early marriages, while frequent, are not met with any noticeable reaction from the French American community other than mild token resistance from the Catholic Church. Nevertheless, the practice does contribute to the negative stigma of the ethnic group held by the dominant Yankee culture and fosters further resistance to interaction and eventual assimilation of the two groups. The impact of such resistance manifests itself in interreligious and ethnic marriage taboos, imposed by both the French Americans and the dominant culture. Catholicism, especially French Canadian Catholicism, has traditionally opposed interreligious marriages. However, Protestant Yankees are opposed to marriages with French Americans on the grounds that it would lower one's social status. French Americans are also opposed to most types of interracial marriages, the exception being between French Canadian and American Indians, since intermarriage between these two groups has existed for over 400 years.

Premarital sexual behavior likewise plays an important part in the mate selection process. It is prevalent among French Canadians in both New England and Quebec and seems to provide one of the few outlets to an otherwise restrictive French Canadian lifestyle. Illicit sexual behavior, officially condemned by the Catholic Church, has nevertheless emerged as a somewhat expectable mode of behavior in French Canadian communities in both countries. And, as matched marriages decrease in popularity, mate selection among French Canadians will become more contingent on change and correspond more closely to the prevailing American patterns.

The substantial incidence of premarital sex without the safeguards of birth control make illegitimacy a common threat to the working-class French Canadian community. However, the situation is usually handled without much conflict. Both abortions and adoptions are frowned upon, so in most cases the unwed mother keeps her child, and if she later marries, the child is generally accepted, taking an unheralded place in the new family. Until she finds a spouse, the participating conjugal family units, comprising the unwed mother's larger extended family, help the mother and child secure a position in the community. Their aid is subtle, so that the unwed mother and her child may appear to be a self-sufficing autonomous social unit, thus improving her chances at marriage. The same holds true when a divorce occurs. Deprived of her husband's status, the estranged wife must revert to her family lineage for social support and identity.

When a couple marries, the new conjugal family unit seeks to establish its own neolocal household. Quite often the family resides in an apartment that belongs to either the husband's or wife's lineal kin. When this situation occurs, it is preferable to reside with the husband's lineage (patrilocal) rather than the wife's (matrilocal), since living with the wife's relatives implies dependency on the wife by the husband. French American communities consist physically of mostly tenements and private homes. A family unit generally starts in a rented apartment, with all eligible family members working and saving so that, if successful, they later will be able to buy their own tenement to live in and rent or to purchase a private home.

The tenements are old, plain, two- or three-story wood-frame units, housing from four to 12 families. These were popular housing units for previous French American generations because they provided a convenient residence for the entire extended family. Large brick or wood apartment complexes, known as "cooperations," still provide housing for the immigrant French Canadian families. Regardless of the nature of the French American family residence, most are adorned with religious objects, personifying the crucifix, child Jesus, and the Virgin Mary. Holy-water receptacles, blessed palms, pictures, and statues are found in most homes. The most affluent families adorn their lawns with larger statues, usually of the Virgin Mary. The function of religious objects in French American families is twofold, providing both religious continuity to their everyday life and relative community status.

Family Life Cycle and Socialization

CHILDHOOD. The birth of a child, since it brings additional social and religious status to both parents, is a significant factor within the working-class family. For the female, childbirth, especially the first born, signifies her *rite de passage* into adulthood. And while both children of either sex are welcomed, male children are more indulged by both parents. The father, as noted above, often gives his first-born son his nickname along with the responsibility for continuing the male lineage and tradition. The result may well be rather heavy pressures brought on the son to excel in the same activities as the father, such as hockey, pool, street fighting, and hunting.

Pregnancy, also discussed above, often precipitates marriages between young couples, or when not followed by marriage, the infant is usually accepted by the woman's family. A third arrangement is to have an unmarried couple live together with their children. After a number of years these arrangements become recognized as common-law marriages subject to the same Church and community expectations as are Church and civil marriages.

Regardless of the father/mother relationship, the child, in order to secure its appropriate position in the hereafter, is baptized as soon as possible. Prebaptismal deaths bring great sorrow to French Americans, mainly due to the belief that the infant's soul will remain in limbo and be denied access to heaven. Considerable affection, attention, and liberties are showered on and made available to surviving children, especially by the mother, grandmothers, and other female relatives. The concern about children, which in its intensity is a relatively new phenomenon, is associated with the smaller French American families and such other factors as pregnancy leaves from work and the greater accessibility to modern conveniences, such as laundromats, diaper services, and the like, which permit more time for the mother to nurture her children.

The preschool child learns both French and English, with its distinctive French American accent, in the home during the first six years. Preschool institutions such as kindergarten, nursery schools, and the like are rare occurrences among this group. Early family socialization is supplemented by the Church activities and involvements, with most young children attending Mass with their mothers on a weekly basis. In all but the high mass, it is not unusual to see numerous mothers holding infants in their arms as well as all other preschool children attending church. School-age children attend mass by class and sit in a special section up front accompanied by their teacher-nuns.

French American children learn quite early the norms of sex peer-group separation. The division is maintained even within the family setting, and early founded peer groups continue to be maintained during the school years. This was especially the case when the parochial school system flourished in New England. The nuns themselves reinforced sexual separation in the classroom, the girls sitting on one side and boys on the other. Similar seating arrangements were made for morning mass, a compulsory daily activity in the parochial school system. Associated with the primary educational process is the child's first communion, which is the first conscious formal activity for the child, and much is still made of it. A new dress or suit for the child and a well-attended ceremony by family, relatives, and friends highlight this activity. In fact, religious ceremonies such as baptism, first communion, confirmation, and marriage have a seemingly far greater significance than civil ceremonies such as convocations and graduation exercises. All in all, the working-class French American child is allowed considerable latitude in his or her behavior within the family, with its patriarchal overtones, and in most community settings. The Church, notably through the parochial school, however, is the stricter disciplinarian. These contravening behavioral expectations sometimes lead to conflict situations, but when this does occur, the person in these days is more likely to reject the proscriptions of the Church.

ADOLESCENCE AND YOUNG ADULTHOOD. Puberty, as a biological phenomenon and confirmation, the social recognition of puberty through a religious *rite de passage,* highlight adolescence in the French American community. Simultaneously, the Church, family, and peer group compete for the youth's attention and devotion. The like-sex peer groups become all the more significant during this period, especially for the males. Within them they find themselves pressured to live up to their father's image. Family expectations are more or less consonant with those of the peer group. To accommodate these demands, the school and Church often become less crucial to the adolescent male. The days of complete integration of all local institutions and associations, if they ever existed, are apparently over.

Dating as well as the establishment of sociability patterns emerge during this period. Although many French American youth have been drinking beer and smoking cigarettes for a few years, the social significance of these activities becomes internalized during adolescence. In fact, most activities, whether they be related to sports, religion, or social events (dating, drinking), are closely tied to the peer-group structure. In this sense, then, the peer group and not the family or Church is the ultimate influence in mate selection. Female youth, however, rely less on the influence of their peer group during this period than do their male counterparts. The family, school, and Church still play an important role for many French American girls; this is evident for one thing in their high educational achievements. Yet the female peer group is an important instrumentality for dating and for determining one's social standing at this time. The main difference, then, between the male and female adolescent peer-group structures is that the former is somewhat more salient and enduring than the latter.

Since it is not unusual for working-class French Americans to marry during their teens, the male's occupational status is often determined during this period. And while the father's occupation is an important consideration, certain occupations are held to be more prestigious than others. Iron workers, truck drivers, machine operators, and construction and mill foremen have considerably more status than unskilled laborers or some white-collar workers. The female's occupational status is less crucial since her paramount role is to raise the children and maintain the household. Many females do work, but sporadically, and the primary consideration is their pay rather than the job itself.

The young married couple often lives in an apartment in a tenement owned by one of their relatives. Their children are indulged by the relatives on both sides, again with the first-born male child shown special attention. The young father continues to associate with his peer group, spending considerable leisure time with them. This is important since the peer group specifies and evaluates his social success. Ritualistic drinking, card and pool playing, along with an avid interest in sports such as hockey, baseball, boxing, hunting, wrestling, and horse racing are all important aspects of the lives of young adult males. And while most still attend church during this period, it is more of a formality than a devotion. Adolescent and young adult males can be seen standing in the back of the church during mass—the last in and the first out. The female, in comparison, establishes a new interaction network—based on her own and her husband's family and relatives, as well as a new cluster of female friends who share a life situation similar to hers.

MIDDLE AND OLD AGE. As the male gets older, he comes increasingly to incorporate into his personality his peer group's perception of him. If this is a positive reflection and is reinforced by his family, community, and Church, then the person usually develops a good self-image, at least within the French American subcultural setting. But not all adult males find themselves in this situation. Numerous interaction confrontations are discernible, the most notable occurring between the peer group and the family. When this situation occurs, the peer group usually emerges the victor, and a breaking of the marital bond results. Dependent children normally remain with their mother, and she continues to receive support from both her family and her estranged husband's family, as well as from the community and Church.

The middle years are a particularly important period for those who have adequately adjusted to the working-class French American lifestyle. This is the time when their years of working and saving finally bring their reward. Unlike their middle-class counterparts, these French Americans seldom get involved in long-term loans and mortgages. Instead, they save their money, rent an apartment, and drive used cars until the time when they can afford to buy their own home, new car, and boat. Such affluence as they enjoy is possible also because French Americans are not traditionally burdened with financing their children through an extended and expensive period of adolescence. They help their children with emotional concern and support but do not see the wisdom or need for mortgaging their own future to assure that of their offspring.

Old age, unlike in the larger dominant American society, brings considerable status on both the French American male and female. If both grandparents survive, it is the female who has the higher status. Most social and religious events as well as Sunday-after-mass visits require a stay with *grand-mère*. When both grandmothers are alive, they share this status. Considerable reverence is also associated with the grandmother's status, and she is the repository of knowledge concerning the entire family kinship network.

Death to the French Americans carries both religious and social significance. The person has borne his or her cross and now awaits God's judgment. With the exception of death prior to baptism (infant death), death is viewed somewhat philosophically by the French Americans. As with baptism, first communion, confirmation, and marriage, it is a time for formality and social interaction. It is often said that the dead are better off now. This refers to passage of the trial of life and the ultimate reward of everlasting peace or punishment, depending on the final judgment. An interesting social ritual associated with the death of veterans who occupy an important male peer-group membership is a military or paramilitary representation at the funeral, accompanied with a rifle salute and an American flag draped over the coffin. After the burial those participating in the burial ceremony go to the local American Legion Hall, VFW, or Lions Club to drink to the deceased. In any event there is little alienation from the dead. Like birth, it is a phenomenon too mystifying to be dealt with rationally and expeditiously. The knitting up of torn social and personal fabric and the reestablishment of social solidarity require ritualization and for some period of time ceremonial remembrance.

The Family and Community

PEER GROUPING. Another interesting and relevant attribute of the French American family structure is also shared by their Canadian relatives, that of like-sex peer-group association. These relationships are fostered early in the primary family setting and endure into adulthood. It is within these peer-group associations that males and females encounter each other, with the success of the relationship often being dependent on the approval of either participant's peer group. The female, once married, most likely forsakes her peer-group interests for that of her new marital role. The male, however, continues his peer-group membership all through his adult life, with peer-group interests often superseding those of his immediate family. Membership clubs, licensed to serve hard liquor as well as beer and wine, consist of numerous ethnic and national organizations, including the Knights of Columbus, the American Legion, and the Veterans of Foreign Wars. These drinking establishments are the central social meeting place for the adult males in the French American community. Many men frequent these establishments daily in a more or less ritualistic pattern. In the winter months the clubs and bars are filled with the seasonal construction workers who draw unemployment during the off season. On weekend evenings group socials highlight the community's weekly festivities. Consequently, the relatively autonomous French American community is organized to provide two opposite but complementary social functions. The Church, through its manifold social and religious activities, provides the moralistic and ideological support for the community members, while the clubs and bars provide acceptable avenues of tension and frustration release. Both functions seem crucial to the maintenance and preservation of the French American subculture.

EDUCATION. As noted above, the French Canadians who originally immigrated to the New England mill communities brought with them their Church and parochial educational system. The French Catholic Church, parochial schools, and the French Canadian language, all closely interrelated, provide the three most crucial cultural institutions responsible for the preservation and perpetuation of the French American subculture. Parochial schools, although currently under considerable economic pressure in New England, still provide the basic educational needs of the Canadian French in both countries. French Canadians have traditionally been opposed to the public educational system, viewing it as an instrument of the dominant Protestant culture. Public schools are viewed, in both countries, as really being "Protestant schools." The French Canadian parochial educational system, through the preservation of its language, culture and Church doctrines, provides the French Americans with their strong sense of ethnocentrism, which in turn keeps them isolated from the larger dominant culture and forestalls assimilation.

OCCUPATION. When the original French Canadians emigrated to New England, their occupational status changed from that of peasant farmers to factory laborers. The occupational transformation was successful due to the minimal degree of specialization and training required for either occupational role. Correspondingly, the low value placed on formal education provided a socioeconomic situation whereby the French Canadians were unprepared to occupy the more specialized and prestigious occupational roles available in the commercial and industrial economy of New England. Lacking the necessary managerial and technical skills, and having failed to attain the educational prerequisites required of these occupations, the French Americans find themselves, for the most part, relegated to marginal occupational roles.

The traditional occupation of French American families has been employment in textile mills. During the early 1950s, after nearly a century of operation, the larger textile industries moved south, seeking lower operational costs. Shoe shops, fiberglass and electronic industries, among others, replaced the departed textile industries in the mill towns throughout New England. In northern New England (Maine, New Hampshire, and Vermont) woodcutting and other lumber- and pulp-related occupations provide employment for French Americans. A third major source of employment is provided through seasonal construction work related to highway, bridge, and building construction.

The abovementioned occupations account for the employment of the majority of the working-class French Americans. Other occupational specialties range from small-business proprietors to professional occupations. Each French American community has its own small ethnic businesses: clothing and shoe stores, small grocery and variety stores, plus an array of other small community enterprises. Other French American families own and operate their own dairy farms, truck gardens, or small-scale logging operations. Professionals of French American heritage provide the necessary medical, dental, and legal services for the community.

The factories, seasonal construction, and lumber-related industries are not high-paying occupations, yet they seem abundant enough to provide the French American families with a somewhat stable and sufficient source of economic support to sustain their lifestyle. Ironically, the areas of northern New England bordering Canada are those with the highest rate of unemployment (at least a percentage point higher than the states' average), and outmigration of young adults. This creates a fluctuating labor shortage, and subsequently bonded and visaed French Canadians have to be imported to rectify the situation. They are needed on a yearly basis as cutters in the lumber industries and on a seasonal basis in the harvesting of apples. This action requires permission from the U.S. Department of Labor, and although extensive efforts are made to recruit native laborers, each year the effort seems in vain. This fresh source of French Canadian contact through the imported laborers reinforces the communication lines between the two French subcultures.

Social and Physical Mobility

Social and physical mobility or the lack thereof reflect the degree of internal cohesion within French American working-class communities throughout New England. Both phenomena are closely related to the high degree of ethnocentrism and the resulting process of "resistance within." Social mobility implies vertical mobility, that is, moving through the various social strata that comprise the larger dominant culture. Physical mobility on the other hand, represents the degree of out-migration from the French American communities to other more integrated communities within the larger culture. As a consequence of their basic value system French Americans are restricted in both forms of mobility. As previously mentioned, the French American socialization process occurs through a cooperative relationship between the parish church and the primary family situation. Education is a quality that facilitates vertical social mobility in our society by preparing its members to enact occupational roles that are highly valued in themselves. It seems apparent that the low level of education among the French Americans can only serve to restrict vertical, social mobility as they compete both socially and economically within the American system. A result of this situation, and in turn contributing to it, is low achievement motivation among French Americans. In one such study they ranked lowest among ethnic groups, with blacks being the only minority group below them (Secord and Backman, 1964:570).

That the most salient criterion for determining high social status among the French Americans, that is, church-related roles, has little relevance to the vertical social-occupational structure of the dominant culture reinforces and intensifies the ecological boundaries surrounding the French American communities. As a result, the French American communites evolved into psychological ghettos that perpetuate the same values that restrict their social and physical mobility, consequently the assimilation of their members into the larger culture. The selective socialization that occurs among the families and institutions within the context of these protective ghetto communities creates in its members both a psychological and sociological dependency on the community for fulfillment of the basic human needs, while at the same time instilling behavioral patterns and mannerisms that account for the negative image of the French Americans in the eyes of the dominant culture. As a result, encounters with the larger culture are often viewed as being negativistic and undesirable and reinforce the desirability of the French American community, whether it be the home community or an adopted one. Voluntary physical mobility among working-class French Americans is mostly restricted to movements to other French American communities or to communities in Canada in which relatives reside. When involuntary physical mobility occurs, such as military conscription, many return to the relative security of their home community, remaining there for the duration of their lives. Hence, low social and restricted physical mobility among French Americans results from a unique socialization process that creates the member's community dependency while instilling those social characteristics that make the French Americans visible as a minority group.

CHANGE AND ADAPTATION

The current situation in Canada has been turbulent. Distinct polar, political, and social boundaries have been drawn and reinforced between the English and French Canadians. French radicals view themselves as being oppressed "white niggers," while a substantial proportion of the less radical French strongly support the separatist policy (Vallieves, 1971). The current political and social indicators seem to imply more chaos and conflict between the French Canadian subculture and the dominant English Canadian culture.

These turns of events minimize the chances for assimilation, convergence, or homogenization of Canada into one mass lifestyle. Yet some feel that French Canada will long resist assimilation and will remain a strong separatist Canadian subculture. Wagley and Harris (1964:200–201) drew this conclusion from their UNESCO study:

> What will be the future of the French Canadian minority in Canada? It is obviously not a group that will be assimilated into English-Canada society rapidly or easily. It is composed of a large population with an exceedingly high birthrate. It has political power in the nation and political control over Quebec. It has its own schools from the primary level to great universities. It takes pride in its French traditions and cultures. . . . French Canada has its national sport and its sporting heroes in ice hockey. The French Canadians as a group have all the elements in a vigorous social unit which cannot easily be overwhelmed even by the more rapidly expanding English-Canadian group.

And as long as these conditions continue to prevail in Canada, their ramifications will be felt among the French Americans residing below the border in New England. The French Canadian parent culture has numerous life lines to its New England relatives, and these continue to nourish the French American subculture. To illustrate the nature of these problems in New England, a year-long study (1978–1979) initiated by the New Hampshire Civil Liberties Union concluded that French Americans are economically and socially disadvantaged and that this discrimination includes educational and occupational opportunities. Some, however, feel that these problems have always existed and that the French Americans even contributed to them by virtue of their isolated and clannish lifestyle. The major reason that these differences are now viewed as reflecting ethnic disadvantages and discrimination is that the French in New England have for the first time fallen behind their French counterparts in Quebec and the Maritime Provinces.

Indeed, a quiet revolution, the *rattrapage,* has occurred in Quebec within the past 20 years and continues today. Under the direction of progressive French leaders such as Trudeau, Pelletier, Bourassa and Levesque, the *rattrapage* has brought about considerable change in French Canada. Moreover, these men have brought about this transformation without sacrificing French Canada's unique ethnic and cultural heritage. This transition, however, did result in a political change, with the Catholic Church now to a considerable extent replaced by secular leaders (Fox, 1978; Trudeau, 1968).

347

Today, French Canadians on both sides of the border are concerned with cultivating their cultural heritage and placing it in a more favorable light. The 1976 election of Rene Levesque and his Partie Quebeçoise government in Quebec clearly accelerated this movement. Many now realize that French Canadians in both Quebec and the United States will be greatly affected by future events in Canada especially if Quebec secedes from Canada, a move that would establish it as the largest French nation in the world.

REFERENCES

Anderson, E. L. 1957. "The French-Canadians in Burlington, Vermont," in M. L. Barron (ed.), *American Minorities*. New York: Knopf.
Beattie, Christopher, and Byron G. Spenser. 1971. "Career Attainment in Canadian Bureaucracies: Unscrambling the Effects of Age, Seniority, Education, and Ethno-linguistic Factors on Salary," *American Journal of Sociology,* 77 (November): 372–490.
Byrne, William D. D. 1899. *History of the Catholic Church in the New England States,* Vol. I. Boston: Hurd and Everts.
Darroch, Gordon A., and Wilfred G. Marston. 1971. "The Social Class Basis of Ethnic Residential Segregation: The Canadian Case," *American Journal of Sociology,* 77 (November): 491–510.
Department of Forestry and Rural Development. 1967. *Development Plan for Pilot Region Lower St. Lawrence, Gaspe, and Iles-de-la-Madeleine.* Ottawa.
Fox, Richard. 1978. "Ethnic Nationalism and Political Mobilization in Industrial Societies," *Interethnic Communication.* Athens: University of Georgia Press.
Giguere, Madeleine. 1979. *La Farog Forum,* 7 (3) (November): 12–13.
———. 1979. *La Farog Forum,* 7 (4) (December):2.
Grayson, L. M., and Michael Bliss (eds.). 1971. *The Wretched of Canada.* Toronto: University of Toronto Press.
Grochmall, Bernard, Jr. 1969. "An Analysis of the Social Stratification of the French-Canadian Community of Newmarket, New Hampshire," unpublished Master's thesis, University of New Hampshire.
Hughes, Everett. 1943. *French Canada in Transition.* Chicago: University of Chicago Press.
Kramer, Judith R. 1970. *The American Minority Community.* New York: Thomas Y. Crowell.
Lieberson, Stanley, 1970. *Language and Ethnic Relations in Canada,* New York: Wiley.
Lines, Kenneth. 1978. *British and Canadian Immigration to the United States Since 1920.* San Francisco: R&E Research Associates.
Metalious, Grace. 1964. *No Adam in Eden.* New York: Pocket Books.
Miner, Horace. 1967. *St. Denis: A French-Canadian Parish.* Chicago: University of Chicago Press.
Minsitry of Industry, Trade and Commerce. 1972. *Canada 1972: The Annual Handbook of Present Conditions and Recent Progress.* Ottawa.

Ministry of Industry, Trade and Commerce. 1971. *Canada Year Book—1970–1971.* Ottawa.

New Hampshire Civil Liberties Union. 1979. *La Farog Forum,* 7 (2) (October): 4.

Newsweek. 1972. (November 13), p. 53.

Ong, Walter J. 1961. *Frontiers in American Catholicism: Essays on Ideology and Culture.* New York: Macmillan.

Piddington, Ralph. 1971. "A Study of French-Canadian Kinship," in K. Ishwaran (ed.), *The Canadian Family.* Toronto: Holt, Rinehart and Winston of Canada.

Rose, Peter I. 1968. *They & We.* New York: Random House.

Ryerson, Stanley B. 1968. *Unequal Union.* New York: International Publishers.

Secord, Paul, and Carl Backman. 1964. *Social Psychology.* New York: McGraw-Hill.

St. John-Jones, L. W. 1973. "The Exchange of Population between the United States of America and Canada in the 1960s," *International Migration,* XI.

Trudeau, Pierre. 1968. *Federalism and the French Canadians.* New York: St. Martin's Press.

Urguhart, M. C. 1965. *Historical Statistic of Canada.* Toronto: Macmillan Company of Canada.

U.S. Bureau of the Census. 1970. *Census of Population.* Washington, DC: U.S. Government Printing Office.

Vallieves, Pierre. 1971. *White Niggers of America: The Precocious Autobiography of a Quebec "Terrorist,"* translated by Joan Pinklam. New York: Monthly Review Press.

Wagley, Charles, and Marvin Harris. 1964. *Minorities in the New World.* New York: Columbia University Press.

The Jewish American Family

The crucial question pursued by the authors in this chapter on the Jewish American family concerns the orientation of Jews toward traditions they brought with them from the European continent. The analysis takes a look at the Jewish family from a generational perspective, pointing out the increasing rates of change and movement away from Jewish tradition in each subsequent generation. In spite of the emphasis on loss of tradition, however, it becomes clear that the Jewish family is still an important unit, and Jewish identity still has an impact on individual behavior.

CHAPTER FIFTEEN
BY

BERNARD FARBER, CHARLES H. MINDEL, AND BERNARD LAZERWITZ

HISTORICAL BACKGROUND

From the earliest days of the Exodus, Jews have been a people on the move. Their settlements may have at times seemed permanent, but time and again political, social, or religious events have conspired to make them a nomadic people. The most remarkable characteristic of these people has been that in spite of the oppressions and persecutions, or perhaps because of them, Jews have retained a remarkable degree of distinct religious and cultural identity.

Judaism, a worldwide religion, embraces about 14 million constituents, tending to be concentrated in a few key areas throughout the world. Until the time of Hitler, the largest concentration of Jews lived in Europe. Presently, approximately 43 percent of the world's Jews, or about 6 million, live in America, where they now constitute a distinct subgroup among world Jewry.

Jews in America

The settlement of Jews in America is an old one. Jews have been in America since the colonial period, though they began arriving in large numbers only 100 years ago. It has been agreed that the immigration of Jews to America occurred in three major historical waves involving people from three national locations: Sephardic Jews from Spain and Portugal, German Jews from the Germanic states, and eastern European Jews, largely from Poland and Russia but also from Rumania, Hungary, and Lithuania. It would be inaccurate to assume that there has been no overlap among these three waves of immigration because there was immigration from Germany at the same time as immigration from Poland and Russia. These three waves of immigration are important because they define three distinct cultural patterns that Jewish communities tended to differentiate in America.

Immigrants from the nearly destroyed Sephardic, German, and eastern European Jewish communities differed for a variety of historical, cultural, and economic reasons. Descendants of migrants from eastern Europe, who were the last to arrive, comprise by far the largest number of America's Jews, probably over 90 percent. The Sephardic Jews and the German Jews are and have been important not for their numbers but largely because of their social position and influence.

The Sephardic Jews

The earliest Jewish settlement in America occurred in 1654 in what was then New Amsterdam (now New York City), a colony of the Dutch West Indies Company. The Jews who settled there followed a circuitous route, ultimately traceable to the large medieval Jewish population of Spain and Portugal. However, the Jews were not particularly welcome in New Amsterdam. Peter Stuyvesant, the governor, resisted and argued that "none of the deceitful race be permitted to infest and trouble this new colony" (Golden and Rywell, 1950:13). However, the Dutch West Indies Company decided to allow the Portuguese Jews to live in New Netherlands "provided the poor among them shall not become a burden to the Company or to the community but be supported by their own nation" (Golden and Rywell, 1950:14). From this beginning there continued a steady flow of immigration of Sephardic Jews, and increasingly, German Jews, who numbered in 1840 around 15,000.

The German Jews

The middle of the 19th century, from approximately 1840 to 1880, saw a second "wave" of Jewish immigration, mostly German Jews. Conditions in Germany, or to be more accurate the collection of Germanic states, at mid-century were quite inhospitable for Jews and non-Jews alike. Anti-Jewish medieval laws of oppression were enacted, especially in Bavaria, which among other things provided for heavy discriminatory taxation, designated areas to live in, restricted occupations, and restrictions on the number of Jewish marriages. These conditions prompted many German Jewish single men to leave for America to seek opportunity. Later on, in the latter part of the 19th century, when these laws were relaxed, immigration of these German Jews slowed down to a trickle (Glazer, 1957; Weinryb, 1958).

Many German Jewish immigrants started out as peddlers, an occupation that did not require great skill or large capital investment. They spread out all over America and gave many non-Jews their first glimpse of a Jewish face. Originally starting out with a pack carried on their back, they traversed the countryside. If they were reasonably successful, they would graduate to a horse and wagon. If they were able to accumulate a little money, they might open a dry goods store in one of the many small towns and cities in which they traded. These were the origins of what later became the great clothing and department stores in America, such as Altmans, Bloomingdales, Bambergers, Gimbels, Goldblatt, Nieman-Marcus, Macys, Mays, Maison Blanche, Stix, Bare & Fuller, and others.

The importance and influence of the German Jews is linked crucially to their spectacular financial success. While certainly not all German Jews became wealthy, the rise of one group of families, many of whom started out as peddlers, had enormous implications for the status of Jews in America. They became important figures in banking and finance in a period of American history when the industrialization of America was just beginning and there was a need for large amounts of capital to feed the growing industrial base.

The German Jewish influx into America was great enough to overwhelm in number the Sephardim. By 1848 there were 50,000 Jews in America, and by 1880 there were an estimated 230,000, largely German Jews (Sklare, 1958).

Eastern European Jews

It was, however, the arrival of the Jews from eastern Europe that has had the greatest impact on Jewish American life. Beginning around 1888 and largely ending by 1930, almost three million Jews immigrated to America.

These individuals and families, though Jewish like their American counterparts, were in fact of another world. Whereas the Germans came from an "enlightened" modern society in which Jews were more often than not integrated into German culture, the eastern European Jews came from a milieu in which the feeling of homogeneity was strongly entrenched, where a set of Jewish values and attitudes prevailed, including religious devotion and observance.

Most of the five million Jews of Russia and Poland had been restricted, from the time of Catherine the Great, to an area established for them known as the Pale of Settlement. The Pale extended from the shores of the Baltic south to the Black Sea. Jews were generally not allowed to settle in the interior of Russia and were limited to this area. The Pale has been described, except for the Crimea, as a 313,000 square-mile, monotonously flat, sand-arid prison (Manners, 1972:30). Within this area, about the size of Texas, 808 *shtetlach* (townlets), each of which was perhaps two-thirds Jewish and 94 percent poor, Jews lived, survived and "attained the highest degree of inwardness . . . the golden period in Jewish history, in the history of the Jewish soul" (Manners, 1972:31).

The concentration of Jews in these areas for hundreds of years led to the development of a culture and civilization grounded in biblical and talmudic teachings that remained to a remarkable degree unchanged until the 20th century. Those who migrated from this society to America and elsewhere have on the whole become prosperous; those millions who remained, including most of the devout, were, for the most part, destroyed.

The mass migration of east European Jews began in the 1880s and continued at a high level until the passage of the restrictive immigration laws in 1924. The chief instigating factors that started the massive flow were the governmentally inspired *pogroms* of the Imperial Russian Government in 1881. *Pogroms* (devastation and destruction) consisted of ransacking, burning, rape, and assorted violence committed in the towns and villages of Russia. The government, driven by an overwhelming fear of revolution, used *pogroms* as a form of diversion and weapon against dissenting minorities (Manners, 1972).

Beginning in 1882, new laws, the so-called "May laws," were issued by the Czar, which severely restricted Jewish rights, such as they were. Thousands were forced to leave their homes, especially those who resided within interior Russia. These laws and the extensions of them left most Jews no choice but to emigrate.

Most emigrants came to America. Some went to Palestine, and some others went to other parts of Europe. Forty thousand came in 1881–1882, another 62,000 came in 1888, and by 1906 the number was up to 153,000 per year (Manners, 1972:57).

The *pogroms* and restrictive laws that forced the migration of these Jews were but the final chapter of a long process of disintegration of Jewish communities that had been going on for more than a century. Antagonisms and tensions had been developing within for a long period of time. Of more importance were the effects from the world outside the *shtetl*. Industrialization and the decline of the feudal system of relations came late to eastern Europe, but by the 19th century its effects were being felt there as well. Thus, by the time of the *pogroms* in the late 19th century and early 20th century social change and social disintegration had already come to this traditional society.

German Jews vs Eastern European Jews

The arrival of this mass of people was not an unmixed blessing to the already established, especially to the German American Jews who feared for their recently achieved middle-class status. However, native Jews and Americans, in general, took a compassionate though largely condescending view toward poverty-stricken immigrants (at least until 1924 when the American government, in the throes of a xenophobic isolationist wave, passed a restrictive immigration law).

Relations between the older established, primarily German American Jews and the newly arrived eastern European Jews were nevertheless difficult. The German Jews were interested in helping the immigrants in order to "Americanize" them so they would not be a source of embarrassment. They saw the strange dress and speech and the poverty as reflecting unfavorably on themselves, feeling that the quicker they became indistinguishable from the rest of America the better. Americanization was made more difficult by the fact that the eastern European Jewish immigrants clustered together in distinct urban neighborhoods, especially in the American northeast, particularly in New York City.

The eastern European Jewish immigrants were usually Orthodox. Though the immigrants tended to be less observant and traditional than their counterparts who remained in Europe, the religious institutions established by them in America were traditional and Orthodox recreations of the institutions that existed in eastern Europe. The immigrants did not recognize the Reform Judaism as it was practiced by the native, predominately German Jews. To them it was unacceptable. "They are Jews," declared Rabbi Dr. Issac Meyer Wise, the leading light of Reform Judaism, "We are Israelites." And the Russian Jews said with equal assurance, "We are Jews. They are *goyim* (Gentiles)" (Manners, 1972:76).

One important ingredient in the continuing vigor of Orthodox Judaism in America was the immigration during the Hitler and post-World War II years of numbers of Orthodox *Chassidic* Jews. The *Chassidic* groups, organized around a particular charismatic leader, the *rebbe,* or *Tzaddik,* are identified by the location in Europe from which they originated. These groups stress a communal life and close-knit group cohesion. They are found generally in the New York area, often in old neighborhoods. One group, however, the Skverer *Chassidim,* has established their own town, New Square, in the suburbs of New York City, in which they have attempted to recreate the traditional life of the eastern European Jew. The impact of these groups has been to bring new life into what was a disappearing branch of Judaism. The close ties of the members and the emotionalism of the religion as they practice it are attractive to many young people who have been seeking more emotion in their religious practices. Others who have not become members of *Chassidic* groups have borrowed much of the emotional content of this movement and put it into their own observance.

The Traditional Family of the East European Shtetl Community[1]

It has been estimated that today over 90 percent of America's Jewish population are or descend from immigrants from eastern Europe. Since their arrival has been relatively recent, family patterns which existed in Europe and were brought to the United States can still be expected to have an impact on present day family lifestyles. In the following paragraphs family life in the small eastern European town—the *shtetl*—where most Jews lived is described.

The *shtetl* was a poor place, a place of unpaved streets and decrepit wooden buildings. It is said that there was no "Jewish" architecture, rather the most noticeable features of the dwellings were their age and their shabbiness (Zborowski and Herzog, 1952:61). Occupationally the Jews were generally tradesmen—dairymen, cobblers, tailors, butchers, fishmongers, peddlers, and shopkeepers.

Social Organization

The marketplace was the economic center of the *shtetl*; however, the synagogue was the heart and soul of the community. The values of the religion infiltrated all aspects of life; every detail of life was infused with some religious or ritual significance. It was impossible to escape and to separate the religious from the secular.

Chief among the values of the *shtetl* and of Jewish culture was the value of learning. One of the most important obligations of a devout Jew is to study and learn. To obey the commandments of the scriptures one must know

---

[1]Much of this discussion of shtetl family structure comes from Landes and Zborowski (1968) and Zborowski and Herzog (1952).

them, and one must study them to know them. Studying and learning *Torah*[2] became the most important activity in which a man could involve himself— more important than earning a good living. Every *shtetl* of reasonable size would contain schools of various levels including the *cheder* for boys as young as three and four years of age. A learned young man was considered the most highly prized future son-in-law. In fact it was considered prestigious for a father-in-law to support his new son-in-law for the first few years of marriage if the son-in-law was bright, so that he could devote himself to full-time study.

The stratification of the *shtetl* was based in large measure on learning and on the tradition of learning in one's family. *Shtetl* Jews were either *sheyneh yidn* (beautiful Jews) or *prosteh yidn* (common Jews). The position of a person in this status hierarchy was dependent ideally on learning but wealth played an important part in determining the *sheyneh*. A third quality, *yikhus*, a combination of family heritage with respect to learning and wealth was also an important criteria in determining social position. A person with great *yikhus* was able to claim many ancestors of great worth particularly with respect to learning and philanthropy. To have *yikhus* was very prestigious.

Life in the *shtetl* was guided by written codes of behavior that derived from the Talmud and other religious sources. These standards ideally had the effect of regulating behavior of all Jewish residents of the *shtetl, sheyneh* and *prosteh* alike. It is in these codes of behavior and the folklore, folksayings, and other customs that grew up around the *shtetl* that we find the unique cultural basis for Jewish family life, important aspects of which still have an impact today.

Marriage

Duties and roles for men and women were carefully detailed by traditional writings and chief among these was the injunction that a man and woman marry. It was said, "It is not good for man to be alone."

Marriage in the *shtetl* was traditionally arranged by the parents of the young couple frequently through the use of a matchmaker (*shadchen*). It was assumed that the "parents always want the best for their children" (Zborowski and Herzog, 1952:275), and the children went along with the match.

---

[2]*Torah* literally refers to the Pentateuch, the five books of Moses, or the written scriptures. However, *Torah* has come to mean much more. It has come to include remaining portions of the Old Testament as well as the whole of the commentaries and interpretations on the Pentateuch which was known as the oral law or the *Talmud*. In addition, the numerous codifications and newer commentaries that appeared during the Middle Ages such as the works of Maimonides in Spain have also come to be included under this rubric. In essence, *Torah* means all the religious learning and literature including and surrounding the holy scriptures.

Since marriage was considered such an important institution, indeed a commandment (*mitzvah*), there was great pressure for marriage and families to remain united. In fact, because divorce reflected badly on one's family and stigmatized the individuals involved, it was a relatively rare occurrence. Marital stability was related to a dominant orientation in Jewish family life, *sholem bayis* (domestic harmony or peace). Only when maintaining a satisfactory family equilibrium became impossible and the *sholem bayis* was broken was divorce considered. The relative infrequency of divorce indicates that adaptations of many kinds occurred with some frequency.

Marital Roles

The injunction that a man should study, learn, and promote the book-learning tradition had important implications for the functioning of the husband in the family. The husband/father was often remote from most domestic concerns. If he was a scholar, much of the economic responsibility of the home was left to the wife. The husband's primary responsibility was in the spiritual and intellectual sphere; only the males were taught to read, speak, and write Hebrew, the sacred language; women who were literate spoke and read *Yiddish*.[3]

In reality, women often played a dominant role in family life and in the world outside. There was a high degree of interchangeability in family roles and wives were trained to be ready to assume the economic burdens of supporting the family. Women often had wide latitude and opportunity for movement to conduct business or seek employment, and in time of emergency or need women were able to partake in any number of "male" activities. It has been argued that women as a consequence of their subordinate status were less regulated than men, and therefore they were able to partake in all activities that were not expressly forbidden to them. As a result they quite often had greater freedom than men, who were bound up very tightly in a highly regulated way of life (Landes and Zborowski, 1968:81).

THE EASTERN EUROPEAN MOTHER. Basic to the eastern European Jewish family with its wide range of rights and obligations was parental love.

---

[3] Yiddish, a middle high German dialect written in Hebrew characters, was the common *mamaloshen* (mother tongue) of most eastern European Jews. Its use can be traced back 1000 years, and though Yiddish varied in form and pronunciation in different parts of western and eastern Europe, it provided a common language for Jews across all national boundaries and was a crucial factor in maintaining the unity of this branch of the Jewish people. The other major Jewish branches are the Sephardim, who spoke a dialect of Spanish written in Hebrew characters, and the Oriental Jews, who usually used Arabic.

357

Seldom demonstrated verbally or physically after the child was four or five, parental affection, especially from the mother, was felt to be an unbreakable bond. "No matter what you do, no matter what happens your mother will love you always. She may have odd and sometimes irritating ways of showing it, but in a hazardous and unstable world the belief about the mother's love is strong and unshakable" (Zborowski and Herzog, 1952:293). The Jewish mother's love was expressed by and large in two ways: "by constant and solicitous overfeeding and by unremitting solicitude about every aspect of her child's welfare" (Zborowski and Herzog, 1952:293). Both paternal and maternal love contain the notions of suffering and sacrifice for the sake of the children. It is said that "she kills herself" in order to bring up her children. She is always worrying, nagging, scolding, and sacrificing for her children and for her husband as well, who also becomes like a child in the family. Her conduct is understood and tolerated by her children who nostalgically idealize it when they get older; she is remembered as a "loving despot."

Affection among the *shtetl* Jews as mentioned was not expressed with kisses and caresses after a child reached four or five and espcially in public. However, a mother was more likely to be demonstrative to her son and a father more demonstrative to his daughter. Furthermore, though much contact between members of the opposite sex was restricted by avoidance etiquette, such as between brother and sister, there is virtually no avoidance between mother and son. It has been claimed that "though marital obligations are fulfilled with the husband, the romance exists with the son" and that "when the son marries, he gives the wife a contract and the mother a divorce" (Landes and Zborowski, 1968:80–88).

The father relates to his daughter like the mother to her son only not with quite the same intensity. With his daughter he is undemanding and indulgent. A father, however, is a distant figure for the most part, one to whom great respect is owned. He is a particularly remote, authoritarian figure for the boy whose growth into a "Jew" and a *mensch* (a "whole person" or adult) was his responsibility.

FAMILY OBLIGATIONS. The *shtetl* was viewed as an extended family, at the very least Jews consider themselves as ultimately related as the "Children of Israel" and often because of extensive intermarriage within the *shtetl* they were closer than that. In any case there were strong obligations and pressure to maintain close ties to kin. Particularly strong was the obligation to take care of elderly parents, although there is great reluctance on the part of the elderly parent, especially the father, to accept aid.

THE MODERN AMERICAN JEWISH FAMILY
Fertility

As families from all branches of world Jewry have become involved in urban, industrial societies, they have rapidly lowered their fertility levels. Indeed, the first birth-control clinic opened by Margaret Sanger was in Brownsville, a Brooklyn Jewish immigrant neighborhood.

Freedman, Whelpton, and Campbell (1959:110) report that the 83 percent of American Jewish women employing contraception start such use before their first pregnancy, while only 52 percent of Protestants start contraception as early in married life. Several national fertility studies (Freedman, Whelpton, and Campbell, 1959, 1961; Whelpton, Campbell, and Patterson, 1966) report that American Jews are the most successful of American major ethnic groups with regard to family planning and birth spacing. Estimates are that from about 1920 to 1940, the Jewish birth rate in America fell almost 40 percent (Seligman, 1950:42).

Reduction in the Jewish birth rate derives not only from effective use of contraceptives but also from late marriage. In the 1957 U.S. Census survey, the median age at first marriage for Jewish women was 21.3 as compared with 19.9 for Protestants and 20.8 for Catholics. Goldstein (1971:24) indicates that "later age of marriage has characterized Jewish women since at least 1920." For Jewish men as well, marriage has been later than it has for Protestants and Catholics. However, the data also indicate that the discrepancies in age at first marriage for Jews and non-Jews are disappearing. Although the high educational levels may be a factor in this tendency for Jews to marry later than others, it is unlikely the only one.

The shift from families characterized by large numbers of children in eastern Europe, North Africa, or the Middle East to families having two to four children may have been a major factor permitting Jewish women to increase their involvement in Jewish communal life, to extend and enlarge their participation in the labor force, and to have less rigid sex work tasks within the home. Furthermore, the rapid fertility reduction characteristic of all the world's Jews who have entered to any extent in modern life seems to reflect extensive communication and decisionmaking with regard to their husband–wife, father–mother roles within the Jewish family (Lazerwitz, 1971). Rapid fertility reduction has also permitted Jewish parents to support the educational desires of their fewer offspring and, thereby, give strong support to the rapid socioeconomic mobility that has been the outstanding achievement of American Jews (Lazerwitz, 1971).

Sergio Della Pergolá (1980) estimates that American Jewish fertility at the start of the 1970s was slightly below the level needed to replace the Jewish population and was still declining. Jewish religious involvement accounts for only a minor portion of the fertility variations among younger American Jewish couples. Nevertheless, slightly more than a quarter of American Jews do have higher fertility than the rest. This quarter consists of frequent synagogue attenders who prefer the Orthodox or Conservative denominations. At the lowest fertility end one finds the infrequent synagogue attenders with moderate to high occupational status. This latter group composes slightly more than 40 percent of younger American Jewish couples (Lazerwitz, 1980).

Characteristics of American Jewish Families

Since historically European Jewish social structure and characteristics are the foundation of the American Jewish family, one is tempted to use number of generations in the United States as a basic variable with which to view American Jewry. However, research by Lazerwitz (1978) and Lazerwitz and Harrison (1979) introduces a more effective, and less time-bound, variable, namely, denominational preference. Denominational preference incorporates historic change, gives a more accurate characterization of tomorrow's Jewry, and simultaneously describes the value stances around which Jewish families are organizing.

Orthodox Jews make up 11 percent of the adult Jewish population. They seek to carry historic Jewish religious practices, value orientations, and social roles into modern life with as few basic changes as possible. Jews preferring the Conservative denomination make up 42 percent of American Jewish adults. As a whole, they seek a balance between traditional ways and the demands of modern life and are more inclined toward basic social change in Jewish life. Reform Jews comprise 33 percent of the American Jewish adult population. As a group, they have given considerable emphasis to doing what they regard as modernizing Judaism. For them traditional practices depend on individual desires, and many practices have been abandoned. They also make the least Jewish educational demands upon their children of the three denominational groups.

At the furthest extreme from the Orthodox are those Jews who regard themselves as "just Jewish" and have no specific denominational preference. This group composes 14 percent of the Jewish adult population and is, as a whole, marginal to the Jewish community and its religious practices.

It seems that denominational orientations are fairly well formed by the time young people start into their twenties. Then, the next crucial step is actually joining a synagogue of their donominational preference. The latest available national data (Lazerwitz and Harrison, 1979: 658) indicate that at the start of the 1970s half of all adult Jews were members of synagogues (see Table 1).

Combining denominational preference and synagogue membership gives an informing picture of American Jewry. Since the heavy majority of those preferring Orthodoxy are synagogue members while the reverse holds among those with no denominational preferences, the information in Table 1 is in six basic categories. The five indices of this table were developed by Lazerwitz (1973, 1978) and represent amount of Jewish education, extent of religious behavior, and the degree to which adults are involved with fellow Jews with regards to family courtship, marriage, and friendship. Jewish and general organizational activity indices measure the degree of involvement in Jewish and non-Jewish voluntary associations. Finally, third U.S. generation refers to those who are native-born of native-born parents.

Clearly there is a rank order, with Orthodox Jews coming first on Jewish education, having kosher homes, religious behavior, Jewish primary groups, and Jewish organizational activities; then come members of Conservative synagogues. On balance, those who prefer the Conservative denomination but are not synagogue members are similar to members of Reform synagogues. Those who prefer the Reform denomination but are not synagogue members are quite similar to those who do not have denominational preferences.

There are some interesting exceptions to those patterns. Note that the re-

TABLE 1

Percent Reaching High Levels on Various Jewish Characteristics by Denominational Preference and Actual Membership

JEWISH CHARACTERISTICS	DENOMINATIONAL PREFERENCE—MEMBERSHIP[a]					
	ORTHODOX MEMBERS	CONSERVATIVE		REFORM		NO DENOM. PREF.
		MEMB.	JUST PREF.	MEMB.	JUST PREF.	
Jewish Education Index	70	50	35	38	14	15
Has Kosher Home	87	42	40	6	6	9
Religious Behavior Index	87	59	25	26	5	3
Jewish Primary Group Involvement Index	71	55	37	22	17	12
Jewish Organizational Activity Index	63	49	16	43	5	7
General Organizational Activity Index	19	32	10	50	37	20
Third U.S. Generation	5	16	13	25	24	27

SOURCE: National Jewish Survey, 1971

[a]Numbers are percentages.

tention of the kosher dietary laws by the Conservative denomination, but not by the Reform, sh' ws up on the differences between their adherents. Also, note that Conserva ive Jews are more likely to be involved in Jewish social networks. Finally, the nearly equivalent activity in Jewish organizations of Conservative and Reform synagogue members, in contrast to those who merely prefer these denominations, shows a major impact of synagogue membership (York: 1979).

Activity in general community organizations is a Reform characteristic. Even those who merely prefer the Reform denomination are considerably more active than those with no preference. Note, too, that on this important characteristic the previous ranking relationships change. Now, Orthodox and no-preference people, previously at opposite extremes, share the same level of activity in general community organizations.

The extent to which these denominational groups attract multigenerational American Jews conforms to the previous Orthodox-to-no-preference ranking scheme. The Orthodox group is least attractive to multigenerational Americans; next come the Conservatives; then the Reform, with 37 percent of no-preference Jews being at least third-generation Americans.

These findings emphasize the diversity among American Jews. While there might be common features, such as support for Israel and aid to Soviet Jewry, it is obvious that it is not easy to speak of American Jewry as a whole. Rather, a better view would focus upon the affinity of Jews to the various religious subdivisions within United States Jewry. In that way, one does encounter more homogeneous components of the American Jewish community.

It is likely that these differences among American Jews, associated with their denominational outlook, apply to additional life areas. One would then expect family patterns, sex roles, leisure time use, and personal norms to reflect the basic value orientations that differentiate these four subdivisions of American Jewry.

Intermarriage

Marriages and conversions among our major religious and ethnic groups have been topics of major social interest for some time. Only recently, however, have reliable national data been gathered on Jewish intermarriage.

In 1971, 7 percent of ever-married, Jewish-born adults were then in, or had been in, an intermarriage (Lazerwitz, 1981). Consistent with historical trends it was found that 10 percent of adult Jewish-born men were currently intermarried in 1971, but only 3 percent of adult Jewish-born women were. In 1971, 14 percent of currently married Jewish-born adults who were under 35 years of age had non-Jewish-born spouses. Among these young adults, 34 percent of the non-Jewish spouses had converted to Judiasm.

In a study by Mayer (1980) it was found in a sample of 446 intermarried Jewish couples, 66 percent involved a Jewish male and non-Jewish female. However, he found an interesting trend appearing. Among those aged 40–49, 80 percent of the out-marrying Jews were men versus 20 percent women. However, for those aged 20–29 the ratio was 46 percent Jewish men marrying out versus 54 percent Jewish women—a significant shift.

What are the outcomes of intermarriage? Table 2 explores this question by contrasting religious characteristics among all currently married Jewish adults, currently married Jewish adults whose spouse has converted to Judiasm, and currently married Jewish adults whose non-Jewish spouses have retained their original religious preferences. Clearly, marriages involving conversions to Judaism are much more involved in rituals than the religiously heterogeneous marriages. Only on membership in Jewish organizations do marriages with conversions attain the marginality to the Jewish community that religiously mixed marriages do.

National data (Lazerwitz, 1981) indicate that both the converts into Judaism and the Christian spouses of Jews tend to have a prior history of marriage and divorce. Rosenthal (1970) reports that those entering a second marriage have high intermarriage rates. The national data reported in Table 2 also show that previously married Jews have a much larger intermarriage rate

TABLE 2
Religious Characteristics Among Currently Married Jewish Adults[a]

RELIGIOUS CHARACTERISTICS	ALL CURRENTLY MARRIED JEWISH ADULTS	CURRENT MARRIAGES WITH CONVERSIONS INTO JUDAISM	CURRENT MARRIAGES THAT ARE RELIGIOUSLY MIXED
Lit *Shabat* Candles	36	63	4
Had Only Matzahs in Home Last Passover	55	22	5
Prefer Reform Denomination	32	43	21
No Denominational Preference	13	5	63
Member of 1–2 Jewish Organizations	35	11	9

SOURCE: National Jewish Survey, 1971.

[a]Numbers are percentages.

than Jews marrying for the first time. Work done by Bumpass and Sweet (1972) show that first marriages in which both spouses were of the same faith had considerably lower divorce rates than those first marriages where spouses were of different faith backgrounds.

The marriages of Jewish women who intermarry tend to break up with greater frequency than those of intermarried Jewish men. The Maller (1975) study of California divorces and the national data introduced here both find about equal numbers of Jewish men and women reporting terminating intermarriages, despite the fact that Jewish men intermarry more than Jewish women. However, these data may reflect the shift mentioned earlier in the sex of Jews who are marrying out. The ever-increasing numbers of Jewish females marrying out are now reflected in the divorce rates.

As would be expected, intermarriage rates reflect denominational orientations. Orthodox Jews report 3 percent with intermarriages; Conservative Jews report 4 percent with intermarriages; Reform Jews report a 9 percent intermarriage rate; and 17 percent of no-denominational-preference Jews report intermarriages [Lazerwitz and Harrison (1979: 663); see also Mayer (1980: 507)]. Jews now marrying, or who will marry in the near future, will be increasingly third-generation Americans, with college degrees, more frequently entering a second marriage, and more often without any Jewish denominational preference. All of those social categories are characterized by high intermarriage percentages. Hence, the Jewish intermarriage percentage is bound to rise.

Family Solidarity

Writers on the American Jewish family have assumed that "solidarity" is a hallmark of Jewish domestic life throughout history. Brav (1940:7) notes, for example, that in the Biblical period "strong family solidarity was a matter of course," and he goes on to state (p.20) that "observers of the modern scene claim to note the existence in the Jewish family of a solidarity or cohesiveness that appears to be unique in degree as well as in quality. Among Jewish writers this is generally admitted as axiomatic." Brav ends by questioning whether this assumption about Jewish family solidarity has "sufficient factual support." This questioning appears to have reflected the concern of those whose family values had been nourished in a European setting but who now found themselves in a society in which less emphasis was placed on family obligations.

The research findings reported by Balswick (1966:167) in his review of studies suggest that although indices of solidarity indicate a greater cohesiveness on the part of Jewish than other families, "it seems obvious that the change has been from the closely knit European Jewish family to the less closely knit American Jewish family." Beginning with Brav's (1940) investigation, there has been little effort by researchers to distinguish between family organization of foreign-born household heads and native-born heads. Many of the findings, however, seem to refer to families of the preholocaust generation. Landis (1960) found, for example, that in families of Jewish college students in the 1950s (as compared with Catholic and Protestant families), the divorce rate of the parents was lowest and the relationship of respondents to their parents was closest. W. I. Thomas's analysis of the *Bintl Brief* in the *Daily Forward* (Bressler, 1952) focused on the immigrant generation. Thomas, too, regarded "the key motif expressed in Jewish family patterns [to be] ... an effort to preserve the solidarity of the family" (Balswick 1966:165). Brav's own conclusions in comparing indices of solidarity among Jewish and non-Jewish families in pre-World War II Vicksburg, Mississippi, were that Jewish solidarity is not markedly stronger than that in non-Jewish families.

But such concepts as solidarity or cohesiveness by which earlier writers sought to explain personal loyalties and the acceptance of familial obligations are vague, and the indicators chosen to measure then do confound various motives, pressures, and meanings. For example, merely because couples do not divorce does not suggest a high degree of "solidarity"; and because people live together or visit or assist one another is not a definite indicator of personal affinity. Be that as it may, disorganizing effects of migration eventually wore off, and family "cohesiveness" ceased to be a primary concern; the next cohort of Jewish families no longer could make a direct comparison between the "solidarity" of the European family and the "individuality" of the Americans.

Kinship and Mobility: Diaspora upon Diaspora

To begin with: Is there a uniquely Jewish approach to kinship? In order to proceed, however, we must first have to answer the questions: How can we identify this approach? What shall we look for?

Anthropologists have used the term *collaterality* to refer to the fact that people regard some types or categories of relatives as genealogically closer than others: For example, in one society a nephew may be regarded as closer than an uncle; in another an uncle may be closer. If families possess limited resources and several relatives have an equal need for them, there must be a set of rules that tells an individual which relatives have greater claim to these resources. Differences in collaterality are important because they express different modes of kinship organization—that is, different ways of figuring which relatives have prior claim to resources and property over others.

Superimposed upon the notion of collaterality, variation in priorities based upon the personal and social qualities of particular relatives is found. While these personal elements would affect the obligations one feels to them, the idea of collaterality is that underlying these personal qualities, there exists for most people a hierarchy of priorities based on kinship status itself. At times, kinship status may override any personal considerations in making decisions; at other times, the personal qualities of the relatives may be the crucial factor. The point is that people discriminate among relatives by kinship status as well as by personal characteristics.

Kinship priorities have been found to be formalized in inheritance laws and in laws defining incestuous marriage. Inheritance laws establish the order and priorities among relatives to a decedent's estate, while incest laws describe the ranges of relatives considered too close to marry. In western civilization, despite great variations in economic and political systems, only a few such priority systems have emerged to accomodate intestacy and incestuous marriage laws. These systems or models are the Parentela Orders model (with origins in ancient Judaism and classical Greece), the Civil Law model (whose source was the Twelve Tables of early Rome), and the Canon Law model, which appeared in the 12th century systemization of Church Law. More recently, proposals have been made to apply genetic relatedness (i.e., shared chromosomes) to inheritance and marriage laws. These different models emerged to meet the specific demands upon family and kinship in the particular social settings in which they originated. As described in the *Mishnah* and the *Talmud,* the Parentela Orders model gives most emphasis to continuity of the family line; while consistent with Church writings, the Canon Law model is least oriented toward familial perpetuation. A translation of these kinship priorities (in terms of distances from EGO, the reference person) for the various models of collaterality are shown in Table 3 [see Farber (1981)]

Recent research (Farber, 1981) has shown that people who conform to these priorities among kin also vary in their family kinship ties. For example, as Table 3 indicates, in decisions on inheritance, comparing claims of siblings and grandchildren of the decedent, choosing siblings would be appropriate for the Canon Law and Genetic models, equal claim would fit the Civil Law model, and grandchildren would be consistent with the Parentela Orders model.

During this research, a fifth model was discovered. This model places its emphasis upon the individual's ancestral line and classifies kin according to whether they are children, grandchildren, great grandchildren, and so on of

366

EGO's (i.e., the individual's) direct ancestors. The rank ordering of kin according to this model is also shown in Table 3. Because the model is most prevalent among white Protestants of high educational and income levels (and with native-born parents and grandparents), it has been called the Standard American model (Farber, 1981: 45–65).

Although people are generally unaware of the kinship priority patterns among religious groups, they tend to be overrepresented in the categories associated with their own religion. Many Catholics fall into the Canon Law category; Jews cluster in the Parentela Orders category. Moreover, a branch of Judaism is itself related to holding a Parentela Orders perspective in kinship collaterality. Persons raised in Orthodox homes show a higher inclination toward the Parentela Orders Model than do individuals from less traditional branches. In contrast, persons brought up in Reform Judaism are likely to develop Genetic or Canon Law patterns of collaterality. But whether we study current affiliation or branch of upbringing, the results are similar: The more traditional the branch of Judaism, the greater is the tendency to conform to the Parentela Orders model of collaterality (Farber, 1979, 1981).

What does conformity to the Parentela Orders model imply about family relationships? Regardless of religious affiliation, people who hold a Parentela Orders orientation exhibit certain characteristics in their family and kinship ties. Compared with persons who conform to other kinship pespectives: (a) their age at first marriage tends to be late; (b) they and their parents and siblings show a high degree of marital stability; (c) their fertility level tends to be above the average for their particular religious group (as does that of their parents and siblings); (d) when they intermarry with persons of other religious backgrounds, both husband and wife adopt the same religious affiliation (their children are raised in the same religion); (e) there is a somewhat greater proclivity to live near the husband's than the wife's parents; but (f) residential distance is not crucial for persons with a Parentela Orders view, since even over great distances, there is intense involvement with relatives (Farber, 1981).

Moreover, holding a Parentela Orders conception of collaterality is related to ethnic identity. A study of the Kansas City Jewish community found that persons with a Parentela Orders orientation tend to live in areas with a high Jewish concentration and to maintain Jewish communal ties more than do Jews with other kinship orientations. They are generally nonmigrants; they tend to have Jewish friends; they are more active than their parents in Jewish matters; and they disapprove of intermarriage (Farber, 1979). The Kansas City findings relating to ethnicity are confirmed in ongoing research on Mexican Americans in Phoenix. The study shows that those Mexican Americans with a highly salient ethnic identity are overrepresented in the Parentela Or-

367

TABLE 3

Distances from EGO of a Set of Relatives as Measured by Different Models of Collaterality, by Generation of Relative[a]

A. Canon Law Model
DISTANCE FROM EGO: DEGREE OF RELATIONSHIP

GENERATION	0	1	2	3
2			Grandparents	Great Aunts and Great Uncles
1		Parents	Aunts and Uncles	
0	EGO	Siblings	First Cousins	
−1		Children	Nieces and Nephews	
−2			Grandchildren	Grandnieces and Grandnephews

B. Genetic Model
DISTANCE FROM EGO: FRACTION OF CHROMOSOMES SHARED

GENERATION	1	1/2	1/4	1/8
2			Grandparents	Great Aunts and Great Uncles
1		Parents	Aunts and Uncles	
0	EGO	Siblings		First Cousins
−1		Children	Nieces and Nephews	
−2			Grandchildren	Grandnieces and Grandnephews

C. Civil Code Model
DISTANCE FROM EGO: DEGREE OF RELATIONSHIP

GENERATION	0	1	2	3	4
2			Grandparents		Great Aunts and Great Uncles
1		Parents		Aunts and Uncles	
0	EGO		Siblings		First Cousins
−1		Children		Nieces and Nephews	
−2			Grandchildren		Grandnieces and Grandnephews

D. Parentela Orders Model
DISTANCE FROM EGO: RANKS BASED ON PARENTELAE
PARENTELAE: LINES OF DESCENT FROM EGO'S ANCESTORS

GENERATION	I	II	III
2			Grandparents (7)
1		Parents (3)	Aunts and Uncles (8)
0	EGO (0)	Siblings (4)	First Cousins (9)
−1	Children (1)	Nieces and Nephews (5)	
−2	Grandchildren (2)	Grandnieces and Grandnephews (6)	

TABLE 3
(continued)

E. *Standard American Model*
DISTANCE FROM EGO: RANKS BASED ON DESCENT DISTANCE FROM EGO'S ANCESTRAL LINE
DISTANCE FROM EGO'S ANCESTRAL LINE

GENERATION	ANCESTRAL LINE	CHILDREN OF ANCESTRAL LINE	GRANDCHILDREN OF ANCESTRAL LINE	GREAT GRANDCHILDREN OF ANCESTRAL LINE
2	Grandparents (2)			
1	Parents (1)	Aunts and Uncles (5)		
0	EGO (0)	Siblings (4)	First Cousins (8)	
−1		Children (3)	Nieces and Nephews (7)	
−2			Grandchildren (6)	Grandnieces and Grandnephews (9)

[a]NOTE: Distances from EGO based on measures in Farber (1981:189).

ders category and have a strong family identification. While the proportion of Mexican Americans falling into the Parentela Orders grouping is smaller than that generally found for Jews, the trends for the two studies are in the same direction.

Collectively, the findings of studies on collaterality support the view that Jews tend to follow an approach to family and kinship, symbolized by the Parentela Orders model, which is rooted in the Pentateuch and later Jewish writings. This approach encourages strong ties with the *mishpokhe* (extended family) despite impediments to interaction. Given this approach, Jewish family and kinship bonds provide a sharp contrast to those of other groups. For example, an investigation of kinship among people aged 21–45 living in Phoenix, Arizona, reveals that:

1. When parents and in-laws live out of state, Jewish respondents have the most frequent contact by telephone and mail; Catholics the least. The gap between Jews and Catholics is especially great when it comes to mothers-in-law. Whereas 65 percent of the Jewish respondents have frequent contact with their mother-in-law, only 35 percent of the Catholics do so.

2. For persons whose close relatives also live in the Phoenix metropolitan area, differences between Jews and other religionists are even clearer. Among religious groups, Jewish respondents exhibit by far the greatest amount of contact with parents and brothers and sisters, and those with no religious preference show the least contact. Roughly 90 percent of

the Jewish respondents have at least weekly contact with their parents, while only about half of the nonreligionists do.

3. While a majority of Jews have known their European-born grandparents well, this is true of only a minority of Catholics or Protestants. The greater dispersion of non-Jewish families had interfered with the development of close bonds with grandparents.

The religious differences in kinship patterns in Phoenix are consistent with empirical evidence derived from studies of other metropolitan areas.

Research in a Chicago suburb indicated that Jewish families during the 1960s showed the greater amount of "familism," that is, more than Protestant and Catholic families: (a) Jewish families had more households of kin in the same metropolitan area; (b) more often the related households of Jewish families consisted of close relatives (often parents or siblings); (c) there was a greater amount of interaction among the related Jewish families; and (d) the Jewish families were more likely to give or receive assistance from these relatives. Holding migratory status constant statistically, the investigators reported that "familism" was more a *basis* for reluctance to migrate than a *result* of residential stability (Winch, Greer, and Blumberg, 1967).

The findings of families in other cities are comparable (Leichter and Mitchell, 1967). Lenski (1961) found, for example, that in Detroit during the 1950s, Jews, much more often than Protestants or Catholics, had relatives living in Detroit and visited with them weekly. Lenski found that Jewish respondents, more often than Christians, reported that their spouse, children, and parents influenced their religious beliefs. Croog, Lipson, and Levine (1972) found, however, that Jews did not differ from non-Jews in assistance given to relatives stricken with heart attacks. However, Wake and Sporakowski (1972) reported Jews are more willing to support aged parents.

Gordon (1959) suggests that movement to the suburbs by Jews during the 1950s did little to damage strong kinship ties. About 60 percent of his respondents reported visiting with parents and other relatives as often as they did while the whole *mishpokhe* (extended kin group) lived in the central city. Most of those who see their relatives less frequently still observe festival and holy days together. In these respects, the move to the suburbs has perhaps had a less disruptive effect than that found in England among lower-middle-class non-Jewish families (Young and Willmot, 1962); findings reported by Gordon are, however, consistent with those that indicate that in highly industrialized societies, when relatives see one another with less frequency, feast days and holy days, for Christians as well, become special days for visiting and celebrating (Lüschen et al., 1971).

A study of Jewish kinship ties in New York also shows the persistence of traditional norms. Leichter and Mitchell (1967) found that a majority of men and women each feel closer to their own relatives than to their spouse's. In general, women interact more often with their kin and have a wider variety of kinds of assistance that they exchange with relatives, much of which involves child care. Yet men interact more often with their own relatives when matters arise pertaining to business or to help in household repairs.

Until the 20th century, Jewish communities in Europe had been organized as corporate bodies (Elazar and Goldstein 1972). The tradition of organizing formal structures has been extended in American Jewish communities to the family as well. William Mitchell (1978) reports that, with the decline of Jewish neighborhoods and the dispersal of kin throughout metropolitan areas, people organize the *mishpokhe* by establishing associations of "cousins clubs" and "family circles." These associations replicate some of the functions of the organized Jewish community—sustaining family identity and solidarity (reinforcing Jewish identity and solidarity), giving to charity, planning festivities, and mutual assistance. Since ties to the descent group can be limited to associational obligations, these "cousins clubs" and "family circles" facilitate perpetuation of the *mishpokhe* without making excessive demands upon members who have diverse professional and social commitments outside the family.

But the very tight integration of the *mishpokhe* may have drawbacks for members. The husband's kindred may attempt to dominate his family, offering unsolicited criticisms and demanding much loyalty from his wife and children. Indeed, Leichter and Mitchell (1967: 177–181) found that there was greater conflict with the husband's kin than with the wife's over interference in internal family matters.

In recent decades, dispersion of Jewish populations, however, has occurred not only within metropolitan centers. It has also redistributed the American Jewish population throughout the country.

Table 4 presents data on trends in the distribution of the American Jewish population from 1900 to 1972. The following movements seem to be occurring:

1. Prior to 1900, the existing Jewish population had spread westward and southward to the east north central and south Atlantic states.
2. Immigration during the first part of the 20th century, however, reconcentrated the bulk of the Jewish population in the northeast. Relative to the middle Atlantic states in particular, by 1928 all other regions showed a smaller percentage of the total Jewish American population.

TABLE 4
Distribution of the Jewish Population, by Regions, 1900, 1918, 1930, 1963, and 1972; and Total U.S. Population for 1972

REGION	1900	1918	1930	1963	1972	TOTAL U.S. POPULATION 1972
Northeast	56.6	69.9	68.3	65.9	62.6	23.9
New England	7.4	8.6	8.4	6.7	6.8	5.8
Middle Atlantic	49.2	61.3	59.9	59.2	55.8	18.1
North Central	23.7	20.2	19.6	13.7	12.2	27.7
East North Central	18.3	15.7	15.7	11.2	9.8	19.7
West North Central	5.4	4.5	3.9	2.5	2.4	8.0
South	14.2	6.9	7.6	9.1	11.8	31.9
South Atlantic	8.0	4.0	4.3	6.7	9.4	15.3
East South Central	3.3	1.3	1.4	0.8	0.7	6.3
West South Central	2.9	1.6	1.9	1.6	1.6	9.6
West	5.5	3.1	4.6	11.5	13.3	17.3
Mountain	2.3	0.7	1.0	0.9	1.1	4.2
Pacific	3.2	2.4	3.6	10.6	12.2	13.1
Total: per cent	100.0	100.0	100.0	100.0	100.0	100.0
Number (in 1000s)	1058	3389	4228	5599	6115	208,232

Data on distribution of Jewish population from *American Jewish Year Book*, 1 (1900), pp. 623–624; 21 (1919), p. 606; 33 (1931), p. 276; 65 (1964), p. 14; 74 (1973), p. 309. The 1972 U.S. data from the U.S. Department of Commerce, *Population Estimates and Projections*, Series P-25, No. 200 (cited in *American Jewish Year Book*, 1973, 74:309). Data for 1900 and 1930 cited in Goldstein (1971).

3. Since World War I, there has been a steady redistribution of the Jewish population, with the major losses in the northeastern and north central states.

4. Dramatic shifts occurred between 1930 and 1972 in the movement of population to the south Atlantic and Pacific states. For the most part, this movement represents large Jewish migrations to more salubrious, warmer climates—to Florida (particularly to Miami) and to California. Writing in 1950, Seligman (1950:45) noted that Miami and Tucson, Arizona, showed "tremendously rapid growth in the last decade."

Despite the findings on the stability of kinship ties, the recent shifts in population to the south and to the southwest may contribute much to the decline in social relationships among family and relatives. In the Lakeville study (Sklare and Greenblum, 1967:252) there was a sharp decline in the amount of time spent with relatives from one generation to the next. Although almost

40 percent of the respondents reported that when they had been children their parents spent more time with relatives than with friends, only 5 percent of the respondents indicated that they themselves spend more time with relatives than with friends. Moreover, while almost 60 percent saw their cousins at least monthly when they were children, only 40 percent of their own children now visit with cousins.

There is also a significant decline in extended family households as families move to the suburbs or migrate to warmer climates. In their study of Providence, Rhode Island, Goldstein and Goldscheider (1968) reported that 85 percent of the Jewish households consisted of husband, wife, and their children, and a mere 8 percent held other relatives as well. The effect of generation on household composition was considerable. When age was held constant statistically, the percentage of nuclear-family households headed by third-generation persons was considerably greater than that for first-generation heads. Since generation is related to religious orthodoxy, one would expect to find more households augmented by relatives among the more orthodox than among the more liberal or among nominal Jewish families.

The Jewish population movement to the south and the southwest has included not only young families but also the elderly. Young families may see in this migration an opportunity to live a more desirable existence away from familial obligations, only to find that their relatives, perhaps now old and retired, wend their way southward and westward. It is difficult to assess fully the implications of this movement. Undoubtedly, it will act to deconcentrate the Jewish community and will likely decompose family obligations still further.

Family Roles

Household division of labor in traditional European non-Jewish families is often associated with an ideology of patriarchial authority and the subordination of women. Yet writers about the Jewish family generally agree that the subordination found in some European systems (e.g., the Italian) has been absent among Jews. Gordon (1959:58), for example, suggests that:

> Historically, the entire responsibility for the support as well as the care of the family often rested on the woman's shoulders. Jewish women, through the centuries, often carried on the business or earned the family's livelihood in order that the husband might devote himslef to the intensive study of Torah. Her influence with respect to her children and her husband was extraordinary.

Even among immigrant families, Gordon notes (p. 59), "there was a far greater degree of equality between husband and wife than is generally assumed. . . . The mother was the homemaker, but it was she whose personal piety and example within the home was expected to influence her children, while winning their love and veneration."

Gordon (1959:59) further suggests that as the Jewish families moved to the suburbs following World War II, "the wife, by virtue of her increased duties and responsibilities within the family, has become the modern matriarch of Jewish suburbia. Her ideas, opinions and values clearly dominate."

One would expect women in traditional homemaking roles to have a strong investment in their children's behavior. In a study of Westchester County, New York, concern over possible deviance in children's behavior was greatest among the more traditional groups. As one might anticipate on the basis of the Jewish mother stereotype, "More Jewish than non-Jewish mothers reported worrying, though their children were no more impaired than those of other religious groups" (Lurie, 1974:113).

The movement by women toward increased labor-force participation (especially in professional and managerial positions) is expected to lead to a growing ambivalence toward maternal roles. [See, for example, Luria (1974)]. In the Phoenix study, as one might expect, the probability of finding the proverbial Jewish mother is quite high among the *parents* of the respondents. Only 25 percent of Jewish mothers worked during the time when the respondents were growing up—in contrast to 35 percent for non-Jewish mothers. But for the respondents themselves, differences by religion disappear; regardless of religion, about 60 percent of the women were working. However, there is a catch: The chances of maternal employment depend in large part on the number of children in the home. Since Jewish women have very few children, we would expect even more Jewish than non-Jewish women to be employed. Since there are not, the data may be well shielding the degree of maternal involvement of Jewish women (Farber, 1981).

Traditionally, the father has had a priestly role in the household. Since the husband had been the link between the family and the religious community, he was responsible for the piety, morality, and ethical standards of the family members. In the contemporary American context, the priestly status of the father is translated into his occupational dedication and his retention of achievement values for his children, especially sons (Strodtbeck, 1958). For whatever reason, Jews have traditionally gone into occupations that require long hours and energy demands—self-employed in business, the free professions—and even in blue-collar occupations they have exerted much dedication toward achieving unionization and increased social welfare. In many instances, participation in social movements apparently substituted for the *shtetl* synagogue. Yet in suburban America, "few mothers or fathers accept easily the role of religious director in the family" (Seeley, Sim, and Loosely, 1956:214). In fact, in religious organizations, Jewish "women are much more in evidence than men and more frequently represent the family" (Seeley, Sim, and Loosely, 1956:2:15). Thus, insofar as men have retained their traditional priestly status in the family, they have, for the most part, shifted their dedication to the mundane.

Sklare (1971:87) points out that in the traditional Jewish family, a child is never considered as truly emancipated from his parents. He suggests that children are seen as extensions of their parents rather than as distinct entities. One of the basic forms of exchange for parent and child is for parents to provide a basis for their children's own success in family and community, while the child has an obligation to supply *nakhus* (pleasure or gratification) for his parents. In providing the conditions for *nakhus,* the parent creates a lifelong obligation for the child.

The decline of the special structure of the Jewish parent–child relationship emanates, according to Sklare (1971:89) from two sources. The first source is the high level of secular educational attainment of Jews, which stresses urbanity and cosmopolitanism. The second source is the affinity of Jews toward those schools of modern psychology that "stress the reduction of dependence (whether on the part of parents or children) [and in doing so] they are necessarily critical of the structure of the Jewish family and of its special culture" (Sklare, 1971:90). Sklare thus sees an escalating estrangement that is destroying traditional family commitments.

Socialization of Children

The parent–child relationship described by Sklare (1971) of creating in the child an obligation to be successful by bringing *nakhus* to the parents makes certain assumptions about the nature of conduct. These assumptions provide a basis for the kinds of socialization practices found in Jewish families. Essentially, one channels behavior rather than "shaping" it. The person is seen not as a responding mechanism or a *tabula rasa* but as someone who has a drive to act requiring controls and outlets. The psychoanalytic perspective is quite congenial to this conception of socialization.

Viewing socialization of children as channelization suggests that personal behavior is the outpouring of a substance (such as water or vital matter) that demands expression in its flow. One can guide the flow or dig new channels, but one cannot dam up the flow indefinitely. Punishment does not inhibit behavior, but only diverts it to other channels.

In the European *shtetl,* the aim of socialization was to make each child a *mensch,* that is, one who does the appropriate things at the appropriate time and place with appropriate persons (Zborowski and Herzog, 1952:335):

> Weeping is accepted as a normal means of expression and, on occasion, a legitimate weapon. . . . Grown men are not expected to weep as often or as freely as women and children, but for them too tears are in order during certain rituals, or as an accompaniment to pleas for help, either for themselves or for their community.

Channelization of behavior, as found in Jewish families, implies that "each year adds new responsibilities in the child's life" (Zborowski and Herzog, 1952:350) as well as fresh forms of tension release. With each special responsibility, the child is seen as becoming more of a *mensch.* "Despite the persisting, but steadily contracting, areas of indulgence, from the moment a child is able to help with the younger ones or with the family *parnosseh* (earning a living), or to go to *cheder* (religious school), it becomes a responsible and functioning member of a group" (Zborowski and Herzog, 1952:331). Especially strong is the separation of male and female worlds in the *shtetl.* As boys and girls mature, they "become more and more aware of the rules against intermingling of sexes" (Zborowski and Herzog, 1952:352). Bit by bit, the individual assumes the "yoke of Jewishness," *ol fun Yiddishkeit,* the discipline imposed by Judaic ritual.

The channeling of behavior in terms of division of labor seems to give rise to a heightened intensity of behavior in specific roles. Indeed, the father is not merely head of the house; he is also its "priest," responsible for its living according to ritual and Jewish law and ideally dedicated to prayer and study. One is not merely a mother; one is instead a *Yiddisheh mahmeh,* with all of the stereotypical nurturance, overprotection, and domineering that the "Jewish mother" implies. The mother–child relationship is "complementary rather than reciprocal. Parents are donors and should not receive from children. The children can make return by passing benefits to their children" (Mandelbaum, 1958:512). In illness, a Jew does not suppress pain; instead, concerned with its symptomatic meaning, he makes the most of it, expressing its intensity at every opportunity (Zborowski, 1969:240–242). In family conflict, one is forbidden to use physical violence; but one may still curse, and Jewish curses contain imaginative invective in their expression—for example, oxen should grow in your belly, or your father's godfather should get a kick. Children are often imbued with the "Protestant ethic," often to a greater extent than Protestants (Slater, 1969). Findings indicate that high-achievement motivation is related to parental praise and expression of parental pride (Rehberg, Sinclair, and Schafer, 1970). Participation thus tends to be unbalanced—perhaps even caricatured—in different spheres of the social world.

Complete dedication to work, to home, or to piety seems to flow from the conception of socialization as the channelizing of energy.

Some balance in behavior is achieved, however, through the ritualization of the rhythms of living. There are religious injunctions covering daily, weekly, monthly, and seasonal rhythms. The daily prayers, the celebration of the Sabbath, and the periodic holidays during which one must turn from the tension of the workaday world, all act as regularized forms of tension release. Ritualization of tension release requires (a) the development of delayed gratification patterns since time and place of rituals are fixed, (b) deflection and sublimation as socialization techniques as opposed to inhibition and negation, and (c) reliance on authority and benefice as justifying conduct rather than seeking reciprocity in all behavioral exchanges. The heavy reliance on ritual thus does not leave even tension release to chance.

The research on drinking supports this conception of child socialization. Without exception, studies of drinking patterns indicate a low rate of heavy drinking among Jews, especially in Orthodox homes (Snyder, 1958). At the same time, cross-cultural analysis of drinking shows that societies that are highly indulgent to their children in the preadolescent years tend to be high in drunkenness, and where there is a general pressure for obedience and responsibility in children, drunkenness tends to be low (Field, 1962). Thus, Jewish families seem to fall into the latter category, characterized by highly controlled tension release, permitting and even encouraging the ritual use of alcohol.

Psychoanalytic concepts seem appropriate to describe what happens when the channelized expression of behavior exceeds acceptable limits or when channels are blocked. Given general socialization data, it does not seem surprising that, in types of mental illness, Jews tend to specialize in neurotic or mild or moderate symptoms of mental illness, whereas Catholic and Protestant populations are more prone to severe mental impairments (Rose and Stub, 1955:112; Srole, Langer, Michael, Opler, and Rennie, 1962:304; Roberts and Myers, 1954). Moreover, unlike Catholics and Protestants, parental religiosity is unrelated to degree of impairment among Jews (Srole, Langer, Michael, Opler, and Rennie, 1962:310). The qualitative difference between Jews, Protestants, and Catholics is expressed further in attitudes toward psychotherapy and psychoanalysis. Among psychiatrists, there is marked tendency for Jews to hold a psychoanalytic orientation (Hollingshead and Redlich, 1958). In general, Jewish individuals are more favorably inclined toward psychotherapy as an effective mode of treatment and are more often outpatients in psychiatric services than are Catholics or Protestants (Srole, Langer, Michael, Opler, and Rennie, 1962:125–318).

As the current generation of adolescents matures, one finds a waning of the modes of socialization that have characterized earlier generations. Boroff (1961) reports that Jewish youth are losing their sense of uniqueness. He finds that the younger teenagers identify strongly with other teenagers as a generation, but that older Jewish teenagers are more college-oriented than their peers. In this generation, when parents differ with friends of their children over such things as the use of kosher meat, the children agree more often with their peers than their parents (Rosen, 1955). The youth seem to have developed a strong bond to the broad American community, with its emphasis on the insulation of youth from family influence.

Despite these shifts in patterns of socialization, however, the emphasis in the family on scholarly achievement remains high. In the Phoenix study, Jewish respondents reveal a strong relationship between kinship collaterality and emphasis upon academic achievement in the teenage years. Eighty-eight percent in the Parentela Orders (i.e., the traditionally Jewish) category regarded high grades as important, as compared with 82 percent in the Standard American class, 63 percent in the Civil Law group, and only 56 percent in the Genetic and Canon-Law approaches to kinship (Farber, 1981). Moreover, significance of this association is brought out by an analysis of scholastic achievement by students at Arizona State University. Those students of all religions who conformed to the Jewish kinship model trended to have the highest cumulative grade point averages (GPAs), and those persons whose pattern of answers resembled the Canon-Law or Genetic models had the lowest GPAs (Farber, 1977).

American Jewry and World Jewry

It is important to realize that American Jewry is but one part, albeit the largest part, of world Jewry. Many of the characteristics that have been presented for American Jews apply in differing degrees to Jews of central and eastern European background or descent who live in other countries. Many of these characteristics do not apply at all to the other major branches of world Jewry: Jews originally from Spain or Portugal who settled throughout the Mediterranean basin after the Spanish expulsion, or Jews from Arabic-speaking countries—the so-called Oriental Jews.

The legend of a "Jewish face" might seem to hold for American Jews. However, Israel, the gathering place of all the different branches and subgroups of world Jewry, presents such a wide variety of "Jewish faces" that one cannot determine who is Jewish by mere appearance. In today's world, it is likely that few traits of any major division of Jewry apply to most of world Jewry. Perhaps, in 50 years or so, when the presently highly varied groups of world Jewry change into fewer types, especially in Israel, more widespread Jewish traits will appear. If so, it seems likely that such traits will be strongly influenced by the traditions of eastern Europe mixed in with a "strong flavor" contributed by Middle Eastern Jewry.

CHANGE AND ADAPTATION

Forecasts of the future of the American Jewish family generally fall into three groups: the pessimists, the ambivalent, and the optimists. Each group has its fervent proponents, and each group establishes its case on different grounds.

THE PESSIMISTS. The pessimists view trends in Jewish family organization as mirroring those of the American middle class. According to this position, the same forces that are weakening traditional family bonds in middle-class society are destroying the Jewish family. This group sees the steady increase in mobility and migration, the continued growth of individualism, and the heightening of cosmopolitanism in American society as undermining the basis for strong family life in American society. For example, Gordon (1959:83) writes:

> It is my belief that, if our suburban communities continue to change internally as they have since 1950 ... Jewish residents will inevitably feel that they are a rootless community. They will not feel "at home" or at ease within any given area. To regard the suburb in which one lives as a *temporary* home is to destroy the sense of permanence that all families need. . . . Jewish family relations, which to date have remained excellent, may not be able to survive another decade of extreme mobility without showing signs of great stress and strain.

Focusing on the role of the family in establishing Jewish identification in children, Sklare also presents a pessimistic stance. He regards the very social and economic success of American Jews as contributing to the downfall of the traditional *mishpokhe,* which long has acted as a bedrock of Jewish community institutions. Sklare proposes (1971:89–100):

> The changing significance of the family, and particularly the fairly recent declines in the frequency and intensity of interaction with the kinship group, means that identity can no longer be acquired through this traditional institution. . . . American Jewry has a highly developed communal structure as well as a firmly established network of Jewish schools. . . . But however significant the communal network and the school system are as building blocks, they are a kind of super-structure resting upon the foundation of the family—for it is the family that has been the prime mechanism for transmitting Jewish identity. This system of identity-formation is currently on the decline. The emerging crisis of the Jewish family in identity-formation is in part due to the newer limitations on the family

as a socialization agent—limitations that affect all other Americans as well. But it is traceable to . . . the high acculturation of many Jewish parents, the diminished interaction with relatives, and the presence of Gentiles in the Jewish kinship network. . . . It is the shrinking contribution of the family to Jewish identity transmission that constitutes its essential weakness.

In summary, the view of the pessimists is mainly that the American family itself is becoming ineffective as a socialization agent, and that by becoming assimilated into the mainstream of American life, the Jewish family has lost its crucial role in identity transmission.

THE AMBIVALENT. Whereas the pessimists emphasize the decreasing differentiation between Jewish and non-Jewish family life in the American middle class, the ambivalent observers regard the survival of the Jewish family as a personal decision. The risk taken by relegating choices in social issues to personal decisions is that many individuals will choose *against* the perpetuation of traditional norms and values.

Charles Liebman (1973:151–152) expresses a pessimism over preference for interaction with other Jews or affiliation with formal organizations in the Jewish community to be effective in the survival of Jewish institutions. He notes, for example, that preferred association with other Jews—as ubiquitous as it is—is uncorrelated with any other index of Jewish identification. Affiliation with Jewish formal organization is of limited interest; Jewish communal organizations are experiencing difficulty in attracting talented and highly educated persons. Liebman thus expresses doubt that communal motives can be induced to strengthen Jewish identification and Jewish family life. His solution rests solely on personal decision.

> Jewish peoplehood is threatened by the growing impulse toward cosmopolitanism and universalism; in a society which increasingly stresses the primacy of conscience and individual freedom against even society's own law, *Torah* and the study of sacred texts become increasingly absurd. The very notion of sacred text is antiquarian, and there is no room for a tradition of study in a culture which affirms the values of sensation and of the individual as the final arbiter of right and wrong. It is, therefore, my strong belief that, at least until we enter a postmodern world, the Jew who wishes to remain in the United States, but who is also committed to the survival of Judaism, has no alternative but to retreat into a far more sectarian posture than has up to this time characterized American Jewish life.

The personal decision to adopt traditional Jewish norms and, by implication, Jewish family norms in particular necessarily assumes the risk that a significant proportion of Jews will make this decision. Otherwise, there can be no survival of the idea of peoplehood, of religious community, or of communal life according to biblical injunctions. Liebman's position thus implies a faith that others will also make a "moral" decision as a resolution of personal ambivalence.

Perhaps the survival of a remnant living according to norms of Jewish family life is all that can be hoped for in modern society. Berman (1968:560) suggests:

> An open society where ethnic boundaries survive because they serve the individual's needs for variety, for belongingness, for continuity of identity, for authenticity—where ethnic boundaries are not prison walls—where those Jews who would rather be Gentiles and Gentiles who would rather be Jews are equally free to cross the boundary and find a more congenial ethnic home—that, in this writer's opinion, is a good society.

THE OPTIMISTS. The optimists believe that modern society sustains ethnic differences by its very composition, and that this persistence of ethnicity will act to sustain traditional Jewish family organization. The argument presented by Glazer and Moynihan (1974) is as follows: (a) More and more modern societies are becoming multiethnic states; (b) diverse ethnic groups occupy different and conflicting positions in modern social structures; (c) because of their opposing positions, ethnic groups become rallying points in the identification of interest groups in the society; (d) in becoming rallying points in relation to political, social, and economic interest, ethnic groups tend to stress those features that define their uniqueness; and (e) features that ethnic groups claim as unique thus tend to survive. One of the features that Jews have claimed as unique is their family life—the *Yiddisheh mahmeh,* the *nakhus,* etc.; hence, the optimist would see a conscious effort to sustain Jewish family norms growing ultimately out of a need to defend Jewish interests (e.g., support of Soviet Jewry, backing of Israel, opposition to quota systems in occupations).

The view expressed by Glazer and Moynihan presupposes that there will always be a series of significant issues to provide for the constant revitalization of ethnic identification. At best, however, one can expect the flow of issues as rallying points to mobilize only segments of the Jewish community, and despite the optimism of Glazer and Moynihan, people tire of mobilization. Thus, without coercive constraints, one would anticipate a general waning in voluntaristic mobilization. Without institutionalized factionalism, one would anticipate a slow languishing of the norms and values traditionally associated with Jewish family life.

All data show that American Jewry has continually shifted away from a traditionalist stance to one involving increasing marginality to Judaism and the organized Jewish community. By the year 2000, it is likely that the Reform denomination will be the largest one, replacing the present leading Conservative denomination. It is hard to predict the growth trend for those without denominational preferences: This category can be self-limiting. Many of those who express such Jewish marginality choose to leave the Jewish community and disappear among the vast numbers of non-Jewish Americans. As they do so, those who chose to remain Jewish and express this with a denominational preference may well become an increasing proportion of American Jewry.

It is also likely that the population exchange between American Jews and non-Jews, produced by intermarriage and conversion, will increase. If so, the religious and communal leaders of American Jewry will need to double their efforts to integrate religiously and communally those new to the Jewish community. Furthermore, American Jews will probably become increasingly like the rest of their fellow Americans, separated only by the strength of their attachment to the Jewish religion and its traditions and by a network of communal services aimed at meeting their religious, educational, and family services needs.

REFERENCES

Balswick, Jack. 1966. "Are American-Jewish Families Closely Knit?" *Jewish Social Studies* 28:159–167.

Berman, Louis, 1968. *Jews and Intermarriage: A Study in Personality and Culture.* New York: Thomas Yoseloff.

Boroff, David. 1961. "Jewish Teenage Culture," *The Annals of the American Academy of Political Science,* 338:79–90.

Brav, Stanley R. 1940. *Jewish Family Solidarity, Myth or Fact?* Vicksburg, MS: Nogales Press.

Bressler, Marvin 1952. "Selected Family Patterns in W. I. Thomas' Unfinished Study of the Bintl Brief," *American Sociological Review,* 17:563–571.

Bumpass, Larry, and James Sweet. 1972. "Differentials in Marital Instability: 1970," *American Sociological Review,* 37:754–766.

Della Pergolá, Sergio. 1980. "Patterns of American Jewish Fertility." *Demography.*

Elazar, Daniel J. and Stephen R. Goldstein. 1972 "The Legal Status of the American Jewish Community," *American Jewish Yearbook,* 73:3–94.

Farber, Bernard. 1977. "Social Context, Kinship Mapping, and Family Norms," *Journal of Marriage and the Family,* 39:227–240.

———. 1979. "Kinship Mapping Among Jews in a Midwestern City," *Social Forces,* 57:1107–1123.

———. 1981. *Conceptions of Kinship.* New York: Elsevier North Holland.

Field, Peter B. 1962. "A New Cross Cultural Study of Drunkenness," in David J. Pittman and Charles R. Snyder (eds.), *Society, Culture and Drinking Patterns.* New York: Wiley, pp. 48–74.

Freedman, Ronald, Pascal Whelpton, and Arthur Campbell. 1959. *Family Planning Sterility, and Population Growth.* New York: McGraw-Hill.

———. 1961. "Socio-Economic Factors in Religious Differentials in Fertility, *American Sociological Review,* 26:608–614.

Glazer, Nathan. 1957. *American Judaism.* Chicago: University of Chicago Press.

Glazer, Nathan, and Daniel P. Moynihan. 1974. "Why Ethnicity?" *Commentary,* 58 (October):33–39.

Golden, Harry, and Martin Rywell. 1950. *Jews in American History,* Charlotte, NC: Henry Lewis Martin Co.

Goldstein Sidney. 1971. "American Jewry, 1970," *American Jewish Year Book,* 72:3–88.

Goldstein, Sidney, and Calvin Goldscheider, 1968. *Jewish Americans: Three Generations in a Jewish Community.* Englewood Cliffs, NJ: Prentice-Hall.

Gordon, Albert I. 1959. *Jews in Suburbia.* Boston: Beacon Press.

———. 1967. *The Nature of Conversion.* Boston: Beacon Press.

Hollingshead, A.B., and F.C. Redlich. 1958. *Social Class and Mental Illness.* New York: Wiley.

Landes, Ruth, and Mark Zborowski. 1968. "The Context of Marriage: Family Life as a Field of Emotions," in H. Kent Geiger (ed.), *Comparative Perspectives on Marriage and the Family.* Boston: Little, Brown, pp. 77–102.

Landis, Judson T. 1960. "Religiousness, Family Relationships, and Family Values in Protestant, Catholic, and Jewish Families," *Marriage and Family Living,* 22:341–347.

Lazerwitz, Bernard. 1971. "Fertility Trends in Israel and Its Administered Territories," *Jewish Social Studies,* 33:172–186.

———. 1973. "Religious Identification and Its Ethnic Correlates: A Multivariate Model," *Social Forces,* 52:204–220.

———. 1978. "An Approach to the Componants and Consequences of Jewish Identification," *Contemporary Jewry,* 4:3–8.

———. 1980. "Religiosity and Fertility: How Strong a Connection?" *Contemporary Jewry.*

———. 1981. "Jewish–Christian Marriages and Conversions," *Jewish Social Studies.*

Lazerwitz, Bernard, and Michael Harrison. 1979. "American Jewish Denominations: A Social and Religious Profile," *American Sociological Review,* 44:656–666.

Leichter, Hope J., and William E. Mitchell. 1967. *Kinship and Casework.* New York: Russell Sage Foundation.

Lenski, Gerhard. 1961. *The Religious Factor.* New York: Doubleday.

Liebman, Charles S. 1973. "American Jewry: Identity and Affiliation," in David Sidorsky (ed.), *The Future of the Jewish Community in America.* New York: Basic Books, pp. 127–152.

Luria, Zella. 1974. "Recent Women College Graduates: A Study of Rising Expectations," *American Journal of Orthopsychiatry,* 44:312–326.

Lurie, Olga R. 1974. "Parents' Atitudes Toward Use of Mental Health Services," *American Journal of Orthopsychiatry,* 44:109–120.

Lüschen, Gunther et al. 1971. "Family Interaction with Kin and the Function of Ritual," *Journal of Marriage and the Family,* 33:755–765.

Maller, Alan. 1975. "New Facts About Mixed Marriages," *Reconstructionist,* 34:26–29.

Mandelbaum, David G. 1958. "Change and Continuity in Jewish Life," in Marshall Sklare (ed.), *The Jews, Social Patterns of an American Group.* New York: The Free Press, pp. 509–519.

Manners, Ande. 1972. *Poor Cousins.* New York: Coward, McCann and Geoghegan.

Mayer, Egon, 1980. "Processes and Outcomes in Marriages between Jews and Non-Jews," *American Behavioral Scientist,* 23:487–518.

Mitchell, William E. 1978. *Mishpokhe.* New York: Mouton Publishers.

Rehberg, Richard A., Judie Sinclair, and Walter E. Schafer. 1970. "Adolescent Achievement Behavior, Family Authority Structure, and Parental Socialization Practices," *American Journal of Sociology,* 75:1012–1034.

Roberts, B. H., and J. K. Meyers. 1954. "Religion, Natural Origin, Immigration, and Mental Illness," *American Journal of Psychiatry,* 110:759–764.

Rose, Arnold M., and Halger R. Stub. 1955. "Summary of Studies on the Incidence of Mental Disorders," in Arnold M. Rose (ed.), *Mental Health and Mental Disorders.* New York: Norton, pp. 87–116.

Rosen, Bernard C. 1955. "Conflicting Group Membership: A Study of Parent–Peer-Group Cross Pressures," *American Sociological Review,* 20:155–161.

Rosenthal, Erich. 1963. "Studies of Jewish Intermarriage in the United States," *American Jewish Year Book,* 64:3–53.

———. 1970. "Divorce and Religious Intermarriage: The Effects of Previous Marital Status Upon Subsequent Marital Behavior," *Journal of Marriage and the Family,* 32:435–440.

Seeley, John R., R. Alexander Sim, and E. W. Loosely. 1956. *Crestwood Heights, a Study of the Culture of Suburban Life.* New York: Basic Books.

Seligman, Ben B. 1950. "The American Jew: Some Demographic Features," *American Jewish Year Book,* 51:3–52.

Sklare, Marshall (ed.). 1958. *The Jews, Social Patterns of an American Group.* Glencoe, IL: Free Press.

———. 1971. *America's Jews.* New York: Random House.

Sklare, Marshall, and Joseph Greenblum. 1967. *Jewish Identity on the Suburban Frontier: A Study of Group Survival in the Open Society.* New York: Basic Books.

Slater, Mariam K. 1969. "My Son the Doctor: Aspects of Mobility Among American Jews," *American Sociological Review,* 34:359–373.

Snyder, Charles R. 1958. *Alcohol and the Jews.* New York: The Free Press.

Srole, Leo, Thomas S. Langer, Stanley T. Michael, Marvin K. Opler, and Thomas A. C. Rennie. 1962. *Mental Health in the Metropolis.* New York: McGraw-Hill.

Strodtbeck, Fred. 1958. "Family Interaction, Values and Achievement," in Marshall Sklare (ed.), *The Jews, Social Patterns of an American Group.* Glencoe, IL: The Free Press, pp. 147–165.

U.S. Bureau of the Census. 1958. "Religion Reported by the Civilian Population of the United States: March 1957," *Current Population Reports,* Series P-20, No. 35. Washington, DC: U.S. Government Printing Office.

Wake, Sandra B., and Michael J. Sporakowski. 1972. "An Intergenerational Comparison of Attitudes Toward Supporting Aged Parents," *Journal of Marriage and the Family,* 34:42–48.

Weinryb, Bernard D. 1958. "Jewish Immigration and Accommodation to America," in Marshall Sklare (ed.), *The Jews, Social Patterns of an American Group.* Glencoe, IL: The Free Press, pp. 5–25.

Whelpton, Pascal, Arthur Campbell, and John Patterson. 1966. *Fertility and Family Planning in the United States.* Princeton, NJ: Princeton University Press.

Winch, Robert F., Scott Greer, and Rae L. Blumberg. 1967. "Ethnicity and Extended Familism in an Upper-Middle-Class Suburb," *American Sociological Review,* 32:265–272.

York, Allen. 1979. "Voluntary Associations and Communal Leadership Among the Jews of the United States," unpublished Ph.D. dissertation, Department of Sociology, Bar Ilan University, Ramat Gan, Israel.

Young, Michael, and Peter Willmot. 1962. *Family and Kinship in East London.* Baltimore: Penguin Books.

Zborowski, Mark. 1969. *People in Pain.* San Francisco: Jossey-Bass.

Zborowski, Mark, and Elizabeth Herzog. 1952. *Life Is with People: The Culture of the Shtetl.* New York: Schocken Books.

The Mormon Family

The concept of family, the foundation of Mormon theology and social structure, is being modified as the Church approaches its 150th anniversary in 1980. Several social scientists have identified certain strains that exist in the Mormon subculture between the routinized charismatic authority of the Mormon Church and the secular urban, industrial American society. In this chapter on the Mormon family, Drs. Campbell attempt to present the normative system that was promoted by Joseph Smith, the founder of the religion, and to examine the developing patterns of Mormon family life, paying special attention to the consequences of beliefs in the lives of those who hold them. Like most of the authors in this book, Drs. Campbell are members of the group of which they are writing. They are aware of the possible sources of bias that may affect the validity of their study. They commented:

> The "insider" has the advantage of an intimate knowledge of his culture that could take the "outsider" years to develop. The structure of relationships, the idiom, or special nuances in a reply are clearer to the insider than the outsider. However, there are certain pressures on the insider which may introduce bias into his study making the role of disinterested scholar difficult to maintain in certain circumstances. The excommunication of Dr. Sonia Johnson and church support of "profamily," antiabortion, and antifeminism political movements has probably influenced how we examined these issues.

The above problems are particularly sensitive with a group such as the Mormons whom Drs. Campbell characterize as possessing "missionary zeal" and concern with "generation of self."

CHAPTER SIXTEEN
BY
BRUCE L. CAMPBELL
AND EUGENE E. CAMPBELL

HISTORICAL BACKGROUND
Emergence of the Mormons as a Minority Group

Mormonism had its beginning in an atmosphere of supernaturalism, millenialism,[1] and religious revivalism that characterized the "Burned-over Dis-

---

[1] A belief that Christ would soon establish an earthly kingdom over which He would reign for a thousand years.

trict" of western New York during the first decades of the 19th century.[2] America, with relative religious freedom and readily available land, has historically nurtured a variety of transplanted European, Christian–Utopian societies and these same elements proved vital in the emergence of Mormonism as an American-born religious movement. The early history of Mormonism can be described as a cycle in which the Mormons created a new settlement, prospered, clashed with their non-Mormon neighbors, and then were forced to create a new settlement. This pattern was repeated in New York, Ohio, Missouri, and Illinois before they were driven out of the United States to the Great Basin, then Mexican territory. For decades the Mormons settled much of the area that later bacame Utah, Idaho, Nevada, Arizona, and parts of California, developing from a "near-sect" to a "near-nation" (O'Dea, 1957:115). In the process of taming this wild and arid land, the teachings of Joseph Smith, the founder of Mormonism, were translated into religious, social, political, and economic systems, forming the basis of Mormonism as it is known today.

Launching an "American Religion"

Joseph Smith, Jr., the founder of the religion, born in 1805, claimed to have experienced a series of heavenly visions, beginning about 1820, near Palmyra, New York. According to the Prophet Joseph, as his followers came to call him, in the first visitation, God the Father and His Son, Jesus Christ, appeared to him and informed him there was no true Church of Christ on the earth, and that he should join none of them.

Other visions revealed the location of golden plates buried by an ancient American prophet on which were written the records and religious experiences of ancient inhabitants of America, including a visit of Jesus Christ to the American continent after His resurrection. After obtaining these plates and some spectaclelike instruments to aid in translating them, Joseph Smith, with the help of several scribes, produced the Book of Mormon, asserted to be an inspired translation of the golden plates. Mormons accept this book as an important "second witness to the divinity of Jesus Christ" and when it was published in 1830, it became an effective missionary tool in the hands of the young prophet and his converts.

Smith also claimed to have received heavenly instructions and authority to reestablish what he said was the true, restored Church of Christ, which he

---

[2]Allen and Leonard describe the Burned-over District of western New York as being intensely affected by a religious awakening " . . . characterized by circuit-riding preachers, fiery-tongued evangelists, new grass-roots religious movements, fervent emotionalism, and the manifestation of certain physical excesses that demonstrated to new converts divine acceptance" (1976:11).

organized in 1830 at Fayette, New York. In 1838, the phrase Latter-day Saints was added reflecting the belief in the imminence of Christ's second coming and the end of the present age.[3] Thus, Mormonism began as a restoration of primitive Christianity with a strong eschatological and millenial flavor.[4]

It may seem incredible that a movement based on such supernatural experiences should attract so many people, but its claim to charismatic authority—a living prophet and a new scripture—seemed to satisfy the religious needs of those who had been disoriented by the religious diversity that characterized 19th-century America. Smith also preached a brand of communitarianism that may have met some of the economic hopes of his followers.

Mormons as a Persecuted Minority

As the Mormon movement began to grow, it attracted enemies, and for several decades Mormons and their enemies, including at times the Government of the United States, clashed. The Mormon assumption that Jesus would soon return to establish His Earthly Kingdom was the basis for their close knit social, economic, and political organization. Mormons believed they were chosen to be instrumental in the imminent establishment of Christ's Kingdom, so they often approached their tasks with fanatical religious zeal. Convinced they were engaged in the work of the Lord, many Mormons were willing to make great personal sacrifices to build the Kingdom of God.

This spirit of cooperation, sacrifice, and religious fervor was fundamental to their success as community builders but it was also threatening to their more individualistically oriented neighbors on the sparsely settled American frontier (Hill, 1978). Conflict was inevitable and in Missouri and Illinois, Mormon and non-Mormon differences escalated to armed conflict. Anti-Mormon mobs (sometimes including elements of the state militia) attacked Mormon settlements—burning homes, murdering religious leaders, raping Mormon women, and threatening the population with death and destruction if they did not change or leave. Mormons felt that government leaders at the state and national level acquiesced in these crimes.

In June of 1844, a series of events led to Joseph Smith's arrest at Nauvoo, Illinois, then the Church's headquarters. Subsequently, Joseph and his brother Hyrum were murdered while incarcerated at nearby Carthage, Illinois. Governor Ford of Illinois tried to prevent this mob action, yet Mormons perceived governmental contrivance in the plot to murder their beloved leader.

---

[3]The official name of the "Mormon Church" is the Church of Jesus Christ of Latter-day Saints.

[4]Eschatology is the doctrine or concept of the last days in a two-stage view of history. This present evil age is to be followed by a "Golden Age" in which Christ will reign.

After the death of Joseph Smith, Mormon leaders concluded that they could not rely on the protections guaranteed by the Constitution and decided to leave the United States to settle somewhere in the Rocky Mountains where they would be free to practice their social and religious beliefs.

This was a fateful decision: If they had remained in Illinois either extermination or gradual assimilation seemed their likely end. In the west, however, they were able to develop for several decades unique social institutions, relatively free from outside influence. As a result, they became a unique and important ethnic group.

In February 1846, the Mormons began their epic trek west. An advance pioneer company completed it's journey to the valley of the Great Salt Lake on July 24, 1847, and established the initial colony of their Great Basin Kingdom in what was then Mexican territory, but which was ceded to America in the treaty with Mexico in February 1848.

Brigham Young and the other leaders were effective colonizers; within ten years approximately 100 towns had been established in Utah, with outlying colonies in California, Nevada, Idaho, and Wyoming. Missionary work continued in many parts of the world, and a steady stream of converts, mainly from the British Isles and northern Europe, poured into the Great Basin, resulting in expanding colonization. By the time of Brigham Young's death in 1877, approximately 300 colonies had been established, primarily in Utah, Idaho, and Arizona.

There were many differences between the Mormons and the other Americans which *might* have been ignored if gold had not been discovered in California. Picked for its isolation and apparent desolation, the valley of the Great Salt Lake was paradoxically located on the best route to the gold fields of California. Mormon theocratic political power apparently threatened federal control of the Utah territory and hence the route to California, so for several decades the government attempted to alter Mormon social, economic, and political institutions. The Mormons resisted and a period of conflict ensued. Federal authorities used the Mormon practice of plural marriage as a means of diminishing Mormon political power.[5] Congress passed laws making the practice of polygamy in the territories illegal and disenfranchising Mormons who supported it. The Church was even disincorporated as a legal institution. The Church capitulated in 1890, ending 40 years of legal struggles with the government.

Presidential amnesty followed, but it was many years before Mormons were regarded as loyal citizens. Mormons faced a political dilemma. They

---

[5]The Mormon practice of plural marriage was widely discussed and deplored in the United States. Perhaps federal authorities focused their attack on Mormon polygamy because it presented an easier target than political or economic practices.

loved the Constitution and were loyal to the principles of the United States, but they felt that state and federal officials had deprived them of constitutional rights to practice their religion freely. Today, many Mormons seem to solve this dilemma by adopting conservative, sometimes ultraconservative political ideas, which allow them to love and support America while they oppose a strong federal government.

THE MORMON FAMILY—HISTORICAL DEVELOPMENTS

It has been asserted that all utopian movements have experimented with the family unit. Though Mormonism was utopian in spirit, as various experiments in communal living testify, it did not begin with a fully developed theoretical or theological blueprint for changing the family. In fact, the Mormon experiment with polygamy and the subsequent emphasis on the family as a divine unit did not appear until the movement was well under way.

There was nothing especially distinctive about early Mormon families. They tended to be large, closely knit, hard-working, and religiously oriented. They reflected the social origins of the converts from Ohio, Pennsylvania, New York, Upper Canada, and the manufacturing, shipping, and mining centers of Great Britain.

Ellsworth's (1951) study of Mormon origins reveals that most of the early converts were proselytized by relatives and friends and came primarily from towns and cities rather than the frontier, as has often been assumed. A considerable number of the important leaders in the Church came from New England stock, including the Smiths, Brigham Young, Heber C. Kimball, and Wilford Woodruff. Most were of the working class: farmers, unskilled and semiskilled laborers. A few were ministers or doctors.

The duty to gather to Zion and the unpopularity of the Church often separated new converts from their family. Many sought to replace such ties within the developing structure of the Church. By the middle of the Nauvoo period (1839–1846), the family was welded to the core of Mormon theology, involving concepts of (1) the eternal family, (2) the extended family by adoption, (3) the patriarchal family, and (4) the polygamous family.

The Eternal Family

The family has long been recognized by religious and secular thought as a basic, if not the basic, institution of society. In Mormon doctrine, however, the family became the basic social organization in the eternal Kingdom of God.

Mormons assert that man is a dual being composed of a spirit body and a physical body, and that God was and is the literal father of the spirit in a preearth life called the preexistence. Thus, God is not the creator of the spirit being but the *literal father* in the *same sense* that earthly fathers are the procreators of physical bodies.

The Mormon view of man asserts that not only is he a spirit child of God, but he is capable of achieving Godhood himself. In the process of becoming a God, a man must enter into the "new and everlasting convenant of marriage" by which he and his wife or wives will be married for all eternity and will have the privilege and duty of procreating spirit children throughout eternity even as God procreated us. Thus, man may become a god when he learns to organize a world and can populate it with his own spirit children. Mormons call this celestial marriage, and *only* faithful members of the Church who can gain authorization from priesthood leaders to enter the sacred temples built for solemnizing such ordinances are so married.

To qualify for participation in temple marriage, one must be a member of the Church in good standing and believe in the charismatic authority of the Church. Some of the more important behavioral expectations are sexual purity, payment of tithing (10 percent of gross income paid to the Church), and obedience to the "Word of Wisdom," which requires abstaining from the use of tea, coffee, alcohol, and tobacco. It should probably come as no surprise that less than half of the membership of the Church obey these requirements. Anything less than a temple marriage, however, is seen by many Church members as failure, and entrance to the temple is one of the most effective sanctions the Church has to exert control over its members. According to Mormon teaching there are millions of spirit children of God who are waiting their chance to come to this earth in their continuing quest for Godhood. Brigham Young (1925:305) said:

> There are multitudes of pure and holy spirits waiting to take tabernacles (bodies), now what is our duty . . . to prepare tabernacles for them, to take a course that will not tend to drive those spirits into the families of the wicked, where they will be trained in wickedness, debauchery, and every species of crime. It is the duty of every righteous man and woman to prepare tabernacles for all the spirits they can.

Such doctrines at the heart of Mormon theology have a compelling impact on the modern Mormon family and account for some of its peculiar characteristics such as attitudes toward birth control and abortion.

The Extended Family

According to Mormon theology, the organizational structure of heaven is the extended family-kinship network. Closely tied to this concept is the Mormon practice of extending and unifying one's family through "sealing ordinances" in the temple for members of the family who did not have the opportunity to embrace the Gospel during their lifetime. This "work for the dead," as it is called, is based on the belief that only by being "born of the water and the spirit," (baptized and confirmed a member of the Church of Jesus Christ) can one gain exaltation in the Celestial World and have the opportunity to be in God's presence and "become as He is." Since most of the human race has lived and died without a knowledge of the "true Church," Mormons are taught that it is their obligation to seek out the names of their dead ancestors and to act as proxy for them by going to the temple and experiencing baptism and other sacred ordinances in the name of deceased relatives. This program has resulted in the building of a score of temples in various parts of the world and the development of one of the greatest and most extensive genealogical library systems in the world. It has also resulted in extended family organizations for the promotion of genealogical research.

An interesting development of this extended family concept occurred early in Mormon history when leading men began adopting others to be a part of their extended family. Since many people had lost contact with their own families because of joining the unpopular movement, and since it was believed that Church members would soon be the governing officials of Christ's millenial kingdom, it seemed to be desirable to regain family ties within the Church through adoption. Thus, Brigham Young, in addition to his own 56 children, had many more by adoption, usually adults. These adoptive family relationships served as a nucleus for groups migrating to Utah and in cooperative efforts for colonizing the Great Basin.

The Patriarchal Family

The Mormon family, whether polygamous or monogamous, was patriarchal in nature. Following the Old Testament pattern was characteristic of the Mormons and is reflective of American religious thought of the time. Every man is expected to hold some office in the Mormon priesthood and to preside over his family. The wife is to be subject to her husband "as he is subject to God." Thus, while the father is expected to preside and rule the family, that rule should be based on religious principles.

The Polygamous Family

The concept of eternal marriage was closely tied to the practice of polygamy, or technically, polygyny. The practice was begun secretly by Joseph Smith and other Church leaders as early as 1842 and was based on the concept that the same God who had approved the Old Testament prophets who had many wives had revealed this principle to his modern prophet, Joseph Smith, with the command that the practice be instituted among the faithful and deserving Saints. Since polygamy remained secret until the public announcement in 1852, it is difficult to describe it in accurate detail. However, there is ample evidence that Joseph Smith married a number of wives before he was killed in 1844, and that Brigham Young and other leaders continued and enlarged the practice.

Since plural marriage in Nauvoo was clandestine, the Church leaders denied the practice on several occasions when asked about such marriages. As late as 1850, representatives of the Church in foreign lands continued to deny the doctrine and practice of polygamy. However, after the Mormons left Nauvoo and began their epic trek to the valley of the Great Salt Lake, this practice could no longer be hidden from the membership of the Church, but it was not until they were established in Utah that the practice was publicly announced and defended.

Some leaders in Nauvoo refused to accept the practice as inspired of God and asserted that Joseph Smith was a "fallen prophet." Opposition to the practice of polygamy was one of the reasons for the foundation of the Reorganized Church of Jesus Christ of Latter-day Saints in 1860.[6]

One of the most prominent reasons given for the institution of polygamy was the need for "righteous" men to bring as many children into this world as possible, and to do this, many wives were needed. It was also claimed that there were more women than men in the Church at that time because women were more receptive to religious convictions than men. These women, from the Mormon point of view, needed protection and help on this earth, and their eternal salvation depended on their having a celestial marriage; thus it was a sacred duty for qualified men to take extra wives. This claim is subject to question since census reports of Utah Territory list more men than women in each decade.[7] There is some evidence that in the heavily Scandinavian sections of Utah there were more women than men, suggesting foreign-born women as a likely source of second and third wives (Mulder, 1957). But there

---

[6]The practice of polygamy not only led to a major schism resulting in the RLDS, but it has led to numerous defections of small groups, since the Manifesto. These latter groups refuse to give up the practice and regard the Mormon Church as having apostatized from the true faith.

[7]The U.S. Census Compendium records the following statistics for Utah Territory:

	MALE	FEMALE
1850	6,020	5,310
1860	20,178	19,947
1870	44,121	42,665
1880	74,509	69,454
1890	110,463	97,442

were not enough foreign-born women to meet the demand for extra wives. This demand was met by allowing young women to marry older men. The number of males in the 30–39 age cohort was significantly smaller than the number of available females in the 20–29 age cohort (Smith and Kunz, 1976).

Orson Pratt, an early Mormon theologian who was chosen by Brigham Young to make a defense of polygamy at the time of the public announcement, asserted that God would need plural wives to procreate all his spirit children. He also argued, and many Mormons have since concurred, that Jesus Christ himself must have been married. Just as Jesus needed to be baptized to set a perfect example for men to follow, the Mormons reasoned, he would need to be married in the celestial way, which presupposed polygamy. Pratt suggested that the miracle of turning water to wine at Cana was the celebration of Jesus' own marriage. Although the New Testament does not directly support this claim, Pratt argued (Young, 1954:37–38)

> One thing is certain, there were several holy women that greatly loved Jesus—such as Mary, and Martha her sister, and Mary Magdalene; and Jesus greatly loved them, and associated with them much; and when he arose from the dead, instead of first showing himself to his chosen witnesses, the Apostles, he appeared first to Mary Magdalene. Now it would be very natural for a husband in the resurrection to appear first to his own dear wife, and afterwards to show himself to his other friends.

While such arguments powerfully influenced and continue to influence Mormon thought, there is little wonder that the Christian world regarded the Mormons as being heretical. Eliza R. Snow (born 1804) wrote in her journal that among other things the practice of polygamy led to an elevation of character and "was also instrumental in producing a more perfect type of manhood mentally and physically, as well as in restoring human life to its former longevity" (Snow, 1971:129–30). She was, no doubt, alluding to the accounts of the Old Testament patriarchs who lived to be hundreds of years old. Heber C. Kimball (1858) made similar claims when he wrote:

> I would not be afraid to promise a man who is sixty years of age, if he will take the counsel of brother Brigham and his brethren, that he will renew his age. I have noticed that a man who has but one wife, and is inclined to that doctrine, soon begins to wither and dry up, while a man who goes into plurality looks fresh, young and sprightly. Why is this? Because God loves that man, and because he honors his work and word. Some of you may not believe this; but I not only believe it—I know it. For a man of God to be confined to one woman is small business; for it is as much as we can do now to keep up under the burdens we have to carry; and I do not know what we should do if we had only one wife apiece.

All such explanations and justifications are "after the fact," however, and the official position of the Mormon Church is that Joseph Smith began the practice because it was a revealed commandment of God. Religious conviction appears to be central to the acceptance of the practice.

As has been stated, polygamy had been practiced from at least 1842 but did not really get under way until after 1847 when the Mormons entered the Salt Lake Valley. Mormon polygamy differed from polygamy in other cultures in that it developed rapidly with little or no chance for the usual norms and other institutions of society to appear and regulate this custom. As a result, Mormon polygamy was not circumscribed by a set of generalized norms as is the case in other cultures allowing for polygamous marriages. There was no limit—formal or informal—as to the number of wives a man might have or any strictly prescribed method of gaining extra wives.

The patterns of housing one's wives were varied. Some families lived under one roof, while others favored separate homes for each wife. At other times, the families were spread throughout the city or even over the thousands of square miles of the Great Basin. The grandfather of a Mormon social scientist claimed he could "catch any streetcar in Salt Lake City and arrive *home.*" Sometimes a man only visited his wives in the outlying regions often enough to bless his newest child and get another one started.

Theoretically, all of the wives in a family were to be social equals; however, in practice, the first wife was usually the most powerful because she was the only *legal* wife. She was also supposed to give her permission before her husband married other wives. Young's (1954) study indicates that in the case in which the man took several wives, he often continued to consult the first wife about subsequent additions but did not feel the need of consulting his other wives on the subject. If the first wife had a more powerful legal position, the second or latest wife often had a position of power owing to her youth, beauty, or the romance of the courtship.

Recent research suggests that first wives in polygamous families generally had more children than either women in monogamous unions or third wives in polygamous unions, suggesting her role as first wife gave her more access to her husband and thus more power than subsequent wives (Smith and Kunz, 1976). There is some indication that second and third wives were females who "survived the monogamous marriage market" in that they tended to be older than first wives when they married (Smith and Kunz, 1976). It may be that second and third wives were at a competitive disadvantage to first wives in the marriage market and thus had less power in these marriages.

Studies of Mormon polygamy by Kimball Young (1954), Ivins (1956), and Anderson (1937) indicate that during the 50-year period that polygamy was practiced, about 10 to 15 percent of the eligible males were polygamous. Ivins' (1956:233) study reveals that:

> ... of 1,784 polygamists, 66.3% married only one extra wife, another 21.2% were three-wife men, and 6.7% went so far as to take four wives. This left a small group of polygamists of less than 6% who married five or more women. The typical polygamist, far from being the insatiable male of popular fable, was a dispassionate fellow, content to call a halt after marrying one extra wife required to assure him of his salvation.

Of those who chose to have five or more wives, Brigham Young was the most prominent. He probably had at least 27 wives, 16 of whom had 56 children. Heber C. Kimball, Young's first counselor, is said to have had at least 35 wives, but there were so many different arrangements that the term "wife" requires definition before totals can be determined.

While at the time it was assumed that sexual desire was the main motive for taking an extra wife, Arrington (1958:152) argues that Church pressure was the strongest motive for practicing polygamy. The coincidence of a rise in the rate of polygamous marriages and periodic religious "reformations" are cited. These reformations generally took place when the Mormons were threatened economically.

How did polygamy work? According to Young (1954:57), 53 percent, or more than half of the cases examined, were either "highly successful" or reasonably successful. One-fourth of them were only moderately successful, and 23 percent were rated as having considerable or severe conflict.

Recent evidence developed by E. Campbell and B. Campbell (1978) suggest more conflict than described by Young. Brigham Young granted nearly 1700 divorces during his reign as President of the Church, and most of these were polygamous unions.

In theory, polygamous families were supposed to be ruled over by a patriarchal father. However, Kimball Young (1954) found that many of the women had considerable power in the home, especially in regard to the rearing of the children. In many cases, the husband was not physically present for much of the year, and the women were forced to take a rather independent, self-confident stance. Frontier living, the demands of the Church on a man's time, and the need for equal interaction with his families tended to remove the man to some degree from the home. He did not exert the day-by-day influence on wife and children that his theology and his western European cultural heritage would suggest. Polygamy, moreover, permitted an intelligent, ambitious woman to marry and bear children to fulfill her religious–social role as a woman and still allowed her some freedom to pursue a career (Arrington, 1958).

The Mormon Church now opposes the *practice* of plural marriage but has never renounced it as a doctrine. In 1890, Wilford Woodruff, the President of the Church, issued the Manifesto announcing the end of the practice of polygamy in the Church. For those already married in polygamy, the Manifesto created an ambiguous situation. Some men ended all contact with their plural wives, while others stopped having intimate relations with their extra wives, but continued to support them financially. Many men, including President Joseph F. Smith (a relative of the founder, Joseph Smith), continued to live with their wives but took no new ones. A few married extra wives after 1890. However, having demonstrated its control over the Utah Territory, the federal government decreased its prosecution of polygamists and winked at its practice in many cases. The government seemed satisfied to let Mormon polygamy die gradually and as a generation passed, so did the practice of polygamy in the Mormon Church.

However, certain persons felt that the Manifesto was not God's will, but rather political expediency, and they determined to keep the practice alive even though it meant excommunication from the Church. Some claimed that Church officials came to them in secret and called on them to carry on the practice of polygamy. As a result, on the fringe of the Mormon subculture there are some persons who marry plural wives, but because of the clandestine nature of their operation there is little reliable information on their marriage and family practices.

Although the Mormon Church no longer allows the practice of polygamy in terms of cohabitation, two situations remain that are polygamous in intent. First, if a Mormon couple is married in the temple, and the wife dies, the husband may marry another wife in the temple for time and eternity, which is a second celestial marriage. She is regarded as a "second" wife joining a polygamous eternal family unit. Second, if a man has a legal but not a temple "divorce" from a woman, he may marry another woman in the temple. Since Mormons see the temple ceremony as an eternal marriage, the man is in effect a polygamist. The Church, however, would feel that he would be committing adultery if he tried to cohabit with his first wife while legally divorced from her.

This view of eternal marriage does have one unfortunate consequence. If a woman is married to a man for eternity and her husband dies, she may have a difficult time finding an orthodox Mormon man who will marry her. The doctrine teaches that in the eternity she would belong to her first husband, as would all of her children, even though they might be fathered by her second husband. Few orthodox Mormon men will deny themselves the right to their own wives and children in eternity. This is especially difficult for a devout young Mormon widow, for she feels she must marry an active Mormon in order to find happiness in a second marriage. In recent years, there seems to be some sentiment among Church leaders to modify this doctrine.

However, polygamy has left its mark on the Church. Those who have polygamous ancestors are proud of this fact and see it as a mark of honor and loyalty. The practice of polygamy also seems to have increased the family orientation of the subculture and made the Mormon religion more family-oriented than most. There remains some bitterness in families that can be traced to the practice. The family of the first wife may not recognize the family of subsequent wives as legitimate heirs to the family name or fortune. It also seems to have created a certain looseness in the marriage system. Some rather strange relationships were formed, and for many years there was a kind of marriage underground. In some ways this may help to account for a higher divorce rate in the Mormon subculture than one might expect.

Polygamy and the Popular Perception of Mormons

The isolation of the Mormons in the American west and their practice of plural marriage caused them to be the source of great national and international interest. Hundreds of volumes have been written by European and American adventurers on what the Mormons were really like—some accurate, some pure fantasy. However, two themes have developed to which Mormons react even today.

Theme one is the Mormon elder as supersexual being with devious and magical ways, which lure women to Utah and into polygamy. The purported, evil animal-like stare of the Mormon man was a result of his debased state. Some scientists of the time noted that Mormon eyes tended to be "almond shaped" indicating sexual wantoness. One writer quoted by Bunker and Bitton said: "The hog, the wild boar, the dog, the cat, every species of serpent, all of the ape tribes, and all those whose eyes exhibit the almond-shaped opening are promiscuous in their attachments" (1979:115–116). Patent medicine producers took advantage of this image and produced such products as Mormon Elder's Damiana Wafers, Brigham Young Tablets, and Mormon Bishop Pill to cure either lagging sexual desire or ability (Bush, 1976b). Mormon men were viewed as evil, cunning, seductive, promiscuous, but above all virile.

Mormon men and women were included in the second theme which assumed that due to the practice of polygamy, Mormons were breeding an inferior species of human beings. Female children were said to exceed male children to a dramatic degree and the death rate among children was said to be high because they were generally of inferior stock, and their parents did not take proper care of them. All—men, women, and children—were described as having a Mormon look, which included an air of imbecility, brutal ferocity, habitual and hardened sensuality, feeble virility, yellow, sunken, cadaverous visage, and low forehead (Bush, 1979). Bush suggests, "Like Blacks, Indians, Jews, Orientals, the Irish, Mexicans and Catholics, the Mormons were stereotyped by the use of theories of behavior popular in the Nineteenth Century. Unprepared for a pluralistic society, Americans sought and found psychological support for their misconceptions" (1979:118). Given this negative picture of Mormons, it is not surprising that they have attempted to adjust to 20th century American society by demonstrating superiority. They cannot be just good citizens, they are superpatriots. They are not just good parents and family members, they are superparents with the best families. As a society they have adopted middle-class norms and striven to be accepted. They adapt by overconforming and so any sign or study that reports them as merely being okay or average or like other Americans in similar circumstances is seen as an attack on them and their Church.

THE MORMON FAMILY TODAY

In many, perhaps most ways the Mormon family of today resembles the stereotyped "white, middle-class American family." The outstanding differences are the attitudes Mormons have about their families and the extension of family life into the hereafter. Other outstanding features include larger family size, low divorce rates (for temple marriages), relative importance of the parent–child relationship, the Church Family Home Evening, and perhaps a greater stressing of sexual "purity" than is found in the general population.

Demographics

There are about three million Mormons living in the United States today, concentrated mainly in the western states. Utah's population of 1,255,000 is about 75 percent Mormon and the adjoining states of Idaho, Nevada, Arizona, and California have significant Mormon populations. The Church is an active proselyting church and is said to be one of the fastest growing in the U.S.A.—if not in the world. Thus the population is expanding. One of the reasons for its growth is that it has a high birth rate and is relatively successful in socializing these children into the Mormon faith (Kunz and Brinkerhoff, 1970).

Urban–Rural Differences

Even with intense irrigation, the semiarid land of the west cannot support a large farming population. In 1850 over 50 percent of Utah's population was employed in agriculture while by 1960, only 5.8 percent were farmers. However, because the Church promotes such practices as keeping a garden, having a year's supply of food on hand, and having large families, Mormons have been characterized as urban dwellers with rural ideals.

Wilford E. Smith (1959) found urban Mormons are less orthodox in many beliefs and practices than rural Mormons. Furthermore, urban Utah Mormons conform substantially *more* to Church practices than urban Mormons on the west coast (Mauss, 1972a, 1972b).

Family Size—Fertility—Contraception

Perhaps no area of Mormon family has received more serious scrutiny by social scientists than Mormon fertility patterns. First, Mormons are proud of their large families and are willing to have this aspect of their lives studied. Secondly, because Mormons believe in an eternal extended family unit as a heavenly structure, they have been leaders in genealogical research. They have collected and validated thousands of detailed family histories covering several generations in some families. These records have been made available to demographers who are beginning to produce excellent multigenerational studies of Mormon fertility patterns (Skolnick et al., 1978). Finally, an important issue of study is how Mormon couples conform to the strongly pronatalist doctrine of the Church.

There are excellent reviews of the position of the Mormon Church on birth control and family size (Hastings et al., 1972; Bush, 1976a), which clearly show Church opposition to birth control, voluntary sterilization, and abortion. Mormons take very literally and seriously the Biblical injunction to multiply and replenish the earth. An official letter issued in 1969 seemed to allow for child-spacing and consideration for the physical and mental health of women in making birth control decisions, but it also proclaimed that those who limit their family would "reap disappointment by and by." Self-control was suggested as the only acceptable means of birth control. The First Presidency of the Church says that in some "rare cases" (rape, danger to the health of the mother) abortion may be acceptable. However, they also state that "abortion must be considered one of the most revolting practices of this day ... (Priesthood Bulletin, 1973:1). President Kimball (1976:2–5) stated:

... the union of the sexes, husband and wife, ... was for the principal purpose of bringing children into the world. ... We know of no directive from the Lord

400

that proper sexual experiences between husbands and wives need be limited totally to the procreation of children, but we find much evidence from Adam until now that no provision was ever made by the Lord for indiscriminate sex.

If this is the ideal, then how have Mormons responded to it? All surveys indicate a declining birth rate among Mormons (Bush, 1976a; Hastings et al., 1972; Skolnick et al., 1978; J. Wise and Condie, 1975; Bowers and Hastings 1970). On the other hand, Mormons tend to want and have more children than other Americans, including Roman Catholics (Thornton, 1979). The birth rates of Mormon leaders have followed the same general Church membership, with the leaders having slightly larger families than Mormons as a whole (Thornton, 1979).

Mauss (1972b) has demonstrated that Mormons living in urban centers on the west coast have fewer children than Salt Lake City Mormons, but they still have more children than their neighbors. Converts to the Church tend to have larger families than those born into the Church (Merrill and Peterson, 1972) while orthodox Mormons have more children than their less committed brothers and sisters.

It appears as though the forces of urbanization and industrialization, which are depressing the general American birth rate, are having the same impact on Mormons. However, Thornton (1979) concluded that if the historical trend were to continue as is, it would be at least 150 years before Mormon and non-Mormon birth rates would converge.

Mormons appear to support their leaders with regard to abortion (Erlend Peterson, 1971); however, on the issue of birth control there appears to be a gap between what the Church teaches and the attitudes and behavior of the members. By and large, Mormons are family members and though they differ from non-Mormons to some degree, they practice birth control using the most effective methods available (Erlend Peterson, 1971; Hastings et al., 1972; Bush, 1976a; Bowers and Hastings, 1970). For many of them, however, this discrepancy is a source of guilt and personal discomfort (Bush, 1976a).

Intermarriage

Generally, Mormons have opposed intermarriage partially because mixed marriages were assumed to be less stable, and partially because they share the racial attitudes of other Americans, but mainly they have opposed mixed religious marriages for doctrinal reasons. Most Utah marriages are racially homogamous partly because of the low concentration of minority members in the population (Galliher and Basilick, 1979).

What percentage of Mormons marry non-Mormons is not known, but Mauss (1976) reports that about 60 percent of the Salt Lake City Mormons thought marrying a non-Mormon to be a serious matter while 40 percent or less of his coastal city respondents accepted this judgment.

Divorce

Divorce rates for the state of Utah and the United States are almost identical. Table 1 indicates that the divorce rate in Utah is rising and is nearly twice what it was in 1940. However, Table 2 suggests that Utah's rate of divorce is relatively low when compared to adjacent states.

However, it is important to compare Mormon temple marriages to nontemple marriages to see how Mormon orthodoxy influences divorce. Harold Christensen (1972:21) clarifies this influence somewhat, reporting the following divorce percentages: Civil marriages 13.4; Latter-day Saint nontemple marriages, 10.2; non-Mormon religious marriages, 5.5; and Latter-day Saint temple marriages, 1.8 percent. Other studies report similar findings (K. Cannon and Steed, 1972; Mitchell and Peterson, 1972).

Apparently, being married in a Mormon temple reduces ones chances of becoming divorced, but the dynamic of this relationship is not clear. Several theories have been advanced to explain this relationship including antidivorce teachings, a selection process that increases the probability of attitudinal and behaviorial homogamy, and support for conservative values which are very compatible with traditional marriage (Cannon and Steed, 1972). Nuttall (1959) found that temple-married Mormons reported higher levels of marital satisfaction accompanied by greater feelings of security and higher levels of empathy than Mormons married outside of the temple. Finally it is likely that given their strongly profamily values Mormon couples may be more inclined than others to *perceive* their own marriages as successful and happy.

Additionally many temple-married Mormons who later divorced contemplated suicide because of their feelings of failure and sin (Hagerty, 1961).

TABLE 1
Divorces per 1000 Population in Utah and the United States (Selected Years)

	UTAH	UNITED STATES
1940	2.7	2.0
1950	3.0	2.6
1960	2.4	2.2
1970	3.7	3.5
1978	5.0	5.0

SOURCE: Utah Department of Health (1976).

TABLE 2
TABLE 2
Selected States and U.S. Crude Divorce Rate

STATE	1970	1972	1973	1974
Arizona	7.2	6.7	6.8	7.9
Colorado	4.7	5.3	5.9	6.0
Idaho	5.1	5.1	5.6	6.0
Nevada	18.7	21.9	18.2	17.5
New Mexico	4.3	NA	NA	7.0
Wyoming	5.4	6.4	6.4	7.0
Utah	3.7	4.4	4.6	4.7
United States	3.5	4.4	4.4	4.6

SOURCE: U.S. Bureau of the Census (1976).

One could not suggest such trauma for all Mormons who divorce, but it suggests strong forces keeping together marriages that may not be satisfying. This may result in increased trauma for Mormon children when divorce does occur, but there are no studies on this issue.

Husband and Wife—Authority and Power

The normative authority pattern in Mormon family life is patriarchal. The man has the responsibility to act as leader of his family and officiates in a number of religious functions in the home. Every orthodox male member of the Mormon Church should be ordained to the priesthood at age 12 and from then on should have increasing responsibilities in the Church. The Mormon father who holds this priesthood (as all active men do) performs such important functions in the religious aspects of family life as blessing and naming of children (christening), baptism of children, priesthood ordination of sons, some temple ordinances, and the blessing of sick family members, as well as leading in family prayers at each meal and on other occasions. In fact, almost all of the religious ordinances that a minister or priest might perform for members of other Christian churches is performed by the Mormon father for his family if he is "worthy." This activity, in addition to the Mormon conception of the eternal family unit, would seem to make the male dominant in the family and much more influential than his wife.

Christopherson (1956) found that the vast majority of Mormon couples believed that patriarchal authority is a divine endowment and is necessary, in this life as well as in eternity, as a system of family government. However, the majority of the husbands and wives felt that "the husband's authority operates chiefly in matters pertaining to religion" (p. 139). Christopherson

(1963:151) makes the conclusion in another article: "the Mormon family has always exercised democracy in its family relations to a very high and pronounced degree." One interesting case that Christopherson (1956:326) reported indicated a curious discrepancy between the norm of male power and the principle in practice as follows:

> Typical of such instances was an interview with one family in which the woman had just finished expressing a point of view to the effect that in her family the husband and father was regarded as the ultimate seat of recourse with respect to most, if not to all, family disputes. Almost in the same breath, she interrupted her husband to correct him with an air of finality with regard to a point of Church doctrine.

Some Mormon women are fond of Eph. 5:22–24, which is interpreted to mean that wives need submit themselves only when the husband is acting "righteously" and that the wife can make such a judgement!

Research findings about the Mormon male's actual power and authority in marriage are contradictory. Mormon women may be rather reluctant to lead in family matters even when their husband appears ineffectual (Christenson, 1970). Furthermore, many Mormon women claim they desire "traditional" rather than "companionate" marriages (Mote, 1961; G. Wise and Carter, 1965). A recent survey reports that in many ways Mormon families are very similar to Protestant and Catholic families but that they were consistently more patriarchal than the other groups (S. Bahr and H. Bahr, 1977). However, other studies indicate a high level of equalitarianism in Mormon marriages (Black, 1969; McBride, 1963; J. Cannon, 1967). Mormons are becoming increasingly accepting of female participation in the provider role, but in the areas of child care, housekeeping, and others, they remain traditional (Albrecht, Bahr, and Chadwick, 1979).

Extended Family Relationships

Mormons see the extended, eternal family unit as being very important. There are, however, no studies that have clarified the actual extent of extended family interaction. Life in the Mormon subculture convinced the observer that the kinship network must be at least as strong as those found by Sussman (1963) or Litwak (1960) in other parts of America.

Living among the Mormons, one is much aware of men who have taken substantial cuts in salary and entered less attractive positions solely to return to "Zion" to be near their families. It is interesting to note that while Mormon doctrine indicates that extended family groups will be the social structure of heaven, very few choose or are encouraged to choose such a living arrangement now. The three-generational household appears to be no more frequent among Mormons than among other Americans.

Status of Women

Mormon women *do not* hold the priesthood, and although women have leadership positions in the Relief Society (woman's organization) and other Church auxiliaries, they are placed in these positions by men who are Church officers. In the past, the Relief Society was rather independent but recently this organization has been brought more directly under the control of the Church's male leadership. Though women participate in Church operations, they lack the priesthood authority to exercise leadership.

Church officials proclaim the role of mother to be the equal of, if different from, the male's priesthood role. Women are urged to make motherhood a career and women who desire other careers are cautioned that it is sinful to place a career above their God-given duty to be a mother.

The leadership of the Church has reacted in an overwhelmingly negative way to the Women's Liberation Movement. The Church leaders seem to see, with some justification, that the aims and goals of some parts of the Women's Liberation Movement are incompatible with their stated doctrine. The Women's Movement is *seen* as antichild and antifamily; proabortion, advocating sexual freedom and a glorification of lesbianism. The movement also presents a challenge to the authority of the male-only priesthood in the Church.

As a result, the Mormon Church has responded by opposing the Equal Rights Amendment (ERA). Warenski (1978) has documented the strong stand Mormons have taken on ERA and suggests that to some degree they have become captives of the far-right wing of the American political spectrum on this issue. The excommunication of Sonia Johnson in December, 1979, received public attention and showed the political organization of the Mormon Church to be in opposition to the Equal Rights Amendment (Sillitoe and Swenson, 1980). The actions of the Church have raised the question of whether or not a woman can be a feminist and an active, believing Mormon at the same time. The answer is not at all clear at this writing.

In the important area of women's employment outside the home, however, it appears as though Mormon women are being affected by the same social and economic forces as their other American sisters. Howard Bahr (1979:2–3) reports:

... over the past generation the labor force participation of Utah women has become increasingly like that of women nationally, and today there is no differ-

405

ence. Utah women are as apt as other women to work outside the home. . . . Both in Utah and in the nation, the position of women relative to men with respect to higher education and to participation in high-status occupations has either remained stable or deteriorated.

Devout Mormon women face a dilemma: Their religious leaders urge them to have large families, to eschew a career, and to follow the lead of their husbands. However, as a group they are having fewer children and increasing their labor participation; both trends likely to increase their relative power in marriage. The resolution of this dilemma is likely to be an important issue in the future.

Family Home Evening

David O. McKay, while President of the Church (1969) said, "No success in the world can compensate for failure in the family." In this spirit, the Church has long provided various organized programs to help *parents* become successful in raising *their* children. Failure, of course, is having a child who is not a "good Mormon." These programs have met with varying degrees of success, but in 1964 the Church instituted a program called "family home evenings." Members of the Church were urged to meet with their families one evening a week to learn about the gospel, using a lesson manual which was developed to aid families in starting this program. Monday evening church meetings were discontinued and all members were urged to set aside Monday as a family night.

Most members appeared to have tried the program, but its regular practice is far from universal. Interestingly enough, it does not appear to be busy teenagers who need to "break away" from home who have undermined the program, for Miller (1969) reports that teenagers express the desire for more regular practice of family home evening than is the practice in their homes.

This attempt to construct a family ritual has received some acclaim outside the Church, but its impact on family solidarity and happiness has been difficult to measure (Larsen, 1967).

Socialization of Children

While most American marriages evolve to be child-centered, Mormon marriages often start out child-centered. Cook (1966) reported, for example, that 45 percent of the young married college-student Mormon couples had a child within the first year of marriage. These are college-educated people who could be expected to be successful in a birth-control program if they had chosen such a course. This desire for children did not insulate the couples from experiencing crises at the birth of the first child. Marlow (1968) found that Mormon couples experience the same loss of marital satisfaction in at least the early stages of the family life cycle that has been reported among other American couples.

When asked to check their primary concern in married life, Mormon homemakers in Wasatch County (Bacon, 1964:84) indicated their first concern to be "helping your children to have faith in God and to be creatively active in Church." Issues centering around the marital relationship per se were near the bottom of the list of concerns. Mormon mothers clearly take childrearing seriously; however, their socialization practices are similar to those of other Americans (Kunz, 1963). It appears that the prime value of Mormon parents is "proper" socialization in terms of end results rather than in terms of method. They do what they think will be effective in terms of making the child a good Mormon. They are, for the most part, quite willing to accept advice from Mormon or non-Mormon "experts" in the area of childrearing.

Adolescence

Since it is well recognized that a restrictive culture can be applied to children more readily than to teenagers, it is important to examine Mormon success or lack of success with teenagers. In some areas this question can be answered, but in other areas—drug abuse, for example—the information is only impressionistic. One piece of data to be examined is the Church's missionary program. Presently, the Church has about 25,000 missionaries in the various missions of the Church, ranging from Japan to South Africa. The vast majority (90 percent) are young men from 19 to 22 years old who have taken this time out of their lives to participate in what is considered a high calling and an honor. They are supported with funds they have saved or through money their parents contribute to them. These young men must meet strict standards of sexual morality, obey the Word of Wisdom, subject themselves to rigid conventions of dress while on the mission, and be willing to go any place the Church calls them. That these young men are willing and able to go suggests they have accepted the standards and values of their parents. A study by Lake (1963) suggests that many Mormon youths are quite willing to accept parental and Church guidance in a wide range of behaviors and expectations.

Mormon youth have not been untouched by the youth culture and its emphasis on drugs and sex. The Church has taken a strong stand against the use of drugs of any sort but in spite of this, some Mormon teenagers have been experimenting with drugs (Galliher and Basilick, 1979). However, Utah was one of the first states to "enact a law reducing the penalty for first-offense possession (of marijuana) from a felony to a misdemeanor" (Galliher and Basilick, 1979:284). Reportedly this was done because "the marijuana problem was hitting middle-class families and Mormon youth . . . (Galliher and Basilick, 1979:291).

The sexual revolution! Has it hit the Mormon youth? Hatch (1968) found that somewhere between necking and light petting was the extent of acceptable sex relations before marriage for Brigham Young University students. A study of single men at the University of Utah shows Mormons with less sexual intercourse than non-Mormons. Christenson (1970), in a longitudinal study of sexual attitudes and behavior, found some increase in the percentage of students in the Utah area approving of sexual intercourse before marriage (males, 38 percent; females, 23.5 percent). As for actually having sex relations, 35 percent of the males and 32.4 percent of the females admitted to the experience. The most dramatic change was that of the females, with only 9.5 percent admitting to premarital sex relations in the 1958 study. These findings suggest that there is likely a great deal of guilt surrounding sexual behavior in the Mormon subculture. In a more detailed analysis of the Mormons in his sample, Christensen (1977) discovered that active Mormons had a much lower rate of premarital sexual activities than inactive Mormons who tended to behave like their non-Mormon friends in Utah. He also found that premarital sexual behavior among Mormon youth may be a form of rebellion or acting-out behavior. He says (1977:4) Mormons as compared to non-Mormons:

> were somewhat more promiscuous once they started with premarital sex; were more apt to have engaged in their first premarital sexual experience as a result of either force or felt obligation; were more apt to have been careless or reckless in their first premarital sexual encounter, in the sense of drinking alcohol and not practicing contraception. . . .

Apparently, however, Mormon youth believe their parents make more attempts to control them and that they show more interest in them than do the parents of other American youth (Evan Peterson, 1977).

The Elderly

Surprisingly, there is little written on the elderly in the Mormon subculture. The top leaders in the Mormon Church keep their positions until they die. A kind of "date of rank" is important in determining who is President of the Quorum of Twelve Apostles, and the head of this quorum normally becomes

President of the Church when the current President dies. This seniority system is not followed elsewhere in the Church, for young and middle-aged men dominate the leadership positions. It seems that the elderly, as in other churches, lose their positions and power.

Temple work, which involves participating in sacred dramas and rituals as proxy for the dead, is doctrinally important in the Mormon Church and is a regular source of activity among the elderly, who have looked forward to the day when they could retire and work in the temple. Since most do not receive money for this work, it is not motivated by a desire for income. The gratifications are religious and social in nature.

Many of the elderly are either not "worthy" or do not find temple work rewarding, so they do not have this outlet. It is difficult for the elderly person who has not been active in the Church to be a part of it in later years. The signs of his former "unworthy" life are all around him, and so he may not be willing to attend church. Recently there have been some centers for the elderly growing up in Utah towns that might fill a need for many non-Mormon or inactive Mormon elderly, although active Mormons also participate in these centers.

A study of intergenerational contact in elderly Mormon families revealed that the Mormon pattern of intergenerational contact does not differ from the more general societal pattern and that this contact "provides no guarantee that there will be an absence of growing feelings of powerlessness and a lack of sense of meaning and purpose in life" (Albrecht and Chappell, 1977:74).

The Church has no specific program designed to meet the needs of its elderly members and stresses the religious obligation of the family to provide for its aging members (Featherstone, 1975). If there are no family members ready or willing to care for an elderly Church member, then the Church may provide for them, but this is no guaranteed retirement plan.

CHANGE AND ADAPTATION

Like the French Canadian Americans and the Amish, there are no external barriers to assimilation of individual Mormons into the larger society. Their predominantly Anglo-Scandinavian ethnic stock coupled with their strong adherance to middle-class norms creates no barriers they must break to be accepted by other Americans.

Thus, how will Mormons maintain their identity while meeting the challenges of a changing society is problematic. At least three factors are important to the future existence of Mormons as a peculiar people: (1) continued acceptance of Church leaders and doctrine; (2) strong families; and (3) a sense of peoplehood. These issues are related but each adds something to our understanding of the survival potential of Mormonism.

Leone suggests that Mormonism has a "capacity to absorb change and exists in a condition of continued renewal . . ." (1974:763). He sees the leaders of the Church being sensitive to their followers and that they make Mormonism more acceptable to the membership by either changing a doctrine or by changing the emphasis given a certain doctrine. For example, the Church has moved from supporting polygamy as a central principle to a glorification of monogamous family life.

Dolgin (1974), having examined the belief system of Mormons, concludes that they have a strong sense of peoplehood which arises from the assumption that they hold similar beliefs. However, she reports that under an umbrella of "official" doctrines, individual Mormons tend to hold widely divergent views (Dolgin, 1974). Apparently many who leave the Church do so for doctrinal reasons, but other issues also influence this decision (Mauss, 1969; Seggar and Blake, 1970).

O'Dea felt that the issue of whether or not black Mormon men would be allowed the priesthood would be a diagnostic issue as to whether or not the Church could adapt to modern realities or remain lost in the past (1972:162). He says:

> The race issue has become symbolic of the entire complex of problems involved in that challenge and the defensive attitude against the idea of change with respect to its stands surrogate for "standpatism" generally in the face of the larger challenge. The church's adequacy to handle the problems of its encounter with modernity will eventually be judged by the adequacy of its response to the problem of racial justice.

Since this article was published, in June 1978, President Kimball announced a divine revelation that blacks were to be given the priesthood. It was an electrifying event and most Mormons hearing of the event called other Mormons they associated with to see if they knew or not. There seemed to be two general reactions: One, they did not think this would happen in their lifetime, and two, relief—it's about time. There was wide acceptance and the Church seems to have adapted without any problems.

Presently Mormonism seems to succeed through a delicate balance between the need to follow powerful authoritarian leaders and a tolerance of divergent individual beliefs. Potentially controversial issues abound which could destroy this balance if care is not exercised by the leaders.

Strong Mormon family life, the second major issue in the future state of Mormonism is profoundly related to temple marriage. An investigation of temple versus nontemple marriages is an interesting case in point. Throughout this chapter a number of Mormon family behavior patterns as encouraged by Church officials have been examined. In *every* case, those married in the temple were much closer to the Mormon official norm than those married elsewhere. Many more cases were examined than can be presented here, but it is quite apparent that the Church is dependent on couples married in the temple for most of its support.

A number of studies indicate that the decision to marry in the temple is powerfully influenced by one's parents and family (Jack W. Peterson, 1969; Rollins, 1958; Mauss, 1972b). For men, serving on a mission is highly correlated with temple marriage, and serving on a mission is greatly influenced by one's family (Mauss, 1972b).

The evidence is clear. The Church is dependent on the family for effective socialization of religious attitudes in the coming generation. Family-orientation and religion courses on the college level appear to have an interactive effect, producing stronger beliefs in the adult, but again the primacy of the home must be acknowledged (Mauss, 1972b).

The Mormon congregation or ward often forms a community approaching the *gemeinschaft* ideal type. Mormons are likely to do business with Mormons when they can and stay within the ward (congregation) if necessary. Because a ward will include a variety of individuals, many primary relationships may be formed even in urban settings. Thus, the Mormon who is active in the Church may have a ready-made community that will support him in his practice of the Mormon religion. Studies indicate that marrying within the Mormon Church is a strong boundary maintenance activity among Mormons (Beckstrand, 1971), while other findings demonstrate that having a high percentage of Mormon friends is associated with having more orthodox attitudes and beliefs (Mortenson, 1972; Anderson, 1968; Allred, 1971).

As the Church membership increases, however, this community feeling may be more difficult to maintain. Until recently, Mormons were white, middle-class Americans, usually from Utah or adjoining states. In a few minutes of conversation, newly acquainted Mormons were likely to find that they were connected through mutual friends or associates or that they held similar positions in the Church. This, plus the factors previously mentioned, has traditionally promoted strong bonds between Mormons. As the Church membership becomes more diverse, such bonds may become more tenuous.

R E F E R E N C E S

Albrecht, Stan L., and Bradford Chappell. 1977. "Intergenerational Contact and Alienation in Elderly Mormon Families," in Phillip R. Kunz (ed.), *The Mormon Family.* Family Research Center, Provo, UT: Brigham Young University, pp. 62–77.
Albrecht, Stan L., Howard M. Bahr, and Bruce A. Chadwick. 1979. "Changing Fam-

ily and Sex Roles: An Assessment of Age Differences," *Journal of Marriage and the Family,* 41:41–50

Allen, Jame B., and Glen M. Leonard. 1976. *The Story of the Latter Day Saints.* Salt Lake City, UT: Deseret Book Company.

Allred, Garth L. 1971. "A Study of Expressed Attitudes of Selected L.D.S. Youth Regarding Social Trends," unpublished Masters thesis, Brigham Young University.

Anderson, Charles H. 1968. "Religious Communality Among White Protestants, Catholics and Mormons," *Social Forces,* 46 (June): 501–508.

Anderson, Nels, 1937. "The Mormon Family," *American Sociological Review,* 2 (October): 601–608.

Arrington, Leonard J. 1958. *Great Basin Kingdom.* Cambridge, MA: Harvard University Press.

Bacon, Mary R. 1964. "Comparative Study of Expressive and Instrumental Concerns of Homemakers in Wasatch County," unpublished paper, Brigham Young University.

Bahr, Howard M. 1979. "The Declining Destinctiveness of Utah's Working Women," Discussion Paper Series, Family Research Institute, Brigham Young University.

Bahr, Stephen J., and Howard M. Bahr. 1977. "Religion and Family Roles: A Comparison of Catholic, Mormon and Protestant Families," in Phillip R. Kunz (ed.), *The Mormon Family.* Family Research Center Brigham Young University, pp. 45–61.

Beckstrand, Therald C. 1971. "Religiously Endogamous and Religiously Exogamous Courtships as Perceived by Male College Students," unpublished paper, Brigham Young University.

Black Marybeth R. 1969. "The Relationships Between Wives' Simfam Relative Effective Power Scores and Husbands' Marital Satisfaction," unpublished paper, Brigham Young University.

Bowers, Donald W., and Donald W. Hastings. 1970. "Childspacing and Wife's Employment Status Among 1940–41 University of Utah Graduates," *Social Science Journal,* 7:125–136.

Brown, Kenneth J. 1961. "Church Participation as a Factor Associated with the Educational Aspirations of Youth in Three Central Utah Counties," unpublished paper, Brigham Young University.

Bunker, Gary L., and Davis Bitton 1979. "Polygamous Eyes: A Note on Mormon Physiognomy," *Dialogue: A Journal of Mormon Thought,* 12(6): 114–119.

Bush, Lester E. 1976a. "Birth Control Among the Mormons: Introduction to an Insistent Question," *Dialogue: A Journal of Mormon Thought,* 10:12–44.

———. 1976b. "Mormon Elder's Wafers: Images of Mormon Virility in Patent Medicine Ads" *Dialogue: A Journal of Mormon Thought,* 10:89–93.

———.1979. "A Peculiar People: The Physiological Aspects of Mormonism 1950–1975," *Dialogue: A Journal of Mormon Thought,* 10:12–44. 12:61–83.

Bushman, Claudia Lauper. 1971. "Women in Dialogue: An Introduction," *Dialogue: A Journal of Mormon Thought,* 6 (Summer):5–8.

Campbell, Eugene E., and Bruce L. Campbell 1978. "Divorce Among Mormon Polygamists: Extent and Explanations," *Utah Historical Quarterly,* 46:4–23.

Cannon, John Q., Jr. 1967. "Traditional Family Ideology of University Students," unpublished paper, Brigham Young University.

Cannon, Kenneth L., and Seymour Steed. 1972. "Relationship Between Occupational

Level, Religious Commitment, Age of Bride at Marriage, and Divorce Rate for L.D.S. Marriages," in *Developing a Marriage Relationship.* Provo, UT: Brigham Young University Press, pp. 285–92.

Christensen, Harold T. 1972. "Stress Points in Mormon Family Culture," *Dialogue: A Journal of Mormon Thought,* 7 (Winter); 20–34.

———. 1977. "Some Next Steps in Mormon Family Research," in Phillip R. Kunz (ed.), *The Mormon Family.* Family Research Center, Provo, UT: Brigham Young University, pp. 1–12.

Christensen Harold T., and C.F. Gregg. 1970. "Changing Sex Norms in America and Scandinavia," *Journal of Marriage and the Family* (November), p. 626.

Christensen, Talmage. 1965. "Exploring the Golden Years of Marriage," unpublished paper, Brigham Young University.

Christenson, Robert A. 1970. "The Effects of Reward and Expert Power on The Distribution of Influence in Mormon Couples," unpublished paper, Brigham Young University.

Christopherson, Victor A. 1956. "An Investigation of Patriarchal Authority in the Mormon Family," *Marriage and Family Living,* 18 (November):328–333.

———. 1963. "Is the Mormon Family Becoming More Democratic?" in Blaine Porter (ed.), *The Latter-day Saint Family.* Salt Lake City, UT: Deseret Book Company, pp. 317–38.

Cook, Carole, I.C. 1966. "The Crisis of Parenthood as Experienced by L.D.S. Couples with One Child," unpublished paper, Brigham Young University.

Dolgin, Janet L. 1974. "Latter-Day Sense and Substance," in Irving I. Zaretsky and Mark P. Leone (eds.), *Religious Movements in Contempory America.* Princeton: Princeton University Press. 519–546.

Ellsworth, S. George. 1951. "History of Mormon Missions in the United States and Canada, 1830–1860," unpublished paper, University of California at Berkeley.

Featherstone, Vaughan J. 1975. "The Savior's Program for Care of the Aged," *Conference Reports* (October).

Galliher, John F., and Linda Basilick. 1979. "Utah's Liberal Drug Laws: Structural Foundations and Triggering Events," *Social Problems,* 26:284–297.

Hagerty, Everett Louis. 1961. "An Exploratory Study of the Effects of the Divorce Process and Post-Divorce Readjustment on LDS Persons," unpublished paper, Brigham Young University.

Hastings, Donald, Charles H. Reynolds, and Ray Canning. 1972. "Mormonism and Birth Planning: The Discrepancy Between Church Authorities' Teachings and Lay Attitudes," *Population Studies,* 26:19–28.

Hatch, Jerry Lee. 1968. "Patterns of Affection in Dating Approved by LDS Students," unpublished paper, Brigham Young University.

Hill, Marvin S. 1978. "The Rise of the Mormon Kingdom of God," in Richard Poll (ed.), *Utah's History.* Provo, UT: Brigham Young University Press.

Ivins, Stanley. 1956. "Notes of Mormon Polygamy," *Western Humanities Review,* 10:224–239.

Kimball, Heber C. 1858. "Temples and Endowments," *Journal of Discourses,* 5:22.

Kimball, Spencer W. 1976. "Marriage the Proper Way," *The New Era* (February), pp. 4–7.

Kunz, Philip R. 1963. "Religious Influences on Parental Discipline and Achievement Demands," *Marriage and Family Living,* 24 (May): 224–225.

Kunz, Philip, R., and Merlin B. Brinkerhoff. 1970. "Growth in Religious Organizations: A Comparative Study," *Social Science,* 45(4):215–222

Lake, Bruce M. 1963. "A Measure of Attitude Change Toward Courtship and Marriage," unpublished paper, University of Utah.

Larsen, Robert E. 1967. "Factors in the Acceptance and Adoption of Family Home Evening in the L.D.S. Church: A Study in Planned Change," unpublished Masters thesis, Brigham Young University.

Leone, Mark P. 1974. "The Economic Basis for the Evolution of Mormon Religion," in Irving I. Zaretsky and Mark P. Leone (eds.), *Religious Movements in Contempory America.* Princeton: Princeton University Press, pp. 722–766.

Litwak, Eugene. 1960. "Occupational Mobility and Extended Family Cohesion," *American Sociological Review,* 25:9–21.

Marlow, Roy H. 1968. "Development of Marital Dissatisfaction of Mormon College Couples over the Early Stages of the Family Life Cycle," unpublished paper, Brigham Young University.

Mauss, Armand L. 1969. "Dimensions of Religious Diffection," *Review of Religious Research,* 10: 128–135.

———. 1972a. "Moderation in All Things: Political and Social Outlooks of Modern Urban Mormons," *Dialogue: A Journal of Mormon Thought,* 7 (Spring):57–64.

———. 1972b. "Saints, Cities, and Secularism: Religious Attitudes and Behavior of Modern Urban Mormons," *Dialogue: A Journal of Mormon Thought,* 7 (Summer):8–27.

———. 1976. "Shall the Youth of Zion Falter? Mormon Youth and Sex: A Two City Comparison," *Dialogue: A Journal of Mormon Thought,* 10:82–83.

McBride, Gary P. 1963. "Marriage Role Expectations of Latter-day Saint Adolescents in Utah County," unpublished paper, Brigham Young University.

McKay, David O. 1969. "Saving the Family," *Improvement Era* (June), pp. 2–5.

Merrill, Stan W., and Evan T. Peterson. 1972. "Some Aspects of Family Size: Stress and Utility," *Institute of Genealogical Studies: Working Papers,* Brigham Young University (4) (August).

Miller, Don LeRoy. 1969. "A Study of Factors Which May Influence Attitudes of L.D.S. Teen-agers Towards Family Home Evening," unpublished paper, Brigham Young University.

Mitchell, Sidney, and Evan T. Peterson. 1972. "A Longitudinal Study of Factors Associated with Divorce Among Mormons," *Institute of Genealogical Studies: Working Papers,* Brigham Young University.

Mortenson, Ramah P. 1972. "Affectional Attitudes and Behavior Patterns of Selected L.D.S. Students from Universities and Colleges in Utah," unpublished paper, Brigham Young University.

Mote, Herbert I. 1961. "The Wife's Role in the Family: A Comparative Study of Three Educational Levels with a Male and Female Group at Each Level," unpublished paper, Brigham Young University.

Mulder, William. 1957. *Homeward to Zion.* Minneapolis: University of Minnesota Press.

Nelson, Lowry. 1952. *The Mormon Village.* Salt Lake City, UT: University of Utah Press.

Nuttall, Paul E. 1959. "Comparison of L.D.S. Couples Married in the Temple in Respect to Marital Adjustment, Feelings of Security and Empathy" unpublished Masters thesis, Brigham Young University.

O'Dea, Thomas F. 1957. *The Mormons.* Chicago: University of Chicago Press.

———. 1972. "Sources of Strain in Mormon History Reconsidered," in Marvin S. Hill and James B. Allen (eds.), *Mormonism and American Culture.* New York: Harper & Row, pp. 147–167.

Peterson, Erlend D. 1971. "Attitudes Concerning Birth Control and Abortion as Related to L.D.S. Religiosity of Brigham Young University Students," unpublished paper, Brigham Young University.

Peterson, Evan T. 1977. "Parent–Adolescent Relationships in the Mormon Family," in Philip R. Kunz (ed.), *The Mormon Family.* Family Research Center, Provo, UT: Brigham Young University. 108–115.

Peterson, Jack W. 1969. "A Study of Selected Family Background Factors Influencing Women to Marry Outside of the L.D.S. Church," unpublished paper. Brigham Young University.

Pratt, Orson. 1954. *Defense of Polgamy* (as cited in K. Young, *Isn't One Wife Enough?*). New York: Henry Holt & Co.

Priesthood Bulletin. 1973. Vol. 9. No. 1.

Rollins, Boyd C. 1958. "Factors Influencing the Decision of Latter-day Saint Youths Concerning the Selection of Temple or Non-temple Type of Marriage Ceremony," unpublished paper, Brigham Young University.

Seggar, John F., and Reed H. Blake. 1970. "Post-Joining Non-Participation: An Exploratory Study of Convert Inactivity," *Review of Religious Research*, 11:204–209.

Sillitoe, Linda, and Paul Swenson. 1980. "A Moral Issue," *Utah Holiday*, 9:18–34.

Skolnick, M., L. Bean, P. May, V. Arbon, K. De Nevhs, and P. Cartwright. 1978. "Mormon Demographic History I. Nuptiality and Fertility of Once-Married Couples," *Population Studies*, 32(1):5–19.

Smith, James, E., and Phillip R. Kunz. 1976. "Polygyny and Fertility in Nineteenth Century America," *Population Studies*, 30:30.

Smith, Joseph. 1846. *History of the Church.*

Smith, Joseph F., Sr. 1917. *The Relief Society Magazine*, 4:318.

Smith, Joseph Fielding. 1966. *Doctrines of Salvation*, 13th ed. Salt Lake City, UT: Bookcraft.

Smith, Wilford E. 1959. "The Urban Threat to Mormon Norms." *Rural Sociology*, 24:355–361.

Snow, Eliza R. 1971. "Sketch of My Life: Reminisances of One of Joseph Smith's Plural Wives." (ed. Spencer J. Palmer), *Brigham Young University Studies*, 12:129–130.

Sussman, Marvin B. 1963. "The Help Pattern in the Middle Class Family," *American Sociological Review*, 18:22–28.

Taylor, Samuel W. 1972. "The Second Coming of Santa Claus: Christmas in a Polygamous Family," *Dialogue: A Journal of Mormon Thought*, 7:7–10.

Thornton, Arland. 1979. "Religion and Fertility: The Case of Mormonism," *Journal of Marriage and the Family*, 40:131–142.

Twain, Mark. 1872. *Roughing It!* Hartford, CT: American Pub. Co.

U.S. Bureau of the Census. 1976. *Statistical Abstract of the United States*, 97th edition. Washington, DC: U.S. Government Printing Office, p. 71.

Utah Department of Health. 1976. Annual Report on Marriage and Divorce. Salt Lake City, UT.

Warenski, Marilyn. 1978. *Patriarchs and Politics: The Plight of the Mormon Woman.* New York: McGraw-Hill.

Whitton, Nathan L. 1928. "Response of a Mormon Village Population to the Reli-

415

gious Institutions as Measured by Attendance at Meetings," unpublished Masters thesis, Brigham Young University.

Wise, Genevieve M., and Don C. Carter. 1965. "A Definition of the Role of Homemaker by Two Generations of Women," *Journal of Marriage and the Family,* 27(4) (November):531–532.

Wise, Jeffery and Spencer J. Condie. 1975. "Intergenerational Fertility Throughout Four Generations," *Social Biology,* 22:144–150.

Young, Brigham. 1925. *Discourses of Brigham Young Arranged by John A. Widtsoe.* Salt Lake City, UT: Desert Book Co.

Young, Kimball. 1954. *Isn't One Wife Enough?* New York: Henry Holt and Co.

The American Ethnic Family: Protean and Adaptive

Most edited works in sociology are without a final, concluding chapter. Whatever the reasons—editor's fatigue, the press of publication schedules, the difficulties of summarizing and integrating materials not one's own, or perhaps the paralyzing suspicion that nothing can be concluded and that no summing of the parts into a greater whole is possible—many scholars have closed up shop with the last contributed chapter to their book. All along we, the present editors, have hoped to write the kind of conclusion that would leave the reader with a somewhat better comprehension of the common, parallel, and more or less shared experiences and contingencies of ethnic life in America, particularly as it gets institutional expression in the ethnic family.

However, rather than engaging in the space-consuming task of summarizing the life history of each of the 15 ethnic families already compactly presented in the book, we have chosen to deal with them first in historical perspective and then more or less analytically, searching for propositions or general statements that might help the reader get some perspective on ethnic family diversity without doing too much violence to the historical uniqueness that each author has taken such pains to depict. Finally, we will attempt a brief discussion of some of the problems that have merged or loom on the horizon as recent social changes bear on current ethnic family organization and lifestyle.

CHAPTER SEVENTEEN
BY
ROBERT W. HABENSTEIN
AND CHARLES H. MINDEL

THE HISTORICAL BACKGROUND

In the century after 1830 about 35 to 40 million immigrants came to America. They came crowded in sailing vessels whose unsanitary conditions and disease-ridden voyages gave rise to the term "fever ships" (Feldstein and Costello, 1974:1–141). The west coast received Chinese by the tens of thousands—"coolie" labor for the building of the transcontinental railroads and for working in the mines. Hispanic peoples were added as America "gained" Texas, and later French Canadians sifted across the northeast border into the New England states.

That abysmal chapter of our nation's history, the two centuries of enslavement and shipping African black peoples to America for plantation and other labor-intensive enterprises, precedes the great ethnic migration. But exploitation of blacks continues throughout this time, emancipation marking a political but not significant shift in economic circumstances as black migrants move toward cities to compete with a growing white urban proletariat.

Scholars have subdivided this century of inpouring peoples into the period 1830–1882 as that of the "new," or early, and 1882–1930, as the "old" immigration. The ten million who made up the first period were predominantly Irish Catholics, Germans, and Scandinavians. The ethnic composition changed after 1882, as did the character of the country's economy, and the great influx of southern, eastern, and central European migrants mostly of peasant stock coincided with the rapid surge of industrial and urban growth in America. No longer needed to build the railroads or settle the virgin land of the western states, the new arrivals, Bohemians, Slovaks, Polish, Russians and Russian/Polish Jews, Czechs, and Italians were directed to the factories and sweatshops of America's slum-ridden cities (Feldstein and Costello, 1974:3). Also, after 1882 federal control replaced that of the states, and immigration became a matter of increasing public concern, eventuating in a social movement after World War I to "Americanize" all immigrants (Hartmann, 1948) and at the same time to change immigration laws (1921, 1924) to the virtual exclusion of all ethnic peoples other than those of Nordic and Anglo-Saxon stock.

The denigration of Asians, Jews, Slavs, and others of southern and central European ancestry resulted to some extent in their sharing the stigma heaped on blacks, enslaved or emancipated; American Indians, decimated, subjugated, and virtually driven into reservations; and Mexicans, whose exploitation for an expanding labor force in the southwest gave rise to a long-lasting form of peonage. It is against this historical backdrop that the authors have chronicled the experiences of the specific ethnic groups, from which groups in most cases they are descended, and on whose family and kinship organization they have focused their scholarly energies and attention.

The Initial Ethnic Family in America

Initially, the ethnic family of mid- and late-19th-century America represents a transplanted, adaptive, primary social unit engaged in the business of conserving and rebuilding ethnic culture, and through a distinctive socialization process, of creating new generations in the image of the old. In its typical form, which might vary somewhat from group to group, we find the patterning of structural characteristics, the operation of distinctive principles of organization, and a set of discernible functions.

Somewhat static, stationary, and resistant to geographical mobility, the initial ethnic family remains kin-involved and community-situated. Families and kin generate neighborhoods, which combine into communities, perhaps better identified as colonies, or in Gans' terminology, particularly appropriate for city-dwelling migrants, "urban villages." Once established, ethnic colonies become known as collective refuges and along with kinship ties attract fellow immigrant countrymen.

STRUCTURE. Prototypically, the family is large, or becomes large, with nuclear units of husband, wife, and children embedded in households comprised of some extended kin and possibly a boarder, some nonrelated compatriot. The norm is three generations under one roof. Family organization consists in the more or less habituated role enactments of the members, with executive command in the male head, management skills developed by the wife and mother, and a division of labor that includes all members of the household.

The initial ethnic family in America, then, is most likely "father-headed and mother-centered." But the long hours of arduous work away from home, often compounded by long journeys to work, meant that many if not most heads of households were limited in their contacts with the family and might remain important yet shadowy figures in the socialization experiences of the children. The reverse, of course, might occur if the family set up a shop or other type of small family enterprise. In such cases the family members would be thrown into almost continuous interaction, the authority becoming more diffuse as personality factors of wife, children, and husband as well would interact with cultural values. In any event, family loyalty, respect for the family name, the adjudicating of squabbles and conflicts within households, or perhaps in the context of extended kin circles, and a rather pronounced authoritarianism were typical organizational features that kept the head of the household in a dominant position.

It is axiomatic that ethnic groups maintain their distinctive character through rules prescribing and proscribing marriage, residence, kinship obligations, and to some extent, division of labor. Endogamy, marrying within the group, is a normative prescription, and as a mode of achieving kinship integration, cousin marriages may also be allowed, or even preferred. For ethnic groups suffering discrimination, exploitation, and sometimes threats to life and property, kinship organization, with its mutual and reciprocal aid system, has operated as a social mechanism for survival. Patrilocality, endogamy, service of daughter-in-law to the mother, some form of dowry system that offered a modicum of protection to the marrying-in wife, and a wide network of kin obligations, all help in structuring and giving viability to a family-centered existence in a new world of strange persons, external institutions, and unforeseeable contingencies.

Uncles, aunts, and cousins interpenetrate the social life of family members, serving as sources for affection, support, advice, and to a considerable extent, control. Mother's sister becomes at times mother's surrogate, father's brother the "dutch uncle" for nieces and nephews. The family remains adult-centered and maintains a place in the sun for the elderly, whose contributions to the household continue so long as they are able to help, and who serve as storehouses of wisdom, legend, and lore, cautionary and exemplary tales all part of the cultural heritage.

CHAIN MIGRATION AND TRANSPORTATION. The initial ethnic family in America cannot, however, be seen as a simple transplant, a family system lifted out of its Old World context and deposited intact in the New. Few if any complete family systems, with all personnel included, would have made the journey. The first moves might be made by single young men seeking opportunities and prospects for better work, jobs that would permit the saving of money for an eventual return to the home community. Or as was very often the case, the young husband would leave first, hoping to be able to bring his family across the ocean as soon as possible—which might turn out to be years rather than months. When intact nuclear families made the crossing, some members of the extended family group might, if able, come to swell the group. But in the context of chain migration, single men, women, families, or parts of families emmigrated in some sort of sequence that seemed to make sense to the family members involved at the time. Thus, families sought to reassemble in the image of family systems left behind. Often single men did not return but married and settle down into an ethnic community. The most important generalization to be made, perhaps, is that immigrants initially, and at least through the first generation, clung to the same family orientation in the New World as they had in the Old, and that this orientation would play a central role in the structuring of the initial New World ethnic family. The family as a primary unit of social organization, as a source of identity and a repository for men's strongest affections and loyalties, could not easily leave the minds of men as they exchanged living in one land for another.

FUNCTIONAL DEPENDENCE AND INDEPENDENCE. Yet the exigencies and contingencies of the new life were as many as they were threatening. The ethnic family was in the first instance a refuge *par excellence,* a place of first and sometimes last resort within which coping responses to threat might be traditional, virtually automatic, and unthinking; or they might be tempered with the realization that things are done differently in America, and that adaptation and accommodation must also be part of the struggle for survival.

The economic factor could hardly have been more important, yet the responses of the ethnic groups and families were never completely captured by nor prefigured in the economic stimulus. The labor-intensive needs of a rapidly developing rational and amoral capitalist economy produced new imperatives, functionaries, and roles. Immigrants were subject to the influence of the recruiting agent, the labor boss, the ethnic labor contractor, the hired strikebreaker, and even the national-guard trooper, all working in the service of a system that had little regard for, if it did not stand in opposition to, the urban villager of peasant stock with his traditional family-centered mores. Yet the economy's demands, no matter how generally they came to be met, never determined in what specific form and in what actual ways ethnic family members would respond. Opportunities might be taken advantage of immediately to dig ditches, carry hod, build, transport, or engage in protective or personal services. An industrial complex would draw many into mills and factories. Nevertheless, the decisions to respond, the strategies of coping and surviving, were ethnic-specific, most often made in a family context or with implications for the family as a first consideration.[1]

Italians in Buffalo at the turn of the century, as Virginia Yans McLaughlin demonstrates, showed "a definite preference for occupations that permitted minimal strain on their traditional family arrangements" (Gordon, 1973:137). Females worked, but only at jobs that could be done in the home—sewing, basting, and artificial flower making; while first-generation Italian males preferred occupations in the fringes of Buffalo's industrial structure "where customary family relationships could be and were effectively maintained" [McLaughlin, in Gordon (1973:137)].

Another more sweeping example of the family's strength in channeling and mediating occupational behavior is found in Richard Sennett's innovative historical research on later 19th century middle-class families in Chicago's Union Park. Rather than pushing the members outward into society to achieve social mobility and societal recognition, the families closed in on themselves, withdrawing to some extent from the fluctuating, potentially dangerous (anarchists were thought to be everywhere) world about them into the sanctuary of their homes. In the process, the father, who does not aggressive-

---

[1]A friend of one editor recounts how after receiving a Ph.D. at Columbia in the late 1960s he worked one year more at his Italian father's family-operated, small grovery store even though there were five other less highly educated brothers available to help out!

ly set a role model as the socially mobile head of the family "on the make," finds his authority eroding, and at the same time the wife and mother's role expands. The result is a form of more or less mother-centered middle-class family, going nowhere in particular, sheltered, nuclear, privatistic, and emanating a "full respectability" [Sennett, in Gordon (1973:111–134)].

IDEOLOGICAL CONTENT. Beliefs tend toward the concrete rather than the abstract. The physical and social world is personalized, suffused with the sacred and a body of folk beliefs expressed in folk sayings, discrete aphorisms, and maxims providing explanation, meaning, and guidance to everyday life. The focal concerns of the initial ethnic family are survival, acquisition of necessities, and, if possible, developing resources against hard times. Kinship, family name, family honor, good marriage, sociability among one's relatives and familiars, wariness in dealing with outsiders who may or may not prove worthy of trust, complete the constellation of focal concerns that consitute early ethnic family ideology.

COHESION AND INTEGRATION. The initial ethnic family develops unity through division of labor and attendant habituated role playing, and significantly through family rituals, ceremonies, and group participation in sacred and pragmatic activities. Holidays, festivals, religious observances, storytelling, with much reference to magic, spirits, and the mysteries of the unknown, draw family members closer and serve to keep alive meanings that undergird the everyday more prosaic practices.

Gatherings of related families for marriages, baptisms, funerals, and other rites of passage are as important as they are ubiquitous. Out-group threats, perceived or real, contribute to in-group solidarity. Such ethnic families have it as an article of faith that they must first and always protect their own. Philanthropy, social and public service conceived of in the abstract, and effort expended for which few if any immediate concrete rewards can be foreseen are all rejected out of hand. The family, kin, quasikin bonded through godparenthood, blood vows, and the like remain insular, resistant to the society of institutional and voluntary associations that mark the structural rearrangements and *gesellschaft* bonds of a developed industrial society with its impersonal market economy.

Institutional Relationships of Early Ethnic Families

Ethnicity presupposes antecedent culture: traditions, symbols, meanings, and practices. But the patterns of behavior that are rooted in and express the emotions, beliefs, and ideals of any ethnic group do not exist inside a social vacu-

422

um. Particularly is this the case where ethnic groups formerly separated by long-secured boundaries are thrown into contiguity, if they are not actually mixed together, in urban milieus. In these cases, local institutions arise; or those that are already present in antecedent Old World societal organization of the ethnic peoples are adopted to ensure some form of cultural and social survival.

The initial ethnic family, then, may further be viewed as a *primary* social unity embedded in a constellation of indigenously developed or adapted limited-purpose local institutions. For example, the ethnic boarding house sheltered, fed, and offered its residents some psychological security, functioning at best as a surrogate family household, at worst as minimum shelter for unattached migrants and sojourners in a land they did not intend to make their own. Since immigrant families often included a lodger, there might be some overlap of function, but for the most part the ethnic family and the ethnic boarding house served complementary purposes.

The neighborhood-tavern relation to the initial ethnic family is more complex. Male members of the family might look to the tavern as a refuge, a source of conviviality with age mates, an interesting social milieu in which the long hours of arduous work, the vexations and troubles, and the coarseness of daily life might be forgotten or put aside. Drunkenness was not invented in ethnic taverns, but by the same token it was not an unexpected nor surprising happenstance. Family visits to neighborhood taverns, on the other hand, as a form of family ritual would likely contribute to cohesiveness and tone up family morale. The services of the saloonkeeper beyond serving drinks to patrons might well include tendering advice and information, and often the keeping of savings for fellow ethnics who found commercial banks strange, if not forbidding.

The settlement house mixed social uplift, training in self-help, and instruction by example with sociability and groupish activities. The family, however, remains the arbiter or medium through which the new learning must pass muster. Along with the boarding house and the tavern the settlement house operates socially at a secondary level of community organization. Labor bosses, on the other hand, span a continuum of relationship to labor gang members. Father figures, operating in highly personalized and particularistic contexts marked one pole; at the other were men whose power over the job could lead to anything from petty tyranny to total and unmerciful exploitation.

Finally, labor unions extended ethnic power but in the course of work-force convolutions interethnic solidarities or accommodations would bring about secondary levels of association. Ethnicity then became only one of many factors in what was eventually to become large craft guilds or industrywide union organizations. In any event family involvement and interchange of influence with, upon, or from unions might be close and supportive, that is, with workers meeting in each others homes at the earlier stage and later separated by formal organizational structures and more universalistic ideologies as big unions rise to meet the challenge of even bigger corporate power.

The Ethnic Family in Modern Perspective

Each of the ethnic families portrayed in this work has its distinctive social biography. By their having taken up existence in America at a particular point in history, and consequently having been exposed to the forces and elements of societal organization extant at that time, the life course of each will not only vary, but will vary in relation to the historical experiences of the others. The composite picture, similar to an automobile race in which some drivers would lap others and in turn be lapped, so that only by each driver's time being kept separately can the winner be determined, is extremely complex. In all candor it must be admitted that the patterning of experiences of the earlier ethnic groups, particularly for those who came during the previous century, seems easier to discern, label, and typify. Generalizations about *the* ethnic family of the present time are not impossible, but at every turn we would be first to note exceptions and to point out that intraethnic differences further compound the problem set by differences that separate one kind of ethnic family from another.

RESIDUAL CHARACTERISTICS OF THE INITIAL ETHNIC FAMILY. Currently, ethnic families in America, excluding Cubans and Vietnamese, are no longer transplanted social entities but have become integral to a distinctive type of pluralist society whose internal differences are more likely to be home grown than imported. The anticipated assimilation of the immigrant groups and the merging of Old World traits into one cultural whole is by no means complete; to the contrary, there are strong recent arguments contending that ethnics, particularly of southern and eastern European provenance, have all the while remained "unmeltable" and are in fact capable of a renascence whereby identities partially lost or obscured by the passage of time may be recovered (Novak, 1973; Greeley, 1969, 1974; Glazer and Moynihan, 1970). While we will have more comment on this matter at the end of the chapter, our present judgment is that although the spirit of ethnicity and ethnic consciousness may vary rather significantly from time to time, many indubitably important changes in ethnic family structure and function *have* taken place, and that when these changes are juxtaposed against the model of the initial ethnic family developed above, it can be argued that what

424

remains is an institutional *residuum*. This residuum of what was a discernible historical type of family in our opinion remains of undeniable social import, but it is neither as unitary and viable as the "unmeltable ethnics" position holds, nor is it a mere vestigial remnant of some bygone set of rapidly fading institutional arrangements, as the assimilationists have wanted us to believe over the past half century.

STATICITY AND MOBILITY. The modern ethnic family remains to a considerable extent place-centered. Geographic mobility in America is high, and it is true that we are indeed a nation of movers. Moreover, today's ethnic family, particularly in urban centers, finds itself subject to ecological and social forces that make clinging to a homestead around which a body of symbols, images, and memories have long developed increasingly problematical. As always, one or more members of the younger generation may be encouraged to strike out for a new location in which prospects for a better livelihood seem possible, or likely. But no ethnic family (except the Gypsy) uproots itself as a matter of course. Home ownership has always been a central value to American ethnics, particularly because saving for, buying, and owning a home, often a dream in their countries of origin, has always been feasible, and thus transformable into a social reality. But, as intimated, there are many contingencies associated with maintaining local community residence in urban milieus: impinging and threatening invasions of other ethnic groups, physical deterioration of neighborhood, declining economic life chances, reduced political power—the Polish in Detroit as a prime example—the demise, flight, or structural change of local institutions, the erosion of civility, that indispensable product of interethnic accommodation, and the suburban movement which in recent times suggests a species of mass collective behavior. All these, and the reader can certainly add more, combine in inner cities in which ethnic colonies traditionally took roots to lay a heavy burden upon the home-centered, place-minded, ethnic family.

The familiar response, migration, through succession, that is, in a slow centripetal movement with families of one ethnic group taking up residence areas of other ethnic groups; or by jumping over these areas to the suburbs; or yet by migrating to more distant places, remains the most viable solution for ethnic youth seeking in the acceptable American style to found their own homes away, but usually not too far away, from the family homestead. For the adults, the old, and the very old, however, mobility with attendant destruction of established neighborhood folkways and the attenuation of kinship and sociability networks, moving out can only mean leaving a lot of one's life behind. Enmeshed in a welter of social and ecological contingencies, the established adult ethnic family, having committed itself to stay in or near the family homestead, can be expected to close in on itself, to resist the blandishments of mobility, to maintain as best it can personal and social ties, and to aid in the structuring of the group solidarity necessary to forestall rapid and destructive neighborhood change. In times of crises, of course, when a "state-of-seige" mentality suffuses an embattled ethnic enclave, efforts to move out inevitably produce charges of disloyalty to one's ethnic heritage; thus, family, neighborhood, and community values converge into a united front against potential leavers.

STRUCTURE. With the passing years, the established ethnic families become smaller in members, the nuclear units of husband, wife, and children become more visible and free-standing, family households are less likely to have three generations under one roof, and other nonrelated members such as boarders become almost nonexistent. Yet in all respects except the last these changes have been at a slower pace than for families in the society at large. Extended family organization, for example, continues to remain important both as a back-up system of social support and as a resource for services, sponsorship, and often financial assistance. Aged parents still find shelter in children's homes when independent living no longer becomes feasible—at least until impairments dictate the necessity for hospitalization or nursing-home care. For many ethnic families the latter is anathema, and resistance to institutionalization of their elderly remains strong.

Meanwhile, the "father-headed and mother-centered" ethnic family has not disappeared even though the roles of both parents, particularly the father's, are becoming less institutionalized. The area of negotiation of internal family matters has expanded at the same time and values of companionship and spontaneity are emerging where once controls and restrictive norms held families together somewhat in a state of compression. But in spite of all this, the truly "equalitarian," "companionship," "democratic," or "open" family is at least one full step beyond the ethnic family as we discern it in the chapters of this work. Granted that street culture, peer groups, nonlocal institutions, and the evocations of mass popular culture create values and structure sentiments that work at cross purposes to ethnic-family cohesion, the total effect of these influences does not seem to jell toward the creation of a new mode or system of family organization. For rather than disorganized or resolutely organized, the ethnic family appears to be somewhat unorganized, susceptible to strain in matters involving the acceptance and enactment of roles, distribution of authority, and recognition of individual rights—drifting rather than headed in any easily chartable direction.

By and large, rules of marriage have tended to be prescriptive rather than proscriptive, with emphasis placed on categories of persons acceptable, even preferred as potential marriage partners. But parents do little if any match-making; they may have strong marriage preferences for mates for their children, but to be effective these must be applied through indirection. Head-on clashes with children over marriage partners are to be avoided, although feelings on the matter need not be hidden. Ethnic endogamy remains a norm, as does marriage within the same religion, but again controls either through sanctions or rewards are at best only partially effective. The chances remain about even that youth will marry within their own ethnic group.

Uncles, aunts, and cousins still continue as important relatives, but the locus of family control seems to be shifting away from them and to a lesser extent from the parents. Socialization of children includes traditional practices, often involving and reinforced by close relatives, mixed with the prescriptions found in the popular culture, in books, manuals, and an infinite number of articles in newspapers, pulp and slick journals. Ethnic families have, then, multiple foci: Parents, grandparents, children, relatives, all find themselves ambivalently involved in each other's personalities; but variation, chance, external factors, the easing of social controls, and a somewhat heightened ego consciousness of all principals make for a blurred rather than a clearly discernible product.

FUNCTIONAL DEPENDENCE AND INDEPENDENCE. Many of the contingencies, even threats to the physical existence of the early arriving ethnics, have over the past century been disposed of or otherwise dealt with successfully. In part through their own efforts, but also in great measure reinforced by a national ideology stipulating an equal chance for all immigrant groups to survive, even prosper, ethnic groups in America have never found themselves permanently locked into a rigidly stratified caste system. Many local institutions—ethnic boarding homes, taverns, groceries, unions, protective associations, cultural organizations, and the like—have either grown and become societywide (the Bank of America, an excellent example), incorporated into broader ranging organizations or continue to exist on a marginal basis. The back-up or bulwarking function of these entities has meanwhile shifted appreciably.

The modern ethnic family becomes much less a refuge and creator of protective, educational, and religious functions. The socialization process has been shared with external, increasingly abstract, and bureaucratic agencies. Within the past several decades millions of federal dollars insinuated into community affairs have had as their goal the development of more viable systems of community organization and the strengthening of the family. Data on the success or failure of literally dozens of plans, demonstration projects, and programs aimed at activizing local citizenry have yet to be decisively analyzed and evaluated. Our perspective, which emphasizes both differentiation and patterning, is not primarily evaluative. We can generalize, on the basis of the data of the contributing authors, that modern as opposed to earlier ethnic families will be likely to have fewer uninterrupted hours together, will be less likely to operate as a social unity, and less likely to keep its members on a short tether, particularly as peer groups, school affairs, and age-specific mass entertainment provide strong inducements for family members to go their own way. Certainly the family is less likely to operate as an economic unity. Paying board is now a rarity, as working youth squirrel away their earnings for purchases in markets that cater to and help define their age groups or save toward acquiring the standard package of household furnishings and other commodities that become part and parcel of their marriages— the business of such sales and acquisitions is estimated at 15 billion dollars a year!

After World War II the educational and training assistance provided service veterans began an enormous expansion of education that was further exacerbated by Sputnik and the subsequent national concern for this country's retaining world leadership in research and technology. And while the initial response was commensurate with the promise that education was infinitely expansible, with the greater payoffs correlated with increasing exposure to education for management, technicians and the professions, the counterculture youth in the 1960s, continuing to the end of the war in Vietnam, questioned both the methods and goals of education and rejected the traditional expectation that one's major portion of his waking life be allocated to participation in the work force.

The role of the ethnic family in all this remains somewhat obscure, but it appears that ethnic family norms have continued to stress the need for ethnic youth to prepare themselves for life with a vocation, a "good steady job," that only as much education as is consistent with this goal is deemed necessary (Jewish families apparently an exception), and that youth should settle down fairly early in life to job, marriage, and homemaking. Moreover, despite the long-held and deep-seated patriotism found in ethnic families, military service has become an object of considerable ambivalence, particularly since the new wars have lost their simple black and white character, and also because the lower the socioeconomic status of the ethnics involved, the higher their apparent casualty rates. In addition, that ethnics, particularly those of darker pigmented skins, are overrepresented on the rolls of the unemployed, with additional prospects for a "permanent army of the underemployed" (O'Toole, 1975a) does little to support the notion that America's ethnics should simply seek to immerse themselves wholeheartedly in the work force and let the problems of the economy be worked out without their attention. If jobs are to remain a central issue to our ethnic populations, one has some right to expect that ethnic youth will reverse the emphasis of the 1960s on doing one's own thing to finding something vocational to do and, not finding it, to find themselves caught up in a new activism.

Again, the internal response of ethnic families to the vagaries of the business cycle and the propensity for many businessmen to subject the disadvantaged to exploitation has not been for these families to become seedbeds of revolt with children socialized toward the acceptance of revolutionary roles. Rather, the family, adapting in a protean manner, tends to reorganize around new modes, some truly innovational, and new values for ensuring continued existence. The ethnic mother with the steady, reasonably well-paying job, by virtue of her new responsibilities in and to an external social world, becomes less a source of nurturance and care, less the heart, and more the operating head of the family. Her mother may now become indispensable to the home, and other blood-related females serve as resources for the reorganization of the family. The resultant product, a matricentric, partially extended family is compounded out of lower socioeconomic class position and an ethnic heritage that contains great latent strengths in females despite the patriarchal overcast of immigrant families. For the modern middle-class ethnics with husband and wife both often holding well-paying jobs, the ethnic family may move toward the equalitarian or companionship mode. Yet as intimated above, all reports seem to suggest that cultural residues still have their effect. Equality in work disposes ethnic families toward sharing in authority, responsibilities, and in relating to external society; but there is no evidence across our broad spectrum of families that all who share roughly the same economic contingencies are headed in a single direction and at the same rate of development.

IDEOLOGICAL CONTENT. Members of the modern ethnic family more or less tenuously hold beliefs that in the larger society have long ago passed into receivership. The expressive dimension of ethnic family life still contains images, symbols, mystical, magical, and folk beliefs, superstitions, religious credulity involving strong beliefs in miracles, the efficacy of prayer, spiritual intercession, patron saints, personalized deities, demonic spirits, evil eyes—an immense and amorphous uncritical ideational mass, the function of which remains as unclear as it is pervasive.

If these are remnants of a sacred society, their presence suggests some well-anchored resistance by the ethnic family and its members to emancipation from nonrational thought. Contrariwise, if the modern freewheeling, secularized, nuclear family that constantly engages in rational decisionmaking turns out to be critically lacking in social and personal bonds, and only with great difficulty reaching consensus on anything, then these same ethnic-related, nonrational ideological elements may exist instructively as resources for other families and persons who as groups and as individuals have reached the end of the line.

Other ideological elements of ethnic families may be viewed similarly: the sense of honor backed up with appropriate codes of prescribed behavior, fierce loyalty toward kin, interfamilial sociability and primary relationships structured along kinship lines, godparenthood, the sanctity of the adult mother, protectiveness toward the female sex generally, respect and fondness for the aged, all still present in some degree or another and well worthy of comparison with those "melted down" ethnic groups whose attachment to such ideological elements are presumably more attenuated.

COHESION AND INTEGRATION. It should be fairly clear to the readers of this work that while the early or initial ethnic family develops considerable unity through division of labor and authority, habituated role-playing, and through family rituals and ceremonial participation in sacred and pragmatic activities, today's counterpart has been unable to display or assemble a clearly agreed upon, integrated set of definitions of what all members might best be doing at all times. Looking at the complexity of American society and its changing position in world affairs, the product of its evolutionary growth and convolutionary spasms remain for students of ethnic families somewhat blurred—as a moving object caught by a camera whose shutter speed is too slow. The outlines are discernible, particularly in our case in which the initial ethnic-family model is available for comparison. Hard thought on the matter suggests difficulty in achieving a sharp analytical focus on the manifold of variables, happenstances, differential rates of change, different things changing (divorce rates, intermarriage, achievement norms, social and geographical mobility) and the effects of large-scale economic and political developments across the land and around the world.

To be an ethnic in America means something different each time a major shakeup occurs in domestic or international affairs. The continuing function of the ethnic family has been to orient its members pragmatically to the here and the now, but always against a cultural backdrop. The culture of the "old country" may lose meaning in one instance, only to gain meaning in another. Old World cultures may become articles for mass consumption by leisured ethnics with money for travel and a curiosity to see the land of their fathers. The revivalistic impulses of some modern ethnics have brought new attention to themselves, and sociological literature expands accordingly. But how to relate what nearly four generations ago E. A. Ross called the "planes and currents" of society to such a stuck-in-place social unity as the family?

430

We have suggested that the ethnic family is adaptive, that it does not lose cultural content and social meanings so rapidly that new meanings, new foci of attention (bussing school children, urban demolition, employment jeopardy, bureaucratic machinations) may not arise, first as problems, then changing to adaptations, then becoming the folkways of groups whose identities may shift and blur only to become reorganized around new foci, and, finally for these folkways as community, neighborhood, and group preoccupations to become central to family belief and behavior.

There is little chance that this process will give way overnight to a new family form expressing the rational-purposeful, means-ends-dominated, instrumentally oriented features of a family that serves only the functional requisites of a corporate-business-dominated society. Neither will the modern ethnic family simply reflect the overarching and homogenizing forces of a mass, consumption-oriented society. Somewhere between these great grindstones that would pulverize traditional family organization a type of family, once consigned to oblivion—being ground or melted down—persists: protean, adaptive, conservatizing, generating meanings, and forming a sense of identity partly from the realities of an earlier time, partly from the exigencies of the present. The bonds of ethnicity are reminiscent of the life forces of those desert creatures that, buried in the earth for years, come "alive" again when it rains. It is not the task of the authors to proclaim nor to look askance at ethnic groups and their constituent families, in their variegated forms, in their dropping from sight, their reemergence, growth, and change. Their existence is *sui generis,* to be studied as our authors have studied them, and to be a continuing object of the thinking sociologist's scrutiny.

REFERENCES

Feldstein, Stanley, and Lawrence Costello (eds.). 1974. *The Ordeal of Assimilation.* New York: Anchor Press/Doubleday.
Fischer, David Hackett. 1978. *Growing Old in America: The Bland–Lee Lectures Delivered at Clark University, Expanded Edition.* New York: Oxford University Press.
Gans, Herbert H. 1962. *The Urban Villagers.* Glencoe, IL: The Free Press.
Gelfand, Donald E., and Alfred J. Kutzik (eds.). 1979. *Ethnicity and Aging: Theory, Research, and Policy.* New York: Springer.
Gersuny, Carl, and William R. Rosengren. 1973. *The Service Society.* Cambridge, MA: Schenkman.
Glazer, Nathan and Daniel Patrick Moynihan. 1970. *Beyond the Melting Pot.* Cambridge, MA: M.I.T. Press.
Gordon, Michael (ed.). 1973. *The American Family in Social-Historical Perspective.* New York: St. Martin's Press.

Greeley, Andrew M. 1969. *Why Can't They Be Like Us?* New York: Institute of Human Relations Press.

——. 1974. *Ethnicity in the United States: A Preliminary Reconnaissance.* New York: Wiley.

Greenstone, J. David. 1975. "Ethnicity, Class, and Discontent: The Case of Polish Peasant Immigrants," *Ethnicity,* 2 (March):1–9.

Handlin, Oscar. 1963. *The American People in the Twentieth Century.* Boston: Beacon Press.

Hartmann, Edward G. 1948. *The Movement to Americanize the Immigrant.* New York: Columbia University Press.

Higham, John. 1968. *Strangers in the Land.* New York: Atheneum.

Horowitz, Irving Louis. 1975. "Race, Class and the New Ethnicity," *Worldview,* 18 (January):46–53.

McLaughlin, Virginia Yans. 1971. "Patterns of Work and Family Organization: Buffalo's Italians," *Journal of Interdisciplinary History,* 2 (Autumn). Reprinted in Gordon, Michael (ed.). 1973. *The American Family in Social-Historical Perspective.* New York: St. Martin's Press.

Novak, Michael. 1973. *The Rise of the Unmeltable Ethnics.* New York: Macmillan.

O'Toole, James. 1975a. "The Reserve Army of the Underemployed: I—The World of Work," *Change,* 7 (May):26–33 *passim.*

——. 1975b. "The Reserve Army of the Underemployed: II—The Role of Education," *Change,* 7 (June): 26–33 *passim.*

Park, Robert E., and Herbert Miller. 1969. *Old World Traits Transplanted.* New York: Arno Press and The New York Times.

Patterson, Orlando. 1975. "Ethnicity and the Pluralist Fallacy," *Change,* 7 (March): 10–11.

Schermerhorn, R. A. 1970. *Comparative Ethnic Relations.* New York: Random House.

Sennett, Richard. 1969. "Middle Class Families and Urban Violence," in Thernstrom, Stephen, and Richard Sennett (eds.), *Nineteenth Century Cities: Essays in the New Urban History.* New Haven: Yale University Press. Reprinted in Gordon, Michael (ed.). 1973. *The American Family in Social-Historical Perspective.* New York: St. Martin's Press.

——. 1970. *Families Against the City.* Cambridge: Harvard University Press.

van den Berghe, Pierre. 1970. *Race and Ethnicity.* New York: Basic Books.

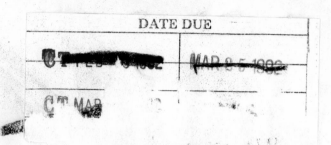